THE SUTTON HOO SHIP-BURIAL

VOLUME 2

THE SUTTON HOO
SHIP - BURIAL

VOLUME 2

ARMS, ARMOUR AND REGALIA

by

RUPERT BRUCE-MITFORD

with contributions by

Mavis Bimson, D. F. Cutler, Katherine East,
S. E. Ellis, Angela Care Evans, Carola Hicks, Michael Hughes,
W. A. Oddy, M. S. Tite, Susan M. Youngs and A. E. A. Werner.

Published for
The Trustees of the British Museum by
British Museum Publications Limited

ISBN O 7141 1335 2 *this volume*
ISBN O 7141 1331 X *the set*

Published by British Museum Publications Limited
6 Bedford Square, London WC1B 3RA

British Library Cataloguing in Publication Data
Bruce-Mitford, Rupert
    The Sutton Hoo ship-burial.
    Vol. 2: Arms, armour and regalia.
    1. Sutton Hoo, Suffolk – Antiquities
    I. British Museum
    942.6'46   A690.59

Set in Linotron Imprint
PRINTED IN GREAT BRITAIN
AT THE UNIVERSITY PRESS, CAMBRIDGE

To

SUNE LINDQVIST

1887–1976

friend and teacher

CONTENTS

List of colour plates   *page* xi

List of figures   xiii

List of tables   xxiv

Preface   xxv

CHAPTER I   THE SHIELD

Section 1	Introduction and primary accounts of the discovery	1
I	The state of the remains in the ground and the evidence available for reconstruction	1
II	Primary accounts of the discovery	7
Section 2	General description of the reconstruction	11
I	The front of the shield	11
II	The back of the shield	15
Section 3	Detailed discussion of the reconstruction	15
I	Size	15
II	Shape	19
III	Construction	21
IV	The rim	29
V	The distribution of features	36
VI	The gilt-bronze 'sword-ring' and its associated strip	45
VII	The boss	48
VIII	The bird	55
IX	The winged dragon	63
X	The eleven small bosses	66
XI	Animal heads on the shield rim	67
XII	Ornamental strips on the front of the shield	67
XIII	The carrying and hanging-up mechanisms	69
XIV	The grip extensions	75
Section 4	Cloisonné work	78
Section 5	Animal ornament and interlace designs	79
A	Designs stamped with dies on to foil	82
B	Designs cast from moulds and tool-finished	90
Section 6	The Sutton Hoo shield in relation to Anglo-Saxon and Continental shields	91

Appendix A Report on the scientific examination of the shield (W. A. Oddy, Mavis Bimson and A. E. A. Werner) 100

Appendix B Backing materials in the garnet inlays and behind bronze foils (Katherine East) 123

Appendix C Identification of wood fragments from the shield material (D. F. Cutler) 127

CHAPTER II   THE GILT-BRONZE RING FROM THE SHIELD

129

CHAPTER III   THE HELMET

Section 1 Introduction and primary account of discovery 138
Section 2 Detailed description 150
    I The cap 150
    II The crest and dragon heads 152
    III The face-mask 163
    IV The cheek-pieces 171
    V The neck-guard 173
    VI The lining and textiles associated with the helmet 179
Section 3 The restoration of the helmet and the making of the replica 181
Section 4 The five dies 186
    1 The dancing warriors 186
    2 Rider and fallen warrior 190
    3 Fragmentary and unidentifiable figural design 197
    4 The larger interlace 200
    5 The smaller interlace 201
Section 5 Summary and conclusions 203
    I Summary of features 203
    II The Sutton Hoo helmet in the Anglo-Saxon and Scandinavian contexts 205
    III The Late Antique background 220
    IV The condition and date of the Sutton Hoo helmet 224
Appendix Report on the scientific examination of the Sutton Hoo helmet (W. A. Oddy, Mavis Bimson and A. E. A. Werner) 226

CHAPTER IV   THE MAILCOAT

Section 1 Introduction and primary account of the discovery 232
Section 2 Description and discussion 232
Appendix Report on scientific examination of fragments of mailcoat (W. A. Oddy and A. E. A. Werner) 240

CHAPTER V   SPEARS AND ANGONS

Section 1 Introduction 241
Section 2 The spears 245

Section 3	The angons	259
Section 4	Ferrules and supposed ferrules	265
Section 5	The ferrules and their relations to the spears	270
Appendix	Botanical report (D. F. Cutler)	272

CHAPTER VI   THE SWORD

Section 1	Introduction and primary accounts of discovery	273
Section 2	The sword, its component parts and the fittings directly associated with it	282
Section 3	Cloisonné work in the sword-pommel, scabbard-bosses and pyramids	303
Appendix A	A note on the pattern-welding of the sword-blade (Angela Care Evans)	307
Appendix B	Reports relating to the sword and scabbard: scientific examinations carried out in the British Museum Research Laboratory (W. A. Oddy and M. S. Tite)	308

CHAPTER VII   THE SCEPTRE

Section 1	Introduction and primary accounts of discovery	311
Section 2	General description	312
Section 3	The human heads: detailed description and discussion	316
I	Heads at the lower end of the sceptre	316
II	Heads at the top of the sceptre	321
III	Discussion	323
Section 4	The two ends of the stone bar contrasted	324
Section 5	The pedestal, iron wire ring and stag assembly	328
Section 6	The stag	333
Section 7	The evidence for connecting the stag assembly with the stone bar	339
Section 8	The implications of the analytical results from the metal fitments of the sceptre	343
Section 9	The ceremonial status of the stone bar	345
Section 10	Contemporary sceptres and the Antique tradition	350
Section 11	Sources, origin and significance	357
I	The human faces and their style	358
II	Whetstones and their possible ceremonial or religious use	360
III	The sceptre's significance	370
Section 12	Conclusions	375
Appendix A	A note on the provenance of the Sutton Hoo stag (C. Hicks)	378
Appendix B	Petrography and provenance of the Sutton Hoo stone bar (S. E. Ellis)	383
Appendix C	Scientific examination of the stag assembly and the bronze fitments of the stone bar (A. E. A. Werner, W. A. Oddy, M. J. Hughes)	385

CHAPTER VIII   THE WOOD, BONE OR IVORY ROD

Section 1   Introduction and primary account of discovery   394
Section 2   Detailed description   397

CHAPTER IX   THE IRON STAND

Section 1   Introduction and primary accounts of discovery   403
Section 2   General description   406
Section 3   An iron object (Inv. 210) possibly connected with the stand   419
Section 4   The function of the stand   422

CHAPTER X   THE GOLD JEWELLERY

                Introduction and list   432
Section 1   The finding of the jewellery and primary account of discovery   435
Section 2   The positions of the individual pieces in the ground   439
Section 3   Description of the individual pieces of jewellery   447
        I   Small cloisonné buckle and two matching strap-mounts (Inv.
                12–14)   449
        II   Two pairs of similar rectangular mounts, a T-shaped strap-
                distributor and a rectangular buckle (Inv. 6–9, 17 and 11)   456
        III   Curved mount (dummy buckle) (Inv. 10)   473
        IV   Triangular zoomorphic strap-mount or counter-plate (Inv. 18)   481
        V   Plain strap-runner in the form of a tongueless buckle, and the
                plain strap-end (Inv. 15, 16)   485
        VI   The purse-lid, sliding catch and purse (Inv. 2, 3)   487
        VII   The shoulder-clasps (Inv. 4, 5)   523
        VIII   The great gold buckle (Inv. 1)   536
Section 4   Comments on the design of the harness and the functions of the
                various pieces of jewellery   564
Section 5   Millefiori and blue glass inlays   582
        I   Introduction   582
        II   The shoulder-clasps   584
        III   Millefiori inlays in the purse-lid   590
        IV   The pyramids   594
        V   Inlays of blue glass in shoulder-clasps, purse-lid and pyramids   594
        VI   General discussion   594
Section 6   Style and technique   597
Section 7   Filigree work   603
Section 8   Gold analysis   611
Appendix A   Weights of the gold jewellery items in the Sutton Hoo ship-burial   615
Appendix B   Types and distribution of inlays   617
Appendix C   Report on the analysis of gold of the Sutton Hoo jewellery and
                some comparative material (M. J. Hughes, M. R. Cowell,
                W. A. Oddy and A. E. A. Werner)   618

Bibliography   626
Index   640

LIST OF COLOUR PLATES

Plate   1   The Sutton Hoo shield.   *between pages* 326 *and* 327

2   Bird's head and leg from the shield.

3   Winged dragon from the shield.

4   The shield-boss: oblique view.

5   The shield-boss: (*a*) a section of the flange showing a design of interlocked horses stamped in gilt-bronze foil; (*b*) disc with zoomorphic ornament from the top of the boss.

6   The shield: handgrip extensions from the back.

7   The shield: (*a*) gilt-bronze ring; (*b*) and (*d*) gilt-bronze strap-ends from the carrying strap; (*c*) anchor fitment for the carrying strap; (*e*) pyramidal studs in gilt-bronze from the back of the shield.

8   The helmet replica made in the Royal Armouries in the Tower of London, in collaboration with the British Museum.

9   Left side of the reconstructed helmet showing rusted original fragments in a modern matrix.

10   The sceptre, with detail of the stag and ring.

11   The sceptre: (*a*) the lower end with the saucer-fitting removed; (*b*) the upper end with iron staining on the tip of the stone bar; (*c*) the stag.

12   The upper part of the iron stand: oblique view.

13   The purse-lid with a detail of the double plaque with animal interlace.

14   The purse-lid: pairs of decorative plaques; (*a*) bird of prey and duck; (*b*) man between beasts; (*c*) hexagonal plaque.

15   The pair of hinged shoulder-clasps.

16   Detail of one end of each of the two shoulder-clasps showing intertwined boars and filigree decoration.

17   Panel of geometric design from shoulder-clasp 5a.

18   The shoulder-clasps: details of the remaining three cloisonné panels.

19   Group of gold jewellery: (*a*) rectangular buckle; (*b*) buckle and pair of matching strap-mounts; (*c*) ring-headed filigree strip and gold foil animal; (*d*) fluted strip with animal head and foil triangle with engraved animals; (*e*) gold loop and strap end.

20   The great gold buckle, with enlarged details.

21   Gold mounts associated with the sword: (*a*) the pommel; (*b*) the pyramids; (*c*) the scabbard bosses and (*d*) mounts of the upper and lower guards.

22   The original elements of the Sutton Hoo sword mounted on perspex (*a*); (*b*) side view of the shoulder-clasps (below), the curved mount, Inv. 10 (top), and a pair of clasps from the Taplow burial (centre); (*c*) interior view of the Sutton Hoo sword pommel and detail of the upper gold plate of the guard to which the pommel was attached; (*d*) gold filigree mounts from a purse, Beckum, Westaphalia; (*e*) one of the gold and garnet pyramids from Sutton Hoo seen in transmitted light. (Photos: *d*, by courtesy of the Westphalisches Landesmuseum fur Vor- und Frühgeschichte, Münster, and *e*, Ian Yeomans.)

23   (*a*) Reconstruction of the Benty Grange helmet; (*b*) interior view of an assembly of Sutton Hoo helmet fragments; (*c*) a transparent red square from a millefiori inlay on one of the shoulder-clasps showing gas bubbles; (*d*) foil, garnet and blue glass inlays from a bird's eye on the Sutton Hoo

purse-lid; (*e*) a garnet on edge in one of the cells of the buckle, Inv. 11; (*f*) millefiori inlay from the purse frame showing a design of four T-shapes in red with stems pointing inwards. (Photos: *c*, *e*, *f*, British Museum Research Laboratory; *d*, Ian Yeomans.)

24   (*a*) Millefiori inlays from the Sutton Hoo jewellery; A–Q the eighteen different patterns used. The monochrome drawings indicate the minimum areas required for the production of millefiori sheet for inlays A and K. (*b*) Detail of the west end of the burial deposit showing the shield remains *in situ*, based on a field plan by Stuart Piggott.

LIST OF FIGURES

Figure 1 Plan of the burial deposit. 2

2 The shield remains *in situ* with the iron boss and the winged dragon in the foreground. (Photo: O. G. S. Crawford) 5

3 The shield remains *in situ* showing part of the rim and the strap-hanger. (Photo: O. G. S. Crawford) 6

4 The shield remains *in situ*: detail showing the boss and the broken handgrip extensions. (Photo: O. G. S. Crawford) 8

5 The shield: explanatory drawing based on figure 2. 10

6 The reconstructed shield: outline drawings. 13

7 The reconstructed shield: cross-section. 14

8 The reconstructed shield. 14

9 The shield: the two largest fragments from the gilt-bronze rim 16

10 One of the two handgrip extensions. 18

11 Outline drawing of the handgrip and its extensions, showing the fractures it sustained in the ground. 19

12 The shield: detail of the remains of the shield in the ground showing the relationship of the boss, the handgrip and the winged dragon. (Photo: O. G. S. Crawford) 20

13 Alderwood underlay of the winged dragon from the front of the shield. 22

14 Alderwood seating for one of the small hemispherical gilt-bronze bosses from the top of the shield. 22

15 Alderwood underlay of the gold-foil tail and wing of the bird from the front of the shield. 23

16 The iron handgrip of the shield. 25

17 Comparative shield designs from figural panels on Swedish helmets. 26

18 The shield: the small hemispherical terminals from the back of the boss flange. 27

19 Cross-section through the central iron boss of the shield. 27

20 Cross-section through the shield-board under one of the small bosses. 28

21 Enlarged photographs of the leather which originally covered the shield-board. (Photos: British Leather Research Association) 28

22 Five of the best preserved animal heads from the shield-rim. 29

23 Drawing of two typical animal heads of different types from the rim of the shield. 30

24 Diagrammatic section through the rim of the shield based on surviving fragments. 31

25 Surviving leather fragments from the rim of the shield with examples of a peripheral bronze clip. 32

26 Fragments of gold foil from the U-shaped bronze channelling on the rim of the shield. 33

27 Outline drawing of the shield from Valsgärde grave no. 8, Sweden. (After Arwidsson) 35

28 Shields with applied motifs found at Stabio and Lucca, Italy. 36

29 The shield with a diameter of 96·5 cm (38 inches) incorporating twelve rectangular panels around the rim. 37

30 The Sutton Hoo shield: reconstruction drawing showing the relative movements in the ground of the surviving elements. 38

31 Alderwood underlay and wood of the shield-board from beneath the small gilt-bronze hemispherical boss IV.12. 41

32 Remains of the shield in the ground, showing the relative positions of the bird's claw and eye, and one of the gold strips. (Photo: O. G. S. Crawford) 43

Figure 33 The shield: disintegrated fragments of a small gilt-bronze boss. 44

34 The shield: the iron and gilt-bronze boss, before and after cleaning. 47

35 The back of the shield-boss, after cleaning. 48

36 The shield: design A8, erect horses with interlacing limbs. 49

37 The shield: design A9, interlace from the vertical collar of the shield-boss. 49

38 The shield: the interlace panel, design A9, and the use of an overlapping die. 50

39 The shield: design A10, zoomorphic interlace design from the lower edge of the dome of the boss. 51

40 The shield: design A11, zoomorphic interlace below the raised central disc of the boss. 52

41 The shield: design B1, zoomorphic interlace surrounding the central cloisonné inlay of the disc of the boss. 52

42 The shield: two animal heads from the boss. 53

43 The shield: detailed drawings of four different heads, from the grip extension and bird. 53

44 The bird from the front of the shield as reconstructed. 54

45 The shield: original fragments of gold foil forming the interlace design of the bird's tail. 56

46 The shield: fragment of leather showing the impression of the bird's leg and claw, with the leg and claw alongside. 57

47 The shield: alderwood underlay of the bird's tail and wing, photographed in 1949. 57

48 The bird from the Sutton Hoo shield with birds from continental contexts for comparison. (After Nerman and Fettich) 58

49 The shield: designs A4 and A5, the interlace designs of the bird's wing and tail. 59

50 The shield: the winged dragon from the front. 62

51 The shield: designs B2–B5, the interlace panels from the body of the winged dragon. 64

52 The shield: impressed gold-foil collar surrounding one of the hemispherical gilt-bronze bosses on the front. 66

53 Decorated shield strips of gold-foil from Sutton Hoo, and of gilt-bronze from Vendel 12, Sweden, shield 1. (After Stolpe and Arne) 68

54 The shield: fragments of gold-foil strip from Area IV.16 in 1945. (Photos: British Museum Research Laboratory) 70

55 The shield: fragments of gold-foil strip from Area IV.17. (Photos: British Museum Research Laboratory) 71

56 The shield: the attachment plate of the strap-anchor. 72

57 The shield: plan and sectional drawings of the strap-anchor. 72

58 The shield: details of the strap-end and the leather strap showing its tooling pattern. 74

59 The shield: one of two pyramids from the strap-hanger. 75

60 Detail of the handgrip extension. 76

61 The shield: designs A14 and A15, the interlace designs of the lunate foils from the handgrip extension. 77

62 The shield: design A13, the interlace pattern from the handgrip extension. 77

63 The shield: cloisonné garnet designs. 78

64 Original fragments of gold foil from a rectangular panel at the rim of the shield. 81

65 The shield: details of design A1. 82

66 The shield: drawings and fragments of gold foil containing designs A2 (compared with A1), A3 and A4. 84

67 Comparative snake motifs from the Bury St Edmunds die, the Franks Casket and the Book of Durrow. 85

68 Interlaced animal from Valsgärde 6 comparable with design B2 from the winged dragon. 92

69 Details of the boss from Bidford-on-Avon, Gloucestershire, the gilt-bronze disc from Barton Seagrave, Northamptonshire, and an appliqué fish found at Kenninghall, Suffolk. 93

70 The boss from shield 1, Vendel 12. 95

71 The boss from shield 1, Vendel 12, an oblique view. 96

72 Outline drawings of the shields from Vendel 1 and Valsgärde 7 for comparative purposes. 98

73 Outline drawing of the shield from Wiesbaden, Westphalia. (Städtlisches Museum, Wiesbaden). 98

74 The Sutton Hoo shield: surviving gold foil from the bird's wing. 99

75 The shield: the bird's head assembly with a section across the junction of the head and crest. 100

76 The shield: enlarged detail of the bird's eye. 100

Figure 77 The shield: diagram of the garnet panel in the tapering crest at the back of the bird's head. 101

78 The shield: diagrams to show sampling positions and garnet panel contained within the bird's thigh and the cell walls of the garnet panel of the bird's leg. 102

79 The shield: radiograph of the gilt-bronze dragon on the front. (British Museum Research Laboratory) 104

80 The shield: diagram to show sampling positions and the garnet panel on the winged dragon. 105

81 The shield: photomicrographs of the stamped foil backings to the garnets of the dragon. (Photos: British Museum Research Laboratory) 105

82 The shield: diagram to show sampling positions on the anchor-plate and strap-ends. 106

83 The shield: strap-attachment plate. 107

84 The shield: diagram to show the sampling positions on the handgrip extensions. 107

85 The shield: the surviving animal heads from the rim. 110

86 The shield: diagram showing sampling positions on the hemispherical bosses. 112

87 The shield-boss: montage to show sampling positions. 115

88 The shield: table showing the different types of punch-marks. 118

89 The shield: photomicrographs of different punch-marks used. (Photos: British Museum Research Laboratory) 120

90 The shield: photomicrographs of the animal heads from the rim. (Photos: British Museum Research Laboratory) 121

91 Diagram to illustrate location of photomicrographs shown in figure 88. 122

92 The shield: detail to show variations in the impressions produced by the large triangular punch. (Photo: British Museum Research Laboratory) 122

93 The gilt-bronze ring from the shield. 129

94 The sword-pommel and ring from Orsay, Seine (Rhein Landesmuseum, Bonn). 130

95 The sword-hilt from Vallstenarum, Gotland. (Photo: Gustavianum, Uppsala) 131

96 Sword-rings from Coombe and Sarre, Kent; Italy (unprovenanced); Grave 20, Chaouilly, Meurthe et Moselle. (After Evison 1967) 132

97 Sword-pommel with attached ring from Snösbäck, Västergotland, Sweden. 134

98 Three views of the gilt-bronze ring found associated with a drinking-horn in Valsgärde grave 7. (Copyright: Gustavianum, Uppsala) 135

99 The Sutton Hoo shield: alderwood underlay of the gilt-bronze ring. 135

100 Anglo-Saxon sword-rings: Gilton, Kent; Faversham, Kent and Dover, grave C. (After Evison 1967) 136

101 Drinking horn from Valsgärde grave 7, with the gilt-bronze ring mounted on a decorative strip. 137

102 Fragments of the Sutton Hoo helmet before work began on a new reconstruction in 1971. 139

103 The helmet as reconstructed in 1971: front view. 141

104 The helmet: right side. 142

105 The helmet: left side. 143

106 The helmet: rear view. 144

107 The helmet seen from above. 145

108 The helmet: distribution of the decorative panels on the front. 147

109 The helmet: distribution of the decorative panels on the side. 148

110 The helmet: drawings of the four designs that are capable of reconstruction. 149

111 The helmet: view of the interior of the cap. 151

112 The helmet: photograph and radiograph of conjoining sections of the crest. (British Museum Research Laboratory) 153

113 The Sutton Hoo helmet: details of the iron crest and its silver inlay patterns. 154

114 The helmet: radiograph details of the ends of the crest. (British Museum Research Laboratory) 154

115 The helmet: drawing showing the original relationship between the fragments that survive from the rear of the crest. 155

116 The helmet: reconstruction drawing of the complete crest, with the bronze crest and comb from Vendel grave 1, Uppland, Sweden. 157

117 The helmet: the three gilt-bronze dragon heads. 160

118 The helmet: the dragon heads, showing decorative details. 161

Figure 119 The helmet: enlarged detail showing gold foil with punched circle decoration from a portion of dragon neck *in situ* at the rear of the crest. 161

120 The helmet: front and back views of the bronze nose and mouth casting from the face-mask. 162

121 The helmet: radiograph of the nose casting. (British Museum Research Laboratory) 163

122 The helmet: enlargement of the nose casting showing the nostril holes. 165

123 The helmet: profile of the nose casting showing the decorative *schema* and the taper of the bronze tang at the top. 166

124 The front of the helmet showing the 'flying dragon' imagery created by the nose, the eyebrows and the dragon head above the nose. 168

125 The helmet: schematic drawing showing applied decoration on the bronze nose casting. 169

126 The helmet: the 'flying dragon' image from the front. 169

127 The helmet: front and rear views of the eyebrows. 170

128 The helmet: the complete boar's head terminal from the right eyebrow. 171

129 The helmet: the right cheek-piece showing the series of fragments which define its shape and the location of design 1. 172

130 The helmet: detail of the neckguard, with individual original fragments numbered. 173

131 The helmet: vertical cross-section of the neck-guard showing the relationship of the two iron parts. 174

132 The helmet: detail of the upper right-hand corner of the neck-guard. 175

133 The helmet: fragment from the upright collar of the neck-guard showing the rivets and reinforcing plate of a hinge and the relation of the hinge to the decorative panel. (British Museum Research Laboratory) 177

134 Roman infantry helmet from Witcham Gravel, Cambridgeshire. 178

135 The Sutton Hoo helmet: rust impression of the textile SH 10 on the inside of fragment 21 from the neck-guard. 179

136 The helmet: detail of a cheek-piece on the modern replica. 182

137 The helmet: the decorative appearance of cap, crest and neck-guard as seen on the modern replica. 183

138 The helmet replica showing the distribution of design 4 panels in relation to the hinges and crest. 184

139 The helmet: section and frontal view of the type of leather hinge thought to have provided flexible links between neck-guard and cap. 185

140 The Sutton Hoo helmet: design 1, showing two dancing warriors. 186

141 The helmet: drawing showing the location of the surviving fragments of design 1 on the reconstructed helmet. 187

142 The helmet: six of the principal fragments which make up design 1. 188

143 The helmet: design 2, the rider with fallen warrior. 189

144 The helmet: drawing showing the location of original fragments bearing parts of design 2. 190

145 The helmet: the principal surviving fragments showing design 2. 193

146 The repoussé gold disc-brooch from Pliezhausen, Kr. Tübingen, Germany. 194

147 Plaster casts of ornament from the helmet found in Vendel grave 14. (Photos: Statens Historiska Museum, Stockholm) 195

148 The helmet: drawings of the seven fragments of design 3. 197

149 The helmet: the two largest pieces of design 3. 198

150 The helmet: reconstruction drawing of the larger interlace, design 4. 200

151 The helmet: reconstruction of the smaller interlace, design 5. 202

152 Drawing of spear-head from Vendel grave 14. 204

153 Drawing from a silver-foil fragment from Caenby, Lincolnshire. 206

154 Fragments of stamped foil showing a varied interlace design and billeted bordering, from the Asthall barrow cremation burial, Berkshire. (Photos: Ashmolean Museum, Oxford) 207

155 Bronze foil fragment with part of the figure of a dancing warrior, from the East Mound of Gamla Uppsala (Sweden). (Photo: Statens Historiska Museum, Stockholm) 208

156 Bronze dies from Torslunda, Öland, Sweden. (Photos: Statens Historiska Museum, Stockholm) 209

157 Representation of a helmet from one of the dies from Torslunda, Öland, Sweden showing cheek-pieces and a broad neck-guard. 210

158 Helmet from Vendel grave 14. 211

159 Helmet from Valsgärde grave 7. (Photo: Per Bergström) 212

160 Helmet from Valsgärde grave 7, viewed from above. (Photo: G. Arwidsson and O. Lindman) 213

Figure 161   Side view of helmet from Valsgärde 7. (Photo: G. Arwidsson)   214

162   Gilded bronze eyebrows and nasal inlaid with garnet, from the helmet from Valsgärde grave 7.   215

163   Distribution of the figural scenes and interlace on the helmet from Valsgärde grave 7. (Drawing by Per-Olof Bohlin)   216

164   Six decorative panels on the helmet from Valsgärde grave 7. (Drawings by M. Roosmay, Per-Olof Bohlin)   217

165   Identical zoomorphic interlace found in two burials in Uppland, Sweden. (Drawing by Per-Olof Bohlin)   218

166   Late Roman helmets from Constantinian workshops: Berkasovo, Yugoslavia, helmet 1, Berkasovo, helmet 2, and the Deurne or de Peel helmet, Holland.   219

167   Late Roman helmets from the Constantinian workshops.   221

168   Late Roman helmets from the Constantinian workshops.   222

169   Early second-century cavalry sports helmet from Ribchester, Lancashire (British Museum) and a cavalry sports helmet with hinged and silvered face mask, from Homs (Emesa), Syria.   224

170   The Sutton Hoo helmet: sampling positions on three foil-covered fragments.   226

171   The helmet: sampling positions on the fluted dividing strips.   226

172   The helmet: sampling positions on a fluted strip flanking the crest and on the rear crest tang.   227

173   The helmet: details and sampling position on U-shaped rim binding.   227

174   The helmet: punched decoration on a gilded bronze dragon head.   228

175   The helmet: views of the front showing sampling positions.   229

176   The helmet: surviving garnet inlays in the eyebrows.   230

177   The mailcoat: plan of the second layer of the deposit beneath the Anastasius dish showing the position of the mailcoat.   233

178   The mailcoat: the upper surface after cleaning.   233

179   The mailcoat: detail of one of the larger fragments showing individual links.   234

180   The mailcoat: radiograph of a selection of loose fragments, showing interlocking rows of links.   235

181   The mailcoat: radiograph of part of the mailcoat, showing a random pattern of dense black spots which are the remains of tiny copper rivets.   236

182   Helmets from Vendel 12 and Valsgärde grave 6, showing the use of mail as protective curtains. (After Thordeman 1941)   238

183   Mailcoated and helmeted warriors from the Franks casket.   238

184   The complex of spears and angons *in situ*, from the north. (Photo: O. G. S. Crawford)   242

185   The complex of spears and angons *in situ* from the north-east. (Photo: O. G. S. Crawford)   243

186   Drawing to show the relative positions within the burial deposit of the six spears and three angons, and the four possible ferrules.   244

187   Spear no. 1 (Inv. 101).   246

188   Spear no. 2 (Inv. 102).   247

189   Spear no. 3 (Inv. 103).   249

190   Spear no. 4 (Inv. 104).   250

191   Spear no. 4: cross-section of the socket.   251

192   Spear no. 5 (Inv. 105) lifted from the complex. (Photo: O. G. S. Crawford)   252

193   Spear no. 5 (Inv. 105).   253

194   Spear no. 6 (Inv. 97).   255

195   Spear no. 6: cross-section through the shaft.   257

196   The six spears (reconstructed): outline drawings.   258

197   Angon no. 1 (Inv. 98).   260

198   Angon no. 2 (Inv. 99).   262

199   Angon no. 3 (Inv. 100).   263

200   The three angons: outline drawings.   264

201   Iron ferrule (Inv. 106).   266

202   Iron ferrule (Inv. 107).   266

203   Iron ferrule (Inv. 108).   267

204   The iron and wood object (Inv. 211), perhaps a ferrule with part of the shaft surviving. (Photo: M. O. Miller)   268

205   The iron and wood object (Inv. 211) from the 1967 excavations.   269

Figure 206 Doubtful 'ferrule' (Inv. 271), found during the 1967 excavations of mound I.   270

207 The sword *in situ*: general view. (Photo: C. W. Phillips)   274

208 The sword: enlarged details showing the gold and garnet scabbard-bosses and their matrices.   275

209 The sword: detail of the badly damaged upper portion as excavated. (Photo: S. Piggott)   276

210 The sword: drawing.   277

211 The sword: photomontages of two faces, with radiograph showing pattern welding. (British Museum Research Laboratory)   278

212 The sword: section cut through sword and scabbard showing the blade profile. (Photo: British Museum Research Laboratory)   283

213 The sword: detail of the top, showing tape bindings and the remains of one of the spare coils of tape found under the sword.   284

214 The sword: enlarged details of animal hairs on the scabbard. (Photos: British Museum Research Laboratory)   285

215 The sword: the upper surface of the scabbard showing the full extent of a superficial tapering wooden feature.   286

216 Detail of sword 1 from Valsgärde grave 7 showing part of the suspension mechanism.   287

217 The sword: details of the gold mounts from the hilt.   289

218 The sword: drawings of the hilt.   290

219 The sword: details of the pommel.   292

220 The sword: oblique view of the pommel and upper guard plates, showing the remains of the high tin alloy which originally filled the lower gold mount.   292

221 The sword: details of the tang and grip.   293

222 The sword: the scabbard-bosses.   295

223 The sword: drawings showing the construction of the scabbard-bosses.   296

224 Drawings of the scabbard-bosses in position.   297

225 The sword: details of two filigree clips of different sizes from the lower and upper ends of the grip.   298

226 The sword: beaded wire collar surrounding the head of an outer rivet and a gold nail from one of the filigree clips on the grip.   299

227 The sword: views of the pair of gold pyramids (Inv. 28 and 29) with a detail of the millefiori inlay in the top of one of them.   301

228 The gold pyramids: drawings showing their structure.   302

229 The Sutton Hoo sword: cell forms in the sword pommel.   303

230 Sword-pommel from Hög Edsten, Bohuslän, Sweden. (Photo: Statens Historiska Museum, Stockholm)   304

231 The sword: cell forms in the scabbard-bosses.   305

232 The Sutton Hoo sword: a garnet and its gold-foil underlay from one of the scabbard-bosses (Inv. 26). (Photo: British Museum Research Laboratory)   305

233 The sword: cell forms in the pyramids.   306

234 The sceptre: enlargement of head A2.   310

235 The sceptre *in situ*. (Photo: S. Piggott)   312

236 The sceptre: the stone bar with the bronze saucer-fitting removed and simplified drawing of the bar with the saucer-fitting in position; both showing areas of dark staining.   313

237 The sceptre reconstructed.   314

238 The sceptre: two pairs of carved faces from opposite ends of the stone bar; heads A1 and B1, A2 and B2.   318

239 The sceptre: two pairs of carved faces from opposite ends of the stone bar; heads A3 and B3, A4 and B4.   319

240 The sceptre: drawing of a head with bearded chin, B1, and of a head with exposed chin, A4.   322

241 The sceptre: end view and profile of the terminal knobs of the stone bar.   325

242 The sceptre: two views of the saucer-fitting and cage.   326

243 The sceptre: the upper and the lower ends, showing constructional differences in the bronze cage mounts.   327

244 The sceptre: bifid motifs carved in the angles between the head frames at the upper end of the stone bar.   328

Figure 245   The sceptre: the bronze pedestal and iron ring that carried the stag.   329

246   The sceptre: suggested construction of the elements comprising the pedestal assembly which carried the stag.   330

247   The sceptre: reconstruction drawing of the iron ring and pedestal with a detail from the replica made in the British Museum Research Laboratory.   331

248   The sceptre: four views of the bronze stag.   332

249   The sceptre: drawings of the stag in its present condition.   333

250   The sceptre: simplified cross-sections of the stag at selected points.   334

251   Three views of the stag as excavated, before conservation.   336

252   Red deer stag in Richmond Park, Surrey; (b) identification of red deer antlers. (After Frohawk)   337

253   The stag: reconstruction drawings of the stag in its original condition.   338

254   The sceptre: the stag-mount pedestal foot.   341

255   The sceptre: replica made in the British Museum Research Laboratory.   342

256   The sceptre: interior view of the pedestal base with iron corrosion products removed.   348

257   Ceremonial staffs and sceptres depicted on late Roman ivory diptychs. (After Delbrueck 1929)   351

258   Wooden sceptre from the sixth century grave of a boy prince in Cologne Cathedral. (After Doppelfeld and Pirling 1966)   353

259   Charles the Bald shown with crown and sceptre. (After a Carolingian psalter of before A.D. 869, Bibliothèque Nationale Lat. 1152, f. 3v.)   355

260   Reconstruction of the head of an Avar sceptre. (After Alföldi 1948)   355

261   A silver sceptre from Taganča, near Kiev. (After Alföldi 1948)   356

262   Edward the Confessor (A.D. 1043–66) and Harold Godwinson (A.D. 1066) in the Bayeux tapestry, showing the use of sceptres by late Anglo-Saxon Kings. (Photos: Victoria and Albert Museum)   357

263   Bronze figure and face from a wooden staff from Søholdt, Denmark; with a bronze mount, thought to be from a wooden staff, from Vimose, Denmark.   359

264   Photographs and drawings of two miniature whetstones from Birka, Sweden.   362

265   Two whetstones from a pagan Saxon burial place at Uncleby, Yorkshire.   363

266   Two stone bars or whetstones from a rath at Coleraine, Northern Ireland.   365

267   Carved stone figure from Hough-on-the-Hill, Lincolnshire.   366

268   A carved face, apparently part of a stone bar, from Lochar Moss, Dumfriesshire.   367

269   Examples of fine-grained stone bars or hone-stones with carved or incised heads or faces and other motifs.   368

270   Human face profiles on a bronze padlock from Dorchester-on-Thames, Oxfordshire. (Drawings by Miss Marion Cox)   370

271   The bronze figure of a stag from Gateholm Island, Pembrokeshire.   379

272   Three bronze stag-head terminals of the Roman period from Lloseta, Mallorca, Rennes, France, and Brampton, Norfolk.   381

273   The Sutton Hoo sceptre: enlarged photographs of the surface of the stone bar of the sceptre. (Photo: British Museum Research Laboratory)   383

274   The sceptre: presumed cross-section of the bronze pedestal from the stag assembly.   385

275   The sceptre: (a)–(e) the stag and enlarged details of the bronze pedestal-fitting and saucer-terminal, showing the positions of drillings taken for analysis. (Photos: British Museum Research Laboratory)   386

276   The sceptre: radiograph of the bronze pedestal of the stag-assembly showing the hollow construction of the curved arm of the bronze Y-piece.   387

277   The iron stand: the upper plate, with drawing showing sample positions.   392

278   Gold filigree strip (Inv. 30).   395

279   Gold filigree strip: detail.   397

280   Gold filigree strip: a detail of the filigree design.   398

281   Gold-foil animal (Inv. 32).   398

282   Detailed drawing of the gold-foil animal (Inv. 32).   399

283   Triangular gold-foil mount (Inv. 33).   399

284   Fluted gold strip (Inv. 31): details.   400

285   Drawing of fluted gold strip with animal head terminal (Inv. 31).   400

286   The wood, bone or ivory rod: suggested reconstruction.   401

Figure 287 Iron clip-like fitting from Hawnby, Yorkshire. 401
288 The iron stand *in situ*: detail (Photo: O. G. S. Crawford) 403
289 The iron stand: detail of the upper plate. (Photo: O. G. S. Crawford) 405
290 The iron stand in its present condition after consolidation and conservation treatment. 406
291 The iron stand with the modern replica made by F. Landon of Jarvis Brook, Crowborough, Sussex. 407
292 The iron stand: lettered sketch. 408
293 The iron stand: drawing of grid showing the sequence of construction. 408
294 The foot of the iron stand. 411
295 The iron stand: radiographs showing the relationship between point B and the tip of strut C, and the welded join between strut D and the lower plate. (British Museum Research Laboratory) 412
296 The iron stand: detail of the cage of the replica. 413
297 The iron stand: details of strut C. (British Museum Research Laboratory) 414
298 The iron stand: sketch of the lower plate. 415
299 The iron stand: radiographs of the grid. (British Museum Research Laboratory) 416
300 The iron stand: radiograph of the edge of the grid, showing double twisted bars. (British Museum Research Laboratory) 417
301 The iron stand: drawing and radiograph of one of the stylised animal heads from the corners of the grid. (British Museum Research Laboratory) 418
302 The iron stand: reconstruction drawing of a corner of the grid. 418
303 The iron stand: the upper and lower plates in their present condition. 419
304 The spanner-like iron object of uncertain use (Inv. 210) found adhering to the stem of the stand. 420
305 The iron object: radiographs and drawing showing its construction. (British Museum Research Laboratory) 421
306 Pottery lamp with spike from Thetford, Norfolk, twelfth century. 424
307 Iron trivet from Lilleberre, Norway, now in the British Museum. 425
308 Iron grid from Veszprem, Hungary, now in the Bakony Museum. (Photo: Bakony Museum) 425
309 Firedogs in iron with stylised heads, from Valsgärde grave 6, and Valsgärde grave 5. 426
310 Iron stands from continental contexts: Klinta, Öland; upper part of the iron strip found in grave 1782, Krefeld Gellep, and Vallstenarum, Gotland. (After Petersson 1958, Pirling 1974 and Nerman 1972 respectively) 427
311 Sketch based on an illumination in the St Gall Psalterium, f. v, 163, showing a rider holding a standard with a fire-breathing 'dragon' emblem. 429
312 Bronze dragon head of a Roman *vexillum* found at Niederbieber, Kreis Neuwied, West Germany. (Photo: Dr H. Eiden) 430
313 Fourth century coins showing examples of different standards. 431
314 The Sutton Hoo ship-burial: plan showing the positions of the various pieces of jewellery, identified by inventory numbers, as they lay in the ground. 434
315 Pencil plan by Stuart Piggott of 'Area A'. 436
316 Field plan of Area III by Stuart Piggott (plan 3). 438
317 Field plan of Area A (fig. 315): redrawn version showing inventory numbers. 440
318 The sword: detail of the under side, the scabbard, showing the impression of the back of the rectangular gold buckle. 443
319 Drawings and photographs of pieces of gold foil, enlarged, showing the different types used in the Sutton Hoo jewellery. 448
320 The cloisonné buckle and two matching strap-mounts (Inv. 12–14): cell forms and characteristic cell patterns. 449
321 The cloisonné buckle (Inv. 12), and two matching strap-mount (Inv. 13 and 14). 452
322 Pair of rectangular strap-mounts (Inv. 6 and 7): cell forms and characteristic cell patterns. 457
323 Strap-mount (Inv. 7): enlarged detail of a terminal rivet-shelf with a drawing of the rivet shelf at the end of the rectangular buckle (Inv. 11), for comparison. (Photo: British Museum Research Laboratory) 457
324 Pair of rectangular strap-mounts (Inv. 6 and 7). 458
325 Strap-mount: early photograph of Inv. 6 or 7 showing the back of the upper cloisonné-bearing plate. (Photo: British Museum Research Laboratory) 459
326 Pair of rectangular strap-mounts (Inv. 8 and 9): cell forms and cell patterns. 460

Figure 327   Pair of rectangular strap-mounts (Inv. 8 and 9).   461

328   Strap-mounts: cloisonné designs of the edge panels of Inv. 6, 8 and 17, for comparison.   462

329   Details of running interlace from panel work in the Book of Durrow and the Echternach Gospels, with a detail from the Sutton Hoo strap-mounts, Inv. 8 and 9.   462

330   Strap-mount: enlarged detail (Inv. 9) showing the use of beaded or sealed cells to bring out the interlace theme.   463

331   Strap-mount (Inv. 9) showing the independent cloisonné-bearing plate removed and cross-sections of the mount with the plate in position.   464

332   Strap-distributor (Inv. 17): cell forms and cell-patterns.   466

333   Strap-distributor: sketch with letters to distinguish the parts of Inv. 17.   466

334   The hinged T-shaped strap-distributor (Inv. 17).   467

335   Strap-distributor (Inv. 17): drawing showing the movement of the hinged and swivelling parts with a detail of the hinge.   469

336   Rectangular buckle (Inv. 11): cell forms and characteristic cell patterns.   470

337   The rectangular buckle (Inv. 11).   471

338   The rectangular buckle (Inv. 11): simplified longitudinal and transverse sectional drawings.   471

339   The dummy buckle (Inv. 10): cell forms.   474

340   The dummy buckle: patterns and themes in the cell work.   474

341   The dummy buckle (Inv. 10): front, back and two profile views.   475

342   The dummy buckle: drawings, including a suggested sectional view.   476

343   Curved clasps from the Taplow barrow, Buckinghamshire.   477

344   The dummy buckle: garnet with curved and stepped sides, and associated foil tray (type A1) from the large boss at the toe (Inv. 10).   477

345   The dummy buckle: theme of interlocked half-mushroom cells and residual cell forms shown with corresponding mushroom cell theme and residual cell from a pair of disc brooches from the burial of Queen Arnegunde at St Denis.   478

346   The dummy buckle: detail of the shoulders and loop.   479

347   The dummy buckle (Inv. 10): the empty cell at the toe from which the garnets and foil illustrated in figure 344 were removed.   480

348   The dummy buckle: details of the toe. (Photos: British Museum Research Laboratory)   480

349   Cell forms and patterns in the triangular zoomorphic mount (Inv. 18).   482

350   The triangular zoomorphic mount (Inv. 18).   483

351   The triangular zoomorphic mount: drawings and photographs of the small animal heads at the upper corners.   483

352   Cell-work details from the zoomorphic mount (Inv. 18) and a scabbard-boss (Inv. 26).   484

353   The plain gold strap-mount (Inv. 15): front, back and end views.   485

354   The small plain gold strap-end (Inv. 16).   486

355   The purse *in situ*, with other pieces from Area A. (Photo: M. Guido)   487

356   The purse: drawing based on figure 355 indicating the possible outline of the bag of the purse.   488

357   The purse-lid: oblique view of the frame as excavated and after straightening.   489

358   The purse-lid, as reconstructed in 1945.   490

359   The purse: cell forms and patterns used in the frame.   491

360   The purse-lid lying upside down in the ground, as drawn in the field by Stuart Piggott.   492

361   The purse: enlarged details of the central hinge and adjacent bar.   493

362   The purse: enlarged detail of the side hinge and the right-hand upper corner of the frame with a back view of the corresponding left-hand corner.   495

363   The purse: drawings showing, *inter alia*, cross-sections of the purse-lid as reconstructed in 1945 and in 1972.   496

364   Two decorative plaques: side views, Inv. 2(a) and Inv. 2(d). (Photo: British Museum Research Laboratory)   497

365   The purse-frame: enlarged detail of the back at the central point of the curved portion.   499

366   The empty purse frame: oblique view.   500

367   The purse-lid: an oblique view showing the decorative studs and plaques free-standing on the surface.   502

368   The purse: cell shapes and patterns of the zoomorphic double plaque, Inv. 2(b).   503

Figure 369   The purse: the front and back of the zoomorphic double plaque, Inv. 2(b), with radiograph print enlarged to the same scale.   504

370   The purse: basic and residual cell shapes of the hexagonal mounts (Inv. 2(c) and 2(d)).   506

371   The purse: cloisonné themes and patterns from the hexagonal mounts.   506

372   The purse: views of the fronts and backs of the hexagonal plaques, Inv. 2(c) and 2(d), with radiograph prints enlarged to the same scale.   507

373   The purse: millefiori details, inlay O with foil underlay and inlay Q.   508

374   The purse: cell forms and themes of the bird plaques, Inv. 2(e) and 2(f).   509

375   The purse: front and rear views of the two bird plaques, with radiograph prints.   510

376   Cell shapes and themes of the plaques depicting a man-between-beasts, Inv. 2(g) and 2(h).   512

377   The purse: front and back views of the two man-between-beasts plaques, with radiograph prints.   513

378   The purse: cell shapes and theme from the border of a stud.   515

379   The purse-lid: the four circular studs, Inv. 2(i)–(l). (Photo: British Museum Research Laboratory)   515

380   The purse: views of the fastening mechanism, with drawings to illustrate its operation.   516

381   Gold purse-lid inlaid with garnets and coloured glass from Apahida, near Cluj, Romania. (By courtesy of Professor K. Horedt)   518

382   Purses and purse mounts from München-Aubing, Köln-Mungersdorf and Harquency-Mülheim.   519

383   The leather purse from Krefeld-Gellep, grave 2268, reconstruction.   520

384   One of the burials of horses in pairs associated with the *Fürstengrab* at Beckum, Westphalia with the design of facing interlinked animals from the Sutton Hoo purse and shield-boss. (Photo and plan: W. Winkelmann, Westfälisches Landesmuseum für Vor- und Frühgeschichte, Münster)   521

385   The man-between-beasts motif as seen on a die from Torslunda, Öland and on the Sutton Hoo purse-lid.   522

386   The shoulder-clasps (Inv. 4 and 5), separated into halves.   524

387   The shoulder-clasps: cells of boar's head and leg in Inv. 4a, numbered to show distribution of foil-types A1 and B1.   524

388   The pair of shoulder-clasps (Inv. 4 and 5), cell forms and patterns.   525

389   Cell forms and patterns in the pair of shoulder-clasps.   526

390   The shoulder-clasps: design of two intersecting boars from the ends.   526

391   The shoulder-clasps: animal interlace designs from the border round the cloisonné panel of half-clasp (Inv. 4a).   528

392   The shoulder-clasps: side view showing attachment staples.   529

393   The shoulder-clasps: fastening-pin from one of the clasps, with details of the two pin-heads.   531

394   The breastplate of the muscle-cuirass from the statue of the Emperor Augustus at Prima Porta (By courtesy of the Vatican Museum).   533

395   Pair of curved bronze clasps with Style I ornament from Grumpan, Västergötland. (Photos: Statens Historiska Museum, Stockholm)   535

396   The great gold buckle (Inv. 1).   537

397   The great gold buckle: profile, with rear view and side view.   538

398   The great gold buckle: technical details of the locking mechanism.   539

399   The great gold buckle: three views of the bosses from the front, with their shanks.   541

400   The great gold buckle: details.   542

401   The great gold buckle: interior and exterior views.   544

402   The great gold buckle, with the backplate fully opened.   545

403   The great gold buckle: views of the loop and tongue.   547

404   The great gold buckle: views with tongue and loop removed.   548

405   The great gold buckle: details of zoomorphic designs of snakes with bird heads from the shoulders of the buckle.   549

406   The great gold buckle: animal ornament from the edges and toe.   551

407   The great gold buckle: details of animal heads, feet and hips.   553

408   Snake themes in interlace from the cup from Farthing Down, Surrey, the bronze mount from Vendel 1, the pyramid from Selsey, Sussex and from the sword hilt and the upper edge of the pommel from Crundale Down, Kent.   554

409   The great gold buckle: details of punch-work.   555

Figure 410   The great gold buckle: impression of the interior, showing a possible method of attachment of a belt to a block.   557

411   Sketches of reliquary buckles from Kaiseraugst, Wahlern-Elisried and Yverdon. (After Moosbrugger-Leu)   559

412   Silver and silver-gilt buckle from Crundale Down, Kent.   561

413   Drawings of the Crundale Down buckle.   562

414   Relief appliqué in the form of a fish from the Crundale Down buckle.   562

415   The large hanging-bowl (Inv. 40), showing the silver patch.   563

416   Three methods of sword suspension in use in the late Roman and early mediaeval periods.   566

417   The sword and scabbard from Valsgärde grave 7, Sweden. (Photos: Uppsala Universitets museum för nordiska fornsaker)   569

418   Suggested suspension method of the sword from Dirlewang 27 as worn: reconstruction by W. Menghin.   570

419   Reconstruction by H. Ament of the sword belts from Sutton Hoo, Altenerding, grave 674, St-Sulpice, grave 168, and Lauterhofen, grave 29.   571

420   Curved scabbard-mount from Donzdorf 66. (After Menghin)   572

421   Ten swords from Continental graves showing fittings of the scabbard and sword-belt as excavated. (After Menghin)   573

422   The Sutton Hoo sword-belt: suggested reconstruction by Ortwin Gamber.   576

423   The Sutton Hoo harness: suggested reconstruction.   578

424   The Sutton Hoo strap-mounts, buckles and other fittings as found in the ground, linked up to show how they relate to the reconstruction in figure 425.   579

425   The Sutton Hoo gold regalia as it may have been worn.   581

426   Details of sword-harnesses and fittings from a Late Saxon manuscript (BM Cotton Tiberius C VI) with bronze pyramidal mounts associated with sword 1 in Valsgärde grave 7.   582

427   Photomicrograph showing inclusions in a garnet from St Cuthbert's Cross. (Photo: British Museum Research Laboratory)   584

428   Shoulder-clasp (Inv. 4): apparent shapes and arrangement of glass rods used for millefiori inlays in the boars' hips (inlay K).   585

429   The shoulder-clasps and the purse-lid: key to the millefiori inlays.   586

430   Cell pattern on a glass inlay from the linked pins found at Roundway Down, Wiltshire.   596

431   Detail from the Kingston (Kent) brooch, showing imitation millefiori and zoomorphic filigree.   596

432   The Sutton Hoo jewellery: enlarged details of filigree.   604

433   The Sutton Hoo gold jewellery: enlarged details of filigree.   605

434   The Sutton Hoo shoulder-clasps: detail of filigree from the half-clasp Inv. 4a.   606

435   The shoulder-clasps: filigree details from Inv. 5a and b.   607

436   The shoulder-clasps: details of filigree.   608

437   The gold buckle from the Taplow barrow, Buckinghamshire: enlarged detail.   609

438   Gold filigree on the ring from Snape, Suffolk, the bird-buckle from Faversham, Kent, a brooch from Dover, Kent and the silver-gilt buckle from Crundale Down: enlarged details.   610

439   Time–fineness graph by Dr J. P. C. Kent showing the changing gold percentage content of Merovingian tremisses by decades from A.D. 580–700.   613

440   Sampling points for gold analyses of objects from the Sutton Hoo ship-burial.   619

441   Anglo-Saxon jewellery analysed for gold content, for comparison with the results from the Sutton Hoo jewellery.   620

442   Anglo-Saxon brooches from Kent analysed for gold content.   621

443   Sampling points for gold analyses of some of the pieces of Anglo-Saxon jewellery illustrated in figures 441 and 442.   622

LIST OF TABLES

———⇒✠⇐———

Table   1   Extracts from Inventory of Material from Sutton Hoo (1945)   *page* 12

2   Shields of the Vendel period from Valsgärde and Vendel, Sweden, showing the relationship between the lengths of the grip and grip extensions and shield diameter.   17

3   Result of analysis of a sample of gold leaf from the bird on the shield.   103

4   Metal analysis of the pins of the handgrip bosses of the shield.   108

5   Metal analysis of a sample from the grip extension of the shield.   109

6   Metal analysis of a sample from one of the bird heads from the grip extension.   109

7   Results of analyses of samples from three animal heads from the rim of the shield.   111

8   Results of analysis of a sample of gold foil from a rectangular panel from the rim of the shield.   112

9   Result of analysis of a sample of one of the hemispherical bosses on the front of the shield.   112

10   Result of analysis of a sample from the fragmentary boss from the shield.   113

11   Result of analysis of a sample of gold foil from a gold strip from the front of the shield.   113

12   Result of analysis of the shank of a rivet from the boss of the shield.   114

13   Result of analysis of a sample from the central disc of the boss.   114

14   Result of analysis of a sample from the gilt-bronze ring from the front of the shield.   116

15   Results of analyses of bronze components from the shield.   116

16   Results of analyses of gold foil from the shield.   117

17   Backing materials found in the shield.   117

18   Distribution of punch-marks on the shield.   119

19   Distribution of medium and large triangular punch-marks.   122

20   Dimensions of angon-heads.   265

21   Result of gold analyses for items associated with the sword.   306

22   Result of analysis of a sample from the stag.   385

23   The sceptre: result of analysis of a sample from the plain bronze loops on the iron ring.   387

24   The sceptre: results of analyses of bronze samples from the Y-piece of the iron ring.   388

25   The sceptre: results of analyses of bronze samples within the Y-piece of the iron ring.   388

26   The sceptre: results of analyses of bronze samples from the collar and pedestal foot.   389

27   The sceptre: result of analysis of a sample from the saucer-fitting.   389

28   The sceptre: result of analysis of a sample from the swaged bronze strips.   389

29   The sceptre: analyses of bronze components.   390

30   Analyses of bronze objects of the Dark Ages.   391

31   Results of gold analyses from the great gold buckle.   545

32   Strap widths and thicknesses accommodated by the plates and loops of the various gold mounts and buckles.   568

33   Weights of the gold items in the ship-burial, other than coins, blanks and ingots.   615

34   Analysis of inlays in the gold jewellery with numbers of covered cells.   617

35   Results of analyses of the jewellery (in percentages by weight).   624

36   Results of analyses of early Anglo-Saxon gold jewellery from other sites (in percentage by weight).   625

PREFACE

VOLUME II covers those items in the burial deposit that may be classified under the headings of *Arms, Armour* and *Regalia.*

The categories *arms* and *armour* include the shield (chs. I and II), the helmet (ch. III), the mailcoat (ch. IV), the spears and angons (ch. V) and the sword (ch. VI). The scramasax (a one-edged long knife or sword) referred to in earlier literature and in *Sutton Hoo* Volume I (pp. 179, 200, 463, 538 and fig. 355), where it appears in the Inventory (p. 441) under the number 97, has proved in the final analysis, thanks to an observation by Miss Angela Evans, to be a spear-head. It is included in chapter V with the spears and angons, and its inventory number is retained in spite of the change of category. This identification has solved some difficulties in the appraisal of the burial deposit— why, for example, the 'scramasax' wholly lacked the ornamental features and decorative sheath-fittings often associated with scramasaxes in many rich Continental mainland and northern burials, when the sword that lay beside it is brilliantly furnished with mounts and associated fitments of gold. The identification also simplifies problems associated with the assembly of the gold harness and the roles played by the minor pieces of jewellery (ch. X, sec. 4), since allowance need no longer be made in the design of the belt or belts for the possible wearing of a scramasax.

The category *regalia* includes the stone sceptre (ch. VII); an inferred wood, bone or ivory rod with ornamental features, presumably a rod of rank or office (ch. VIII); the tall iron stand with a spike at the bottom which, although deprived of the stag once thought to surmount it, may still be a kind of standard (ch. IX); and the gold jewellery, regarded as part of a ceremonial outfit rather than as items of personal adornment.

Vital work of revision and reconstruction has gone into the most important pieces described in this volume, notably the helmet, shield and sceptre.[1] The new reconstructions are here fully documented, the evidence for each aspect of the reconstructions being set out, and the margins of uncertainty made clear, so that readers will be able to judge the reconstructions critically. It gives me great pleasure to pay a special tribute here to the exceptional work of Mr Nigel Williams, Senior Conservation Officer, in connection with the creation of the new versions of the helmet and shield.

[1] The measurements given in this volume are exact as far as the condition of the material permits. If any discrepancy is noted between these figures and those given in the Inventory in Volume I, the figures in Volume II will be authoritative.

In preparing this volume I am very greatly indebted to the help and guidance provided in every respect by the Research Assistants on the Sutton Hoo team—Miss Angela Care Evans, F.S.A., Mrs Katherine East and Mrs Susan Youngs. They have read the text critically and made many helpful suggestions. Our colleagues in the Research Laboratory have been of great assistance throughout, as the scientific contributions to the volume indicate. Mr Andrew Oddy, F.S.A., of the Research Laboratory has helped us extensively in connection with conservation problems and all scientific requirements. My wife, formerly Miss Marilyn Luscombe, supervised the colour photography and prepared an initial descriptive account of the gold jewellery, which included numerous interesting observations subsequently incorporated in the jewellery chapter.

Help from foreign colleagues in the form of photographs and information is acknowledged at appropriate points in the text. I would particularly express the Trustees' thanks to Professor G. Arwidsson (Stockholm), Professor J. Werner (Munich) and M. Albert France-Lanord (Nancy); and to Drs Birgit Arrhenius and Agneta Lundström (Stockholm), Dr Wilhelm Winkelmann (Münster), and Dr K. Horedt (Cluj), Dr H. Dannheimer (Munich), Dr H. Ament (Frankfurt), and Dr H. Erden (Mainz), Dr H. Vierck (Münster). The authorities of the Römisch Germanisches Zentralmuseum, Mainz, particularly Dr Konrad Weidemann, have been unfailingly helpful, and I am indebted to them for letting me have prints from their negatives of late Roman helmets and for supplying a facsimile of the leather purse from the Krefeld-Gellep grave, figure 383. I am also much indebted to Dr Renate Pirling (Krefeld) and Professor Bertil Almgren (Uppsala), and to Mr H. Russell Robinson, F.S.A., of the Royal Armouries in the Tower of London, for advice in connection with the helmet and arms and armour generally.

Mr John Hopkins, M.A., the Librarian of the Society of Antiquaries, and his staff, have been most helpful over bibliographical problems, as have the staff of a number of other libraries.

The drawings in Volume II are the work of the Museum's chief illustrator, Miss M. O. Miller, and of the full-time illustrator in the Sutton Hoo unit, Mr Eric Eden, with assistance from Mr Michael Grogan.

The British Museum   *Rupert Bruce-Mitford*
June 1976

CHAPTER I

THE SHIELD

—————⟪✦⟫—————

1. *Introduction and primary accounts of discovery*

I   THE STATE OF THE REMAINS IN THE GROUND, AND THE EVIDENCE AVAILABLE FOR RECONSTRUCTION

THE SHIELD as found lay flat in the burial deposit. It was close to the western end wall of the chamber, with its centre slightly to the north of the keel-line (fig. 1). Its condition as it was uncovered by the excavators is illustrated in plate 24b; by photographs (figs. 2–4) and by the elucidatory drawing, figure 5. The coloured plan (pl. 24b), and the corresponding areas of the 'fair copies' of the burial deposit plan in colour prepared by Stuart Piggott in 1939 (plans 7 and 8)[1] are the sole graphic record of the shield remains in the ground.

Extracts from Phillips's diary referring to the shield, together with relevant passages from his log and from his published report,[2] are given below. These are valuable first-hand evidence, subject to the proviso that phenomena are not always recognised in the process of excavation for what they really are, so that Phillips's account has to be used critically, in the light of subsequent knowledge.

The above records, written and graphic, are supplemented by nine photographs of the shield in the ground taken by O. G. S. Crawford. These are indispensable for the interpretation of the plan (fig. 5), and they supply a great deal of additional and indeed crucial information.

In plate 24b the excavators' packing-numbers (IV.6, IV.13, etc.) are attached to individual elements on the plan. As each box thus marked by the excavators was opened in the British Museum Research Laboratory in 1945 a brief description of the contents was made by the Laboratory staff. The list made then is printed here (table 1). Questions of identity and mistaken identity of fragments will arise in the discussion that follows. With the exception of clearly recognisable features, such as the winged dragon, the central boss, or the grip extensions, the location in the ground of individual elements of the shield can only be established or confirmed by means of this list, used as a key to the numbers on the plan (pl. 24b), and it is thus vital in the reconstruction process. Identifications are made using photographs, packing

---

[1] For a discussion of these plans see *Sutton Hoo*, Vol. I, 141–2. [2] Phillips 1940a, 165.

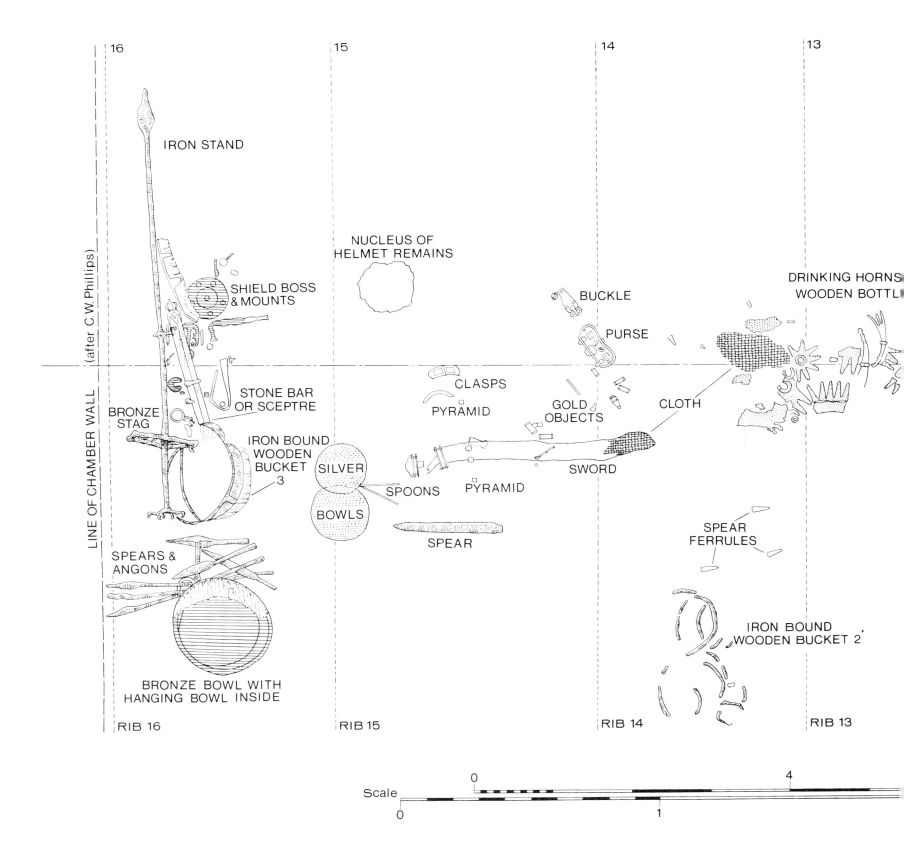

16   15   14   13

(after C.W. Phillips)

IRON STAND

NUCLEUS OF
HELMET REMAINS

DRINKING HORNS
WOODEN BOTTL

BUCKLE

SHIELD BOSS
& MOUNTS

PURSE

LINE OF CHAMBER WALL

CLASPS

STONE BAR
OR SCEPTRE

PYRAMID

GOLD
OBJECTS

CLOTH

BRONZE
STAG

IRON BOUND
WOODEN
BUCKET
3

SILVER

PYRAMID

SWORD

SPOONS

BOWLS

SPEAR FERRULES

SPEAR

SPEARS &
ANGONS

IRON BOUND
WOODEN BUCKET 2

BRONZE BOWL WITH
HANGING BOWL INSIDE

RIB 16   RIB 15   RIB 14   RIB 13

Scale 0   4
       0   1

FIGURE 1   The Sutton Hoo ship-burial: plan of the burial deposit.

2

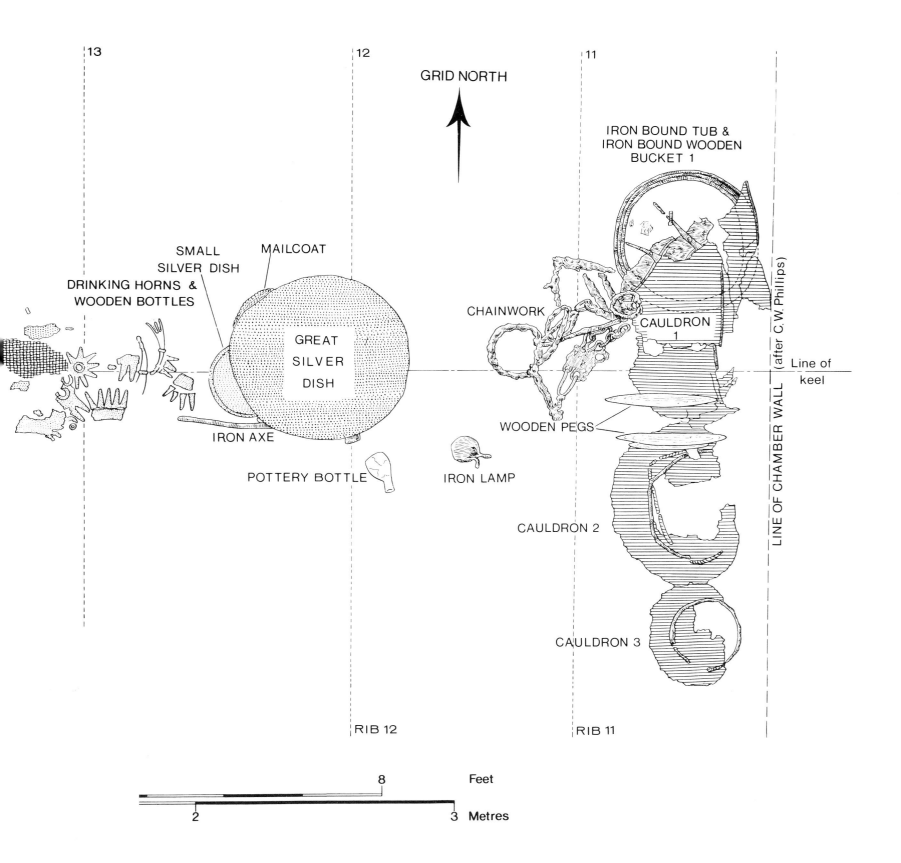

13

12

11

GRID NORTH

IRON BOUND TUB &
IRON BOUND WOODEN
BUCKET 1

SMALL
SILVER DISH

MAILCOAT

DRINKING HORNS &
WOODEN BOTTLES

CHAINWORK

GREAT
SILVER
DISH

CAULDRON
1

IRON AXE

WOODEN PEGS

POTTERY BOTTLE

IRON LAMP

CAULDRON 2

CAULDRON 3

LINE OF CHAMBER WALL (after C. W. Phillips)

Line of
keel

RIB 12

RIB 11

8   Feet

2   3   Metres

3

list and plan together. W. F. Grimes's brief account of his salvage work on it in the field, which contains useful observations as to its physical condition, completes the evidence (p. 11).

Even with these records reconstruction is difficult and not every feature of the shield can be recaptured. Without the excavation photographs the task of reconstruction would be impossible. Plate 24 *b*, valuable though it is, provides no more than a partial plan, and is inevitably an imperfect record because at that stage the nature and even the shape of what was being drawn was often not clear. It corresponds closely with the photograph, figure 2. Many of the elements of the shield cannot be recognised on any plan or photograph.

Figures 2, 3 and 4 are three views of the shield in the ground, each taken from a different angle. As analysed in section 3v (p. 36 below) and in figure 30 they make it possible for us to reconstruct the sequence of movements to which the shield remains were subjected in the ground; and they illustrate the highly confused state of the remains, as a result of which careful analysis is necessary before any feature of the shield, except the boss and its attachments, can be assigned to its original position on the shield-board.

We cannot say whether or not the burial party had placed the shield upright[1] against the end wall of the chamber, but it seems clear at least that before its disintegration began the shield had assumed the horizontal position in which it was found, even if this were not its position from the outset. The boss, as Phillips's account implies, had dropped through the shield-board to a lower level. This fact alone might be taken as evidence for curvature of the shield-board. Had the shield been flat it is doubtful whether there would have been a large enough cavity below it for the boss to disappear into.[2] The boss remained the right way up and the rest of the shield, although laterally compressed and driven inwards, remained centred upon it. This could only have happened with the shield lying flat. Had the shield collapsed whilst standing vertically its remains would have been in an even more chaotic state than they were when found; all displacement can be logically explained by detectable lateral movements that took place subsequent to its disintegration when in a horizontal position (p. 38 ff. and fig. 30).

It will be seen from plate 24 *b* and figure 5 that the shield-rim to the left of the boss had been pushed back into a long, thin, almost straight-sided loop. The straight line effect can be seen again to the right of the boss; and this straightness and, on the extreme right, rectangularity in the visible outline, together with the apparent lack of any connection between the rim elements and the underlying boss, led the excavators to mistake the shield-board for a wooden tray (fig. 5 shows a further length of shield-

---

[1] Cf. the shields in the rich Morken chamber grave and in Niederstotzingen, grave 9 (Böhner 1959; Paulsen 1967).

[2] Much would depend on whether the ship had bottom boards, or whether the flooring of the burial chamber, or the platform on which the body (if present) and centrally placed grave-goods lay, extended far enough to underlie the shield. Had such flooring collapsed, or had there been no flooring, the shield would probably have spanned adjacent ribs and the boss could have sunk in the space between the ribs.

4

FIGURE 2 The shield: the remains *in situ*. The ornamented iron boss lies tilted towards the bottom of the picture. The winged dragon can be seen to the left of the boss, while to the right and slightly below lies one of the small gilt-bronze hemispherical bosses and the tip of one of the handgrip extensions. To the left of the dragon the distorted shield-rim is visible and also to the left, above the iron boss, are the second handgrip extension and the strap-hanger. (Photo: O. G. S. Crawford)

rim to the north of the boss, on an east–west alignment, based on an addition to the Piggott plan by Phillips; diary entry for 21 August, see p. 8). Because of their freedom from the boss and grip extensions, which had fallen to a lower level, and perhaps because certain fittings had fallen off the back of the board or become loose, the board and its surface appliqués, when lateral pressure was applied, moved to a considerable extent independently of these basic fittings. Figure 5 shows to what extent the fittings were found lying outside the limits of the inward-driven board as defined by its rim. The reconstruction process consists in interpreting and identifying individual features; working out from where, in view of movements in the ground, they have come; and restoring them to their original positions in relation to the boss and grip extensions.[1]

II PRIMARY ACCOUNTS OF THE DISCOVERY[2]

(1) *Extracts from C. W. Phillips's Excavation Diary*

Sunday July 23, 1939 '... The partition [the west end wall of the chamber] was seen to have consisted of planks laid horizontally edge to edge one above the other to make a vertical wall. Naturally only the two lowest planks were observed, and these had been pressed into the burial chamber to a depth of nine inches eastwards.[3] ... In removing the whetstone remains of wood decorated with gold leaf over hollow clay cores and strips of decorated gold leaf were observed. Their condition was very bad and their examination was deferred until the area could be approached with more ease and safety.'

Friday July 28, 1939 'The day was devoted to the complete clearance of the western end of the burial deposit.

A large shield boss (IV.8) was revealed by brushing the western edge of the burial deposit. *A long strip of wood edged with gold leaf, with gold leaf panels of interlace decoration and the wood itself panelled out into impressed (?) rectangles partly overlay the boss on the western side and extended further to the north and south* (IV.6). It was of generally similar character to the aforementioned strip,[4] but was probably not part of the same object. Other small pieces of generally similar character (IV.10, IV.16) were found, IV.16 to the south-west of the boss, underlying IV.9 described below, and IV.10 to the north-east.

There were four bronze zoomorphic mountings with gilt hemispherical bosses and facings near the shield-boss. IV.9 lay to the south-west face downwards. It consisted of a central spine with zoomorphic head and side volutes at the base of which was a circular gold-leaf covered boss of

---

[1] The 184 surviving fragments of the shield, or items each comprising a number of fragments, are individually described, numbered and drawn in a checklist in typescript begun in 1963 by Mrs V. H. Fenwick (nos. 1–107) and continued by Miss E. Pye (nos. 108–84). A copy of this list is kept with the material in reserve. Only crucial fragments are illustrated and discussed here.

[2] Throughout this section various passages have been put into italics for emphasis. R.B.-M.

[3] The full extent of this movement can now be shown to have been as much as 46 cm (p. 39, n. 2).

[4] Apparently the strips referred to on 23 July.

FIGURE 3 The shield: the remains *in situ*. In the foreground part of the shield-rim and the strap-hanger are clearly visible. Above the strap-hanger, part of the broken handgrip extension can be seen sticking up in relation to the general lie of the remaining features. The dragon and the iron boss are in the background. (Photo: O. G. S. Crawford)

FIGURE 4 The shield: detail of the remains *in situ*. To the right of the iron boss, the angle of the broken handgrip extension can be clearly seen. To the right of the handgrip extension and slightly above lies the strap-hanger. (Photo: O. G. S. Crawford)

similar type to IV.2. IV.7 lay to the south-east of the boss and roughly at right angles to IV.9. It was face upwards, and near it, on the south, was IV.15, another boss, lying upside down. IV.11 lay on its edge to the north of the boss. It was much corroded and damaged. It was decorated on both faces, but the gold leaf mounted face and boss were to the west.

Beneath IV.11 and obliquely to it was IV.12, a similar mount to IV.9 except that the boss, instead of being at the base, was immediately behind the zoomorphic terminal. The mounting [IV.13] was face downwards. Beneath IV.12 again were several fragments of embossed gold leaf mounted on thin wood of generally similar character to IV.6.

The whole area surrounding the shield boss was covered with thin wood exhibiting a silky texture, but hopelessly contorted.

IV.7 was partly covered at its east end by a big piece of wood.'

Monday August 21, 1939 '. . . Otherwise the main feature of the day was more local clearing in which it was found that a fragment of the elongated thin wooden object with gold leaf edge-binding and gesso zoomorphic decorations [i.e. the shield-rim] continued from the north end where it was last seen during the removal of the burial material, turned a right angle, and ran east for nine inches before finally petering out. The remains were in the usual desperately bad condition but were removed.'[1]

[1] This entry explains the addition to Piggott's field record made by Phillips (Phillips 1940a, pl. xxxvii) and recorded in the archaeological plan, *Sutton Hoo*, Vol. 1, fig. 112; here figs. 5, 30.

(2) *Extracts relating to the shield from C. W. Phillips's first continuous account* (*prior to publication in* Antiquaries Journal)

'Partially under the N. edge of this bucket (bucket no. 3) and stretching along the east side of the line of the "lampstand" [the iron stand] was a miscellany of objects comprising a large ornamented whetstone, a large bronze shield boss, bronze and gilt mounts of various kinds from the shield, a small bronze figure of a stag mounted on an iron ring and *some tantalizing remains of a large and fragile wooden object like a thin tray or gaming board* (?) *lavishly decorated with gold leaf enrichment round the edges and gesso zoomorphic work.* This was in a hopeless condition, but appeared to have lain on top of the other objects, and especially on top of the shield. The remains of its wood exhibited a silky surface very unlike that of any other wood found in the burial.

There were signs that in the collapse the lower part of the W. wall had bulged into the chamber leaning over all these objects north of the Coptic bowl.'

(3) *Extracts from C. W. Phillips's first published report* (Phillips 1940a)

THE TRAY

'East of the flambeau and partly under and to the north and east of the whetstone was perhaps the most difficult complex of objects in the whole grave. It consisted of objects in which both wood and metal were used, and with the complete decay of almost all the wood their interpretation must be uncertain until all the finds have been completely examined. The essentials of the deposit were the remains of a grandiose and very decorative shield, probably a parade piece, upon which there were the remains of what appears to be a sub-rectangular (?) tray-like object *elaborately decorated round the edge with gold-leaf work on gesso as well as impressed rectangles which may have been produced by poker-work.* The dimensions of this affair was at least 2 ft. × 1 ft. [61 × 30·5 cm], and all its central and eastern parts were missing, assuming that it was really rectangular to begin with.

Among the wreckage of this 'tray' and the shield there were a few pieces of gold-leaf covered wood which did not appear to belong to either, but rather to some sort of small box, but it would be difficult to imagine anything much more fragile than these wafer-thin pieces of rotted wood decorated with gesso and gold leaf which was liable to curl off the moment after the uncovering of the object. . . .

To deal with the 'tray'-remains first, since they definitely overlay those of the shield, an interesting point was that its wood was little thicker than card and had a silky sheen on its surface. *The edge had a continuous plain beading of thin gesso covered with gold leaf, and at intervals there were heads of animals in low relief on gesso also covered with gold leaf, projecting at right angles from the beading* beautifully executed with tiny round inset eyes made of garnet discs backed by *pointillé* gold leaf. *The 'poker-work' rectangles formed a continuous band along the edge of the 'tray' between the animal heads* and as far as anything of the field of the object could be seen at all it appeared to be plain wood. Making every allowance for decay it seems certain that this was always a fragile object, and for this reason alone it would not appear to have been either a gaming board or any part of the shield. In the east part of the 'tray' region a few featureless flakes of what is probably ivory were found when cleaning up the area later.'[1]

THE SHIELD

'This contained no recognizable traces of its board work, but consisted of a great bronze boss in an upright position surrounded by elaborate mounts tumbled about, all obviously disturbed by the fall.

[1] Fragments of the gaming-pieces, Inv. 172 (*Sutton Hoo*, Vol. I, 444).

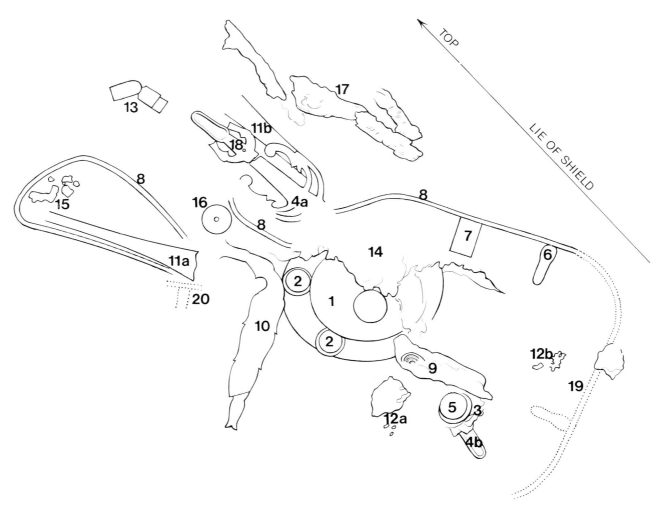

1   Shield boss
2   Flange bosses
3   Wooden underlay for foil strip
4   (a and b) Grip extensions
5   Gilt-bronze boss from a
    gold strip
6   Peripheral animal head in
    position
7   Gold foil panel
8   Shield rim

9   Bird head and leg
10 Dragon
11 (a and b) Two pieces of a
    gold foil strip
12 (a) Gold foil fragments (IV 10)
12 (b) Gold foil fragments
13 Bronze strap-mounts
14 Shield board wood
    overlying the boss
15 Fragments of a gilt-bronze boss

16 Gilt-bronze boss from a gold
    strip, upside down
17 Iron concretions, not
    connected with the shield
18 Rivet hole in grip extension
19 Further length of shield rim
    described by Phillips
20 Gilt rim fragment and
    ?animal head

FIGURE 5 Explanatory drawing based on figure 2 identifying the
elements of the shield as seen in the photographs.

The central boss is an object of great size and weight of domed form with a circular stud at the apex, whose form and decoration is not yet known. The main body of the boss has an elaborate interlace in good condition. . . . and there appear to be signs of gold-leaf enrichment. The boss rim carries five large symmetrically disposed domed studs, and the iron hand grip behind has almost completely rusted away.'

(4) *Extracts from W. F. Grimes, ' The salvaging of the finds'* (Grimes 1940)

'The greater part of 28 July was devoted to what was perhaps the most intricate piece of cleaning, that of the remains of the shield. The central feature was the massive boss, which was solid and unlikely to cause trouble. But radiating irregularly from it were several richly decorated bronze mounts. Some of almost paper thinness, some face upwards, some reversed, at all angles and presenting a picture of complete confusion. . . . To add to the difficulties this complex was partly covered with the remains of a fine wooden object ornamented with gold leaf. None of the material of the shield itself appeared to remain. The *umbo* was lifted without difficulty, but freeing the various adhesions of the mounts was a slow and tedious business. Each was lifted separately on two or more trowels after it had been drawn in on the plan.'

2. *General description of the reconstruction*

Plate 1 and figure 6 show the front and back of the shield as reconstructed in 1972. It is circular. The shield-board, like a watch-glass, is curved back at the edges but flat in the middle (fig. 7). The curvature of the outer parts of the board would tend to envelop the body and provide added protection; the edge is bound and reinforced with a metal rim.

I THE FRONT OF THE SHIELD (fig. 6*a* and pl. 1)

On the convex side is mounted a large dome-shaped central boss of iron, covered with many elaborate gilt-bronze embellishments. Five large hemispherical gilt-bronze ornamental rivet-heads occur, evenly spaced, on the flange of the boss. They are the heads of the rivets that attach the boss to the shield-board. Above the central boss, at the top of the shield as carried, are three hemispherical bosses of gilt-bronze, of the same size and appearance as the large rivet-heads of the central boss, arranged in an inverted triangle. Below the central boss is a similar small hemispherical boss of gilt-bronze. This boss and the lowest of the triangle of three are equidistant above and below the central boss; each appears at the centre of a long, horizontally set ornamental gold strip which tapers at each end. Below the lower of these two strips at the bottom of the shield there is a similar but shorter strip, at the centre of which is mounted a gilt-bronze casting having the general form of a sword-ring (figs. 6*a* and 93).

These motifs on the front of the shield are related to its vertical ornamental axis, and their position is determined by the alignment of the handgrip and its extensions on the back (fig. 8). They are, therefore, like the handgrip, slightly off centre. The small bosses at the centre of the tapering strips are the heads of rivets which fasten

TABLE I EXTRACTS FROM 'INVENTORY OF MATERIAL FROM SUTTON HOO'[1]

Reference no.	Description	Comments by H. Maryon with subsequent comments by R. Bruce-Mitford, and annotations taken from Stuart Piggott's plan of area IV
Area IV.11	Gold complex spiral, hemisphere etc. (very frail)	1. This must be the remains of the bird, and the hemisphere behind it (H.M.) 2. 'On edge facing east, boss face west, gold leaf on under (W) face. Under it was a similar mount to IV.9, also face downwards, and connected with IV.12.' (Endorsement on field plan by Stuart Piggott. This must be the small boss from the back of the shield at the base of the grip extension. R.B-M.)
IV.16	Gold leaf complex	This lies under the whetstone and is a piece of the gold strip. See Laboratory photographs (H.M.)
IV.15	Gilt copper hemisphere and fragments	'Face downwards' (S.P.)
IV.12	Gilt copper hemisphere and large fragments	'Face downwards' (S.P.) but the photographs show the boss (hemisphere) to be right way up—the 'fragments' (grip extensions) face downwards (R.B-M.)
IV.2	Pyramidal stud	Far to the south, near hanger. (H.M.) Phillips's Diary for 28 July suggests there was a gold boss in IV.2 (p. 8 above) (R.B-M.)
IV.14	Three pieces of bronze, one with handle attachment	At extreme south of complex. Fitting anchoring end of narrow strap (H.M.), and one mount from the broader tooled strap (R.B-M.)
IV	Pyramidal stud attached to gilt copper hemisphere	There is no way of identifying this important element (fig. 20) on the plan (R.B-M.)
IV.3	Bronze evidently related to area IV.2, 6, 17 and 2 below	
IV.2	Gold complex	U channelling (i.e. bronze shield-rim. H.M.)
IV.6	Gold complex	U channelling (H.M.)
IV.17	Gold fragments in glass-covered box	U channelling (H.M.) This comment by Maryon probably refers to the T-shaped element (pl. 24b and fig. 2) which was included in 'IV.17' as well as the foil strip (R.B-M.)
IV.2	Gold band complex (fragment of gold leaf)	U channelling (H.M.)
IV.6	Gold complex with garnets (very frail)	Probably a dragon head and edging (R.B-M.)
IV.9	Gold object with garnets and gilt hemisphere	Grip extension and attached gilt boss (R.B-M.) 'Face downwards' (S.P.)
IV.13	Gold complex (very frail)	Presumably wood, foil etc., attached to IV.12 (R.B-M.)
IV.12	Gold object (see area IV.9)	Apparently a second item from this box (see above). The reference to IV.9 indicates that it is part of the grip extension: 'face downwards' would then be correct (R.B-M.)
IV.10	Frail gold fragments	Not a boss (H.M.). Probably either part of a gold-foil strip, or a rim panel (R.B-M.)
IV.17	Gold complex (a powdery mass: very frail)	Gold-foil strip (R.B-M.)

The following items are not included in this unpacking list:

IV.1 Unidentified: drawn as though iron (i.e. coloured black) and described as 'iron fastening'. Probably not shield. (R.B-M.)

IV.7 Dragon.

IV.8 Shield-boss.

IV.5 Stag.

[1] An unpacking list compiled in 1945 in the Research Laboratory.

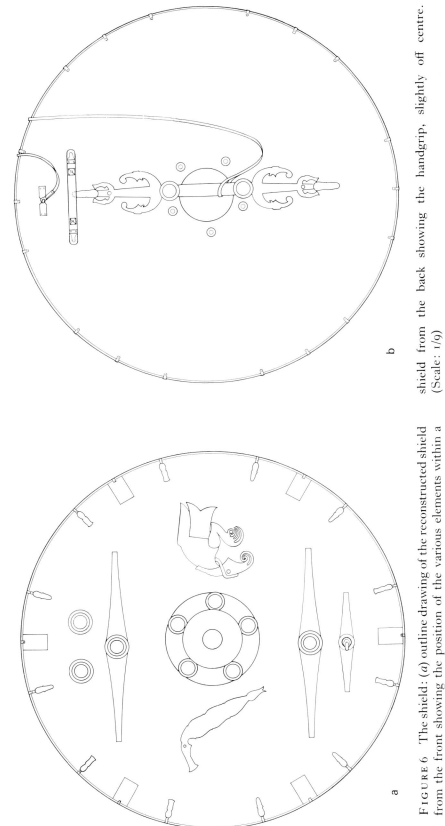

b

a

FIGURE 6 The shield: (*a*) outline drawing of the reconstructed shield from the front showing the position of the various elements within a 91·5 cm (36 in.) rim diameter; (*b*) outline drawing of the reconstructed shield from the back showing the handgrip, slightly off centre. (Scale: 1/9)

13

FIGURE 7 The reconstructed shield: cross-section. (Scale: 1/6)

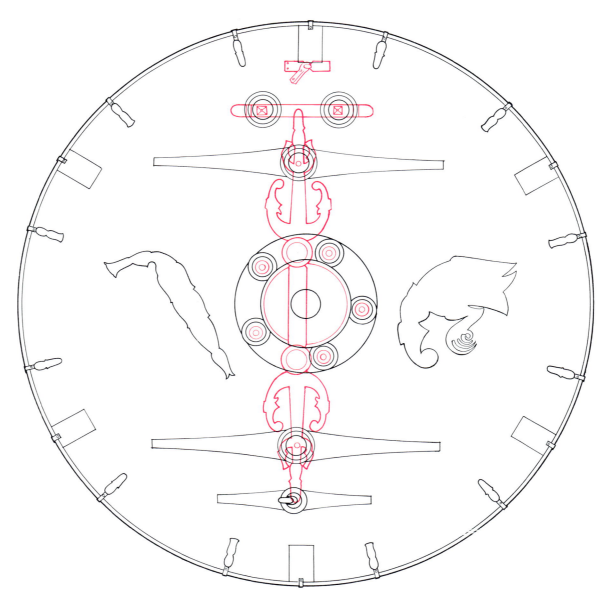

FIGURE 8 The reconstructed shield: drawing showing the relationship of the features on the front of the shield (in black) to those on the back (in red). (Scale: 1/6)

14

the grip extensions on the back of the shield to the shield-board. On the decorated gilt-bronze surface of the grip extensions, at the back of the shield, the ends of these same rivet-shanks are finished off as small domed studs (pl. 6a).

Two striking devices complete the treatment of the central flat area of the shield-board: the figures of a winged dragon and of an eagle or hawk, both in flight (pls. 1, 2 and 3). The dragon is entirely in cast bronze. Only the head and leg of the bird are cast; the rest was executed in thin gold foil mounted on cut-out wooden shapes. This only partial use of casting for the bird figure is an original feature of the design and does not indicate damage or loss.

All the elements so far described on the front of the shield lie on the flat central area of the board. The rim region or edge of the shield, which curves backwards, is decorated round the circumference with twelve inward-facing animal heads cast in two designs. Rectangular panels of zoomorphic interlace in gold foil, with their long axes pointing inwards, are spaced between them. From fragments of gold foil that survive and are believed to come from these peripheral panels two slightly different designs can be reconstructed (p. 82 ff., figs. 64–66). It is possible, indeed it seems probable, in the light of observations made at the time of excavation by Phillips, that there were originally twelve of these foil panels, although the surviving fragments do not represent more than six, as shown in the 1972 reconstruction (pl. 1, fig. 6a). A drawing of the shield showing twelve foil panels, which may well give the true aspect of the shield, is provided in figure 29.

II   THE BACK OF THE SHIELD (fig. 6b)

On the back of the shield an iron handgrip crosses the opening of the central boss and this grip is extended in a straight line out across the shield-board above and below the boss, in the form of an iron strip which is covered over and developed ornamentally with gilt-bronze. The grip, and consequently its extensions, are set off-centre (fig. 8). Each extension terminates in a cast bronze animal head and has identical decorative pendant projecting animal and bird heads on each side.

In addition to the grip and its extensions, the back of the shield bears metal fittings for straps both for carrying the shield on horseback and for hanging it up when not in use (p. 69 ff.).

3. *Detailed discussion of the reconstruction*

I   SIZE

Because of its compressed state (figs. 2–4) it was not possible to establish the diameter of the shield by excavation alone, as it has been in the cases of several of the Vendel-period shields in the Valsgärde boat-graves.[1] Very little of the Sutton Hoo shield-board

[1] Cf. Arwidsson 1954, Abb. 32, 33 and *Sutton Hoo*, Vol. I, figs. 369, 372.

remained in solid form, as the excavators' accounts cited above make clear, although wood was preserved here and there, particularly where closely associated with metal fittings. This has enabled the placing of several of these fittings in relation to the grain of the wood to be determined, and in one instance has given us the thickness of the board (fig. 20). The woods employed for the shield-board and for the cut-out surface underlays on which most, if not all, of the applied gold-foil sheeting was mounted, have been identified as lime and alder (p. 127 ff.).

The fact that the shield was circular is established by the surviving fragments of its gilt metal rim (fig. 9) and by impressions of the rim in certain pieces of wood not belonging to the shield.[1] The two largest fragments of rim are no more than 5·2 and 5·7 cm long and these only allow the diameter to be calculated approximately. These two pieces, when the curves are drawn out, do not give identical results. One fragment, that used by Plenderleith and Maryon in 1945 to determine the diameter in the first reconstruction, has a curvature which gives a diameter of 83·8 cm (33 in.); the other gives a diameter of 96·6 cm (38 in.).[2] The new reconstruction (1972) has been built with a diameter in between these two figures, at 91·5 cm (36 in.).

FIGURE 9 The shield: the two largest surviving fragments of the gilt-bronze rim. (Scale: 1/1)

Various factors influenced us in choosing this intermediate figure. The 83·8 cm diameter (33 in.) proves to be the smallest practicable size for the elements, decorative and functional, that have to be accommodated. The largest diameter (96·6 cm, 38 in.) gives a more spacious visual effect, but the extra 12·5 cm (5 in.) implies greater depth in the curvature of the shield, and so additional thickness in the block of wood from which the boards were cut. This may have been the true size of the shield, but the compromise diameter (91·5 cm, 36 in.), while giving a comfortable visual distribution of ornamental features, would involve less wastage of wood, and the shield would be lighter to carry.

The diameter of a shield may be expected to be appreciably in excess of the overall length of the grip and its extensions (in the Sutton Hoo shield, only 63·5 cm). Little evidence to demonstrate this is available from Anglo-Saxon graves, since there is no shield that can be reliably restored, and grip extensions in Anglo-Saxon shields show minimal development. Since the Sutton Hoo shield, as suggested in the subsequent discussion (p. 91 ff.), is not Anglo-Saxon but in all its essential characteristics an East

---

[1] Notably the fragment numbered 94 J4 (12) (maplewood, and thought to be part of the lyre) in which gold leaf traces remain in the depression left by the shield-rim. The registration number was allotted at a time when the fragment was believed to belong to the shield (Inv. 94).

[2] Maryon's statement (1946, 21 ff.) that the rim fragments all exactly fitted a circle of 33 in. diameter is inaccurate.

16

TABLE 2 SHIELDS OF THE VENDEL PERIOD FROM VALSGÄRDE AND VENDEL, SWEDEN, AND SUTTON HOO AS RESTORED, SHOWING THE RELATIONSHIP BETWEEN THE LENGTHS OF GRIP AND GRIP EXTENSIONS AND SHIELD DIAMETER

Burial	Length of grip extensions	Shield diameter	Difference	Distance between grip extension terminations and rim
Valsgärde 6				
Shield 1	53 cm	95 cm (minimum)	42 cm	21 cm
Valsgärde 7*				
Shield 1	fragmentary	96 cm	unknown	unknown
Shield 2	71·5 cm	108 cm	36 cm	17·5 cm
Shield 3	57 cm	100 cm	43 cm	19 cm unmounted
Valsgärde 8				
Shield 1	69 cm	110 cm	41 cm	20·5 cm
Shield 2	70 cm	108 cm	38 cm	19 cm
Sutton Hoo				
(as restored, 1973)	63·5 cm	91·5 cm	28 cm	14 cm
Vendel 1		115 cm (41 in.)		

* By kind courtesy of Professor Greta Arwidsson, in anticipation of her own publication.

Scandinavian shield of Vendel type, it is directly relevant to compare the factor we are considering in the reconstruction (shield diameter in relation to length of grip and extensions) with this factor in its East Scandinavian counterparts from the Valsgärde cemetery. The relatively recent Vendel 12 shield reconstruction[1] may also be taken into consideration, in spite of the fact that it is based largely on the evidence of the Valsgärde shields.

For the Sutton Hoo shield, we know that we must add to the length of its grip and extensions at least twice the length of the rectangular gold-foil panels that were spaced round the rim (p. 29 ff.). These panels, set with their long axes pointing radially inwards towards the shield-boss, need not have fallen on the alignment of the grip and its extensions (as they are shown to do in our drawing, fig. 8) but, even if they were staggered in relation to it, they were carried, like the peripheral animal heads, wholly on the backward curving rim zone and it is clear that this backward curve of the shield board only began at the extreme limits of the grip extension (fig. 7).

The relationship between the fittings on the front and the back of the shield is shown in figure 8 where the grip, grip extensions and suspension devices on the back are superimposed (in red) on the fittings of the front. The functions of the three small bosses grouped together in the upper part of the front of the shield can be seen. In considering the shield diameter in relation to the fittings of the back, it will be seen that space is needed between the end of the grip extensions and the rim, and clear of the transverse hanging-up strap, for the small metal fitting that anchors the narrow shoulder-strap (p. 72, figs. 56 and 57) to be fitted in. The general location in the ground

[1] See Lindqvist 1950a.

of the anchor-fitting and of the two strap-ends from the transverse hanging-up strap, in line with the grip extension, can be seen in figure 5 (no. 13) and in figures 2–4.

As figure 11 shows, the under-surfaces of the two gilt-bronze animal-head terminals of the grip extensions begin to curve backwards.[1] There can be no doubt of this curve, since the two terminal heads are castings in sound condition (pl. 6, fig. 11). At this point above and below the boss, then, the shield-board began to curve back; and from there outwards a gradual curve may be envisaged to complete a rim to accommodate the rectangular foil panels and the cast animal heads comfortably. Nothing smaller than 84 cm (33 in.) is practicable. The diameter of 91·5 cm (36 in.) selected for the reconstruction avoids an appearance of congestion. The largest size, 96·6 cm (38 in.), gives a slightly more spacious effect, but, as has already been said, it would imply the use of a deeper block of wood from which to cut the boards which made up the shield and would increase its weight.[2]

It may be argued that if only one of the two rim fragments is distorted then the 84 cm (33 in.) indicated by the curvature of the one, or the 96·6 cm (38 in.) indicated by the curvature of the other, will be correct, and that a compromise diameter must be wrong. But as the rim was hand-fitted to the edge of the board complete accuracy in the reconstruction of the circle from such short lengths cannot be guaranteed. The difference between the radii arrived at by estimating the circumference from the curvature of these two rim-fragments is 6·3 cm. In selecting a diameter of 91·5 cm (36 in.), we have adopted an increase in the radius of 3·75 cm over the possible minimum and a diminution from the maximum (96·6 cm) of 2·55 cm. The margin of error in the diameter of the reconstruction is reduced from what it would have been (some 6–7 cm) had either the minimum or maximum size been adopted.

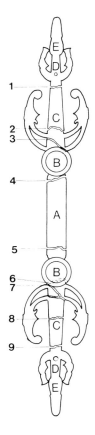

FIGURE 10   The shield: the handgrip and its extensions, showing the fractures it sustained in the ground. (Scale: 1/6)

---

[1] The profile of the grip extension as a whole, with the evidence for its flatness over the central area, is discussed in the following section.

[2] The smaller diameter of the Sutton Hoo shield in relation to most of those from Valsgärde may be related to the fact that it was curved whereas they appear to have been flat. The one Valsgärde shield which is thought to have had a curved board, Valsgärde 6, shield 1, was of approximately the same diameter as the Sutton Hoo shield (95 cm, Table 2).

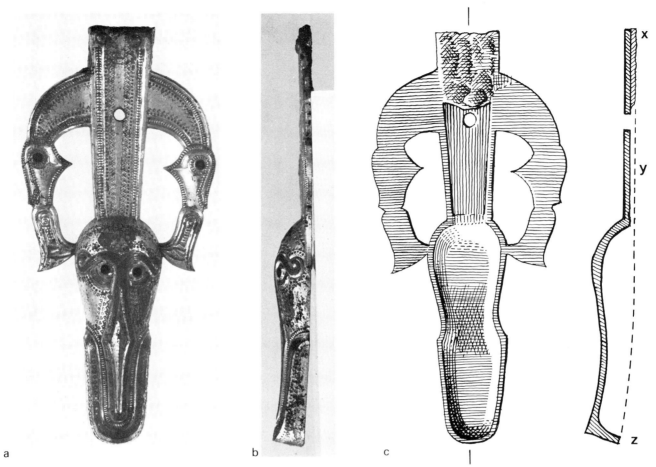

a b c

FIGURE 11   The shield: one of the two handgrip extensions: (*a*) plan view; (*b*) profile showing the divergence of the end of the grip; (*c*) drawing based on (*b*). (Scale: 1/1)

11 SHAPE

As we have seen, the shield is circular in plan. But how can we establish whether it was of flat, conical or curved section? The grip extensions continue outwards from the grip across the back of the shield in opposite directions and each terminates, well beyond the single rivet by which it was fastened to the shield-board, towards their outer ends, in a solid cast bronze animal head. The iron grip itself, across the opening at the back of the boss, has the usual bent-back flanges. It shows a curve (fig. 16*c*), but an inconsistent one, having a definite sag as compared with its extensions. The iron grips of the Vendel and Valsgärde shields also sag slightly along their lengths. The shield-boards have nevertheless been reconstructed by their Swedish excavators as flat.

Maryon and Plenderleith stated in 1945 that the fragments of the grip and its extensions, 'when stuck together at clean fractures', formed 'a curve which must have corresponded with that of the back of the shield'.[1] Certain of the key fractures in the iron are, however, not clean but corroded; and it is also evident from Maryon's own notes that the fragments were not truly joined during this experiment but 'built up on strips of plasticine'.

[1] Maryon 1946, 23 and fig. 4.

19

Figure 10 shows all the fractures in the main straight element of the grip and its extensions, numbered serially from top to bottom. Fractures 2 and 3 on one side of the boss and 5, 6, 7 and 8 on the other make perfect joins. Both sequences, and the longer sequence 5–8 in particular, which includes the transition from grip to extension, yield a completely straight line. The surface of the back of the iron strips constituting the grip extensions is everywhere masked by a corrosion layer, but the general straightness is clear and can be checked against a straight edge. The true line of the under-surface can indeed be seen in a non-corroded substance: gold. The patterned gilt-bronze foil which covers and decorates the visible surface of the grip extension (fig. 60) is just wide enough to allow its being wrapped round the sides of the iron strip and then folded over under its back. The clean and absolutely straight line of the rear angle of the grip extension can be seen in thick gilding.[1]

Fractures 4 and 9 (fig. 10) are poor and cannot be joined. Fracture 1 does indeed make a perfect join; but when this join is effected the end of the grip extension can be seen to lean in the wrong direction, against the supposed backward curve of the shield. This join is that of the fracture seen at the south end of the grip extension where the terminal can be seen sticking up at a sharp angle in the ground (figs. 2–4). There is no evidence in the grip extensions for any curvature of the shield until the points marked D in figure 10 are reached. Here the dragon-head terminations of the grip extensions show a definite curve in the casting. They are flat from x to y (fig. 11c), but curve from y to z. The drop is measured at 5 mm over a length of 7·5 cm. It can be seen therefore that the shield-board is flat over its central area as far as points x–y but from there curves back towards the rim (fig. 7). The length and depth of the curved portion depend on the diameter of the shield. Any increase in the diameter would increase these factors, and conversely any reduction in the diameter would reduce them, the point at which curvature begins being constant. The curvature appears to agree in general terms with that adopted in the reconstruction of shield 1 from Valsgärde 6, on the similar evidence of the backward curve of the ends of the grip extensions.[2]

III CONSTRUCTION

The shield may be accepted as being of lime wood (*Tilia* sp.), although the condition of surviving wood fragments led Dr David Cutler of the Jodrell Laboratory, Kew Gardens, to qualify this identification in his report by the word 'probably'. Although identification was not absolutely certain from botanical examination, all examined

[1] Analogies to the folding over of the edge of the foil under the back of the iron strip occur in both shields in boat-grave 8 at Valsgärde (Arwidsson 1954, 55 and Abb. 36, 38).

[2] Arwidsson 1942a, 35, Abb. 29 and Taf. 6.

FIGURE 12   The shield: detail of the remains *in situ*, showing the relationships of the boss, the handgrip and the winged dragon. (Photo: O. G. S. Crawford)

FIGURE 13 The shield: leather and wood from beneath the winged dragon. (Scale: 1/1)

fragments gave the same result (probably lime) and other types of wood could be ruled out (App. C, p. 127 ff.). The identification is of special interest if the shield is Swedish-made since the Vendel-period shields excavated at Valsgärde, in those cases in which it has been possible to identify the wood, have proved to be of pine.[1]

The board was covered front and back with leather, an important element in shield construction (p. 28 ff.).

The castings which we may provisionally describe as of gilt-bronze[2] on the front and back of the shield—the winged dragon, the head and leg of the bird, the twelve animal heads round the rim, and the iron and gilt-bronze grip extensions on the back—were mounted directly on the leather of the shield-board. The patterned gold foils on the front of the shield were mounted on a separate thin layer of wood on top of the leather. These wood underlays, which were cut to shape, have been in a number of cases wholly or partially preserved by the overlying metal. The pair of small bronze bosses with foil collars at the top of the reconstructed shield had circular wood underlays (discs) (fig. 14). These were identified by the Jodrell Laboratory as 'most probably' alder wood (*Alnus glutinosa*, Gaertner). Similar fragments (App. B, nos. 94 and 95), now identified as the underlays of the bird's tail and wing (fig. 15), are of the same wood.

FIGURE 14 The shield: alderwood seating for one of the small hemispherical gilt-bronze bosses from the top of the shield. (Scale: 1/1)

A problem is posed by fragments 12–15 (App. C, p. 127). These were regarded in 1945 as part of the rim of the shield. They had been packed as part of the supposed

---

[1] For example, Valsgärde 8, shields 1–3, Valsgärde 6, shield 3; Vendel 14, 12, 1 (Stolpe and Arne 1927).

[2] The highly corroded condition of some of these items makes identification of the exact nature of the original substance by chemical analysis difficult to establish. See App. A, especially p. 111.

FIGURE 15 The shield: alderwood underlay of the gold-foil tail and wing of the
bird from the front. (Scale: 2/1)

'tray or box complex' (i.e. shield, p. 9 above). They are of a third wood, maple,
and are now considered likely to be pieces of the lyre,[1] whose surviving remains were
found in the Coptic bowl some 75 cm to the south of the shield. The missing sound
box of the lyre ran out in the direction of the shield.[2] Another piece now identified
as maple, thought at the time to consist of two different pieces of wood pressed
together, was photographed on edge in 1945 to show supposed differences in graining.

[1] To be published in *Sutton Hoo*, Vol. III.
[2] The arms of the lyre were fractured across the northern
rim of the Coptic bowl, close to their roots, and the whole
of the sound box had broken off outside the bowls on this
side. A thin fragment of maplewood, apparently from the lid of
the sound box, infused with iron corrosion products, survives
attached to the shaft of angon no. 3 (p. 264 below).

23

This was held to be the evidence for the thickening of the rim, by an additional ring of wood which was incorporated in the 1945 reconstruction.[1] The wood, when sectioned, was shown to be a single thickness which had split along the grain, the difference in angle of the grain in the two halves seen from the end being due to twisting of the wood.

There is no direct evidence as to how the shield-board was built up. Three boards, a broad central board with narrower boards to either side, as observed in the remains of shield 1 from Valsgärde 8,[2] were probably used. This method of construction can be inferred in numbers of large shields of the period and in particular in Swedish shields. The three-board make-up is indeed implied by the occurrence of long grip extensions on the backs of shields, coupled with the presence of small bosses, placed equidistant above and below the central boss, especially when these are associated with horizontal metal strips on the front of the shield. These small bosses are the umbrella-like heads of rivets which pass through the wood of the shield, clamping the grip extensions firmly to the shield-board. The rivets are far enough out from the central boss to pass through the two outer boards at a safe distance beyond the line of junction of these boards with the central plank. They thus serve to hold the outer boards against the central board, assisting in the binding together of the shield-board as a whole, which is also accomplished by the leather covering and by the metal rim or other edge-binding. If the rivet and its boss-like head are associated with a horizontal solid metal strip on the front of the shield and this strip is in turn held to the board by rivets at its outer ends, a more comprehensive purchase by the grip extensions on the outer boards is ensured. The grip extensions in the Sutton Hoo shield would indicate a three-board construction, but in this instance the horizontal strips on the front seem to have been decorative only, at least in the form in which they existed on the shield when it was buried. They appear to have had no rivets at their outer ends.

In no case do the metal strips which commonly appear on the front of the Swedish shields run at right angles to the grain. They are not there to prevent splitting, which, if anything, they could be said to encourage;[3] nor do they serve to hold the boards together except, in subsidiary fashion, in the two 'structural' strips attached to the grip extensions. They run parallel with the grain in all cases; this fact alone suggested that the original reconstruction of the Sutton Hoo shield, in which the one strip then recognised was placed vertically across the grain, was incorrect.

Low down inside the iron hand-grip itself (fig. 16) are remains of wood with grain at right angles to the length of the grip. This indicates, as can be seen in shield grips from Vendel 11, 12 and 14[4] and from Valsgärde 8,[5] that two lunate openings were cut

[1] Maryon 1946, 23, fig. 4 and pl. III.
[2] Arwidsson 1954, figs. 33 and 35.
[3] Particularly in cases where a great many such strips are used, as in one of the shields from Valsgärde 7 where no less than fifty-eight are employed, representing very many rivet-shanks (174) piercing the grain of the wood.

[4] Stolpe and Arne 1927, pls. XXIX, fig. 1, XXXIV, fig. 2 and XLIII, fig. 2.
[5] Arwidsson 1954, fig. 35; also shield 3 from Valsgärde 7 (unpublished).

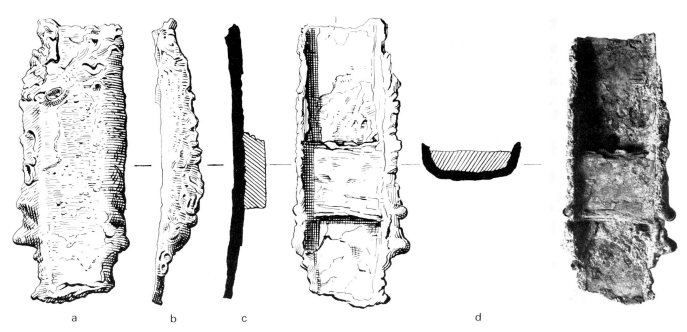

FIGURE 16 The iron handgrip of the shield: (*a*)–(*c*) plan, profile and cross-section; (*d*) drawing and photograph of the inside of the handgrip with cross-section. (Scale: 3/4)

in the centre of the shield-board with a bridge consisting of the wood of the board left between them. A separate billet of wood with rounded back, cut with the grain along its length, was added to the inner face of the bridge, and the iron flanges of the grip were then hammered back round it. This is implied both by the fact that the flanges are deeper than the thickness of the shield-board and by their shaping (fig. 16*d*).

Lunate openings of different sizes to either side of the grip (covered from the front by the boss) are the standard arrangement for accommodating the back of the hand when the grip is grasped. The difference in size of the two openings arises from the fact that the back of the hand requires more accommodation than the fingers. The grip is therefore slightly off centre and so in consequence are its extensions. The extensions in turn are reflected on the front of the shield by the small bosses associated with the horizontal strips. We have no evidence for the exact placing of the two additional small bosses at the top of the Sutton Hoo shield but they would seem to call, visually, for a symmetrical arrangement in relation to the small boss immediately below them, which is attached to the grip extension.[1] All known parallels have this symmetry (fig. 17).[2] The extra strip added, tentatively, at the bottom of the front of the shield, which carries the gilt-bronze ring (p. 45), would seem also to call for lining up on the same vertical axis. The effect is that all these elements of decoration or design on the front of the shield are off centre, and not in line with the central disc that

[1] We know of the two additional small bosses that they came from this part of the shield, and that the strap-ends belonging to the strap that ran horizontally between them were found mixed up with the pieces of the anchor-fitting (p. 44 ff.).

[2] Cf. Valsgärde 8, shield 1 (Arwidsson 1954, Abb. 31, 33 and Taf. 10); Niederstotzingen, grave 3b (Paulsen 1967, Abb. 61).

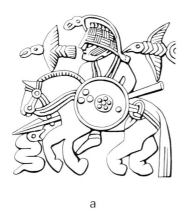 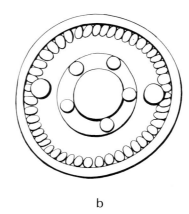

a   b

FIGURE 17   Two shield designs from the figural panels on the helmet from the Vendel
I boat grave. (Scales: *a*, 1/1; *b*, approx. 3/1) (Based on Stolpe and Arne).

surmounts the great boss. The design of the rim is free to move independently. The rim is concentric with the disc at the centre of the central boss, and its ornaments have consequently, in the reconstruction, been aligned in relation to this centre point, unaffected by the off-centre line of the grip and its extensions and the shift this imposes on the motifs just referred to on the front of the shield.

On the back of the shield (figs. 6*b*, 8) the ends of the grip proper are marked by two large hemispherical gilt bronze domes or bosses (rivet-heads). These are in sharp contrast to the small domed heads and washers that terminate the rivets which come through from the five flange-bosses on the front (fig. 18). It is clear from the fixed spacing of the five flange-boss washers that a central placing of the grip would bring its larger terminating bosses into conflict with them. It follows that the five flange-bosses on the front must fall into the positions shown in plate 1 in relation to the top of the shield, the shield being held on the left side of the body with hand and forearm approaching from the left. Finally, confirming the off-centre placing of the grip, Maryon records the early observation of rusty marks left by the iron grip 'beside two of the subordinate bosses, not straight across the middle of the opening as might have been expected'.[1]

Although the main central area of the shield-board is seen to have been flat, an unsolved constructional problem is presented by the profile of the central boss (fig. 19). Its flange slopes downwards, definitely and uniformly, and not as the result of pressure or damage. There must therefore have been either a wedge-shaped gap between the flat board and the sloping flange of the boss, which would seem both clumsy and avoidable, or else, to fill this space, a raised wedge-shaped wooden ring, perhaps cut out of the solid along with the rest of the board, on which the boss was seated. No evidence is recorded in the Laboratory notes of 1939, made before the cleaning of the boss, to indicate that there was any evidence for such a separate ring

[1] Maryon 1946, 24. For the off-centre placing of grips in Anglo-Saxon shields see R. J. C. Atkinson in Leeds and Shortt 1953, 57.

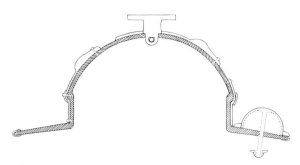

FIGURE 18 The shield: small hemispherical bosses from the back of the iron boss. (Scale: 1/1)

FIGURE 19 The shield: cross-section through the central iron boss, showing *inter alia* the downward sloping flange and a section through one of the five flange-bosses. (Scale: 1/3)

of wood added to the board as a seating for the boss. The effect of the sloping flange would be to set off the ornament and form of the boss, especially when viewed from the side. The majority of the shield-boss flanges from Vendel and Valsgärde, and that of the shield from the well-known burial at Vallstenarum, Gotland,[1] are flat, but those of Valsgärde 6, shield 1, and Vendel 12, are sloped. The sloped flange in a pronounced form is known from both earlier and later periods,[2] and is a common feature in Anglo-Saxon material. This sloping of the boss flange does not necessarily imply a conical form for the shield.[3]

The thickness of shield-board

The maximum thickness of the Sutton Hoo shield-board at the point where the hanging-up strap of the shield (p. 73) was placed, and where (fig. 20) the cross-section of the shield is completely preserved, is 7 mm. This figure is given by the spacing between the under-surface of the fluted strap held by the gilt pyramid at the back of the shield and the wood disc underlying the gilt boss on the front, and includes the leather that covers the board front and back. It is a valid figure in that it is independent of any shrinkage factor in the wood.

It is necessary for a shield-board to be thin to keep down its weight. The thickness of the published Valsgärde shields is given as only 5 to 6 mm—a quarter of an inch or less. Shields like that from Valsgärde 7, loaded with fifty-eight iron strips, tend to be smaller in diameter or to carry a lighter boss in compensation for the extra weight of metal, indicating an awareness of the need to keep down the overall weight.

[1] Nerman 1969, pls. 70 and 142, nos. 621–30, and 1237–9.
[2] Izikowitz 1931, 189, fig. 76; Evison 1963, figs. 11–14; see also Izikowitz, 187–8. For shield with dropping boss flanges on Gotland, Almgren and Nerman 1923, text fig. 209 and figs. 641–5.
[3] Furthermore the slope of the flange of a boss may affect the accuracy of deductions as to the thickness of the shield-board made from the length of rivets remaining in position in the flange; cf. Evison 1963, 45 and fig. 3; also the calculation of the thickness of the board of the shield from Ischl (1·5 cm) based on the same evidence (Werner 1951/2, 46).

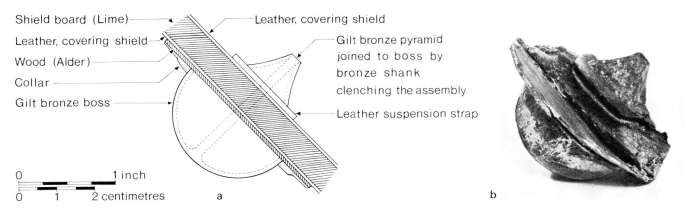

Shield board (Lime)
Leather, covering shield
Leather, covering shield
Wood (Alder)
Collar
Gilt bronze boss

Leather, covering shield
Gilt bronze pyramid joined to boss by bronze shank clenching the assembly
Leather suspension strap

0   1 inch
0   1   2 centimetres   a   b

FIGURE 20   The shield: (*a*) cross-section through the shield-board of one of the small bosses, based on surviving fragments; (*b*) the fragments reassembled.

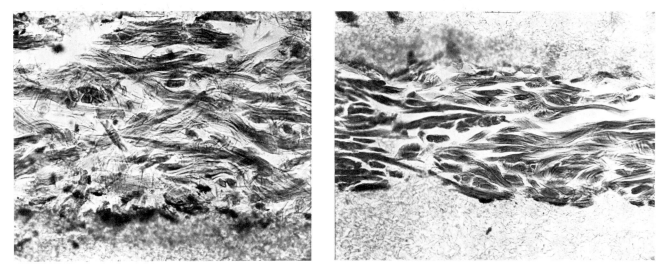

FIGURE 21   The shield: photomicrographs of selected fragments of the leather which originally covered the shield-board. (Scale: 55/1) (Photos: British Leather Manufacturers Research Association)

Leather covering

The effective resistance of a shield to blows may have come not so much from the wood as from its leather covering. This in later shields is known to have been of *cuir bouilli*, leather boiled and then stretched while soft over the board. When dried and after suitable treatment the leather can become extremely hard. This can also be effected by impregnation of the leather with hot wax.[1] The hardness factor cannot be established from excavated shields because the leather when it survives is found soft as a result of prolonged burial in the soil. The Sutton Hoo shield was leather-covered on both sides (figs. 21 and 25), the leather being cattle skin.[2] No evidence for glueing or for staining or colouring has been recovered from laboratory examination. The

[1] Coles 1962, 178.
[2] Identified by Dr R. L. Sykes, Director of the British Leather Manufacturers' Research Association, in a letter dated

15 November 1971: 'The large size of the leather fibre bundles indicates that the pieces are from cattle hide.' Photomicrographs illustrating the fibre structure are shown in fig. 21.

FIGURE 22 The shield: five of the best preserved animal heads from the rim.
For the remainder of the heads see figure 86 below. (Scale: 1/1)

leather which survives from the Sutton Hoo shield is preserved in fragments derived from the edge of the shield and under metal fittings. It is soft but, as has been indicated, its hardness in use may have been counteracted by chemical reactions in the ground. Scientific examination has revealed what appears to be evidence of vegetable tanning.[1] The supposed traces of tanning may, however, have been derived from the wet oak of the hull of the ship and its flooring, with which the shield was surrounded. The leather might have been hardened by boiling or by impregnating with wax, but no evidence of this can be detected.

IV THE RIM

The shield-rim as seen in the ground is recorded in figures 2–4 (cf. pl. 24b and fig. 5). In these illustrations a considerable length of the shield-rim can be seen. To the south of the central boss it is compressed into a narrow loop with almost parallel sides. One of the animal heads is visible in position on the rim above and to the right of the boss in figure 2 and is indicated in plate 24b. Another is recorded by Phillips as occurring in the middle of a long length of rim added by him to Piggott's plan, well to the north of the boss (fig. 2). These are shown in figure 5. A third may be represented by a T-shaped gold appearance (?rim and head) seen, in what would be an inverted position in the bottom right hand corner of the area marked IV.17 (pl. 24b and fig. 5, immediately below 11a).

Plate 24b also shows a substantial patch of gold foil associated with the rim just

[1] Dr R. L. Sykes, in the letter previously quoted, reports that the leather samples gave no distinct reaction for vegetable tan with ferric alum. It was however his opinion that, with the possible exception of the leather from beneath the bird which was very much paler in colour, the samples were 'obviously vegetable tanned'.

above and to the right of the boss. The plain gold foil which coated the bronze rim itself came off readily and a good deal of it was found lying about loose and more was blown away by the wind in tiny fragments (fig. 26 and p. 33, n. 1). The size and the rectangular shape of this particular patch, however, and its sharp inner edge as seen in the photographs (e.g. fig. 2) show that it is something different. It does not correspond either in position or size with one of the twelve gilt animal heads that were mounted on the rim. It may therefore be taken as representing an additional area of gold foil in this position (fig. 5, no. 7).

The excavator's field impressions of the rim confirm this. They are given in Phillips's entry in his diary for 28 July (p. 7 above): 'A long strip of wood edged with gold leaf [the gilding of the shield-rim] *with gold leaf panels of interlace decoration, and the wood itself panelled out into impressed(?) rectangles,*[1] partly overlay the boss on the western side and extended further to the north and south (IV.6)' (pl. 24b). His *Antiquaries Journal* account augments this description: 'The "poker-work" rectangles formed a continuous band along the edge of the tray [i.e. shield] *between the animal heads.*'[2]

In conjunction with the visual and graphic records these statements make it clear that the rim of the shield, besides peripheral animal heads of the types seen in figures 22 and 23, had on it what appeared to be other ornamental features ('poker-work rectangles'), including rectangular panels of gold foil with interlace patterns, occurring between the animal heads.

These references in Phillips's diary to 'impressed rectangles' on the wood, and 'poker-work rectangles', present some difficulty. Since the board was leather-covered the foil would not have come into contact with the wood of the board. Yet the diary refers to the 'wood itself' as 'panelled out into impressed(?) rectangles'. We have seen above (pp. 26–7) that there is no evidence for any separate wooden rim reinforcing the shield-board, let alone one exposed above the leather, on which foil might have been directly laid. None of the fragments of alder wood underlays that survive from the shield with the impress of interlace patterns from stamped foil have any marks which might indicate that they had been under the interlace panels said to be associated with the rim. Certain fragments preserve a complete cross-section of the edge of the shield with the metal rim in position (fig. 24). In these no extra wood is trapped between the metal rim and the leather. Since the bird, which consisted in part of foil on wood underlays,

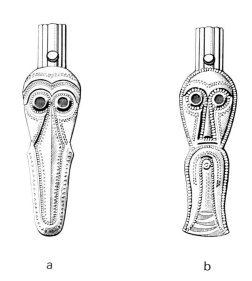

a   b

FIGURE 23 The shield: two typical animal heads of different types from the rim. (Scale: 1/1)

---

[1] My italics, R.B.-M.   [2] Phillips 1940a, 164.

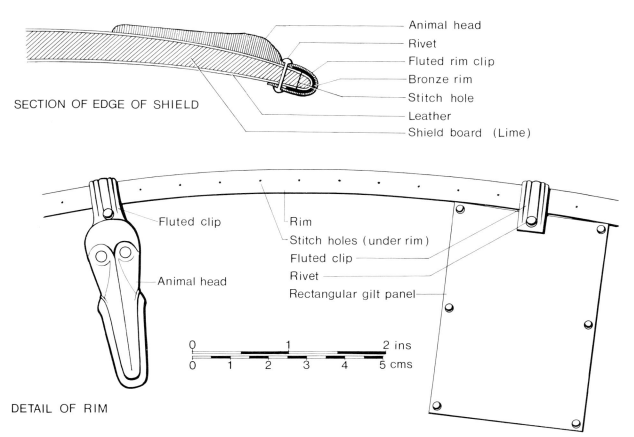

SECTION OF EDGE OF SHIELD

- Animal head
- Rivet
- Fluted rim clip
- Bronze rim
- Stitch hole
- Leather
- Shield board (Lime)

Fluted clip

Animal head

Rim
Stitch holes (under rim)
Fluted clip
Rivet
Rectangular gilt panel

0   1   2 ins
0 1 2 3 4 5 cms

DETAIL OF RIM

FIGURE 24   The shield: diagrammatic section through the rim,
based on surviving fragments.

can be shown to have been originally in this quarter of the shield (p. 42) it is perhaps possible that the excavators may have seen the wooden underlays of the bird's patterned foil body and tail, but this seems unlikely as nothing resembling them can be seen in the photographs. Furthermore the head and leg of the bird, accompanied by gold foil, were found elsewhere (pl. 24 b, IV.11, and fig. 2).

The excavator's observations might be thought to support the statements of Maryon and Plenderleith, when the original reconstruction was published, that the shield-rim was thickened by the addition of a ring of wood.[1] If this were so, we would not have separate underlays cut for each individual foil rectangle but a continuous added ring of wood, on which the rectangles were mounted at intervals. The presence of such a rim on the Sutton Hoo shield would be the first archaeological evidence that shields with raised rims, such as seem to be represented in certain depictions in Vendel art (fig. 17), really existed. No such rims have been recorded amongst excavated materials, and their apparent rendering in Vendel graphic representations of shields could be no more than an artistic emphasising of a metal rim or decorative zone. Alternatively, they could represent a leather edging on the rim of a shield whose boards were not themselves covered.[2] Plenderleith and Maryon seem to have misinterpreted the excavation photographs (figs. 2–4), which they cited as evidence, taking for a

[1] Maryon 1946, 23.   [2] Paulsen 1967, 124.

31

a

b

c   d

FIGURE 25   The shield: (*a*) and (*b*) surviving leather fragments from the rim, (*a*) showing the impression of one of the clips that held the rim to the board; (*c*) and (*d*) examples of a peripheral bronze clip (front and back views). (Scales: *a* and *b*, 2/1; *c* and *d*, 5/1)

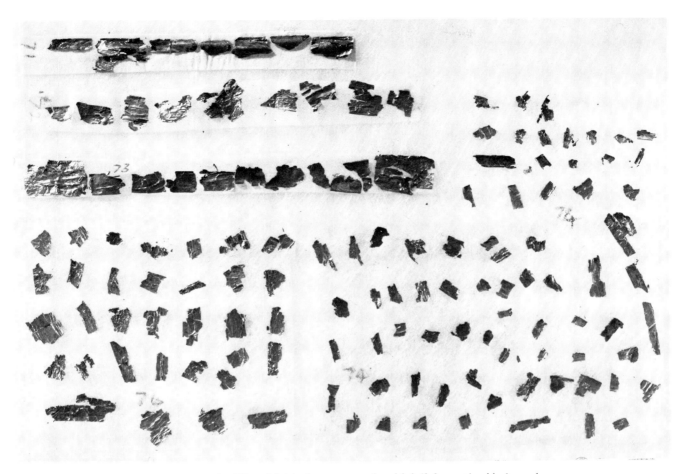

FIGURE 26   The shield: fragments of gold foil from the U-shaped
bronze channelling on the rim. (Scale: 4/5)

continuous raised rim what was in fact the broken edge of the board, held together
by the mechanical support of the bronze rim, animal heads and other mounts. They
also appear to have taken for a double thickness of wood what was in fact a single
piece split along the grain and contorted (pp. 23–4).

Figure 25 shows some wood and leather fragments from the edge of the shield,
and figure 9 the two largest surviving fragments of bronze channelling—the coating
of gold foil is almost wholly absent; figure 26 shows loose undecorated gold foil which
had come off the rim and was collected separately. There is no doubt that the rim
was gilded with leaf and not by mercury gilding. This plain foil, so readily detached
from the metal rim, to which it must have been fixed by size and heat, may have
accounted for the gold foil which continually blew away while the shield was being
excavated.[1]

The circumference of the reconstructed shield is 290 cm, thus the rim would have
carried a plain gold foil strip nearly 3 metres long and when flattened out 2·2 cm wide.

[1] Verbal statements from the excavators spoke of a 'snow
storm' of gold leaf, which it was impossible to stop. In the
re-excavation of 1965–7 an appreciable quantity of plain gold leaf
emerged from the soil at the point where the shield had lain.

Figure 24 gives a section of the rim and figure 25 shows surviving leather (p. 28 above). One leather fragment (fig. 25 a) shows a group of three holes, the central one marking the point of fastening of a metal clip which held the bronze rim in position. The clips, which were fluted, were bent round the rim, the two opposite ends being riveted together through the shield-board. A round convex plain gilt rivet-head appeared on the front of the shield while at the back the point of the rivet was burred over on the metal clip. Equally spaced to either side of the central hole were two more rivets. The tops of rivet-shanks in position, or rivet holes, can be seen. It is clear from fragments of foil adhering to the rim, and from subsequent reconstruction work, that two rivets spaced to either side of the clip held the corners of rectangular gold foil panels of stamped interlace and also that these panels were set end-on to the rim, that is, with a narrow end of the rectangle at the rim and the length of the panel running inwards towards the boss. The number of the panels is uncertain. There is evidence from rim fragments for not less than six; to judge by the excavators' descriptions, the quantity of gold foil spoken of, and the even, continuous spacing of such ornaments on Swedish shields, there could have been twelve, and only the fact that so little panel material has survived prevents one from claiming this.

Fragments survive of twelve animal heads from the shield-rim (fig. 86; no. 12 is from the 1967 excavations). These are of two types, shown in figure 23 a and b. It seems likely that if there were six rectangular foil panels they would be associated with pairs of matching heads, the six panels going with six pairs of heads, and that where the different head types were adjacent there was no panel in between. This is the arrangement adopted in the reconstruction (fig. 6 a). It is possible that there may have been more panels. One factor that might be thought to suggest this is the evidence (p. 83 below) that two different dies of the same size and shape were employed, their designs apparently very similar but differing somewhat in detail (fig. 66). The only place available on the shield-board for such panels seems to be the rim. If two variant dies were employed, it might seem more appropriate to vary the design if it occurred twelve times than if it only occurred six times. Twelve panels of two designs would then match with twelve animal heads of two designs (cf. fig. 29).

The Valsgärde shields, though inferior to the Sutton Hoo shield in richness and in workmanship, offer parallels to its rim decoration which the finer Vendel shields do not. Several of the Valsgärde shields have decorative iron appliqués round the rim (fig. 27). All the shields so provided have metal rims, the appliqués being functional in the sense that, like the animal heads round the Sutton Hoo shield, they were developments of clips which held the metal rim to the board at intervals. The number of rim motifs, where it can be computed, is between seven and sixteen.[1] These shields do not assist us in establishing the number present on the Sutton Hoo shield, which, if the animal heads and the flat foil panels are taken together, must number

[1] Valsgärde 6, shield 1 (restored as convex)—at least 7; Valsgärde 7, shield 2, 10; Valsgärde 8, shields 1 and 2, 16 and 15. Several different designs of rim appliqués are employed on each shield, and as many as four on shield 1 from Valsgärde 8 (Arwidsson 1942 a, 1954 and Valsgärde 7, forthcoming).

34

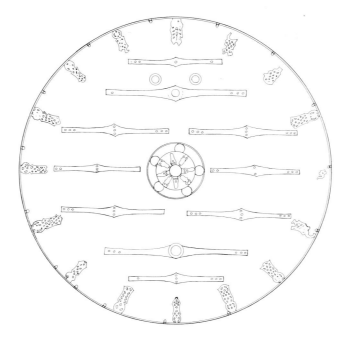

FIGURE 27   Shield I from Valsgärde grave 8.
(Scale 1/13) (After Arwidsson)

not fewer than eighteen. The question is whether there were, as is quite possible, another six foil panels, making, in the case of the Sutton Hoo shield, twenty-four elements in the rim-decoration (twelve animal heads of two types and twelve panels of two types). If this was so the two types of animal heads would no doubt be arranged alternately, not in pairs.

In the Valsgärde shields the peripheral mounts are evenly spaced, as we assume the twelve heads round the edge of the Sutton Hoo shield to have been. The effect of inserting six foil panels into the series of animal heads on the Sutton Hoo shield is to group the rim ornamentation into sets of three, two matching animal heads flanking each foil panel. The resultant ornamental effect is suggestive of the grouped impression given by the rim ornaments of certain shields of Swiss or north Italian provenance (fig. 28 a and b) where, although the peripheral ornaments have been evenly spaced in the reconstruction, the impression is of a series of isolated images flanked by circles. The Sutton Hoo shield, if East Scandinavian, might be expected to derive influences in design from early Lombardic or (as the Sutton Hoo helmet does) Late Antique models (p. 96 below). We need not expect this piece of royal equipment to be influenced by the Valsgärde shields, which are not only inferior in quality but also later in date.

To summarise, the factors affecting our estimate of the number of panels on the shield-rim at Sutton Hoo are, first, the knowledge that two different dies were used, and second, the excavators' explicit accounts of what they saw. Neither is decisive. The two panel designs should relate to the two types of animal head; these are shown in the reconstruction as alternating in matching pairs round the circumference of the

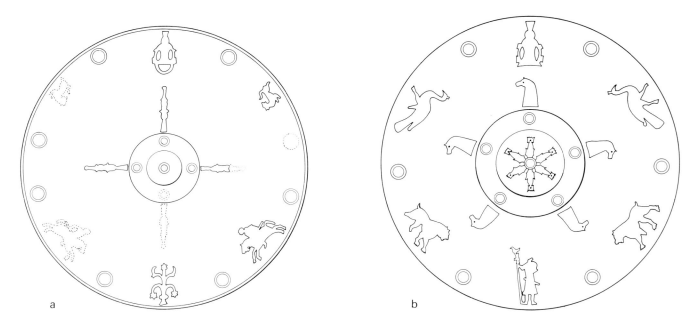

FIGURE 28 (*a*) The shield with applied motifs found at Stabio, Italy; (*b*) the shield with applied peripheral mounts and large central boss from Lucca, Italy.

shield. There is no evidence for this, but if it was so the two foil patterns no doubt alternated similarly, for the shield gives evidence of purposeful and consistent design. If there were twelve panels as well as twelve heads, this would undermine the suggestion of a grouped rim design and imply a continuous one, adding decorative weight and richness to the rim and to the shield as a whole. The more conservative solution, six panels only, has been adopted in the British Museum reconstruction; but, in further support of the twelve-panel uninterrupted sequence, we have Phillips's statement that the 'poker-work panels [i.e. the rectangular impressions of pattern on ?leather] formed a continuous band along the edge between the animal heads'. The 'grouped' reconstruction leaves gaps which do not seem to fit this description, and twelve panels might also accord better with the general abundance of foil which so impressed the excavators.

The main rim panel design (A1), which can be completely reconstructed, is shown in figure 64 *b*; fragments of the second panel design (A2) are shown in figure 67. A drawing of the shield as it would appear in an alternative reconstruction, which may be correct, with slightly larger diameter (96·5 cm, 38 in.) and twelve rim panels, is given in figure 29.

V   THE DISTRIBUTION OF FEATURES

The original distribution of features on the front and back of the shield is discussed here in the light of the positions in which they were found by the excavators. All the elements of the shield, in addition to the decomposition and disintegration that has occurred, appear to have been pushed out of place, or out of shape, or both, as they

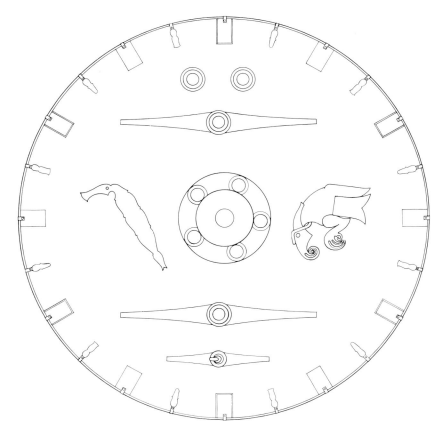

FIGURE 29 The Sutton Hoo shield, with a diameter of 96·5 cm (38 in.) incorporating twelve rectangular panels around the rim. (Scale: approx. 1/9)

lay in the ground, by lateral pressures operating in various directions. In addition some elements belonging to the shield cannot be identified on any plan or photograph. Its design can consequently only be recovered by a close analysis of all the observable phenomena and of such records as there are.

The general nature of the problem with which we are confronted in our attempt to restore the design of the shield can be gauged from contemporary photographs (figs. 2–4). A key to the appearances on these photographs is given in figure 5. This is drawn as far as possible from almost vertical views, but before using it for the purpose of following the detailed argument about to be undertaken it should be checked against Piggott's field plan (pl. 24b). Figure 30 shows the shield remains in relation to the original line of the end wall of the burial chamber and to the limits of the wall's subsequent inward bulge. The position of the shield remains in relation to the keel-line is shown in the burial deposit plan (fig. 1). Figure 30 also seeks to show how the positions in which the various elements were found can be explained, in relation to the places they are held to have occupied on the intact shield-board, by detectable or inferred lateral movements within the burial chamber. It is through the process of recognising features seen in the plan and photographs for what they are, and by

37

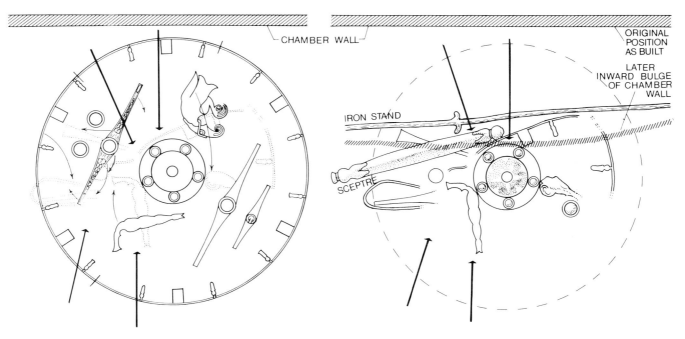

FIGURE 30   The Sutton Hoo shield *in situ:* reconstruction showing the
relative movements of the surviving elements.

defining the movements that must have taken place in the burial chamber, that it is
possible to recover the design of the front and back of the shield with a high degree
of certainty.

It is possible that, in addition to lateral pressures, a part of the shield may have
been struck by some falling element and distorted or thrown out of place. Assuming
the shield to have been lying flat at the time, this would account for the upward-
projecting position of no. 4a (fig. 5)—the southern end of the grip extension. However, all the movement which resulted in the compression and confusion seen in
the plan and photographs (pl. 24b and figs. 2–4) must have taken place before the
final collapse of the chamber, as a general collapse would smother the remains and
prevent further movement.

The first thing to be established, if we are to speak of lateral pressures, is that the
shield must have been lying flat in the burial chamber, and that it had not been placed
in an upright position, leaning against the wall, as in the warrior's chamber-grave at
Morken,[1] or at least, however the funeral party may have left it, that it must have
assumed a horizontal position in the chamber whilst still essentially intact.

The shield-boss, facing upwards, was found lying virtually flat (horizontal); and
so, face downwards (as they should be) were the grip extensions. They maintained
a correct straight line in relation to the grip at the back of the boss. It is difficult to
see how the shield-boss and grip could have maintained this relationship, or ended
up lying flat, if the shield had been standing vertically when it began to disintegrate.

[1] Böhner 1959.

38

That the shield was lying flat at an early stage is also indicated by the fact that the boss and grip mechanism had fallen to a lower level, leaving the board in position above it. This must have occurred when the shield was horizontal. If, then, we accept that the shield was lying flat, as the excavators themselves inferred,[1] it can be seen from figures 2–4 that it had been exposed to lateral pressures from the south-west, and to lesser extent from the west. The inferred directions from which the pressure came are indicated by arrows in figure 30. It will be seen from plate 24 b and from figure 30 that the west end wall of the chamber, encountered by the excavators at a higher level, above the deposit, bulged under pressure into the chamber for a distance of at least 23 cm, right up to the flange of the shield-boss.[2]

Plans and photographs show how the grip extensions from the back of the shield, riveted to the flange of the boss, themselves robust and held down by the weight of the boss, have remained in position at their low level, detached from the shield-board; while the shield-board, lent substance by its metal rim, has in its southern half been independently pushed across this once central axis into a loop almost parallel with the exposed (southern) grip extension, but lying away to the east of it.[3] The line of the rim (shown in pl. 24 b as gold and iron, in reality gilt-bronze) can be followed in figure 4 (cf. fig. 5) where it can be seen to be associated with a mass of dark earth and some fragmentary material, presumably the compressed remains of the board. That this part of the rim should be found running parallel with the grip extension and not at least obliquely across it, indicates a clean fracture. The break is recognisable in the plan (pl. 24 b), where the close inward turn of the gilt rim around the south side of the boss is shown. A further intermediate length of rim (IV.6) is also seen lying parallel with the grip extension, again on the wrong side of it, to the east, and between it and the head of the winged dragon.

The long, compressed loop of shield-rim lying to the south of the boss stands in marked contrast with the relatively undisturbed area of the shield-board to the north. The direction of lateral pressure on the shield-board was evidently from the west and south-west (fig. 30). Its ultimate agency was evidently the bulging inwards of the end wall of the chamber. This seems to have swept before it the iron stand and the other grave goods that had been ranged against the wall. At a lower level, below and unaffected by all this movement, the position of the boss, grip and grip extensions remained unaltered, establishing the position in the ground of the vertical axis of the shield.

---

[1] Phillips 1940 a, 165.

[2] *Sutton Hoo*, Vol. I, 733 and fig. 112. The evidence suggests that the probable line of this wall was originally some 23 cm further west than fig. 112 indicates, so that an overall inward bulge of as much as 46 cm may be in question. Whatever the degree of movement, its direction is plain, and the position in which the bulge ended in relation to the objects is fairly clear (cf. fig. 30).

[3] It does not seem likely that the movement of the board of the shield, its pushing away to the east, was caused by the sceptre, because the bottom end of the sceptre, anchored under the remains of the iron-bound wooden bucket no. 3, lies further east than the upper end. One would have to suppose the whole whetstone to have been lying obliquely south-east to north-west, and to have been moved, with the bucket, uniformly along its length in a north-east direction. This may have been the case; the iron stand, if then horizontal, would have been the main source of pressure, causing the movement of other grave-goods interposed, and ultimately the squashing-up of the shield.

Although the vertical axis of the shield in the ground can thus be easily determined it remains to establish which direction represents the top and which the bottom of the shield. It can be shown that the triangle of three small bosses occurred to the south of the boss. The two outer bosses cover rivets holding the ends of a horizontal strap which, placed as these bosses indicate across the axis of the shield, can only have served for hanging the shield up. Assuming that it would be hung the right way up and not upside down, this should be the top of the shield. This triangular grouping of three small bosses is indeed taken to be at the top in the Vendel and Valsgärde shield reconstructions where this feature occurs. But is it necessarily so? Since the three small bosses are in no known instance combined with figural devices which have a top and a bottom, like the standard-bearer on the Lucca shield (fig. 28 b), a clear answer can only be provided if the excavators at Valsgärde were able to record how these bosses lay in relation to the off-centre position of the grip. The direction from which the left hand approached the boss, and accordingly the side on which the larger of the two lunate openings lay, would indicate which really was the top. Unfortunately, if a shield is lying in the ground face upwards the lunate openings are concealed from view by the boss. At Sutton Hoo the boss itself has travelled a little away northwards from the southern grip extension, and, as figure 3 shows, it was tilted. The whole west edge of the shield seems to have been lifted up with the tilting of the boss. The boss however has not *rotated*. It can be seen from figures 2–4 that, with the grip extension axis established and the grip positioned as in the reconstruction (fig. 6b), we have two flange-bosses parallel with it on one side and one directly opposite them on the other. Figure 2 shows that the two flange-bosses are on the same side as the dragon and this arrangement (fig. 6a) brings the triangle of bosses to the top. If this is correctly seen, the top of the shield must be to the top left of figure 2, that is to the south. How the dragon can have reached the position seen in figure 2 (upside down in relation to its position as shown in our reconstruction) is discussed on page 43 and indicated in figure 30.

The next point to establish is the number of decorative foil strips on the shield and their positions. Figures 2–4 reveal some strange movements and circumstances which cannot be readily explained. Figures 2 and 5 mark the line of the shield-rim, and the plan (pl. 24 b) shows at this point (IV.17) an expansion of the area of gold. This might be expected to be one of the rectangular panels on the rim. Item 'IV.17' is described in the Research Laboratory's unpacking list as 'gold fragments' and 'gold complex (a powdery mass: very frail)' (p. 12 and fig. 55). The T-shaped appearance near IV.17 is probably one of the animal heads attached to a length of rim, but switched round the wrong way. The illustrations (figs. 2 and 5) show the gold expansion on the rim alignment to be a foil strip, tapering from right to left. Its borders, with rivet-heads in position, can be recognised. The interlace pattern and the clustered spots of an animal's head and jaw (p. 87) can be seen in the photograph. In the same way part of a similar strip can be identified at IV.16 (pl. 24 b and fig. 54), but here the

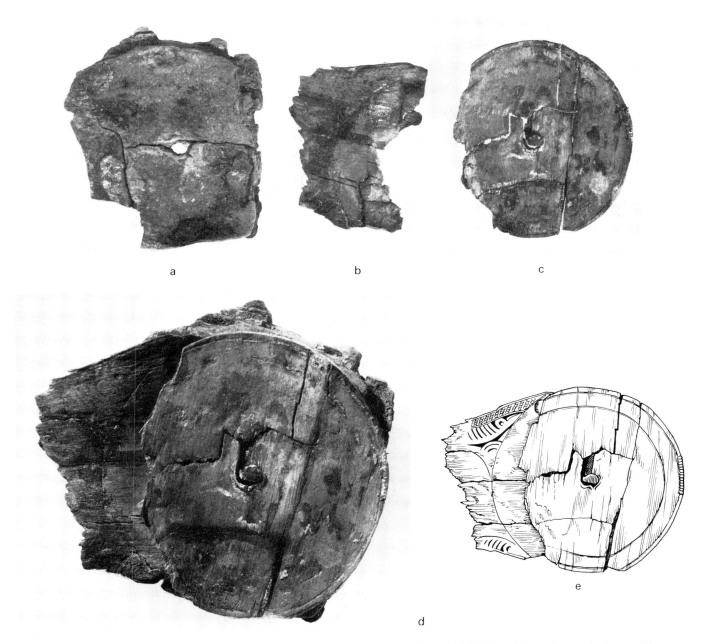

FIGURE 31 The shield: (a)–(c) alderwood underlay and wood of the shield-board from beneath the small gilt-bronze hemispherical boss IV 12; (d) underlay and wood reassembled: (e) drawing of alderwood underlay. (Scale: a–c, e, 1/1; d, 3/2)

taper is from left to right. Clearly these two gold residues are parts of a long strip which lay to the left-hand side of the shield-boss in the photograph. This is the upper half of the shield, as we have just shown. The two pieces therefore represent a gold-foil strip above the boss. The position of the rivet hole on which this strip was centred is shown in figure 5 as no. 18. The board itself has been pushed clean away from the grip extension in an easterly direction. Half the strip has been left behind, and lies parallel with the grip extension on its west side (fig. 30). The other half has moved with the board. No. 16 (fig. 5) marks a gilt boss upside down (IV.15, pl. 24 *b*, figs. 2–4). It would not be surprising if the boss from the rivet hole at no. 18, mounted on the front of the shield as the innermost of the triangle of bosses, had moved with the board and, once broken off its rivet-shank, had turned over in this way. The strip must have fallen into two parts as the boss broke away, one part (11 b) remaining on the west of the grip extension, being caught up against it and in some way underneath it. It was pushed or turned north-west. The other half (11 a) travelled with its gilt boss to the point shown. The position of 11 b in figure 5, *under* the grip extension, is an inversion of the natural order since the strip was on the upper surface of the shield and the grip extensions on the back.

If we now turn to study the shield to the north of the central boss (fig. 32), a small boss is seen in this area. It is the right way up, still in position, attached to the grip extension. It has a raised collar round it and wood can be seen under the collar. This wood, an alder underlay, is reproduced in figure 31. It shows and fits the impression of an identical gold-foil strip (fig. 53). More gold can be seen in the ground to the north and south of the collared boss (figs. 2, 3, cf. fig. 5). This probably represents parts of the strip. It is at this point, under the collared boss, that the shield-board itself is preserved, and by reassembling the fragments (fig. 31), it can be seen that the grain of the shield-board is running across the grip extension at right-angles and that the gold strip itself ran parallel with the grain of the shield-board. We thus have in all evidence for two horizontally placed strips; one broke into two parts which drifted apart, above the iron boss; the other remained on its correct alignment, still centred on the grip extension, below the boss. The positioning of these strips on the central axis above and below the boss, effectively excludes the dragon and bird from these positions. They must therefore have been situated on each side of it. It is fairly clear that the dragon must have been situated on the east side of the boss. It could scarcely have worked its way round the boss to the place where it was found from any position to the west. In the case of the bird, on the other hand, the general inward movement of the shield-board and its fittings towards the north-east from the south-west (fig. 30), suggests that the bird figure must have occupied a position to the west of the boss, somewhere near where the large gold patch appears on the rim at IV.6 on plate 24 *b*, moving as shown in figure 30. On this assumption it is easy to explain how the fragments of the bird reached the position in which they were found.

Figure 32 shows us the elements of the bird figure in the ground as Phillips described them (p. 8 above): 'IV.11 lay on its edge to the north of the boss. It was much corroded and damaged. It was decorated on both faces, but the gold-leaf mounted face and boss were to the west.' The bird's foot is here seen pointing south, and the head, identified by the eye, the cloisons of the garnet-inlaid eye surround, and the edge of the crest at the back of the head, points the same way. Both these elements face eastwards. Phillips, however, speaks in addition of 'the gold-leaf mounted face [of IV.11]

FIGURE 32 The shield: remains of the front of the shield *in situ* showing the relative positions of the
bird's claw and eye, and one of the gold strips. (Photo: O. G. S. Crawford)

and boss' being to the west. The gold-foil covered wooden elements of the bird's body
must have moved along with the cast elements (head and foot) and ended up in the same
spot but facing west.

It is difficult, at first sight, to reconcile the precise positions assumed by these bird
elements (the head and the foot both pointing south) and by the dragon (its jaws
pointing south), with the figures as reconstructed on the shield (fig. 6a). The
directions in which these cast-bronze fittings were found to be facing in the ground
would be more easily explained had the bird and dragon been the other way up on
the board. If the top of the shield is to the south, however, as has been established,
this cannot have been so. We must suppose the cast parts of the bird to have been
turned right round and then pushed up into a vertical position. Equally, in the case
of the dragon, we must suppose its head to have moved southwards and westwards
through an arc of some 90 degrees (fig. 30). We can in fact see that the eastern rim
of the shield has moved inwards in this westerly direction, directly opposite to that
of the general pressure from west to east. This can be seen from the location taken
up by the length of rim, IV.17 (pl. 24b). Some resistance to the eastward movement,

43

a corner of some sort it seems, must have forced the rim on this side of the shield inwards at this point. Following this trend, the movement of the dragon from the position shown in the restoration (fig. 6a) to that in which it was found (fig. 2) presents no difficulty.

The positions of the remaining two small gilt bosses can also be deduced. One is clearly shown on the plan (pl. 24b, IV.17) as a gold circle just inside the southern tip of the loop formed by the rim. On the photographs, however, we do not see a boss at this point but a group of small fragments (figs. 2–4). These fragments are curved and gilded with gold leaf. They assemble to the correct size and shape of a small boss (fig. 33). The boss, evidently intact when the plan was drawn, was in a highly fragile state, and it must have broken into pieces before the photographs were taken.[1]

The second of the strap-holding pair of bosses may have been at IV.2 (pl. 24b). A statement in the diary for 28 July (pp. 7/8 above) indicates that there was a boss at IV.2, but this may perhaps be an error. The presence in IV.2 of a 'pyramidal stud' is attested (p. 12), and pyramidal studs (fig. 59) held the rear ends of the rivets of which these bosses formed the heads (p. 73). But this pyramidal stud could have belonged to the plaster-like boss from IV.17, and close by. The unpacking list reference to what should be this boss (table 1, under IV) unfortunately does not help us. It seems clear however that in IV.14, mixed up with the remains of what can be identified as the anchor-fitting for the carrying strap, is one of the strap-ends associated with the tooled strap which ran between the two bosses (p. 73). It is possible also that a rectangular appearance on the photograph (fig. 2) to the right of the piece of metal that projects from under the mount with cut-away shoulders, and between it and the tip of the grip

FIGURE 33 The shield: disintegrated fragments of a small gilt-bronze boss. (Scale: 5/3)

extension, represents a square of shield leather preserved under a pyramid, and that from beneath this in turn, correctly placed, part of the tooled leather strap can be seen emerging. There is therefore clear evidence that the hanging-up strap with the two bosses that mark its position on the front of the shield was situated in this region, well to the south of the central boss.[2]

[1] The gilt fragments are to all appearances not bronze, and they are not plaster (gesso) as at one time suggested. They prove, on analysis, to be of a corroded high tin alloy (App. A, p. 111), with the appearance of plaster, being white in colour and of plastery consistency. It seems that the excavators, who took the object initially for a gilt bronze boss, changed their idea after it had broken into pieces that appeared not to be of bronze but looked like plaster. One of the plans (plan no. 3; *Sutton Hoo*, Vol. I, p. 236) bears an endorsement in Piggott's writing, attached to this appearance, 'not a boss', implying that it had been earlier thought to be one. This is another instance of bronze subjected to an exceptional degree of corrosion.

[2] The necessity of establishing this can be seen in the light of the very different placing of these bosses in the first reconstruction of the shield, issued from the British Museum Research Laboratory (Maryon 1946, plate III).

The location of the anchor-fitting for the thin carrying strap requires some discussion. It seems clearly identified as IV.14 by the unpacking list ('IV.14: three pieces of bronze, one with handle attachment').[1] Any possible ambiguity in the unpacking list description is eliminated by the simple fact that the fragments can be recognised on the O. G. S. Crawford photographs (figs. 2–4). The rectangular attachment plates of the anchor-fitting have cut away shoulders, the two round-ended strap-ends associated with the broader hanging-up strap do not. The assembly of fittings seen in these photographs clearly includes both a round-ended strap-end and one of the attachment plates, with cut away shoulders clearly visible, of the anchor-fitting. The second attachment plate of the anchor-fitting can be seen protruding from beneath the first, recognisable by its strictly rectangular shape. The presence of a strap-end (and it may seem also of a pyramid, as just discussed above) together with the remains of the anchor-fitting in IV.14 confirms the close association of hanging-up strap and the anchor-fitting of the carrying strap as seen in the reconstruction, together, at the top of the shield (fig. 6b).

VI   THE GILT-BRONZE 'RING' AND ITS ASSOCIATED STRIP

The association of what appears to be a sword-ring or similar object (p. 129, pl. 7a and fig. 93) with a shield is unique. The object was not seen by the excavators and is nowhere recorded. Its association with the shield is supported by the following factors:

(a) It was found among boxes of material from the shield complex. It fell out of a lump of sand in the Laboratory when shield material was being examined. Though not at the time thought by the Laboratory staff to belong to the shield, and though subsequently separated from it and exhibited as an individual object, it was nevertheless noted in the Laboratory as having come 'from the shield region'.

(b) It is gilt-bronze and its characteristics indicate that it is East Scandinavian in type. The fittings and general design characteristics of the shield are also of East Scandinavian type.

(c) The seating for the ring (fig. 99) has been recognised on a piece of alder wood underlay found amongst the shield remains in the reserve collection. This alder wood is identical in character with the underlays associated with the gold-foil elements and the small bosses on the shield. Not only is the shape of the ring with its projecting nose outlined in greenish-whitish discoloration of the wood (caused by corroding bronze) but the narrow edging of the hollow ring has left its complete impression in the wood, and fragments of gilding survive in the impression in two places (fig. 99a, b). The central rivet hole in the alder wood corresponds exactly with the projecting rivet-shank at the back of the ring.

[1] Maryon took this location to be the bottom of the shield and consequently mounted it below the boss in his reconstruction.

The association of the ring with the shield is thus firmly established: its position on the shield remains unknown. There are several possibilities, but it seems that, by a process of elimination, these can be reduced to a single probability (fig. 6).

Figure 99 a shows the wooden seating of the ring. It can be seen from the elucidatory drawing (fig. 99 b) that the ring-shape is surrounded by a circular area of wood with no patterning; and that the ring itself occupies an elongated space with its nose pointing to the bifurcation of a pattern of symmetrical type. The symmetrical outward development of the pattern resembles this appearance at the base of the zoomorphic pattern of the large strips (fig. 53 a); but the sword-ring cannot have come from either of these, as they already have central features (the small bosses). It thus seems likely that it formed a central feature of another strip, but one smaller in scale, as the smaller diameter of the circular area in which the ring was set and the apparently smaller scale of the pattern both show. If we look for other possible positions for the ring, it seems that it cannot have occupied the area of the bird's body (for which there is no information). For one thing, its attachment to the bird would tend to confuse both the imagery of the bird and the significance of the ring. But, primarily, there is no room for the ring in the area of the bird's body: if the necessary circular space is left around the ring the residual shape is both irregular and insufficient for the development of a pattern of the kind indicated—a symmetrical pattern of a narrow, long form.

We can also say that the ring did not come from one of the rectangular foil panels around the flange or rim of the shield. These were apparently not mounted on wood backings and their designs were overall patterns (fig. 64). The ring was mounted, and on such a panel would have covered up the ornament; whereas we can see that the pattern associated with the ring was directly related to it, that is, it began outside the limits of the circle surrounding the ring and developed away from it.

Again, the ring, if mounted on a foil strip, as it seems to have been, does not appear to be capable of a position near the winged dragon without a loss of general effect and balance. It seems natural to put the ring and its inferred strip (which should run horizontally, as all strips do) in the only remaining place suited to the generally symmetrical design of the shield, as shown in figure 6, strengthening the vertical decorative axis and helping to balance the triangle of bosses at the top. The indications that the Sutton Hoo ring came from a strip are perhaps supported by the fact that the only other similar ring known, demonstrably not from a sword (p. 134)—that from the drinking-horn in the Swedish boat-grave, Valsgärde 7—was mounted on a silver strip apparently[1] of general shield type, tapering to the ends, which were squared off. The strip was set lengthways along the drinking horn (fig. 101).

The ring from the Sutton Hoo shield is described and discussed in detail in chapter II below.

---

[1] The original strip, with the Valsgärde 7 finds in the Gustavianum, Uppsala, is in a very fragmentary condition and it is not clear from the fragments themselves how far there is evidence for the shape given to it on the reconstructed horn.

46

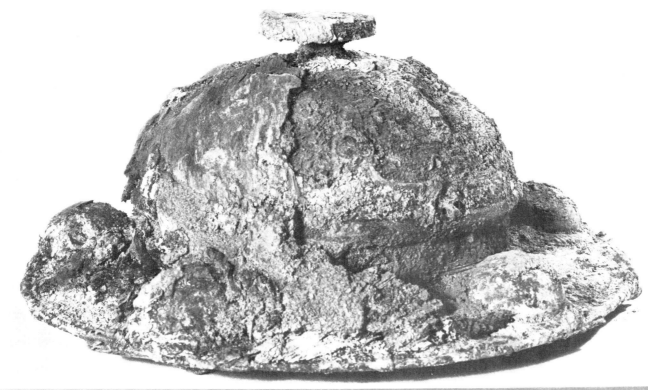

a

b

FIGURE 34   The shield: the iron and gilt-bronze boss, (*a*) before and (*b*) after cleaning. (Scale: 3/4)

47

The boss (pl. 4 and figs. 19, 34 and 35) is of iron. Its top is slightly crushed or depressed, presumably from the weight pressing on it since the collapse of the chamber.

Dimensions

Width overall	21·5 cm
Width of dome	13·5 cm
Width of flange	4·5 cm
Height overall	10·0 cm
Diameter of central disc on top	4·0 cm

The boss is of domed form. It has an internal depth, measured from a flat surface (including the downward slope of the flange), of 8 cm. The opening (fig. 35) originally crossed by the grip has a width of 12 cm. Above the opening is a vertical collar or cylindrical neck of the same diameter, and 2·5 cm in height. Immediately above this the boss expands and then turns back inward on itself to form a rather shallow overhanging dome. This is in turn crowned by a thick solid central cylindrical stem

FIGURE 35   The back of the shield-boss, after cleaning.
(Scale: 1/2)

surmounted by a flat circular disc (pl. 5 *b*). The flange of the boss is broad and carries five large equally spaced gilt-bronze hemispherical rivet-heads, each surrounded by a raised collar. Between the rivet-heads are five sheets of stamped bronze foil, heavily gilded and bearing identical designs of two pairs of horses, erect and interlinked (pl. 5 *a* and fig. 36). The outer edge of the flange is bound with gilt-bronze edging held by five fluted gilt-bronze clips each of which is placed midway between a pair of bosses (figs. 34 *b* and 36). The designs on the flange are complete in themselves and were designed for the space they occupy. The collars round the hemispherical flange-bosses, however, impinge on the foil, covering the extremities of the design. The design is iconographically related to that of the double plaque in cloisonné-work on the lid of the purse (pl. 13, fig. 369). Both depict quadrupeds erect with interlacing limbs and with bodies interlocked. The only difference, allowing for scale and the fact that one is executed in cut garnets and the other in the much more naturalistic foil medium, taken (to judge from its refinement of detail) from a *cire-perdue* cast die, is that in the design on the shield-boss flange a facing pair of animals (horses) occupies the centre of the field. Each of their bodies, canted sharply outward, interlocks with a single outward-facing horse. In the purse-lid plaque the facing pairs are interlocked, the centre of the design being occupied by their intersection.

FIGURE 36 The shield: design A8, erect horses with interlacing limbs impressed in gilt-bronze foil, from the flange of the iron shield-boss. (Scale: 1/1)

FIGURE 37 The shield: design A9, interlace from the vertical collar of the shield-boss. (Scale: 1/1)

The iron boss is embellished with carefully designed applied bronze features which cover most of its surface, leaving the iron exposed only in the middle zone of the dome. The vertical collar between the flange and the overhang of the dome is covered by five sheets of tinned-bronze each bearing an impression from the same die (fig. 37)—an interlace, made up from three animals, in a convoluted style. The die was not tailormade to fit the collar space for, as figure 38 shows, the impressions are cut short at the join. Below them can also be seen the top of repeat impressions, proving that the sections of the collar band have been cut from sheets stamped with two or more

49

FIGURE 38 The shield: detail of the vertical collar of the shield-boss, showing the interlace panel, design A9, and the use of an overlapping die. (Scale: 2/1)

parallel die impressions (fig. 38). (The designs and styles of the interlace on the shield are discussed in more detail below, p. 88 ff.) The die used on the collar is close to one on shield A1 from Valsgärde 7. As figure 34a suggests, the dome of the boss has been crushed slightly downwards, and the panels of bronze sheet on the collar appear to have been pushed up, their lower borders being exposed but the upper borders concealed. A fluted gilt-bronze strip held by rivets conceals the junction between the foil sheets of the flange and those of the collar (fig. 34b). Round the overhang of the dome is riveted a broad, V-sectioned, plain bronze edging, part of which is tinned and part gilded (parcel-gilt). This strong bronze edging holds both the upper edges of the foil panels on the collar and the lower edges of the sheets of the lowest zone of applied foil decoration round the dome. This lowest decorative zone on the dome is made up of five abutting panels of gilt-bronze foil each carrying the impression of an interlace design of horse-like heads and feathered feet (fig. 39b), the horse heads resembling those of the horses on the flange (fig. 36). From the central upper edge of each panel (fig. 39a) a neck develops which supports the base of the skull of an upward-pointing animal head modelled in relatively high relief (fig. 42a). Close examination indicates that the animal head, in spite of its higher relief, was part of the same die as the running zoomorphic pattern below it. The design of horse-like creatures is seen upside down if the boss is looked at from the side. It is meant to

50

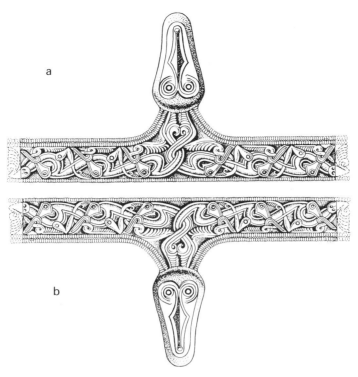

a

b

FIGURE 39 The shield: design A10, zoomorphic interlace design from the lower edge
of the dome of the boss, (*a*) seen from the
side, (*b*) as described in the text. (Scale: 1/1)

be read as it would appear if the shield were viewed from the front, and is shown
thus in figure 39 *b*. The design is completely symmetrical, consisting of backward-turned
animal heads facing outwards on either side of a central linking theme. The running
pattern of backward-turned animal heads with split necks, showing penetration of the
body by a leg terminating in a fern-like foot, is closely paralleled by material found
in Sweden. The lower jaw of each animal is converted into a feathered foot, turned
backward, with the big toe curling back again through the jaws. The whole design
of the panel springs from two bands or bodies ending as feet at the centre. These feet
are cut short by the sharp elevation of the base of the animal head, but this truncation
it seems was part of the design. These bodies or bands cross over and develop each
into three outward-looking horse heads. The two outside end animals must have
terminated in hindquarters with rear legs as shown in the figure. The one strip in
a condition to be drawn, however, has been trimmed at one end and passes under
the neighbouring strip at the other, so that only part of the face in each rear hip can
be seen (fig. 39). The front hip of each animal carries a central spot. Each of the
upward-pointing animal heads modelled in relatively high relief terminates in a neatly
set rivet with round gilded head through the point of the snout. Such rivets, thickly
gilded, are used throughout the work on the shield, and make a distinct contribution
to the decorative effect.

51

The upward-pointing heads round the base of the dome occur midway between the flange-bosses. In between each two upward-projecting heads, one of five animal heads of a different design (fig. 42b) radiate downwards from a central decorative feature at the top of the boss. This consists of a much damaged broad collar of bronze foil of which the stamped pattern can fortunately be recovered (fig. 40). It is not possible to say by visual inspection whether the downward-pointing animal heads are impressed in separate sheets of foil from that bearing the pattern round the disc. The upward-pointing and downward-pointing heads on the dome overlap, so that the ornamental schemes round the base of the dome and round its top interlock, the ten animal heads at the level at which they sit each being a tenth of the circumference apart.

FIGURE 40   The shield: design A11, zoo-morphic interlace below the raised central disc of the boss. (Scale: 1/1)

FIGURE 41   The shield: design B1, zoomor-phic interlace surrounding the central cloi-sonné inlay of the disc of the boss. (Scale: 1/1)

The disc at the top is a solid bronze casting in good condition. It is supported on a solid cylindrical column which is held to the boss by a projecting loop which penetrates the top of the boss and is held in place by an iron pin (fig. 19). Round the outer part of the flat top of the disc, in chip-carving technique, is a procession of five linked animal heads on split necks, the heads doubled back flat over their bodies, and each head having a flat countersunk garnet eye (fig. 41). The interior of the disc is filled by a circle of garnet cloisonné work (fig. 63e) employing four simple cell-shapes.[1] The two ornamented fields are separated and enclosed by borders of two lines of inward-pointing impressed triangles, creating a reserved zig-zag ribbon.[2] The condition of the animal bodies is somewhat worn, the bare metal being exposed through the gilding. The plain outside edge of the disc, 4 mm in depth, is also gilt. The workmanship of the whole boss is of the highest quality. Control of design extends to the placing of the last small rivet-head (fig. 34b).

[1] The cell walls had very largely disintegrated and were replaced in the immediate postwar period in modern metal.

[2] The application of the silver and niello employed in these fields is discussed in App. A, p. 114.

The five lower heads on the boss, as has been said, were part of the same die that produced the running horsehead pattern. All ten were mounted on cores of bees-wax (App. A, p. 114). The animal heads modelled in relief, pointing alternately upwards and downwards, on the dome of the boss, are drawn in figure 42. Other heads from the shield, in high relief, are illustrated in figures 43*a* and 22. Those on the boss are of different construction from the others; whereas the others are cast, these are of thick bronze foil, apparently struck from dies. The analytical results obtained by the Laboratory from other relief heads on the shield, and from the winged dragon, all of which have been cast, are given in Appendix A. The difference in condition, appearance and composition between three of the animal heads round the rim of the shield and the remaining nine, and of parts of the rear end of the winged dragon from the rest of it, were noted at an

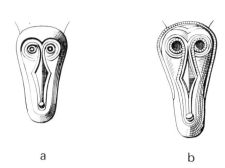

FIGURE 42   The shield: two animal heads, (*a*) and (*b*), from the boss. The heads are raised in gold foil over a wax base. Head (*a*) is thought to be an integral part of design A10, the two being incorporated in a single die. (Scale: 1/1)

early stage. Combined with other indications, such as the presumed substitution of gold foil strips on wood for original strips probably of gilt-bronze, this led to the view that the shield had been in a very delapidated condition when it was buried, with the features referred to either missing or badly damaged.

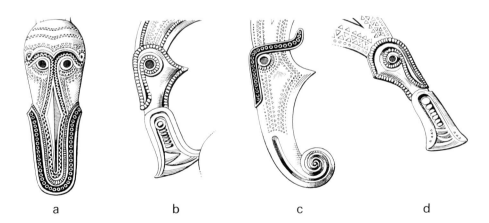

FIGURE 43   The shield: detailed drawings of four different heads; (*a*)–(*c*) from the grip extension; (*d*) from the bird on the front. (Scales: *a, c* 3/4; *b, d* 1/1)

It now seems evident that the remarkable differences in condition and chemical composition of the items and elements cited above are due to differential corrosion and to segregation of constituents of the bronze (p. 111 below). The differences noted can no longer therefore be regarded as evidence for repair or replacement, and do not

FIGURE 44   The shield: the bird from the front as reconstructed, the head and leg elements are original, the body, wing and tail modern reproductions. (Scale: 1/1)

indicate that the shield was delapidated at the time of the funeral, and so an heirloom.

The date of manufacture of the shield will, it seems, remain a matter of analysis of its formal characteristics and ornamental styles.

VIII   THE BIRD

The original elements available for the reconstruction of the bird are:

(*a*) two elements in cast bronze, well-preserved, comprising a leg with large curled foot and a Style II bird's head, from the back of which projects a crest which terminates in an animal head with gnashing teeth (fig. 44).

(*b*) gold foil, detached in 1945 from fragments of wooden underlay then incorrectly assembled as a wing (fig. 45 *a*), but which are now seen to have formed the bird's tail. In 1945 the gold foil detached from this wooden underlay was stuck down, arranged in the supposed wing shape, to a piece of modern leather cut to this shape. As a result of the use of a leather and adhesive backing the foil in the course of time has been contracted and shrivelled almost to total illegibility. Its original quality and the clarity of the design stamped into it may be seen in a fine photograph made before it was attached to the leather (fig. 45 *a*). The photograph also shows a number of small but diagnostic details very clearly.

(*c*) fragments of original wooden underlay, incorrectly assembled in 1945 as a wing which, when correctly reassembled, can be seen to form a bifid tail (fig. 15).

(*d*) mounted alongside the upper edge of (*c*), another narrower piece of alder wood, part of the underlay for a foil wing.

(*e*) a fragment of gold foil depicting a running sequence of animal heads and large frond-like feet, with human faces forming hips (fig. 74).

Items (*c*) and (*d*) as originally found joined were photographed in the Research Laboratory in 1945 (fig. 47). When the photograph was taken the gold-foil fragment (*e*) was still attached to the narrower piece of alder wood (*d*); the photograph also records the true relative positions of the smaller piece of alder wood (wing) and the larger (tail). The two subsequently became separated, but are shown reunited in figure 15. In figure 47 the correct relative positions of the rivet holes in the abutting borders of tail and wing should be noted. The photograph further shows that the leather (and wood) of the shield-board ran continuously beneath the two alder underlays, establishing beyond doubt that these belonged together.

The imprint of the cast leg of the bird survives directly on the shield leather (fig. 46) which is still backed by the wood of the shield-board; there is no trace of an underlay for the leg, nor for the bird's head. The cast bronze elements, in fact, had no wooden underlays, but were fixed directly on to the leather covering the shield-board. The relationship of the hip impression on the leather to the grain of the shield-board beneath shows that the hip lay horizontally on the shield-board. This fact conditions the attitude of the reconstructed bird.

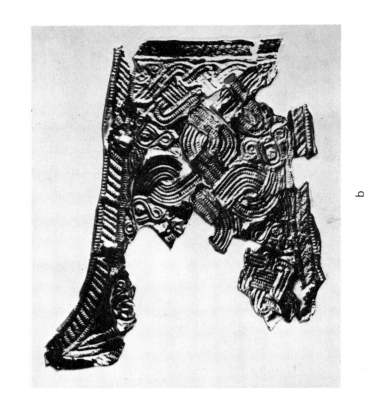

FIGURE 45   The shield: (a) original fragments of gold foil now identified as forming the interlace design of the bird's tail, incorrectly assembled as a wing; (b) photomontage of the same fragments of foil correctly arranged. (Scale: 1/1)

a

b

56

FIGURE 46 The shield: fragment of leather showing the impression of the bird's leg and claw, with the leg and claw alongside. (Scale: slightly over 1/1)

FIGURE 47 The Sutton Hoo shield: alderwood underlay of the bird's tail and wing, photographed in 1949. Traces of the interlace designs of the gold foil that covered the underlay may be seen and a fragment of gold foil still adheres to the surface. (Scale: 2/1)

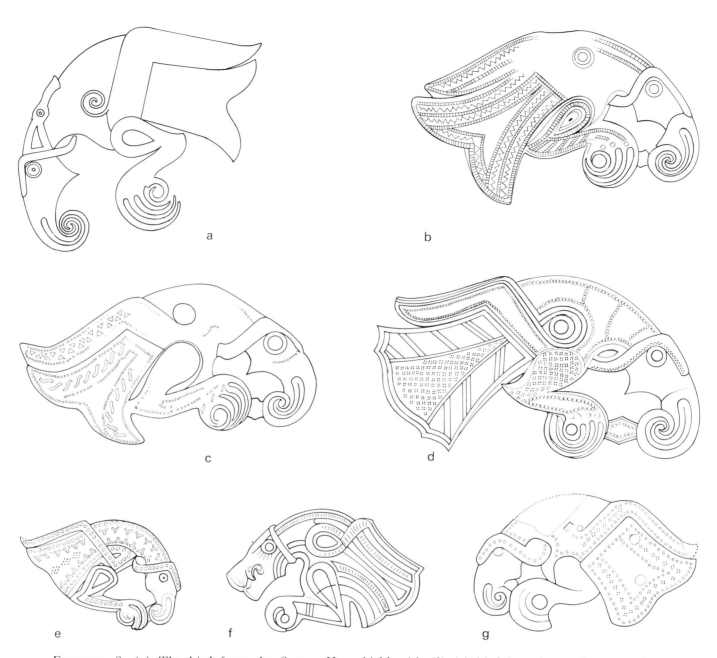

FIGURE 48 (*a*) The bird from the Sutton Hoo shield with (*b*)–(*g*) bird brooches and mounts for comparison; (*b*)–(*e*) and (*g*) are Gotlandic, (*f*) is unprovenanced, now in the Hungarian National Museum. (Scales: *a* 1/3, *b*–*g* 1/1) (*e*, B.M. reg. 1921, 11–1, 251; *b*, *c*, *d*, *g* after Nerman, *f* after Fettich)

The shape given to the bird in the reconstruction (fig. 44) working from these five elements, has been determined by two factors; first, that the tail was of a re-entrant, bifid form, as the correct assembly of the wood underlay fragments showed (fig. 15); and secondly that the wing lay directly against the tail, as shown by the abutting wood fragments (fig. 47), and did not lie detached from it as is the case with the birds on the shield from Valsgärde 7 (fig. 72 *b*) used as evidence for the reconstruction of the Vendel 1 shield (fig. 72 *a*). These features of the bird, the bifid tail and the wing held

58

close against it, are to be found in a bird form commonly used for Gotlandic brooches of the period (fig. 48), and this, rather than the form of the Valsgärde 7 birds, was adopted for the bird on the Sutton Hoo shield. With the thigh set horizontally, as the evidence requires, the effect was automatically to drop the head so that it hung down beneath the foot, as seen on the reconstruction. There is no direct evidence for the shape of the bird's body. The shape adopted follows generally that found in the Gotlandic brooch-type bird, at the same time seeking to link our particular head, leg, tail and wing in a plausible manner.

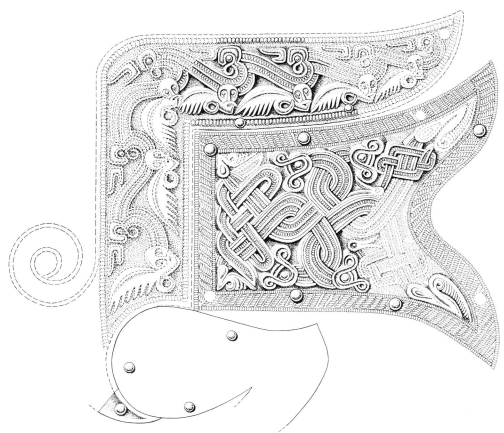

FIGURE 49   The shield: designs A4 and A5, the interlace designs of the
bird's wing (A4) and tail (A5). (Scale: 1/1)

The gold foil from the tail ((b) p. 55 and fig. 45 a) is shown correctly reassembled as a tail in the new photomontage from the 1945 photograph, figure 45 b. This corresponds with the correct reassembly of the fragments of the wood underlay, figure 15. The decorative design of the tail is drawn in figure 49, with the design of the abutting wing in position above it. The evidence for the continuance of the wing down across the bird's body at right-angles to the preserved portion, as shown in reconstruction in figure 49, is slender but definite. The gold foil can be repositioned on its wooden underlay by matching up the rivet holes on tail and wing as they are to be seen, undisturbed, in the 1949 photograph. It will then be seen that whereas

59

the faces in the hips of the animals along the straight middle part of the strip come down in each case to the frame, interrupting the continuous line of feet, on the extreme left the face is smaller, is set higher and leans slightly outwards, and the heel and toe of successive feet come together beneath it. This variant occurs exactly at the corner of the tail at the point where, if it were going round the corner, the pattern should turn. As design is so competent and controlled throughout the shield and its foil corpus, we must suppose that this shift is intentional and significant. The line curling outward at the bottom of the supposed return of the wing across the bird's body is hypothetical, but echoes a feature common in bird brooches where the wing is treated as we suppose that of the Sutton Hoo bird to have been.

The bird's leg

The bird's leg and hip castings have gently rounded (i.e. slightly convex) upper surfaces and are gilt. The foot is flat, and is partly tinned and partly gilt. The leg and hip castings are decorated with broad bands of punch work, consisting of two lines of inward-pointing triangles with a zig-zag ribbon of reserved metal between them (pl. 2 and fig. 46). The curved talons of the bird are tinned but the nails that terminate them are gilt. The hip contains a cloisonné face in garnet-work set in a pear-shaped field. The cell forms (fig. 63 c) are simple. The eyes are of solid bronze (reserved metal) while the mouth is represented by an opaque orange coloured inlay (cuprite). Round the cloisonné face is a border of simple cells, the whole of the field within this border being filled by the face. An analogy with the treatment of the faces on the stone sceptre springs to mind (pp. 358 and fig. 238).

The punched decoration on the bird's leg (figs. 46 and 89 f) consists of broad borders of punched triangles and dots which run parallel with the outlines of the leg. Round the cloisonné face in the hip are two such bands of punched work separated by a narrow plain gilt zone. Each band consists of two facing lines of staggered inward-pointing triangles, with a line of punched dots outside the outer and inside the inner band. The two bands behave similarly. The inner band gives the effect of a reserved zig-zag ribbon with a line of punched dots inside it. Where its two ends meet, just below the point of the chin of the cloisonné face, the lower or left-hand ribbon butts against the upper or right-hand one which straightens out at the point of abutment and then curves back, slightly tapering to a point at the rivet situated in the knee of the bird's leg. On the left, the outer band butts against the passing inner band; on the right it continues as a slightly backward curve to merge with the inner band at the point of the bird's knee. The line of dots inside the inner band runs through, closing off the work and marking one end of the decorative field represented by the leg below the knee. On this lower portion of the leg the decorative treatment is similar except that, to suit the broader area to be decorated, an extra line of inward pointing triangles is added to the inside of the two parallel bands. The lines of dots form the outer margins of the bands. The spacing and lining up of the dots and

60

triangles has been done with great care (fig. 89 f). The punched triangles throughout this work are very small (though the largest of those used on the shield) and each contains a cruciform pattern which must have been cut in the point of the punch (fig. 92). In addition to the added lines of triangles in the lower leg, the gilded space separating the marginal bands of punched work is broader.

The toes of the bird's foot are clearly separated from each other by spaces of equal or greater width than the toes themselves. They curve round and develop into long pointed claws while the rear toe or spur curls tightly in the opposite direction. The foot carries linear punched ornament of a design different from that on the leg, and consisting of double bands of the smallest triangles alternating with rows of dots (pl. 2, fig. 44; App. A, figs. 89 g and 91).

The bird's head

The bird's head is richly gilded and decorated with punch-work and cloisonné garnets. The triangular and round punches employed are those employed on the leg. The punch-work design is identical with that on the flat part of the bird's leg—a line of inward-facing triangles with reserved zig-zag ribbon between them, a further line of triangles pointing inwards and an outer border of dots. This design is used unmodified round the central cloisonné field in the projecting crest, which, unlike the rest of the head, is flat. The design is modified round the eye and on the crest, against the angled cloisonné membrane, where space is restricted and the inner border of dots is omitted. The coiled or spiral beak is plain. It is carinated throughout, like the claws, not flat, like the toes. Behind the eye the angled membrane is wholly in cloisonné work, employing the simplest of cell forms (fig. 63 a), as is normal where the cloisons are in bronze. The cell walls have disintegrated (p. 52, n. 1). The cloisonné work in the crest, filling a triangular field, is again rudimentary (fig. 63 b). It may be intended to suggest a face. A yellow crescentic inlay (pl. 2) matches in shape and substance the mouth of the cloisonné face in the bird's hip, and the one circular cell suggests an eye. The cloisonné work on the head thus provides a sketch equivalent to the extreme zoomorphic shorthand notation found in Style I and traced by Arrhenius in the cloisonné work of the sixth and seventh centuries.[1]

The eye of the bird (fig. 76) was apparently made of two concentric bronze cells, the outer one bordered with filigree work in beaded and twisted wire. The filigree bordering consists of an inner and outer beaded wire ring, with two beaded wires twisted to form a braid between them. The original substance of the eye has not been identified; it was largely missing or disintegrated and was replaced in a modern material in 1945. The central cell, containing the pupil of the eye, appears to have disintegrated, like the cell walls in the angled cloisonné panel behind the eye. It seems to be represented by a circular depression in the modern plaster. The central inlay (pupil) is again a modern replacement (for analytical details see App. A, pp. 100, 101).

[1] Cf. Arrhenius 1970, figs. 12–14.

FIGURE 50 The shield: the winged dragon from the front (Scale: slightly over 1/1)

A detailed analysis of the punched decoration on the bird and elsewhere on the shield, made by Mr W. A. Oddy of the British Museum Research Laboratory, is given in Appendix A (p. 121 ff). The study was suggested in the hope of perhaps identifying individual punches for purposes of close comparison with similar work, particularly East Scandinavian material.

IX   THE WINGED DRAGON

The dragon (pl. 3 and fig. 50) was excavated in a fragile condition and was backed with net and adhesive in the Research Laboratory at an early stage. It has not since been possible to remove all these backings to examine the original rear surface in detail. The head and body were cast separately in bronze (fig. 79). At one point near the middle of the body on the upper edge is an incrustation of iron corrosion which cannot be removed; it was probably derived from the shield-boss (figs. 2 and 3). A piece of the wing on which this corrosion rests is missing. At the tail end of the dragon the tip of the lower of the pair of feet (which resemble a bifid tail) is damaged. This whole terminal element was separated from the rest of the body when found and was in a very poor state. Otherwise the surface condition of the dragon though fragile is good to excellent, and the high quality decoration clear and well preserved.

The length of the dragon in a straight line between extreme points is 27 cm. Along the curve from the outer tip of the jaw to the points of the pair of feet at the other extremity it measures 33 cm.

The head and the body fit to each other in congruent curves. The angle at which the head should be set in relation to the body, adumbrated by the downward turn of the neck, can be exactly determined. The head is fixed to the neck by a rectangular tenon countersunk into the neck, allowing no movement. This is well seen in the radiograph (fig. 79). The join is held by a single rivet. The head of this appears on the front of the dragon at the end of the neck, outside the limits of the decorative panel (fig. 50).

The body, disregarding the wings, is thin and narrow, expanding only at the pair of powerful shoulders, marked by spirals each with a central garnet, from which the first pair of wings develop. The two subsequent pairs of wings also spring from spiral joints, similarly set with a flat garnet. The wings are held close against the body, as if the dragon were coasting through the air looking downwards for a victim. The neat symmetrical composition of the pair of feet which terminate the dragon adds to this streamlined effect. The look and treatment of the feet is the same as that of the wings, especially that of the lowest pair of wings next to them, which is smaller than the other two pairs. The fact that they are feet and not wings is made clear by the presence in each case of big toes (compare the animal feet in the two central panels on the body, especially fig. 51 *b* and *c*). The body proper may be said to consist of the curved neck, of expanded subtrapezoidal shape, and the three narrow panels with their narrower joining necks. The last panel tapers more sharply than the others and is squared off

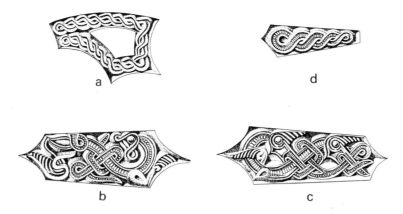

FIGURE 51 The shield: (a)–(d) designs B2–B5, the
interlace panels from the body of the winged dragon.
(Scale: 3/2)

at the outer end; beyond this the pair of feet and their twisted spiral joint develops. The whole of the body so defined is enclosed by a tinned border carrying two continuous lines of inward-pointing punched triangles (App. A, p. 105). The wings and feet and their joints all develop outside this tinned border. The body thickens slightly towards the middle and tapers off towards the foot. The expanded sub-trapezoidal fields represented by the neck on the one hand and narrow tapering field between the bottom pair of wings on the other are both decorated with a filling of pure (non-zoomorphic) interlace consisting of two-strand and three-strand interlaces continuously twisted, like skeins of wool. In the neck panel the interlace surrounds a small trapezoidal space filled with simple cloisonné work set with garnets (figs. 51 *a* and 63 *d*).

The two larger central panels are identical in size but taper slightly in opposite directions. They contain very fine cast and tooled animal ornament (pl. 3, figs. 50 and 51 *b* and *c*). The panel nearest the head contains a single complete animal in profile, logically set out. The middle panel shows an interesting variant treatment, which illustrates the liberties with logic and zoology that could be taken in zoomorphic interlace. Since there are two well-finished heads of equal prominence one would suppose this panel to contain two animals. In fact it contains a single animal, whose hindquarters are turned into a second head and jaws (figs. 50 and 51 *c*). A further unusual feature is the way in which the jaws of the principal animal are ultimately combined into a single strand. This terminates with a twist at the right-hand end of the panel.

The border, tinned and with linear punched decoration, which encloses the dragon's body, is itself edged on the inside with a fine continuous beading. This edging, as distinct from the border itself, is pinched out between the shoulder spirals of the lowest pair of wings for lack of space, but starts again immediately and continues round the lowest field. The strand of interlace which makes up the tapering *guilloche* or 'skein of wool' pattern inside this lowest field (fig. 51 *d*) consists of plain outer elements with a beaded element running between them—a three-strand interlace; this central element is dropped for the last twist of the skein, in the same way that the beaded border-edging is pinched out between the lowest pair of wings. The designer did not attempt to keep the pattern intact as a three-strand interlace because in so doing he would have had to reduce it, where the field contracts, beyond the point of legibility. Instead he reduced the interlace on this terminal section to two strands, thus keeping the pattern both clear and effective. Decisiveness of this kind shows the touch of a self-assured master-craftsman. The interlace skein in the relatively narrow fields round the cloisonné panel in the dragon's neck is a plain two-strand interlace throughout, without central beading. Beading is, however, used to help pick out the spiral wing joints down each side of the body. In the upper two pairs of wings the beading encloses a curled strip which carries a single line of punch-marks from a square-headed punch, impressed in diamond fashion. The head of the punch has been cut to diversify the effect (figs. 89 and 91, d and h). The punch-marks show a central raised spot set on a square platform which is not congruent with the sides of the square punch but is set at an angle of 45 degrees to them. The spiral elements forming the wing and foot joints are gilded throughout. In the centre of each of these seven spirals is a flat circular garnet with a pointillé patterned foil underlay. The wings are minutely feathered with some thirty lateral strokes which run inwards from a continuous backbone. The feet at the dragon's lower extremity are similarly treated but are slightly different as is required by the area they have to fill and the need to accommodate the big toes. The careful and symmetrical decorative use of hemispherical gilt rivet heads throughout, from the jaws to the tips of the last pairs of wings, should be noted.

The dragon's head which, as has been said, is a separate casting, has no interlace and, unlike the rest of the dragon figure which is flat, is modelled in light relief. It has a garnet eye consisting of a single cabochon stone. The appearance of the body is strongly affected by the tinned border that surrounds it. There is no tinning on the head; this further differentiates it from the body and it might be thought to be secondary. There is no technical evidence to support this and the alloys of the two castings are essentially the same (App. A, p. 103). The types of beading and punch work used on the body are used also on the head (figs. 89 and 91 i), the same punches being employed (p. 105). The head must be accepted as contemporary with the body and the markedly different ways in which head and body are treated must be a deliberate feature. In the jaws the incisor and molar teeth are distinguished and at the inner corner of the mouth is a prominent single bead which is a rivet head (fig. 50). This rivet and the single rivet through the tang (fig. 79) are the sole means by which the dragon's head is fixed to the shield-board. But, unlike that which holds the tang, the rivet in the mouth is an integral part of the design of the head and has been gilded over so as to be indistinguishable to the naked eye as a separate object.

In addition to the five prominent hemispherical bosses on the flange of the central boss, there are four more identical bosses on the front of the shield and two on the back. All have a diameter of 3·5 cm and a height of 2·2 cm. The visual effect of the small bosses on the front of the shield is striking. Those on the flange of the central boss (p. 115, fig. 34 b) have collars of thick ribbed and tinned bronze foil over a paste backing. The four gilt bosses out on the board, however, in addition to rounded collars, in these cases not ribbed and tinned but covered all over with fine dots and gilt (fig. 52 a), are surrounded by gold-foil discs stamped with animal ornament. These zoomorphic discs are all struck from the same die (fig. 52 b and c). The two bosses on the back of the shield cap the rivets which fix the handgrip to the shield-board and to the flange of the boss. They are mercury gilded and have tinned bronze collars, decorated with a twisted rope or ribbed design like those of the flange bosses.[1]

A decorative distinction is thus made between the small bosses associated with the central boss, whether on the front of the shield or back, which have ribbed collars that are tinned, and the four outlying bosses on the front of the shield which have inner gilded collars covered with fine dots and outside these a ring of gold foil with zoomorphic decoration.

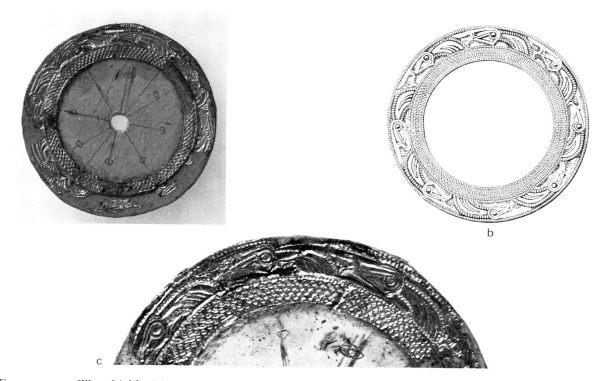

FIGURE 52   The shield: (a) impressed gold-foil collar surrounding one of the hemispherical gilt-bronze bosses from the front; (b) A6, the zoomorphic design of the collar; (c) enlarged detail of part of the gold-foil collar. (Scales: a and b, 1/1; c, 2/1)

[1] For the identical collar design on the shield from Valsgärde 8 see Arwidsson 1954, Taf. 18, no. 264.

XI ANIMAL HEADS ON THE SHIELD-RIM

These are of two types, seen in plate 1 and figures 22, 23 and 85. Punched decoration and beading are used as seen on the dragon and, for punched ornament, on the bird, and similar or identical punches are employed (fig. 90). The garnet eyes countersunk in the bronze are flat, with gold-foil backings. The clips fixing the heads and panels to the shield-rim are of two patterns (fig. 6b). The heads have presented metallurgical problems discussed below (App. A, p. 110 ff.). They are all likely to have been of bronze, showing dramatic differences in condition and terminal composition.

The two types are of the same length: in one, the animal head is seen frontally and has a long slightly tapering muzzle with central carination (fig. 23a); the eyes and forehead of the other type face forward, above a short squared nose and a mouth seen in profile with jaws open, showing four teeth (fig. 23b). The inner angle of the mouth has a circular stop or moulding. The whole outline of the head, except for the opening of the mouth, is bordered with beading. Round the base of the mouth is a loop of zig-zag ribbon, reserved between two rows of staggered triangular punch-marks, as seen on the bird's head and leg. This feature is only carried down a certain distance on each side of the mouth and then stops. In some of the heads (fig. 90) it is carried down further than in the example shown in figure 23b.

XII ORNAMENTAL STRIPS ON THE FRONT OF THE SHIELD

The two long horizontal strips on the front of the shield (p. 40, figs. 6a and 53a) were of gold foil and were mounted directly on strips of alder wood (figs. 54 and 55) cut to their shape. They were held to the alder wood by pins or small rivets concealed by decorative nail or rivet-heads down the sides of the strips (fig. 53a). Pin-holes can be seen in these positions in the wooden underlay (e.g. fig. 55). The two strips were apparently identical in the animal ornament design they carried, since none of the surviving foil fragments that can be attributed to these strips seem to show any variation.

It has been supposed that these fragile gold-foil strips mounted on thin alder wood underlays on top of the leather covering the shield must be secondary—replacements for lost original foil-clad metal strips, probably of iron, which could have performed a practical function, such as strengthening the holding of the two outer boards to the centre board (p. 24) or providing some degree of protection against the effects of weapons. However, the high quality of workmanship which the gold-foil strips exhibit and the fact that the animal ornament designs were worked out for strips of this exact size and shape, and that the strips are complete, so far as we can tell (i.e. not trimmed or cut away anywhere), together with the fact that the central width of the foil and the circle marked out on the wood at the centre of the underlay exactly match in width the existing bronze boss, raise the possibility that they are the original strips designed

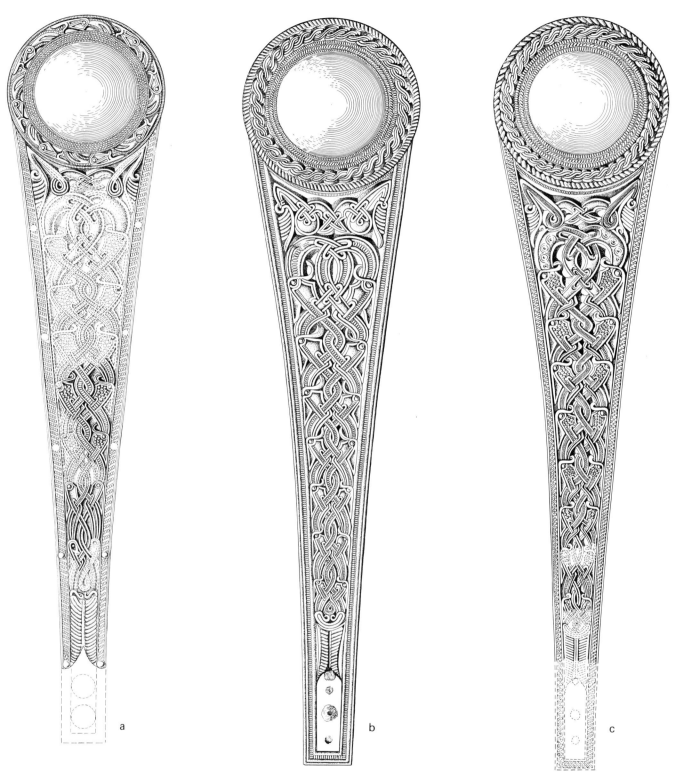

FIGURE 53 Shield strips decorated with gold foil from Sutton Hoo (*a*), with (*b*) and (*c*) closely similar strips from the Vendel 12 boat grave. (Scale: 4/5) (*b* and *c* after Stolpe and Arne)

for this shield. There is no trace where the wood of the shield-board is preserved from beneath the strip (fig. 31) of any lost metal element which the alderwood underlays might be replacing. There is thus no evidence to indicate that the strips are secondary.

If these gold-foil strips are indeed the original ornaments designed for the shield a number of interesting points arise. The Sutton Hoo shield would in this particular differ from surviving East Scandinavian shields, where such strips are almost invariably of solid metal.[1]

The use of non-functional strips on the Sutton Hoo shield might suggest it was for ceremonial use rather than for battle. A further point in favour of this is that whereas the strips on the Sutton Hoo shield terminate, like the bronze strips of almost identical design from the Vendel 12 boat-grave (fig. 53b and c), in a flat bare length which carried two circles (fig. 56a), they are unlike the Vendel 12 strips, in that they have no rivet shanks penetrating these circles—the proper mechanism for attaching the iron strip with its foil covering firmly to the shield-board. The fact that these circles, designed to carry central rivets, are included in the design of the Sutton Hoo gold foils but not used, again stresses the non-functional nature of these strips on the Sutton Hoo shield, suggesting either that this was a ceremonial shield not meant for use in battle, or that the foil strips are replacements whose purpose was to restore a defective shield to its pristine appearance, probably in this case for the funeral.

The similarity of the design used for the strips on the Sutton Hoo shield with those used for the similar strips (bronze foil on iron?) from the Vendel 12 boat-grave is remarkable (p. 88 below, fig. 53a–c). The quality of both is also the same, and they must have emanated from the same hand.

XIII THE CARRYING AND HANGING-UP MECHANISMS

The carrying mechanism

The anchor for the carrying strap at the top of the shield is well made and technically in keeping with other metal fittings of the shield, such as the strap-ends of the hanging-up strap. It consists of two elements, an anchor mechanism of two flat bronze plates which were riveted to the shield-board, with an upstanding loop between them and, attached by a ring to this upstanding loop, a long narrow strap-terminator which is free to move both up and down and sideways on the loop of the anchor-fitting. This fitting has been broken, one of the anchor plates being loose and having a piece missing where it joined the loop (pl. 7c, figs. 56 and 57).

There is no reason to doubt either the connection of this fitting with the shield or its position on the shield-board (pp. 18 and 44 and fig. 8). The fitting is parcel-gilt in the bold and effective manner of the bird's leg, the strap-ends of the hanging-up strap and other fittings. The flat surfaces are all thickly tinned, while the six small

---

[1] The only instance known to me where the use of another substance (wood) is reported is the topmost strip out of the ten which reinforce the front of shield 1 from Valsgärde 8. Arwidsson 1954, 55.

a

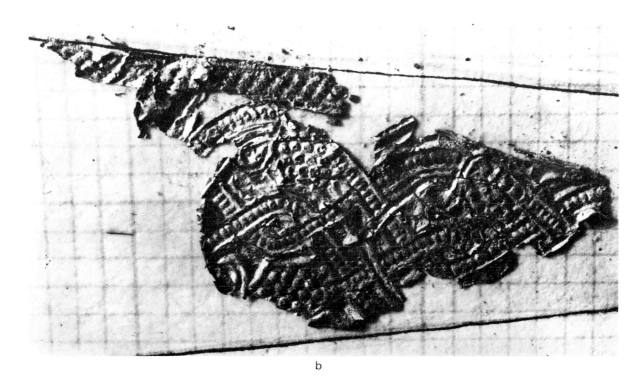

b

FIGURE 54 Gold-foil strip from the Sutton Hoo shield: (*a*) fragments from Area IV. 16 (p. 12) as unpacked in the British Museum Research Laboratory in 1945, (*b*) detail from *a* remounted and enlarged. (Scales: *a*, approx. 1/1; *b*, 4/1) (Photos: British Museum Research Laboratory)

a

b

FIGURE 55 The Sutton Hoo shield: second gold-foil strip; (*a*) fragments from Area IV.17 and (*b*) the largest surviving area of crumpled gold foil. (Scales: *a*, approx. 3/4; *b*, approx. 5/2) (Photos: British Museum Research Laboratory)

hemispherical rivet-heads and at the centre the two interlinked loops are heavily gilded. The strap-end and the plates of the anchor-fitting are both decorated with punch-work apparently identical in general design with that on the bird's leg, but obscured by corrosion. The same individual punches were apparently also used (App. A, p. 107 and fig. 91). The anchor-fitting is evidently the product of the same workshop as the bird's head and leg. An interesting point in its decorative design is the manner in which the rivets in the outer corners of the attachment plates are separated from the field of the plate and from the pattern of triangular punch-marks by a quarter-circle of punched dots. Gold rivets in the jewellery are treated in much the same way except that quarter-circle cell walls containing garnets are substituted for punched dots (see pp. 450, 456 and figs. 320 *n* and 323 *a*).

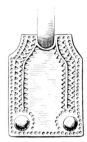

FIGURE 56 The shield: attachment plate of the strap-fitting from the back. (Scale: 1/1)

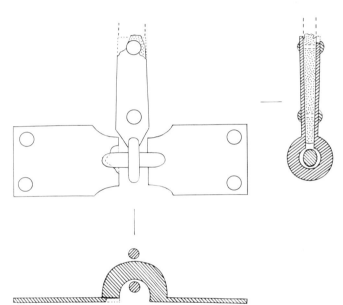

FIGURE 57 The shield: plan and sectional drawings of the strap-fitting. (Scale: 1/1)

The measurements of the fitting and plates are: length 6·2 cm; width 2 cm. The narrow free-moving strap-end attached to the anchor-fitting tapers slightly, giving a width for the emergent strap of only 4 mm. Remains of leather, considered to be the other end of this strap, still remain corroded to the upper end of the iron grip. The reconstruction shows the restored strap thus attached at its free end to the grip. Its overall length in the reconstruction, the result of practical experiments in carrying the shield reconstruction, is 134 cm (fig. 6*b*). Presumably this thin strap was found sufficient to carry the weight of the shield and because of the nature of garments worn (?mailcoat or leather tunic?) did not cut into the neck or shoulder. The narrow strap is evidently that depicted in the Vendel 1 helmet panel designs and on the Valsgärde 7 helmet (figs. 17*a* and 164*a*) as used by horsemen carrying shields.[1]

[1] For a discussion of the use of carrying straps in East Scandinavian shields, with literary references, see Arwidsson 1954, 60–1.

72

The fitting is drawn in figure 57 in section and in plan. It cannot be precisely reassembled from the existing pieces. One plate now seems lower than the other, but this was probably not so originally: it depends whether the loose plate with a piece missing at one end fitted against the end of the vertical connecting loop, or beneath it. In the present cleaned state of the fitting this cannot be established, but the flat, symmetrical version is probably correct. The curvature of the fitting envisaged by Maryon in the old reconstruction, in which both plates tipped slightly downwards, was contrary to the curve of the back of the shield. Maryon was obliged to build up the fitting on wedges of wood.[1] A natural position, especially in relation to the space that we can calculate to have been available for it, is horizontal as shown in the reconstruction. In this position the flat fitting can be mounted without difficulty.

The hanging-up mechanism

The relatively broad transverse strap seen on the reconstructed shield (fig. 6 *b*) just below the anchor-fitting appears to have performed an independent function, unconnected with the long and narrow carrying strap attached to the anchor-fitting. It was probably used to hang up the shield when not worn.[2] There are four metal fittings associated with it—two gilded bronze pyramids and two parcel-gilt bronze strap-ends (figs. 58 and 59). Portions of the leather strap are preserved in good condition between one of the pyramids and the shield-board and attached to one of the strap-ends (fig. 58 *b* and cf. fig. 20). It was tooled in parallel grooves, much in the manner of the fluted bronze clips that hold the bronze rim to the shield-board. The gilt pyramids are rear terminals of the rivet-shanks capped by the two uppermost hemispherical bosses of the triangle of bosses at the top of the shield (p. 44 above).

There is no direct evidence for the overall length of this strap or for the spacing of the two bosses between which it ran. An arbitrary spacing has been chosen for the two bosses that show on the front of the shield in relation to the third boss, the position of which is fixed. The resultant triangle of bosses has much the same spacing as depicted in the Vendel 11 helmet panels (e.g. fig. 17 *a*) and seen in the Valsgärde shields which have this hanging-up mechanism, but the bosses may be too close together and the strap made slightly too short. The relation of the strap to the wood grain of the shield-board can still be seen. This establishes that the strap must have run horizontally across the shield. The strap is not adjustable and the purpose of the parcel-gilt strap-ends (pl. 7 *b* and *d*) is presumably to prevent the ends of the strap from fraying or pulling out.

The two delicate gilded pyramids have concave sides and are 1·2 cm high and 1·5 cm wide (pl. 7 *e* and fig. 59). Fittings of this kind are extremely rare, whereas the

[1] Maryon 1946, pl. 11 (the old reconstruction, back view) where the fitting is shown at the bottom of the shield and incorrectly aligned in relation to the grip extensions.
[2] Izikowitz 1931, figs. 79, 80; Maryon 1946, pl. 11. A similar

leather strap but provided with stamped foil ornament in iron and bronze was found in position on shield 1 in Valsgärde 8 (Arwidsson 1954, 56, 60–1, Abb. 35, Taf. 18).

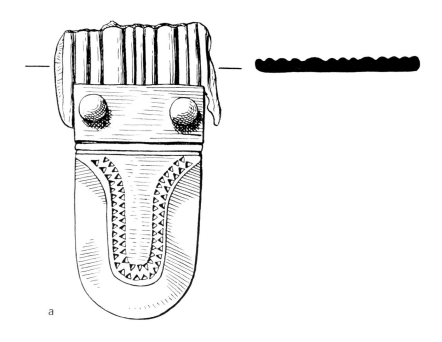

a

b

FIGURE 58 The shield: (a) drawing of the strap-end
and the leather strap, showing its tooling pattern; (b)
enlarged detail of the leather strap. (Scales: a, 2/1; b, slightly
under 5/1)

74

FIGURE 59 The shield: the two pyramids
from the strap-hanger. (Scale: 1/1)

richer pyramids, quite different in function, associated with swords, are relatively frequently encountered (pp. 301, 570 and pl. 22 *e*).

XIV THE GRIP EXTENSIONS

These are rich and elaborate fittings with many interesting features. They are identical, apart from very minor decorative variations. At the base of each extension a gilt boss surrounded by a tinned-bronze ribbed collar, modelled with close-set oblique strokes, caps the rivet that fastens the grip to the flange of the shield-boss. These two gilt bosses and their collars are identical with the five on the upper surface of the flange. The iron of the grip extensions continues for a distance of 20 cm beyond these bosses, tapering all the while. The first 13 cm are covered in gilt-bronze foil stamped with a zoomorphic interlace (fig. 60). Where the foil ends, hollow-cast bronze terminal fittings are riveted over the continuing iron strip; these end in a large animal head, seen from above. Lower down, two animal heads, seen in profile, develop from the fittings on each side, forming symmetrical projections which curve up to meet the terminal large animal heads. Two small rivets with gilt hemispherical heads, side by side, affix these terminal fittings at their bases to the iron strips of the grip extensions. They are placed in a plain zone of the bronze, before the punched decoration begins. A short way above these there is a larger centrally placed domed rivet-head (missing on one of the two grip extensions). These masked the major rivets whose heads are the rounded bosses seen on the front of the shield at the centre of the long horizontal strips (pl. 1 and fig. 6*a*). The hole through which this rivet ran can be clearly seen in photographs of the shield in the ground, where the bronze terminal element of the southern grip extension is seen sticking up at a sharp angle (figs. 2–4).

At the base of each extension large cast bronze bird heads in profile develop symmetrically to either side, immediately above the bosses at each end of the handgrip (fig. 60). These bird heads are nearly twice as large as the upper pair of animal heads.

75

FIGURE 60   The shield: detail of the handgrip extension. (Scale: 3/2)

The various types of heads are drawn in figure 43. The expanding necks of the birds
are split to provide decorative interior fields of sharply tapering and curved form. These
openings were filled with stamped bronze foil bearing a zoomorphic interlace designed
to fit the space (fig. 61).

The large bird heads have the typical Style II form with the membranes at the back
of the garnet eye forming a right-angle, and with sharply pointed chins. The animal
heads (dragon heads) in profile have chins pointed no less sharply than those of the
birds' heads (fig 43b and c). They do not, since they are not birds, have the angular
membrane at the back of the eye, but instead have a rounded profile in cast beading
which is thrown forward to make a triangular flap over the eye. In the mouth, the
molar teeth are distinguished from the canines, as in the winged dragon on the front
of the shield, and in the inner corner of the mouth, also as in the dragon, is a pellet,

76

here given the form of an eye in a setting or socket. All the animal and bird heads and necks have stamped decoration similar to that on the leg of the large bird on the front of the shield, already described in detail (p. 59 ff). The large bird heads at the base of each of the grip extensions show triple lines of stamped triangles, carefully imposed. The two inner rows have their points turned inwards and are slightly staggered, creating between them a reserved zig-zag ribbon which stands out prominently. The beaks run out into tight spirals, the elements representing the upper and lower parts being sharply carinated in a chip-carving technique

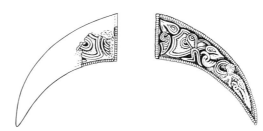

FIGURE 61 The shield: designs A14 and A15, the interlace designs of the lunate foils from the bird-headed side-pieces at the base of the handgrip extension. (Scale: 1/1)

(fig. 60). In the finial (the large terminal animal head) the extent of the stamped patterns is reduced; there are two rows of triangles instead of three. The lines of triangles are again outlined with a single line of punched dots down the outside (fig. 89 a).

The grip extension heads introduce into the Sutton Hoo material, on the large birds' heads in the eyebrow membranes, and in the large terminal head on a raised lip round the jaw, a new form of decoration—annulets of metal in a sunken ribbon of niello (fig. 89 e). The distinctive treatment of the mask of the animal heads, especially the eyes, may be seen in figure 43. It compares closely with the treatment of the peripheral heads round the rim of the shield.

The gilt-bronze foils with zoomorphic interlace which cover the lower portions of the grip extensions between the birds' heads are noteworthy (figs. 60 and 62). The interlace terminates symmetrically towards both the outer ends of the foil. Just beyond the outer end of the interlace pattern there occurs a plain circle with a central dot. This circle fits exactly the space between the rope-like beaded borders. Beyond this circle, contiguous with it, is the greater part of a second similar circle, with a segment at the outside edge cut off. This circle also shows a central dot. The presence of these two circles, combined with the fact that one has been slightly cut short, shows that the die used was designed for a long strip of the kind set horizontally on the fronts

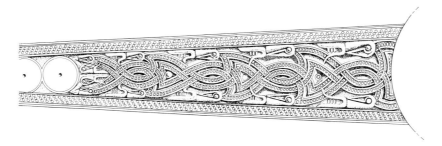

FIGURE 62 The shield: design A13, the interlace pattern from the handgrip extension. (Scale: 1/1)

77

of so many Swedish shields, two examples of which are seen on the front of the Sutton Hoo shield (but in gold foil on wood, not the usual functional iron with decorative foil cover). A detail from the restored Vendel 12 shield (fig. 53*b*) shows that these circular spaces were designed to receive large ornamental rivet-heads.

The two corresponding interlace patterns from the bases of the two grip extensions are illustrated in figure 61. They are not identical and are discussed below (p. 90).

4. *Cloisonné work*

This occurs on the front of the shield in five places (fig. 66):

(1) on the bird's head the angular feature or cere at the back of the eye is completely rendered in cloisonné garnet work;

(2) on the crest or projection from the back of the bird's head, which has a small cloisonné panel in its expanded portion;

(3) on the bird's leg, which shows a cloisonné human face within a cloisonné surround;

(4) on the winged dragon, a panel in the expanding field of neck-and-shoulder;

(5) on the shield-boss, at the centre of the central disc.

In addition to this cloisonné work, individual garnets are employed as eyes or wing joints on the dragon and as eyes on bird and animal heads on the front and back of the shield. The exception is the bird on the front of the shield where the centre of the eye does not appear to have held a garnet (p. 100). In most examples the eye garnets are flat-cut stones inset in individual cast sockets. In the case of the winged dragon the garnet is convex. Where preserved, the cell walls of the cloisonné work are seen to be of bronze, but much of the bronze has crumbled.

A technical examination has been undertaken of the paste employed as backing material beneath the foil underlays of the garnets. The results are discussed in Apendix B (pp. 123–26), and are further referred to in chapter X (p. 599).

The five cloisonné patterns are illustrated in figure 63*a–e*, to which the following points relate:

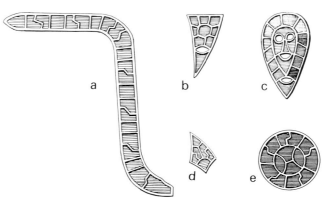

FIGURE 63 The shield, the cloisonné garnet designs: (*a*) angular membrane over the bird's eye; (*b*) triangular setting within the 'crest' projecting from the back of the bird's head; (*c*) pointed oval setting forming a simplified human face contained within the bird's thigh; (*d*) simple geometric pattern from the neck of the winged dragon; (*e*) the central disc from the great iron boss. (Scales: all 1/1)

(1) The bird's eyebrow shows a simple variation of the basic line of plain rectangles. It consists of a regular series of interlocked one-stepped stones, giving the effect of a series of rectangles broken with a zig-zag, with plain squares between them.

(2) There is sufficient differentiation in the cell work and use of colour on the crest to suggest that this is intended to suggest a human face. One of the light-coloured stones is a modern replacement (p. 101).

(3) The use of the pear shape of the hip to enclose a human face with pointed chin is a familiar theme in Vendel art, for example in such well-known pieces as the bridle-mount and shield-boss from Vendel 12 (fig. 70).[1] On the Sutton Hoo shield the theme occurs in the interlace animal ornament of the bird's wing and on the boss (figs. 49 and 39). The cloisonné panel on the bird's hip shows a point of difference: it is not merely a face, but one within a border, 'stopped' below the chin by a semicircular opaque yellow inlay. The analogy with the faces on the sceptre, in frames stopped below with circular pads (figs. 238 and 239), is notable. The repertoire of cell shapes employed can be seen in figure 63c.

(4) The cloisonné inclusion in the dragon's shoulder is a simple mosaic of coloured stones used for relief.

(5) The disc of the great boss round the outside shows the simple theme of interlocked one-step stones (fig. 41) used in the bird's eyebrow.

The all-over style is typical of East Scandinavian cloisonné decoration (see pl. 5b and fig. 230). The cell walls had disintegrated and have been replaced by a grid executed in modern metal. The stones and their foil underlays are original.

The cloisonné inlays are remarkably similar in technique and in cell forms to those on the tongue-plate and loop of the belt buckle from the Åker burial (Hedmark, Norway), although this, while using bronze cell walls on the tongue-plate, employs gold for the cloisonné work in the loop.[2]

5. Animal ornament and interlace designs

The decorative designs on the shield fall technically into two groups:

A—designs stamped with dies into thin gold foil, or into bronze foils, some of which are gilded.

B—designs cast from moulds and tool-finished, in the chip-carving tradition.

The individual designs or patterns are as follows:

CATEGORY A. *Stamped with dies on to foil*
There are fifteen different designs, all zoomorphic.

From the front of the shield

A1 Rectangular panel, capable of complete restoration, from the rim of the shield (perhaps three or six impressions).

A2 Fragment of a second rectangular pattern, closely similar to A1 (perhaps three or six impressions).

[1] Stolpe and Arne 1927, pl. xxxviii, 1, 2 and pl. xxxiii, 2, 3.   [2] Gjessing 1934, 25–32, pl. 1.

A3   Fragment of a zoomorphic pattern with one straight edge preserved.
A4   The bird's tail (unique).
A5   The bird's wing (unique).
A6   Rings round the small independent bosses from the front of the shield (four impressions).
A7   Long tapering strips from the front of the shield (four impressions).
A12 Pattern (uncertain) perhaps from a foil strip associated with the gilt-bronze ring.

From the shield-boss

A8   Design of interlocked, erect horses on the flange (five impressions).
A9   From the constriction or neck below the overhang of the dome (five impressions).
A10 Procession of horse heads and feet from the base of the dome (five impressions).
A11 Circle of foil or collar below the central disc (single sheet).

From the back of the shield

A13 Foil covering central length of the grip extensions (two impressions).
A14 Lunate panels in the bird-headed side-pieces at the base of the grip extension, left side with the extension pointing upwards (two impressions, one only preserved).
A15 Lunate panels in the bird-headed side-pieces at the base of the grip extension, right side with the extension pointing upwards (two impressions, fragment of one preserved).

CATEGORY B. *Cast designs*
These occur on the front of the shield only.

B1   Shield-boss: ring of zoomorphic ornament surrounding the circle of cloisonné garnets on the central disc.

Patterns on the winged dragon

B2   Two-strand plain interlace round the garnet cloisonné field in the shoulder of the dragon.
B3   Smaller zoomorphic panel (one animal).
B4   Larger zoomorphic panel (two animals).
B5   Plain interlace at the tail end of the dragon.

These twenty designs are individually illustrated and described below, in so far as the condition of their surviving fragmentary remains permits. In addition to the zoomorphic and interlace ornament, decorative effects are achieved by the use of garnet inlays and punch work. The garnet inlays and the punched ornament are discussed in Appendix A.

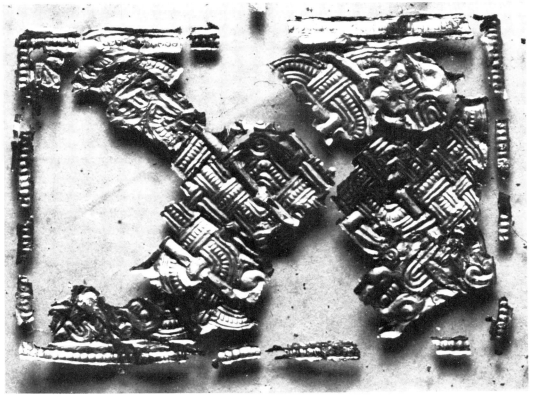

a

b

FIGURE 64 The shield: (*a*) original fragments of gold foil from a rectangular panel at the rim; (*b*) design (A1) of the rectangular panel based on the fragments in (*a*). (Scale: 5/2)

CATEGORY A. *Designs stamped with dies on to foil*

From the front of the shield

A1   *The completely restorable rectangular design of panels from the shield-rim (fig. 64a and b).* The design, which is in general symmetrically balanced, is composed of six animals and two snakes, all intertwined and interlinked (fig. 65). Three animal heads and three hind feet are lined up along the top of the panel, and three along the bottom. Both the snake heads, seen facing inwards, are at the bottom of the panel as we have drawn it (fig. 64b). The snakes have plain rounded bodies which contrast with the flat but broader and more elaborate ribbon-bodies of the interlinked animals. These animal bodies are composed of a line of close set billets with double borders on each side. The bodies of the two snakes cross at the centre of the panel and are tightly stitched on to the other elements in the design. The snakes have narrow jaws, turned sharply outwards at their ends into a gape. They bear a close resemblance both to the snakes' heads in the bird's tail design on the front of the shield (A4) and the inward-pointing triangular foil mounts on the terminals of the two Sutton Hoo drinking horns.[1] The snake theme, with a different head type, is a prominent element also in the design of the plate of the great gold buckle (again associated with quadrupeds), and monopolises the buckle loop. A remoter but nevertheless interesting analogy to the snake heads as we have them in design A4, with small round skulls and splayed jaws, is the snake or goose head attached to the ribbon-like neck bound round the closed muzzle of the seated figure with horse's head on the left of the Bargello panel of the Franks Casket (fig. 67b). The rolled up animals in A4 are in effect ring-chain animals similar to those of the Bury St Edmunds die[2] and the Book of Durrow animal folio (fig. 67a and c) but for their angularity.

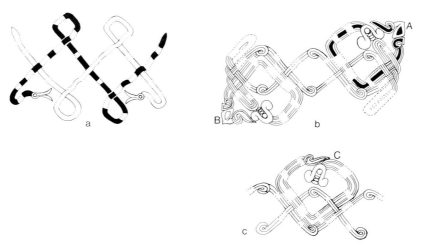

FIGURE 65   The shield: details of design A1 extracted from figure 64. (Scale: 1/1)

---

[1] Fully illustrated in Volume III.
[2] For the Bury St Edmunds die, Leeds 1936, plate XVIII *e*; Capelle and Vierck 1971, fig. 22.

Although the design A1 can be completely restored (fig. 64 b), it is not readily analysed and in several respects is ambivalent. A series of extracted details may serve to illustrate its peculiarities (fig. 65). First, it is easy to extract the two snakes (fig. 65 a). Figure 65 b then takes two animals (A and B) from diametrically opposite corners of the design. Like all the four animals that occupy the corners of the design, these have, pressing against the frame, a rear leg with spiral joint, pear-shaped hip, and foot. From the rear leg the body is rolled into a ring, taken out to a central point, with the clearly depicted head facing outwards. If the jaws of animal A are traced it will be seen that they begin as three-strand elements and then change to two-strand elements. The latter soon enter a twist, which in the case of the upper jaw is attached to the angular point of the body of the parent animal itself. The lower jaw can be seen to run into the lower jaw of the animal which lies upside down below A, it then becomes the upper jaw of this animal and behaves as does the upper jaw of A. From the twist the element that descends from the upper jaw of A passes through two more twists or spirals, finally attaining three strands again where, in the opposite corner of the design, it becomes the lower jaw of the B animal at the other end of the panel. The fact that the six twists in the design, each sited exactly at the pointed extremities of the rolled-up bodies (fig. 64 b), break the borders of these bodies, indicates that the twists are conceived in some way as integral with them. They can only represent the front hips of the animals and, seen as such, the two-strand elements proceeding from them are the front legs of the animal of whose body the twist is part. The design then is one which the jaws and front legs of different animals fuse together. At the centre of the design (fig. 65 c) the two inward-facing animals (C is the upper one) appear to have no jaws. Opposite their heads, though somewhat dissociated from them, are two twists, from which two-strand elements move in opposite directions. Although two-strand and not three, these are presumably intended to serve as jaws for the two middle animals.

A2 *Fragment of a second rectangular zoomorphic panel from the rim of the shield.* Small fragment showing a rear joint spiral, hip and foot, part of an animal body, interlacing jaws and the end of a plain snake's tail (fig. 66 a and b).

This fragment shares the border pattern of A1 and has a closely similar design, but one which appears slightly larger in scale. At first sight it seems possible that the fragment might be the top left-hand corner of A1 (fig. 65 b), but a detailed comparison of the two designs shows significant differences (fig. 66 b and c). In the top left-hand corner of A1 the body of the animal can be seen to emerge from interlacing elements that run across it and then to continue by itself for a short distance before developing the joint spiral at the hind quarters. In A2 the body is seen to be cut off immediately from the joint spiral by an element of two-strand interlace that is not present in A1. We must therefore accept A2 as being from a die closely similar to A1 in conception but different in detail.

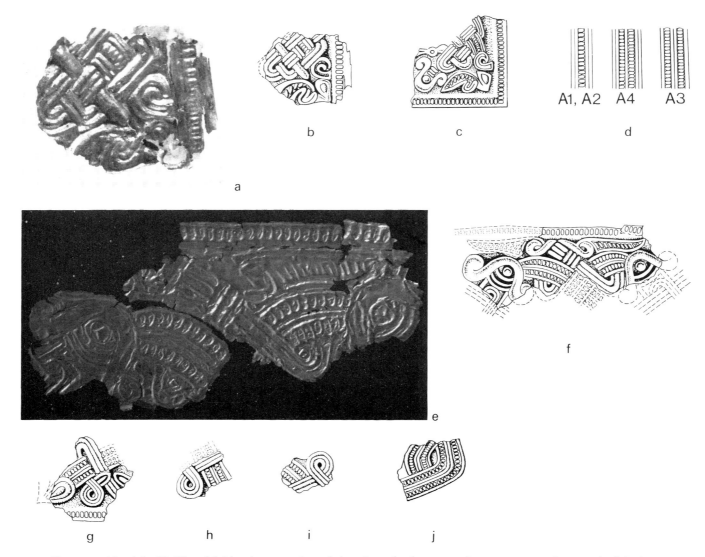

FIGURE 66   (a)–(b) The shield: photograph and drawing of a fragment from a rectangular panel of design
A2; (c) corner from the completed panel of the closely similar design A1; (d) designs of billetted borders
from the shield, A1 and A2 from rectangular panels, A4 from the tail of the bird and A3 from fragments
considered as a possible design for the body of the bird; (e)–(f) fragment and drawing of design A3; (g)–(j)
further fragments of design A3. (Scale: photographs 3/1; drawings 3/2)

It must be pointed out here that the design of the top left-hand corner of A1, with
which we have been comparing the fragment of A2, is almost wholly restored, the
original foil of the panel being defective at this point. The restoration is based on the
evidence of both the upper and lower animals at the right-hand end of the panel, where
the animal body is completely preserved from its emergence from the crossing
elements of interlace to the spiral joint. There is no sign of the additional element
of plain two-strand interlace that cuts off the joint from the body in A2. The principle
of symmetry and logical development seen in the A1 design implies the same situation
at the more defective end of the panel, the top right-hand corner being particularly
relevant as it is in these top corners that the snakes' tails similarly emerge, their heads
both occurring at the bottom of the panel (fig. 65) as already pointed out.

84

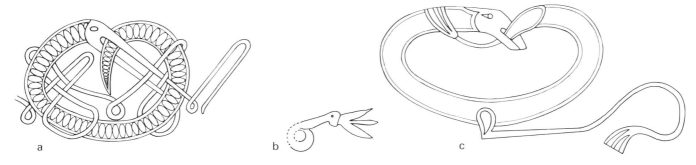

FIGURE 67 Snake-like motifs and a ring-chain animal from (a) the Bury St Edmunds die; (b) the Franks Casket, (c) the Book of Durrow. (Scale: 1/2)

A3a *Fragment of a zoomorphic pattern* (*fig. 66e–f*). Fragment showing parts of two outward-facing animal heads. These, like the heads in A1, have rounded U-shaped plain mouldings forming the backs of the heads which end in plain outward-curling swellings, but here the eye is sealed off by three concentric curves instead of three straight bars. The jaws, abnormally in the Sutton Hoo material, do not form a separate design element detached from the head, but run straight out from the curves that enclose the eye. The necks or bodies belonging to the heads are composed of two parallel billeted ribbons separated by a double plain moulding and bordered externally by a single plain moulding. Behind the heads and turned to face into the panel are two feathered or frond-like feet, with the big toes emphasised and turned backwards. The feet are attached to legs made up of three plain parallel strands, in contrast with the orthodox treatment of the feet seen in A1, 2 and 4, where the feet are joined either to pear-shaped hips or to curls that are in turn attached to cross-billeted bodies. These three-strand legs or elements with which the feet of A3a are associated cross (under and over) the broad necks above and then appear to turn back and vanish behind the necks.

The outer border of the panel consists of a single line of straight transverse billets.

A3b–d (*fig. 67g–i*). These additional fragments, considered to be of A3, show parts of animal bodies composed, like A3a, of two ribbons separated by a double plain moulding and bordered by a single plain moulding. The panel borders where preserved consist, as in A3a, of a single line of straight transverse billets. These fragments A3b–d seem therefore to belong to the same die-struck design as A3a.

If these fragments of A3 are compared with the completed rectangular design, A1 (seen at the same scale, fig. 66), it can be seen that the border, a single line of straight transverse billets, is the same; the general scale of the pattern is more massive. The animal heads have the same plain U-shaped moulding forming the back of the head, with outward-curling expanded or clubbed ends, but the design itself is different. The animal bodies in A1, unlike those of A3, are composed of a single ribbon of billets, within double borders. The eyes are sealed off, as in A3a, by three strokes but these are straight, not, as in A3*a*, curved. The distance apart of the backs of the two animal heads in A3, as measured on the original foil, is 18–19 mm, as against 12 mm in A1 and 8·7 mm in A4. If we regard A3 as being yet another rectangular panel, as its straight, plain line of billet border suggests (cf. the borders of A1, figs. 65*b* and 66), there would seem no place for it on the shield except round the rim. It is, however, possible that A3, with distinctive double-ribbon body matching those of A4, may, like A4, come not from a rectangular panel but from the bird.

The bird's wing, where it turns downward across the body, provides a straight edge and a billeted border. A3 could therefore be part of the presumed missing foil pattern from the bird's body. If we compare A3 with all other patterns from the shield, it can be seen that it shares with A4 and A5 a feature seen nowhere else, namely the two-ribbon bodies just referred to. The two-ribbon bodies in the two designs however are not identical. Whereas in A3 the ribbons are separated by a double moulding and bordered by a single one, in A4 this is reversed. In each case, rounded U-shaped mouldings form the back of the animal heads and curved lines seal off the eye; but whereas in A3 the U-feature is one solid moulding, in A4 it is a double line; and where three curved lines seal off the eyes in A3, in A4 there are only two. The A4 design shows no feet behind the heads, and the outer border, showing a continuous series of long oblique strokes between beaded borders, is also different.

A4   *The bird's tail (figs. 45a, b and 49)*. This pattern is made up of four animals and is unique, in the sense that it is not designed for general repetition, but to fit the symmetrical but irregular shape of this particular bird's bifid expanding tail. Each of the four animals has one short rear leg. The two animals at the right-hand bifid end of the design, while having identical heads and bodies, are adapted to the differently shaped space by having narrower jaws; these are interlaced round their lower bodies in a box form and turned into complete snakes by terminating one jaw of each pair with the snake's head used in A1 (fig. 65). The pear-shaped hips which develop just beyond this interlace of jaws are elongated; the feet are prolonged and bent back to fill up the points of the bifid tail-shape. The other two animals in the design have similar heads and interlacing bodies and jaws. The upper jaw is common to both heads. The rear limbs are tightly composed to fit the corners of the design and are considerably smaller than those filling the tips of the tail.

The tapering of the relatively thick bodies as they join heads and hips is noticeable. Front legs and hips are not present. The thick bodies consist of plain double outer mouldings containing two broad lines of transverse billets separated by a single plain central moulding. The jaws are outlined by a single plain moulding and carry one line of transverse billets down the middle.

These are again the ring-chain animals referred to in connection with design A1. The four broad animal bodies interlink and interlace at the centre of the design. The bird's tail has surrounding it a broad border of oblique billeted strokes.

A5 *The bird's wing (figs. 49, 74).* This shows a distinctive theme, a linear repeat pattern of backward-turned animal heads on split necks, each animal having one front hip and foot, large in proportion to the rest of the design and feathered in style, but turned the wrong way, pointing backward like the head and not forward as front feet should.

The animal bodies consist of a double row of billets separated and bordered by single mouldings. The jaws are short and straight, the lower jaw being shorter than the upper, reflecting the smaller space available. The eye-surround ends in a curl.

There are human faces of pointed oval shape in the hips. They have moustaches, and above and below the pupil of each eye is a tiny spot. The big toes of the feet curl backwards across the leg.

A6 *The foil rings surrounding the outlying small bosses on the front of the shield (fig. 52a–c).* The patterns of the foil collars round the bosses appear all to be the same, and from the same die. The design is a simple procession of split necks and heads, the heads having rather short stubby jaws, the upper straight, the lower turned down, mouth open, showing three teeth (fig. 52b). No head impinges on any other; all are detached. The jaws are slightly pointed. The necks have billeted edges, and the animals have pointed chins. Inside the outer zone of animal ornament is a broad border consisting of a twist or rope-pattern made from dots between inner and outer billeted borders (cf. the borders in A4, A7, figs. 49 and 53a). The rope pattern inner zone and the outer zoomorphic zone are at different levels, the inner one being slightly raised, but they were struck from the same die.

A7 *The long tapering gold-foil strips on the front of the shield (fig. 53a).* This is a remarkable design, the association of which with A6 is seen from the drawing (fig. 53a). There were two identical impressions of the die, running out in opposite directions from a common central boss bordered with A6. The second strip on the front of the shield was of the same design, a symmetrical double procession of fourteen animal heads, seven a side, tapering outwards from the boss. The design begins and ends with feet. The legs associated with the feet at the broad end of the strip were designed to allow for and fit the curved outer border of A6. These legs belong to animal necks or bodies which turn outwards, the heads facing down the length of the strip. The jaws of the initial animal bite across its own body, which then becomes the neck of the succeeding head. The lower jaw runs into the back of this head; the upper jaw passes through the mouth of the second head and becomes the neck of the third. The jaws of the last two animals' heads on the strip join up to become a leg from which an elongated terminal foot develops. This design is repeated in mirror image down the two sides of the strip, the two processions of heads being interlinked by the crossing of the upper jaws of each of two opposed heads to form a succession of small twist themes down the central axis of the design. The animal heads, except for the last pair, have pointed jaws. The first five on each side have their cheeks filled with pellets; the sixth and seventh, which are too small, are plain.

The outer border is a twisted rope pattern in raised dots, the border, as elsewhere on the foil decoration of the shield, carrying convex gilt rivet-heads which add to the decorative effect. In design and execution this long strip bears a remarkable resemblance to that from the Vendel 12 shield (shield 1) reproduced alongside it in figure 53b. The chief difference is that the pellets in the cheeks of the animals in the Sutton Hoo strip are not seen in the strip from Vendel. This detail, however, does appear in a second, otherwise almost identical, strip from Vendel 12, perhaps from the second shield in that boat-grave. This appears in our illustration (fig. 53c). This strip, of which only a fragment was published in Stolpe and Arne 1927 (pl. XXXIX, 9) has since been reconstructed in its entirety, and the restoration is mounted on the same reconstructed shield as is figure 53b.

There can be no doubt that these three strips on the Sutton Hoo and Vendel 12 shields not only emanated from the same workshop, but that the dies are the work of the same hand.

A8 *Design from the flange of the shield-boss (pl. 5a, fig. 36)*. This design is intricate, highly competent, and one of the finest artistic elements in the ship-burial. Its quality and general effect may be inferred from plate 5a. Its relationship with the double plaque in cloisonné on the purse-lid has been discussed earlier (p. 49).

The centre of the field contains a pair of inward-facing horses which interlace back to back with two similar outward-facing animals whose extremities are partly obscured by flange bosses. The animals are drawn in a naturalistic manner. The heads and the necks, on which manes are depicted, stand out clearly. The hip and shoulder joints are strongly demarcated and stylised and the fore and hind legs have feathered feet with the big toe curled back. The front legs of the central pair interlace and the front foot of every animal is gripped by its own jaws. The U-shaped mouldings of the joints contain a central pellet[1] which is separated from the limb by three smaller pellets in the case of the two central animals and two in the case of the outer animals. The shoulders of the central animals are elaborated with a petal-like arrangement of billets. In all four animals a collar of billets marks the junction between head and neck. The bodies show a central line of beading between plain bands. As in A1 and A4, the bodies taper towards their junction with the hip. Double contours outline each body, neck and head, and one of these lines is used on the head to define the eye and sweeps back to form the ear. From the back of each front foot a finger-like element projects and passes under the point of the chin. The design is curved to match the boss flange and is bordered along its inner and outer edges with a single line of beading.

A9 *Design from the neck of the boss (fig. 37)*. This design occurs five times in slightly overlapping impressions. The stamped bronze foil was not gilded, but tinned, creating,

[1] Cf. Arwidsson 1942a, Abb. 83.

88

with the angled edging of the overhang of the boss (p. 50) a parcel-gilt appearance, used also with great effect on the strap-anchor and strap-ends on the back of the shield (p. 69) and elsewhere. The interlace, more confused or turbulent than that of other designs, seems to have affinity with a pattern from Valsgärde 6.[1] Three animals are involved in the design. The animal bodies and their jaws and legs are all of the same weight and an element from each animal flows smoothly into the adjacent animal. Two adjacent animals are one way up, the third is the other way up, giving a twist or inversion to the usual processsional theme. Bodies, jaws and limbs alike consist of a central row of pellets between plain borders. The panel is edged on three sides by a border of transverse billets between two raised mouldings, and the pattern appears to continue beyond the long lower mouldings (fig. 38), as though the die were broader than the one pattern selected for use, or else that the same die had been very carefully repeated on a sheet of foil in such a manner as to give a continuous ornamented surface (cf. the treatment of the face-mask of the helmet, p. 164).

A10 *Procession of horse heads and feet from the base of the dome (fig. 39)*. The design has affinities both in style and execution with A8. It is of the same quality. The upward-facing animal heads, in much deeper relief (fig. 42 a), which surmount these patterns on the boss are struck from the same sheet of metal, and are evidently part of the die. A detailed description of the design is given on page 51. The die included billeted borders; that of the upper edge of the design (as seen in fig. 39 b) is single, while that of the lower edge is double.

A11 *Circle of foil below the disc on the boss (fig. 40)*. The design consists of a procession of five animal heads on split necks. Each has a forward and upward-turned curl or crest above the forehead. The head, or its muzzle, passes in front of one element of the split neck which moves forward to form the upper part of the neck of the next animal head. The jaws, which are plain, cross each other. The split halves of the broad bands comprise two lines of billets separated by a plain moulding and bordered by single outer mouldings, as in the bird wing, A5 (fig. 49). The animals' heads face down the boss, in the opposite direction to the horses heads of the zone of ornament (A10) round the base of the dome, which face upwards.

A12 *Fragmentary design, perhaps from a strip associated with the gilt-bronze ring (fig. 99b)*. This survives only as an impression on a fragment of alder wood underlay. The right-hand portion of the wood is shrunken and distorted. Little of the design can be recovered. A pattern of four lines is recognisable, as shown in figure 99. The left-hand one curls outwards and encloses faint marks.

[1] Arwidsson 1942 a, Taf. 8, 119 b.

89

From the back of the shield

A13 *Foil covering the straight portions of the grip extensions nearest to the boss (figs. 60, 62).* The pattern, a double procession of animal heads diminishing in size, one side of the strip exactly mirroring the other, is akin in the principles of its layout to A7 (fig. 53a). The bodies consist of two borders of beaded ribbon with a plain area in between. The heads have shortish jaws: the lower turn down, and three teeth hang from the straight upper jaws. The outer edges of the necks are billeted or beaded. The neck splits, one border coming forward under the head to rise to the back of the head immediately in front. There are no feet or limbs, except at the extreme point of the strip (its narrower end) where hips develop symmetrically; the feet are replaced by two more heads, back to back, of the same type as those already discussed.

The surge of the pattern, which takes off or thrusts from a circular shape, resembles that seen on the great buckle (figs. 396, 405).

At the upper or broad end of the strip the two elements or strands of the design change over in a simple curve. Pellets occur in the gaps along the central axis of the interlace. The design is completely symmetrical.

A14, A15 *Lunate fillings in the bird-headed side-pieces at the base of the grip extensions (figs. 60, 61).* These patterns decorate the openings in the necks which support the birds' heads to either side of the base of the grip extensions. They were designed for the space they occupy. The two patterns were similar but reversed, since the fields to be decorated are mirror images. Within the billeted borders of the crescentic field lie two separate and distinct animals. The larger has two legs, each of which has a pear-shaped hip and feathered or pectinated feet with an exaggerated backward-curling toe. The head turns back across the body, which is outlined with a double contour. The jaws are simple, but the lower turns back at a sharp angle. The smaller animal is similar but simpler, its design adapted to the sharply reducing field.

CATEGORY B. *Designs cast from moulds and tool-finished*

B1 *From the cast-bronze disc on the shield-boss (pl. 5b, fig. 41).* This occupies a broad ring surrounding the central cloisonné circle. Five animal heads are linked by split necks or bodies, one element of which is cut across by the downward turning lower jaw. The pattern is in chip carving style. The recessed parts retain heavy gilding. The flat upper surfaces in which the design is realised were gilt, but the zoomorphic forms are picked out by linear inlays in metallic silver.[1] The zig-zag between the inner and outer borders may have held an inlay of niello.

B2–5 *Four designs from the body of the dragon*

[1] App. A, p. 114.

90

B2 *Interlace from the neck and shoulders (fig. 51 a).* A simple regular non-zoomorphic skein, in chip carving, surrounding the garnet panel.

B3 *The zoomorphic panel nearest the dragon's head (fig. 51 b).* A single animal, logically deployed, with backward turned head, designed to fit the unique shape of its field. The animal has many points of similarity with those in designs A1 and A4. The head-type is that of A1 and A4. The neck, the jaws and the rear spiral joint contain pellets or small billets, while the broader body is filled with a line of larger billets. The jaws are knotted in an angular manner about the body. The front leg develops from a pear-shaped hip and ends in a rather shortened blunt-ended foot with a small backward-curling toe. From the terminal twist of the body (cf. A1, p. 82) a pear-shaped hip and thin leg develop into a large foliate foot with an exaggerated curled-back toe, designed to fill out the point of the field and the space remaining between the hip and the jaws.

B4 *The zoomorphic panel nearest the dragon's tail (fig. 51 c).* As explained on page 64, although two heads identical in style and of almost equal weight appear in series, point the same way and dominate the panel, the design is really of one animal, with head and leg on the left, whose ribbon body terminates in a second head. The animal's head is turned back and bites across its body; as in B3, the lower jaw forms an angular knot around the body and then runs into the upper jaw, fusing with it to form a single ribbon which continues to pass through the jaws of the second head.

As in B3 the jaws in both heads have a single contour and contain a line of billets smaller than those of the broader body. Each of the two heads has a prominent round eye, a pointed chin and a forelock feathered like a foot. The leg, beginning in a pear-shaped hip, passes under the animal's body and turns, at the point of the chin, to develop into a long feathered foot. This lies across the body and neatly fills the pointed left-hand end of the field.

B5 *Interlace twist from the end panel on the dragon (fig. 51 d).* This simple tapering skein motif has outer borders containing a pattern of transverse billets, which are omitted from the last twist (see also p. 65).

6. *The Sutton Hoo shield in relation to Anglo-Saxon and Continental shields*

The references already made to East Scandinavian shields presenting close parallels to the Sutton Hoo shield may be thought sufficient indication that the latter is of East Scandinavian origin. The deeper the analysis proceeds, the closer the links, both technical and artistic, will be seen to be. From figure 53 a–c the inference was drawn that the dies employed for the long strips on the Sutton Hoo shield and that from Vendel 12 were the work of the same man. The repertoire of animal ornament in the twenty different designs on the Sutton Hoo shield is tightly packed with intimate stylistic and iconographic points of resemblance with East Scandinavian animal ornament (e.g. fig. 68). On the Vendel 1 and Valsgärde 7 shield-boards we see together both the bird and the dragon devices that are so prominent a feature of the Sutton Hoo shield (figs. 72, 6a). The peculiarity seen on the Sutton Hoo shield that only the leg and head of the bird are in solid metal, the rest of the bird being of more fragile substances, is found again on the shield from Vendel 1 (fig. 72a). The gold foil on thin wood backings which supplies the wing and tail of the Sutton Hoo bird helps us to visualise how elaborate the absent elements of the Vendel 1 birds may have been, with zoomorphic detail perhaps tooled or painted on the leather of the shield-board. Even the more mundane milled or 'twisted rope' collars round the small bosses on the flange and grip of the Sutton Hoo boss are seen again round the small bosses on the front of shield 1 from Valsgärde 8.[1]

FIGURE 68 Interlaced animal from Valsgärde 6 which may be compared with design B2 from the winged dragon. (Scale: 1/1)

The similarity of the turbid zoomorphic interlace on the neck of the boss with that of foil covering one of the iron strips on shield 1 from Valsgärde 6,[2] and of the single animal in one of the panels of the winged dragon (fig. 51b) with the animals on the flange of the shield-boss from shield 1, Valsgärde 6,[3] are further instances of the natural context of the Sutton Hoo shield in Vendel-period Swedish art. The bird, also, as reconstructed, is typically East Scandinavian in formal characteristics and details of design.

If we ask, can the Sutton Hoo shield be Anglo-Saxon, and the source of influence on the design of the later Swedish or East Scandinavian examples, the answer is no. The shield, in spite of stylistic affinities here and there with East Anglian finds, is an entirely exotic piece in the Anglo-Saxon milieu—the distinctive, typically East Scandinavian heavy boss type of the Sutton Hoo shield, for instance, with overhanging dome and constricted neck, and with massive hemispherical gilt rivet-heads in the flange, so close to those from Ulltuna (Uppland)[4] and Vendel 1 and 12 (figs. 72a, 70 and 71), is unknown in Anglo-Saxon contexts. Even the two leading Anglo-Saxon princely graves of the first half of the seventh century, Taplow[5] and Broomfield,[6] produced only routine and featureless shields, with unimpressive bosses. It is not that the Anglo-Saxon craftsmen-armourers were incapable of fine decorative work, as details of some of the most impressive Anglo-Saxon shield finds so far show (fig. 69a–c), but that the boss type and the elaborate shield that goes with it is unknown.[7] If the

[1] Arwidsson 1954, Taf. 18, 264.
[2] Arwidsson 1942a, Taf. 8, 119b.
[3] Arwidsson 1942a, Abb. 82c; here fig. 68.
[4] Ekholm 1917.
[5] Victoria County History: Buckinghamshire, Vol. I, 199–204.

[6] Victoria County History: Essex, Vol. I, 320–6.
[7] The elaborate metal appliqués, once supposed to be from a shield, found in a tumulus at Caenby, Lincolnshire, now in the British Museum, can be shown not to have been from a shield, as first noted by Mrs V. H. Fenwick. For these mounts,

a

b

c

FIGURE 69 (a) Detail of the shield-boss from Bidford-on-Avon, Gloucestershire; (b) gilt-bronze disc from a shield-boss, Barton Seagrave, Northamptonshire, with interlace design; (c) the appliqué fish, probably from a shield, found at Kenninghall, Norfolk (see p. 92, fn. 7). (Scales: a, 3/5; b and c, 1/1) (Copyright (a), Trustees and Curator of the Birthplace, Stratford-upon-Avon)

93

Sutton Hoo shield is to be thought of as made in England then it must have been made by an East Scandinavian armourer working here with dies and punches brought from his native land, and exclusively in the manner and traditions of that land.[1]

A more precise discussion of the shield and its position in relation to Continental examples, in particular those referred to below, both of Late Antique and of Lombardic origin, from northern Italy, is a matter for future studies. Meantime, as it bears on the general shield-boss design and on the validity of significance of major features in the reconstruction, it is necessary to draw attention to the relationship of the Sutton Hoo shield with others of East Scandinavian origin. Not only is this the milieu from which, it seems clear, the Sutton Hoo shield comes, but the boat-grave excavations, in Uppland particularly, have produced an unparalleled series of reconstructable shields with much informative detail.

On the reconstruction of the Sutton Hoo shield there are eighteen peripheral ornaments, and, as has been said (p. 34), it is possible there may have been twenty-four: twelve animal heads, of two types, and twelve rectangular panels of animal ornament, also of two types (fig. 29). Of the Valsgärde shields, Valsgärde 8, shield 1, has sixteen peripheral ornaments of four types (fig. 27), and shield 2 has fifteen.[2] Valsgärde 6, shield 1, has a number of similar large open-work iron rim ornaments—including not less than seven which were not included in the restoration of the shield.[3] In the case of Valsgärde 7, one shield, which has fourteen horizontal metal strips, has ten rim ornaments all of the same form.[4]

The Sutton Hoo shield, allowing for the margin of uncertainty as to its precise diameter, is of average size, perhaps on the small side, in relation to the Vendel and Valsgärde shields and other Continental examples whose dimensions are fixed or can be reasonably estimated. The shields from Niederstotzingen, in Württemberg, if anything a little smaller than the Sutton Hoo shield, are thought to have varied between 80 and 90 cm in diameter.[5] That from grave 145 at Oberflacht is given as 88 cm.[6] The Valsgärde shields have the following range:[7]

and an account of the excavation of the tumulus in 1850, see British Museum 1923 (R. A. Smith) and the primary account by the Rev. Edwin Jarvis (1850). The fish illustrated in figure 69 c, from Kenninghall, Norfolk, in a collection presented to the British Museum by A. W. Franks in 1883, shows a rivet clearance at the back of 7 mm, exactly corresponding with the thickness of the Sutton Hoo shield-board. Its length, 15·1 cm in its slightly incomplete state, makes it suitable in scale for a shield ornament. It was found with remains of a shield-boss, with a disc on top; the shield grip, six silver-plated discs 3·8 cm in diameter, probably from the flange of the boss, and one similar disc 4·3 cm in diameter. The Kenninghall fish must certainly be regarded as a shield mount. Somewhat similar fish-mounts are cited by Reginald Smith in the *Victoria County History: Suffolk*, 342, from Mildenhall, Suffolk (length 7 cm) and Kempston, Bedfordshire (British Museum, length 10·4 cm). These are smaller than the Kenninghall fish; but that

from Kempston is said to have been found with the remains of a shield, which included two tinned or silver discs.

[1] Although comparative data are as yet very limited, the employment for the Sutton Hoo shield-board of lime wood and not conifer, the type of wood which seems to have been regularly used in East Scandinavian shields in which wood identification has hitherto been possible, should be noted. It could be compatible with the notion of manufacture in England from local woods by an East Scandinavian armourer. For Swedish shields where pine has been identified see Ardwidsson 1942 a, 35, 40 and 1954, 54 (Valsgärde 6, shields 1 and 3; Valsgärde 8, shield 1).

[2] Arwidsson 1954, Taf. 10, 11, 16, 17.

[3] Arwidsson 1942 a, 38–9, Abb. 31; Taf. 9, 143 and Taf. 10.

[4] Unpublished.

[5] Paulsen 1967, 123, col. 1.

[6] Veeck 1934; mentioned by Paulsen 1967, 123.

[7] Arbitrary numbering since the shields are not yet finally published.

FIGURE 70   The boss from shield 1, Vendel 12. (Scale: 2/3)

Valsgärde 6
Shield 1   95 cm
Shield 2   not determinable
Shield 3   84 cm

Valsgärde 7
Shield 1   96 cm
Shield 2   108 cm
Shield 3   100 cm

Valsgärde 8
Shield 1   110 cm
Shield 2   108 cm

FIGURE 71   The boss from shield 1, Vendel 12, an oblique view showing the similarity of profile with that of the Sutton Hoo shield. (Scale: 2/3)

The restored shield from Vendel 1, with the birds and dragons on its front, has a diameter of 104 cm. The Sutton Hoo shield as restored with a diameter of 91·5 cm would be among the smaller shields. If 96·5 cm were chosen it would still seem of modest size amongst these great shields.

Several European shields have been reconstructed as having curved boards, including five of the nine from the rich graves at Niederstotzingen,[1] and shield 1 from Valsgärde 6. On the other hand Vendel shields originally reconstructed as curved[2] have since been re-made as flat. The Sutton Hoo shield appears to be the only one to give clear evidence of a curvature that starts only at the extreme ends of the grip extension (fig. 11, p. 18 ff.). The Sutton Hoo shield, in the version adopted in the reconstruction, with only six rectangular panels (pl. 1), gives an impression of a grouped decorative rim treatment—spaced panels flanked by pairs of heads. Although these are in a northern zoomorphic manner, and although the shield includes a striking use of figural elements (bird and dragon), the general concept and design seem to bear affinities with the remarkable Lombardic or sub-Byzantine group of shields, attributed to the early seventh century, which include those from Ischl-an-der-Als

[1] Paulsen 1967, 123.   [2] Izikowitz 1931.

96

(Bavaria), Lucca (Italy) and Stabio (Canton Tessin) (fig. 28 *a* and *b*).[1] These shields, strongly influenced by the late Roman or Byzantine tradition, with devices of peacocks, lions, chalices, standard bearers and riders on horseback, are the product of a workshop or workshops in a Late Antique figural style making only limited concessions, if any (e.g. the horses' heads on the Lucca shield), to the Germanic manner, although in the ornamental field the extensive use of surface decoration of punched triangles and dots (in one version exactly matched on the Sutton Hoo shield) must represent a Germanic element. The Sutton Hoo type, which must have had behind it an already well-established tradition, may have originated in the Lombardic/South Germanic areas, where the heavy 'Swedish' boss-type (if less developed), Style II interlace, often surprisingly similar to Swedish interlace, an almost identical use of punched ornament, and the manner of decorative treatment with appliqués on the front of the shield, are all to be found. On the other hand, the fact that the Sutton Hoo shield seems to be probably contemporary with or earlier than these Italian and Swiss-found examples, as they are at present dated, places difficulties in the way of such a theory.

An important and distinctive feature of the Sutton Hoo shield which cannot at present be paralleled elsewhere is the use of applied zoomorphic patterns in thin gold foil on wood backings. We see the use of foil, moreover, not confined to the horizontal strips, grip extensions and boss flanges, where patterned bronze foil performs a similar function in other shields, but used in the large bird figure and in panels round the rim. The use of gold foil on the Sutton Hoo shield may be merely an expression of the richness sought for in the design of a royal shield, pure gold being employed as well as gilt-bronze. But against this it must be said that pure gold is not consistently employed, for there is much gilt-bronze foil as well, in basic features such as the boss and grip extensions. The use of gold foil for the long strips, the panels round the rim and the bird's body and wing, might suggest that the shield was a ceremonial or parade piece not intended for battle, or else that these are replacements or repairs on a shield originally furnished throughout with more conventional materials. If the gold foil were mounted on metal strips this would not affect the basically functional character of the shield. Its mounting on thin veneeers of soft wood, as seen on the Sutton Hoo shield, however, abandons any functional pretensions, but is entirely effective ornamentally; and as apparently not very robust it would suit the idea of repair or making good for a special ceremonial occasion such as a grand royal funeral, as well as it would the idea of a parade shield.

The cast bronze leg and head of a bird figure in the shield from Vendel grave 1 (fig. 72 *a*) is of much the same size and style as the Sutton Hoo bird. With them were found traces of the body, tail or wing in iron. This bimetallism occurs again on the same shield in a second motif, the dragon. This parallels strikingly the use of these two themes on the Sutton Hoo shield, but on the Vendel 1 shield the bird and dragon occur not once but twice.

[1] Werner 1951/52 (Ischl and Stabio) and Fuchs 1940 (Lucca).

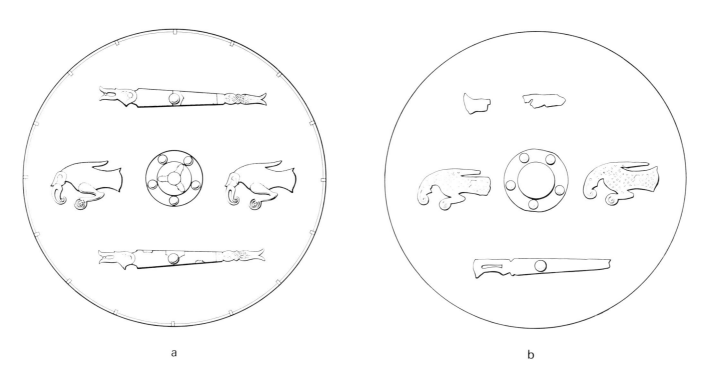

FIGURE 72   The shields from (*a*) Vendel 1 and (*b*) Valsgärde 7 for comparative purposes.

The use of these two themes as joint devices on the front of a shield, and again of two of each, as in the Vendel 1 shield, occurs on a much cruder shield from the Valsgärde 7 boat-grave. This shield was expertly excavated and so could be validly reconstructed, and it was used as the basis for the new reconstruction of the Vendel 1 shield.[1] In the shield from Valsgärde 7 the birds and dragons are wholly executed in iron and their bodies are in an open lattice pattern. It is noticeable that in both shields[2] the dragons take the place on the front of the shield of the two conventional strips, with small bosses at their centres, that are riveted through to the grip extension on the back, and help to hold the two outer boards to the centre board. As has been demonstrated (p. 24 ff.) this cannot have been the role of the dragon on the Sutton Hoo shield, where this function is performed by the gold strips of conventional form, if not of conventional substance. It is noteworthy also that in the Vendel 1 shield, whatever may have been the case with the birds' bodies, of which nothing survives, in the case of the dragons' bodies enough survives to be recognised as an iron strip edged with gilt-bronze on both upper and

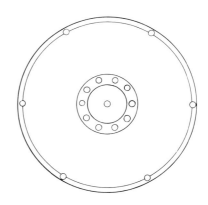

FIGURE 73   The shield from Wiesbaden now in the Städtlisches Museum, Wiesbaden (drawing based on photographs). (Scale: 1/9)

[1] Lindqvist 1950*b*, figs. 4, 5 (here fig. 72*a*).
[2] In that from Vendel 1 the length of the dragons would seem to preclude any other positioning; cf shields 1 and 2 from Valsgärde 8, Arwidsson 1954, Taf. 10, 11, Abb. 33.

98

FIGURE 74   The Sutton Hoo shield: surviving gold foil from the bird's wing. (Scale: 3/1)

lower edges. In the Vendel 1 shield both dragons fly in the same direction and are the same way up. In the Valsgärde shield the uppermost dragon appears to be upside down, lying on its back. This would yield two inner straight edges to match the lines of the board edges (fig. 72 a and b).

The Sutton Hoo shield shares with several of the Valsgärde shields a notable feature that is not found on the finer Vendel shields, namely, ornamentation round the circumference of the rim (figs. 6 a, 23 and 27). The rim-ornaments of the Valsgärde shields are in iron openwork and are devolved and schematic to the point of obscurity. This is no doubt to be explained by the relatively poorer Valsgärde social level (rich indeed though it is) as compared with Sutton Hoo, and by the manifestly later date of the Valsgärde shields. Nevertheless these shields offer many interesting analogies.

Manuscript illustrations show that both curved and painted shields were in use in Carolingian times, and elaborate surface decoration of the shields of dignitaries was evidently established in the Imperial bodyguard and in court circles in the Eastern Empire. Unfortunately no trace of paint or staining of the leather can be detected on the Sutton Hoo shield remains. In the reconstruction (pl. 1) a natural oak-bark tanned leather has been used.

APPENDIX A

REPORT ON THE SCIENTIFIC EXAMINATION OF THE SHIELD[1]

by

W. A. ODDY, MAVIS BIMSON, M. J. HUGHES AND A. E. WERNER

1. *The bird ornament from the front*

The head

This appears to be made from one piece of bronze and examination of the radiograph shows no evidence for joins. However, the possibility that there were joins along the lines *a–b* and *c–d* (fig. 75) cannot be ruled out. These possible junctions are now obscured by copper corrosion products but it can be seen that the back is not flush across the line *a–b* (fig. 75, section).

76. The inner and outermost rings are single beaded wires and the join in the circle can be seen in each case. Between these circles is a ring composed of two beaded wires twisted together; in this case the join cannot be detected. The wire assembly has been mercury gilded after being assembled, presumably by soldering.

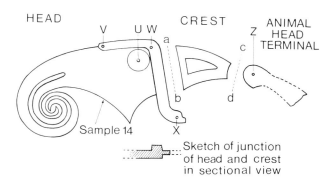

FIGURE 75 The shield: exploded diagram of the bird's head assembly with a section across the junction of the head and crest. (Scale: 1/2)

FIGURE 76 The shield: enlarged detail of the bird's eye. (Scale: 3/1) (Photo: British Museum Research Laboratory)

The top surface of the bird head assembly has been mercury gilded. A sample from position 14 (fig. 75) was examined by emission spectrography and shown to contain gold, silver, copper and mercury, with traces of some other elements. The punched decoration was almost certainly applied to the head and tapering crest after the gilding had been carried out, but the decorative work on the terminal head must have been completed before gilding.

The components of the eye are shown in figure

Repairs in gypsum were made to the material of the eye setting in 1945. The original central setting is absent, although a ring of dark grey-green material surrounds the cavity for the missing pupil. An attempt to identify this by X-ray diffraction analysis failed because the sample proved to be amorphous; X-ray fluorescence analysis on the scanning electron microscope revealed the presence of tin containing smaller amounts of several other elements, including copper. At the bottom of the pupil cavity is a yellow

[1] This report records the work carried out during the period 1971–5.

deposit which also failed to give a meaningful pattern when examined by X-ray diffraction, but which was shown by X-ray fluorescence to contain aluminium and silicon with minor amounts of other elements. The possibility that this is soil contaminated by corrosion products cannot be excluded, although an identification as a packing material containing clay, and perhaps quartz, is consistent with the analytical results.

The eyebrow contains twenty-three garnets. These are all backed with stamped gold foil, having the depressions pointing upwards, except for numbers 7, 12 and 20 (counting from the front end of the eyebrow) which have the depressions pointing downwards.

There is no evidence, either visual or by radiography, for cell walls between these garnets, although in a few places there are traces of bronze corrosion round the edge.

Garnet 4 was removed from the eyebrow, together with its gold foil backing, to reveal a soft greenish material in the bottom of the setting. This backing material was examined by X-ray diffraction analysis and shown to consist mainly of calcite. A small amount of some other material is present which could not be positively identified, but which does not seem to be wax. Hence this material belongs to Arrhenius's Group 1.2.a.[1] Garnet 4 was identified as almandine by X-ray diffraction analysis.

The tapering crest is decorated with an approximately triangular garnet panel. The cell walls now consist of corroded bronze and the positions of existing ones are shown on figure 77. Microscopic examination of both the back and the front of the panel reveals no evidence for any others.

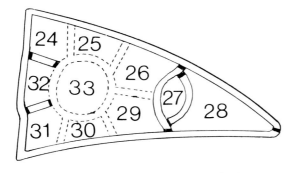

FIGURE 77 The shield: diagram of the garnet panel in the tapering crest at the back of the bird's head. (Scale: 4/1)

Inlay 25 is an imitation garnet inserted in 1945 and inlay 27 has been shown by X-ray diffraction analysis to be cuprite glass. Inlay 33 is made of a brown material which could not be identified by X-ray diffraction analysis as it proved to be amorphous. All the other inlays are garnets backed with stamped gold foil with the depressions pointing upwards. The back of the foil below the garnets appears to be coated with a pale green paste. Under the microscope this paste is seen to be non-homogeneous and to consist of a white matrix containing a green crystalline material. Analysis by X-ray diffraction has shown that the major constituents are wax and malachite (basic cupric carbonate) respectively, but that other unidentified materials may be present in smaller amounts. The analyses of similar backing materials reported by Arrhenius do not contain a mixture of wax and malachite. It is probable that a backplate has been lost from this garnet panel and that the pale green mixture is a packing material from the bottom of the cloisonné cells.

The animal head terminal is set with one thick, almost opaque garnet (the eye) which does not appear to have a stamped gold-foil backing.

Two punches have been used for the surface decoration of the head and tapering crest. One is triangular with a cross within the triangle (fig. 89a) and the other is a small circular one, which is probably the same as one used on the leg of the bird. The punch-marks are quite crisp, and were added after the mercury gilding.

Radiography has revealed five rivets on the head of the bird (fig. 75), three behind the eyebrow (v, w and x), one behind the eye (u) and another possible one behind the eye in the animal head terminal (z).

The leg

The bird's leg is made of bronze. Part of the foot (shaded on fig. 78a) is tinned and the rest of the leg and the claws are mercury-gilded.

A qualitative spectrographic analysis of the bronze from which the bird's leg is made revealed the presence of minor amounts of several other metals in the alloy as would be expected. An examination of the tinned surface of the foot by emission spectrography (sample 24) showed that the main metals present in the sample were copper, silver, gold, tin, lead and iron. This analysis indicates that the

[1] Arrhenius 1971.

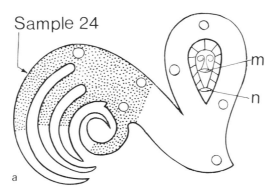

FIGURE 78 The shield: (*a*) diagram to show sampling positions and garnet panel contained within the bird's thigh; (*b*) diagram showing the cell walls of the garnet panel of the bird's leg. (Scales: *a*, 3/4; *b*, 2/1)

presumed tinning of the various parts of the Sutton Hoo shield may not consist of pure tin.

Eight samples from different tinned ornaments on the shield were examined by X-ray diffraction analysis. This showed that the white decoration on the surface is, in fact, an alloy of tin and copper. The proportions of the two elements differed from one object to another, but varied between a ratio of tin:copper of approximately 2:1 and 1:4. Tin/copper alloys of these compositions are very hard and have a high melting point. It is not possible to use them to coat a base metal in a similar manner to a normal tinning process. However, experiments have shown that if bronze is tinned in the normal way with pure tin and flux and then heated in a reducing atmosphere (e.g. a charcoal fire) there is interdiffusion of the tin on the surface with the underlying copper which leads to the production of a layer of tin/copper alloy on the surface which is very strongly bonded to the base metal. This process makes the layer of tinning very durable, but in the case of the Sutton Hoo shield ornaments there is a second reason for doing it, as most of the pieces are gilded as well. As the gilding has been carried out by the process of fire-gilding, ordinary tinning would have been damaged by the flame because of the relatively low melting point of the tin. The tin/copper alloys, with their much higher melting point, can withstand the application of gilding to adjacent areas of the base metal.[1]

The leg of the bird is decorated with an inlaid panel, consisting mainly of garnets arranged in the shape of a human face. The bronze cloisonné walls have been attached to a bronze back plate. No join is visible in the circumference of the outermost cell wall. The joins in the cloisonné walls are shown in figure 78*b*. The eyes now consist of green corrosion products of copper. It is not possible to determine whether they were originally made of (gilded?) copper or bronze, or perhaps of red cuprite glass. They are not preserved in the same condition as the inlays marked *m* and *n* on figure 78*a* which give a cuprite pattern when examined by X-ray diffraction, indicating that these are made of cuprite glass.

Traces of gilding are visible on some of the cell walls and in view of its very fragmentary nature it was probably applied as gold leaf after the garnets had been fitted into the cells, rather than by the process of fire gilding. This would suggest that the cloisonné cell walls of the other garnet inlays on the bird's head and the dragon plaque may have been gilded in a similar manner, although no traces of gold are now visible.

The rest of the inlays in the hip are garnets backed with gold foil, having the depressions of the stamped design pointing upwards except for the garnet forming the nose. This does not have a stamped foil backing; it may originally have had a plain foil, but if so it is now very damaged.

An attempt was made to secure a sample of the backing material from the garnet panel in the bird's leg by excavating through the corroded backing plate from behind, but this had to be abandoned in the interests of safety.

The gilded part of the leg was decorated using the same (or a very similar) triangular punch with a cross

[1] W. A. Oddy, Gilding and tinning in Anglo-Saxon England in *Aspects of Early Metallurgy* (ed. W. A. Oddy), London 1977.

102

in the centre, as was used for the bird's head and the head of the dragon on the shield front. In addition a small round punch was used which is probably the same as the one used to decorate the bird's head. The tinning on the foot is decorated with similar round punch-marks, and also with some very small triangular punch-marks (fig 88 c and g), which are probably the same as those on the head of the dragon.

The tail and wing

A sample of the stamped gold foil was submitted to a qualitative spectrographic analysis. The pattern of trace elements detected is similar to that obtained from layers of mercury gilding. It included a trace of mercury, although it is clear from a visual examination that this section of the bird could not have been fire-gilded.

Quantitative analysis was carried out on a small fragment of the gold leaf weighing only 7 mg; the result is given in table 3.

TABLE 3   RESULT OF ANALYSIS OF A SAMPLE OF GOLD LEAF FROM THE BIRD

		%
Copper	(determined by polarography)	2·27
Silver	(determined by atomic absorption)	1·30
Lead	(determined by atomic absorption)	< 0·11
Gold	(determined by difference)	96·4

2. The dragon ornament from the front of the shield

The dragon (fig. 50) is made in two sections; a head and a body, which are joined at the neck by a rivet which passes through the body section and into a tang projecting from the head. This is shown in the radiograph, figure 79.

Both parts of the dragon are made of bronze, the surface of which has been decorated by several different techniques. The bronze is completely mineralised.

There is a slight change in the colour of the gilding about half way along the body which is reflected in the radiograph (fig. 79) by a sharp change in density of the corroded metal. The reason for this change in radiographic density is not clear, since there is no visible discontinuity of the decoration on the front of the dragon, and it seems certain that the whole of the body was made at the same time. The lower half of the body is much more fragile than the top, and on the back it is a paler green than the upper half. These four observations suggest two possible explanations. One is that two different pourings of metal, of significantly different composition, were used in the casting process; the second is that the two ends of the dragon ornament have been subject to different conditions of corrosion. Emission spectrography has shown (samples 30 and 31, fig. 80) that

the lower part of the dragon and the head section contain a similar series of minor and trace elements, and X-ray diffraction analysis of samples 32, 33 and 35 (fig. 80) gives the same very diffuse patterns of cassiterite (tin oxide, SnO_2). Further samples from two other positions gave X-ray diffraction patterns of brochantite [basic copper sulphate, $Cu_4(OH)_6(SO_4)$], and azurite [basic copper carbonate, $Cu_3(OH)_2(CO_3)_2$]. A sample (weight 11 mg) of the pale green material, taken from the edge of one of the breaks in the dragon's body before it was conserved, was subjected to quantitative analysis by atomic absorption spectrophotometry and was found to contain 15% copper, 24% tin, 6% lead and 1% zinc. The analysis does not total 100% because the sample consisted entirely of corrosion products. Hence, although the actual magnitude of these figures is meaningless, it is clear that the pale green material is merely the corrosion product of a tin bronze. It is not possible to determine the ratio of copper to tin in the original bronze from these figures, because of the differential rates of corrosion of the two elements in the same alloy.

The terminal section of the dragon was restored in the immediate postwar period. Careful examination of the radiograph (fig. 79) shows that virtually

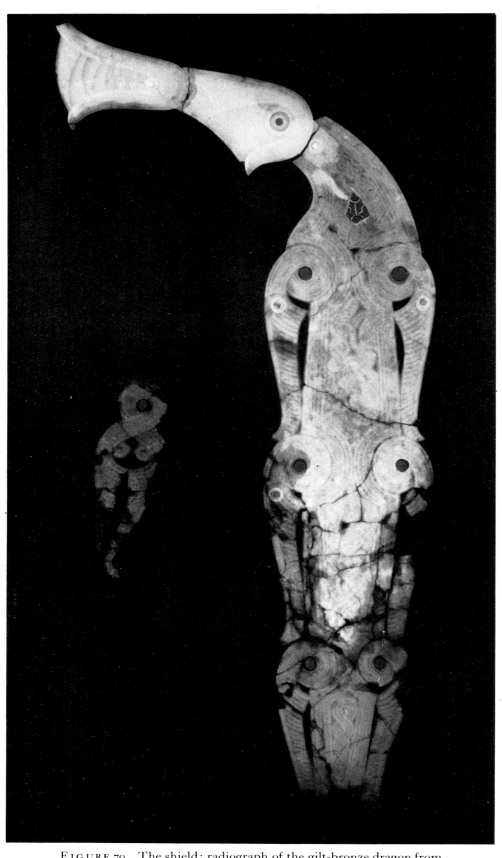

FIGURE 79   The shield: radiograph of the gilt-bronze dragon from
the front. (Scale: 1/1) (British Museum Research Laboratory)

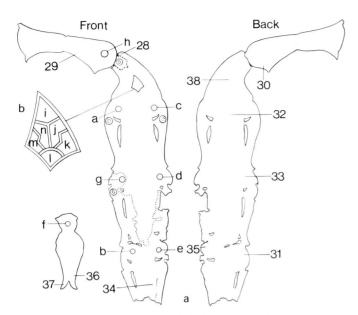

FIGURE 80 The shield: diagram to show (a) sampling positions and (b) the garnet panel on the winged dragon. (Scales: a, 2/5; b, 2/1)

the whole of the feet consists of original fragments. Some of these fragments are very faint in figure 79 because the gilding is missing from the surface. The postwar restoration of the section was carried out using plaster of Paris and then the surface was tinted with a yellow paint containing white-lead pigment. These two identifications were made by X-ray diffraction analysis (samples 36 and 37 respectively, fig. 80).

The front of the dragon is gilded, and the presence of mercury in the gold, detected by emission spectrography (sample 29, fig. 80), suggests that the fire-gilding technique was used. In addition there is a ribbon of tinned decoration on the body of the dragon, which has been further embellished by the use of a triangular punch; the same, or a very similar punch has been used on the head of the dragon and on the anchor-fitting and strap-ends. This ribbon of tinning was shown by emission spectrography to contain some copper, together with traces of other metals, and it is clear that it was produced by first tinning the bronze and then heating under a reducing atmosphere to form a hard tin/copper alloy, which would withstand subsequent mercury-gilding, as has already been described (p. 102). The gilding of the shoulder whirls of the dragon's body has been decorated using two punches; a very small triangular one, used also on the head section and on the tinning of the leg of the bird, and a lozenge-shaped punch used only on the two upper pairs of shoulders and not elsewhere on the shield. Besides the very small triangular punch, the dragon's head is also decorated with two other triangular punches, which have been used on other parts of the shield. The larger one has a cross cut in its end. A fuller description of the punched decoration follows on page 121 and some of the impressions on the dragon are illustrated in figure 89 (b–d, h, i).

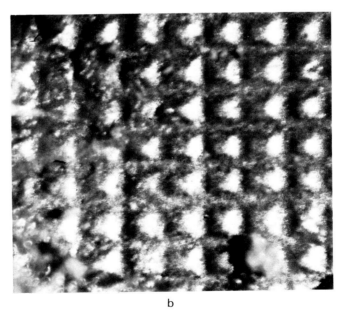

a   b

FIGURE 81 The shield: photomicrographs of the stamped foil backings to the garnets of the dragon. (Scale: 24/1) (Photos: British Museum Research Laboratory)

Fourteen garnets, labelled *a* to *n* on figure 80, are set into the dragon, one in the eye, seven in the shoulder and terminal joints and six in a lozenge-shaped cloisonné panel in the neck. All are backed with stamped gold foil, the reverse of which is visible on the back of the dragon for garnets *a* and *b*. The indentations in the gold foil point upwards behind garnet *a* and downwards behind *b*. This is illustrated by the photomicrographs in figure 81 which show the reverse of these two gold foils as photographed using oblique lighting. The way the light is reflected is different in the two photographs because the depressions in the foil point away from the camera in the case of garnet *a* and towards the camera in the case of garnet *b*.

The foils behind the other garnets were examined microscopically and *c*, *d*, *e*, *g*, *i*, *j*, *m*, *n* (?) and *l* (?) were found to have the depressions pointing upwards like *a*, while *f*, *k* and *h* (?) had the depressions pointing downwards like *b*.

The cloisonné cells for garnets *i* to *n* are made of copper or bronze, arranged as shown in figure 80. No trace of gilding remains, but it is possible that the cell walls were originally leaf-gilded by analogy with the similar cloisonné panel on the leg of the bird.

A sample of the backing paste was obtained from behind the lozenge-shaped cloisonné panel by excavating from the back (sample 38 on fig. 80). The material was not homogeneous and was shown by X-ray diffraction analysis to consist mainly of α-quartz with a small amount of clay mineral and possibly a little wax. This analysis puts the material into Arrhenius's Group II.1.b.

Garnets *a*, *c*, *d*, and *g* are set in single cells made of bronze. Garnet *e* is surrounded by a gap and garnets *b* and *f* are set in a white material which was not analysed.

3. *The strap-ends mounted on the short strap on the back of the shield*

The matching pair of strap-ends (fig. 82) is made of bronze which is partly gilt and partly tinned. In places where the gilding has been lost the bronze has corroded to give cuprite in a massive crystalline form. The gilding has not adhered to the underlying metal as well as on many other pieces of the shield ornaments, but as mercury was detected by emission spectrography in samples of the gilding from one of the strap-ends (sample 8, fig. 82), and in the gilding of one of the rivets (sample 9, fig. 82) there seems little doubt that the technique of application was fire-gilding.

A sample of the tinned decoration was examined by X-ray diffraction analysis and shown to be a white copper/tin alloy (cf. p. 102). The tinned area is further decorated with triangles made with the medium triangular punch.

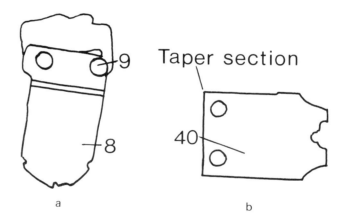

FIGURE 82   The shield: diagram to show sampling positions on (*a*) a strap-end and (*b*) the anchor plate.

4. *The carrying-strap assembly on the back of the shield*

This consists of a strap attachment and a pair of anchor-plates joined by interlocked loops (fig. 57). Both sections are made of bronze, tinned and gilded so skilfully that any joins in the assembly have been completely obscured.

The strap attachment consists of two plates joined

to a loop. Between the two plates is a double thickness of leather, mitred as shown in figure 83. The leather is held between the plates of the strap attachment with rivets, the heads of which are gilded. Both parts of the strap assembly have their rivet-heads, their interlocking loops and the slightly be-

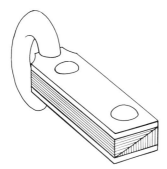

FIGURE 83 The shield: strap-fitting plate, simplified drawing showing mitred section of leather.

velled edges of the plates gilded. This gold has not been analysed, but it has the appearance of having been applied by the process of mercury-gilding. The upper surfaces of all four plates are tinned and decorated by punching. X-ray diffraction analysis (sample 40, fig. 82) confirmed that the tinning is a copper/tin alloy. The strap attachment has medium-sized triangular punch marks, similar to those decor-

ating the ribbon of tinning on the dragon, and each anchor-plate has both the larger triangular, and also small circular impressions (figs. 56, 88 and 89a, and table 18).

A taper section was polished on one corner of the anchor-plate (fig. 82) and a metallurgical examination was made to ascertain the structure of the metal. This clearly showed a twinned equiaxial structure superimposed on dendrites, indicating that the anchor-plate was made from cast sheet metal which was cold worked and annealed into its final form. The twinned grains were slightly distorted, showing that some cold working had been carried out after the final anneal. Particles of the α- and δ eutectoid and also lead are visible, and it is likely that the bronze contains about 8% of tin. At the corner of the anchor-plate there are adjacent layers of tin and gold, and the metallographic examination showed that the thickness of the layers is very similar in both cases.

5. *The handgrip and grip extensions*

The grip and its hemispherical bosses

The core of the handgrip is a strip of iron to which the various decorative elements are attached. The iron core is extensively corroded. Figure 84 illustrates the handgrip and indicates the sample positions referred to below.

Section A and B of the iron grip are covered with a mercury-gilded stamped foil. Analysis of this foil by emission spectroscopy (sample 18, fig. 84) suggests that it is a conventional bronze, as zinc and lead were not detected. The gilding (sample 12, fig. 84) contains mercury. The foil is wrapped over the edges of the iron strip and overlaps the underside by 1 to 1·5 mm. The outer ends do not overlap the rebates of the terminal fittings and each inner end is obscured by a large hemispherical boss. The bosses, labelled C and D are, by analogy with other similar ones on the shield, presumably hollow. They have projecting pins to act as rivets. These pins have been analysed quantitatively, using atomic absorption spectrophotometry, by drilling samples from where they project through the iron strip. The results are given in table 4.

These totals do not add up to 100% as a small amount of corrosion product was present in the sample. The analyses show several elements present

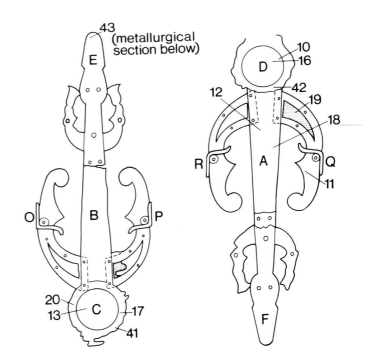

FIGURE 84 The shield: diagram to show the sampling positions on the handgrip extensions.

TABLE 4   METAL ANALYSES OF THE PINS
OF THE HANDGRIP BOSSES

	Boss C %	Boss D %
Copper	77·7	75·9
Tin	6·7	4·4
Lead	2·15	1·75
Zinc	8·3	9·6
Iron	1·07	0·87
Silver	0·12	0·11
Antimony	0·03	0·04
Gold	not detected	0·04
Arsenic	trace	trace
TOTAL	96·1	92·7

in significant amounts and in particular zinc is present in both samples as nearly 10% of the total.

Qualitative analysis of surface samples (13 and 16, fig. 84) of the two bosses revealed the presence of traces of a few expected elements, not listed above, together with mercury, suggesting that the bosses were fire-gilded.

In the area of boss D, the surface has been eroded away to reveal a fairly soft white material below. Emission spectrographic analysis of a sample of this white material (sample 10, fig. 84) indicated the presence of all the elements which had been determined in the boss pin, together with traces of others whose presence as soil contaminants could be expected. This suggests that the white material is a corrosion product of bronze. This was confirmed by X-ray diffraction analysis which showed that it consists of a mixture of cuprite, cassiterite and basic lead carbonate. Microscopic examination of the white material shows it to have a crystalline form, but it was not possible to determine whether this was due to a 'ghost' dendritic pattern preserved after corrosion to the oxides, or to crystals of the oxides themselves.

The two bosses are surrounded by collars with a rope-work of milled decoration. These collars are made of copper or bronze foil and plated with a white metal which was shown by X-ray diffraction analysis to be one of the tin/copper alloys (or more correctly intermetallic compounds) which had been encountered on other tinned areas of the shield. This shows that the collars were tinned in the normal manner and then heated to form the alloy by interdiffusion of tin and copper.

These foil collars are backed with a white material. Emission spectrography of samples from both the surface (sample 20, fig. 84) and interior (sample 17) of this milled collar show the same distribution of elements, namely copper, silver, gold, tin, lead, iron, magnesium and calcium, but zinc was not detected in either sample.

X-ray diffraction analyses on samples from the backing material of both these collars show that one (sample 42, fig. 84) consists mainly of calcite and that the other (sample 41) contains chiefly calcite with perhaps a small amount of wax. These backing materials probably belong respectively to Arrhenius's groups I.2.a and I.1.c.

The grip extensions

At the extremities of the grip extensions are large animal heads (fig. 84, E and F) each of which is fixed by two rivets to the iron tang extending from the handgrip. The iron tang fits into a recess on the underside of each terminal section.

Animal head E is only superficially corroded; a taper section was polished below the snout and the structure of the metal examined under a microscope. The presence of a cored dendritic structure proves that the head was made by casting. There is no sign of recrystallisation, although the animal head has obviously received some heat treatment subsequent to the casting, when it was mercury-gilded.

A sample (43, fig. 84) was taken for quantitative analysis by atomic absorption from the area of the taper section. The results are given in table 5.

The other terminal animal head (F) is much more corroded, and in places the corrosion products are very pale green or white.

At the base of the handgrip extensions are pairs of openwork gilded bronze birds' heads. The tri-

TABLE 5   METAL ANALYSIS OF A SAMPLE FROM THE GRIP EXTENSION

	%
Copper	73·7
Tin	8·2
Lead	2·86
Zinc	7·0
Iron	0·65
Silver	0·23
Antimony	0·16
Gold	1·34
TOTAL	94·1

angular open areas were originally filled with stamped bronze foil, running under the back of the plaques. Emission spectrography (sample 19, fig. 84) has shown that the bronze foil contains all the usual trace elements except zinc, and X-ray diffraction analysis has detected the presence of a copper/tin intermetallic compound, which suggests that the surface of the foil was originally tinned, although there is no visual evidence for this. The foil was probably riveted in position, as no trace of solder can be seen on the back of the bird O which is in good condition. Birds O and P have five rivet holes around the open neck area, while Q and R have only four rivet holes. In each case two of the rivet holes were used to fasten the plaque to the underside of the iron handgrip extension; in view of the fact that this was extensively corroded, it cannot be stated with certainty that the plaques were laid in rebates in the extension, but this seems likely.

Each bird head has a garnet as an eye. The garnets on Q and R are backed with stamped foil, but it is not possible to determine which way up the stampings are. Garnets O and P are not backed with stamped foil.

TABLE 6   METAL ANALYSIS OF A SAMPLE FROM ONE OF THE BIRD HEADS

	%
Copper	80·8
Tin	7·5
Lead	2·86
Zinc	6·9
Iron	0·81
Silver	0·16
Antimony	0·18
Gold	not detected
TOTAL	99·2

A sample was removed, for quantitative analysis by atomic absorption spectrophotometry, from the back of one of the birds (Q or R). The result is given in table 6.

Both the terminal animal heads (E and F) and all the four bird heads (O, P, Q and R) are decorated with punched designs using the large triangular punch with an incised cross together with a circular punch. One of the terminal animal heads is also decorated with the medium triangular punch. This punched decoration is dealt with more fully later; a portion of the decoration from the neck of one of the animal heads is illustrated in figure 89 a.

The terminal animal heads and the bird heads are all further decorated with ribbons of white metal inlaid with a dark material. This dark material is contained within channels in the original bronze castings although it now stands proud of the surrounding white metal surface, no doubt because of chemical changes which have taken place since the handgrip was made (fig. 89 e). The ribbon round the snout of each of the terminal heads contains decorative rings, coated with white metal, which was shown by microscopic examination to be part of the original casting. These chemical changes which have caused the expansion of the dark inlay are reflected in its chemical analysis. Four samples, from one of the animal heads (E, two samples) and from two of the birds (Q and O), were examined by X-ray diffraction and found to consist of silver chloride, silver (twice) and a mixture of copper/silver sulphides (Mckinstryite and Jalpaite). The dark inlay is shiny and brittle and was originally niello. Samples of the white metal of one of the terminal heads (F) and two of the birds (R and O) were also examined by X-ray diffraction analysis and shown to consist of tin/copper alloys, indicating that the ribbons of white metal were originally tinned and then heated. This would have been carried out first and the niello applied in a subsequent operation. Microscopic examination of the ribbons of tinned decoration, inlaid with niello, have revealed conclusive proof that the tinning was applied before the mercury gilding, as postulated above (p. 102). In two positions on animal head E the gilding can be seen spreading over the tinned ribbons, and in places where the tinned surface is damaged, red copper oxide (cuprite) is visible beneath.

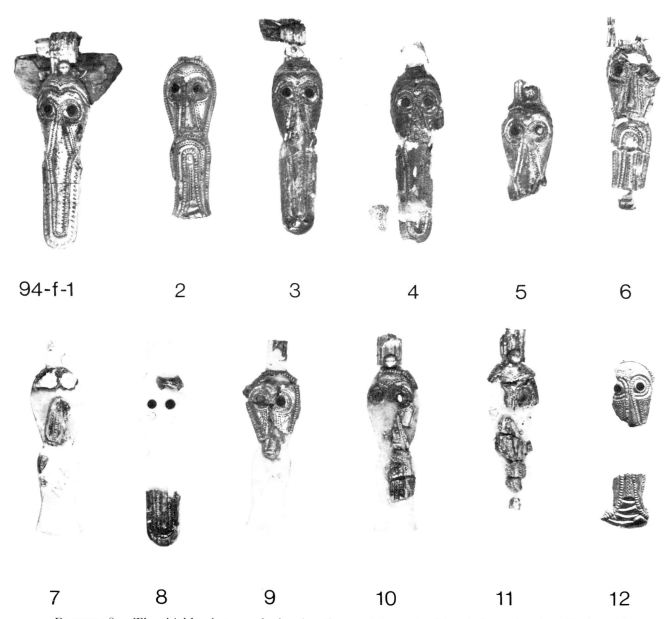

94-f-1   2   3   4   5   6

7   8   9   10   11   12

FIGURE 85   The shield: photograph showing the surviving animal heads from the rim. (Scale: 1/1)

6. *The animal heads from the rim of the shield*

The nature of the composition of these decorative features on the rim of the shield has been a matter of some discussion in the British Museum in recent years. Plenderleith[1] originally thought that three were made of bronze and eight made of gesso, and this identification was repeated by Maryon.[2] Subsequent examination by X-ray diffraction analysis showed that those animal heads which had originally been identified as gesso are in fact mainly composed

of tin oxide (cassiterite, SnO_2). Recent microscopic examination has shown that the shapes of dendrites are preserved within the body of the white material from the animal heads, showing that the material was cast from the molten state.

Samples were taken from three of the animal heads, which seemed to consist mostly of tin oxide, for a full quantitative analysis. The samples were taken from animals 94–F–4, 94–F–8 and a small

[1] Dr H. J. Plenderleith, Keeper of the British Museum Research Laboratory 1949–59, in his laboratory notebook.

[2] Maryon 1946, 21–30.

110

TABLE 7 RESULTS OF ANALYSES OF SAMPLES FROM THREE ANIMAL HEADS

	% 94-F-4	% 94-F-7	% 94-F-8
Acid-insoluble residue	3·5	4·8	6·4
Tin oxide (SnO_2)	60·0	46·0	47·5
Copper oxide (CuO)	3·2	2·8	5·0
Magnesium oxide (MgO)	0·04	0·03	0·04
Calcium oxide (CaO)	0·14	0·12	0·18
Iron oxide (Fe_2O_3)	4·9	2·1	3·0
Lead oxide (PbO)	0·95	1·3	2·0
Zinc oxide (ZnO)	0·4	0·54	0·67
Aluminium oxide (Al_2O_3)	2·1	2·2	6·2
TOTAL	75·2	59·9	71·0

detached piece of 94–F–7 (fig. 85). They were first washed with acetone to remove the remains of adhesives used in their original conservation, and then treated with a mixture of hydrochloric and nitric acids. The insoluble residue was determined gravimetrically and the metals in solution were analysed by atomic absorption spectrophotometry. The results are expressed conventionally as percentages of the most common oxides, as no free metal remained in the samples (table 7). However, the calcium, magnesium, copper and lead would actually be present as carbonates or basic carbonates.

A further sample was taken from the animal head 94–F–4 and washed with acetone. It was then ignited at 600 °C to constant weight, and the percentage loss in weight, due to evaporation of moisture and decompositon of carbonates was calculated. The result was 20%.

Hence the total analysis for this head 94–F–4 is about 95% and it is clear that this head must have been cast from tin, containing smaller amounts of other elements, provided that no preferential leaching of any of the metals has taken place during burial. The use of tin would be unusual but not impossible, as the Anglo-Saxons had access to supplies of tin and used the metal extensively as a surface decoration for bronze. Assuming that the other two animal heads contained similar proportions of combined water and carbonates, their analysis totals come to significantly less than 100%, but there is no reason to think that they are different in composition from head 94–F–4. Microscopic examination of the surviving animal heads from the rim of the shield suggests that 94–F–2 was definitely made of copper or bronze and that 94–F–1 and 94–F–5 may also be similar. However, the other eight heads (94–F–3, 4 and 6–11) now consist predominantly of tin oxide and it seems unlikely that this could be the corrosion product of a normal bronze (i.e. one containing less than about 15% tin). It is not possible to determine scientifically whether these animal heads are original decorations or later replacements, but as three at the most are made of bronze it is possible that the apparent use of a high tin alloy for the casting is an original feature.[1]

Spectrographic analysis of samples of the gilding of some of the tin animal heads indicates that a trace of mercury is present in the gold. In this case it cannot definitely be taken as an indication that the tin animal heads were mercury-gilded, because tin melts at a lower temperature than is required to effect the fire-gilding process. However, tin containing at least 20% of copper has a melting point in excess of 500 °C and objects cast in such an alloy could probably be mercury-gilded without melting the original casting. Examination under the microscope reveals that the gilding can be seen to be much thicker than the layer normally produced by mercury-gilding. Figure 90 a–f shows detailed photographs of several of these animal heads. Differences in the punched decoration clearly show that it must have been applied after the heads were cast.

---

[1] Recent work (1977) on the hanging bowls has provided an example of a cast bronze suspension ring which has corroded to give white tin oxide in one area and red cuprous oxide and green basic cupric carbonate in another. As this ring was obviously cast in one piece it strongly suggests that some rather unusual segregation effects have occasionally taken place when bronze has corroded at Sutton Hoo and it hence seems likely that the so called 'high tin alloy' which has been postulated in several places on the shield (e.g. animal heads round the rim) and helmet (e.g. left eyebrow) is more likely to be a normal tin bronze. This is fully described in the hanging-bowl appendix in *Sutton Hoo*, Volume III.

7. *The rectangular panels from the rim of the shield*

A quantitative analysis has been carried out on a fragment of gold foil from one of the rectangular panels round the rim of the shield. In Table 8 the results are expressed as percentages, the gold being calculated by difference.

TABLE 8 RESULT OF ANALYSIS OF A SAMPLE OF GOLD FOIL FROM A REC-TANGULAR PANEL

	%
Gold	91·9
Silver	1·72
Copper	6·30
Lead	<0·07

8. *The small hemispherical bosses*

The shield is decorated with eleven small hemispherical bosses. Two of these are attached to the handgrip on the back of the shield, and five others to the main shield-boss on the front. The other four all decorate the front of the shield, two being at the centre of elongated strips of decorated gold foil while two are mounted on the shield-board above the upper strip.

Of these four bosses, one (boss 1, fig. 86) is in good condition and is made of gilt bronze. It is mounted on the shield at the centre of the upper gold foil strip (fig. 6a). Quantitative analysis by atomic absorption and polarography of a sample of metal drilled from the pin at back of the boss showed the metal to have the percentage composition shown in table 9.

TABLE 9 RESULT OF ANALYSIS OF A SAMPLE OF ONE OF THE HEMISPHERICAL BOSSES

	%
Copper	78·5
Lead	5·7
Tin	4·5
Zinc	11·5
Silver	0·08
Iron	0·63
Antimony	trace
Nickel	0·11
Gold	0·05
Cadmium	trace
Arsenic	trace
TOTAL	101·07

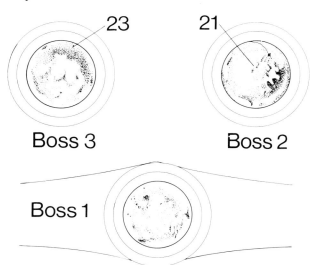

Boss 3   Boss 2

Boss 1

Foil collar

FIGURE 86 The shield: diagram showing sampling positions on the hemispherical bosses.

The other three bosses are in an advanced state of corrosion. Two (2 and 3, fig. 86) are those mounted at the top of the shield. Both these bosses are light in weight and pale in colour while a third is in a fragmentary condition, consisting of lumps of an almost white material, about 1·5 mm thick, with traces of the original gilding on one side. Samples from all three bosses were taken for quantitative spectrographic analysis (21 and 23, fig. 86). They all showed the same pattern of elements as boss 1 (table 9 above) with the exception that in no case were cadmium and nickel detected; zinc was only detected at trace level.

A further sample was removed from the fragmentary boss for quantitative analysis. The sample was washed with acetone to remove traces of organic consolidants applied during a former restoration and then treated with a mixture of hydrochloric and nitric acids. The insoluble residue was filtered off and determined gravimetrically. The metals which had dissolved in the acid were analysed by atomic absorption spectrophotometry. The results are expressed conventionally as percentages of the common oxides, as no actual metal remained in the sample, but the calcium, magnesium, copper and lead would be present as carbonates or basic carbonates (table 10).

TABLE 10 RESULT OF ANALYSIS OF A SAMPLE FROM THE FRAGMENTARY BOSS

	%
Acid-insoluble residue	5·6
Tin oxide (SnO_2)	65·0
Cupric oxide (CuO)	3·8
Magnesium oxide (MgO)	0·02
Calcium oxide (CaO)	0·12
Iron oxide (Fe_2O_3)	4·6
Lead oxide (PbO)	1·6
Zinc oxide (ZnO)	0·67
Aluminium oxide (Al_2O_3)	3·0
TOTAL	84·4

The remaining 15% of this analysis is probably water and carbonate ions as the weight loss on ignition of the similar white material from one of the animal heads from the shield-rim was about 20% (p. 111).

Microscopic examination of the pieces of fragmentary boss revealed the remains of dendrites within the body of the white material, and so it is concluded that this boss was originally cast metal. Assuming that there has been no preferential leaching of any particular constituents of the alloy, the above analytical results indicate that this boss was cast from tin or a high tin alloy containing small amounts of other elements.[1]

This result shows that, if preferential leaching of the copper salts has not taken place here, at least two different alloys were used for the various small hemispherical bosses. The two other bosses, which are light in weight and pale green in colour, were not analysed quantitatively. A sample from just below the gilding of one of the bosses from the handgrip was shown by X-ray diffraction analysis to be apparently very similar to the fragmentary boss, which has been shown to be mostly tin oxide; quantitative analysis of the pins from the back of both the bosses on the handgrip has shown that they are a normal bronze (p. 108). One other problem is the nature of the gilding on those bosses which are apparently made of tin or a high tin alloy. If the alloy contains less than about 20% of copper it cannot have been gilded by the fire-gilding technique as the temperature required for this process would be greater than the melting point of the alloy. Presumably if these bosses did consist mainly of tin they would have been gilded with gold leaf.

Bosses 2 and 3 are surrounded by circles of stamped gold foil, which has been shown by emission spectrography (sample 7, fig. 86) to contain small amounts of silver, copper and mercury. It is not clear why mercury is present in this sample, as it is not an example of mercury-gilding, but it acts as a warning that the presence of a trace of mercury in gilding is not necessarily indicative of mercury-gilding (cf. p. 103).[2]

9. The gold strips on the front of the shield

A sample of gold foil from one of the elongated strips on the front of the shield was analysed by atomic absorption spectrophotometry and polarography. The results are expressed in table 11 as percentages, the gold being calculated by difference.

TABLE 11 RESULT OF ANALYSIS OF A SAMPLE OF GOLD FOIL FROM A GOLD STRIP

	%
Gold	93·4
Silver	1·31
Copper	5·32
Lead	<0·05

[1] But see p. 111, n. 1.

[2] Lins and Oddy 1975.

This is secured onto the shield-board with five gilded brass rivets, which are visible from the back of the shield. The shank of one of these has been analysed quantitatively by atomic absorption spectrophotometry and by polarography. The results are given in table 12.

TABLE 12 RESULT OF ANALYSIS OF THE SHANK OF A RIVET FROM THE BOSS

	%
Copper	70·0
Lead	1·7
Tin	0·6
Zinc	27·1
Silver	0·17
Iron	0·36
Antimony	0·15
Nickel	0·16
Gold	0·13
Cadmium	trace
Arsenic	trace
TOTAL	100·4

The central decoration of the boss is a large flat disc, decorated with animal ornament and a circular panel of cloisonné garnets. A sample was obtained from the body of this disc for quantitative analysis of the metal, which has been inlaid with a dark material which now stands proud of the surface (cf. the dark inlay in the tinned strips or the terminal animal heads from the handgrip extensions). The results, expressed as percentages, are given in table 13.

TABLE 13 RESULT OF ANALYSIS OF A SAMPLE FROM THE CENTRAL DISC OF THE BOSS

	%
Copper	76·0
Lead	1·7
Tin	9·1
Zinc	10·9
Silver	0·1
Iron	0·44
Antimony	trace
Nickel	0·01
Gold	0·04
Cadmium	trace
Arsenic	trace
TOTAL	98·3

The top surface of the central disc is covered with a layer of silver (identified by X-ray diffraction analysis) which is about 0·6mm thick. It was not possible to discover how this is attached to the disc, but it was almost certainly applied after the chip carved decoration was carried out. This silver surface and the edges of the central disc are partially gilded by the fire-gilding technique (sample 5, fig. 87) and the silver is inlaid with niello in overlapping triangular punch marks, which form circles near the edge of the disc and also round the central garnet-inlaid panel, the cell walls of which are a modern restoration.[1] The inlay in the animal ornament was also indentified by X-ray diffraction analysis as niello, and the pattern suggested that a mixed silver/copper sulphide had been used. One of the garnets was removed from this setting and beneath it was a piece of stamped gold foil resting on a green waxy-looking material which was shown by X-ray diffraction analysis to contain calcite (calcium carbonate). The green coloration is probably due to the presence of traces of corrosion products of copper. It is possible that some wax is present in this green backing material, but it was not detected. This backing material thus belongs to either Group I.1.c or Group I.2.a of the classification proposed by Birgit Arrhenius (1971). The garnet which was removed was identified as almandine having a refractive index of 1·809.

The shield-boss is illustrated in figures 34 and 87. The upper and lower rings of animal heads consist of copper or bronze foil shown by emission spectrography (samples 44 and 45, fig. 87) to be mercury-gilded, resting on a white material which was identified (samples 46 and 47, fig. 87) by X-ray diffraction analysis as wax. For the samples described in this report the X-ray diffraction patterns were not sufficiently clear to identify the type of wax used but the most likely material is beeswax. Emission spectrography showed that calcium is also present and the X-ray diffraction pattern indicates the possibility that calcite may have been mixed into the wax. As the wax is the main constituent this backing material belongs to Arrhenius's Group I.1.a.

The panel bearing the upward-pointing animal heads is held by a ring of bronze edging which is partly gilded, presumably by the mercury-gilding

---

[1] The restoration was made in the Research Laboratory by H. V. Batten during his work on the Sutton Hoo material in the immediate postwar years.

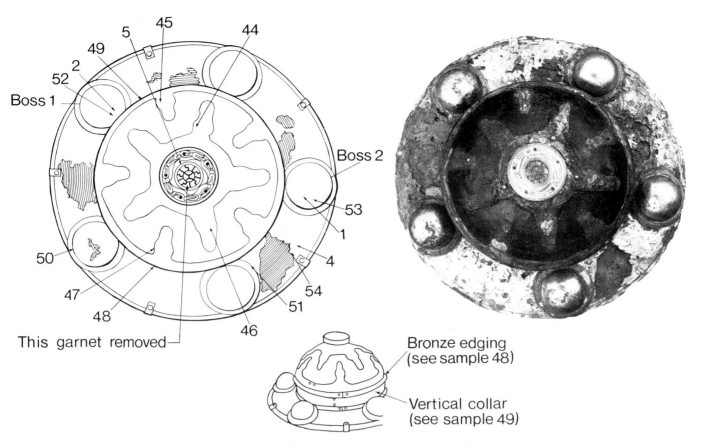

Boss 1
Boss 2

This garnet removed

Bronze edging
(see sample 48)

Vertical collar
(see sample 49)

FIGURE 87   The shield-boss: montage to show sampling positions.

technique, and partly tinned. X-ray diffraction analysis (sample 48, fig. 87) has shown that the tinning now consists of an alloy of copper and tin containing about 25% of tin.

A metallurgical examination was made on a small fragment of the stamped foil from the neck of the boss. A layer of tinning rests on a corroded copper or bronze foil. X-ray diffraction analysis (sample 49, fig. 87) has indicated that the surface layer corresponds to the ε copper/tin intermetallic compound which contains 38% of tin by weight. The foil does not appear to have been supported on any soft backing material, and in many cases the spaces behind have become filled with the corrosion products of iron. Below the collar is a swaged bronze strip whose surface has been shown by emission spectrography to contain gold and mercury and which has the appearance of being mercury-gilded.

The flange of the boss is decorated with five gilded hemispherical bosses surrounded by raised and decorated collars. These bosses appear to be bronze, and not of the tin alloy variety, with the possible exception of boss 1 (fig. 87), although qualitative

emission spectrography of the body material of bosses 1 and 2 (samples 52 and 53, fig. 87) showed the same elements to be present in both bosses. Emission spectrography on samples of the gilding from two of these bosses (samples 1 and 2, fig. 87) indicated the presence of a trace of mercury in the gold. The five collars round the hemispherical bosses are made of tinned copper or bronze foil resting on a white backing material. Samples from the white backing material of two of these collars (samples 50 and 51, fig. 87) were shown by X-ray diffraction analysis to consist mainly of calcite but a small amount of α-quartz may also be present. (This should be compared with the results on the similar collars surrounding the small bosses on the hand-grip.) Hence the backing for these collars belong to Arrhenius's Group I.2.a or I.2.b.

Between the hemispherical bosses are panels of decorated gilded bronze foil. Qualitative emission spectrography (samples 4 and 54, fig. 87) has shown that the foil was originally copper or bronze and that the gilding was applied by the fire-gilding technique. A metallurgical examination of a fragment of this foil suggests that the copper is fairly pure and shows that it is well worked, consistent with the design having been stamped onto it. Copper foil would be preferable to bronze for decoration in this way as it is softer and would take the details of the die more easily.

This foil, like the vertical collar, does not appear to rest on any soft backing material. In fact there are hollows below it in many places, while in other areas these voids have become filled with the corrosion products of iron which have taken the shape of the reverse of the foil, thus giving the impression of being backing material.

11. *The gilt-bronze ring from the shield*

The shield ring is made of bronze and is decorated with a thick layer of gilding on the surface. Qualitative emission spectrography has revealed the presence of traces of tin, iron, zinc, mercury, silver and copper in the gold. The presence of mercury suggests that the gold was applied by the fire-gilding technique.

A sample was obtained by drilling from the back of the shield ring and was analysed by polarography and atomic absorption spectrophotometry (table 14, expressed as percentages).

TABLE 14 RESULT OF ANALYSIS OF A SAMPLE FROM THE GILT-BRONZE RING

	%
Copper	83·5
Lead	2·2
Tin	4·7
Zinc	6·85
Silver	0·04
Iron	0·4
Nickel	0·18
Cobalt	0·04
Gold	trace
TOTAL	97·91

All the quantitative bronze analyses which have been carried out on the different components of the shield are collected together in table 15 for ease of reference. Gold analyses are given in table 16 and those for backing materials in table 17.

TABLE 15 RESULTS OF ANALYSES OF BRONZE COMPONENTS FROM THE SHIELD

	Ring %	Handgrip: pin of boss C %	Handgrip: pin of boss D %	Handgrip: dragon E %	Handgrip: bird %	Small boss 1 %	Centre boss: rivet %	Centre boss: central disc %
Copper	83·5	77·7	75·9	73·7	80·8	78·5	70·0	76·0
Tin	4·7	6·7	4·4	8·2	7·5	4·5	0·6	9·1
Lead	2·2	2·15	1·75	2·86	2·86	5·7	1·7	1·7
Zinc	6·85	8·3	9·6	7·0	6·9	11·5	27·1	10·9
Iron	0·4	1·07	0·87	0·65	0·81	0·63	0·36	0·44
Silver	0·04	0·12	0·11	0·23	0·16	0·08	0·17	0·1
Gold	trace	not detected	0·04	1·34	not detected	0·05	0·13	0·04
Nickel	0·18	not analysed	not analysed	not analysed	not analysed	0·11	0·16	0·01
Antimony	not analysed	0·03	0·04	0·16	0·18	trace	0·15	trace
TOTAL	97·87	96·1	92·7	94·1	99·2	101·0	100·4	98·3
Weight of the sample (mg)	2·38	9·65	15·97	3·05	1·44	10·29	9·63	10·41

TABLE 16 RESULTS OF ANALYSES OF GOLD FOIL FROM THE SHIELD (in percentages)

Location	Sample wt (mg)	Gold	Silver	Copper	Lead
Foil from bird wing	0·69	96·4	1·30	2·27	< 0·11
Foil from rectangular panel	1·07	91·9	1·72	6·30	< 0·07
Foil from longitudinal strip	1·52	93·4	1·31	5·23	< 0·05
Sample from shield-rim	3·65	93·8	0·86	5·29	< 0·04

TABLE 17 BACKING MATERIALS FOUND IN THE SHIELD

Location	Components	Corresponding Arrhenius paste number
Bird eyebrow	Calcite+small amount of unidentified material, not wax	I.2.a
Bird, tapering crest	Wax (+malachite)	
Dragon, garnet panel	α-quartz+small amount of clay mineral+possibly a little wax	II.1.b
Handgrip, boss collar (1)	Calcite	I.2.a
Handgrip boss collar (2)	Calcite+a little wax	I.1.c
Shield-boss, central disc	Calcite+possibly wax	I.1.c or I.2.a
Animal head of boss	Wax+some calcite	I.1.a
Boss, under collar of a flange-boss	Calcite+small amounts of α-quartz	I.2.a or I.2.b

12. *Punched decoration*

Punched decoration occurs on both tinned and gilded areas of the dragon and bird on the front of the shield; on the peripheral animal heads; on tinned areas on the strap-anchor and strap-ends; and on gilded areas of the handgrip and of the rivets on the back of the shield which secure the shield-boss. Five punches were used, a circular one, a lozenge-shaped one and three triangular ones of different sizes, the largest of which had a cross cut in the end. The two larger triangular ones were used most frequently.

The punched decoration is arranged in strips consisting of between one and four rows of impressions. These are catalogued in figure 88, and table 18 indicates the distribution of the different punch marks on the various parts of the shield, some of which are illustrated in figures 89 and 90.

Comparisons of the impressions produced by the medium triangular punch suggest that the punch was sharpened at least once during the work (or that two very similar punches were in use). The distribution of impressions produced by these two punches, designated B.i and B.ii is given in table 19. Similarly the impressions made by the large triangular punch which has a cross cut into the triangle, can be divided into three groups, A.i, A.ii and A.iii, representing either two successive sharpenings of the same punch, or the use of three almost identical punches. Two slightly different impressions (A.i and A.iii) produced by the large triangular punch are illustrated in figure 92. It is possible that a more extensive examination of the punched decoration on the various components of the shield would reveal evidence of more variations of the five basic punches.

Acknowledgement. Thanks are due to Margaret Sax, Janet Lang, P. T. Craddock, M. R. Cowell and N. D. Meeks who carried out some of the experimental work.

Location	Decoration	Punch used	Comment
Dragon, head section	▽ ▽ ▽ ▽	Large triangular punch	On gilding
	▽△▽△▽△▽ ▽▽▽▽▽▽▽	Large and medium triangular punches	On gilding
	△△△△△△△△ ▽△▽△▽△▽ ▽▽▽▽▽▽▽▽	Large and medium triangular punches	On gilding
	▽△▽△▽△▽△▽△▽	Small triangular punch	On gilding
Dragon, body section	⋈⋈⋈⋈⋈⋈	Medium triangular punch	On the ribbon of tinning
	◇ ◇ ◇ ◇	Lozenge shaped punch	On the upper two pairs of gilded shoulder joints
	▽△▽△▽△▽△▽△	Small triangular punch	On the lower pair of gilded shoulder joints and the single gilded hip joint. The strip of stamped decoration on one of the shoulder joints is unfinished.
Bird, head section	○○○○○○○○○ ▽△▽△▽△▽ ▽ ▽ ▽ ▽	Large triangular and circular punches	On gilding
	▽△▽△▽△▽ ▽ ▽ ▽ ▽	Large triangular punch	On gilding
Bird, leg section	○○○○○○○○○ ▽△▽△▽△▽	Large triangular and circular punches	On gilding
	○○○○○○○○○	Circular punch	On tinning
	▽△▽△▽△▽△▽△	Small triangular punch	On tinning
	○○○○○○○○○○ ▽△▽△▽△▽△▽△ ○○○○○○○○○○	Small triangular and circular punches	On tinning
Carrying-strap attachment, anchor-plate	○○○○○○○○○ ▽△▽△▽△▽ ▽ ▽ ▽ ▽ ▽	Large triangular and circular punches	On tinning
Carrying-strap attachment, strap-holder	▽▽▽▽▽▽▽ △△△△△△△	Medium triangular punch	On tinning
Strap-ends	▽▽▽▽▽▽▽▽ △△△△△△△△	Medium triangular punch	On tinning
Boss, rivets on back of shield	○○○○○○○○○ ▽▽▽▽▽	Large triangular and circular punches	On gilding

Punched decoration on the shield (*cont.*)

Location	*Decoration*	*Punch used*	*Comment*
Handgrip extension, profile bird heads at sides	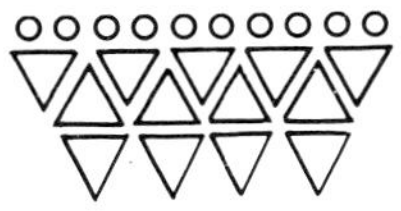	Large triangular and circular punches	On gilding
Handgrip extension, terminal animal heads	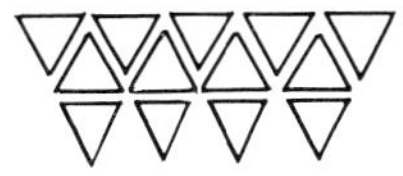	Large triangular punch	On gilding of both heads
	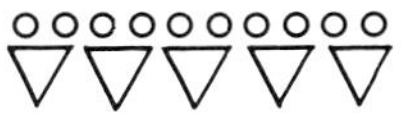	Large triangular and circular punches	On gilding of both heads
	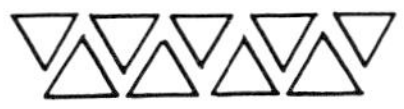	Large triangular punch	On gilding of one of the heads
	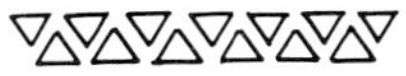	Medium triangular punch	On gilding of one of the heads
Handgrip extension: neck of terminal animal heads	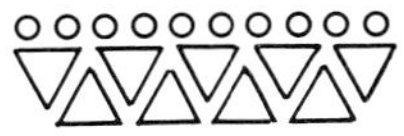	Large triangular and circular punches	On gilding
Handgrip extension: neck of profile animal heads	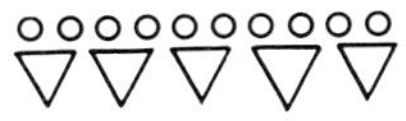	Large triangular and circular punches	On gilding
Animal heads from shield-rim	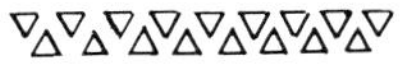	Small triangular punch	On gilding
	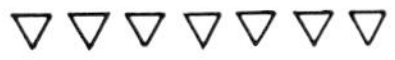	Medium tringular punch	On gilding
	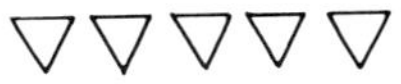	Large triangular punch	On head of 94 F.1 only, on gilding

FIGURE 88 Table showing the different types of punch-marks used on the Sutton Hoo shield.

Table 18 distribution of punch-marks (1)

	Dragon on shield front: head	*Dragon on shield front: body*	*Bird on shield front: head*	*Bird on shield front: leg*	*Strap-anchor fitting and strap-ends*	*Central boss: rivets on back of shield*	*Handgrip extensions*	*Animal heads from rim*
Large triangle	G		G	G	T	G	G	G
Medium triangle	G	T			T		G	G
Small triangle	G	G		T				G
Circle			G	G T	T	G	G	
Lozenge		G						

Note: The letters G and T indicate whether punch-marks are on gilding or tinning respectively.

FIGURE 89   The shield: (a)–(d) photomicrographs of different punch-marks used on the shield. (a) large triangular and circular punches; (b) medium triangular punch; (c) small triangular punch; (d) lozenge-shaped punch; (e) rings of metal surrounded by niello from the snout of a terminal animal head from the handgrip extension; (f)–(i) different decorative patterns produced by the use of punch-work. The locations from which the photomicrographs were taken are shown in figure 91. (Scales: a–e, 25/2; f–i, 3/1) (Photos: British Museum Research Laboratory)

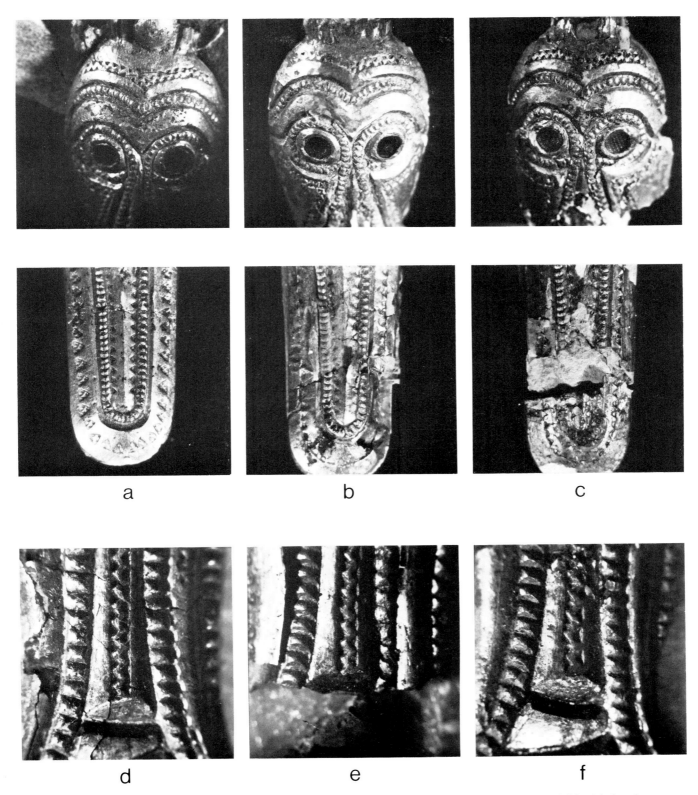

FIGURE 90 Photomicrographs of some of the animal heads from the rim of the shield. (*a*) head 1; (*b*) head 3; (*c*) head 4; (*d*) head 2; (*e*) head 6; (*f*) one of the fragments found in 1967. (Scales: *a–c*, 3/1; *d–f*, 6/1) (Photos: British Museum Research Laboratory)

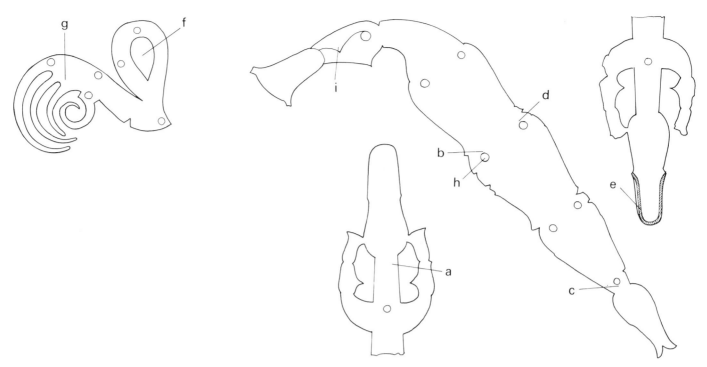

FIGURE 91   The shield: diagram to illustrate location of photomicrographs shown in figure 89.

TABLE 19   DISTRIBUTION OF PUNCH-MARKS (2)

Medium triangular punch-marks

B.i   Strap-attachment, tinning
      Dragon, body, tinning

B.ii Strap-attachment, tinning
      Strap-attachment, tinning
      Dragon, head, gilding

Large triangular punch-marks

A.i   Bird, head, gilding
      Bird, leg, gilding
      Bird, leg, gilding
      Strap-attachment, tinning
      (The identification of the stamps
      here as A.i is only tentative, but the
      impressions match this stamp more
      nearly than those of A.ii or A.iii.)

A.ii Handgrip, gilding
      Dragon, head, gilding
      Dragon, head, gilding

A.iii Bird, head, gilding
      Bird, head, gilding
      Bird, leg, gilding
      Bird, leg, gilding
      Dragon, head, gilding

FIGURE 92   The shield: detail to show variations in the impressions produced by the
large triangular punch (p. 117 and table 19).
(Scale: 24/1)   (Photo: British   Museum
Research Laboratory)

122

BACKING MATERIALS IN THE GARNET INLAYS AND BEHIND BRONZE FOILS ON THE SUTTON HOO SHIELD

by

KATHERINE EAST

In the course of her work on garnet jewellery and gem stones, Dr Birgit Arrhenius[1] has investigated the cements or pastes which underlie the stones in cloisonné work and are used as filler material in disc brooches. One hundred and nine samples of these backing materials were analysed by X-ray diffraction and classified according to composition. Five main classes of substances are employed: carbonates, silicates, gypsum, sulphur and organic materials. These groups are further subdivided according to the nature and quantity of the subsidiary materials incorporated.[2]

Dr Arrhenius discusses the occurrence of the different pastes in relation to the inlay technique used and the size and shape of the garnets in the jewellery concerned and attempts to correlate the use of specific techniques and characteristic pastes with the chronological and geographical distribution of the jewellery. Seven different inlay techniques are described and differentiated according to certain criteria such as the height and thickness of the cell walls, the way in which the cellwork is built up, how the backplate, where present, is affixed and whether the garnets are set in from the front (as, for example in the sand putty technique) or from behind, before the application of backing material and attachment of the backplate (e.g. the cement technique). Well-defined groups of backing materials are considered by Dr Arrhenius to be diagnostic for specific inlay methods. Four of the techniques are described below in relation to the analytical composition of the pastes found in the Sutton Hoo shield which were analysed by the British Museum Research Laboratory (App. A and table 17).

Backing materials occur in two situations on the shield; in the cells of the cloisonné work as a bedding beneath the gold foils which underlie the garnets and as a backing for decorative bronze foils. The gilt-bronze animal heads on the shield-boss and the collars surrounding the small bosses on the handgrip, as well as those on the flange of the shield-boss, are supported on various types of cement or putty.[3]

Backing materials analytically comparable with those used on the Sutton Hoo shield have been associated by Dr Arrhenius with four different inlay techniques: the cement technique using calcite with a wax overlay; the sand putty technique in which calcite or calcite and quartz is used without wax; a method involving the heating of wax in quantities of up to 50% with calcite or quartz; and a later and very widespread variant of the cement technique in which wax is the predominant component.[4]

Groups based on composition of pastes (*Arrhenius classification*)

I. Carbonate group
   1. Calcite with wax
     (*a*) Wax predominant
     (*b*) Wax less than 50%
     (*c*) Wax as a minor constituent
   2. Calcite without wax
     (*a*) Pure calcite (sometimes with traces of other substances)
     (*b*) Calcite with little quartz
     (*c*) Calcite with larger amounts of quartz and mixed silicates
   3. Aragonite with wax as a secondary constituent
   4. Aragonite without wax
II. Silicate group
   1. Quartz with wax
     (*a*) Wax predominant
     (*b*) Wax less than 50%

---

[1] Arrhenius 1971.
[2] Ibid., 216–19, table II.
[3] The collars of the four similar small bosses on the shield

front are made of gold foil mounted directly onto thin pieces of alder wood backing, cut to shape (p. 22, figs. 14, 31).
[4] Arrhenius 1971, 80, 85, 90 and 94.

2. Quartz without wax
    (a) Quartz with mixed silicates
    (b) Quartz with clay minerals
3. Cristobalite
III. Gypsum group
    (a) Gypsum with wax as a secondary constituent
    (b) Gypsum without wax
IV. Sulphur group
V. Organic group
    (a) Calcium oxalate
    (b) Plant material
    (c) Charcoal

1. *Cement technique (Group I.1.c)*

This is the oldest of the inlay methods which employ a backing material and was in use in Frankish areas from before A.D. 482 until around 540.[1] There is no known occurrence of this technique in Scandinavia, nor does Dr Arrhenius cite any from Anglo-Saxon material, though the characteristic cell shapes of the period are found in both places. These include stepped cells with 1·2 mm steps and cells with U-shapes or S-curves, including quatrefoils.

Analysis of the paste behind the garnets in the disc of the Sutton Hoo shield-boss gave a result consistent with a place in this group (calcite with a little wax), but it is not now possible to be sure whether the garnets were originally mounted in the manner typical for this technique. This involves preparing the cloisonné cells as for an openwork setting and backing the stones with a thin layer of wax[2] followed by a thick layer of the cement; the bronze backplate is added afterwards.

A backing material of the same type as in the boss disc came from under the collar of one of the handgrip bosses. A paste without wax occurs under the other handgrip boss collar and is discussed below.

2. *Sand putty technique (Groups I.2.a, I.2.b)*

Here the cell walls, which tend to be rather thin, were soldered to the base plate initially and the putty, foil and inlay put in afterwards.[3] The tops of the cell walls were then flattened out over the edge of the garnets to retain them. The characteristic putties employed (of quartz or calcite or a mixture of the two) were also used as infilling in some disc brooches. Analysis results would imply that this technique was used in the Sutton Hoo shield in three instances: as a backing to the garnets of the decorative membrane or 'eyebrow' behind the bird's eye, behind one of the handgrip boss collars and under the collar of one of the flange bosses of the central shield-boss. In the first two cases calcite was the only material positively identified but analysis of the paste of the flange boss collar showed it to contain a small quantity of α-quartz with the calcite (table 17).

Dr Arrhenius suggests that this technique developed in the Rhineland, and she distinguishes between the brown sand used in the upper Rhineland and the sand and calcite mixture of the middle Rhine area. However the putty which is predominantly calcite, as in the Sutton Hoo examples, occurs not only from the cemetery at Köln Müngersdorf but also in objects from Gotland, eastern Sweden and eastern Norway, and in the Dover composite brooch and the Taplow buckle (figs. 442 c, 441 a). One of the Gotlandic round *pressblech* fibulae[4] in this group is decorated with interlaced limbless animals with pointed chins and teeth, closely similar to the heads on the gold-foil surrounds to the small bosses on the front of the shield (fig. 52) and to the design on the handgrip (fig. 62).

In the Rhine–Frankish areas an earlier and a later period using the same sand putty technique can be distinguished by the cell shapes used; the earlier period (about A.D. 510–600) is characterised by the use of stepped rhomboids, oval cells, wedge-shaped cells and wedges with curved sides; in the later period (about 540–630) wing shapes[5] and mushroom cells appear.

3. *Melting or fusion technique (Group II.1.b)*

Quartz and wax were the components of the paste behind the garnets of the inset cloisonné panel of the shield dragon. Similar putty was found in Dr

---

[1] Ibid. 120.
[2] A note in H. J. Plenderleith's laboratory notebook (1945) records the presence of a 'wax base' behind the garnets in the Sutton Hoo shield-boss disc. The cell walls had corroded away and were replaced (p. 114, n. 1).

[3] Arrhenius 1971, 85.
[4] Nerman 1969, Taf. 11, 90.
[5] Arrhenius 1971, fig. 133, 1–4.

Arrhenius's analyses of material from Gotland and east Sweden. A putty of calcite and wax, used in a technically similar way to that of quartz and wax has been identified in an Anglo-Saxon disc brooch from Kingston, Kent,[1] and also in objects from Gotland, eastern Sweden and Italy. Amongst the Swedish objects investigated the use of calcite precedes the use of quartz which is not found in connection with this technique until Nerman's period VII.3 in Gotland and contemporaneously on the relatively late (Vendel style D) disc-on-bow brooches in east Sweden.[2]

4. 'Later' wax technique (Group I.1.a)

The use of this method for holding garnets was widespread and is found in objects from workshops which were using other techniques at the same time. Wax is the main constituent of the paste, mixed with a little calcite or quartz.

In the Sutton Hoo shield, wax with a little calcite formed the backing material to the bronze foil animal heads in high relief on the shield-boss. This paste does not occur as a garnet backing on the shield though there is a possibility that the wax contaminated with malachite found in the cloisonné panel on the bird's crest originally contained, or overlay, small amounts of calcite. This could have disappeared in the acid soil since the backplate of the panel was either absent or corroded away.

The composition of the pastes and the garnet inlays on the shield

The acid burial conditions would favour the differential disappearance of calcite but wax is well preserved.[3] There is thus every reason to suppose that where calcite alone does occur or where it occurs with wax, the present analysis result is either substantially applicable to the original cement or else the proportion of calcite is now diminished. Calcite is the commonest component of the backing materials found in the shield and this agrees well with results

of investigations on Anglo-Saxon material.[4] Calcite, used with wax in the fusion technique, is also diagnostic for Scandinavian material in an early period, contemporary with the older Rhine–Frankish cloisonné work. The use of quartz with wax in the cloisonné panel of the dragon represents a much earlier use of this variant than has previously been reported.[5]

The Sutton Hoo shield has every appearance of being an entity and not an assembly of parts from different periods or geographical areas. It is difficult to reconcile this with the idea that the different pastes represent significantly different techniques. Clearly there was considerable diffusion of influence and technical knowledge between workshops yet it is to be expected that one particular technique or variants of it would be favoured for a single object. The pastes cannot be treated in isolation and consideration must also be given to the cloisonné work, the foils and the garnet shapes. Of the five cloisonné panels in the Sutton Hoo shield the backing materials of four have been examined (pp. 101, 106, 114). All four were different and each is typically associated by Dr Arrhenius with a different inlay technique. Unfortunately the poor condition of the bronze cell-walls, many of which have disintegrated completely, and the absence of a backplate in one case (the bird crest) and its inaccessibility in another (the shield disc) make it impossible to be sure from direct evidence whether different methods were used for inlaying the garnets. However the rather substantial cast trough of the bird's eyebrow indicates that in this case the garnets must have been set in from the front. When the bird's leg is seen from the back, it is clear that the cloisonné panel was made separately from the rest of the leg and inserted into position when complete. This was probably also the case for the crest panel of the bird head and perhaps for the dragon panel but there is no evidence to show how the cloisonné work of these panels was made up.

The gold foils used throughout the shield are of a plain pointillé pattern. This is a characteristic foil for the cement technique but not for the older Rhine–Frankish material for which the sand putty tech-

[1] Arrhenius 1971, 92; Avent 1975, pl. 37. This is a brooch of Leeds's Class I(d) (Leeds 1936, 117).

[2] I.e. not before A.D. 700 and continuing through the eighth century; Arwidsson 1942b, 28 and 60.

[3] A beeswax cake remained in the iron lamp and wax is preserved in the shield especially in the case of the relief animal heads on the boss.

[4] In objects from Melton, Suffolk; Kingston and Dover, Kent; Taplow, Bucks; also in the composite brooches from Sarre and Leighton Buzzard. Certain objects from Gilton and Faversham, Kent had quartz pastes. Arrhenius 1971, table II and British Museum Research Laboratory analyses (unpublished).

[5] Arrhenius 1971, 202.

nique was being used.[1] The grid pattern foil was found by Dr Arrhenius to be common in Anglo-Saxon disc brooches of Kendrick's Style A[2] though both main types occur; brooches of Style B use both foil types[3] and both are represented amongst the composite brooches; they occur together on the Dover brooch (fig. 442c).

Cell shapes used in the Sutton Hoo shield are simple. Single steps are found in the bird's eyebrow and as a border on the boss disc but the steps are never crisp or right-angled. Curved walls, both concave and convex, are found and there are pointed oval cells in the boss disc. The pattern in the centre of the disc (fig. 63e) is exactly paralleled in a number of circular brooches from the Rhineland,[4] and on a relief brooch with late Style I ornament from Hällan, Hälsingland;[5] the design evidently remained popular, or was revived two hundred years later, to reappear on the Tuna disc-on-bow brooch.[6] The Sprendlingen brooch,[7] cited as using the sand putty technique, carries a central pattern developed from one like that on the shield-boss and also a similar border of steps. The face motifs which are a feature of the shield cloisonné work have already been discussed (p. 79). Such faces are also seen in Gotlandic material from a period around 570–650. The cell repertoire of the shield lacks the typical keystone wedges, triangles, roundels and T-steps which are characteristic of early Anglo-Saxon jewellery but includes patterns found on Frankish and Gotlandic objects from the middle of the sixth century.[8]

Conclusion

The diversity shown in the composition of backing materials from the Sutton Hoo shield precludes any attempt to localise the place of manufacture on the basis of Dr Arrhenius's system for correlating composition with technique and distribution. However,

the use of calcite and wax or calcite alone is consistent with an English or Scandinavian origin and these are the materials found in the shield, with the occasional addition or substitution of quartz.[9] Ground quartz would produce a clear, hard powder which would be an ideal alternative to ground shell or limestone in districts where the latter were not readily available, but there is no apparent reason why it should have wholly taken the place of the traditional calcite in one situation only (the dragon) on the Sutton Hoo shield.

Classification of the cements and putties into groups which are characterised by the relative proportions of their components has formed the basis for the foregoing discussion of the four different inlay techniques which could have been used on the shield. Although several different techniques may well have been simultaneously in use at the time the shield was made,[10] the idea that four were used on the one object seems untenable. Technical reasons could account for the different backings for the bronze foils but not for variation in inlay technique used in the garnet panels. The use of a particular inlay technique should not therefore be inferred from the paste alone but sought in additional evidence provided by the structure of the cloisonné work. Such evidence is not obtainable from the corroded bronze panels on the shield.

It seems reasonable to assume that not more than two basic techniques were used for all the garnet inlays on the shield, the cast trough of the bird's eyebrow possibly necessitating a different inlay method from that used in the cloisonné panels. If so, and despite the accepted possibility of some differential deterioration or contamination of the mixtures, the variation in composition suggests that the proportions of calcite, wax and quartz used in the preparation of these garnet backing materials were somewhat arbitrary.

[1] Arrhenius 1971, 117 and 128. It is described as 'waffle' pattern in contradistinction to a ring pattern or a chequered (grid) design.

[2] Ibid. 136.

[3] Avent 1975, nos. 25, 69, 73, 78 *inter alia*.

[4] Rupp 1937, Taf. XVI, 2, 5, 11, 13, XVII B.

[5] Arrhenius 1971, fig. 87.

[6] Ibid. fig. 190c.

[7] Ibid. fig. 71.

[8] Rupp 1937, 72; Arrhenius 1971, 186 and figs. 183–5.

[9] Some contamination by silicates might be expected from the sandy soil but the disparity in the occurrence of quartz in the shield pastes suggests that soil contamination is not sufficient explanation.

[10] Arrhenius 1971, 95 and 203.

IDENTIFICATION OF WOOD FRAGMENTS
FROM THE SHIELD MATERIAL

Twenty-six selected fragments from the shield and shield area were sent to the Jodrell Laboratory, Royal Botanic Gardens, Kew, for identification of the wood. The examinations were carried out by Dr D. A. Cutler and his reports received in September and December 1971. Ten of the fragments could not be identified because they were too small and decomposed and in some cases identifications were tentative only because of the condition of the specimens.

The sample numbers are those allocated to pieces of shield material listed by Mrs V. H. Fenwick (p. 7, n. 1). In the majority of cases the position of the wood fragment on the shield, or its relationship to a fitting, could be established with certainty because of the shape of the piece, adhering gold foil, bronze staining, rivet holes or the impression of a recognisable fitting. The fragments are described and Dr Cutler's identifications are given below.

Nos. 3, 8, 9

The underlay of a small boss (no. 3) with the underlying wood (no. 8) and a small square (no. 9) which has the impress of the base of a pyramid on it. A section through the shield showing both a small boss and a pyramid is shown in figure 20.

Wood identifications

No. 3 ? Alder, *Alnus glutinosa* (Gaertner)
No. 8 Probably lime wood, *Tilia* species
No. 9 ? Animal hide, probably leather

Nos. 4, 7, 11

The underlay of a small boss (no. 4) with a fragment of the underlay of a gold strip (no. 7) and a piece of wood 6 mm thick at its thickest part (no. 11). These three pieces can be assembled as shown in figure 31. The grain of the wood of no. 11 is in the same direction as the axis of the strip.

Wood identifications

No. 4 ? Alder, *Alnus glutinosa* (Gaertner)
No. 7 ? Alder, *Alnus glutinosa* (Gaertner)
No. 11 May be ? lime wood, *Tilia* species, badly decomposed, most of the finer structure is broken down but spirals still in evidence were not identified.

Nos. 12–15

Fragments from the shield area now believed to be part of the lyre (p. 23).

Wood identification All probably a maple, *Acer* species.

No. 23

A fragment 7×6·5 cm and 3 mm thick showing impressed lines and traces of gold foil. It has not been finally identified.

Wood identification Probably lime wood, *Tilia* species.

No. 24

A fragment 7×5·5 cm and 6 mm thick. On one surface is a well preserved green-stained piece of leather which has a clear impression of the bird's leg on it (fig. 46).

Wood identification Probably lime wood, *Tilia* species.

Nos. 93, 94, 95

A fragment 3·5×1·5 cm and 4 mm thick (no. 93). It has two rivet holes 9 mm apart, one of which has the shank of a bronze rivet in it. Nos. 94 and 95 can be joined and they fit on top of 93. There is an impressed pattern on 94 and 95, 94 has fragments of gold foil adhering to it: these pieces are from the underlay of a gold strip and 93 is a fragment of the shield-board from beneath the strip.

Wood identification
- No. 93   Probably lime wood, *Tilia* species.
- No. 94   Probably alder, *Alnus glutinosa* (Gaertner)
- No. 95   Probably alder, *Alnus glutinosa* (Gaertner)

No. 35

This fragment, 17 cm long and 4 cm at its widest, is the wood from beneath the dragon (fig. 13). At the back is some textile which has small fragments of wood embedded in it.

Wood identification The main wood from the specimen is lime, *Tilia* species. The small fragment of very decomposed wood, which was difficult to identify, is oak, *Quercus* species.

CHAPTER II

THE GILT-BRONZE RING FROM THE SHIELD

A SOLID gilt-bronze ring of sword-ring type (Inv. 206, fig. 93), but not from a sword, was mounted on the front of the shield (fig. 6*a*). The ring with its attachment tang and ornamental detail is cast in one piece.

Dimensions

Length	27·0 mm
Width	19·0 mm
Overall height with projecting tang	17·5 mm
Projection of tang below the flat basal plane of the ring	8·0 mm

Weight in present condition 30·8 g

Note. The tang is defective at its lower end, apparently disintegrated rather than broken. It tapers towards its lower end.

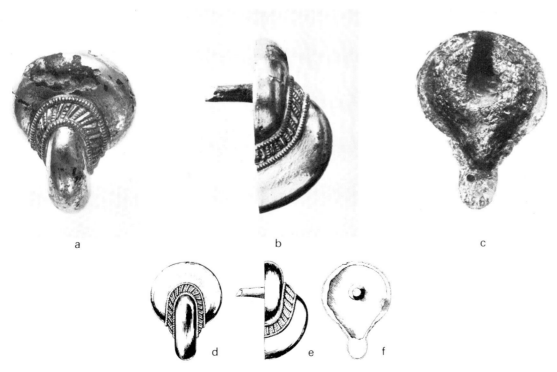

FIGURE 93   The shield: the gilt-bronze ring (*a*) from the front; (*b*) profile; (*c*) back view showing the remains of the single rivet that fastened it to the shield; (*d*)–(*f*) drawings of the gilt-bronze ring. (Scales: *a–c*, 2/1; *d–f*, 1/1)

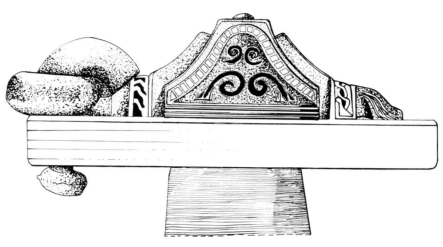

FIGURE 94 Drawing based on photographs of the sword-pommel and ring from Orsay, Seine, now in the Rheinische Landes-museum, Bonn. (Scale; approx. 1/1)

The ring consists of a flat circular lobe or 'button' 4 mm thick, which merges with a vertically set lobe of approximately the same thickness (5·5 mm at the level of the horizontal plane of the ring, fig. 93 *a*). The vertical lobe joins the button at its centre and projects to one side in a 'beak', which comes down to end flush with the base of the button and projects 10 mm beyond its circumference. The horizontal 'button' part is hollowed out at the back but the projecting vertical beak is solid (fig. 93 *c, f*). The junction of the horizontal and vertical portions of the ring is masked by a broad band of imitation filigree 3–4 mm wide and cast in one piece with the rest of the ring; this band consists of two beaded borders, the narrow space between them hatched with seventeen oblique and roughly parallel plain bars with lines of beads, varying in number from four to six, between them; the angle at which the bars are set varies with the varying slopes of the filigree band. The centre point of the tang occurs about one-third of the way along the long axis of the ring, 18 mm from the tip of the beak, 8·5 mm from the rear.

The ring is similar to others associated with the type of weapon to which the characteristic name 'ring-sword' is applied, but differs in one important particular from all known sword-rings save perhaps one exceptionally small example (fig. 96 *d*) discussed below. In sword-rings fitted to the pommels of swords the vertically set lobe

a

b

FIGURE 95 The sword-hilt from Vallstenarum, Gotland: (*a*) view of hilt showing the guards, a single clip, handgrip collars, pommel with attached ring decorated with plaited filigree binding; (*b*) detail of the pommel and ring from above. (Scale: 1/1) (Photo: Gustavianum, Uppsala)

rests on the slope of the pommel, being cut away obliquely to fit on to the slope (fig. 94). The end of the pommel that carries the ring is usually either designed from the outset or later adapted to accommodate the cut-away end of the vertical lobe. In the Sutton Hoo ring the vertical lobe is not cut away but continues down to the horizontal plane of the undersurface of the circular button.

The imitation filigree band which masks the junction of the vertical and the horizontal lobes is also carried down at the sides to the general horizontal level of the undersurface of the ring. This band occurs on true sword-rings, but only on a limited number of East Scandinavian examples (p. 134 below); the leading examples show it in gold filigree, not in cast gilt-bronze. There are gilt-bronze rings from Vallstenarum, Gotland (fig. 95), Karleby, Östergötland and Snösbäck, Väster-gotland (fig. 97). The latter is so similar to that on the Vallstenarum sword that they were probably both made by the same craftsman, or copied

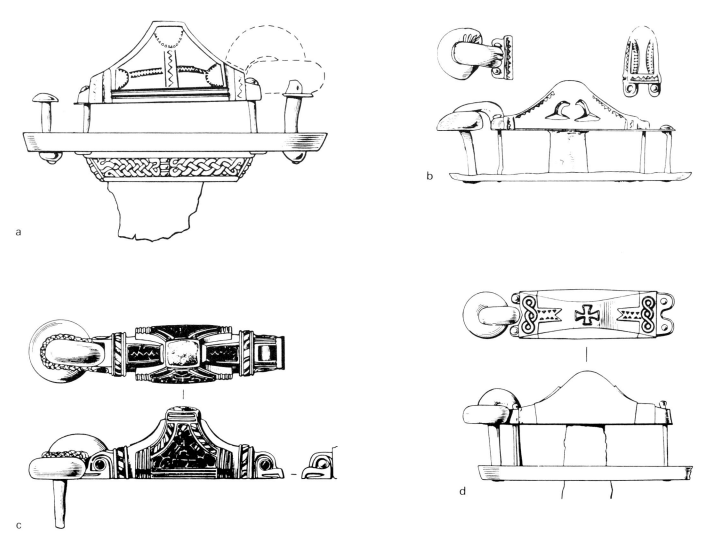

FIGURE 96 Sword-rings from (*a*) Coombe; (*b*) Sarre; (*c*) Italy (unprovenanced, now in the British Museum); (*d*) grave 20, Chaouilly, Meurthe et Moselle. (Scale: 1/1) (After Evison 1967)

132

from one another.[1] Theoretically a sword-ring might be mounted alongside the pommel, on the projecting end of the upper guard, but normally there is no room. Only one ring-sword apparently so designed survives, the exceptionally small example referred to above, that from grave 20 in the cemetery at Chaouilly, Meurthe-et-Moselle (fig. 96d).[2] In this the tip of the vertical lobe of the ring appears, to judge by the published drawings, to meet the upper surface of the guard between the pair of collared rivets which fix the pommel on to the guard at this end. Even in this case the pommel was designed from the outset to receive the projecting ring-lobe, for the collars which hold the rivets are reduced in size and spaced more widely than they are at the other end of the pommel; and the end of the pommel itself between the rivets is further given a re-entrant shape to take the projecting nose of the ring (fig. 96d). In this unique case the sword-ring is a very small one, 1·55 cm in length as against the 2·7 cm of the Sutton Hoo ring. If a larger ring is to be accommodated alongside the pommel instead of overlapping it either a much greater overall length of quillon would be required (as the increase on one side would have to be balanced by an equal increase on the other), or the pommel itself would need to be much reduced in proportion to the guard as a whole. The general trend for the sixth to the eighth centuries is for a marked increase in size of pommel, guard and ring together.[3] Only one ring with uncut vertical lobe (of the design and size of the Sutton Hoo ring, but without the decorative band of imitation filigree), exists. It was found in the boat-grave, Valsgärde 7, and is discussed below (p. 134, fig. 101).

It should be made clear that the Sutton Hoo ring never belonged to the sword contained in the Sutton Hoo burial deposit; that is, it was not transferred from this or any other sword to the shield. In the first place, the materials differ, the pommel and upper guard mounts of the sword being gold, while the ring is gilt-bronze. Secondly, the Sutton Hoo sword is not a ring-sword: the pommel was neither designed nor later adapted to receive a ring, and the projection of the upper guard mount beyond the pommel to either side is only 1 cm. There would be no room to house this ring, which is 2·7 cm in length and does not overlap the pommel, even allowing for the normal projection of the horizontal portion of the ring beyond the end of the guard (e.g. figs. 95, 97 and 219). Since the tang at the back of the ring is at the centre of its circular portion, and when the ring is mounted must be stationed a little way in from the end of the guard for adequate purchase, a minimum clearance of 2·2 cm is needed. This does not exist on the Sutton Hoo sword.

Although the Sutton Hoo ring can now be shown to come from the shield (p. 45 above), and not to have been made for the sword, we should still ask whether it originally came from another sword or was made for mounting on a sword; or whether

[1] For the Vallstenarum sword see Arrhenius 1970, 193–209: for the Vallstenarum find, see Nerman 1969, figs. 264, 479, 523–4, 654, 675, 677, 6ç°–9, 1178, 1260–3, as cited by Arrhenius 1970, 1.

[2] Evison 1967, 117, fig. 14a; a profile of the ring itself is not given in this drawing but from the view in plan it appears that the vertical element falls between the two rivets at its end of the pommel and presumably therefore continues down to the base plate. (Evison 1967 is brought up to date in her 'Sword rings and beads', *Archaeologia* cv, 1976, 303–15.)

[3] Cf. Behmer 1939, passim and pls. XLII and XLVIII; Evison 1967, pl. XIIIb (the sword from Vallstenarum, Gotland and the swords from Valsgärde 5 and 8).

FIGURE 97 Sword-pommel with attached ring from
Snösback, Västergotland. (Scale: 1/1)

it was intended from the first as a device to be mounted on the shield. Böhner and
Davidson[1] have reviewed the special social significance of the sword-ring and the
custom of the giving of rings as a reward for distinguished service. Evison has
suggested that the Sutton Hoo example might have been a 'spare', available for
presentation by the king when the occasion arose; after presentation, it would be cut
or adapted by the recipient to fit his own sword.[2] This is reasonable in principle and
may well seem a practical procedure, but it does not seem likely here, for a number
of reasons. If the ring were of gold or silver it would be relatively easy to cut it. Cast
bronze is not so readily cut, so that it would seem unlikely that a ring given with a
view to adaptation to the individual sword of the recipient would be of bronze. No
surviving bronze ring shows signs of having been cut back secondarily in this way,
though some gold ones do. If it were intended to be added without cutting, it would
need a sword with an abnormally large or long upper guard to accommodate it
alongside the normal pommel without overlap, but swords with long upper cross-guards
are a late development and associated with very large rings. The abnormal feature
of the Sutton Hoo ring calls for explanation in some other way. The explanation seems
to be that it was designed from the outset to be mounted on the shield.

It is relevant, as has been said above, in the context of the Sutton Hoo burial with
its East Scandinavian elements, that the only other known example of a sword-ring
in which the vertical lobe is not cut to fit the pommel (apart perhaps from that cited
from grave 20 at Chaouilly), comes from boat-grave 7 at Valsgärde (fig. 98). Like
the Sutton Hoo ring, this ring is of bronze and cast in one piece, and has the same
flattening of the horizontal lobe and narrowness in the vertical lobe. It is of similar
size. It is not gilt. Moreover, it was not from a sword at all, but was mounted on
a drinking horn (fig. 101).

The fact that the Valsgärde 7 example showed that rings could be mounted on
objects other than swords, and that the Sutton Hoo ring, like the shield, is East
Scandinavian in character, led me to place it among the shield material when the new

[1] Böhner 1949, 167–70, Ellis Davidson 1962, 75–7.   [2] Evison 1967, 72.

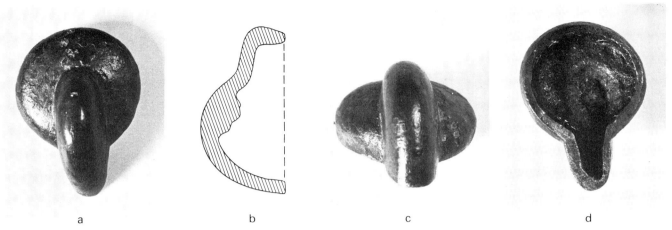

FIGURE 98 Välsgarde grave 7: (*a*), (*b*), (*d*) three views of the gilt-bronze ring found associated with a drinking-horn in this burial; (*b*) cross-section through the ring. (Scale: 2/1) (Copyright: Gustavianum, Uppsala)

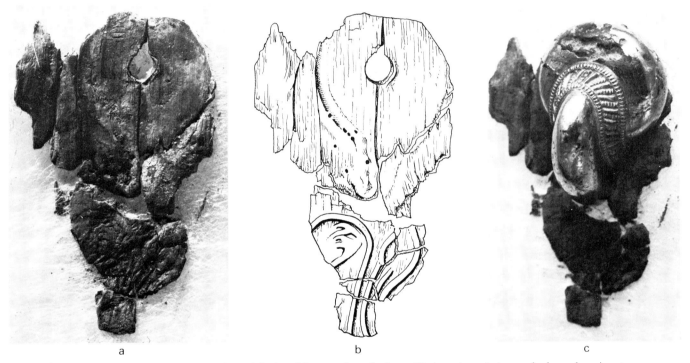

FIGURE 99 The gilt-bronze ring: (*a*) the alderwood underlay; (*b*) drawing of the underlay, showing traces of a pattern from the decorative strip at the centre of which the ring was mounted; (*c*) the ring mounted on the underlay. (Scale: 2/1)

reconstruction was being worked on in 1971, and to see that a close lookout was kept for any evidence that it might belong to the shield. The seating of the ring was duly recognised in a fragment of thin wood backing with a central hole (p. 45, fig. 99).

Evison lists all the ring-swords known from Anglo-Saxon sites. There are eighteen; of these, seven at least had rings of a different kind, consisting of two loose interlinked movable rings.[1] The loose ring type is confined to Anglo-Saxon England (fig. 100). In

[1] Evison 1967; these seven are Petersfinger grave 21, Faversham 951.70 and 954.70, Dover grave C, Bifrons graves 39 and 62, Gilton reg. 6650 M.

135

FIGURE 100 Anglo-Saxon sword-rings: (*a*) Gilton, Kent; (*b*) and (*c*) Faversham, Kent; (*d*) Dover, grave C. (Scale: 1/1) (After Evison 1967)

only one of the other Anglo-Saxon ring-swords has the ring survived. This is the sword from grave 88, Sarre, Kent (fig. 96*b*); it has a small ring 1·8 cm long, crudely shaped and very heavily worn. The vertically set lobe is cut to fit between two rivets on to the shelf which carries the rivets. The two lobes of the ring, horizontal and vertical, are said to have been made separately and soldered together; and they are presumably of silver like the pommel and were probably gilt, though no gilding survives. The ring has been cut back from the circular to give a flattened surface against the pommel, which in fact it does not touch. Though resembling that from Sutton Hoo in being of the solid or fused type, as distinct from the movable type, this ring offers no parallel, even allowing for the fact that its shape has been much altered by cutting and wear. (It had been cut back to fit the Sarre sword and had presumably initially been mounted on another.) The missing ring of the Coombe sword (fig. 96*a*) is recorded in the drawing by J. Y. Akerman in the possession of the Society of Antiquaries.[1] It

[1] Ellis Davidson and Webster 1967; Evison 1967.

136

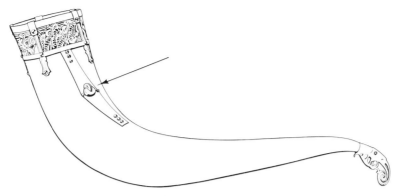

FIGURE 101 Valsgärde grave 7,: drinking horn from the burial with a gilt-bronze ring mounted on a decorative strip, similar to the mounting of the Sutton Hoo shield-ring (drawing based on photographs). (Scale: 1/4)

was of the solid type but in a transitional phase from the loose form being made of two rings soldered together but not fused into one casting. It was certainly mounted on the sword hilt, the end of the vertically set lobe being cut away to fit against a space designed to receive it on the sloping side of the pommel. It is described by Akerman in his sketch as bronze-gilt, but was probably of silver, since it was designed to go with a pommel which on cleaning in the British Museum proved to be of silver, though before cleaning it had appeared to be of bronze.

From this survey it will be seen that the English material does not offer a parallel for the Sutton Hoo ring in general characteristics, let alone in the peculiar feature of not being cut to fit on to a pommel. Even the Coombe ring, the nearest approach to a solid ring among the Anglo-Saxon material, is made in two open pieces and soldered together, not wholly fused. The Sutton Hoo ring, then, has no analogies among Anglo-Saxon traditions and few among those of the Continent.

It could be thought that the Sutton Hoo ring represents a phase in ring development (Evison's phase 3) later than that of the loose or soldered rings, a phase in which the horizontal and vertical elements are cast in one piece; indeed, it is expressly cited by Miss Evison to demonstrate this phase. It seems, however, that her phase 3 is a Continental and notably Scandinavian development which, Sutton Hoo aside, does not occur in the context of Anglo-Saxon archaeology. It is clear from its construction and formal parallels alone that the Sutton Hoo ring is East Scandinavian. It might have been thought that phase 3 is not apparently represented in Anglo-Saxon archaeology because it belongs to the later seventh or eighth century and occurs after the cessation of the burial of grave-goods, and so is concealed from us. The importance of the Sutton Hoo ring lies in the fact that it shows this development to have taken place already before A.D. 625, while grave-goods were still being deposited in Anglo-Saxon graves. Since the development is not found in the Anglo-Saxon material, this tends to confirm the view that it is a Continental development and helps to establish the date when it took place.

137

CHAPTER III

THE HELMET

1. *Introduction and primary account of discovery*

PHILLIPS, in his diary,[1] described the finding of the helmet as follows:

Friday July 28 1939. The crushed remains of an iron helmet were found four feet east of the shield boss on the north side of the central deposit. The remains consisted of many fragments of iron covered with embossed ornament of an interlace type with which were also associated gold leaf, textiles, an anthropomorphic face-piece consisting of a nose, mouth, and moustache cast as a whole (bronze), and bronze zoomorphic mountings and enrichments.

Saturday July 29. A few more fragments of the iron helmet came to light and were boxed with the rest found the day before.

Tuesday August 1. The day was spent in clearing out the excavated stern part of the ship and preparing it for study. Before this a final glean and sift in the burial area had produced a few fragments which are probably to be associated with the helmet and the chain mail respectively.

GENERAL DESCRIPTION

The remains of the helmet as uncovered in the burial deposit consisted of a great many fragments of corroded iron, among which there stood out some better preserved and immediately recognisable elements in cast bronze: a modelled nose and mouth with 'toothbrush' moustache, gilt-bronze animal heads and a pair of eyebrows. The iron of the helmet had completely oxidised before the final collapse of the burial chamber, or before some object or element in the chamber fell on it; as a result the helmet shattered, and clean fractures have made possible its restoration to shape. Had the helmet been crushed while the metal was pliant, as might have happened if the chamber had fallen sooner, it would not have been possible to examine the remains with the same freedom, or to restore its shape perfectly.[2] Unfortunately no photographs were taken of the remains of the helmet in the ground and no plans were made showing the relative positions of the fragments; only the general area of its remains

---

[1] *Sutton Hoo*, Vol. I, 741, 742, 743.

[2] Such distortions have hampered the restoration and study of several of the Vendel and Valsgärde helmets, cf. Arwidsson 1954, 27, writing of the helmet from Valsgärde 8, 'Noch ehe die Metallbleche ihre Elastizität verloren hatten, geriet der Helm in der Erde unter starken Druck, der die ganzen Kalotte stark deformiert hat.' The Valsgärde 7 helmet (fig. 160), as exhibited in the Gustavianum at Uppsala, is built round a cork hatter's former itself cut away and pared down from the regular shape to take the distortion of the crushed helmet. For distortions to the Valsgärde 6 helmet, see Arwidsson 1934, 243–5 and Arwidsson 1942a, 30, 31; for similar effects in the Vendel helmets, Lindqvist 1950a, 3 and 24.

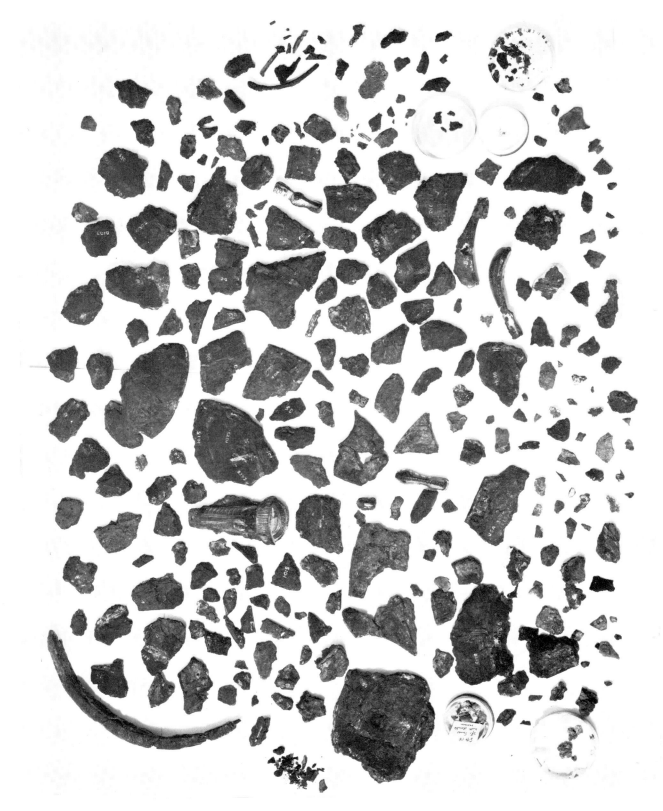

FIGURE 102 The helmet: fragments before work began on a new reconstruction in 1971.
(Scale: slightly under 1/3)

was recorded. It lay north of the keel-line and about 70 cm east of the shield-boss, as seen on the general plan (fig. 1). The task of reconstruction was reduced to a jig-saw puzzle with, as it proved, a great many of the pieces missing (fig. 102). The resultant reconstruction is based exclusively on the information provided by the surviving fragments, guided by archaeological knowledge of other helmets, particularly those from the East Scandinavian milieu to which the Sutton Hoo helmet belongs (sect. 5, II, p. 208 ff.).

The helmet was first reconstructed, and a detailed account of it published in 1947.[1] This reconstruction, which was made without archaeological direction, was never felt to be wholly satisfactory; in 1970 it was finally taken to pieces for re-examination, a difficult operation.[2] The new reconstruction, described here, was completed in 1971 and incorporated extra pieces from the reserve collections, in particular part of a third gilded dragon head matching one already known to belong to the helmet. The reconstruction was carried out in the workshop specially built in the Department of Medieval and Later Antiquities for the conservation and study of the Sutton Hoo material. The process of physical reconstruction was spread over eighteen months in all, and, allowing for other tasks interspersed at times when some waiting was necessary, represents a year's full-time work by Mr Nigel Williams, at that time Conservation Officer in the Department of Medieval and Later Antiquities. Subsequently (1973) a modern version was made, under British Museum direction, in the Royal Armouries in the Tower of London, with the kind permission and cooperation of the Master of the Armouries, A. R. Dufty, by two of his senior Conservation Officer armourers, E. H. Smith and A. Davis. The British Museum supplied electrotypes of the decorative stamped bronze sheets that covered the surfaces of the helmet (made from dies based on reconstructed designs) and of the associated cast bronze parts. The reconstructed helmet is illustrated in figures 103–107 and plate 9. The Tower Armouries' version is shown in figures 136–138 and plate 8. I am indebted to Mr Russell Robinson of the Royal Armouries for his help and advice in connection with some residual problems arising over the 1971 reconstruction and for supervising the making of the modern version.

The original fragments (fig. 102) have been incorporated in the reconstructed helmet only when they join established features or previously placed pieces, or can be seen to belong in a particular position because of their decorative theme, distinctive shape or curvature (e.g. recognisable corners or curves of the neck-guard or cheek-pieces, eye-openings etc.). Some thirty or forty pieces of iron, either devoid of any distinctive features or, if they have any character, incapable of being positioned with certainty, have been omitted. Thus the correct placing of all original fragments incorporated can be demonstrated, and all uncertain elements are expressly excluded from it.

The helmet was made of sheet iron and consisted of a cap to which, below the level

[1] Maryon 1947; for a critique of the old reconstruction and comparison of it with the new, see Bruce-Mitford 1974, 198–209.

[2] Bruce-Mitford 1974, 207.

FIGURE 103   The helmet as reconstructed in 1971, front view.

FIGURE 104   The helmet: right side.

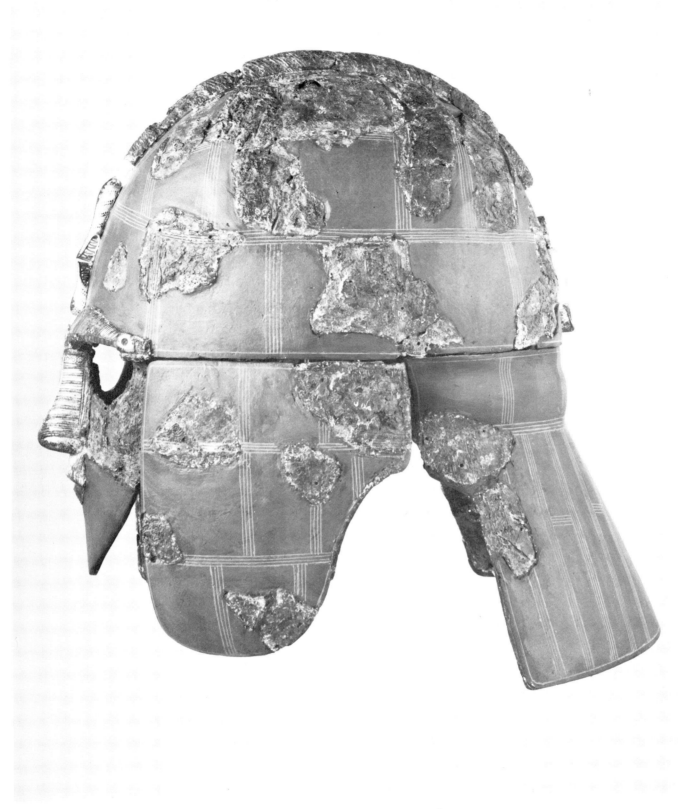

FIGURE 105 The helmet: left side.

FIGURE 106 The helmet: rear view.

FIGURE 107 The helmet from above. The hole in the centre of the crest is clearly seen.

of the brim, were affixed two cheek-pieces, a face-mask and a neck-guard. It was, apparently fitted with a leather lining (p. 179 below). Nothing of this lining survives but its presence is inferred from the peculiar colour and configuration of the iron corrosion inside the cap. A lining of some kind is essential and leather linings are normal in late Roman helmets. The Sutton Hoo helmet cap had not been lined with any kind of textile, since traces of replaced textile impressions would inevitably have remained.

All these iron component parts of the helmet had been covered externally with thin decorated sheets of bronze, held in place by fluted and riveted bronze strips. These foil sheets were tinned and the fluted bronze strips were made of a white alloy (p. 226), giving the helmet a silver appearance. The whole of the outer surfaces of the face-mask and cheek-pieces had been covered with these applied sheets, whereas certain symmetrically disposed areas on the cap and neck-guard had been left bare (figs. 108, 109 and 138; pl. 8). The bare areas could be readily recognised by the uncontrolled development from their surfaces of corrosion products, which had bubbled out into cauliflower-like excrescences that often overflowed on to the adjacent fluted strips and patterned foil, as is still to be seen here and there on the reconstructed iron helmet. Elsewhere corrosion from the iron cap was contained by the overlying bronze sheets. In the present reconstruction the corrosion is seen mechanically reduced (largely filed away in the 1946–7 reconstruction) over the originally bare areas, which can nevertheless still be recognised by their surface texture.

The edges of the cap, neck-guard and ear-flaps were bound with U-shaped brass tubing held in place by fluted bronze clips (p. 227). These edge bindings served also to retain panels of decorative bronze sheeting where these came up against the edges of the different portions of the helmet. The surviving fragments of applied sheeting reveal the use of five decorative designs.[1] Very little remains of this sheeting, or of the fluted bronze strips riveted to the helmet to hold it in place, to frame the individual panels and to bring out a sense of controlled order in the helmet's outward appearance. The few surviving fragments of bronze sheeting are wholly mineralised and are fused with the underlying iron.

All the tinned sheets of bronze foil that were fastened to the helmet's outer surfaces were stamped with scenic or zoomorphic interlace designs. These are fully described in section 4 (p. 186 ff.) and can be identified briefly as follows:

Design 1: Scene of dancing warriors (p. 186; fig. 110a)

Design 2: Scene of rider and fallen warrior (p. 190; fig. 110b)

Design 3: Hardly any of the design of this scene survives and confident reconstruction is impossible, but there is enough of it left to establish that a third figural subject occurred somewhere on the cap of the helmet (p. 197; fig. 148)

Design 4: Large zoomorphic interlace; rectangular, 5×3.3 cm (p. 200; fig. 110c)

Design 5: Small zoomorphic interlace; long and narrow, c. 5×1.3 cm (p. 201; fig. 110d)

---

[1] Discussed on p. 186 ff. The recognition of a fifth scene is a development since the account of the new reconstruction in Bruce-Mitford 1974.

146

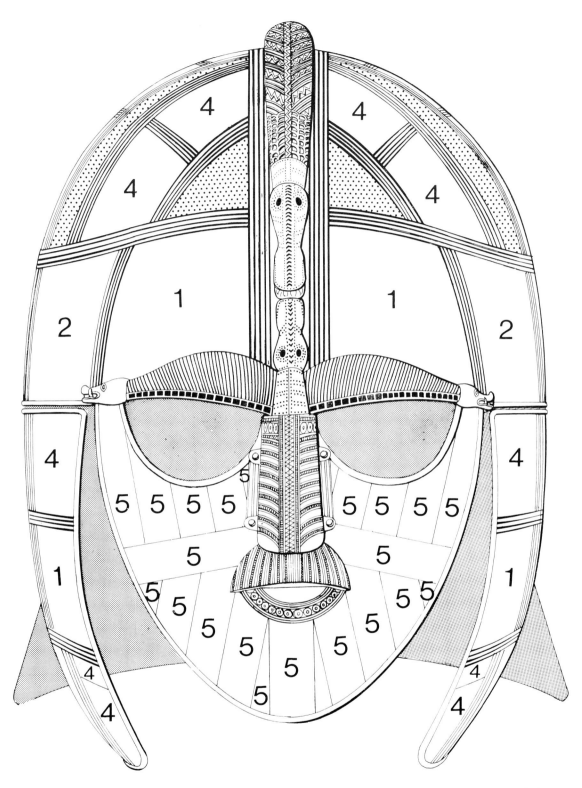

FIGURE 108   The helmet: distribution of the decorative panels on the front of the helmet.
Possible occurrences of design 3 are discussed on pages 197–99.

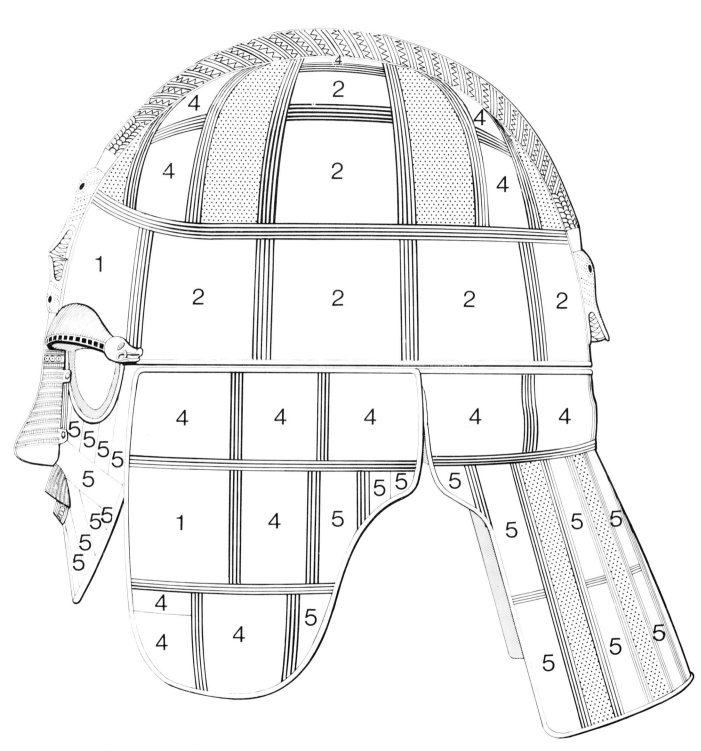

FIGURE 109 The helmet: distribution of the decorative panels on the side of the helmet.
Possible occurrences of design 3 are discussed on pages 197–99.

The neck-guard, regular and symmetrical in shape, carried only impressions of the two interlace dies, designs 4 and 5 (p. 200-1 below); and except in the everted upper corners of the projecting portion of the guard, only complete impressions from the dies were used. The cap carried impressions of four out of the five dies (designs 1–4). Also regular and symmetrical in shape, it carried only complete impressions of the figural panels (designs 1 and 2), and only impressions of the large interlace (design 4) that are either complete or nearly so. This interlace design filled the four ornamental bands that run obliquely between the crest and the horizontal zone of panels round the base of the cap (fig. 109). The foil sheets were trimmed obliquely at the upper and lower ends of these oblique bands to fit against the straight lines of the crest above and the top of the horizontal zone of panels below; the only other occurrence of design 4 on the cap is where halves of the design were used on each side of the crest, at top centre, to fill the residual spaces above the three vertically aligned impressions of design 2, the rider and fallen warrior scene. The inclusion of bare spaces in the design of the cap and the neck-guard (figs. 108 and 109) made it to a large extent unnecessary to fit bits of the designs into corners in order to cover the entire surface. The irregular shapes of the face-mask and cheek-pieces, on the other hand, were made decoratively

FIGURE 110   The helmet: the four designs that are capable of reconstruction: (a) design 1; (b) 2; (c) 4; (d) 5. (Scale: 1/1)

149

effective by covering the whole of the external surface with bronze sheeting. On the cheek-pieces the interlace designs are trimmed and sometimes turned on edge to fill awkward spaces, but on the face-mask, only one design, the long narrow interlace (design 5), has been used, set repeatedly at different angles on a single sheet of bronze foil to fill the awkward space. In spite of this slightly patchwork approach the work is carefully executed and there is nothing slipshod in the final appearance.

The face-mask is a short face-shaped sheet of iron furnished with a gilded cast bronze nose and mouth, and on the cap, above the eye openings, two cast bronze eyebrows; to judge from the Tower Armouries version it seems to have been particularly effective. It has no fluted bronze strips to separate or frame the individual impressions of the die used on it, giving a close surface spread of rich texturing (pl. 8).

Only part of design 2 can be reconstructed with certainty but it has been possible to restore design 1 in its entirety. Designs 4 and 5 are variations of early Germanic Style II (Vendel Style A), and it has been possible to restore both dies completely.

An iron crest, inlaid with silver wires and terminating at each end in a cast bronze dragon head, ran over the crown from front to back. It was flanked by extra-wide fluted bronze strips which were heavily gilded. The helmet did not carry the flamboyant boar or bird crest often seen depicted in the art of the Vendel period in East Scandinavia (cf. figs. 157 and 164e). A third gilded cast bronze dragon head was placed facing upwards on the top of the nose, confronting the dragon head facing downwards at the front end of the crest. The hollow cast bronze eyebrows, inlaid with silver wires and picked out along the under edge with a line of small rectangular garnets, terminate at their outer ends in gilded boars' heads, recalling *Beowulf*, 303–4:[1]

Eoforlīc scionon

ofer hlēorbergan gehroden golde

(Above the cheek-guards shone boar images adorned with gold.)

2. *Detailed description*

I THE CAP

The shape and size of the cap have been arrived at solely on internal evidence. The backs of the fragments, which show distinctive corrosion patterns (pl. 23b), had not been recorded in 1947. They first became available for study in 1970 when the old helmet was dismantled.[2] A whole series of new joins not previously observed could then be established. The fractures are clean and sharp and there was no doubt about the majority of the joins (fig. 111; pl. 23b). A sufficient number of joining fragments of the helmet's top (figs. 107, 111) and crest (fig. 112a), of part of the helmet's left side and of a large piece of the helmet's right side, at the front (fig. 104), could be assembled to enable the cap to be reconstructed completely.

[1] Klaeber 1941, 12. [2] Bruce-Mitford 1972b, reprinted in Bruce-Mitford 1974.

150

FIGURE 111　The Sutton Hoo helmet: view of the interior of the cap. All original assembled fragments are mounted in a jute and resin base. (Scale: slightly over 1/2)

As figure 104 shows, surprisingly little survives that can be allotted to the right-hand side of the cap. Fortunately such fragments as can be allotted to it do not merely confirm but also supplement the record of the left-hand side: where pieces are missing on the one side the corresponding pieces are in some cases present on the other; elsewhere the occurrence of fragments that correspond tends to confirm that the decorative treatment of the two faces is symmetrical, although the occurrence of design 3 presents special problems (p. 199).

The curvature of the cap of the helmet in a front to back direction is established by the crest. This was a separate entity (p. 152 below, figs. 112 and 116a) and, in contradistinction to the first restoration, where sections of plaster had been inserted to fill supposed gaps,[1] it was possible to build up the whole of it, except for a short length at the rear, with perfect joins. With this small section restored, on evidence discussed below (p. 156), and allowing at either end for two dragon head terminals of equal size (p. 159 below), the crest still did not occupy the whole of the distance

[1] See comments in Bruce-Mitford 1974, 123–4.

between the front and the back edges of the cap. A third dragon head (figs. 117*b* and 118*a*), positioned on the top of the nose of the face-mask and pointing upwards, was subsequently found to have taken up this extra length.

Dimensions

The outside dimensions of the reconstructed cap are as follows:[1]

Circumference at brow level (disregarding the eyebrows)	75·5 cm
Length from edge of cap between eyebrows over the top to centre back (disregarding the crest)	44·0 cm
Width at rim level	21·5 cm
Length at rim level	25·5 cm

The cap was beaten up out of a single sheet of iron. Radiographs show no rivets and there is nothing to suggest that the cap was made in strips, sections or halves, methods found in the East Scandinavian helmets of the Vendel period, in the late Roman Constantinian group, from which the East Scandinavian helmets appear to have derived some of their main characteristics, and in the large group of *Spangenhelme* of the sixth–seventh century.[2] The joining of certain fragments at the crown of the helmet demonstrates that the iron sheeting of the cap ran continuously through under the crest. Radiography of these joined fragments gives no indication of any welded, forged or riveted join. In the modern version made in the Tower Armouries the cap has accordingly been raised without joins from a single sheet of metal.

11   THE CREST AND DRAGON HEADS

The crest is a thick iron tube of D-shaped or approximately semicircular cross-section, tapering evenly to each end (fig. 112). It is made from two pieces of iron, a flat bottom strip and an inverted U-shaped upper one, the edges of which came down on each side of the bottom strip (fig. 113*a*). As assembled on the reconstructed helmet the crest occupies a length of *c*. 28·5 cm. With the gilt-bronze dragon heads added at each end its overall length, as restored, is 38·5 cm (fig. 116*a*).

---

[1] The Tower of London modern reconstruction can be worn and experimented with, and its relationship with the reconstruction which incorporates the original pieces, and on which it is based, should be stated. The corresponding dimensions of the replica are:

Circumference at brow level (disregarding the eyebrows)	74·00 cm
Length from edge of cap between eyebrows over the top to centre back (disregarding the crest)	44·0 cm
Width at rim level	21·5 cm
Length at rim level	24·5 cm

The Tower replica was made deliberately slightly smaller in brow-level circumference and length from front to back at rim level to discount a slight inflation of dimensions in the original which was attributed to corrosion.

[2] S. V. Grancsay, 'A barbarian chieftain's helmet', *Metropolitan Museum of Art Bulletin*, June 1949, 272–81. Klumbach, *Spätrömische Gardehelme*, Munich 1973, 14. For the *Spangenhelme* group J. Werner, 'Zur Herkunft der frühmittelalterliche Spangenhelme', *Praehistorische Zeitschrift* 34/5, 1949/50, 178–93. See also section 5 below.

FIGURE 112   Photograph and radiograph of the joined fragments of the Sutton Hoo helmet crest.
The complete front end complete with tang is to the left in both views. (Scale: just under 1/1)

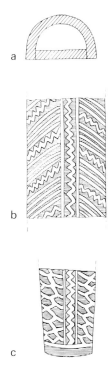

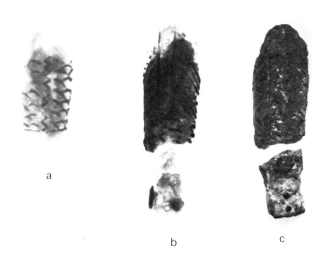

FIGURE 113 Details of the iron crest of the Sutton Hoo helmet and its silver inlay patterns: (a) cross section of the crest at its centre; (b) the principal chevron design; (c) the scale pattern employed at both ends of the crest. (Scale: 1/1)

FIGURE 114 The helmet: (a) radiograph of the front end of the crest; (b), (c) radiograph and photograph of the detached rear portion of the crest with tang fragment. (Scale: 1/1)

The determination of the length of the crest

The crest, built up from fragments in a succession of perfect joins, is complete from its front end for a length of 25·5 cm. At this point in the crest on the reconstructed helmet there is an irregular gap of 19 to 20 mm (fig. 104). The gap should perhaps be fractionally longer, since the two terminal animal heads have been restored to the same length, 4·8 cm, from the tip of the snout to the back of the skull, whereas the rear head may have been slightly smaller overall (p. 159). Nonetheless the crest length shown in the reconstruction, based on the following evidence, will be nearly exact. The iron crest was inlaid with silver wires as a form of decoration and over the main middle portion of the crest these form a running chevron pattern which changes at the ends to a scaly pattern (figs. 112, 113c, 114a). At the incomplete rear end of the reconstructed continuous length of crest (fig. 114b and c) is a fragment where the chevron pattern can be seen to have come to an end and the scale pattern to have begun. This is clear on the radiograph (fig. 114b), though not apparent to the naked eye. With a small margin of error (p. 156 below) we know the length of the scale pattern (assuming that, as seems evident, the two ends of the crest behaved symmetrically), thus we can calculate the length of the missing portion of the crest.

The crest terminated at each end in a projecting iron tang through which a dragon head was riveted. The front tang is in place, and a detached portion of the rear tang has survived (fig. 114b, c). In the latter are two rivet holes, marking the point of attachment of the collar of the rear animal head. The holes show clearly in figures 114b and c. On this iron tang, and registering in the radiograph (fig. 114b), is a small piece of paste-like substance, identified by the British Museum Research Laboratory as a decomposed high tin bronze (p. 228). This bears on its surface a solitary surviving fragment of gold leaf decorated with a punched circle. This corresponds with, and is indeed all that is left of, a larger and very fragile area of gold foil with punched circle decoration, mounted on the same paste-like substance; this was placed between the main part of the crest and the rear animal head in the first reconstruction (fig. 119), but has since been almost entirely lost in the process of dismantling and remaking the helmet. The situation at the rear end of the crest is illustrated in figure 115.

The iron tubing of which the crest is made is 3 mm thick. Its outer surface carried a running chevron design inlaid in silver wire. The chevrons are spaced and each consists of a group of three parallel lines on both sides of the crest, converging towards the centre line, where they abut on the central decorative features, a narrow band running from end to end of the crest, carrying a continuous inlaid zig-zag of silver wire. This central band continues beyond the chevron zone and through the scale patterns to meet the collars of the terminal dragon heads. Figure 113b, c shows a reconstructed detail of the patterns at the two ends of the crest. Each chevron is

FIGURE 115 The helmet: drawing to show the original relationship between the fragments that survive from the rear of the crest. The head shown does not belong to the neck. (Scale: 1/1)

separated from those next to it by a zig-zag silver wire. The chevrons are assumed to point towards the front of the helmet as is the case in those Vendel-type helmets where junctions of eyebrows and crest are preserved.[1] In the Sutton Hoo helmet the scale pattern is relatively well preserved at the front end of the crest, where it appears on the iron fragment with projecting tang which terminates the crest. It can be seen to end in a straight transverse silver wire inlaid across the end of the crest (figs. 112 and 114a). The length of the scale pattern preserved on this terminal fragment from

[1] For example, Vendel 1; and also Valsgärde 5, 6, 7 (fig. 159) and 8, where the mutual relationship of crest and eyebrows was also recorded in the ground.

155

the front end of the crest is 2·5 cm. At this point there is a gap of 7·5 mm in the upper surface of the crest on the far side of which is the chevron pattern. The two patterns must have met in this gap, and if we allow 7 mm for the completion of the scale pattern, we have its length as some 32 mm.

At the rear end of the crest the transition (without any line of demarcation) between the chevron inlays and the scaly pattern, lacking at the front of the crest, is preserved (fig. 114b and c). We have only to complete the gap to make the length of about 32 mm which the scale pattern has at the front end and join up with the surviving tang to arrive at the complete length of the crest, assuming that the two dragon heads were of the same size. The necks that projected from the backs of these dragon heads have not survived; the size chosen for them in the restoration is based on the length of the iron tang at the front end, and on the proportion of the collar or neck to the size of the head seen in similar complete heads on the Vendel and Valsgärde helmets[1] (fig. 116a). All told, it seems clear that the overall length of the crest with the two terminal dragon heads attached will have been almost exactly that shown in the reconstruction.

No additional fragments that might affect the length of the crest came to light in the excavations of the 1939 spoil heaps carried out in 1968–9, although a piece of the surface of the crest was found with certain other fragments.[2] The missing portion of the animal head from the back of the crest was not in the dumps. As it appears to have been of a different more brittle alloy (largely tin) it might have broken up and disintegrated more readily than ordinary bronze if struck a blow in the burial chamber (but see also p. 44, n. 1).

The establishment of the original length of the crest is important, because, with the animal heads at each end in position, it still falls short by some 5 cm of the measurement from back to front over the crown, discussed in the previous section. This residual space is exactly right for the inclusion of a feature new to this class of helmet—the third (complete) head (fig. 117b). The size and bevelled external profile of its projecting collar (fig. 118a), and the lack in the collar of any rivet hole, show that this third head cannot have been attached to the crest, and cannot be exchanged with either of the two heads placed at the ends of the crest in the reconstruction.

It seems clear that the more complete of the two defective heads (the one that lacks only its collar) came from the front of the helmet. The damage at the rear end of the crest, and the fact that the remains of the collar (carrying gold foil with the punched circle ornament) on the tang and the fragment of muzzle are of the same high tin alloy, seem to link the dragon head of which only the muzzle survives, to the back end of the crest.

At the top of the crest in its exact centre is a small circular hole, 1·5 mm in diameter

---

[1] For example, Valsgärde 8 (Arwidsson 1954, Abb. 11, right); Stolpe and Arne 1927, pl. v, fig. 3, pl. vi, figs. 5, 6, xxxvi, fig. 7).

[2] *Sutton Hoo*, Vol. I, figs. 242, 243, 244, 245.

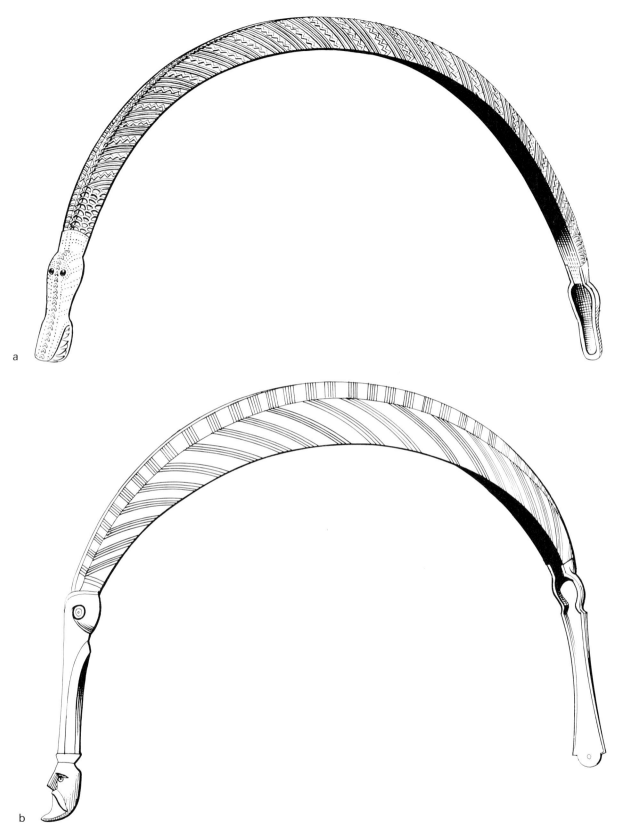

FIGURE 116 Reconstruction drawing of the complete crest of the Sutton Hoo helmet (*a*), compared with (*b*) the bronze crest and comb from grave 1, Vendel, Uppland, Sweden.

(fig. 107). As there is no corresponding hole in the bottom plate of the crest this cannot have served to attach the crest to the cap of the helmet. The hole seems too small to have held a fitment for a plume; nor can it have anything to do with the possible attachment of a central vertical comb such as Vendel-type helmets normally have (fig. 116b). There are no additional holes or any marks to suggest that the Sutton Hoo helmet carried such a crest.[1] In any case, the fact that the median line of the crest of the Sutton Hoo helmet is decorated with a silver wire inlay shows that it was not meant to be covered.

The crest of the Sutton Hoo helmet has made clear for the first time the meaning of the unique Anglo-Saxon word *wala* in *Beowulf*, 1031. The whole passage (1030–34) reads:

> Ymb þæs helmes hrōf   hēafodbeorge
> wīrum bewunden   wala ūtan hēold,
> þaet him fēla lāf   frēcne ne meahte
> scūrheard sceþðan,   þonne scyldfreca
> ongēan gramum   gangan scolde

(Round the helmet's crown a ridge bound with wires protected the head from without so that the sword, hard in battle, might not cause too grave an injury when the shield-warrior went forth against his enemy.)[2]

The Sutton Hoo helmet, alone among Scandinavian helmets, shows a crest or projecting ridge inlaid with wires,[3] a decorative technique invited by its iron construction. The strength derived from its iron construction also seems unusual. An iron crest, in this case plain, occurs on the helmet from Valsgärde 6 (Arwidsson 1942a, 27), but other East Scandinavian helmets have bronze crests, in which the chevron patterns, in the Sutton Hoo crest inlaid in silver wire, are only imitated in the cast bronze.

If the crest was strong and performed the vital protective function described in *Beowulf* it must have been securely attached to the cap of the helmet. Since there is no trace of riveting either in the crown (p. 152 above) or in the crest itself, it must have been attached by soldering or forging. Chemical analysis has reinforced the visual evidence that there is no trace of solder on either crest or cap, so the crest must have been forged on (or possibly, as the Research Laboratory believe, shrunk on). This implies that the silver wire inlays, which would have melted or become discoloured with the heat, were not put in until after the crest was in position; this in turn means

---

[1] The comb of the Valsgärde 8 helmet was held to the crest by at least five pins (Arwidsson 1954, 24–5) and the comb of the Valsgärde 7 helmet by at least two. The cast bronze dragon head at the rear of the Valsgärde 7 helmet in its projecting collar, if not the front one as well, also showed a special adaptation to accommodate the end of the upstanding comb, as well as the end of the crest.

[2] Bruce-Mitford 1974, ch. 9; Anglo-Saxon text from Klaeber 1941.

[3] The pair of helmet eyebrows from Lokrume, Gotland, which are also of iron, are silver plated (Lindqvist 1925a, 194, fig. 97). Silver wire inlays in bronze eyebrows can be seen in Nerman 1969, Taf. 66 (the similar looking decoration in Taf. 67, 607, is cast).

158

that the crest cannot, as in many of the Vendel-type helmets, according to Lindqvist (1950a), be a re-used piece taken over from another helmet and reinforces the impression of homogeneity conveyed by close familiarity with the Sutton Hoo helmet. As would be suited to its quality and royal context, it seems clear that it was designed and made *de novo* for its owner, and that the armourer did not utilise pieces of old or captured helmets.

It is also of importance that, as the absence of rivets and the evidence that the cap was raised from a single sheet of metal show, the crest did not perform the structural function of holding together the two halves of the cap. This is one of the essential elements in the construction of the Constantinian class of helmets from the Eastern Imperial workshops. This remarkable group of Late Antique helmets, studied afresh in a volume edited by Klumbach,[1] includes the de Peel (Deurne) helmet cited by Lindqvist as the kind of prototype from which the Vendel (or East Scandinavian) type must have derived (p. 210 below) and others which offer significant parallels in detail to the Sutton Hoo helmet.[2]

The three dragon heads (figs. 117 and 118)

Two of these (the more complete) are of cast bronze. The third, of which portions only survive (figs. 117c and 118c), was evidently of a different alloy, and now consists largely of tin oxide (p. 228 below). One of the three heads (figs. 117b and 118a) is intact. In this the head-element proper is 23 mm in length and hollow cast, and projecting from the back of the skull, cast in one piece with it, is a strong bronze neck or collar 17 mm in length; this is angular externally, round internally and has slightly bulging or convex sides (figs. 117b and 118a). Seen in profile the projecting neck also has lightly concave lower edges. A second head (figs. 117a and 118b) is complete as far as the point where the neck should develop, but at this point is broken across, and the neck or collar is missing. The head portion, 45 mm in length, is hollow cast (fig. 117a). The third head, of which portions only survive, is represented by the muzzle and jaws, and a small piece of the neck (fig. 119). The dimensions of the muzzle part correspond closely with those of the second head, the muzzles of these two heads being 14 and 15 mm thick respectively, as compared with 10 mm for the first head. The applied decoration, consisting of patterns built up from lines of very small punched circles on a gilded surface (fig. 118) seems to have been identical on all three.

Down the centre line of each complete head, from top to bottom and down the centre of the surviving portion of the third head, runs a band of close-set small chevrons of stamped decoration made by impressions from a V-shaped punch which contained seven circles (fig. 174). All the chevrons point up the head and the band is flanked on each side by a single line of similar circles slightly more openly spaced. Another line of small close-set circles outlines the extreme edge of the muzzle round its upper

[1] Manojlović Marijanski 1964, and the same and other authors in Klumbach 1973.
[2] For helmets of this type in Norway see S. Grieg, 'Norske hjelmer fra folkevandringstiden', *Bergens Museums Aarbok*, 1922–3, Hist. Antikv. Raekke Nr. 3, 3–12.

159

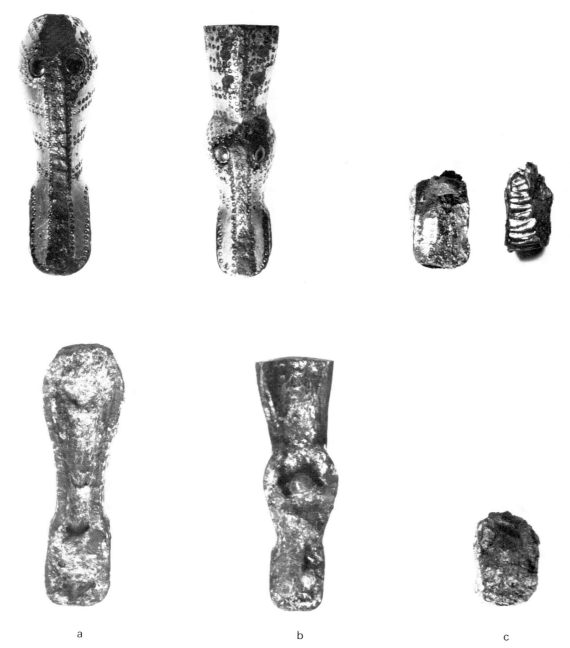

a   b   c

FIGURE 117   The Sutton Hoo helmet: three gilt-bronze dragon heads: (*a*) and (*c*) crest terminals, (*b*) the head placed facing upwards above the nose. (Scale: 3/2)

surfaces and the back of the open mouth. Pairs of parallel lines of circles decorate the cheeks; these parallel lines point forwards towards the muzzle, and when the head is seen frontally give the effect of large chevrons disrupted by the central band.

More punched circles cluster in two rows round the eyes, which are convex garnets countersunk in the bronze castings. Three of the four eyes of the two complete heads have foil backing (simple dots). The left eye of the long head at the front of the helmet does not.

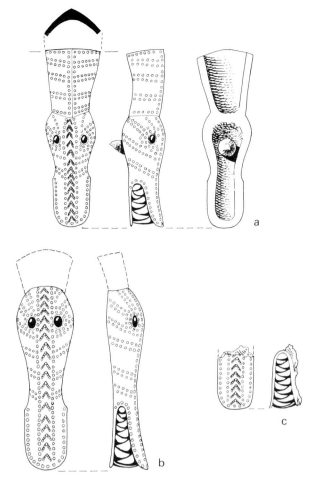

FIGURE 118 The helmet: dragon heads, showing decorative details, front, back and profile views. Variations in the treatment of the teeth prove that no two are from the same mould. (Scale: 1/1)

FIGURE 119 The helmet: enlarged detail from the first reconstruction showing gold foil with punched circle decoration from a portion of dragon neck *in situ* at the rear of the crest. Little of this foil survives.

The theme of pairs of parallel lines of punch-work circles converging to form chevrons is continued on the neck of the smallest head, that which (for reasons given below) has been placed pointing upwards on top of the nose of the face-mask. Since the collar of this head is carinated and has no central stripe of punched chevrons, the lines of close-set circles that flank the central stripe on the other heads are here applied immediately to each side of the carination, and the parallel lines of punched circles forming the large chevrons run directly up to them.

The cast head which points upwards between the eyebrows differs radically in form from the other two. Projecting from its centre at the back, at a point between the eyes, it has a massive rivet-shank (fig. 118 a), and was evidently intended to be fastened directly to the cap of the helmet. As the view in figure 118 shows, the lower edges of its collar form in profile a longitudinal concave curve. This curve corresponds with the convex curve of the surface of the inner ends of the eyebrows. The length of the collar is also equal to the breadth of the eyebrows at their inner ends. The other heads were both riveted by their collars to the tangs at the ends of the crest, and by their noses to the cap. The distinctive long collar of the projecting complete head has no

b

a

FIGURE 120   The helmet: front and back views of the bronze nose and mouth casting from the face-mask. The hole cut into the iron sheeting of the mask to correspond with the open back of the bronze nose casting can be seen in (*b*). (Scale: 3/2)

rivet or rivet hole in it and as has been said (p. 156) cannot have been attached to the crest, so that a position had to be found for it elsewhere. The location chosen, between the eyebrows and resting on the top of the nose, is inevitable because of the dimensions and profile of its projecting neck, and because placed here it fills a vacant space in the design. Its placing here explains also the absence of gilding from the rear portion of the top of the nose casting which is concealed when the head is in position.

III THE FACE-MASK

The face-mask (figs. 103, 120–124) is 12 cm in length as reconstructed and comes to a point. It is curved laterally to match the curvature of the cap of the helmet. Its breadth at the top in a straight line from corner to corner across the curve is 13·5 cm. It was attached to the cap at three points, by riveting: centrally (above the nose) and on each side where the iron sheeting of the mask rises to enclose the eye openings and is continued up a short way inside the cap.

At the central point of attachment a solid bronze plate, cast in one piece with the nose, projects upwards for a distance of 1·5 cm from the top of the nose. This plate is 2 cm wide at the bottom, tapering to a width of 1·7 cm at the top; it tapers also in thickness from bottom to top, and its edges are bevelled (figs. 120 and 123). This tang has a large central hole in it, 3·5 mm in diameter. In the 1945 reconstruction of the helmet this hole was used to carry a modern screw, but there is no record to confirm that it was drilled for the purpose, and it could be an old hole re-used. To the (helmet's) left of this hole, below it and above it, are two small holes; to the right of it and below it there is another small hole matching that in the corresponding position on the left. No second hole on the right to balance the upper small hole on the left can be detected on the radiograph. The radiograph (fig. 121) reveals another central hole, near the bottom of the projecting plate or tang, between the two small holes and larger than them. This hole cannot be seen in figure 120 a, being concealed by corrosion, nor is it visible at the back, for the same reason. The large hole referred to earlier does not show up clearly on the radio-graph, although its position can be seen, because the photograph was taken with the modern screw in position. The inner end of each eyebrow, as seen in section,

FIGURE 121 The helmet: radiograph of the nose casting. (Scale: 1/1)

terminated in a bevelled step below (fig. 127b), above which a short bronze shelf projected. The bevel of the step fitted against the bevel of the side of the projecting tang at the top of the nose, and the projecting shelves (in both eyebrows unfortunately almost completely broken away) would have fitted over the outer edges of the tang. These projecting plates presumably had in them small holes which would have coincided with those in the nose tang. The eyebrows were thus riveted at their inner ends to the nose tang and the tang itself was riveted to the cap, forming a rigid assembly.

The upper outer iron elements of the mask, strips 15 mm wide continuing a short way up inside the cap, were held in place on each side by a large rivet whose end shows behind or below the eyes of the boars' heads that form the outer ends of the eyebrows; this rivet-shank thus held together the eyebrows and two thicknesses of iron sheeting. Only one of these extensions from the face-mask survives, fixed inside the cap. It can be recognised in figure 127d. Thus the eyebrows were riveted to the face-mask at both ends; at the inner end they were attached to the tang rising from the nose; behind the boar's head at the outer end, to the cap and to the side pieces coming up from the mask.

The mask carries a nose in high relief, with short 'tooth-brush' moustache, and mouth. Its shape, as newly reconstructed, has the authentic outline of a face (figs. 103 and 124),[1] and with the eye-openings, eyebrows and general head shape of the helmet, gives a realistic anthropomorphic impression to the helmet.

The mask was completely covered with bronze sheeting decorated with design 5, the smaller interlace. One impression of the die is set more or less horizontally on each side of the moustache, sloping slightly down towards the outer edges of the mask (fig. 108 and pl. 8). Above these the impressions of the die run almost vertically upwards but lean slightly outwards, as though with the backward curve of the mask. Below the transverse impressions of the die more impressions of it are set vertically, leaning slightly inwards. While in the reconstruction the areas of the mask above the transverse impressions of the die can each be seen to carry four vertical impressions set contiguously, the area below is only represented by one surviving fragment of original helmet (fig. 103); this, as far as it goes, shows three contiguous die impressions. In spite of this lack of completeness in the material the overall design has been restored as shown in figure 108, wherein the angles at which the various impressions of design 5 are set may also be seen.

The treatment of the mask is different from that of the rest of the helmet's surface. There are no bronze fluted strips to separate the impressions of the die; its double border (fig. 151) however, brings out the axes on which the patterns are set. Radiographs of the original fragments that composed the face mask show no rivets or rivet holes at all in the interior fields, and it seems clear that a relatively large sheet or sheets of metal were used, on which the die impressions were applied contiguously with very

[1] For comparison with the mask of the first reconstruction see Bruce-Mitford 1974, pl. 46a.

164

FIGURE 122   The helmet: enlargement of the nose
casting showing the nostril holes.

great precision to form continuous running patterns. The use overall of the small-scale interlace gives a uniform textured effect, so that in the face-mask the panelled effect of the rest of the helmet surface is abandoned. The mask however was tinned so that the shining white appearance characteristic of the rest of the helmet would extend to it.[1]

The edges of the mask and of the eye openings were bound with brass U-section tubing held in by short lengths of fluted bronze strip set at right-angles to the edging, as is normal (for example on the shield-rim, or drinking-horn or maplewood bottle mouth mounts), and riveted in place. The U-tubing served not only to finish the edges of the mask but also and in particular to retain the decorated bronze foil sheeting. On each side of the nose, both at the bottom, opposite the point where the patterning on the nose ends, and also above, where the eye openings meet the nose, are two small round projecting plates, cast in one piece with the nose. These hold rivets whose prime function was to attach the nose-casting to the mask. Between these two plates, on each

---

[1] Cf. Beowulf, 2256–7, 'feormynd swefað, / þā ðe beadogrīman bȳwan sceoldon' (the polishers sleep who should make the war-mask shine), ed. Klaeber 1941. I am grateful to Mrs Susan Youngs for drawing my attention to this passage.

FIGURE 123   The helmet: profile of the nose casting showing the decorative
schema and the taper of the bronze tang at the top. (Scale: just under 2/1)

side of the nose, run fluted strips which must have assisted in retaining the applied bronze-foil sheeting.

At the back of the nose the iron sheet from which the mask is made is cut away to expose the hollow of the nose casting (fig. 120 b). Although the wearer's nose would not enter the hollow casting and the mask stands clear of the face, the opening is functional in the sense that it would assist breathing, for two holes like nostrils under the tip of the nose open into the hollow casting, providing a direct supply of air (fig. 122). This would appear to be a practical measure, as with clothing around the neck and the cheek-pieces tied against the mask, extra air might well have been needed.

The dismantling of the former reconstruction in 1970[1] enabled the correct dimensions, shape and ornamental treatment of the mask to be established. On both sides of the mask the line of the under edge of the eye openings, and their depth, width and exact relationship to the nose, are firmly fixed by a series of reliable joins, and the profiles of the mask have only to be extended to arrive at the lowest central point. The relationship of the mask to the cheek pieces can be appreciated from the front view (fig. 103). The curved sides of the shortened mask match exactly the curves of the longer cheek-pieces, so that they fit when brought together and the lower ends of the cheek-pieces are tied together under the chin. A single corrosion fragment (limonite, p. 192) preserves both an original piece of the edge of the cheek-piece and a reverse impression of the edge of the mask practically touching each other.

The bronze castings associated with the face mask
The nose and mouth. Details of the nose casting are shown in figures 122–126 and plate 9. Figure 123 shows the flat top of the nose. The nose is hollow (fig. 120 b) but the hollow is too small to accommodate a real nose, so that the mask must stand well clear of the wearer's face. The hollowness of the nose-casting was presumably intended to reduce weight and save metal, as well as to facilitate breathing (above). The moustache and mouth are cast in one piece with the nose. Some of the decorative details may be studied in the enlarged detail, figure 123. The greater part of the surface of the nose is gilded but gilding covers only the front part of the flat top of the nose (p. 163). The ridge is decorated with triangular punch-marks forming zig-zag ribbons inlaid with silver and this central strip is tinned and enclosed by beaded borders. On each side of the bridge lies a band of three punched circles, again inlaid with silver and enclosed between decorative borders. Below these bands the sides of the nose are embellished with alternate rows of plain flutings and billeted strips which run obliquely between the central strip and a billeted lower edge. The nose is outlined on both sides by a swaged strip running between the two small projecting plates which secure the nose to the mask (p. 165 and fig. 124). The billeting of the lower edge of the nose stops where these plates develop. The ornamental details are drawn out in figure 125. The moustache stands out in relief as a solid casting and is ornamented in the same

[1] Bruce-Mitford 1974, 198–209; and see Maryon 1947, 137–44.

FIGURE 124 The helmet: detail of the front, showing the 'flying bird' imagery created by the nose, the eyebrows and the dragon head above the nose.

manner as the sides of the nose, but with the pattern running vertically. Below the moustache the mouth is represented by a plain heavily gilded flat surfaced crescent, whose lower edge is bevelled and carries, between light mouldings, a line of circles inlaid with silver as on the bridge of the nose (figs. 122 and 125 b).

Eyebrows

The eyebrows (fig. 127 a–d) are hollow cast in bronze, and parts of the helmet cap still adhere to their backs (fig. 127 d). The rivets by which they were fixed at their

168

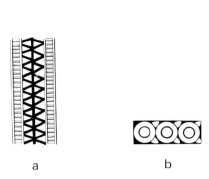

a   b

FIGURE 125   The helmet: schematic drawing showing applied decoration on the
bronze nose casting. (*a*) rows of silver triangles inlaid in punched depressions in the
tinned central strip on the ridge of the nose;
(*b*) concentric circles and triangular punch-
marks inlaid in silver, used on a tinned ground
at the top of the nose and on the mouth. In
both drawings black shading represents a
tinned bronze surface. (Scale: 3/2)

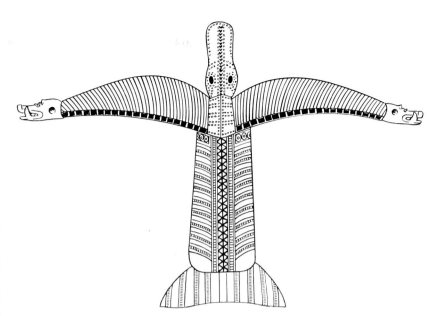

FIGURE 126   The helmet: the 'flying dragon' image
extrapolated from the helmet. (Scale: 2/3)

outer ends to the cap and to the upper frame of the face-mask can also be seen, as
can a rebate or step which fitted against the tenon at the top of the nose (fig. 127*b*).
The eyebrows are inlaid with silver wire lying in close-set parallel grooves which occupy
the full width of the eyebrow.[1] The castings terminate in gilded boars' heads (fig. 128).
The boar's head on the helmet's right side (fig. 127*a*) is complete, that on its left side
is broken across at the tusk. Leaving aside the boars' heads the two brows are not
of the same length. The right brow, which has the complete boar's head, is shorter;
between the inner end and the beginning of the boar's head it measures a little over
61·5 mm, while the helmet's left brow measures 66·5 mm (fig. 127*c*). The complete
boar's head terminal measures 19·5 mm in length. The under edge of each brow is
picked out with a line of plain rectangular garnets in individual bronze cells. Apparently
there were originally twenty-five garnets on the left brow and twenty-three on the right,
but some are now missing: fifteen survive on the left side, twelve on the right. Gold
foil underlies all the garnets in the right eyebrow but none of those in the left. The
left eyebrow carried an estimated forty-six silver wires as against forty-three in the
right. The broad under surfaces of the brows are plain and heavily gilt (for comments
on the garnets, see App., p. 230).

The two eyebrows are kept apart structurally by the tang projecting upwards from
the top of the nose, to which their inner ends are riveted. The resulting gap is filled
by the neck of the upward-pointing dragon head positioned on the top of the nose
(pp. 161/3).

The introduction of this upward-pointing dragon head in this position brings into
being on the front of the helmet the complete image of a winged dragon (fig. 126).

[1] For a pair of bronze eyebrows from Gotland similarly inlaid with silver wires see p. 158, n. 3.

169

a

b

c

d

FIGURE 127   The helmet: front and rear views of the eyebrows, (*a*), (*b*) the helmet's right eyebrow; (*c*), (*d*) the left eyebrow. (Scale: 3/2)

The anthropomorphic impact of the helmet and its human face is scarcely affected by the placing of the third animal head above the nose, or by the concealed dual imagery thus brought about (fig. 124). If visually detached from the human face the flying dragon is readily comprehended and effective. The eyebrows appear as wings springing from its shoulders, while the nose and mouth form its body and tail.

FIGURE 128 The helmet: the complete boar's head terminal from the right eyebrow. (Scale: 1/1)

The effect of the third dragon head placed between the brows is to carry the line of the nose up on to the cap, so that the flying dragon straddles both cap and mask, the visual break coming higher up, where the dragon head rising from the nose comes up against the dragon head directed downwards from the front end of the crest. The strong vertical line of crest with its dragon head terminals is none the less accentuated and carried through to the mouth of the mask.

IV   THE CHEEK-PIECES

The cheek-pieces, like the cap, are made from sheet iron with an outer surface of applied decorative bronze-foil panels. Like the foil on the face mask, these were held in position by a bronze rim-binding with fluted clips. The edge binding is now largely missing and only rivet holes survive. However, further rivet holes show that, unlike the mask, fluted bronze strips once framed the decorative panels and secured them to the cheek-pieces. The shape of the cheek-pieces (figs. 105 and 109) is established solely on internal evidence. A continuous area of joining fragments on the right cheek-piece makes this possible (fig. 129). The fragments preserve almost the entire edge of the cheek-piece with the exception of the upper edge which lies against the cap. This is largely supplied by a substantial fragment on the left cheek-piece comprising its complete upper rear corner; on it are remains of foil which show that the fragment carried a complete impression of the larger interlace design 4. The bottom of the decorative panel (design 4) also occurs in the uppermost fragment of the right cheek-piece. This evidence establishes the overall height of the cheek-piece.

Evidence for the attachment of the cheek-pieces to the cap is provided by a crucial fragment found during the 1968 excavations.[1] This joins an existing fragment from the top of the right cheek-piece. In figures 104 and 129 one original fragment can be seen towards the upper right corner of the restored cheek-piece. Two rivets on the right of the fragment associated with fluted clips that run at right-angles to each other indicate that the whole piece must have been positioned near the upper right-hand corner of the cheek-piece. Two additional rivets can be seen on the left of the fragment and these are evidently from a hinge. The fact that the fragment is not

[1] *Sutton Hoo*, Vol. I, fig. 242.

171

FIGURE 129 The helmet: the right cheek-piece showing
the series of conjoining fragments which define its shape
and the location of design 1 (see also fig. 141). (Scale: 2/3)

central to the top of the cheek-piece indicates this must have had two hinges. The
location of a hinge in this position would seem to be confirmed by the corresponding
fragment of the other cheek-piece (fig. 105), where one of the hinge rivets seems to
survive, but the evidence is ambiguous because of heavy corrosion. This in turn would
imply that the hinges were of leather, as two rigid hinges cannot operate on a curve.

The cheek-pieces have concave inner faces curved both longitudinally and laterally.
The front edges of the cheek-pieces, which are longitudinally curved (fig. 103), fit
closely to the profile of the face-mask when the cheek-pieces are pulled in towards
the chin (cf. the Tower replica, pl. 8). The cut-away shape at the rear of the cheek-pieces
combines with the shape cut away in the opposite direction, of the neck-guard, so
providing a continuous opening which accommodates the movement of the shoulder.

The corrosion in the inside of the cheek-pieces suggests that they were lined with
leather and to this lining, at the point of the cheek-pieces, tapes (p. 180) were probably
sewn so that the two cheek-pieces could be tied together beneath the chin. Designs
4 and 5 (the two interlace designs) are both used, and where necessary the foil sheet
struck from the die is cut to fit awkwardly shaped spaces.

An important new result of the 1971 survey of the fragments is the discovery that

172

an impression of design 1 (the dancing warriors) was located on the front edge of the right-hand cheek-piece (fig. 141). Presumably it also appeared in the corresponding position on the left-hand cheek-piece. In contrast with the neck-guard and cap, where bare zones occur, the surfaces of the cheek-pieces are completely covered with decorative foil.

V THE NECK-GUARD

Most of the original substance of the neck-guard is missing from the reconstruction (fig. 106). The large blank spaces of painted fibreglass devoid of any original material will no doubt give rise to scepticism as to both the breadth and the depth to which it has been reconstructed. In this connection figures 104 and 107 may be cited, for the right side of the reconstructed cap is almost equally devoid of original fragments.

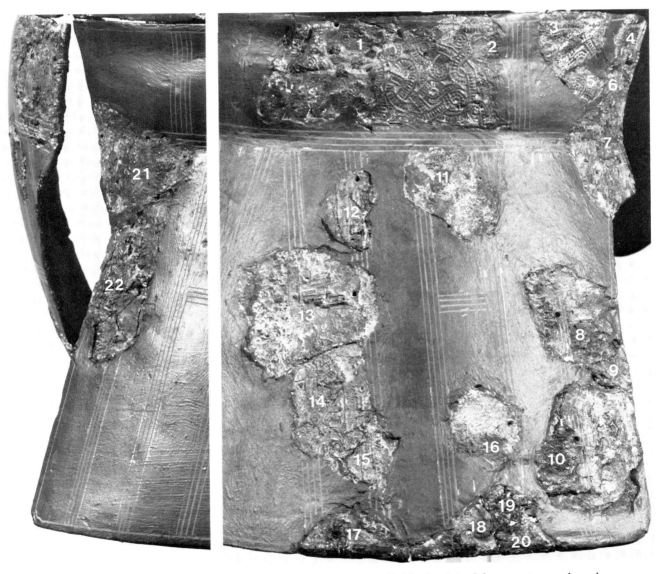

FIGURE 130   The helmet: detail of the neck-guard with individual original fragments numbered.

What then is the evidence for the size and shape adopted for the neck-guard? Many featureless original fragments of rusted iron that cannot be positioned on the helmet may have come from the neck-guard, but there are no grounds for building them into the reconstruction. Figure 130 shows the restored neck-guard in which the original fragments incorporated are individually numbered. Figure 131 gives the profile of the neck-guard and shows the angle of its outward projection. Figure 132 shows some original fragments from the upper right corner showing the use of designs 4 and 5.

The neck-guard consists of a collar-like upright zone at the top (fig. 131 A–B) which fits inside the cap of the helmet and follows its curvature, and a broad fan-like portion (C) below, which is straight from top to bottom but curved laterally to follow the line of the neck. B and C are one piece of metal, but A is a separate strip of iron forged on to the inside of B. The element A–B thus has a step laterally along its length where the overlap occurs, A, as seen from the outside, being recessed. This recession, which can be observed on the fragments 1, 3, 6 and 21 (fig. 130), was at first a puzzling feature but the experiment of making a modern reconstruction has shown that its purpose was to allow the top of the neck-guard to be inset inside the rim of the cap and so to enable the neck-guard to move up inside the cap, even if only minimally, the movement being limited by the play in the leather hinges. It may be noted here that this

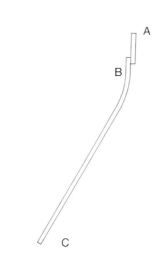

FIGURE 131 The helmet: vertical cross-section of the neck guard showing the relationship of the two constituent iron parts, A and B–C. (Scale: 3/8)

flexibility requires that the hinges should be of leather; metal hinges would not only be rigid but would call for the surfaces of the elements joined by the hinge to lie in the same plane.[1]

Because of the 'step' or change in surface level between A and B in figure 131, the several fragments ornamented with design 4, which show this curious dip halfway up the pattern, can be identified as having come from this top section of the neck-guard. The fact that all the fragments showing the double thickness and stepping represented by the A–B join are covered with design 4 suggests that this pattern exclusively was used on the A–B zone, with the rectangle set lengthways along the neck line. As fragment 1 shows, the depth of the panel equals that of the depth of the zone. Fragments 3, 4, 5, 6 and 7, which join (fig. 132), give one upper corner of the neck-guard at the right-hand end of the A–B zone and seen in profile show that immediately below the zone the neck-guard is canted out at an angle and then runs straight. Fragment 7 (fig. 130) carries two parallel impressions of design 5, separated vertically

[1] Leather hinges, as Mr Russell Robinson tells me, even without such overlaps, are normal in Roman helmets; metal hinges occur in some of the Scandinavian helmets of the Merovingian period, but only in a minority.

FIGURE 132 The helmet: detail of the upper right-hand corner of
the neck-guard.

by the matrix or impression of a fluted bronze strip (now missing), such as are used
elsewhere on the helmet to frame panels and define the ornamental scheme. A central
rivet hole occurs in the line of the strip.

The patterns lie parallel with one another and, with the profile of fragment 7 which
can be seen to be turning through an obtuse angle, suggest the alignment of the
neck-guard. While the outer of the two impressions of design 5 fills up the projecting
corner of the C zone, the inner impression clears the corner and can be seen to have
constituted the decoration of the right-hand edge of the guard, as shown in figure 104.

Fragments 8, 9 and 10, also decorated with design 5, have on the right an apparently finished edge which does not show the bed or marks of a fluted strip (fig. 130). They come therefore from the right-hand edge of the lower part of the guard, which presumably carried the bronze tubular edging, held in place by fluted clips, seen in fragments 17, 18 and 20. A rivet hole (in fragment 8) which does not line up with those of the fluted strip to the left, also suggests a different form of edging (i.e. not a fluted strip) here; presumably it held a clip which bound the U-channelling in position. Immediately above the rivet hole on fragment 8, and aligned on the inner rivet hole, can be seen the mark of a transverse framing strip dividing vertically aligned impressions of design 5.

The same can be seen on the right-hand side of fragment 13 in figure 130. On this fragment a transverse fluted strip can be seen and part of another impression of design 5 is recognisable above it. These fragments show that the design 5 panels on the neck-guard combined two impressions of the design, one above the other. Using the evidence from all the neck-guard fragments, including those from the centre, it can be reasonably deduced that two full impressions of the die were used, and the length of the straight, canted-out portion of the neck-guard is determined solely by the assumption that these two impressions were indeed of the complete die.[1] The die having been defined (fig. 151) the length arrived at with two impressions of the die meeting end to end is that shown in figure 138. Though abnormally long by Roman standards this length seems to be matched in Vendel period graphic representations on the Vendel 14 helmet and one Torslunda plate (fig. 157) and, as the wearing of the replica demonstrates, is quite a practical length (i.e. is not excessive and does not hamper the wearer).

Only design 5 can be seen to have been employed on zone C of the neck-guard. The eruptions of corrosion, seen in residual form (as left after cleaning in 1946–7), on the left-hand edges of fragments 10 and 13, and spreading over the tops of the fluted bronze strips adjacent to the rivet holes, show that the marginal fluted strip of two panels was flanked on the left by a plain undecorated zone without foil covering such as occurs on the cap. The same can be seen on the right-hand side of fragment 22 in figure 130.

There remains the problem of the breadth of the neck-guard. This depends in the first place on the assumption that there must have been two hinges to hold it to the

[1] The 1971 reconstruction (using the original fragments) needs revision in this respect. It shows more space below the lengths of transverse fluted strips than above them. The space left below is greater than the length of the die, while the space above is less than the length of the die. This should be adjusted to equal lengths above and below as shown in the Tower replica. The evidence for two complete die impressions is obtained from fragments 7–10 on the right side of the straight part (zone C) of the neck-guard. Fragments 8, 9, 10, which demonstrably belong to the lower portion of zone C, are together long enough to account for one whole impression. At the top of 8 is the matrix of a transverse fluted strip, marked by a rivet hole. Above this again, with no billeted border showing, is a fragment of interlace corresponding with the left-hand end of the die, figure 151. At the top of zone C, at this same edge of the helmet, is a fragment (7) which carries an interlace element corresponding with the right-hand end of the die. The whole die, without its end border, was evidently visibly exposed here. Fragment 13 shows the end border of the design exposed above the transverse fluted strip, the two running at slightly divergent angles. The Tower reconstruction is probably not correct in showing billeted borders at both ends of the die, and in showing uniformly visible borders clear of the transverse strips.

a

b

FIGURE 133 The helmet: photograph and radiograph
of the large piece (no. 1) from the upright collar of the
neck-guard showing the rivets and reinforcing plate of a
hinge and the relation of the hinge to the decorative panel.
(Scale: 1/1)

cap. A single hinge would seem to be unnecessarily vulnerable and mechanically weak. The large fragment, figures 130 (1) and 133, contains a hinge plate. If this fragment is not placed centrally below the line of the crest, but to one side, as seen in figure 106, and if the truncated panel on the left of fragment 1 is completed inwards, then we have, to the right of the crest, as shown in figure 138, two and a half design 4 panels. This would be balanced by two and a half to the left, making five in all. Five panels exactly fill the space round the back of the helmet between the two cheek-pieces. The only alternative, if some symmetrical arrangement of complete panels is to be envisaged, would be three panels. This narrower width for the neck-guard would leave panel-length gaps between the guard and the cheek-pieces exposing the neck. It would also require that the central panel of the three be centred on the crest, with the other two panels, each of which would show a corner of the neck-guard, and the hinges, disposed symmetrically to either side. The corner of the right-hand panel of the guard is shown in figures 130 and 132. The complete panel on fragment 1 (fig. 133) must, if there are three panels, be the centre one, but as it has a hinge at one corner there should be a second one at the other. There is not. If, on the other hand, there were to be only one hinge attaching a three-panel neck-guard, then that should be in the

177

FIGURE 134 Roman infantry helmet from Witcham Gravel, Cambridgeshire, showing a broad and deep neck-guard analogous to that on the Sutton Hoo helmet.

178

centre of the complete panel which, again, it is not (figs. 133 *a*, *b*). The arrangement adopted in our reconstruction of a five-panel two-hinged form should accordingly be correct.

It will be noted that the cut-away curves of cheek-pieces and neck-guard appear to correspond and when they are brought together form a continuous opening to accommodate the movement of the shoulder (fig. 109). In spite of the lack of original fragments, then, the broad neck-guard must be correct.

Broad neck-guards of the form shown, joining closely with the cheek-pieces, are to be seen on one of the Torslunda plates (fig. 156). We may also note that in Vendel-type helmets the protection of the whole of the neck, even if by different means (mail curtains) was evidently normal practice.[1] The broad fan-tail neck-guard is a feature to be found in Roman infantry helmets, of which that found at Witcham Gravel, Ely, Cambridgeshire, is a convenient example (fig. 134).

VI THE LINING AND TEXTILES ASSOCIATED WITH THE HELMET

We have postulated a leather lining. Softened hide has been used in the Tower Armouries version, giving the feel and effect of chamois leather. The existence of a leather lining is unsupported by any positive evidence; the fragment of leather boxed with 'helmet remains' (79 below) is only loosely associated and is not apparently affected by the characteristic corrosion products of the helmet. It is deduced from the peculiar corrosion found all over the inside of the helmet. This is only to be explained in terms of the interaction of some organic substance with the natural rust formation (the natural formation could be seen on the plain panels—those areas that had no covering of bronze sheeting—of the outside of the helmet). Plate 23*b* and figure 111 show typical areas of the corrosion on the inside of the helmet; it is black, bubbly, grained and striated in a manner suggesting here and there an organised structure although scientific examination is negative on this point (p. 231). That it is not caused

FIGURE 135 The Sutton Hoo helmet: rust impression of the textile SH 10 on the inside of fragment 21 from the neck-guard. (Scale: 1/1)

by a textile lining is clear, as there are no textile impressions associated with the interior of the helmet, except on the neck-guard at one edge, an occurrence which, as it is not matched elsewhere, seems to be accidental (fig. 135, an impression of SH 10, a textile considered by Miss Crowfoot as unsuited for lining material).[2] No

---

[1] Cf. Arwidsson 1954, Taf. 1; 1942*a*, Taf. 3; Thordeman 1941, figs. 2–5.

[2] *Sutton Hoo*, Vol. I, 447.

less than six different textiles have left their impressions on fragments from the helmet, but all except this externally.[1] They are SH 2, 7, 8, 10, 13 and 24.[2] They presumably represent wrapping-cloth or other textiles with which helmet fragments may have come into contact.[3]

The six different types of textile which, as indicated above, are associated with the helmet remains, occur as follows.

(1) A limonite fragment or mould showing interlace pattern seen from the back has on its outside (or front) surface traces of a textile which is probably SH 2.

(2) A helmet fragment from the upper edge of the neck-guard shows a fine rust impression of SH 10 on its inside surface.

(3) A helmet fragment in contact with the crest, which can be localised at the back of the helmet, where the scale pattern (p. 154) occurs, carries traces of SH 7 and 8.

(4) One small helmet fragment and one larger one both show SH 8 folded (i.e. two layers of SH 8 representing a fold of the cloth).

(5) A limonite mould showing an interlace pattern seen from the back has SH 7 on the outside.

(6) A limonite mould with hinge impression from the helmet has replaced textile SH 7 on the outside.

(7) One small helmet fragment with interlace shows a plain weave, SH 10, the same cloth as is left impressed on the fragment of neck-guard, 2 above.

(8) Many small fragments of textile contained in a pillbox labelled by the excavators 'helmet and shield material'. The pillbox has earth, wood, gold and iron as well as textile scraps in it. The tiny textile fragments in the box include SH 8 and 13 (tape).

(9) A small fragment of leather boxed with the helmet remains has on it an impression of SH 24.

The cheek-pieces were probably tied under the chin with linen tapes, sewn into the leather lining. There is no direct evidence for this, although fragments of SH 13, a fine linen tape, occur in the pillbox referred to in 8 above and a replaced fragment has been found on the piece of leather (9 above) which bears the impression of SH 24 on its opposite face. Fine linen tapes of different grades (SH 13, 16 and 23) were plentiful in the burial deposit and were found in association with the mailcoat, sword and shoes.[4] The helmet-associated textiles mentioned above are SH 2, wool from a blanket or cloak(?); SH 7, soumak pattern, twill base from the 'tapestry'; SH 8, (? linen) a soft fabric suitable for wrapping weapons; SH 10, probably a woollen cloak; SH 13, tape; SH 24, a coarse plain weave occurring on a piece of leather,

[1] For superficial textile impressions or replaced textile on helmet outer surfaces, see Arwidsson 1942a, Taf. 1–5 (Valsgärde 6). A slightly better reproduction of the same photo from this point of view is *Acta Archaeologica* v, 1934, pl. xv. There are also abundant textile replacements of at least two types on the Vendel 12 helmet. Vendel 1 helmet has coarse textile round the rim inside; Vendel 12 has replaced textile all over the inside, as well as on the outside.

[2] See *Sutton Hoo*, Vol. I, ch. vi, figs. 327, 332, 333, 335, 338, 349.

[3] The extensive textile residues on the top of the helmet from Valsgärde 6 (Arwidsson 1942a, Taf. 5) may owe their preservation to the fact that this helmet also had an iron crest, and that its iron framework was exposed.

[4] *Sutton Hoo*, Vol. I, figs. 341, 354, 359 and p. 465 ff.

which may be just an impressed pattern and not a textile. Apart from SH 24, all these survive as mineral impressions or replaced textiles and their identification as woven objects of a particular type, such as a cloak, is therefore conjectural but based on comparative evidence. With the exception of the tape (SH 13) none of the cloths thus provisionally identified in association with the helmet fragments are of types that might have had any functional connection with the helmet.

3. *The restoration of the helmet and the making of the replica*

The British Museum reconstruction of the helmet, with original fragments incorporated in it (figs. 103–107) is built of strips of a resin-impregnated jute. The original fragments, their sharp edges carefully preserved, are let into openings cut to their shapes in the resin surface, so that their backs can be seen inside the reconstructed helmet. The surfaces, where no helmet fragments were inserted, were covered with a light coat of plaster, to provide a smooth finish which could be painted and drawn on. The original helmet fragments were edged with resin before the plastering occurred to protect them against the water in the plaster. Acetone or other solvents may be used to remove any fragment or to dismantle the reconstruction, if required, without difficulty.

The Tower Armouries replica (figs. 136–138, pl. 8)

The making of the Tower Armouries version of the helmet enabled a number of technical points to be clarified and certain departures have been made from the design of the 1971 reconstruction. The chief of these relates to the neck-guard. The profile view of the reconstruction (fig. 104) shows that the projecting corner of the cheek-piece and the neck-guard, which adjoin, are not at the same level. This has been corrected in the Tower replica, as it became apparent that the neck-guard must have fitted inside the cap. This off-setting in the line of cap and neck-guard lifts the latter slightly and allows it to ride up, bringing the corners to the same level (fig. 136). This provides the smooth curves at the top of the openings to accommodate the lift of the shoulder or arm.

The cheek-pieces (15 cm) are relatively longer than the mask (12·5 cm), but as the two curved sides of the face-mask measure exactly 15 cm along their curves, which is precisely the length of the inner edge of the cheek-pieces, when the latter are drawn in to the mask they fit closely and provide complete protection.

The greater length (and perhaps width) of the skull-cap of the Sutton Hoo helmet is probably due to the fact that both neck-guard and face-mask were affixed to the inside of the cap, the face-mask rigid but the neck-guard with enough clearance to allow it to move with freedom. In wearing the Tower Armouries version it has been found that it will go on almost any size of head with comfort, but requires varying degrees of padding for a firm fit. There is considerable room for variation, depending

FIGURE 136   The helmet: detail of the left cheek-piece on the modern replica.

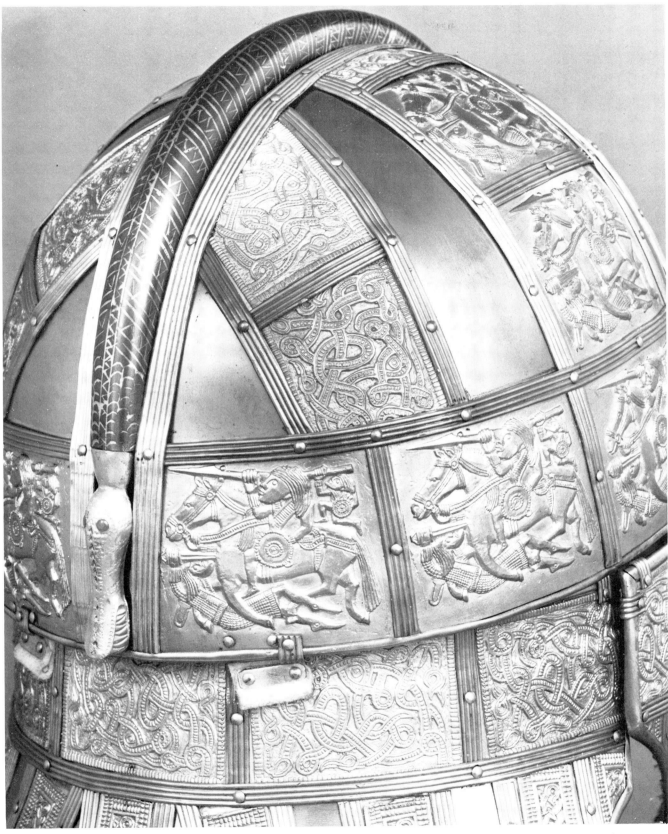

FIGURE 137 The helmet: the decorative appearance of cap, crest and neck-guard as seen on the modern replica; the photograph also shows the type of leather hinge thought to have been used on the original.

FIGURE 138 The helmet: rear view of the replica showing the distribution of design 4 panels in relation to the hinges and crest.

on the quantity of hair to be accommodated and different owners could have used the helmet without alteration by redesigning the padded lining. The soft leather skin by itself seems insufficient for the average head.

As the Tower replica shows (pl. 8), the helmet had a strong vertical and central decorative axis, the strong effect of the line of nose, dragon heads and crest being reinforced by the extra-broad and heavily gilded fluted bronze strips that flank the crest. It can be seen how the trellis-work of applied fluted bronze strips articulates and states the decorative *schema* (figs. 136–138). The fluted strips were made of a hard tin alloy and the applied bronze plates were tinned (App., p. 226–7), giving a white finish. The colour effect seen in the Tower replica thus appears valid. The archaeological implications of this achievement of white and gold surfaces are discussed below (p. 205).

The replica is made of iron and raised from a single sheet. The crest is solid, instead of hollow and the technique of the original was also not followed for the inlays of silver. The eybrows, nose and mouth, and the applied decorative sheets are electrotypes in copper backed with lead solder. The copper was subsequently tinned to secure the white effect, the strips flanking the crest being gilded. The recreated helmet, with lining, weighs 3·74 kg. This is more than the original can have weighed, because of the factors given above (the lead backings for the applied foil and the solid crest, for example). The original must have been lighter, and an estimate of 2·5 kg is suggested.

The attachment of cheek-pieces, face-mask and neck-guard to the cap

The face-mask, as we have seen (p. 163), was riveted rigidly to the cap. The neck-guard was hinged. Figure 133 clearly shows one of the hinge-panels with the two rivets and a metal plate (concealed in corrosion or under the superficial bronze sheeting) revealed by radiography and we have postulated two such hinges. It is clear because of the curvature that they were not of metal; the evidence suggests that, as is the case with many late Roman helmets, they were probably of leather. The Tower of London Armourers, using leather for the hinges of their modern recreation of the Sutton Hoo helmet, have employed a traditional technique of folding back the end of the leather strap so that the rivets pass through a double thickness. A metal plate between the two rivets prevents the leather from tearing away from the rivet-heads in an upward direction, while a metal rod, inserted into the loop of the folded back leather, would tend to prevent its tearing sideways (fig. 139). Though there is no evidence of such rods in the original, a detached piece of metal would not be retained once the leather had perished and might have disintegrated.

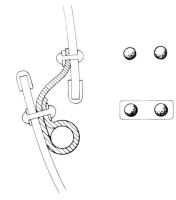

FIGURE 139   The helmet: section of the type of leather hinge thought to have provided flexible links between neck-guard and cap. (Scale: 1/1)

Following the evidence already cited (p. 171) the replica uses two leather hinges to each cheek-piece. The visual evidence is for rivets only and not for more complex hinges of metal.

4. *The five dies*

All the details in the drawings, figures 140, 143, 150, 151, which attempt to define the dies, may not be recognisable on the photographs of the surviving fragments here published as the evidence on which the reconstructions are based. The drawings were in all cases made from the original fragments, except for one detail of design I discussed below. To achieve the final result the fragments have been scrutinised and rescrutinised over a period of years in every variety of lighting.

DESIGN I   THE DANCING WARRIORS

The die bearing this scene (fig. 140) was used four times on the helmet, twice on the cap, at the front on either side of the crest immediately over the eyebrows, and once at the front edge of each of the two cheek-guards (fig. 109). In none of these four instances is the complete scene preserved; indeed, only six fragments among all the helmet remains show any part of it. These six fragments are illustrated in figure 141. From them it has been possible to restore the scene completely (fig. 140). The restoration gains general iconographic support from the closely similar version of the same scene which occurs on the helmet from Valsgärde 7 (fig. 164 c).

FIGURE 140   The helmet: design 1, showing two dancing warriors; heavy lines and shading show details recovered established from surviving fragments or from casts taken from limonite moulds; broken lines indicate the design inferred from what has been established. (Scale: 2/1)

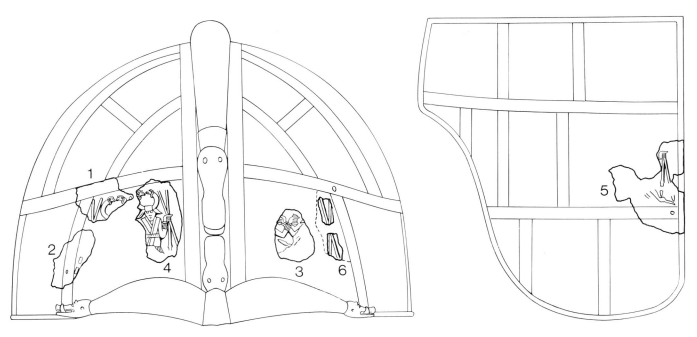

FIGURE 141   The helmet: drawing showing the location of the surviving fragments of design 1 on the reconstructed helmet.

In figure 140 the details preserved on the six fragments are drawn in firm lines and firm shading, while those parts of the design that are reconstructed are shown in broken outline and lighter shading. The space occupied by the figures is 5·6 cm×4·6 cm. There is no evidence surviving that this die included a border, such as can be recognised along the lower edge of the die of design 2 (p. 196 below).

The two men, although carrying sword and spears, seem to be dressed in civilian or ceremonial dress and not in war gear. The figure on the left of the scene is represented only by the upper ends of the two spear shafts, parts of the horns of his headgear and the point of the other man's sword, which appear on fragment 1 (figs. 141 and 142 a); by short lengths of one of his spears which can be distinguished on fragment 2; and by his left arm and the hilt of his sword, which appear on fragment 3 (fig. 142 b). The figure on the right is preserved on fragment 4 (fig. 142 c) from the top of the horns on his headgear to the edge of the skirt of his coat, with his left arm and most of the shafts of his two spears. His right forearm is to be seen in fragment 3 (figs. 141, 142 b) and the tip of his sword in fragment 1 (figs. 141, 142 a). The points of his spear blades, parts of the two shafts and his left hand grasping them, his left leg and foot and a fragment of another spear shaft which rises obliquely between his legs, are seen on fragment 5 (fig. 142 d). Below the elbows and crossed wrists on fragment 3 (fig. 142 b), can be seen the blade of a spear (that of which a portion of the shaft appears on fragment 5) and the matrix left in the rust of another at right-angles to it. The right flap of his headdress is complete (fig. 142 c). The key fragment, however, which shows the crossed wrists and links the two men (fragment 3; fig. 142 b) also carries part of the right flap of the headdress of the figure to the right of the

187

FIGURE 142   The helmet. Five of the principal fragments
which make up design 1. (Scale: 1/1)

composition. It must therefore belong to a second impression from the die. Fragment 6 (fig. 142e) shows the shafts of the spears held by the figure to the right of the composition.

The elements common to the two warriors (headdress with horns, arms and wrists, tops of spears), are identical but reversed and this indicates the reconstruction shown in figure 140. The only major iconographic difference (as distinct from differences in style and drawing) between the Sutton Hoo scene and that on the Valsgärde 7 helmet, used in arriving at our reconstruction, is the presence on the Sutton Hoo scene of the loose crossed spears (i.e. not held), seen below the elbows of the two men and between their legs. This detail, which does not occur on the Valsgärde 7 helmet, suggests that they are performing a spear dance, the crossed spears being conceived as lying on the ground.[1]

The more or less completely preserved figure is wearing a knee-length wrapover coat with elaborately quilted or otherwise decorated facings along the whole of the visible edge right up to the shoulders, evidently continuing round the back of the head, like a collar. The coat is held by a belt and has full-length sleeves ending in elaborate cuffs defined by two transverse lines and a series of parallel billets of equal length running up the arm. It has a heavy hem, beaded below and with a border apparently matching the complex decoration of the facings above. The figure is wearing a horned headdress of which the distinctive features are the downward-tending flaps or points

[1] See Holmqvist 1960 for a discussion of scenes representing the dance and for references to the performance of weapon dances.

188

on each side, the central rectangular shape above the eyes, and the pair of broad upward-sweeping horns which curve inwards at the top and end in inward-pointing birds' heads. The birds' beaks touch, as they can be seen to do also in the Torslunda, Ekhammer, Caenby and Finglesham[1] versions of this figure (figs. 153 and 156a). The birds' heads do not have the characteristic Style II pointed jaw and straight-sided right-angled membrane at the back of the eye; the membrane is curvilinear, or S-shaped. The horns are filled with cigar-shaped billets set obliquely between outer borders. The two drooping ears or flaps of the headdress appear to have concave upper surfaces. Three small transverse billets occur in the inner end of the concavity, just below the horns. The rectangular shape which forms the centre-piece of the headdress was originally filled with ten small billets, in two groups of three and two of two, pointing alternately horizontally or vertically. The decorative edging of the coat has a beaded outer edge and a chevron pattern, built up from groups of billets, inside it; small solid triangles fill up the vacant spaces left by the chevrons. The edging of the length of coat which folds inside seems to be made up of smaller billets than those seen on the outer edging, probably an accidental effect. The belt consists of a line of billets set vertically between single raised plain borders.

The fragment which shows the leg and foot (figs. 141,5, 142d) has surface damage and it is not easy to read the features depicted on it. The two spear points and shafts help to fix its position and it is also clear that the foot is trailing with the sole and heel uppermost (cf. Valsgärde 7, fig. 164c and the bronze die from Torslunda, fig. 156a). The two men are shown moving towards each other in a dance movement, perhaps in the climax of the dance, with their sword-arms crossed. The outward curve of the dancers' hips no less than the trailing outer leg suggest this inward movement.

Each dancer measures 44 mm to the top of his headdress. The exaggeration of the thumb and the treatment of the fingers is distinctive. The swords are short and have triangular pommels with straight sides. The one human face to survive was subsequently damaged and the nose and mouth are now restored, but an early photograph of the original before damage (fig. 142c) was used for the reconstruction drawing. The face is clean shaven. The spear blades seem to be slightly bevelled (fig. 140). The swellings at the base of the blade shown in the drawing can be clearly seen. They may indicate bosses such as are seen on the downward-pointing spears carried by walking warriors on the Vendel 14 helmet[2] and on one of the Torslunda plates (fig. 156b) and indeed on the Sutton Hoo helmet, in the second figural subject, design 2 (fig. 143);[3] a similar but broader swelling profile would be yielded by modifications to spear-head designs such as survive in the bears that flank the exceptionally fine spearhead from Vendel 12 (fig. 152), a spear-head which also provides, incidentally, a close parallel for the distinctive employment of punched circle ornament as it appears on the three dragon heads of the Sutton Hoo helmet (pp. 159-61 above).

[1] Discussed and illustrated in Bruce-Mitford 1974, 207/8, pls. 53, 54; see also p. 207 below.
[2] Stolpe and Arne 1927, pl. XLII, fig. 1; cf. fig. 147a.
[3] This portion of the outer spear of the two held in the hand is not preserved, so that we cannot state positively that they are identical. The corresponding scene on the Valsgärde 7 helmet appears to show spears of different types (fig. 164c).

FIGURE 143   The helmet: design 2, the rider with fallen warrior.
Some of the restored detail, shown in light shading, is based on
continental versions of this scene. (Scale: 2/1)

DESIGN 2   RIDER AND FALLEN WARRIOR

This design (fig. 143), like design 1, is not found in anything approaching completeness.
Its use was confined to the cap. Eight occurrences can be demonstrated; six of these
are on the helmet's left side (fig. 144 a), where they account for all the vacant panel-spaces
available for figural subjects after the impression of design 1 has been placed over the
eyebrow. On the right side (fig. 144 b) details showing the use of design 2 survive only
in two positions. One of these, 6, is joined to a half-panel of the larger interlace (design
4) which in its turn can be shown to be attached to the centre of the crest, thus
establishing design 2 in the third zone of panels up from the bottom of the cap, where
it exactly balances an occurrence of the same scene on the helmet's left side (fig. 144 a,
fragment 3) and showing that in this respect the ornamental layouts conform
symmetrically on both sides of the helmet. The regular layout of design 2 panels on
the left side of the helmet and the use of the same design in at least two of the
equivalent positions on the right side suggests that the ornamental layout was symmetrical throughout and that design 2 was probably used twelve times originally, as
assumed in figure 109. However, the picture is complicated by the survival of some
additional fragments, discussed below (p. 197), which must represent the presence
of one or more further designs on the cap of the helmet. The scene or scenes

190

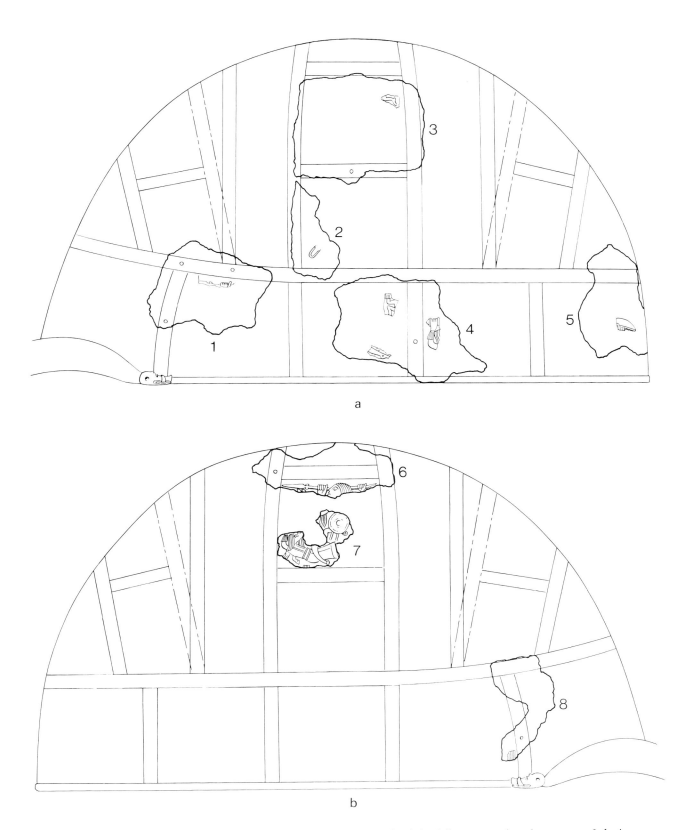

a

b

FIGURE 144   The helmet: drawing showing the location of original fragments bearing parts of design 2.

represented by these fragments must have occupied some of the remaining positions on the right side of the helmet-cap, for which we lack specific information.

The second demonstrable occurrence of design 2 on the helmet's right side is in the lowest ornamental zone of the cap conjoint with the design 1 panel above the eyebrow (fig. 144 b, fragment 8). The surviving iron fragment which held this impression of design 2 is big enough to take the complete scene, but only one very small piece of bronze sheeting remains on it, at one edge. This shows, uniquely, a short section of the horse's tail. As this is at the right of the panel, it indicates that the horse is here moving to the left. This movement of the horse to the left is also to be seen in the other fragment of the rider panel preserved on this side of the helmet, in the third or uppermost of the decorative zones, as well as in all six instances on the left side of the cap. This suggests that the eight known occurrences of the rider scene were struck from a single die, the riders all moving clockwise round the helmet-cap; on the left they move towards the front of the helmet but on the right away from it. In certain other helmets of the Swedish Vendel period group to which the Sutton Hoo helmet belongs reversed dies are used on opposite sides of the helmet. Thus in the Vendel 14 helmet,[1] files of identically dressed foot-soldiers advance from opposite directions on each side of the helmet, as though to join forces at the front; and the scene of a wolf or bear-like animal being led by a man who carries an axe is also reversed on the two sides of the helmet. In the helmet from Valsgärde 7,[2] a rider scene similar in many respects to that on the Sutton Hoo helmet is found in two slightly different versions, with the rider moving to the right in one die and to the left in the other (fig. 164 a and b). This sophistication (the use of two different dies of the same or similar scenes reversed for use on opposite sides of the helmet) does not occur on the Sutton Hoo helmet.

Figure 143 offers a reconstruction of the design 2 die employed on the Sutton Hoo helmet. As in figure 140 (the die of design 1, the dancing warriors) the portions of the design for which there is direct evidence are drawn in solid lines and firm shading, those which are reconstructed or hypothetical are shown in broken lines and lighter shading.

The evidence for the reconstruction of die 2 is of three sorts.

(1) Original stamped foil sheeting still surviving on fragments of the iron cap.

(2) Details recovered by taking plaster casts or plasticine squeezes from lumps of iron corrosion (limonite) derived from the outer surface of the helmet, in which portions of bronze sheeting from the helmet surface are embedded, so that the pattern is seen from the back, in intaglio. Excellent casts can be obtained from some of these, but in other instances, where the sheeting bedded in the corrosion lumps is broken or damaged, or where the corrosion lumps do not contain original sheeting but only an impression from it, the resultant casts can be illegible or misleading.

(3) Comparative evidence of similar scenes on helmets or other objects of the period,

[1] Stolpe and Arne 1927, Lindqvist 1932.   [2] Here reproduced in certain details by kind permission of Professor Greta Arwidsson.

by reference to which elements missing from our scene can be supplied or restored with a degree of probability. Figure 145 shows the largest of the original stamped foil fragments that carry elements of the scene.

The die fills a rectangle 58×52 mm. It shows a rider on horseback, with bare head and flowing hair, carrying a very small[1] shield held in his left hand, and in his right brandishing a spear at head-level. He is riding down a fallen opponent, likewise bareheaded with flowing locks, who is armed with a sword and wears a three-quarter-length coat, which because of its surface texture superficially resembles a mailcoat. The fallen warrior is shown stabbing the rider's horse in the chest with his sword while holding the horse's rein with his left hand. His left forearm is to be seen lying horizontally immediately on top of the sword blade, pointing outwards, with the wrist bent up to grasp the rein. The sword has sunk into the horse for almost half its length, but the horse appears unaffected. It is shown with reins, girth, crupper and bridle or head-stall; the strap running down the exposed side of the neck between the horse's ear and rein is difficult to explain, for a strap in this position is no part

FIGURE 145 The helmet: the principal fragment showing design 2. (Scale: 2/1)

of a normal harness. The use of a back-strap or crupper, proved by the small mould-fragment which carries a knot, shows that the rider has a saddle, as Mrs Susan Youngs has pointed out to me. A third diminutive human, or at least anthropomorphic figure is shown kneeling on the horse's rump. He grips the rear end of the shaft of the rider's spear as though directing it or reinforcing the throw. Very little of this figure survives and many of its details remain uncertain. The following are, however, clear. The face is seen in profile and is turned upwards towards the horizontal spear-shaft above; as in the corresponding form in the iconographically closely similar gold disc brooch from Pliezhausen (fig. 146),[2] and as in the face of the fallen warrior against his sword blade in the Sutton Hoo panel. The kneeling man is not shown with his face turned frontally towards the observer, or with a horned headdress and spear in the outer hand, as is the case in the related scenes on the helmets from Valsgärde 7 (fig. 164 a, b) and 8.[3] In the Sutton Hoo version the straight profile not only turns towards but is pressed up against the spear-shaft, just as is the similar profile of the fallen warrior in the same scene against the horizontal line of his own sword-blade. The kneeling figure has a coat with V-neck and decorated facings, as have the two dancers in design 1 and the fallen warrior in the rider panel. He has a decorated cuff,

[1] In relation to the known dimensions of East Scandinavian shields, p. 17.
[2] Paulsen 1967, Abb. 56; also discussed and drawn by

Moosbrugger-Leu 1971, 117–18, Abb. 46 (one drawing is reversed).
[3] Arwidsson 1954, Abb. 79.

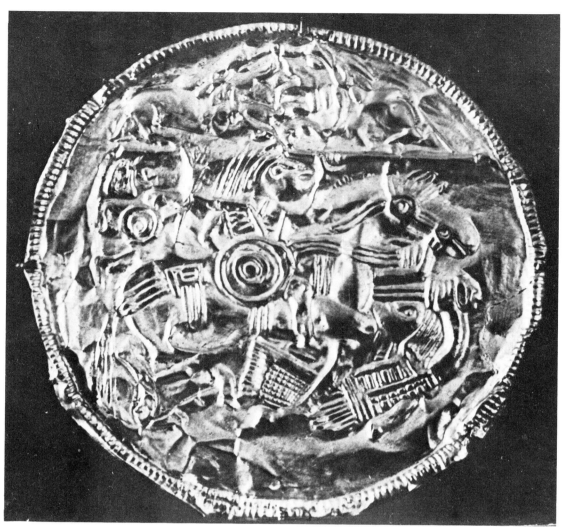

FIGURE 146 Repoussé gold disc-brooch from Pliezhausen, Kr. Tübingen, Germany, bearing a rider scene iconographically very close to that of Sutton Hoo design 2, except for the added element of the facing lions above. (Scale: 2/1)

and on his feet the ankle bones are apparently clearly marked, as with the corresponding figure on the Pliezhausen disc brooch (fig. 146) as drawn by Paulsen. The trailing leg is the more completely preserved of the two. The middle part of the body is missing, but there is just room for a small shield and in the suggested reconstruction one has been included, on the analogy of the Pliezhausen brooch.

The central and dominant feature of the design is the rider. His head and hand are out of all proportion to his leg and to the other figures in the scene. His face is raised as though contemplating the target at which he aims the great spear raised in his right hand. He shows no recognition of the presence of his fallen opponent. The one cuff that is preserved, below the hand that holds the spear, indicates that he is wearing a coat. The small kneeling man behind him, as we have seen, has a similar cuff.[1] No further details survive to indicate whether the rider is wearing a coat with

[1] The cuff of the arm of the fallen warrior which holds the sword, in contrast, is narrowed to the wrist. Close attention has been directed to this detail by arms and armour specialists concerned to establish whether or not a gauntlet is intended (cf.

194

a   b

FIGURE 147   Plaster casts of ornament from the helmet found in Vendel 14: (*a*) two of a procession of walking warriors, showing mailcoats and spear-heads with side bosses, as in design 2, on the Sutton Hoo helmet; (*b*) two bare-headed warriors fighting, showing angons, possible mailcoats and a shield with triple bosses at the top. (Scales: *a*, 3/2; *b* 5/3) (Photos: Statens Historiska Museum, Stockholm)

decorated revers like those of the dancing warriors, but the cuff on his arm is similar and two surviving billets in this position on the figure on the horse's rump suggest that he too had such a collar. The rider carries a spear with large collared rivet-heads behind the blade.[1] A round shield with a decorated rim covers the lower body; the portion that would hold the central boss does not survive, but enough of the rest of the shield-board is preserved to show that it lacked the outlying small bosses in triangular formation (fig. 6*a*) or single, decorative devices known in particular from the shields of East Scandinavia (figs. 7, 27, 147*b*). Projecting from behind the shield is a rounded shape which suggests the chape of a scabbard (cf. the scabbard of the fallen warrior). A version of a similar scene (fig. 164*b*) on the Valsgärde 7 helmet shows the tip of a sword in this position, with the hilt emerging from behind the shield's

Post 1944), and in view of this great care has been taken over the interpretation of this detail in our attempt to define the die. The original was carefully scrutinised by the authority on arms and armour Riksantikvarien Bengt Thordeman of Stockholm. He and I were agreed that the appearances favour a cuff on the arm holding the sword which is long and apparently tapering,

while the fallen warrior's other cuff is shown as much shorter and does not taper. This difference between the depictions of the fallen warrior's two cuffs should be noted.
[1] Cf. e.g. this feature on spears depicted on one of the Torslunda dies and on the Vendel 14 helmet (figs. 156*b*, 147*a*).

upper edge; the sword in figure 143 has been restored on the basis of the Valsgärde 7 scene. The Pliezhausen brooch, which is in other respects so closely related iconographically to the Sutton Hoo scene, lacks this element, it also lacks the scabbard of the fallen warrior (fig. 143).[1] The chape-like protrusion from the shield in the Sutton Hoo scene seems to imply the sword. The space diametrically opposite to it on the other side of the shield-board offers no room for a sword-hilt, but it could have fitted comfortably into the vacant area of design immediately adjacent, as shown in figure 143, if a slight shift in alignment between the two portions of the sword can be allowed. Such a shift in alignment can be seen to occur between the front and rear portions of the spear carried by the rider.

The fallen warrior is the most completely preserved of the three figures in the panel. His coat is held fast by a belt similar to that which holds the quilted coats of the dancing warriors in design 1. The coat is knee-length. It has a broad boarder showing simple lines of straight billets, not the elaborate chevron patterns seen in figure 140. As we have seen, the wrists of the fallen warrior show cuffs. These cuffs, the trimmings of the coat and its wrapover design indicate that, in spite of its all-over surface texture of round dots which might suggest otherwise, this is not a mailcoat.[2]

The fallen warrior's left forearm lies directly along the upper edge of the sword blade, with cuff and hand pointing outwards towards the left edge of the panel. His shortish flowing hair is neatly drawn in parallel curving lines; the face is beardless and the features are cleanly modelled in the firm convention also used for the face of the rider. The point of a scabbard, apparently furnished with a metal chape, is seen in the bottom left-hand corner of the panel. It is presumably the tip of the scabbard from which the warrior has drawn the naked sword held in his right hand.[3] The scabbard, though in a somewhat abnormal position in relation to the wearer's body, neatly fills the empty space that would otherwise exist under the fallen warrior's back in this corner of the panel.[4]

The die used in making the impressions of design 2 had along its lower edge the matrix for a billeted border (fig. 143). Evidence for this survives in fragment 7 which preserves many details of the fallen warrior (figs. 144 and 145). When the impressions from the die were mounted on the helmet this border may have remained visible above the plain bronze rim that edged the bottom of the cap, but it was probably trimmed off the four impressions of the die which rise towards the crest in the second and third zones of decoration on either side of the cap. The edges of the foil sheets carrying

[1] Paulsen 1967, Abb. 56.

[2] For mailcoats see ch. IV. Mail shirts are, as the name implies, shirts, seamless and with a hole for the head. The two types of garment under discussion may be compared in the combat scene from the Vendel 14 helmet (fig. 147 b, Stolpe and Arne 1927, pl. XLI, fig. 3). The use of surface texturing with round dots in circumstances where mail cannot be intended may be seen in two of the Torslunda dies where such texturing is used for a pair of trousers worn by a man the upper part of whose body is bare, and to represent hair on human and animal heads (fig. 156 c and d).

[3] For a scabbard-tip of similar form see the ring-sword held by the warrior with animal mask on the scabbard of the Gutenstein sword (cf. Paulsen 1967, Abb. 52). It is typical of fifth-century swords of the Brighthampton type (Baldwin Brown 1915, pl. XXVII, 8).

[4] The position of the scabbard may have relevance to the method by which the sword was suspended. It is explicable if the sword was carried on a baldric or shoulder strap, but not if attached at or below the waist (cf. p. 567 ff.).

the design would have been covered by the fluted bronze strips that held them to the cap. The occurrence of borders on one or two sides of a helmet-die only, and of no borders on a helmet-die at all, is to be seen on the four Torslunda plates (fig. 156 a–d), no two of which are alike in this respect.[1]

The chief problems associated with the reconstruction of design 2 relate to its central area. The details of the rider's dress are not clear; the 'hair' which seems to fall in profusion across the horse's body just in front of the rider's shield, though clear to see, remains enigmatic. Since the same appearance occurs in the rider scenes on the Valsgärde 7 and 8 helmets, as well as on the Pliezhausen brooch, it is evidently based on some original element in the composition. It does not represent the horse's mane, which is shown separately.

DESIGN 3   FRAGMENTARY AND UNIDENTIFIABLE FIGURAL DESIGN

The third design used on the Sutton Hoo helmet (figs. 148 and 149) can be recognised in seven small fragments only and was not capable of restoration. One of these is of reasonable size (length, 20×11·5 mm), the others are much smaller. The fragments are drawn in figure 148. The principal fragments show the following features.

Fragment D3 (i), 20×11·5 mm. An original piece of helmet-sheeting in excellent condition with sensitively preserved detail (fig. 149 a). It shows a human leg longer than any on the fallen warrior panel (design 2). The toe is pointed so that the front of the leg forms a straight line; the ankle bone is not marked; the knee can be seen, and the thigh lies at an obtuse angle to the lower leg. The modelling of the leg seems thin and angular. Since the surface of the sheeting appears undamaged, this matchstick-like treatment of the leg seems to reflect the original modelling, which may be contrasted with the fuller, chubbier modelling of the legs of the fallen warrior and the kneeling man on the horse's rump in design 2 (fig. 143). Below and to the left of the leg as drawn in figure 148 a, the surface of the panel evidently rose into a convex form and groups of more or less parallel raised lines are to be seen on the convexity. The

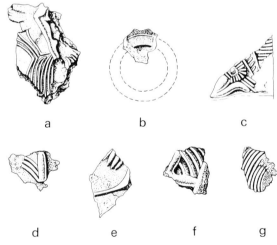

FIGURE 148   The Sutton Hoo helmet: drawings of the seven fragments of design 3. (Scale: 3/2)

different directions in which these groups of parallel raised lines run correspond with changes of angle or direction in the modelled surface, which on the analogy of

[1] Bruce-Mitford 1974, ch. 10. It is possible that the die of design 2 may have had borders on one or more of its other sides, but no trace of this remains.

197

the Sutton Hoo and other rider scenes in Vendel art, strongly suggest the body of a horse.

Fragment D3 (ii), 5×5 mm. A tiny original fragment (fig. 148 b) showing two concentric raised lines two millimetres apart. The outer line is more strongly emphasised than the inner one. This appears to be a segment of the rim of a shield which would be of the same diameter as that held by the rider in design 2, but it lacks the beaded border detectable on that shield. The shield is too big to have been carried by the kneeling man on the horse's rump in design 2.

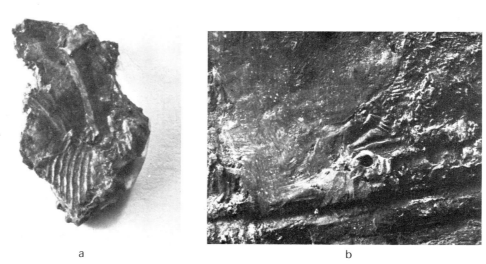

a   b

FIGURE 149 The helmet: the two largest pieces of design 3, (*a*) the slim leg and flutings of design 3 i; (*b*) the stylised hip joint of design 3 iii, photographed in 1947 before deterioration. (Scales: *a*, 3/1, *b*, 2/1)

Fragment D3 (iii). An iron fragment matching other helmet fragments in all physical respects but showing a design which seems unrelated to the other fragments of design 3 or any of the others in the helmet (fig. 148 c). It apparently shows the treatment of a hip broadly analogous to that of the horses on the flange of the shield-boss (fig. 39). The fragment is mounted in the present helmet reconstruction on the right side towards the back (visible in fig. 106) and was present in much better condition on the 1947 reconstruction (fig. 149 b). It is an edge-piece associated with a rivet and fluted strip; this may be not a rim clip but part of a fluted strip which would have covered most of the design. It seems possible therefore that this could be a fragment of a spare foil sheet used merely to fill up a gap, having been tucked under the edges of two sheets showing the recognised helmet subjects. It seems otherwise inexplicable, as an isolated element quite out of context with any other surviving fragment and with what appears to be the subject matter of the design 3 panel.

198

Fragment D3 (iv), 9×7 mm. A fragment of limonite mould (fig. 148*d*) fitted originally by Maryon in the first reconstruction in the neck of the rider of design 2, but apparently making no sense in such a position. It shows a straight raised bar or rod with hair-like lines running obliquely to it. There is nothing to indicate which way up this reversed pattern is to be read (fig. 148) but probably that shown in the drawing is correct. The relief modelling with its change of planes, on which the groups of parallel lines occur, strongly suggests the body of a horse. As has been said in the discussion of design 2, such groups of parallel lines form a regular feature of all the known rider panels that resemble design 2 (Pliezhausen, Valsgärde 7, 8, Vendel 1). It seems therefore that what we have is part of a rider scene, with the parallel lines representing perhaps part of head hair, or a mane, or saddle cloth. The irregularity with which this feature occurs in different versions of this rider can be seen by comparing figures 143, 164*a* and *b*. The pointed foot and angle of leg and thigh suggests a man not kneeling but in the attitude of the warrior with horned helmet or the man in front of the horse's head (fig. 164).

We cannot say precisely how many times design 3 may have been used on the Sutton Hoo helmet; not more than four times, and perhaps only once. Three of the four panel-spaces on the right side of the helmet in which the presence of design 2 cannot be demonstrated are total blanks. The fourth contains only one piece of iron and this has no surviving surface foil (fig. 104). The occurrence of a third figural scene at all upsets the symmetry of design which would otherwise appear absolute in the Sutton Hoo helmet. This consideration alone suggests that the third design may have been employed to repair the helmet; if so this would perhaps suggest that the die used in the original manufacture (design 2) was not available, and that a broadly similar die, from a variant rider scene, was used. The cap was probably originally symmetrical with six impressions of design 2 on each side, of which one, perhaps two, may have suffered damage, and as the scene must have occurred towards the rear of the helmet it may have been connected with damage sustained by the crest at this point and by its subsequent repair.

An alternative solution compatible with the preservation of symmetry would be that the rear panel on both sides of the crest bore this scene as part of the original design, but this appears capable of disproof. The rear panel on the helmet's left side shows a detail of the horse's rump, which is all that can be recognised on it. This detail (fragment 5, fig. 144*a*) exactly corresponds with the horse's rump in design 2 both in dimensions and location, and it is highly improbable that scenes from different dies would correspond so exactly. We have indeed (p. 190), taken this as proof of the presence here of design 2. The third scene, design 3, should be regarded as having been confined to the helmet's right side, and because of the breach of symmetry which its occurrence represents, it should be regarded as a replacement or repair, and it may have occurred no more than once, against the crest at the rear of the helmet's right side. It would, if correctly read, indicate a horse moving to the left, thus maintaining the clockwise procession of rider scenes.

Figure 150 is a reconstruction of the complete die. It shows a single quadruped in ribbon style. The head, with a prominent eye, occupies the upper part of the centre of the panel. The mouth and jaws stand detached from the head and cross over one another. The lower jaw, as it emerges from beneath the upper jaw, is abruptly narrowed and forms a twist. In this twist the ribbon representing the jaw is shown as a line of pellets between strongly defined borders. Where this jaw subsequently emerges from the twist it again changes character and terminates in a length, maintaining the reduction in width, which is filled with lateral billets smaller than those seen in the main body-ribbons and in the rest of the jaw element. The upper jaw passes first under a ribbon which is part of the animal's own body, and then turns downwards, passing over the lower jaw, and under the body again. It then interlaces with the prolonged cere or contour-line of the back of the head, forms a twist filled with thirteen circular beads between firm borders, resumes its cross-billeting and finally terminates in a foot. The body of the animal develops from the back of its head as a neck which runs down to a bead-filled twist, representing the animal's front hip.

This twist has a double outer border. From it develops one front limb, immediately truncated by the frame but carrying a line of dots continuing those in the twist. The other front limb moves upward, interlaces with the descending neck and ends up in the top corner of the panel, illogically, not with a foot but with a hip which develops into a further leg and foot. From the front hip-joint the body crosses the panel from right to left interlacing with the jaws, and proceeds to the top left-hand corner of the panel where it ends in a twist representing the rear hip. This twist-hip again has double outer borders with a line of

FIGURE 150 The helmet: reconstruction drawing of the larger interlace, design 4. (Scale: 3/2)

contained pellets and develops into two legs, one of which has a line of pellets like the front hip and is similarly immediately truncated by the border. The other leg that develops from this rear hip-joint behaves exactly like the corresponding leg from the front hip-joint, ending up in the bottom left corner of the panel in a second hip from which a beaded leg and twisted foot develop.

The rest of the panel is filled up by extensions of the billeted curve which encloses the eye: this develops from its lower end to terminate above the head in a slender elongated point, having changed to a filling of pellets and formed two twists, between which it passes under the neck. The upper end of the billeted curve continues as a billeted ribbon for a short distance until it terminates in a twisted pellet-filled element.

The animal design is a good example of Vendel Style A. Its most marked characteristics are:

(1) a ribbon-style treatment of the body, jaws and limbs, with a filling of transverse billets or bars in the ribbons;

(2) the differentiation of all twists at which the ribbon changes direction, and of most terminations or appendices, by abandoning the transverse billets as a filling and substituting a line of pellets;

(3) the making of an exception to this rule in the case of the jaws, which terminate in billeted lengths;

(4) the abrupt truncation at the edge of the frame of one of the two limbs which emerge from each main hip-joint;

(5) the detachment of the animal's jaws from the rest of its head;

(6) the rendering of feet as a plain twist with two pointed extremities (one, in the case of the foot-like termination of the upper jaw);

(7) the development of the animal's extremities in an unrealistic fashion; jaws, legs and the extensions of the eyelid end in hip, leg and foot or else in a single foot or twist.

The pear-shaped second hips seen in the top right and bottom left corners of the panel, and the feet, have hollow central depressions between raised borders (fig. 150). It had a billeted border at each edge. The billeting, which may be compared stylistically with that seen on the various dies employed on the shield (figs. 27 b and 29) is similar to that preserved along the lower edge of design 2 (p. 196, fig. 143). The die appears to have been freshly cut and in excellent condition when used.

Whereas on the Sutton Hoo helmet the figural panels are in all cases used whole, design 4 is cut and used in incomplete form as occasion requires, particularly on the cheek-pieces. In some cases (fig. 109) these partial occurrences of design 4 are set up on end: in other words, sheets bearing impressions of the main interlace die were liable to be cut and used incomplete to fill up awkward spaces, but this liberty was not taken with the figural panels. The principal surviving areas of design 4 are to be found in the vertical portion (A–B) of the neck-guard (fig. 133 a), and in panels in figure 129.

DESIGN 5   THE SMALLER INTERLACE

This design (fig. 151) is long and narrow. Details of its employment on the face mask (p. 164) appear to indicate that it had a double border of transverse billets down one edge (fig. 124). The evidence for a similar border at one end survives in one place only, on fragment 13 in the neck-guard (figs. 130–32 and see p. 176, n. 1).

The design consists of two animals, upside down and reversed in relation to each other, whose backward-turning heads lie towards the centre of the panel. The two animals are separate and complete but are interlinked at their necks. Their design is complex and difficult to read. The lower jaws move upward, crossing with an element that drops downwards like a forward-flopping lappet; the lower jaws are then prolonged and interlace with the body to its full length. The other elements in the design seem to be the forelock or flopping lappet which passes across in front of the lower jaw before running under the animal's body, and an element which might either represent the upper jaw, although it comes from the head at an unexpected, illogical angle,

FIGURE 151 The helmet: reconstruction drawing of the smaller interlace, design 5. (Scale: 3/2)

or the vestige of a split-neck theme (cf. fig. 40). The design is simplified. The element which may represent the upper jaw crosses the animal's body in a downward direction (fig. 151) and then passes up behind the forelock or lappet to terminate in a point. The outer, tail ends of each animal form a twisted hip from which two short elements of approximately equal length (legs?) emerge. While one of these elements behaves normally like the forelocks of the two heads, the other seems to leave the hip at a contrary angle that breaks the flow of the design, but exactly balances the peculiar behaviour of the upper jaw or 'split neck' element previously discussed.

It is possible that an explanation of the obscurities of the pattern lies in faulty die-cutting. The twist at the right end of the die (fig. 151) is preceded immediately by a splitting of the body mentioned above. If this is regarded as a simple split, the two elements can be seen to develop from it in curves of unbroken fluency. Had such a split been used at the left-hand end of the die the elements here could be similarly rationally explained, but at this end of the die there is no split. The picture is further confused at the left-hand end of the die by the inclusion of an eye in the twist, giving it a close resemblance to the animal's head. The design seems deliberately cryptic, perverse and contradictory.

The central portion of both the animals' bodies and their interlacing lower jaws are solid, and the rest of the bodies and the limbs are depicted as a groove between single outer mouldings. The heads have small round repoussé centre spots for eyes.

The impression from this die used singly, or rather in pairs spaced one above the other, on the neck-guard appears to have borders of billets at both sides (fig. 138). It seems improbable that two separate but otherwise identical dies were used, the only difference being that one had billet borders on one side only, while the other had them on both sides. If the die was applied not one impression at a time but as seen on the face-mask, as a continuous series of impressions carefully juxtaposed, on a large sheet of foil, this could be cut in such a way as to leave the pattern with double borders down each side. It seems that this was the method used on the neck-guard, where the impressions were separated by blank areas, and so had to be made self-sufficient.

5. *Summary and conclusions*

The Sutton Hoo helmet has an iron cap of roughly hemispherical form which has been beaten up out of a single piece of metal. The cap shows no tendency to the conical shape and is not of flatter-than-hemispherical form.

Over the cap, from front to back, is a strong iron crest, of D-shaped cross-section and hollow. It is riveted to the cap only at its ends by the collars of the terminal dragon heads. The inlaid part was not riveted to the cap at any point. The flat bottom plate element of the crest (fig. 113 a) fits wholly inside the inverted U of the convex portion, and there is consequently no projection to either side of the upstanding portion to form flanges or shelves, such as might have held rivets. The crest must, it seems, have been forged or welded to the cap or else, it is suggested (p. 228), made too small, fitted to the cap while hot and in an expanded condition, and allowed to contract into position as it cooled. The crest did not serve the purpose of holding the two halves of the cap together, which is its essential role in the helmets of the Constantinian group from which the Vendel-type helmets are primarily descended (pp. 220-24 below); it is nonetheless functional in the sense that it would perform perfectly the defensive role of the *wala*, to which attention is drawn in *Beowulf* 1030-4 (p. 158).

Attached to the under edge of the cap of the helmet are a face-mask, two cheek-pieces and a neck-guard. These are attached directly to the cap, not to a separate iron band interposed between them and the cap, as is the invariable rule with late Roman cavalry officer helmets of the Constantine type (figs. 166 and 167) discussed below.

The face-mask is rigid, being riveted at three points to the cap. The neck-guard and cheek-pieces, on the other hand, were hinged and movable. The hinges were made of folded strips of leather reinforced with bronze bars and riveted (p. 185, fig. 139). No metal hinge-plates or buckles were found in association with the helmet.

The neck-guard is solid and beaten out of two sheets of metal. It is long from top to bottom, and also broad. It was held to the cap by two riveted leather hinges with metal reinforcing bars (fig. 137). It has a spreading fan-shaped portion, canted out at an angle, which forms the main protection for neck and shoulders, and a short upright collar-like section at the top, which follows the curve of the cap and fits loosely up inside it. The leather hinges give a certain flexibility so that the guard is free to ride up minimally inside the cap. The helmet did not have a permanent textile lining or any padding in textile covers. It can be assumed to have been lined with soft leather or calf-skin. A leather lining is suggested also by the peculiar nature of the corrosion inside the cap (pl. 23b), although no organic structure survives in the rust formation (p. 231); by the evidence for the use of leather otherwise in the helmet construction (for the hinges) and by the effective elimination of textile (p. 179).[1] Leather linings are, moreover, standard in late Roman helmets.[2]

---

[1] The lining may have been removed.

[2] Klumbach 1973, 9-14. For helmet linings see also Robinson 1975, 144. The objections there made to leather linings may perhaps be countered by the possibility that additional padding

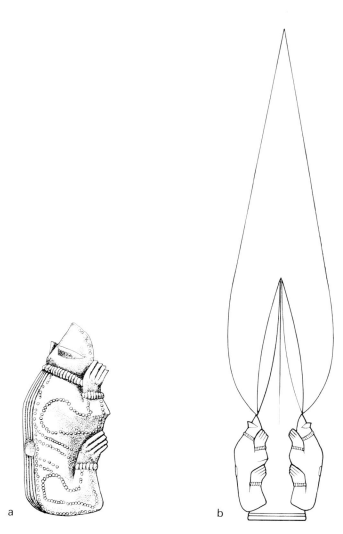

FIGURE 152 Drawing of spear-head from
Vendel 12. The flanking bears are gilded, and
show punched circle decoration analogous to
that on the dragon head of the Sutton Hoo
helmet. (Scales: *a*, 1/1; *b*, 1/2)

The cheek-pieces are heavy and completely protect the side of the face. They
show no cut-out areas, designed to leave the ear exposed, nor does the cap. When
the cheek-pieces are drawn in to meet the face-mask the wearer's face is completely
enclosed.

The surface of the helmet is almost wholly covered with figural or interlace
ornament applied to the surface of the iron cap in the form of tinned bronze sheeting,
into which the ornament has been stamped with dies. The bronze sheeting is held
to the cap, cheek-pieces, neck-guard and mask by fluted strips of bronze riveted
through the edges of the foil to the cap of the helmet.

The helmet is jewelled, if only in a minor way. The eyebrows carry a line of square-

of a removable kind was used, which protected the leather from
the effects of heat and moisture referred to. Mr Robinson, for
whose assistance I am much indebted, himself proposed the use

of the linings of fine calf-skin that have been provided in the
Tower Armouries reconstruction.

cut flat garnets along their lower edges and the dragon heads have cabochon garnets for eyes.

The whole exterior of the helmet had the rich look of silver, with golden touches (pp. 146-50) giving, with the garnet inlays, the appearance seen in the Tower Armouries replica (pl. 8), concisely illustrating *Beowulf* 'se hwita helm...since geweorðad'.[1] In addition, the iron crest and the bronze eyebrows were inlaid with silver wire. The boar and dragon heads, the nose and mouth of the face-mask, the plain under-surfaces of the eyebrows, and the broad fluted strips that flank the crest, were all thickly gilded. The fluted strips which held and framed the decorative panels generally and which were bronze (though scientifically the evidence for this is confused) were also tinned; there is no evidence that they were gilt. The rivet-heads in general use over the helmet do not seem to have been exploited decoratively, though they must have had an appreciable visual impact (pl. 8).

The cut-away rear profile of the cheek-pieces, and the corresponding and opposite cut-away shape of the neck-guard sides, when brought together form a rounded opening which gives freedom of movement to the shoulder.

The front of the helmet shows ambivalence and dual imagery in the realisation of major traits of its design of the bird or winged dragon theme. The effect of the bird or winged dragon with spread wings is simply produced by the introduction of a third dragon head, of special design (p. 161). This has the effect of overriding the transition between cap and mask since the winged dragon-image so created straddles both.

11   THE SUTTON HOO HELMET IN THE ANGLO-SAXON AND SCANDINAVIAN CONTEXTS

Only two helmets that can be dated between the fourth and the fourteenth centuries have been found in Britain: those from Sutton Hoo and Benty Grange in Derbyshire. Both are from seventh-century graves. The Sutton Hoo helmet, like the more incomplete and fragmentary example from Benty Grange, consequently ranks as an object of the greatest archaeological rarity and importance. The two helmets, though roughly contemporary, are yet totally different in construction and detail. The Benty Grange helmet is structurally and ornamentally unique. An attempt has been made to reconstruct its appearance and structural details from the surviving fragments (pl. 23 a).[2]

It has been universally assumed both that the Benty Grange helmet is Anglo-Saxon, and that it is a helmet; these assumptions might be questioned but are probably sound. The helmet as reconstructed makes a satisfactory piece of defensive armour; its iron-strip framework, the tough plates of horn which covered it, the nasal, the protection for the nape of the neck and the jaw-line (the horn plates at the rear continued below the level of the cap), together with a presumed lining of leather, would give an

[1] Klaber 1941, lines 1448–50; there is apparently no philological reason why 'hwit' should not be rendered in English literally as 'white'.

[2] For a full account of the Benty Grange helmet, and other finds that have been claimed as Anglo-Saxon helmets, see Bruce-Mitford 1974, ch. 11.

effective degree of protection while at the same time being light in weight. The strip framework, the nasal, neck-guard and boar crest, and the Christian cross are all features found in continental helmets.[1] Horn plates (in twelve panels) form the outer surface of the small helmet of unusual form found in the young prince's grave under Cologne Cathedral.[2]

The possibility that the Benty Grange remains could represent some sort of priestly or ceremonial headgear has nothing to recommend it. As for its Anglo-Saxon origin, general topographical and archaeological considerations,[3] and the fact that this was a richly furnished burial, are against British origin for the grave. The mound had been robbed and amongst the slight remains that survive from the burial there is indeed an absence of anything (apart from the helmet) that might be called Germanic. Turning to the helmet, the gold and garnet eyes of the boar that stands as a crest, with beaded gold wire collars round the garnets, are pure Germanic goldsmith's work.

a

b

c

FIGURE 153 (a) Drawing of a silver-foil fragment from a seventh-century tumulus at Caenby, Lincolnshire, showing a man in a horned headdress with bird head terminals, holding a sword in his right hand; (b) and (c) show the silver fragment before and after cleaning and with slightly different lighting. (Scale: 2/1)

[1] For crosses on Spangenhelme see the helmets from Vézeronce (Grenoble Museum), in the zone of vine and bird ornament at the base of the cap; and in particular from Planig in the Römisch-Germanisches Zentralmuseum, Mainz, where two sizeable crosses are traced in panels on each side of the crest at the front of the helmet (P. Bouffard, *Revue Suisse d'Art et* *d'Archéologie* x, 1948/9, pl. 64a). See also S. Grieg 'Norske hjelmer fra folkevandringstiden', *Bergens Museums Aarbok* 1922–3 (Hist. Antikv. Raekke Nr. 3), fig. 8.

[2] Doppelfeld 1964, 3–45 especially 18–24, Taf. 39, and 37–45; also Doppelfeld 1960b, 1963 and especially 1961/2.

[3] Ozanne 1962–3.

The substance in which the silver studs that covered the boar's flanks and the hip-plates (cut down from late Roman silver) were embedded appears to have been iron. The boar need not be an original feature of the helmet; it is an appendage rather than structurally integrated with the design. Its construction is complex and remains enigmatic.[1]

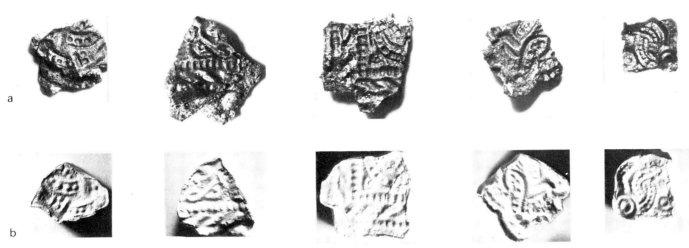

FIGURE 154 (a) Fragments of stamped foil showing varied interlace design and billeted bordering from the barrow cremation at Asthall, Berkshire, with (b) plasticine casts taken from the backs of the fragments. (Scale: 3/2) (Photos: Ashmolean Museum, Oxford)

Apart from the Benty Grange helmet there are only the smallest indications which could possibly suggest the original presence of helmets in two other aristocratic burials, those from Caenby in Lincolnshire and Asthall in Berkshire. The Caenby barrow had been ransacked.[2] A small fragment of silver foil that survives from it was recently recognised by Mrs Leslie Webster F.S.A. as carrying part of an impression of a man with sword and horned headdress with bird's head terminals (fig. 153), resembling one of the twin dancing figures on the Sutton Hoo helmet. This fragment of foil could have come from a helmet though nothing survives from the burial beyond the fragment itself to support the suggestion. Attention should perhaps also be drawn to some hitherto unpublished bronze foil fragments with zoomorphic interlace, showing a rectangular border (fig. 154), and possibly reminiscent of our design 4, from the débris of the cremation in the Asthall barrow excavated by E. T. Leeds, now in the Ashmolean Museum, Oxford.[3] There is nothing further to suggest that a helmet might be involved, and the rectangular panels evidently represented might equally have come from a drinking horn, though no other trace of either horn or helmet survived the cremation.

[1] Bruce-Mitford 1974, 237–40. The body of the boar is primarily composed of two D-shaped hollow bronze tubes set back to back. The iron sheeting which apparently held the studs must have been added to the flanks.

[2] Jarvis 1850.
[3] Leeds 1924.

In contrast with a lack of knowledge of Anglo-Saxon helmets from archaeological sources that is almost total, there is a prodigal amount of evidence for helmets from East Scandinavia. The material is dominated by the finds from the Vendel and Valsgärde boat-graves, in which a considerable number of restorable helmets have come to light, but it has a much wider East Scandinavian distribution. In Uppland sites more or less complete or restorable examples have been recovered from boat-graves 1, 12 and 14 at Vendel, a site some 34 km north of Uppsala, and from boat-graves 5, 6, 7 and 8 at Valsgärde, some 10 km north of Uppsala and only 3 km from the temple and royal mounds at Gamla Uppsala. A similar helmet must it seems have occurred in Vendel 11, from which part of the comb, a hinge and a nasal with attached chain mail survive, with foil fragments carrying a zoomorphic design that matches exactly similar foil on the helmet from Valsgärde 7 (fig. 165).[1] There may have been a similar helmet also in Vendel 10.[2] In addition to these there are seventh- or eighth-century helmets of different construction (built up of a close trellis-work of strips) from Ulltuna, also in Uppland, and Valsgärde 6 (fig. 182 b), and a fragment of stamped foil from the great cremation in the East Mound at Gamla Uppsala (fig. 155, part of a dancing warrior scene) so close in every respect to the corresponding warrior on the Sutton Hoo helmet as to appear at first glance to be from the same die.[3] The close similarity of the East Mound scene in scale and detail to Sutton Hoo design 1 may indicate that it too is from a helmet. The die, though not identical with the one used at Sutton Hoo, was certainly cut by the same man. In addition to these twelve Uppland helmets, there are fragments from Gotland (chiefly eyebrows or dragon-head fittings from the ends of crests) representing more than twenty others.

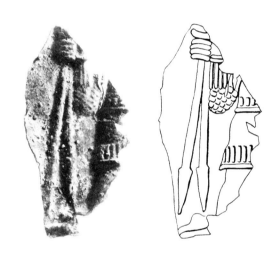

FIGURE 155 Bronze-foil fragment with part of the figure of a dancing warrior, from the East Mound at Gamla Uppsala (Sweden). (Scale: 2/1) (Photo: Statens Historiska Museum, Stockholm)

Beyond these physical remains of over thirty helmets, the range is considerably extended by pictorial representations. In the scenes in stamped foil on their caps the Vendel and Valsgärde helmets depict an abundant use of helmets worn by warriors on foot and on horseback, in considerable variety of form and design, some furnished with massive-looking bird or boar crests. The Torslunda dies from Öland (fig. 156), used specifically for the decoration of helmets, which come from a habitation site yielding hearths and some slag,[4] seem to demonstrate the manufacture on Öland or

---

[1] Stolpe and Arne 1927, pls. xxx, fig. 4, xxxiii, fig. 2 (nose-guard fragment). I am indebted to Professor Greta Arwidsson for drawing my attention to the parallel of the foil fragments and allowing me to reproduce the drawing which is to appear in her forthcoming publication.

[2] Ibid. pl. xxvii, figs. 11, 16, part of mail curtain.
[3] Lindqvist 1936 b, 171. Cf. also Bruce-Mitford 1974, 40 and pl. 14.
[4] Bruce-Mitford 1974, 219–22; Hagberg 1976.

FIGURE 156 Bronze dies from Torslunda, Öland, Sweden, used for stamping foil for helmet decoration. (Scale: 4/3) (Photos: Statens Historiska Museum, Stockholm)

at least in the region, of helmets of the same general character as those found in Uppland, and one of the dies (figs. 156 b, 157) itself depicts helmets that seem to possess some of the distinctive features of the Sutton Hoo helmet, in particular its broad neck-guard. The designs of the helmets from which the many Gotlandic fragments come are not recoverable[1] but certain fragments, such as the eyebrows from Högbro, Halle, and from Lokrume, and another pair from an unknown site in Gotland, suggest that they were similar to the complete examples found in some variety in details of design, in Uppland.[2]

Although helmet remains have been found in Norway, the material is not particularly

[1] For the Ulltuna and other Scandinavian helmets see Thordeman 1941, 90 ff. For Ulltuna, Arwidsson 1935, 243; *Acta Archaeologica* III, 29 ff. For some of the Gotlandic helmet-fragments, Nerman 1969 (Tafeln), Taf. 65–9. For the Vendel helmets, Stolpe and Arne 1927, pls. V, VI; XXVI, figs. 11, 16; pl. XXX, figs. 4–6; pl. XXXVI, figs. 4–8; pls. XLI and XLII, fig. 1. Also (for an account of the new restorations) Lindqvist 1950a, 1–24 (Vendelhjälmarna i ny rekonstruktion). Arbman in Lundberg 1938, 1–28, especially grave inventories, pp. 23–8; Lindqvist in Lundberg 1938, 29–46.

[2] Lindqvist 1925a, figs. 97–99; Thordeman 1941, 96.

informative.[1] The Gjermundbu helmet fragments, said by Grieg to resemble the Valsgärde 6 helmet,[2] are from a tenth-century burial. A terminal dragon head from Øvre Stabu, Toten, Opland[3] is entirely typical of Swedish-found examples. No trace of any helmet of the Vendel period has yet been found in Denmark.[4] The relative mass of evidence surviving from the east of Scandinavia must at least reflect a readiness, arising from established custom, to consign such objects to the grave, as well as their widespread use there.

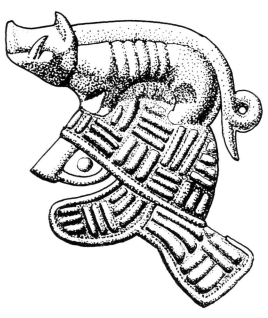

FIGURE 157 Representation of a helmet from one of the dies from Torslunda, Öland, Sweden (fig. 156b) showing cheek-pieces and a broad neck-guard. (Scale: 4/1)

The helmets from East Scandinavia all have rounded caps, distinct in form from the conical *Spangenhelme* of central Europe, and show a highly distinctive system of extensive external decoration by the covering of the helmets with interlace and figural scenes stamped in added foil. They also have well-marked crests or combs. To this the helmet from Vendel 14 (fig. 158) is the solitary exception, since it alone seems to have been designed without a comb, or at least to have been buried without one. Apart from these common factors, the East Scandinavian helmets seem to show an unorganised variety. Some have mail curtains to protect the neck and face (fig. 182), others have spaced iron strips, turned out at the bottom to protect the neck (fig. 158). Only the Vendel 14 example has cheek-pieces (fig. 158). Some like those from Ulltuna and Valsgärde 6 have caps built up from strips in an open trellis. All that are complete enough to enable the point to be established have decorative foil surface overlays. The Sutton Hoo helmet clearly belongs in this context. But in what relationship does it stand to the other helmets found in East Scandinavian sites?

If we compare the Sutton Hoo helmet with the Vendel and Valsgärde groups and other Swedish helmet remains differences are at once apparent. The Sutton Hoo example (like the silver-gilt surfaces of the Deurne and Augsburg-Pfersee helmets, figs. 166 and 167) is silvery, or silver-gilt in outer appearance. It is richer and of higher quality than any other helmet yet found and closer to the late Roman prototypes visualised by Lindqvist, Werner, Thordeman and Klumbach as lying behind the Vendel type.[5] A feature of the Sutton Hoo helmet possessed by no other Vendel helmet type yet discovered is the solid neck-guard, though this is known from Swedish pictorial representations, notably that on one of the Torslunda plates (fig. 157). The

[1] Grieg 1922–3 and 1947.
[2] Grieg 1947, 41–2.
[3] Grieg 1922–3, 7, fig. 5.
[4] The well-known find from Thorsberg, a bog find, and the earliest Scandinavian found helmet, is of Roman Iron Age or early Migration Period date, and of uncertain affinities.
[5] Lindqvist 1925a, 201 ff. and 1950a, 18–21; Werner 1949/50, 192; Thordeman 1941; Klumbach 1973, 14.

FIGURE 158 Helmet from Vendel 14.

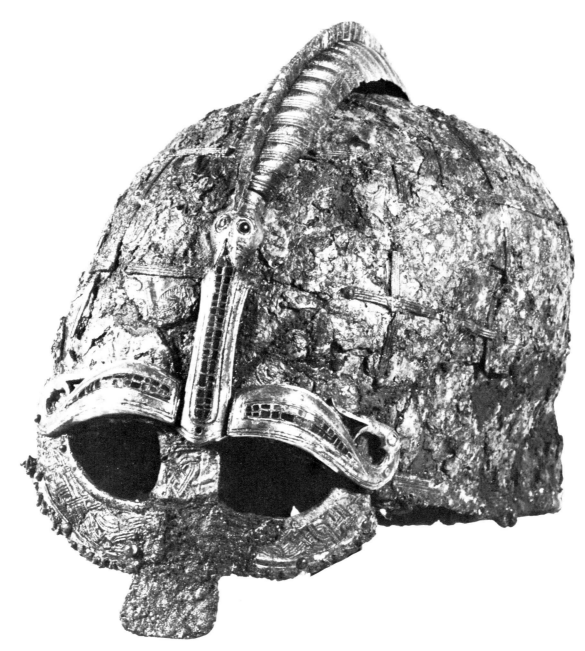

FIGURE 159   Helmet from Valsgärde 7. (Photo: Per Bergström)

surviving Vendel- and Valsgärde-type helmets seem without exception to have had
as neck-guards either iron strips or protective mail curtains—mail curtains in Vendel
10 (probably), 11 and 12, and in Valsgärde 6 (fig. 182 a and b) and 8; iron strips,
curving outward at the bottom, in Ulltuna, Valsgärde 5 and Vendel 14.[1] It is possible
that the Vendel 10 helmet had a solid neck-guard as a hinge seems to have belonged
to it.[2]

These differences from other known examples may express a difference in social

[1] Cf. Thordeman 1941, 'Dräkt', pp. 90, 91, 92, figs. 2–6;
Arwidsson 1942 a, 27–35, Taf. 1–5; 1954, 22–8, Taf. 1–6.
[2] Arwidsson 1935, 254, fig. 10. Although the idea seems to

have been abandoned for the Vendel 1 helmet, cf. Stolpe and
Arne 1927, pl. VI, fig. 8; but see Lindqvist 1950 a, 9–11.

FIGURE 160 Helmet from Valsgärde 7 viewed from above.
(Photo: G. Arwidsson and O. Lindman)

FIGURE 161   Helmet from Valsgärde 7: side view (Photo: G. Arwidsson)

level, as the Sutton Hoo helmet is uniquely from a royal burial, but they could also express a typologically earlier phase in the development of the Vendel type. It is because the solitary helmet fragment (fig. 155) from Gamla Uppsala is also from a royal grave that its virtual identity with the Sutton Hoo fragment is so interesting, the dies seemingly cut by the same hand.

The Sutton Hoo helmet differs from other East Scandinavian helmets in the following respects: (i) it has a solid neck-guard; (ii) it has cheek-pieces, otherwise occurring only in the Vendel 14 helmet, in a differing version well forward on the face (fig. 158); (iii) it has an iron crest inlaid with silver wire, and the eyebrows, of bronze, are also inlaid with silver wire (parallels are cited for the brows on p. 158, n. 3); (iv) it has a face-mask;[1] (v) it has a cap made from a single sheet of metal, without joins, a feature not established as yet in other helmets: that from Valsgärde 7 (fig. 159), which might appear to be in one piece, is in fact made up of eight; (vi) it was tinned all over its bronze sheeting externally, giving the completely silver effect seen in the Tower Armouries replica (pl. 8, figs. 137, 138). The extent to which this may have been so in other East Scandinavian helmets is not clear.

The helmet from Valsgärde 7 is illustrated here in some detail by courtesy of Professor Arwidsson (figs. 159–165 a), because in several important respects it serves,

[1] Amongst the Gotlandic material is an object of bronze sheeting also identified as a face-mask (Nerman 1969, no. 616). It is not clear that this formed part of a complete helmet. I am indebted to Mrs Susan Youngs for this reference.

FIGURE 162 Gilded bronze eyebrows and nasal inlaid with
garnets, from the helmet from Valsgärde 7. (Scale: 1/1)

along with the Vendel 14 helmet (fig. 158), the fragment from the East Mound at Gamla
Uppsala (fig. 155) and the Torslunda dies, better than any of the other helmets of
its type to make explicit the East Scandinavian context of the Sutton Hoo helmet,
and also its differences from other examples found there so far.

In the matter of differences, it had no neck-guard, cheek-pieces or face-mask, these
areas of the body being protected by a mail curtain. The succession of holes by which
the mail rings were attached can be seen along the bottom edge of the cap in figure
161. The crest (fig. 160) is bronze, with cast chevron ornament, and not, as in the
Sutton Hoo helmet, iron inlaid with silver wire.

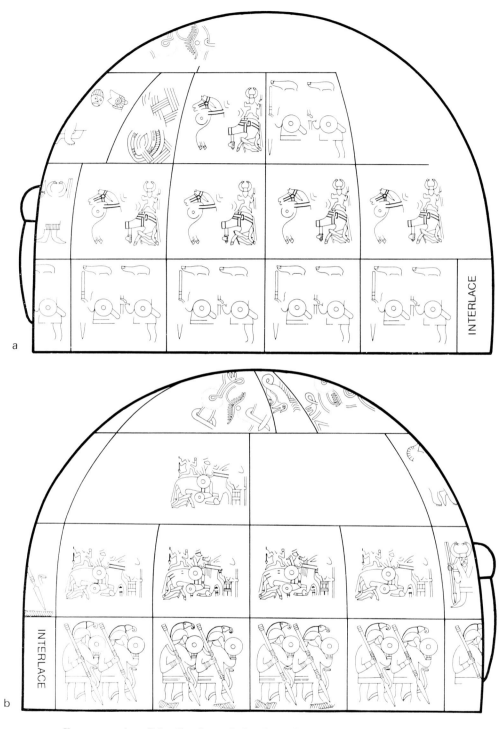

FIGURE 163 Distribution of the figural scenes and interlace on the
helmet from Valsgärde 7: (a) the helmet's left side; (b) the right side.
The simplified animal head in profile marks the front of the helmet.
(Drawing by Per-Olof Bohlin)

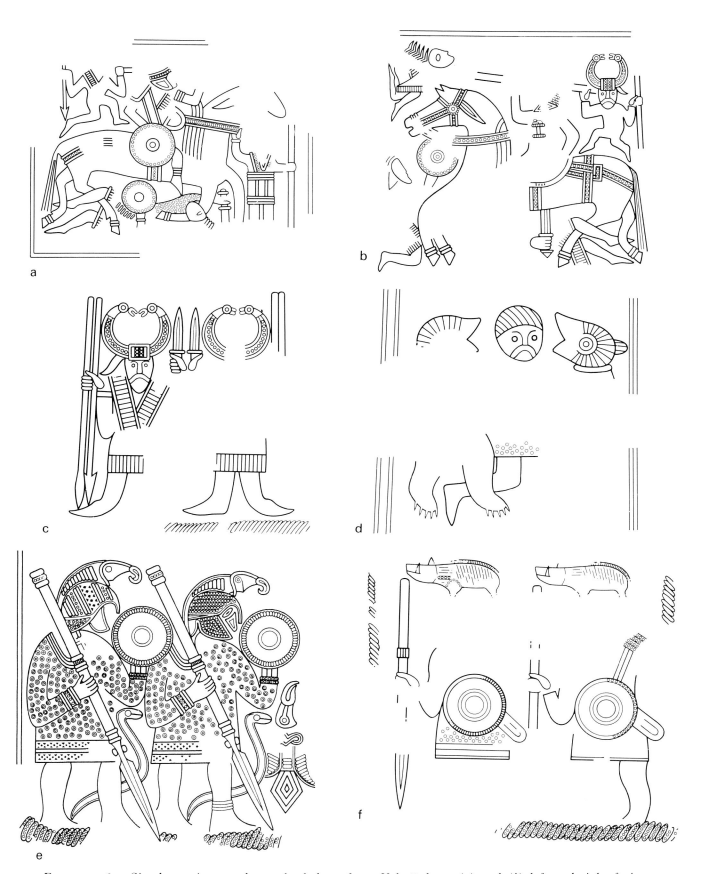

FIGURE 164 Six decorative panels on the helmet from Valsgärde 7: (*a*) and (*b*) left and right facing versions of a riding warrior scene; (*c*) dancing warriors; (*d*) man between bears; (*e*), (*f*) warriors in procession. (Scale: 3/2) (Drawings by M. Roosmay, Per-Olof Bohlin)

217

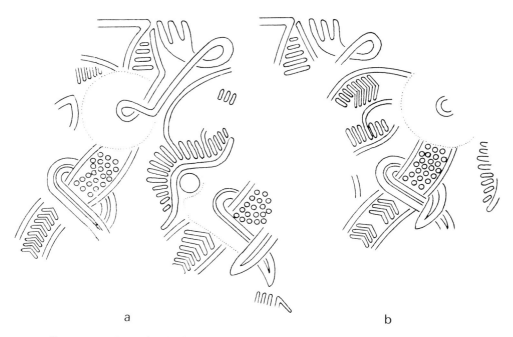

a   b

FIGURE 165 Identical zoomorphic interlace found in two burials in
Sweden: (*a*) employed on the helmet from Valsgärde 7; (*b*) used on the
helmet from Vendel 11. (Scale: 2/1) (Drawing by Per-Olof Bohlin)

On the other hand, the Valsgärde 7 helmet has closer similarities in some respects
with the Sutton Hoo helmet than others of the East Scandinavian helmet finds. It
is 'jewelled', like the Sutton Hoo helmet, but showing a greater use of garnets; and
it is even more extensively covered with figural and zoomorphic foil (figs. 163*a* and
b, and figs. 164*a*–*f*, and fig. 165*a*). There are no plain zones at all, the whole of the
surface being covered. The accumulation of patterns at the top of the helmet against
the crest is well seen in figure 160. An unusual range of dies is also employed on the
Valsgärde 7 helmet (figs. 164 and 165*a*), providing further links with Sutton Hoo. The
rider and fallen warrior scene occurs on it in two versions, though with differing and
additional elements (cf. figs. 164*a* and *b*). The dies are reversed, so that on both sides
of the helmet the riders are moving to the front, instead of circulating in one direction
round the helmet in a continuous procession, as in the Sutton Hoo helmet. The
differences in these and other East Scandinavian rider scenes from the Sutton Hoo
version, serve only to emphasise the remarkable closeness of the iconographic parallel
between the Sutton Hoo version and the stylistically much more disintegrated version
on the Pliezhausen gold disc brooch (p. 193 and fig. 146).[1] Apart from the rider scenes,
the Valsgärde 7 helmet has a version of the dancing warriors scene (fig. 164*c*) of the
Gamla Uppsala and Caenby fragments and of the Sutton Hoo helmet, placed as in the
Sutton Hoo helmet above the eyebrows. In addition there is on the Valsgärde 7 helmet
a version of the man-between-bears scene of the Torslunda die (figs. 164*d*, 156*d*) which
may, in spite of all the differences seen in the Torslunda and Valsgärde versions (p.

[1] Cf. Bruce-Mitford 1974, 37–9.

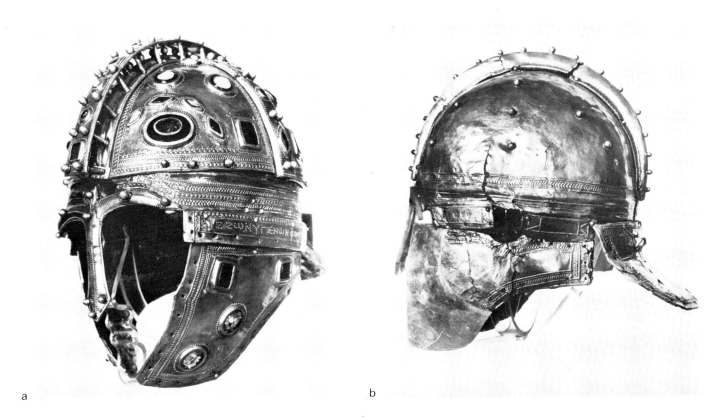

a

b

c

d

FIGURE 166   Late Roman helmets from the Constantinian workshops; (*a*) Berkasovo, Yugoslavia, helmet
1: (*b*) Berkasovo, helmet 2; (*c*) and (*d*) the Deurne or de Peel helmet, Holland.

219

522),[1] be related to the man-between-wolves scene in gold cloisonné work on the Sutton Hoo purse-lid (fig. 377). The Valsgärde 7 and Sutton Hoo helmets between them serve to emphasise the East Scandinavian context against which the scenes on the Sutton Hoo purse must in the first instance be considered, and the wealth of the East Scandinavian indigenous repertoire of representational scenes.

III   THE LATE ANTIQUE BACKGROUND

The differences between the Sutton Hoo helmet and its Vendel-type counterparts serve to make the origins of the type more explicit. First, the crest or comb relates the helmet to the Constantinian group of fourth–fifth century helmets, surveyed in newly cleaned and restored form under Klumbach's editorship (cf. figs. 166, 167 and 168); so do the white or tinned surface of the helmet (figs. 166, 167 b)[2] and the use of semi-precious stones. The Budapest and Berkasovo I (fig. 166 a) helmets[3] illustrate encrustation with precious or semi-precious stones from which may derive the garnet inlays in the eyebrows and animal heads of the Sutton Hoo helmet, and, more prominently, the inlays in the eyebrows and front dragon head of the Valsgärde 7 helmet (fig. 162).

The Sutton Hoo crest form is characteristic of this late Roman group. The Intercisa 2 helmet (fig. 168 b) is a good example in which the iron core is seen free of superficial plating or other features and the crest, like that on the Sutton Hoo helmet, is a hollow iron tube. Many of the Constantinian helmets show the solid projecting neck-guard with vertical or upstanding flange at the top seen in the Sutton Hoo helmet (fig. 166 b, c, d). This was in most cases also attached by leather hinges, since no other means of attachment is indicated (fig. 166 d).[4] The Augst and Intercisa helmets illustrate the same points, and on these helmets in particular we see the solid iron cap, characteristic of Sutton Hoo, Vendel 14 and Valsgärde 7, but distinct from the strip type of construction of Benty Grange, Valsgärde 6 or Ulltuna type helmets. The Intercisa 4 helmet, besides illustrating some of the basic features of the Vendel type, has a high upstanding crest, which may be the prototype of those helmets of the Swedish group that are dominated by huge bird or boar images (figs. 157, 168 a).

The Augst, Intercisa and Worms helmets are infantry helmets.[5] Their cheek-pieces are carried well back and have reciprocal half-openings that correspond for the ears in both cap and cheek-piece. The latter tend to be scalloped or cut away at the front edges. The Sutton Hoo helmet also has certain features comparable with the distinctive cavalry type in the Constantinian group. It lacks the extra iron band interposed in these Cavalry helmets between the cap and the dependent neck-guard, nasal and cheek-pieces (fig. 166), but it shows the cheek-piece design cut away at the back, and the eyebrows cut out of the cap and formed by a separate attached piece

[1] Cf. Bruce-Mitford 1974, 43–5.
[2] Klumbach 1973, Taf. 1–5 and 12–16. Figs. 166–8 are reproduced by courtesy of the Römisch-Germanisches Zentral museum, Mainz.

[3] For Budapest see Thomas in Klumbach 1973; Berkasovo, Manojlović-Marijanski 1964, Taf. I–IX.
[4] Klumbach 1973, Taf. 45, 46.
[5] Klumbach 1973, Taf. 45–64.

a

b

FIGURE 167 Late Roman helmets from the Constantinian workshops:
(*a*) Conçesti, Romania; (*b*) Augsburg Pfersee, Germany.

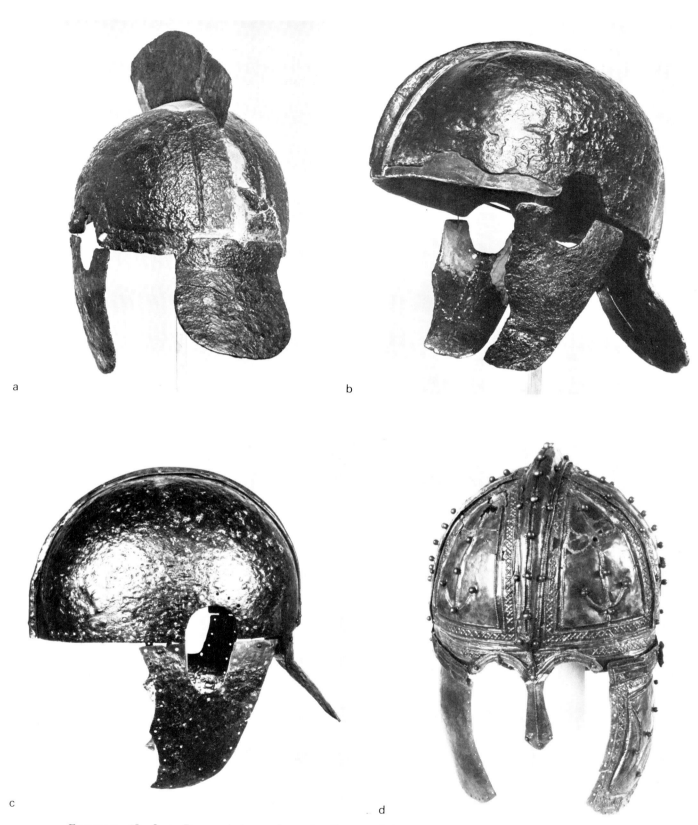

a

b

c

d

FIGURE 168 Late Roman helmets from the Constantinian workshops: (*a*) Intercisa, Hungary, no. 4; (*b*) Intercisa, no. 2; (*c*) Augst, Switzerland; (*d*) Deurne or de Peel helmet.

of metal. The prominent spherical rivet-heads seen on such helmets as Berkasovo 2 and Deurne (fig. 166 *b–d*) could well be the source of the prominent rivet-heads as they appear on the helmet from Valsgärde 8. The Deurne helmet, of which only the silver outer shell was found, also had the solid neck-guard (fig. 166 *d*). The silver and gilt effect of our helmet echoes the rich silver-gilt effect typical of the Constantinian group, well seen on one of the helmets from Augsburg-Pfersee.[1] The Conçesti helmet, like the Sutton Hoo helmet, was 'parcel-gilt'. Finally, we can refer to the preserved leather lining of the Deurne (de Peel) helmet.[2]

The late Constantinian infantry and cavalry helmets are clearly the principal source of the Vendel group, which to this extent can be said to be derived primarily from the Eastern Empire. It is part of the significance of the Sutton Hoo helmet that it makes this derivation much more evident and explicit.

Some minor observations may be added. The face-mask of the Sutton Hoo helmet is not a complete casing-in of the face like that of the Ribchester helmet (the cavalry sports or parade helmet, fig. 169 *a*). It is more akin to the mask of the Homs helmet, which was coated with silver, and hinged at a single central point above the nose (fig. 169 *b*). The Sutton Hoo mask, as we have seen, was rigid, but was a separate element like that of the Homs helmet.

One fact is clear. The Sutton Hoo helmet owes nothing to the large class of *Spangenhelme*, probably of Ostrogothic origins, widespread in the Rhineland and Danube areas, as in Switzerland and North Italy.[3] Yet other East Scandinavian helmets appear to draw from this source at least their mail curtains and their ribbed construction. The fact that two *Spangenhelme* are recorded in Sweden itself may indicate how this came about.[4]

The ring punch ornament of the dragon heads on the Sutton Hoo helmet is distinctive (fig. 117). It is closely matched not only in concept but in its application to sculptural form on the spear-head from Vendel 12 (fig. 152). The use of lines flanking the backbone, and of parallel lines of ring punches forming chevrons to either side, and of wandering lines of ring punch marks outlining the edges and shapes of the anatomy, are exactly matched. We may then compare the pectinated, rigid toes of the Vendel 12 spear-head bears with those of the bears on the Torslunda die (fig. 156 *d*) and seen in miniature on the matching pair of Torslunda dies (fig. 156 *c* and *d*), are the nose, toothbrush moustache and small semicircular mouth of the Sutton Hoo helmet.

These observations on the Sutton Hoo helmet and its East Scandinavian analogies have not included consideration of the animal interlace or the figural scenes. These matters are to be the subject of more detailed study when the East Scandinavian affinities of the burial as a whole are given special consideration against the Continental background.

---

[1] Klumbach 1973, 38, 39.
[2] Ibid. Taf. 26.

[3] Werner 1950 *a*, 164–7.
[4] Thordeman 1941; Arwidsson 1934.

FIGURE 169 (a) Early second-century cavalry sports helmet from Ribchester, Lancashire (British Museum);
(b) cavalry sports helmet with hinged and silvered face mask, from Homs (Emesa), Syria

The consistent and intimate correspondence between details found in the Sutton Hoo helmet and passages describing details of helmets in the Anglo-Saxon poem *Beowulf* have been indicated by citations in the course of this chapter, but must be the subject of a separate study.

IV THE CONDITION AND DATE OF THE SUTTON HOO HELMET

The Sutton Hoo helmet was no doubt of some age when buried, particularly if it is of East Scandinavian manufacture, and so quite likely to have been brought to this country long before its burial in A.D. 624–5. It appears all to have been constructed by one armourer, or one armourer and an assistant, at one time. The only element that might on grounds of style be thought possibly to have been re-used and (since it is an integral part of the Sutton Hoo helmet) taken over from an earlier helmet, is the nose-and-mouth casting.

The same extremely high quality of design and technique is maintained throughout. The four dies used in the stamped foil decoration that are capable of restoration all appear contemporaneous, the work of one man or workshop; and the stamped panels appear all to be the original covering of the helmet. There is no double riveting. There are signs of repair suggested by the use of design 3. It also seems that the gap in the crest at the back, and the decomposed high tin alloy with gold-foil covering with punched circle decoration, which formed the neck and snout of the second dragon head at the rear in the reconstruction (p. 155), could be evidence of damage and replacement, although the dragon heads are all stylistically similar. To this extent the helmet was perhaps not new when buried. From the context we can say, subject to agreement with the identification with Raedwald,[1] that its burial took place in A.D. 624–5. If, as seems likely, it was made in Sweden, it could well have been brought to England much earlier, in the early days of the East Anglian royal dynasty. If it was made locally in Suffolk it can only have been made by armourers fresh from Sweden as, in spite of the differences already described from the Vendel-type helmets so far known, it shows no concession to any other influence than those at work in the Vendel milieu, and dies brought from Sweden would certainly have had to be used in its decoration. The helmet is certainly closer to the late Roman Constantinian workshop prototypes than any other Vendel-type helmet; it could date back into the second or even first half of the sixth century, and the identity of the dancing warriors design with that of the fragment of the East Mound at Gamla Uppsala would be compatible with this; and a date as early as *c.* A.D. 500, proposed by Lindqvist for the Vendel 14 helmet, which he regarded as the earliest of the Vendel/Valsgärde group of seven restorable examples, cannot be excluded.[2]

---

[1] *Sutton Hoo*, Vol. I, ch. x.

[2] Lindqvist 1950*a*, 12; for early dating of the Vendel helmets see Almgren 1948, 81–103.

REPORT ON THE SCIENTIFIC EXAMINATION
OF THE SUTTON HOO HELMET

by

W. A. ODDY, MAVIS BIMSON and A. E. WERNER

The decorative panels, fluted strips and edging

In a paper on his restoration of the Sutton Hoo helmet H. Maryon[1] states that the panels of decoration which covered the helmet were made of tinned bronze separated by swaged strips of tin. No analytical evidence to support these statements can be found in the archives of the Research Laboratory, and it seems likely that Maryon made an educated guess about the composition of the final decoration of the helmet. Analytical samples (fig. 170, 1, 2 and 3) were therefore taken from traces of the foil plaques remaining on three fragments of the helmet and were shown, by emission spectrographic analysis, to contain copper and tin, together with traces of several other elements. This supports the suggestion that the decorative plaques are made of bronze, but there is now no unambiguous appearance of surface tinning. A further sample (fig. 175, 4) was taken from the surface for analysis by X-ray diffraction and shown to consist chiefly of the ϵ-copper/tin intermetallic compound (Cu_3Sn). Analysis of areas of undoubted tinning on the shield (see App. A, p. 101 ff.) have shown that this compound occurs there also, having been produced in situ by the tinning process (p. 102). It is concluded that the decorative panels on the helmet were made of bronze, tinned in the normal way and then heated in a reducing atmosphere, producing an intermetallic compound on the surface which is white in colour and very hard.

The fluted strips between these panels have corroded to a white material which was shown by X-ray diffraction analysis (fig. 171, 5) to contain cassiterite

FIGURE 170 The Sutton Hoo helmet: sampling positions on three foil-covered fragments.

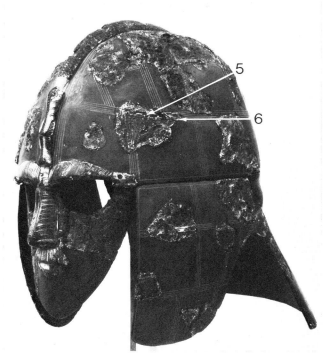

FIGURE 171 The helmet: sampling positions on the fluted dividing strips.

[1] Maryon 1947, 137–44.

(tin oxide, SnO_2). Microscopic examination has revealed slight traces of an ordered structure in the white material, although the indications are so faint that it is impossible to determine whether it represents a 'ghost' dendritic pattern. A surface sample from the same strip (fig. 171, 6) was shown by X-ray diffraction analysis to consist mainly of ϵ-copper/tin compound (Cu_3Sn) and under the microscope the surface has the apearance of being distinct from the main body of the strip. The two broader fluted strips which run from front to back of the helmet on either side of the crest show remains of gilding and emission spectrographic analysis of a sample from the surface of one of these strips (fig. 172, 7) shows it to contain mercury, suggesting that the gilding was carried out by the fire-gilding process.

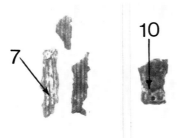

FIGURE 172 The helmet: sampling positions on a fluted strip flanking the crest and on the rear crest tang.

These observations are apparently mutually incompatible because on the one hand the presence of tin oxide as a major component of the corroded strip suggests that the original metal was tin, or at least a very high tin/copper alloy,[1] the colour of which would have been white, and on the other hand the apparent presence of ϵ-copper/tin on the surface of these strips suggests instead that the surface of a bronze alloy containing at least 62% of copper had been coated with tin and heated (see above). Furthermore as pure tin melts at 232 °C and the fire-gilding process requires a temperature of at least 360 °C, any tin alloy which was gilded by this method would have to contain at least 20% of copper in order to raise the melting point of the alloy above this latter temperature. Tin/copper alloys remain white in colour up to about 75% copper and 25% tin.

Similar fluted strips occur on the sceptre where they are made of bronze and the method of manufacturing was probably by swageing, but in this case, if the strips were of high tin alloy throughout,

swageing would be impossible as copper/tin alloys containing more than 20% of tin are very brittle. The edges of the helmet are bound with a U-shaped metal channel held in place by swaged clips. Microscopic examination of these suggests that they are made of a copper alloy and analysis by emission spectrography of a sample from a fragment of the U-shaped channelling (fig. 173) indicates that it contains both

FIGURE 173 The helmet: details and sampling positions on U-shaped rim binding.

zinc and tin (fig. 173, 8). It was impossible to obtain a sample of this edging channel for a full quantitative analysis, but it was possible to obtain semi-quantitative figures from a very small sample taken from the same place, by atomic absorption spectrophotometry. The results indicate that the alloy consists of about 70% of copper and 20% of zinc with small amounts of tin and lead and a trace of silver. It is therefore best described as a brass.

The crest

The crest consists of a D-shaped iron tube inlaid with corroded metallic wires, a sample of which was identified by X-ray diffraction analysis as mainly silver chloride, indicating that the original wires were made of silver. At the end of the crest at the

[1] But see also p. 111, n. 1.

back of the helmet is a tang in which there are two rivet holes. On this tang there are two patches of a pale coloured material (fig. 172, 10) which were shown by X-ray diffraction analysis to be mainly cassiterite (tin oxide, SnO_2). Microscopic examination shows that traces of a dendritic structure remain in this white material, proving that it was originally cast, and it seems likely that it was cast in a high tin bronze. Traces of gilding occur on one of these patches of corroded tin alloy.

Associated with the helmet is a fragmentary animal snout consisting of a similar white material with a gilded surface. Analysis of the white material by emission spectrography showed that the main metallic element present is tin and X-ray diffraction analysis proved that the tin is present as cassiterite (SnO_2). Microscopic examination showed a residual dendritic structure to be present in this white material, proving that it was originally cast, probably in a high tin alloy.[1] In this respect the structure and composition of this fragmentary snout are identical with the traces of white material on the rear end of the crest. The gilded surface layer of the snout has been shown by emission spectrographic analysis to contain mercury. If the gold here was applied by the fire-gilding process, it seems probable, for the reasons explained above, that the snout was cast in a tin/copper alloy containing at least 20% of copper.

The method by which the iron crest was constructed and attached to the helmet cannot be determined scientifically. No solder has been detected. It is possible that the crest was made slightly too small and that it was heated until large enough to fit on and shrunk into position on cooling. Whatever method was used it cannot have been forged to the skull cap as a complete unit because the crest is a hollow D-shaped tube and hammering would have not only damaged the grooves for the inlay but flattened the hollow section. The flat base strip, however, could have been forged on and the U-shaped piece added later.

The two animal heads at the front of the helmet

The animal head at the front of the crest is similar in construction to that between the eyebrows. Both are of bronze, and they were probably cast. The surface is partially gilded, and the detection by emission spectrographic analysis of mercury in the gold (fig. 175 a, 11) suggests that this was applied by

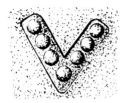

FIGURE 174 The helmet: impression of a punch used on a gilded bronze dragon head. (Scale: approx. 10/1)

the fire-gilding technique. Both animal heads have a central strip, running from the back of the head to the tip of the snout, which is not gilded, but which is decorated with V-shaped punch marks. The punch was decorated with seven circular depressions, so that these V-shaped marks contain seven pellets (fig. 174). This punch-marked ungilded strip is tarnished to a dark colour, but when freshly cleaned it is white. A sample from its surface was analysed by X-ray diffraction (fig. 175 a, 13) and found to be chiefly a copper/tin alloy with some cuprite (Cu_2O). This analysis suggests that the central strips down these two animal heads had been tinned and then heated in a reducing atmosphere to form a hard white alloy before the application of gilding to the areas adjacent to the strip. Within the depressions of the V-shaped punch marks the tinning retains its white colour. A sample from one of the punch marks was analysed by X-ray fluorescence in the scanning electron microscope; the main elements detected were tin and copper.

The eyebrows

The method of construction of the eyebrows cannot be determined with certainty. Both the terminal animal heads are gilded, but the gilding of the right one is reddish in colour while that of the shorter left one is yellowish. Emission spectrographic analysis (fig. 175 b, c, 14 and 15) shows that mercury is present in the gilding on both. The main part of the right eyebrow is bronze, now corroded, which has been inlaid with wires of a white metal to give a striped effect. This white metal was identified as silver by X-ray diffraction analysis (fig. 175 b, 16). Below the inlaid wires is a groove which now contains twelve roughly square garnets, although originally there were probably twenty-one. There is now no evidence of cloisonné walls between the garnets. The lower edge of the eyebrow, which forms the top

[1] But see also p. 111, n. 1.

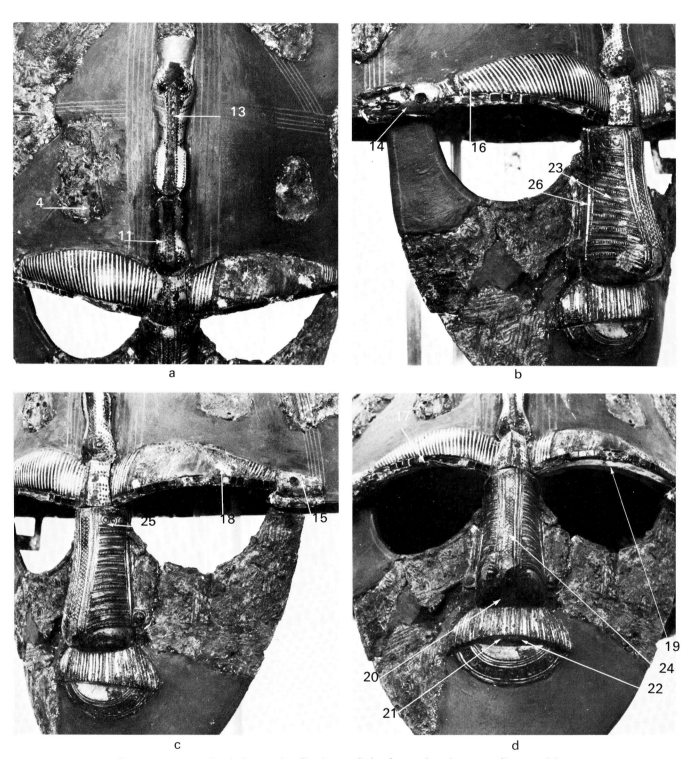

a

b

c

d

FIGURE 175   The helmet: (*a–d*) views of the front showing sampling positions.

edge of the eyehole in the helmet, is gilded and emission spectrographic analysis of a sample (fig. 175 *d*, 17) from this gilding showed that mercury is absent, hence the gilding cannot have been applied by the mercury-gilding technique.

The main part of the left eyebrow is different in appearance from the right one. At its two ends are areas of corroded bronze inlaid with silver wires. However the silver wires are missing from the centre of the eyebrow, though vertical marks remain. The corrosion products which are visible are not the normal cuprite and malachite which would indicate that the metal was originally made of bronze, but are white in appearance. X-ray diffraction analysis has shown that this white material is principally cassiterite (tin oxide) (fig. 175 *c*, 18) and a microscopic examination has revealed the presence of residual dendrites in it showing that it was originally a cast alloy. The presence of this tin corrosion product is very difficult to interpret. It may result from an ancient repair using an alloy differing from the original bronze but the same.product has also been found in analyses of the shield (dragon, p. 103; hemispherical bosses, p. 112/3 and peripheral animal heads, p. 110/1), where evidence for repair is much less certain.[1]

The underside of the left eyebrow is gilded and the gilding was shown by emission spectrographic analysis to contain mercury (fig. 175 *d*, 19). This should be compared with the other eyebrow on which the similar gilding did not contain mercury. Microscopic examination of the gilding of the underside of the eyebrows and of the terminal animal heads reveals none of the features which are characteristic of mercury-gilding.[2] As the physical appearance of these four areas of gilding is very similar apart from the differences in colour, it seems likely that all of them were gilded with gold leaf (cf. pp. 111 and 113.

Along the lower edge of the proper left eyebrow is a groove now containing fifteen garnets out of a likely original total of twenty-two. The garnets in the two eyebrows have been numbered as shown in figure 176. Two red forms of garnet are known, almandine ($Fe_3Al_2(SiO_4)_3$) and pyrope ($Mg_3Al_2(SiO_4)_3$) and both are commonly found in jewellery. These formulae represent the 'pure' or 'ideal' compositions of the minerals, but in nature they are always mixed, having a formula represented by $Fe_x Mg_{3-x} Al_2(SiO_4)_3$. The two types can be dis-

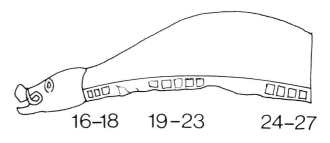

Left eyebrow

Right eyebrow

FIGURE 176   The helmet: surviving garnet inlays in the eyebrows. (Scale: 1/1)

tinguished by measurement of the density or the refractive index (RI), or by chemical or X-ray diffraction analysis. The RI of pyrope is in the range 1·714 to 1·760 and that of almandine 1·760 to 1·830. The measurement of refractive index is difficult for mounted stones, and in the case of the eyebrow garnets an identification was made by observing the absorption spectrum of reflected plane polarised light with a direct vision spectroscope mounted on a Vickers projection microscope.

All the stones in the left eyebrow (1–15) were shown to be almandine and a similar result was obtained with stones 16–25 of the right eyebrow. Numbers 26 and 27 are probably almandine, but the absorption spectrum was very faint and so the identification should be regarded as tentative. The identification as almandine was confirmed by X-ray diffraction analysis for garnet numbers 1 and 24. The stones were examined under a binocular microscope. Stones 19, 20, 21, 23 and 24 in the right eyebrow are backed with a stamped gold foil but none of the stones in the left eyebrow now has a stamped foil backing.

[1] P. 111, n. 1.

[2] Lins and Oddy 1975.

The nose, moustache and mouth

X-ray diffraction analyses of samples from inside one of the nostril holes and from a damaged area on the upper lip (fig. 175 d, 20 and 21) were shown to consist essentially of cuprite, but in another damaged area of the upper lip the body material of the nose was found to be soft and white in colour. An X-ray diffraction analysis (fig. 175 d, 22) showed that it consisted chiefly of cassiterite containing some cuprite. The major part of the surface of this part of the mask is gilded and emission spectroscopic analysis has shown that the gold contained mercury and was probably applied by the fire-gilding technique (fig. 175 b, 23).

Down the ridge of the nose are strips of triangular punch marks which are inlaid with a white metal, shown by X-ray diffraction analysis to be silver (fig. 175 d, 24). Similar triangular inlays, together with circles and dots are located in a strip on either side of the bridge of the nose and on the lower lip; these also were shown to be silver by X-ray diffraction analysis (fig. 175 c, 25). The metal of which these inlays are made is compact and is not corroded. In view of its condition it must be interpreted as a metallic inlay and not as niello which has subsequently been reduced to silver metal.

This silver is inlaid into a surface which was originally coated with a white metal. Traces of this surface layer are clearly visible under the microscope and a sample was analysed by X-ray fluorescence in the scanning electron microscope when the main elements detected were tin, copper and zinc. An X-ray diffraction analysis suggested that the sample consisted of a copper/tin alloy containing 25 % of tin. It can be concluded that the silver was inlaid into a tinned strip.

Down either side of the nose is a plain border coated with a white metal which was also shown by X-ray diffraction analysis (fig. 175 b, 26) to be a copper/tin alloy containing approximately 25 % of tin. The fluted strips running down either side of the nose on the face mask are similar to the strips which separate the decorative panels. They were not gilded.

The helmet lining

The skull cap was examined to determine why the corrosion on the inside is very black and different from that on the outside. The black material gives the appearance of being a distinct layer, but under the microscope no structure reminiscent of leather or textile is visible. In places where blisters of the black layer are fractured, an orientated structure is visible across the layer suggesting that it is the product of a very slow corrosion process. X-ray diffraction and analysis of a sample from this layer showed that it contains an amorphous iron compound.

Acknowledgements. We would like to acknowledge the assistance of M. R. Cowell, P. T. Craddock and N. D. Meeks, who carried out some of the experimental work.

CHAPTER IV

THE MAILCOAT

—————⟫✦⟪—————

1. *Introduction and primary account of the discovery*

PHILLIPS describes the discovery thus:

'At the bottom of the south-west part of the deposit was a scattered mass of pieces of rusted iron which were the remains of a coat of mail. Its condition was interesting evidence of the state of the deposit as a whole at the time of the fall of the roof. It has already been stated that there is reason to believe that the burial chamber held up a long time after the completion of the barrow. It is unlikely that chain armour would have reached a glassy condition in which it readily broke into many pieces without the lapse of many years.'[1]

2. *Description and discussion*

Dimensions

Length of rusted ring mass	60·0 cm
Greatest width	30·0 cm
Maximum thickness of rusted ring mass	10·5 cm
Minimum thickness of rusted ring mass	1·5 cm
Original ring-width, estimated (one size only apparent)	0·8 cm

Weight of whole remains in present condition   11·23 kg

The heavily oxidised lumps of small interlocked rings which are thought to be the remains of a mailcoat lay beneath the Anastasius dish directly on the wooden floor of the burial chamber (perhaps separated from it by a linen cloth)[2] as shown in figure 177.[3] It lay as a coherent though fractured whole, which projected at a low level from beneath the western edge of the Anastasius dish. A considerable variety of textiles and tapes was represented by iron oxide replacements of their fibres on its upper surface, on the exposed western edge and in the deep groove on the underside.[4] There were also extensive remains of leather, thought by the excavators to belong to a bag. Neither textile nor leather can be shown to have an integral connection with the

---

[1] Phillips 1940a, 173; see *Sutton Hoo*, Vol. I, fig. 148 for a photograph of the mailcoat *in situ*.
[2] *Sutton Hoo*, Vol. I, 213–14 and 472, 474.

[3] Cf. *Sutton Hoo*, Vol. I, figs. 141 and 354.
[4] For a fuller discussion see *Sutton Hoo*, Vol. I, 461 ff., figs. 354, 359 and 360–1.

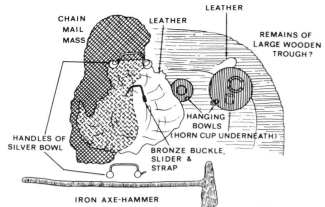

CHAIN MAIL MASS

LEATHER

LEATHER

REMAINS OF LARGE WOODEN TROUGH?

HANDLES OF SILVER BOWL

HANGING BOWLS (HORN CUP UNDERNEATH)

BRONZE BUCKLE, SLIDER & STRAP

IRON AXE-HAMMER

FIGURE 177 Plan of the second layer of the deposit beneath the Anastasius dish showing the position of the mailcoat in relation to the adjacent finds. The 'wooden trough' is probably part of the burial chamber floor.

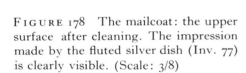

FIGURE 178 The mailcoat: the upper surface after cleaning. The impression made by the fluted silver dish (Inv. 77) is clearly visible. (Scale: 3/8)

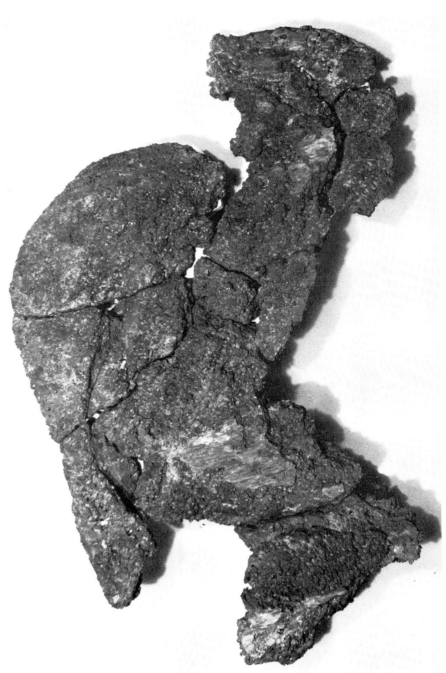

mailcoat, although, as discussed below, two of the textiles might possibly have had a connection.

The quantity and bulk of mail suggests that this was a full-size coat or shirt, probably of knee length. There is nothing either in variation in the size of rings or from the physical disposition of the remains to suggest that the corroded mass includes the remains of more than a single garment, or more than one item of mail construction. There is far too much of it to represent a protective curtain for neck and face, such as are associated with helmets in the Vendel and Valsgärde boat-graves,[1] or a mail coif of the kind seen in use in the Bayeux Tapestry and (coincidentally) suggested by the hair-treatment of one of the heads on the Sutton Hoo sceptre.[2]

Figure 178 is a photograph of the mass of rusted links, showing the upper surface and a detail of one edge. Figure 177 reproduces a redrawn section of the field plan showing the outlines of the mail lump as drawn by Stuart Piggott.[3] Figure 178 is similarly aligned with the long axis vertical on the page. This is as the mailcoat lay in the ground with its long axis north/south, at right-angles across the keel-line.

FIGURE 179 The mailcoat: detail of one of
the smaller fragments, showing individual
links. (Scale: slightly under 1/1)

The mass of rusted mail (figs. 178–80) is made up of nine or ten smaller lumps. There are some twenty lesser fragments kept loose in reserve from the main mass, and some of these are illustrated in the radiograph, figure 180. The rusted mass is wholly non-magnetic, indicating the absence of metal and showing that the process of rusting or oxidisation has proceeded to finality.

[1] Arwidsson 1934, 243 ff.; Thordeman 1941, figs. 4, 5 (here figs. 182a and b); Arwidsson 1954, Abb. 10, 12. The mail curtains in the Swedish boat-graves are associated with helmets and in the large group of helmets known as *Spangenhelme* they are a normal feature. The Sutton Hoo helmet lay at the opposite end of the burial deposit from the mail and in any case had no mail-curtain, the protective function here being performed by neck-guard, face-mask and cheek-pieces.
[2] Head B.3, fig. 239. For coifs see Thordeman 1939, 98 ff.
[3] *Sutton Hoo*, Vol. I, 141, plan 6.

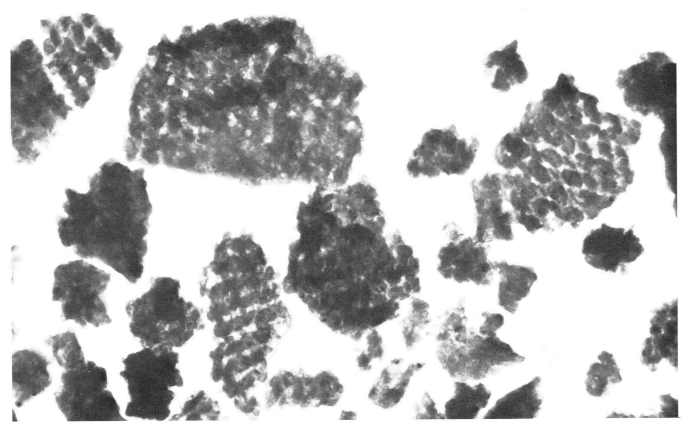

FIGURE 180 The mailcoat: radiograph of a selection of loose fragments showing interlocking rows of links. (Scale: 1/1)

The mailcoat appears to have been folded a number of times, the longest dimension of the resultant mass being now 60 cm. It appears to have been pushed out of alignment and squashed up at one end, the end now 10·5 cm thick. If straightened the mass would be some 65 cm in length. This dimension if covering the distance from neck to hem would reach well down the hips of a six foot man. No edges can be detected, however, so that this 60–65 cm need not give the maximum length of the garment. The 10·5 cm thickness at the north end could conceal extra length. The coat could also equally have been folded lengthways, with the skirt turned upwards again and the sleeves folded in at the other end, partly accounting for the additional thicknesses at each end. The 60–65 cm length, on the other hand, may seem too great to represent the width of a mailcoat.

The rough curve now described by the remains (fig. 178) is probably a reflection of the pressures caused by the forcing down on to the folded but flexible mail and the textiles above it of the rounded shape and circular base-ring of the fluted silver bowl, Inv. no. 77.[1] The marks of the base-ring and the flutings of the bowl can be clearly seen in the remains of leather on the upper surface of the mail.

[1] The silver is described in detail in *Sutton Hoo*, Vol. III.

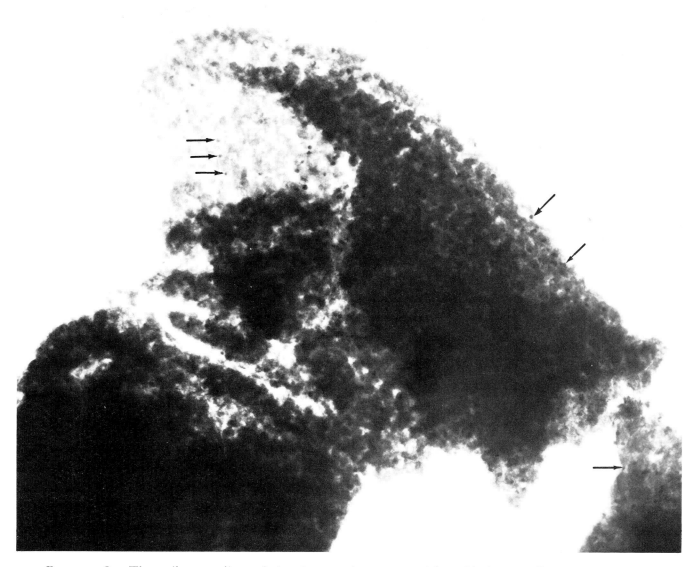

FIGURE 181   The mailcoat: radiograph showing a random pattern of dense black spots, illustrated by arrows; the black spots have been shown by analysis to be the remains of tiny copper rivets. (Scale: 1/1)

No recognisable feature, such as a finished edge, is visible. The right-hand side in figure 178, 1·5 cm thick, appears to represent a single fold of a double thickness of mail; elsewhere the thickness varies, the lower portion and end in figure 178 being 10·5 cm thick and the top end, where again a fold can be seen, 3 cm. A stereo-radiograph has failed to reveal folds in the mail shirt; revelation by radiography of folds might have enabled the size and construction of the coat to be more accurately ascertained. Radiography has revealed no buckles or other metal fitments that could have been connected with the mailcoat, perhaps belonging to a belt. It does, however, clearly show, contrary to previously published statements,[1] that the mail was made of

[1] E.g. Sir James Mann, referring to riveting of mail as universal in the west, says the 'only exception in Europe' is the mail shirt found at Sutton Hoo. 'Minute examination has shown that in this case the ends of the rings are merely butted together as

236

alternate rows of welded or forged links and of riveted links. Hundreds of faint black spots can be seen on the radiographs, indicating denser points in the oxide (figs. 180, 181). Laboratory examination of some of these occurrences has shown that the dense points are probably corroded copper (App., p. 240). The pattern can be distinguished in figure 180, where the riveting of alternate rows of links can be clearly seen. Several well-preserved rings were sectioned, but the total corrosion of the iron makes it impossible to establish the original ring thickness.

DISCUSSION

No single find of mail, however small or fragmentary appears to have been recorded from any pagan Anglo-Saxon grave or context.[1] Nevertheless, mailcoats are a consistent phenomenon in Germanic contexts. They range from the Early Iron Age examples with riveted links, claimed to have been provided on the scale of one for each crew member in the Hjortspring (Als) boat,[2] to the complete shirt of mail that survives with fragments of others from Vimose (Fyn).[3] Other examples include those of the Roman Iron Age from Gammertingen, Bavaria,[4] and Gränby in Uppland, Sweden,[5] throughout Vendel period archaeology (helmet-curtains and body armour from Vendel and Valsgärde); remains from Gotland, where a *Spangenhelm* has been found, and the Fullerö site close to Valsgärde, where Greta Arwidsson thought she could recognise, in some rather crude fragments of mail, the first northern attempts at native manufacture. The Valsgärde and Vendel helmet-curtains are certainly, like the helmets they serve, locally made, as are the fine complete coat, unfortunately folded into a rusty mass of links, together with separate fragments showing riveted links of varying sizes, from the Viking town defences of Birka.[6] In addition we have the standard use of mail for defensive curtains for the *Spangenhelme* group; graphic representations in Vendel art (fig. 147) and, clearly intended as a mailcoat, a depiction in a combat scene from Germanic mythology on the Franks Casket of *c.* A.D. 700 (fig. 183). All these, so far as we can interpret some of the graphic versions, are knee-length coats with short sleeves.

Care has to be taken before we can positively identify mail in graphic representations. The texturing of the coat of the fallen warrior of design 2 of the Sutton Hoo helmet, for example, strongly suggests mail. The bronze figural dies from Torslunda, Öland,

---

in much mail of Oriental origin . . . Rings joined in this way could be easily torn apart and the only excuse for this weak construction is that it is easier and quicker to make' (Mann, in Stenton 1957, 62). This is a good illustration of the obligation of thorough examination before publication and the danger of premature pronouncements. Experience of the Sutton Hoo burial deposit, moreover, makes it clear that only the very best in craftsmanship is represented in it. Inferior workmanship would be wholly out of place. The idea that the Sutton Hoo mailcoat was composed of links with butted joints had been formulated by the Research Laboratory as a result of visual examination, and only recent radiography has disclosed the true construction.

[1] The sole possible instance cited by Baldwin Brown, from the Benty Grange tumulus (Baldwin Brown 1915, 194), is incorrectly identified (Bruce-Mitford 1974, 226–7 and 250, n. 6).
[2] Apart from the Hjortspring publication itself (Rosenberg 1937), see Thordeman 1941, 96; Cederlöf 1955, 155.
[3] Thordeman 1941, 97, fig. 9.
[4] In the Pierpont Morgan Collection, New York; Gröbbels 1905, 132–3.
[5] Arwidsson 1934, 256 and fig. 12.
[6] Mann 1957, figs. 34, 38.

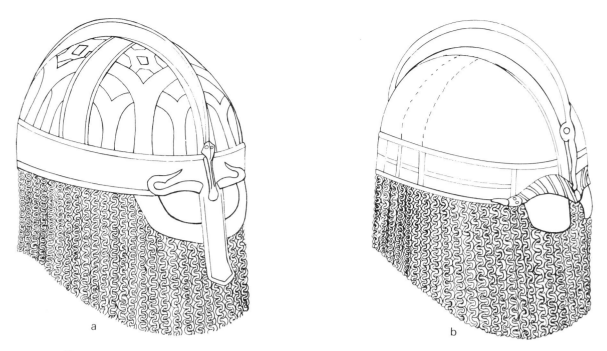

FIGURE 182 (*a*) Helmet from Vendel 12 and (*b*) helmet from Valsgärde 6, showing the use of mail as protective curtains. (After Thordeman 1941)

however (fig. 156), show this surface treatment used as no more than a texture convention for the trousers of the man holding a beast by a rope, and used equally, without any differentiation, for the hair and heads of the humans and animals. The same is found in the version of the scene of the man with roped beast above the left eyebrow on the Vendel 12 helmet, where this pellet-like convention is seen in the trousers or kilt of the man to the right of the panel, who is bare from the waist up, like the man leading the animal in figure 156*c*. The fallen warrior in design 2 on the Sutton Hoo helmet is not wearing mail, but a coat with edgings and wrapover style like that seen in figures 140 and 155. The true mail shirt, on the other hand,

FIGURE 183 Mailcoated and helmeted warriors from the Franks Casket. (British Museum)

238

is seen in examples on the Vendel 14 helmet (fig. 147), in particular in the line of walking warriors; here the actual rings are shown and the garment is seen to be a one-piece shirt-like affair closed up to the neck.

Apart from the relative frequency of the occurrence of mail in the Vendel and Valsgärde boat-burials, relevant references are to be found in *Beowulf*. Although the poetic descriptions are general, expressions such as 'befongen frēawrāsnum' (encircled with lordly chains—line 1041, with reference to a helmet), and references to the 'tangled war-net' (line 552), 'armour of net-like cunning linked by the smith' (lines 405–6), and 'the riveted shirt of mail' (line 1505), are sufficient to indicate the use of mail in Scandinavian aristocratic warrior circles at this period.

REPORT ON SCIENTIFIC EXAMINATION OF FRAGMENTS OF MAILCOAT

by

W. A. ODDY and A. E. A. WERNER

All the fragments of mail were radiographed. This failed to reveal the presence of any buckles or other fittings. A stereo-pair of radiographs was made on one fragment, but this failed to reveal folds in the mail.

Some dense spots were visible on the radiographs of several pieces. These were tentatively identified as rivets on some links. In order to prove this a small fragment was mounted in resin for metallographic examination. A cross-section was ground with frequent examination of the polished surface but the mail was found to be completely corroded. The corrosion products were identified by X-ray diffraction as a hydroxy iron oxide known as goethite. Green spots were observed in the body of the mail. These spots resembled the normal corrosion products of copper or bronze and careful examination revealed the presence of traces of uncorroded metal among the green corrosion products. One of the spots was examined by the LMl Laser Microanalyser (by the firm of C.Z. Scientific Instruments Ltd). The spot was found to be mainly copper, containing lesser quantities of iron, lead, silver, silicon, magnesium and calcium. These elements are mostly derived from the soil and the rivets were probably made of copper containing small amounts of lead and silver.

Because of the totally corroded state of the mail it was not possible to estimate link-size from the metallographic cross-section.

It can be concluded that some links in the Sutton Hoo mailcoat were fastened with copper rivets.

June 1969

CHAPTER V

SPEARS AND ANGONS

———————⫸◆⫷———————

1. *Introduction*

T H E H E A D S of five spears (inv. 101–5) with blades and of three barbed throwing-spears (angons: Inv. 98–100) lay rusted together immediately north of the Coptic bowl (fig. 184). The wooden shafts had disappeared but remains of wood survive in several sockets (e.g. spears 2 and 3, and angons 1–3). The wood remains are substantially mineralised but identification has proved possible in the case of one of the spears and one of the angons (Inv. 103 and 98). In both cases the wood is ash.[1] A sixth bladed spear-head (Inv. 97) lay parallel with the sword and with the keel-line, beside the body-space. No trace of a shaft or of wood or of a ferrule associated with this spear appears to have survived. This spear-head has until now been incorrectly identified as a scramasax, and in *Sutton Hoo*, Volume I appears as such both in the Inventory and in the burial deposit plan, figure 111.

The three iron angon-heads had been thrust through the drop-handle on the north or inner side of the Coptic bowl (fig. 185). One of them (Inv. 99) was firmly attached to the side of the bowl by an iron corrosion development, or rust formation. This angon-head was detached from the bowl in the Research Laboratory in the British Museum in 1939, leaving a circular stain on the side of the bowl. The rust formation remains attached to the angon-head. It shows a flat circular outer surface with a diameter of 2·2 cm (the size of a 5p piece). If this angon-head is repositioned in relation to the Coptic bowl, by placing the rust formation against the stain on the bowl, the exact lie of all the spears and angons as they were found in 1939 can be reconstituted, since the other two angon-heads, two spear-heads and the socket of a third remain attached to the first angon-head by corrosion. The remaining spear-heads can then be related to these from plans and photographs.

Several supposed iron ferrules, or ferrule-tips, were found in the burial chamber. They are not marked on Stuart Piggott's field plans (Plans 1–3) nor on the two composite tracings of the whole deposit subsequently prepared by Piggott (Plans 7 and 8).[2] Three 'ferrules' (Inv. 106–8) are, however, shown by Phillips on Plan 9.[3]

---

[1] See Appendix (p. 272) for the report by Dr David Cutler of the Jodrell Laboratory, Kew Gardens. In the case of Inv. 101 the socket is incomplete and no wood remains survive.

[2] For details of these plans see *Sutton Hoo*, Vol. I, 140–2.

[3] Phillips 1940a, pl. xxxvii; *Sutton Hoo*, Vol. I, 142.

FIGURE 184 The complex of spears and angons *in situ* from the north. The spears are numbered in sequence from 1 to 4 (Inv. 101–104) to distinguish them from the angons (Inv. 98, 99, and 100). Spears 5 and 6 (Inv. 105, 97) are not visible on this photograph. (Photo: O. G. S. Crawford)

The 30 cm long 'wood and iron object', of uncertain use, found in 1967 (Inv. 211)[1] may represent another, with shaft-wood still attached. The identification in this instance of the associated wood as ash supports the possibility that this object is part of a spear.[2] Another apparent ferrule (Inv. 271) was found in the 1967–8 excavation of the 1939 dump. The 'ferrules', and their possible relationships to the spears and angons, are discussed below (pp. 267-71). One of the five supposed ferrules, Inv. 108, which has a blunt end and does not taper, may not be a ferrule. If it is, it is of unorthodox form.

Figure 186 shows the layout of the spears as uncovered, and the positions of the four ferrules, or possible ferrules, whose locations were recorded. The three angons and four out of the six spears may be assumed to have been laid east–west, with their heads near the west end wall of the chamber, their shafts running more or less parallel

[1] *Sutton Hoo*, Vol. I, fig. 199; here fig. 205.   [2] See p. 268 below and Appendix, p. 272.

FIGURE 185   The complex of spears and angons *in situ* from the north-east. (Photo: O. G. S. Crawford)

with the keel-line, and passing just south of the sixth spear (Inv. 97, the former scramasax) on the right side of a presumed recumbent body on its back. One of the spears can never have occupied this position. It must have been laid from the outset transversely across the end of the chamber. This is spear no. 4 (Inv. 104; fig. 190). It lay at a low level, anchored in position by the Coptic bowl and by the shaft of spear no. 5 (Inv. 105) and the blade of spear no. 2 (Inv. 102). Spear no. 3 (Inv. 103), the only spear-head which, as found, still lay parallel with the keel-line, apparently undisturbed, must have been held down and kept in position by the shaft of spear no. 4, which crossed its blade at right-angles. No ferrule that might have belonged to spear no. 4 is recorded from the area in the north-west corner of the burial chamber, near the spike of the iron stand, where it would be expected to have lain had there been one.

In considering the following account of the spears and angons allowance must be made for the condition in which they have survived. All are very heavily corroded, consequently exact dimensions, except perhaps as to length, cannot be given, and outlines, as figures 187 to 199 indicate, tend to be masked or obscured. Radiography,

243

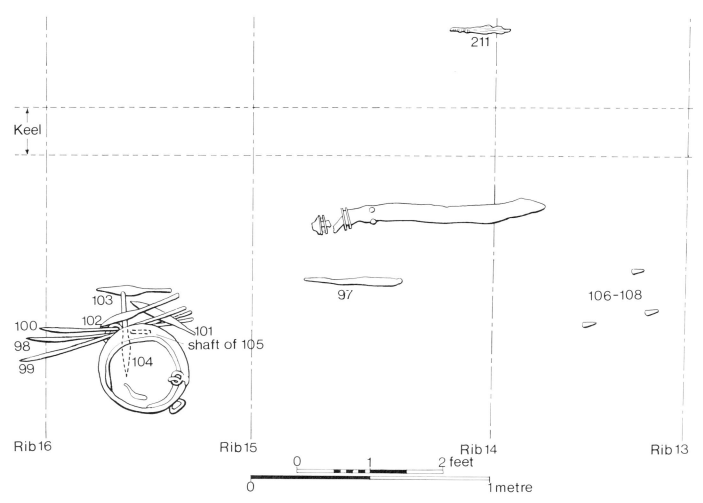

Keel

211

103
100
102
98 101
99 shaft of 105
104

97

106-108

Rib 16   Rib 15   Rib 14   Rib 13

0   1   2 feet

0   1 metre

FIGURE 186   The complex of the six spears, three angons, and four possible ferrules. Relative positions within the burial deposit.

which has been systematically applied to all the spear-heads, helps in arriving at the original profile in some cases, but not in all; for each the most revealing of several radiographs taken has been chosen for illustration. The sections given in the drawings (e.g. fig. 187 *b*) are those of the corroded object, not the section of the original spear as it was in use. Thickness of surface corrosion varies and is difficult to assess: in some cases it seems minimal. In the reconstruction drawings (figs. 196 and 200) an attempt has been made to assess these factors and to give a reliable statement of the original size and shape of the individual pieces in this important closed group of weapons. Miss M. O. Miller, the Museum's senior illustrator, and I have discussed each spear and its radiographs in detail and we are in agreement that the resultant reconstruction drawings represent the best estimate we can give.

A *corpus* of Anglo-Saxon spears, covering between three and four thousand examples ascribed to the pagan period, with over three thousand measured drawings, has recently been compiled by Dr Michael Swanton.[1] The Sutton Hoo spears can thus be seen in the full context of Anglo-Saxon material.

[1] Swanton 1973; see also Swanton 1974 *a*.

244

The bladed spears are described first, followed by the barbed spears, or angons; and finally the 'ferrules' are described.

2. *The spears*

Spear no. 1 (Inv. 101; fig. 187)

Incomplete, the end of the socket and a small fragment from the tip of the blade is missing.

Dimensions

Length, in present state	38·5 cm
Length of blade portion read as	33·0 cm
Width of blade	3·7 cm
Width of top of stem where blade begins to develop	1·5 cm
Diameter of socket where broken off	1·5 cm
Suggested original length of spear-head	46·5 cm

Some 0·5 cm appears to be missing at the tip of the blade. The length of socket that is missing cannot be stated with confidence. The closest parallel to Inv. 101 appears to be a complete spear-head in the British Museum from Kempston, Bedfordshire (BM 91, 6–24, 82; Swanton 1973, fig. 27 c). This is virtually identical in form to Inv. 101; its overall length is 42·5 cm. If this spear can be taken as a guide, the original length of stem and socket of Inv. 101 could have been 13 cm; with the 0·5 cm added at the tip, an overall length of 46·5 cm, as conjecturally restored in figure 187 d.

The broken end of the surviving stem is covered on one side with wood. On its opposite side the edge of the surviving stem is broken away, exposing the hollow interior of the top of the socket. This break is no indication that the socket was split, though the break could have coincided with the tip of a split, the existence of which would thus be concealed if it had reached up as far as this, as it could well have done. The close parallel to Inv. 101 from Kempston has a welded socket, but this does not make it possible to deduce the type of socket used for Inv. 101, as in two otherwise virtually identical Sutton Hoo spears (nos. 2 and 5, Inv. 102, 105) one has a split socket, the other a welded socket.

From a stem-width of 1·5 cm at the head of the socket the blade widens over a length of some 5 cm to a width of 3·7 cm, thus developing to its widest point with some gradualness, and cannot be classified as of any definitely angular form, although there is a distinct, unobtrusive angularity. From the point at which maximum width is reached the sides of the blade run parallel for a distance of 10 cm and the blade then tapers to a pronounced point (fig. 187 d).

Spear no. 2 (Inv. 102; fig. 188)

Complete spear-head, but with the stem largely disintegrated between the tip of the socket-split and the base of the blade.

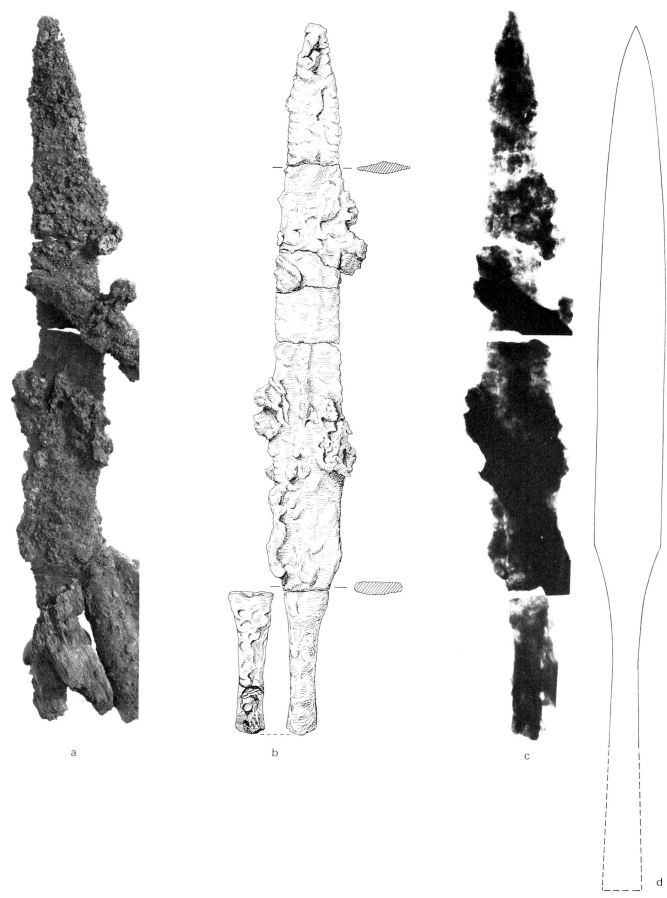

FIGURE 187 Spear no. 1 (Inv. 101): (*a*) photograph in present state after conservation; (*b*) drawing; (*c*) radiograph; (*d*) reconstruction drawing based on radiographic evidence. (Scale: 1/2)

246

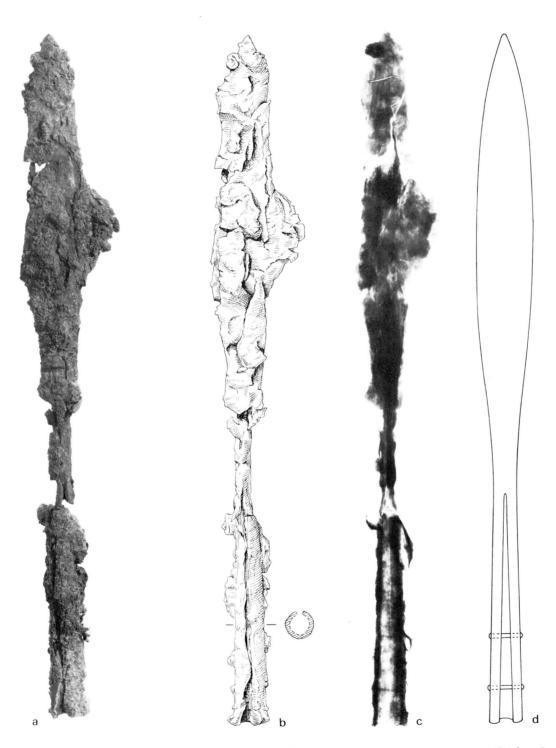

FIGURE 188 Spear no. 2 (Inv. 102): (*a*) photograph in present state after conservation; (*b*) drawing; (*c*) radiograph and (*d*) reconstruction drawing based on radiographic evidence. (Scale: 1/2)

Length	37·5 cm
Length of blade, estimated	23·5 cm
Length of socket and stem	14·0 cm
Length of socket-split	12·5 cm
Width of blade	3·0 cm
Diameter, exterior, at mouth of socket (approx.)	1·8 cm
Narrowest point of stem (approx.)	1·2 cm

Spear-head with leaf-shaped blade and split socket. The length of the blade (from the tip to the point where expansion from the stem can first be detected) approaches twice the length of socket and stem (23·5 cm to 14 cm). The exact point at which the blade begins to develop is a matter of judgement; but at all events the blade is considerably longer than its socket and shank, not less, as Swanton's drawing (his fig. 56, *a*) suggests. The maximum width of the blade is at its middle. The radiograph (fig. 188 *c*) shows two rivet-shanks crossing the socket 2 and 5 cm respectively up from its mouth. The spear-head is probably to be classed with Swanton's D2 group as he suggests, but it is in some ways not unlike his C2 group.[1] It lacks the elongation of blade that is characteristic of his class C3.

Spear no. 3 (Inv. 103; fig. 189)

Complete spear-head with small projection of wood from the socket.

Dimensions

Length (excluding wood projection)	31·5 cm
Length of socket	10·5 cm
Length of blade	21·0 cm
Width	4·0 cm
Width of socket mouth (estimated original)	1·9 cm
Width of socket or stem at narrowest point	1·0 cm

The socket is split. The split extends for some 6–7 cm up the socket. The radiograph (fig. 189 *c*) shows the hollow socket itself to extend for 8·7 cm. It is filled with mineralised wood, which has been identified as ash (App. p. 272 below). The radiograph reveals one rivet crossing the socket at a point 1·7 cm up from its opening; there is perhaps a suggestion of a second at 7·2 cm from the socket mouth. The blade is of an elegant leaf-shaped type, with no suggestion of angularity, and there is a prominent midrib on both faces. The midrib does not appear as a development into the blade of the tapering tube of the socket but is a solid raised central reinforcing or decorative fillet of uniform height and width from end to end of the blade.

The centre of gravity of the blade is below the middle point (fig. 189 *d*) and the taper to the point is long and elegant. The point is very sharp. The socket opening is not quite circular, being 19×17 mm. The split of the socket occurs in one of the slightly flattened sides. The slight flattening is probably accidental, caused by pressure

---

[1] Swanton 1973, fig. 66 and fig. 11, *a*.

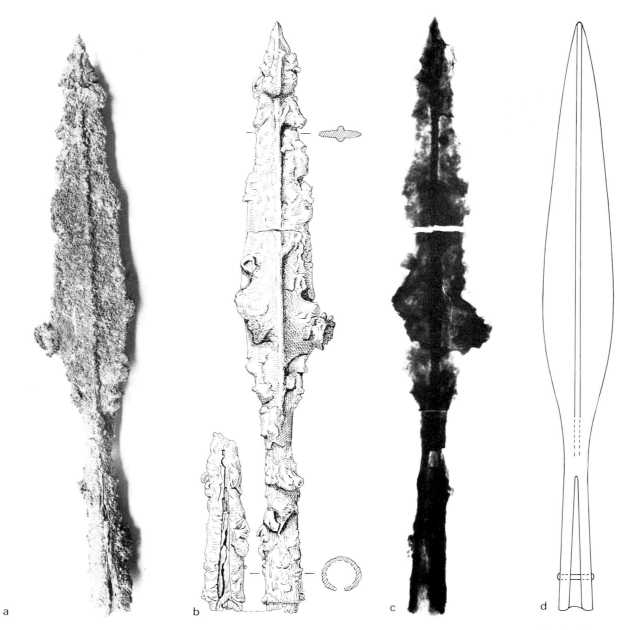

FIGURE 189 Spear no. 3 (Inv. 103): (*a*) photograph in present state after conservation; (*b*) drawing;
(*c*) radiograph and (*d*) reconstruction drawing based on radiographic evidence. (Scale: 1/2)

when the chamber collapsed. This spear-head seems to resemble Swanton's types B2
and C2 in general form.

Spear no. 4 (Inv. 104; figs. 190, 191)
   Spear-head with split socket, apparently complete.

Dimensions
   Length   44·5 cm
   Length of stem   19·0 cm
   Length of blade   25·5 cm

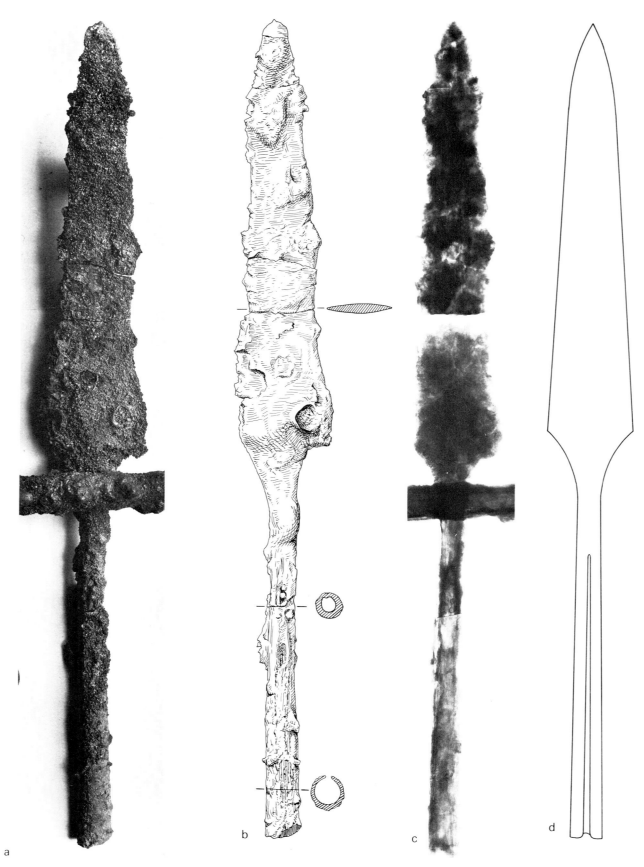

FIGURE 190 Spear no. 4 (Inv. 104): (*a*) photograph in present state after conservation; (*b*) drawing;
(*c*) radiograph and (*d*) reconstruction drawing based on radiographic evidence. (Scale: 1/2)

Width (estimated original, allowing for corrosion)	4·5 cm
Width of stem at broken end	1·7 cm
Width of stem at narrowest point	1·1 cm

The second largest of the six spears. The extreme edge of the socket may be missing. The stem portion of the spear-head is long in proportion to the blade, 19 cm compared with 25·5 cm. The blade develops abruptly from the stem, widening out from an estimated narrowest point of 1·1 cm to 4·5 cm within a distance of 3·5 cm along the length of the spear. The shaft appears to taper very slightly to a narrowest point whence the blade begins to develop. The curved expansion to the point of maximum blade width suggested by the present corroded profile, which is also seen in the radiograph (fig. 190b, c) may not represent the true profile: the shoulders may have been straight, as in most other spears of angular form. The proposed reconstruction drawing (fig. 190d) shows curves at the base of the blade; this seems the inevitable reading of the radiograph.

FIGURE 191   Spear no. 4: cross-section of the socket. The socket was sliced through in the British Museum Research Laboratory to confirm whether it was split and hollow; in the photograph the split may be seen at the top edge of the cross-section. The socket itself is completely filled with corrosion products. (Scale: 2/1)

In the radiograph (fig. 190c) the lower part of the socket or shaft, detached from the spear-head, is slightly rotated in relation to the head, thus when the two radiographs are mounted together there does not appear to be the perfect fit which is in fact present in the original.

Spear no. 5 (Inv. 105; fig. 193)
Incomplete spear-head, comprising a detached blade, not recorded *in situ*, and the lower end of the socket from which this blade evidently derived. This spear is not referred to by Phillips in his original account[1] and not included in Kendrick's

[1] Phillips 1940a, 163.

FIGURE 192 Spear no. 5 (Inv. 105): photograph
taken from the south, showing the spear lifted from
the complex and placed to one side while work
continued on cleaning and lifting the remaining
spears and angons. (Photo: O. G. S. Crawford)

inventory of the 1939 finds.[1] Nevertheless the location of the socket and its alignment
in the ground can be exactly fixed, and the original length and location of the
spear-head in the burial deposit can be re-established, leaving only a small margin of
error as to the length of the complete spear-head.

Dimensions

Length (reconstructed)	(approx.) 36–37 cm
Length of blade	22·0 cm
Length of detached socket portion surviving	13·0 cm
Width of blade	3·2 cm
Diameter (external) of socket at its mouth	1·7 cm
Diameter of socket or stem at narrowest point	not determinable

Leaf-shaped spear-head with welded socket. The diameter of the stem as it can be
seen at the broken-off end of the blade appears, when allowance is made for the effects
of corrosion, to be somewhat less, perhaps by 1 or 2 mm, than that of the broken end
of the surviving socket portion. In calculating the original length of the spear 1–2 cm
has been allowed to cover the supposed gap between the two, thus 36 or 37 cm seems
likely to have been the original length of the whole. This may be compared with an
actual length of 37 cm for spear no. 2 (Inv. 102), which is virtually identical, except
that its socket is split, and that the blade appears somewhat more pointed and very

---

[1] Phillips 1940*a*, 195, xxxi.

252

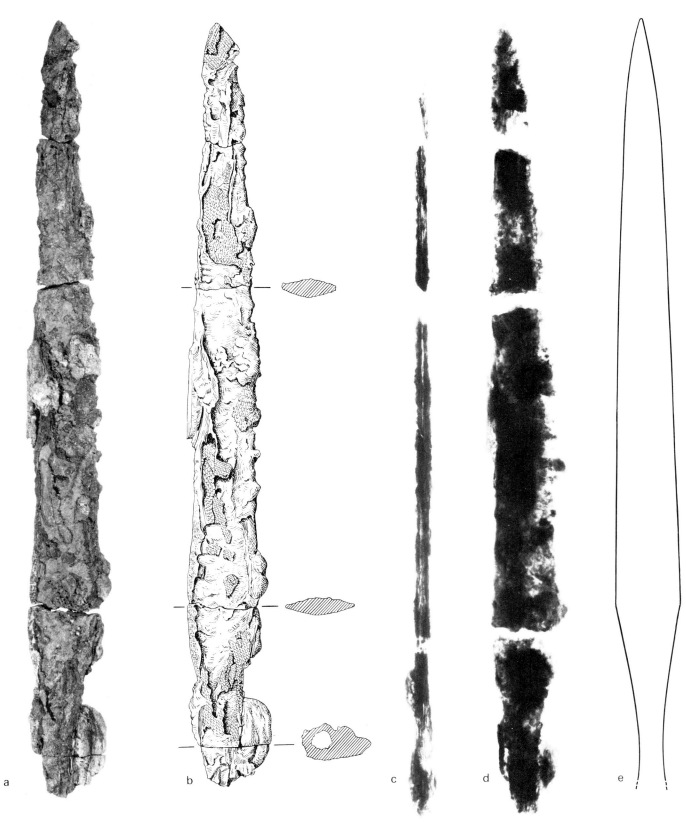

FIGURE 194 Spear no. 6 (Inv. 97): (*a*) photograph in present state after conservation; (*b*) drawing; (*c*) radiograph of the blade on edge; (*d*) radiograph of the spear overall; (*e*) reconstruction drawing based on radiographic evidence and the cross-section, figure 195. (Scale: 1/2)

a   b   c   d   e

255

It lay to the south of the sword and parallel with it, at a distance of some 25 cm (fig. 1). Its point was level with the tips of the handles of the two silver spoons. The object is not mentioned in the excavator's diary, but is identified on Piggott's field plan as 'iron blade'. Hitherto it has been accepted as a scramasax; it is inventoried as such in *Sutton Hoo*, Volume I (Inv. 97, p. 441) and is referred to and illustrated as a scramasax elsewhere, notably in Volume I, figures 352 and 355, and on the burial deposit plan (Vol. I, fig. 111).[1]

It seems possible that the blade was wrapped in cloth, a considerable quantity of which is retained in close association with it through corrosion, in the form of iron oxide replacements, which retain the form and arrangement of the weave, though no actual fibres survive. Remains of three different textiles, SH 2, 7 and 8, are to be found on the blade.[2] A correct though not a fully complete record of the distribution of these three types of textile impressions on the blade and on the fragmentary socket is given in *Sutton Hoo*, Volume I, figure 355. SH7 (a decorative hanging or tapestry) appears in a very small patch at one point only, on the under-surface of the socket as it lay in the ground.[3] Of the other two cloths, SH 8, a soft 2×1 linen twill, appears next to the blade, while SH 2, a coarser fabric, a woollen 2×2 broken chevron twill, 'probably a blanket or cloak', seems to have formed an outer wrapping. Wood remains appear outside the SH 2 textile at one point on the back of the blade. The occurrence of these textiles in the burial-chamber generally is discussed in *Sutton Hoo*, Volume I, chapter VII.

Both superficially and in the radiograph the blade seemed to have the characteristics of a scramasax, that is to say, a broad straight back, forming a blunt angle with the tang, narrowing down to a sharp cutting-edge which tapers inwards to the point and towards the line of the straight back. The apparent thickness of the back in relation to the cutting edge is due to adhering cloth and other material, lacking on the opposite side of the blade. The section of the oxidised blade, at two of the three main fractures which occur along its length, does not have the wedge-like appearance of the scramasax section, but the regular diamond shape typical of spears (fig. 194b). The iron at the centre of the blade has migrated, leaving a hole at the middle of the section, but the even tapering to points away from this on each side is clear. Although the external shape resembles a scramasax, more particularly some of the Continental and East Scandinavian examples as those illustrated by Olsen,[4] a specially cut section through the end (fig. 195), at the point indicated in figure 194b, clearly shows the circular section of a spear shaft and not the flat section of a tang. Although the blade has been submitted to thorough radiographic examinations, no decorative or structural features have been revealed (inlays, welding marks, appliqués or edgings), beyond a suggestion of rapidly expanding lines near the end of what was supposed to be the tang (fig. 194d).

[1] It is listed in Kendrick's inventory in Phillips 1940a, 195, under 'VII, Miscellaneous Ironwork', as 'no. xlviii, blade or batten, l. 18 in.'
[2] *Sutton Hoo*, Vol. I, figs. 327, 332 and 333.
[3] Ibid. fig. 363.
[4] For example, Olsen 1945, figs. 109, 188, 206, 215, 243, 245, 246.

256

FIGURE 195 Spear no. 6: cross-section through the shaft. Like spear no. 4 this was sectioned by the British Museum Research Laboratory, in this case to confirm the evidence suggested by one of the ragged breaks in the blade, that the cross-section was consistent with that of a spear rather than a scramasax which it was formerly considered to be. (Scale: 2/1)

In one of the radiographs (fig. 194c) a series of close-set lines at right-angles to the blade can be seen at one point on the back of the blade and external to it. The spacing equates these lines with textile threads in iron oxide which show up because they are seen here end on (in depth, running round the back of the blade). The textile at this point is not visible except in the radiograph since it is covered by wood.

The identification of Inv. 97 as a spear-head and not a scramasax is due to Miss Angela Evans. It is of considerable general interest and solves several difficulties. The absence of a sheath or of any metal mounts such as could be expected to accompany a scramasax and its sheath in a rich or royal burial is explained.[1] So also is the fact that the blade points in the opposite direction to the sword. It tells us, in terms of the furnishing and layout of the burial deposit, that what was presumably the king's favourite spear, perhaps his boar spear, had been laid beside him, close by his sword, in addition to the one spear laid across the end of the burial chamber and the group of seven associated with the Coptic bowl. It also simplifies the problem of the uses of the various mounts comprising the gold jewellery as it is no longer necessary to allow for the possibility that a scramasax has been worn on the sword-belt or some other part of the harness.

The spears as a group

As belonging to a group of diverse spears from a royal burial the Sutton Hoo examples may not be typical of the general run of Anglo-Saxon spear types. Nonetheless the group as such must be of great importance and interest to the study of the subject, because of the close dating of the deposit and the important associations.

According to Swanton, only two other instances are recorded of Anglo-Saxon burials accompanied by more than two or three spears.[2] A young warrior's grave from

[1] Cf. Olsen 1945, passim.

[2] Swanton 1973, 15, and 1974a, 53, with a reference to Mortimer's Forty Years Researches 1905, 53.

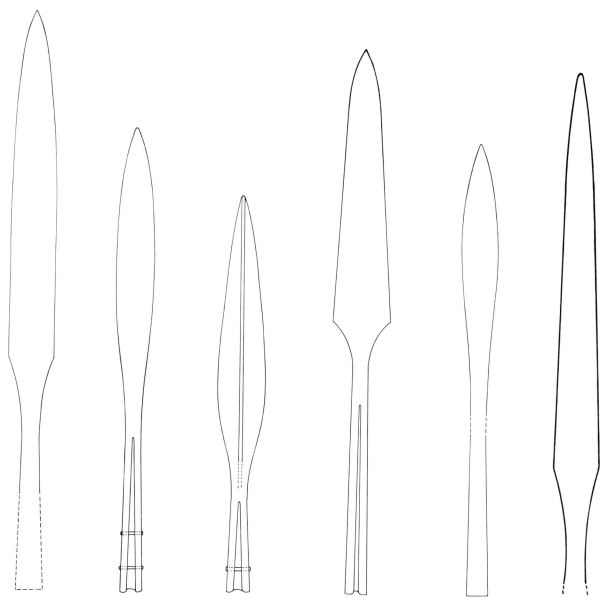

FIGURE 196   The six spears: reconstruction drawings. (Scale: 1/3)

Garton, Yorkshire (Hull Museum), contained seven spear-heads, but they were all of the one type—small leaf-shaped types between 9 and 18 cm in length. Only three of them can now be identified. A barrow burial at Hardown Hill in Wiltshire (Dorchester Museum) 'seemed to have been accompanied by some five angular and three leaf-shaped blades, ranging in size from about 15 to about 31 cm in length', the largest engraved with a fish.[1] Neither of these finds seems particularly well documented.

It will be observed that the shapes here arrived at for the Sutton Hoo spears (fig. 196) do not all agree, in varying ways, with those given by Swanton.[2] In any

[1] Swanton 1973, 15; 1974, 55, with a reference to *Proceedings of the Dorset Archaeological Society* LIII, 1931, 248, plate.

[2] Swanton 1973, fig. 56.

258

case, the categories overlap to some extent and there are intermediate forms whose classification remains unclear.

Two of the Sutton Hoo spears, nos. 2 and 5, are leaf-shaped blades, a type otherwise not found in East Anglia, according to Swanton.[1] The leaf-shaped blades are carried fairly high on the stems, and the type seems to fall somewhere between Swanton's D2 (for outline only) and K2.[2] They seem close to examples from Droxford (Hampshire) and Prittlewell (Essex), classified as D1 and D2 respectively, and another D2 example from Dover B, Grave 96.[3] No. 2 has a split socket, no. 5 a welded socket, an unusual feature at this late date in the pagan period when split sockets seem to have become almost universal in Anglo-Saxon spears. No. 3, a third leaf-shaped form, with a pronounced midrib is discussed at some length by Swanton.[4] Its split socket 'betrays insular workmanship, however skilful'. The point about this spear-head, which cannot, according to Swanton, be matched on the Continent, is that the midrib is no more than a decorative fillet, and is not an extension into the blade of the line of the socket. This is made clearer by comparing the drawing shown in figure 189 d with Swanton's figure 56, c. A number of other instances of this decorative type of midribbing, applied to spears of different forms, are cited by Swanton, notably a fine example from Welbeck Hill, Lincolnshire.[5] This purely decorative midribbing on late forms is of rare occurrence.

Three of the remaining spear-heads in the Sutton Hoo group (nos. 1, 4 and 6) are long-bladed angular forms. Numbers 1 and 6 are much the same as examples in Swanton's E3 group from Barham (Kent) and Kempston (Bedfordshire)[6] or his E4 group. One of the latter comes from the rich burial at Broomfield in Essex.[7] Sutton Hoo spear-head no. 4 was thought by Swanton to have no insular parallel, and to have been imported.[8] Its nature has since been clarified (fig. 190). It has a split socket and is complete; it is probably to be classified in Swanton's group E3, being close to an example from Prittlewell Priory in Essex.[9]

The Sutton Hoo group, to summarise, shows two main forms, leaf-shaped and angular, and all are of native manufacture. The spear-head lengths of between 30 and 46 cm show a size range characteristic for the early seventh century.

3. *The angons*

Angon no. 1 (Inv. 98; fig. 197)

Angon-head, in poor preservation, in two main pieces which do not join; a socket-and-shaft assembly (a composite construction of several fragments joined) 30 cm in length; and an assembly, including point and barbs, 32 cm in length. The point of this angon-head was the middle one of the three as found (fig. 184).

---

[1] Swanton 1973, 141: 'In East Anglia leaf-shaped forms seem to have been avoided at all times.'
[2] Swanton 1974 a, 12 and 23.
[3] Swanton 1973, fig. 66, 1.
[4] Ibid. 43.

[5] Ibid. fig. 82, e.
[6] Ibid. fig. 27, b and c.
[7] Ibid. fig. 71.
[8] Swanton 1974 a, 86.
[9] Swanton 1973, fig. 27, d.

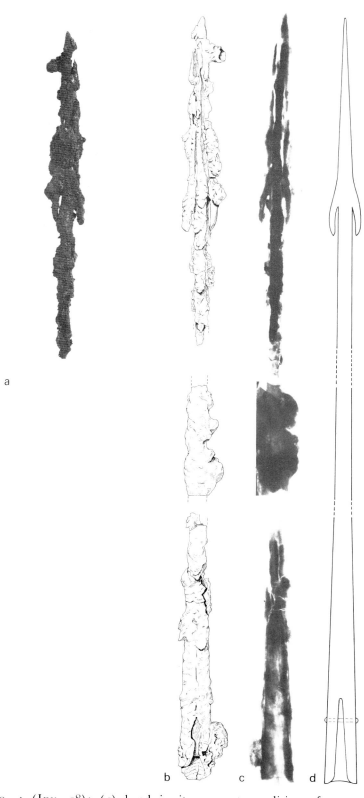

a

b c d

FIGURE 197 Angon no. 1 (Inv. 98): (*a*) head in its present condition after conservation; (*b*) drawing; (*c*) radiograph; (*d*) reconstruction drawing based on radiographic evidence. (Scale: 1/3)

Dimensions

Length overall (minimum, with no extra length allowed to compensate for the lack of join between the two assemblies)	62–63 cm
Length of spear-point, from the tips of the barbs to the point of the spear	18 cm
Length of barbs (externally)	4·5 cm
(internally)	2·5 cm
Projection of point beyond the initiation of the barbs	13·5 cm
Diameter (external) of socket opening	(approx.) 2·5 cm
Diameter of stem	1·2 cm

The socket, starting from a diameter at its mouth of nearly 2·5 cm tapers markedly to a diameter of about 1·6 cm at a distance from the socket-mouth of 16·5 cm finally settling down to 1·2 cm as the diameter of its long straight run up to the spear-point. The socket was evidently split for a short distance. Radiography reveals a rivet with rivet-head.

Angon no. 2 (Inv. 99; fig. 198)

Angon-head, complete except for the beginning of the socket, which is missing.

Dimensions

Length overall (minimum, with no allowance for the missing end of the socket)	77 cm
Length of spear-point, from the tips of the barbs to the point of the spear	13·2 cm
Length of barbs (external)	6·5 cm
(internal)	5 cm
Projection of point beyond initiation of barbs	7 cm
Diameter of incomplete end of socket	2 cm
Diameter of stem	1·2 cm

If the socket-mouth was of the same diameter as those of angon-heads nos. 1 and 3 (2·5 cm) it would seem that to reach this diameter between 5 and 7 cm should be added to the length, giving it a calculated original overall length of 82–84 cm. This angon-point was the most southerly as excavated (fig. 184) and has on its shaft the circular rust formation which developed against the side of the Coptic bowl, as described above.

Angon no. 3 (Inv. 100; fig. 199)

Angon-head, with point bent downwards. A gap in the shaft occurs 30 cm from the opening of the socket but the length of the gap is exactly determined by the rigid assembly of the rusted-together stems. The angon-head is thus complete in the sense that its original length can be exactly determined.

FIGURE 198 Angon no. 2 (Inv. 99): (*a*) head in its
present condition after conservation; (*b*) drawing; (*c*)
radiograph; (*d*) reconstruction drawing based on
radiographic evidence. (Scale: 1/3)

262

a

b   c   d

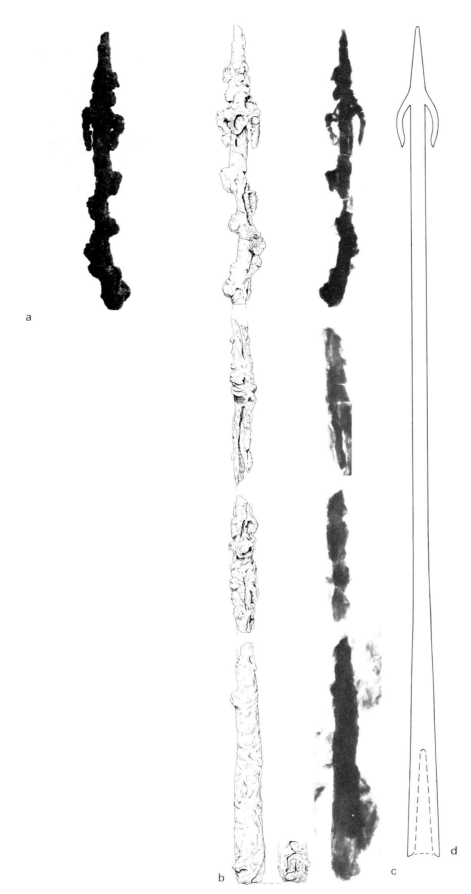

FIGURE 199 Angon no. 3 (Inv. 100): (*a*) head in its present condition after conservation; (*b*) drawing; (*c*) radiograph; (*d*) reconstruction drawing based on radiographic evidence. (Scale: 1/3)

Dimensions

Length (with the bend of the point straightened)	68·0 cm
Length of spear point from the tips of the barbs to the point of the spear	10·0 cm
Length of barbs (external)	4·5 cm
(internal)	3·5 cm
Projection of point beyond the initiation of the barbs	5·5 cm
Diameter of socket-mouth	2·5 cm
Diameter of stem	1·2 cm

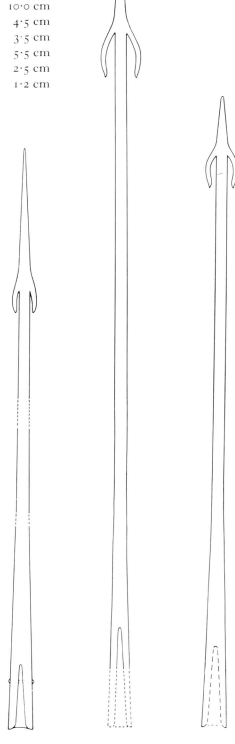

The tip of this angon-point was the most northerly of the three as found, nearest to the keel-line and furthest from the Coptic bowl. On the upper surface of the stem, at the point where the downward bend occurs, is a piece of maplewood sheeting derived from the lyre. This can be seen in several of the photographs of the complex of Coptic bowl, spears and angons in the ground. The downward bend is another indication of the weight that fell on the burial deposit with the collapse of the chamber. In contrast, it would seem, to that of spear 5, the metal still retained some tensile strength when hit, as it did not fracture but was bent.

The angons as a group

All three angon-heads have split sockets, as can be seen in the radiographs (figs. 197c, 198c, 199c), and each socket contains mineralised wood from the shaft. Comparison of the points shows that they differ from each other in type. No. 1 has small, light barbs set well down the point, which projects for a distance of 13·5 cm beyond the roots of the barbs. The splintering of the iron makes it impossible to be certain, but it seems that the projecting point may have been slightly flattened and expanded into a more blade-like form, the plane of the blade coinciding with that in which the barbs lie. The barbs of no. 1 also seem to lie flatter to the shaft than in the cases of the other two. The maximum distance of its barbs clear of the stem is some 5 mm, as against 7 or 8 mm in the case of nos. 2 and 3. In these respects—length of projecting point, smallness of barbs, and, if correctly read, the slight

FIGURE 200 The three angons.
(Scale: 1/4)

264

flattening to a blade-like shape—angon-head no. 1 seems to have affinity with fourth-century Nydam types (Swanton 1973, fig. 3, *e, g*) or those from Northumberland (Carvoran) or Abingdon listed by Swanton as derivatives from the Nydam types. Angon-head no. 2 is longer and heavier than 1 and 3. With a calculated original length of 84 cm it is at least 15 cm longer, and its barbs are almost twice the size of those of 1 and 3. The length of barbs and point together, however, falls 5 cm short of the corresponding dimension of the smaller angon-head 1. No. 3 seems to be a lighter, smaller version of 2. None of the angon-heads has the flattened triangular-shaped barbs or point seen in some of the angons of the Nydam or late Roman phase (Swanton 1973, fig. 3, *d, f, g*; fig. 4, *b, c, e*).

These factors may be judged in figure 200, and are conveniently expressed in figures in table 20. A distinctive feature of all three is that the barbs are rounded, i.e. of circular cross-section, and that, especially in nos. 2 and 3, they diverge from the shaft at an angle of about 20 degrees and then turn and run parallel with it. In the case of nos. 2 and 3 the barbs stood almost 8 mm clear of the shaft—almost twice the distance to be observed in no. 1, where the barbs lie somewhat flatter to the stem.

TABLE 20   DIMENSIONS OF ANGON-HEADS (cm)

Angon-head	Length	Length of barbs	Projection of point	Over-all point length
No. 1 (Inv. 98) (Estimated complete)	66	4·5	13·5	18
No. 2 (Inv. 99) (Estimated complete)	84	6·5	7·5	13·5
No. 3 (Inv. 100)	68	4·5	5·5	10

4. *Ferrules and supposed ferrules*

Ferrules (or more properly ferrule-tips, since none is complete) and other items that are possibly ferrules or ferrule-tips, are listed in the Inventory in *Sutton Hoo*, Volume I under the numbers 106–8, 211 and 271. The three recorded by Phillips in 1939 (see p. 241 above) and mentioned by Sir Thomas Kendrick in his provisional inventory in Phillips 1940 *a* (p. 195, item xxxi) are described first. The two items found subsequently and put provisionally into this category, are then described and discussed (Inv. 211, 271).

Ferrule no. 1 (Inv. 106; fig. 201)

Ferrule-tip, damaged at the point.

Dimensions

Length 5·5 cm

Diameter of mouth 1·4 cm

The object tapers regularly and sharply to a point. The edges of the open mouth are irregular, indicating that this is a broken off ferrule-tip, not a complete ferrule.

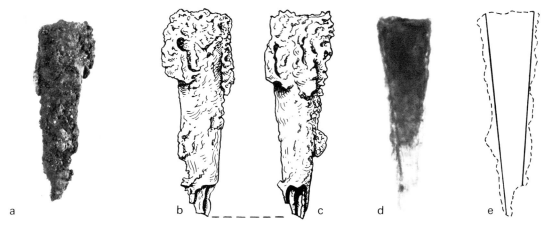

FIGURE 201 Iron ferrule (Inv. 106): (*a*) photograph; (*b*), (*c*) drawings; (*d*) radiograph; (*e*) reconstruction based on radiographic evidence. (Scale: 1/1)

A rivet-shank can be seen crossing a diameter near the opening. No wood structure is to be identified in the interior. The socket end is filled with a yellowish, completely mineralised iron-corrosion product.

Ferrule no. 2 (Inv. 107; fig. 202)

Ferrule-tip (doubtful). The shape is masked by corrosion.

Dimensions

Length	5·0 cm
Diameter of mouth	1·0 cm

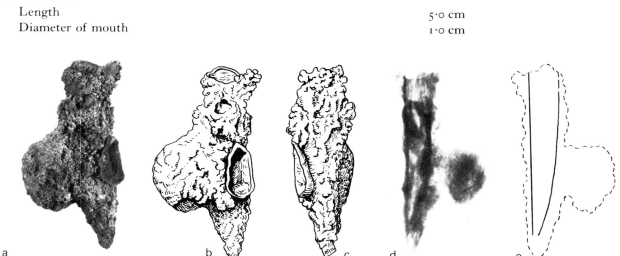

FIGURE 202 Iron ferrule (Inv. 107): (*a*) photograph; (*b*) (*c*) drawings; (*d*) radiograph; (*e*) reconstruction based on radiographic evidence. (Scale: 1/1)

The taper is much less sharp than in the case of ferrule no. 1, and were it not for apparently somewhat excessive length this would seem more likely to be the tip of a nail or spike. It is almost certainly the point of a gunwale spike.[1]

[1] Cf. *Sutton Hoo*, Vol. I, fig. 278, B. Not illustrated by Swanton.

266

Ferrule no. 3 (Inv. 108; fig. 203)

Labelled '(?) ferrule' by Phillips, indicating that it was somewhat different in character from Inv. 106 and 107 and that he had noted the difference.

The ferrule identification cannot be sustained.

Dimensions

Length	5·4 cm
Maximum diameter (excluding obvious corrosion)	1·3 cm
Diameter at end immediately prior to oblique break	1·3 cm

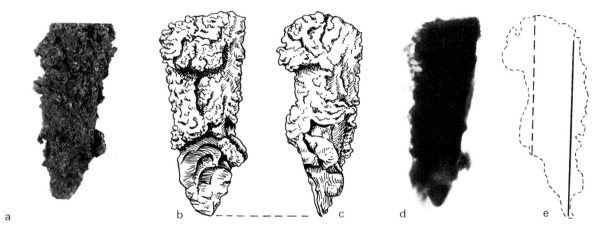

FIGURE 203 Iron ferrule (Inv. 108): (*a*) photograph; (*b*) (*c*) drawings; (*d*) radiograph; (*e*) reconstruction based on radiographic evidence. (Scale: 1/1)

The object is solid and does not taper, in spite of superficial appearances.[1] It appears to be part of a slightly bent angon-shaft or the solid stem part of a spear-head, but cannot be related to any of the spears or angons here described. Wax on one end (the end that is broken straight across as distinct from the oblique break at the other end) reflects the fact that at some phase in the general reconstruction work on the iron items in the burial deposit, its character as a ferrule being in doubt, it was joined to some other iron element. The join was subsequently not validated and the object was returned to its original box. It should be stressed again that Phillips himself had doubts as to its identity. It could easily in its excavated state have been given the provisional identification of 'ferrule' by the excavators; as a result of the oblique break it appears to taper, and it is similar in size to the two other ferrules, and was, according

[1] It is illustrated in Swanton 1973, fig. 56, *h*, from a point of view which does not give the true character of the object. Swanton (p. 151) refers to 'three butt ferrules' at Sutton Hoo, and gives their lengths as '5·6, 5·4 and a fragmentary 4·8 cm long. This agrees with the (marginally different) dimensions in our Inventory of 5·75 (Inv. 106), 5 (Inv. 107) and 5·7 (Inv. 108).

The two illustrated by Swanton are Inv. 106 and Inv. 108 (his fig. 56, *g* and *h* respectively). Swanton, assuming the natural association of the three 'ferrules' with the three angons, says that their position in the chamber indicates an average length for the angons of 2·5 m.

to Phillips's plan, found near them. A small lump of wood is attached by corrosion near the beginning of the oblique break. The grain of the wood lies obliquely across the object.

Ferrule no. 4 (Inv. 211; fig. 205)

Object of uncertain identification, found in the burial chamber during its re-excavation in 1967, consisting of a single straight object of wood and iron, now in two pieces, but conjoint when uncovered and when planned and photographed *in situ* (fig. 204).[1] Probably part of a spear, as discussed below.

FIGURE 204 The iron and wood object (Inv. 211), perhaps a ferrule with part of the shaft surviving, found during the 1967 excavations; photographed *in situ*. (Photo: M. O. Miller)

Dimensions

Length of whole as found	30·0 cm
Length of wooden portion	20·0 cm
Length of iron portion	10·0 cm
Diameter of mouth or opening of iron portion	approx. 2·0 cm
Diameter of tip of iron portion (broken)	approx. 1·0 cm

The iron portion, which is hollow, tapers. The narrow end appears damaged and incomplete; it could well have continued into a point such as in Inv. 106 (fig. 201). In identifying Inv. 211, the diagnostic feature, which is clear from the lie of the object as uncovered, is that the iron portion was attached to the wood and tapered away from it. The wood has been identified as ash (App., p. 272 below). The object as a whole seems to represent the (flattened) wooden shaft of a spear entering either the socket of a spear-head, or a large ferrule.

[1] *Sutton Hoo*, Vol. I, figs. 112 and 398. A fragment has been lost from the end of the wooden part that joined the iron, so that the wood and iron elements do not now seem to be related plausibly to each other.

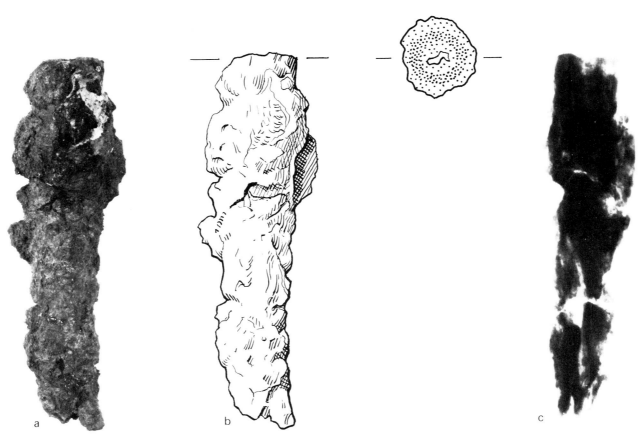

FIGURE 205 The iron and wood object from the 1967 excavations: (*a*) the remaining iron in its present condition after conservation; (*b*) plan and section; (*c*) radiograph. (Scale: 1/1)

The damaged smaller end of Inv. 211 suggests that the object was still hollow at the point to which it survives. If it continued to taper to a point like ferrule no. 1, this would give the iron portion an overall length of about 15·5 cm, which is longer than almost any recorded Anglo-Saxon spear-butt. Well-preserved angon ferrules in the Nydam and Thorsberg bog finds, however, show lengths of 14 to 19 cm, a length which seems to be quite possible for a Saxon spear ferrule.

Ferrule no. 5 (Inv. 271; fig. 206)
  ? Ferrule-tip (doubtful).

Dimensions
  Length   5·4 cm
  Diameter of broad end   1·3 cm

This object was found in Dump β in the 1968 excavation.[1] The depth and distribution of finds in the dump show that it lay in close relationship to fragments of the ten silver bowls, part of an escutcheon rim from hanging-bowl I, a twisted iron element from the iron stand, and a bucket fragment. This suggests that the object came from the

[1] Small find 16 *a*, *Sutton Hoo*, Vol. I, ch. IV, App. E, 339, 343 and fig. 257; see scatter diagram, Vol. I, fig. 235.

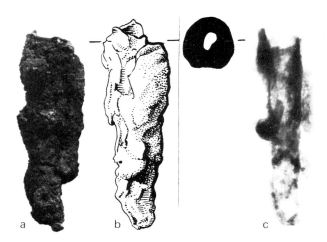

FIGURE 206 Doubtful 'ferrule' (Inv. 271),
found during the 1967 excavations of Sutton
Hoo, mound 1: (*a*) present condition; (*b*) plan
and section and (*c*) radiograph. (Scale: 1/1)

Coptic bowl complex/silver bowls/bucket no. 3 region, rather than from the part of
the burial deposit that contained ferrules 1 to 3.[1] The radiograph suggests that the
object may not taper at all sharply. Its hollowness may be due to the outward
migration of corrosion products. It may not qualify as a ferrule.

5. *The ferrules and their relation to the spears*

As has been said above, the straight ash shaft associated with the tapering iron
element 'ferrule' no. 4 may be part of a spear. If so it must represent the wooden
spear-shaft entering either a ferrule or the socket at the base of the blade. As the join
of iron to wood was undisturbed when found, it follows that the mouth of the iron
object which meets the wood is present and complete. Its diameter is 2 cm. This is
compatible with the likely diameter of a spear-shaft, to judge from the socket openings
of spears nos. 2, 3 and 5 (socket diameters 1·8, 1·9 and 1·7 cm).

Spear no. 1 lacks a socket. The diameter of the broken end of the portion of the
stem attached to the blade is 1·5 cm. Because of corrosion it is difficult to establish
the diameter of the narrow end of the iron element of 'ferrule' no. 4, with which the
blade should be linked, but allowing for damage a diameter of only about 1 cm seems
indicated. It is suggested in the description of spear no. 1 that the length of socket
and stem, on the analogy of the parallel from Kempston, could be about 12 cm. The
stem element still attached to its blade is approximately 4 cm, so that if it connected
directly with the iron portion of Inv. 211 (10 cm) we should have an overall socket
and stem length for spear blade no. 1 of 14 cm. However, the difference in diameter
of the two exposed ends seems to make the connection impossible, for it seems clear
that the length of stem attached to the blade of spear no. 1 has passed its narrowest

[1] For the tipping sequence in Dump *β* see *Sutton Hoo*, Vol. I, ch. IV, App. F, 344.

point and is expanding rather than contracting (fig. 187*b*, profile view), whereas the point of the iron element of 'ferrule' no. 4 seems to be still reducing in diameter.

If therefore Inv. 211 belongs to any of the spears or angons in the burial deposit it must be a ferrule, not a socket. Assuming that it tapered on to a point, this would give us the probable length of some 15 or 16 cm for the complete ferrule. It has the importance of thus being the only ferrule represented in the ship-burial of which the original length can be approximately calculated. It compares well with a ferrule from grave C in the Buckland, Dover, cemetery, in the British Museum, which is also intact. This has a length of approximately 14·5 cm. If we then accept Inv. 211 ('ferrule' no. 4) as the lower end of a spear with ferrule in position, which spear did it belong to? It is noteworthy that it lies the opposite way round to the main group of spears. The ferrule points west and the shaft runs away to the east of it. This fact, and the association of a length of shaft-wood with the ferrule, suggests that it was thrown or flipped to this position, before the chamber collapsed, by a sharp blow which snapped the still resilient shaft. It could belong to any of the spears, including no. 4 which was placed along the west end wall of the chamber at right-angles to the other spears. It might equally have belonged to one of the angons.

BOTANICAL REPORT

Report on wood from a spear socket, an angon socket and from an unidentified object found in 1967 (Inv. 211)

by

D. F. CUTLER

(Plant Anatomy Section, Jodrell Laboratory, Royal Botanic Gardens, Kew)

Our identifications of wood from the spear and angon complex are as follows:

1. Angon socket, Inv. 98: Ash, *Fraxinus excelsior* L.

2. Spear socket, Inv. 103: Ash, *Fraxinus excelsior* L.

3. Wood from Inv. 211: These fragments are completely mineralized. There are no diagnostic characters left in the cell walls, but the general arrangement of the cells is similar to that found in ash, *Fraxinus excelsior* L.

14 October 1974

CHAPTER VI

THE SWORD

⎯⎯⎯⎯⎯⎯⎯⎯⎯⟫◆⟪⎯⎯⎯⎯⎯⎯⎯⎯⎯

1. *Introduction and primary accounts of discovery*[1]

THE SCABBARD containing the blade was initially encountered on 19 July[2] but was not cleaned, photographed and lifted until 27 July. Phillips in his diary describes the sword complex thus:

'Progressive cleaning revealed...(6) An iron sword with gold mounts laid with hilt to the west along the middle line of the boat. The sword was sheathed, but nothing remained of the sheath but much decayed wood with a coating of a whitish substance (ivory?). The sword had a gold and garnet cloisonné pommel, gold fittings at each end of the grip, and two gold and garnet cloisonné hemispherical studs side by side across the scabbard six inches from the hilt. The sword was broken into many pieces, presumably by the fall of the burial chamber roof. It had been swathed in cloth of at least two weaves, many well-preserved fragments of which remained, the finer weave inwards. If there was a chape it is still involved in a mass of cloth and corrosion at the end of the blade.'[3]

W. F. Grimes wrote of the condition of the blade and of its excavation:

'The sword presented an insoluble problem. Its hilt was decayed and corroded beyond hope of recovery except in detached fragments. Its blade, scabbard and covering of fabric were corroded into a solid mass which had been badly damaged in the collapse of the chamber and was otherwise curiously brittle, cracked and fissured in many places. We were obliged to take it up piecemeal.'[4]

The sword (Inv. 95 and 19–21, pls, 21, 22*a*, *c*, *e*, figs. 210 and 211) lay slightly to the south of the keel-line and parallel with it; its pommel was only a few centimetres from the handles of the pair of silver christening spoons and close to the nest of cross-inscribed silver bowls. The position of the sword, the right way up and on the right side of a presumed recumbent body, is a normal one in princely burials,[5] but in view of the cross theme incorporated in the design of the scabbard-bosses (fig. 222) its juxtaposition with the elements in the burial that have specifically Christian significance should be noted.[6] A spear-head[7] lay parallel with it, 25 cm to the south;

---

[1] *Sutton Hoo*, Vol. I, 196–200 and pl. G. The excavation of the sword and its position in relation to the items of jewellery, strap-mounts, etc., is discussed in ch. x, sections 1 and 2.

[2] Ibid. 736 (Phillips's entry for 21 July).

[3] Ibid. 741.

[4] Grimes 1940, 72.

[5] For example, at Morken, Beckum and Krefeld-Gellep, grave 1782 (Böhner 1959, Winkelmann 1962 and Pirling 1964).

[6] Cf. *Sutton Hoo*, Vol. I, 708–9.

[7] Spear no. 6, pp. 254–57 above; formerly incorrectly identified as a scramasax.

FIGURE 207   The sword: general view *in situ*. The nest of silver bowls is seen above the pommel; the shoulder-clasps are to the right. (Photo: C. W. Phillips)

a

b

FIGURE 208 The sword: enlarged details showing: (*a*) the gold and garnet scabbard-bosses accurately re-positioned in the remains of their settings: the grain of the superficial wooden feature that runs between the bosses (p. 288) can be recognised; (*b*) the matrices of the bosses: the marks left by the ends of the staples can be seen in circular spaces at the centres. (Scale: 2/1)

275

FIGURE 209 Detail of the badly damaged upper portion of the Sutton Hoo sword as excavated. The filigree clips (Inv. 24 and 25) lie at the ends of the grip, both on the same side: below the scabbard bosses can be seen part of the rectangular buckle Inv. 11, upside down, and remains of the wooden box (p. 282). (Photo: S. Piggott)

judging by the photographs its point lay to the west, as did those of the spears and angons in general, and was thus pointing in the opposite direction from the sword. Closely associated with the sword in the ground (fig. 207) was the gold and garnet T-shaped strap-distributor (Inv. 17, fig. 334) and a single rectangular strap-mount (Inv. 6 or 7, fig. 324). Lying on top of the middle of the sword, obliquely across it, was a gold filigree strip with ring-head set with five cabochon garnets (Inv. 30, figs. 207 and 278). Close to the ring-head of this was a similar cabochon garnet in a detached setting. Attached to the scabbard 15 cm below its mouth was a pair of hemispherical gold and garnet bosses (Inv. 26 and 27, fig. 208), and to either side of the sword, at some distance, lay a pyramidal gold, garnet and millefiori mount (Inv. 28 and 29, pls. 21 b, 22 e, fig. 227).[1] Adhering to the scabbard, but not part of its construction, were traces of at least two medium-weight textiles[2] and bound tightly around it, near the hilt,

[1] Also *Sutton Hoo*, Vol. I, pl. G.   [2] *Sutton Hoo*, Vol. I, 461 and fig. 353.

were remains of a fine linen tape, in closely overlapping turns (fig. 213).[1]

Attached to the iron tang of the sword, which had been broken off from the blade, is a small fragment of wood from the grip (fig. 221). The cross-guards at the upper and lower ends of the grip were of some organic substance which has wholly disappeared; each was covered above with a gold sheet and fitted beneath by a gold tray with sides turned up all round. These tray-like gold fittings were filled flush with a metallic substance discussed below (p. 292). Two handsome clips, closely similar but of different sizes, decorated with filigree and each originally held by three gold nails, were attached to the leading edge or front face of the grip at its upper and lower ends (figs. 221, 225).

The pommel is of gold, set with cloisonné garnets, and is of 'cocked-hat' form, with concave upper surfaces and convex sides. At each end of the upper guard are three rivets which hold the upper gold sheet to the lower tray; the outermost rivet is clenched on the underside of the guard below a small circular washer but the inner, paired rivets share a common long oval washer (fig. 218, i). The upper ends of the paired rivets pass through tall filigree collars which are attached to vertical plates closing the ends of the pommel (p. 291 below). The oval gold plates of the lower guard are held by a single gold rivet at each end. On the upper face of the gold plate which forms the upper surface of the lower cross-guard and on the under-face of the gold plate which forms the lower surface of the upper guard are oval ropes of filigree, consisting of tightly twisted gold wires closely wound round a central core of indeterminate nature. The inner apertures of these filigree loops give the dimensions of the hand-grip at its two ends. There was no trace of a chape, although the cloth wrapping of the point of the scabbard might have been expected to preserve at least metallic traces. The badly crushed buckle with rectangular plate (Inv. 11) was trapped upside down below the blade, beneath the point where the two bosses occur on the front. Its rear end can be seen protruding in figure 209. It was pressed

FIGURE 210 The Sutton Hoo sword. (Scale: 1/4)

[1] Ibid. 465 and fig. 357.

277

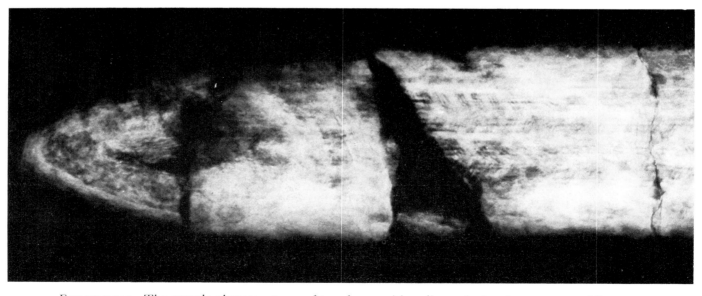

FIGURE 211   The sword: photomontages of two faces, with radiograph showing pattern welding.
(Scale: 1/1) (Radiograph: British Museum Research Laboratory)

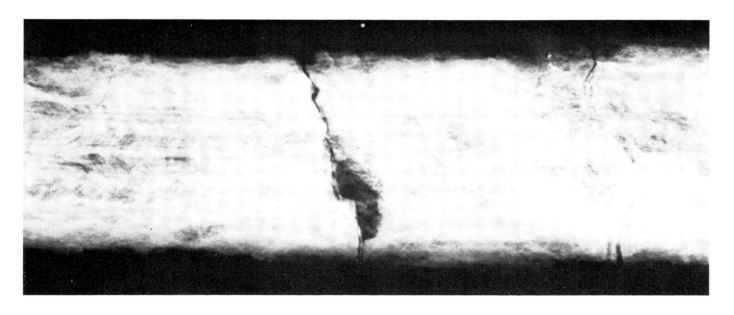

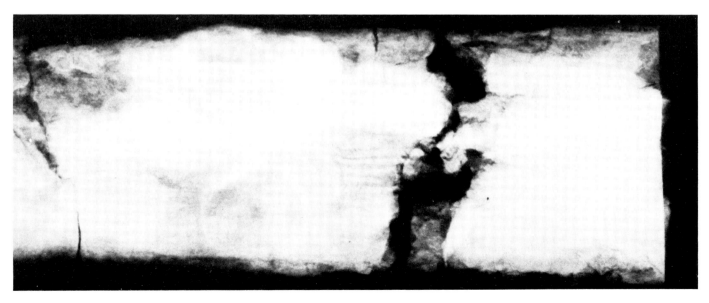

directly into the under-surface of the scabbard, where its glassy impression was clearly to be seen (fig. 318). It had pushed in the side of the lid of the wooden box that lay below the sword.

Figures 207 and 209 show the condition of the scabbard and grip as they survived in the ground, and they show that the blade had been severely damaged either in the collapse of the burial chamber or through some other agency prior to the collapse. The upper part of the blade in particular was badly broken. Remains of the wooden box which lay beneath it, associated with which were coils of spare binding tape for the scabbard,[1] can be seen in figure 209.

2. The sword, its component parts and the fittings directly associated with it

Inv. 95: The sword blade and scabbard

Dimensions

Length of sword blade, with scabbard, and hilt overall	85·4 cm
Length of hilt overall	13·4 cm
Length of blade	72·0 cm
Position of centres of scabbard bosses from the gold cross-guard at the top of the blade	10·5 cm
Length of external tapering wooden grooved feature running from the top of the scabbard between the bosses	17·5–18·5 cm
Width of scabbard at its mouth, i.e. immediately below gold cross-guard	7·3 cm
Width of scabbard of 10 cm below the mouth	6·9 cm
Width of scabbard 10 cm from the tip	5·5 cm

The blade

The blade, badly corroded, is inextricably concealed within the scabbard, which is also severely damaged by corrosion. Rough sections of the corroded blade and scabbard are to be seen in several places where the sword is fractured, but corrosion has proceeded so far that the sections are almost unintelligible. A ground-down section of the blade has been prepared in the British Museum Research Laboratory (fig. 212): this casts some confirmatory light on the welding process employed in the construction of the blade (p. 307 below), and also confirms the presence of a lining of animal skin between the wooden outer part of the scabbard and the blade. Radiography has been very successful in revealing the pattern-welded structure which can be seen from end to end of the blade. The radiographs also show that the tip of the sword is intact within the corrosion (fig. 211). Stereo-radiographs of the blade were made which have helped in the interpretation of its construction. This is discussed by Angela Care Evans in Appendix A (p. 307).

[1] Ibid. 465.

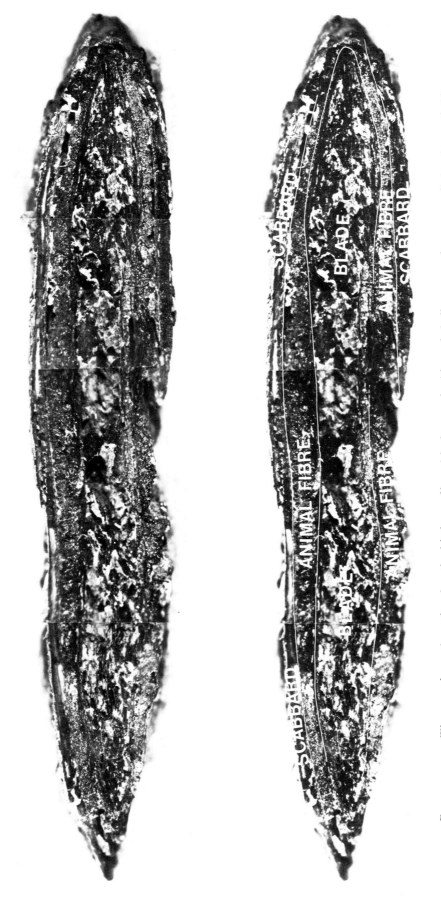

FIGURE 212 The sword: section, showing the blade profile, with the usual wide and shallow central groove, a lining layer of skin and outside this the wood of the scabbard. (Scale: approx. 4/1) (Photo: British Museum Research Laboratory)

FIGURE 213   The sword: Detail of the left-hand corner of the top of the sword,
showing tape bindings and the remains of one of the spare coils of tape found
under it. (Scale: 2/1)

The scabbard

The construction of the scabbard is difficult to establish because of its condition.
The upper surface presents a different superficial appearance from the lower, and both
faces should be studied (fig. 211). The difference in colour and condition of the two
is not due to conservation processes, but must be due to differing conditions affecting
the two surfaces as the sword lay in the burial-chamber.

There is no trace of any leather associated with the scabbard. It was composed of
a very fine-grained wood layer, the thickness of which appears to have been about
2 mm. At the upper end the wooden surface was tightly bound from the mouth
downwards with overlapping bands of very fine linen tape.[1] This binding can be traced
down the scabbard for a distance of 16 cm from its mouth. No similar binding can
be identified at the point of the sword. This is intact, and as radiographs of it reveal

[1] SH 16; *Sutton Hoo*, Vol. I, 465 and fig. 341. The fineness of this tape is indicated by Miss Crowfoot's count of
64 warp threads per centimetre.

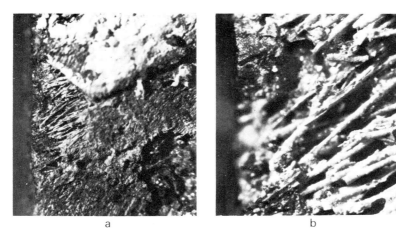

FIGURE 214   The sword: (a) and (b) enlarged details of
animal hairs on the scabbard. (Scales: a, 6/1; b, 24/1)
(Photos: British Museum Research Laboratory)

no trace of any metal edge-bindings or chape, although the point of a scabbard
normally calls for reinforcement, the extension of the tape bindings to this portion
of the scabbard might perhaps have been expected. It is possible that there was a chape
of some organic substance which has disintegrated and left no trace.

Inside the wood of the scabbard evidence provided by layers of what appear to be
hairs or hair roots, seen in some places and at a lower level than the wood of the
scabbard, seems to indicate that the scabbard was lined with soft skin or fur, the hairs
seen being interpreted as the root-lengths lying obliquely in the thickness of the skin
layer (figs. 212 and 214). The appearance of the small patches visible is superficially
like that of the densely packed spreads of beaver hairs, similarly interpreted as lengths
lying obliquely within the thickness of the skin, found adhering to the outer surfaces
of the maplewood of the lyre (Inv. 203).[1] The oblique direction of the supposed hairs
(not parallel with the grain of the scabbard wood which runs lengthways up and down
the sword), their relative disorganisation and their lower depth than the wood of the
scabbard, indicate that they are not wood grain, although their superficial appearance
without magnification is not dissimilar. The totally oxidised condition of these hair-like
or fibrous elements precludes their identification as the hair of a specific animal. Their
presence is confirmed by the prepared cross-section of the blade, in which a uniform
distribution pattern for the hairs on both sides of the blade can be recognised. The
scabbard therefore was of wood (unidentifiable as to species) with a skin or wool lining
next the blade.[2] The wooden scabbard would require a lining of some sort.

Two gold bosses of intricate construction, set with cloisonné garnets, were attached
to the scabbard, side by side, at a point 10·5 cm below its mouth. They are described
in more detail below. For immediate purposes it may be said that they were set on
long staple-like shanks, so that their under-surfaces stood at a height of 1·2 cm above

[1] To be described in detail in *Sutton Hoo*, Vol. III; see also
Sutton Hoo, Vol. I, 452 (Inv. 208).
[2] Cf. the views expressed on the scabbard of the Coombe

(Kent) sword—wood, with lambskin lining (Ellis Davidson and
Webster 1967, 17); and swords from the recent excavations at
Finglesham and Holborough in Kent (Chadwick 1958, 21–2, 28).

FIGURE 215 The sword: the upper surface of the scabbard, showing the full extent of a superficial tapering wooden feature (indicated by arrows) running from the top and between the bosses. (Scale: 1/1)

FIGURE 216 Detail of sword 1 from Valsgärde 7, showing part of the suspension mechanism. The metal supports seen above the zoomorphic mounts to either side are part of the modern mount. (Scale: approx. 1/1)

the scabbard surface, and that they were mounted in high collars of a white substance. The remains of this show no identifiable structural features but chemical analysis (App. B, p. 308) is compatible with a possible identification as bone or ivory. Although the two bosses are of slightly different sizes the shanks on which they stand are of the same height. The collars in which they were set, the matrices of which remain on the surface of the scabbard, show the same difference in diameter as do the bosses.

These matrices measure 25·5 and 27·5 mm respectively. The larger boss is on the left of the photograph in figure 208. It will be seen that the outline or matrix of its missing (? ivory) setting is broken inwards on the inside. Its position is well out towards the edge of the scabbard. The second and smaller boss is further in from the edge of the scabbard. Its matrix is not only intact but can be seen to impinge on the space between the bosses. It seems that both bosses have been shifted together to the left. The significance of this is discussed below (p. 297).

Running down from the mouth of the scabbard, tapering and passing between the bosses, is a wooden feature which, while clearly associated with the sword, is not an integral part of the scabbard. The fine overlapping tape bindings round the upper part of the scabbard pass underneath it (figs. 211, 215). The upper surface of the wooden element is dished. The feature appears to come to a point some 17·5–18·5 cm below the mouth of the scabbard. As it passed between the scabbard bosses this tapering feature would have been some 1·5 cm in width. There are no metal elements (e.g. rivets or clips) associated with this feature, and neither its method of attachment to the scabbard nor its purpose is apparent. The fact that it tapers steadily from the top and the apparent lack of any firm means of attachment do not seem to suit a possible role as a bed for a clamp or bridge operating in connection with the suspension mechanism of the sword (fig. 216), as is known from a number of instances elsewhere (p. 570 below). It may have been purely ornamental.

At each end of the grip are the guards, which must have been of some organic substance such as horn, wood or ivory, no trace of which survives. They were furnished with gold mounts held by gold rivets. In each case the gold fitting which covered the under-surface of the guard is shaped like a tray of slim long oval form, with rounded points at either end (pls. 21 d and 22 c, figs. 217 and 218). The mouth of the scabbard bears the direct smooth and polished-looking imprint of the under-surface of the gold tray of the lower guard, indicating that the mouth of the scabbard, where the tang is broken across and detached, is otherwise intact.

The upper guard and pommel (Inv. 19 and 20; pl. 22 a,[1] figs. 217, 218, 219 and 220)

Dimensions
Upper guard

Length of upper plate	6·3 cm
Width	1·7 cm
Length of lower gold tray element (fig. 218 j)	6·5 cm
Width	1·8 cm
Gold content of upper plate	93·5 %
Gold content of lower tray	91·7 %
Internal length and width of the filigree rope loop on the under surface of the lower gold plate or tray (fig. 218 i). (This gives the dimensions of the upper end of the grip.)	2·8 cm × 1·3 cm

[1] Also *Sutton Hoo*, Vol. I, pl. G.

The pommel

Length	4·0 cm
Width at middle	1·7 cm
Width at each end	1·4 cm
Height	1·5 cm
Gold content	97·0%

Weight of pommel with upper guard (in present condition, with fragments of bronze lining adhering)   51·287 g

The cloisonné and garnet work of the pommel is described separately below (p. 303).

a

b

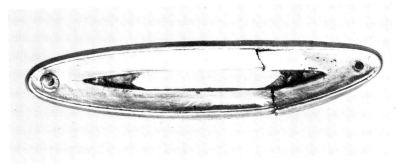

c

FIGURE 217 The sword: details of the gold mounts from the hilt: (*a*) the under surface of the upper guard; (*b*) the upper surface of the lower guard; (*c*) the lower surface of the lower guard. (Scale: 1/1)

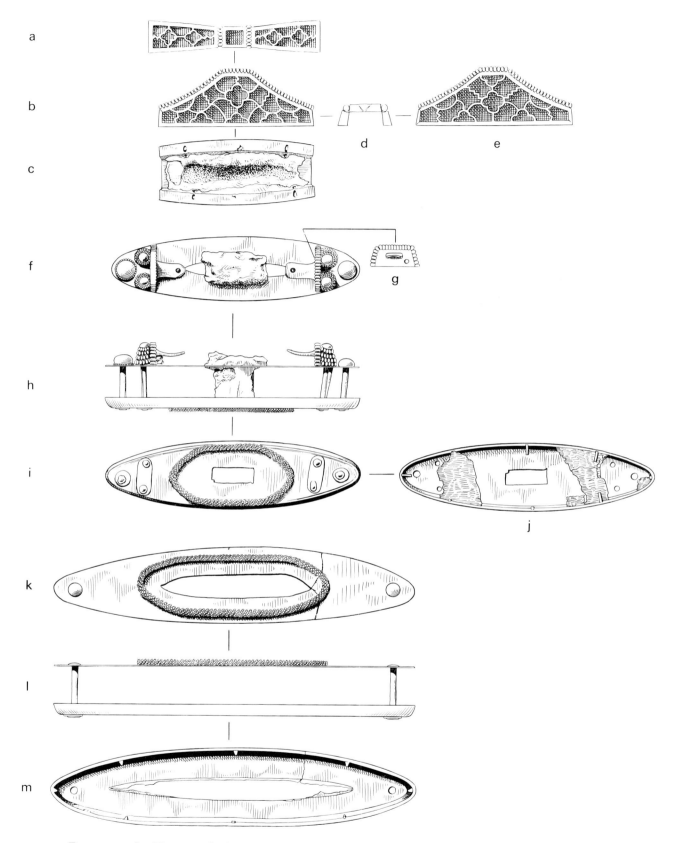

a

b

c

d

e

f

g

h

i

j

k

l

m

FIGURE 218   The sword: drawings of the hilt showing: (*a*)–(*e*) details of the cloisonné work on the pommel, with interior and end views; (*f*)–(*i*) the upper surface, side view and under surface of the upper guard; (*j*) interior view of the lower gold 'tray'; (*k*)–(*m*) three views of the lower guard. (Scale: 1/1)

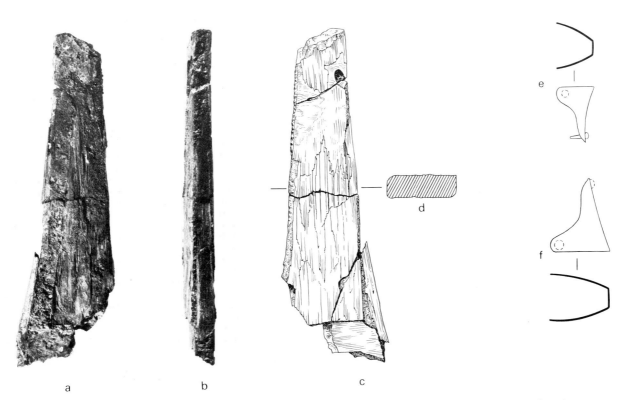

FIGURE 221   The sword: (*a*), (*b*) views of the surviving portion of the tang, showing wood grain
and a fragment (left edge, below) of the wood of the grip; (*c*), (*d*) drawings of the tang fragment:
(*e*), (*f*) outline drawings of the two filigree clips. (Scale: 1/1)

end. The thickness of the iron strip is 4·5 mm, and it tapers in width from a little
over 2 cm where it enters the lower guard to a little over 1 cm where it enters the upper
guard. As reconstructed from the available evidence the length of the grip is 9·2 cm,
a comfortable fit for a man's hand (pl. 22 *a*). The wooden grip itself, as built round
the iron tang must have been oval in cross section. The dimensions at its upper and
lower ends are given by the size of the filigree loops that evidently surrounded it like
close-fitting collars, at the points where the grip abutted on the inner gold plates of
the guards at the ends. The dimensions must have been 4·6 cm × 1·25 cm at the lower
end and 2·8 cm × 1·3 cm at the upper end (fig. 218 *i*, *k*). The shaping of the grip is
further indicated by the filigree clips mounted on it at the inner edges of the filigree
loops (fig. 221 *e*, *f*).

Inv. 21: The lower guard (figs. 217 *b*, *c*, 218 *k–m*)

Dimensions

Length of upper plate	9·4 cm
Width	2·1 cm
Length of opening in upper plate	3·9 cm
Length of lower gold tray element	9·4 cm
Width	2·1 cm
Length of opening in lower element	6·0 cm

Interior dimensions of filigree rope loop on inner surface of
upper gold plate of the guard, giving dimensions of lower
end of handgrip   4·6×1·25 cm
Gold content of upper plate   90·1%
Gold content of lower tray   93·6%

Weight of lower guard (both plates and
the filigree rope)   20·905 g

The guard is not symmetrical, being slightly flattened at one side, rounder on the other (fig. 217 *b, c*). The openings cut in the upper and lower gold sheets reflect this asymmetry. A single long gold rivet at each end held the two plates together, yielding an overall thickness of the cross-guard of 1 cm.

No trace of the filling of the lower tray-shaped gold mount survived. Its walls however show the lower ends of several vertical flat gold strips of the kind present in the tray of the upper guard. The bent-over tops of these strips are broken off (fig. 218 *m*), but their evident presence suggests that this tray carried a metal filling similar to that of the upper tray, which was of a high tin alloy.

Inv. 26, 27: The scabbard bosses (pl. 21 *c*, fig. 222)
Dimensions

	Inv. 26	*Inv. 27*
Overall height	2·0 cm	2·0 cm
Diameter	2·3 cm	2·0 cm
Shank projection from main back plate	1·2 cm	1·2 cm
Width of staple loop	0·9 cm	0·7 cm
Width of the circular raised platform under the base plate (fig. 224 *c*)	0·8 cm	0·8 cm
Gold content	86·5%	89·0%
Weights	17·725 g	14·886 g

These bosses are most remarkable examples of the virtuosity and skill of the master goldsmith and are of strong construction. The rounded ends of the long thick gold staples that supported the domed cloisonné tops have left clearly preserved impressions in the surface upon which they rested (fig. 208 *b*); these show that the two bosses, when in position on the scabbard, were orientated in relation to their cloisonné cruciform designs as shown in figure 208 *a*.

Figure 223 illustrates the construction of the bosses in so far as it can be established. The main constructional components are listed below:

(1) thick gold staple projecting 1·2 cm from the main under-surface of the bosses, to which surface it is attached (fig. 223 *a*);

(2) a circular raised platform 2 mm thick, formed in two halves, fastened round the ends of the shanks of the staple (fig. 223 *a*);

(3) a thin circular base plate (0·2 mm thick) to which the staple is attached (fig. 223 *a*). The plate is 2·3 cm in diameter for the larger boss, Inv. 26, and 2 cm in

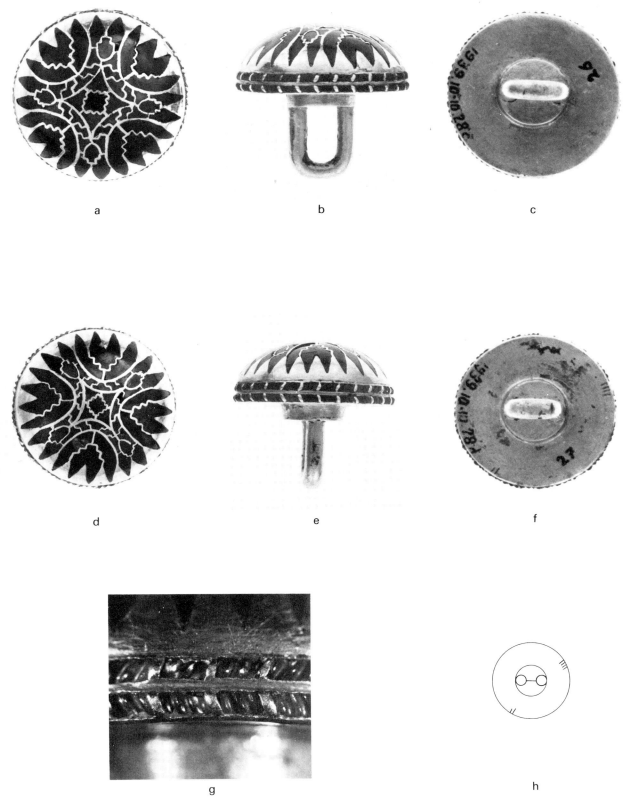

a   b   c

d   e   f

g   h

FIGURE 222 The sword: the scabbard-bosses: (*a*)–(*f*) general views; (*g*) detail showing carved garnets, set in the edges of the boss; (*h*) drawing showing marks cut on the edges of the smaller boss. (Scales: *a–f*, 2/1; *g*, 6/1; *h*, 1/1) (Photo: British Museum Research Laboratory)

diameter for the smaller boss, Inv. 27. This plate carries the cell walls for the rows of serrated garnets round the lower circumference of the boss and the walls of the inner cells (see 5 below).

(4) a thick incurved gold ring in the form of an upstanding gold wall shaped inwards and cut into a continuous series of sharp triangular teeth (fig. 223 *b*, *c*);

(5) a cluster of cell walls set vertically on the base plate (3) within this thick outside *chevaux-de-frise* (4), rising to varying heights to suit the domed design. These walls, with the thick outer serrated wall, held the stones.

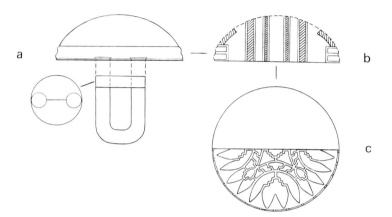

FIGURE 223 The sword: (*a*)–(*c*): drawings showing the construction of the scabbard-bosses, Inv. 26. (Scale: 3/2)

All the cells under the garnets and their gold foil backings, so far as can be ascertained, were and are completely empty. A continuous open gallery runs all the way round the outer edge of the circular plate that carries the vertical cloisonné cell walls. It can be seen in figure 223 *b*.

The construction is broadly similar to that of the boss on the toe of the curved dummy buckle-mount, Inv. 10, but of much greater complexity.

The smaller of the two bosses shows two groups of firmly incised marks on its under surface, at the rim on opposite sides. One has four short strokes, the other two (fig. 222 *f* and *h*).

For details of the garnet cloisonné work and its style see below, page 304.

The under-surfaces of the domed gold and garnet bosses were set, as has been said, at a level of 1·2 cm above the surface of the scabbard, and their domes rose from that height for another 0·8 cm, to 2 cm overall. The bosses were surrounded by and set into high collars of a substance which was probably bone or ivory. The remains of this show no trace of the pronounced graining to be seen in the white settings on St Cuthbert's cross, and the Kingston brooch[1] and on a disc brooch from Faversham[2] and elsewhere which has been identified as shell or 'cuttle-fish bone'. Figure 224 shows

[1] Bruce-Mitford 1974, 283 and 295.　　[2] Evison 1951, 199.

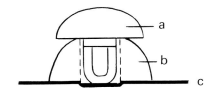

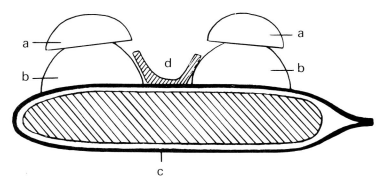

FIGURE 224 The sword: reconstruction drawings of the scabbard-bosses in position. Above, section of one of the bosses, a, mounted on its ?bone or ivory collar, b, on a hypothetical leather strap, c; below, the two bosses shown in section mounted on the leather strap which is fastened round the scabbard. Item d represents the superficial grooved wooden feature which is shown in figure 215. (Scale: 1/1)

the suggested cross-section of the bosses in their settings. The fact that the marks left by the rounded tips of the gold staples (fig. 208*b*) rest in a circle of exactly the same diameter as the raised circular platform at the base of the staples on the under-side of the stud (8 mm in the case of both studs) suggests that a cylindrical shaft occupied the centre of the collar in which the studs were set. If the studs were not purely ornamental, but intended to function as buttons to engage a strap from which the sword was suspended, they must have been firmly attached to the scabbard. Their shanks did not go through the scabbard but only left impressions on its surface. We therefore suggest that the button shanks were sewn on to a leather loop which ran round the scabbard. This could have been added after the binding tape had been applied. The tapering wooden feature which runs down between the bosses could then have been superimposed (fig. 208). Such an arrangement would account for the uniform shift of the two bosses—the loop sliding around slightly while the scabbard remains rigid.

In the lower side edges of the bosses are set two rows of serrated garnets in small cells. These are the only instances in the Sutton Hoo jewellery of garnets carved in this manner, as distinct from being engraved or faceted (fig. 222*g*).

Inv. 24, 25: Filigree mounts on the hilt (figs. 221 *e*, *f*, 225)[1]
Dimensions

	Inv. 24	Inv. 25
Height	1·9 cm	1·3 cm
Width	1·4 cm	1·3 cm
Depth from front to back	1·5 cm	1·0 cm
Gold content	74·6%	70·0%
Weight	2·035 g	1·133 g

Two filigree-covered gold clips each held by three gold rivets (fig. 226 *b*) decorated the ends of the handgrip. They are of different heights and depths but of the same width (fig. 221 *e*, *f*). The smaller clip came from the upper end of the grip, and the larger from the bottom; both were on the same side. Their original locations at each end of the grip are clear from a number of photographs taken during the excavation (fig. 209).[2]

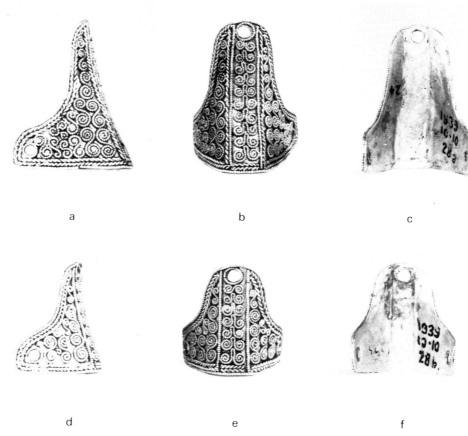

a b c

d e f

FIGURE 225 The sword: (*a*)–(*f*) side, front and back views of two filigree clips of different sizes from the lower and upper ends of the grip. (Scale: 2/1)

[1] See also *Sutton Hoo*, Vol. I, pl. G (iv).
[2] See also photographs (now held in the British Museum) by O. G. S. Crawford, no. 156, M. Guido, no. 1 and C. W. Phillips, no. 47. For an account of the photographic records of the 1939 excavation see *Sutton Hoo*, Vol. I, 139 and 142.

Clips of this kind are familiar from several swords, and the development of such decorative elements on the hilt is part of an evolution which leads to the florid and ornate handgrips of the later swords of the eighth century. Examples from the Lombardic necropolis of Nocera Umbra, and from Vallstenarum (Gotland)[1] may be cited; these swords, while possessing earlier features, were probably not buried until the mid-seventh century or later, and show secondary elements. In some swords, including that cited from Vallstenarum and a second sword from Nocera Umbra,[2] the ends of the handgrip are encased in decorative metal collars which seem to be an evolution from an initial pair of clips.[3] Further clips may then appear on the shoulders of these collars, as at Vallstenarum (fig. 95). Such clips do not appear to have been found on any Anglo-Saxon swords and they could be compatible with the East Scandinavian background for the Sutton Hoo sword that is suggested by its pommel and other features of the Sutton Hoo jewellery (p. 304 below). Nevertheless the clips were certainly made locally in Suffolk for the Sutton Hoo sword. The gold analysis of the two clips (74·6 and 70%, p. 306), suggests that they are to be placed in chronological relationship with the latest coins in the purse (Inv. 14, 71·6% and Inv. 34, 69·2%; *Sutton Hoo*, Vol. I, 652). Apparently no other sword has yet been found in Europe that shows one clip only at each end of the grip. The filigree decoration is well seen in figures 225 and 432 d, e. It is of the finest quality, giving an all-over effect of delicate surface incrustation. The curved sides are tightly filled with S-scrolls of beaded wire, sometimes reversed S-scrolls, and the flat narrow outer faces show a line of hook motifs one above the other, all close-set. The outer edges of the mounts have a beaded wire edging, inside which runs a chevron-like pattern consisting of two wires twisted in opposite directions placed side by side. The hook and eye panels on the narrow outer face are edged by a plain wire, flanked by single wire with a right-hand twist; each rivet is surrounded by a beaded wire collar; only one original rivet survives (fig. 226 b).

a   b

FIGURE 226   The sword: (a) beaded wire collar surrounding the head of an outer rivet on the upper surface of the upper guard; (b) gold nail from one of the filigree clips on the grip. (Scale: 6/1)

[1] Behmer 1939, pls. XLI, 6 and XLII, 1.
[2] Ibid. pl. XLI, 7.
[3] Cf. ibid. pl. XLI, 6 and 7.

Inv. 28, 29: The pyramids (pls. 21 *b*, 22 *e*, figs. 227, 228)[1]
Dimensions

The two pyramids, unlike the pairs of scabbard bosses and of filigree clips, have identical dimensions. They are exactly square in plan.

Height	1·2 cm
Width and depth (external)	1·8 cm
Interior aperture: minimum dimension at base level (fig. 231 *d*)	1·2 cm
Maximum width accommodated at top level of internal crossbar (estimated) (cf. fig. 228 *e*) (reducing steadily with inward slope of the rising pyramid walls)	1 cm
Gold content	76·8% and 77·8%

Weights

Inv. 28, 14·253 g
Inv. 29, 14·121 g

The pyramidal mounts are completely covered externally with cloisonné garnets and blue glass inlays and with a millefiori inset in the top.

The pyramids and their construction are illustrated in figures 227 and 228. They are among the most astonishing examples of technical virtuosity seen in the Sutton Hoo jewellery. The gem-cutting is of a particularly high order. Like the scabbard bosses, the pyramids are of solid, strong construction. In connection with their use, the drawings are of importance (fig. 228 *d*, *e*), as is their situation to either side of the sword. Their construction shows that, while the mounts have an external breadth of 1·8 cm, the apertures by which they were attached to the strap or whatever they were mounted on, reduces from 1·3 cm by means of an inner step (fig. 228 *d*) to 1·2 cm at base level. The bars across the base of the pyramids are flat at the base, where they are 5 mm wide, leaving a maximum width of aperture to either side, at base level, of 4 mm. The bar however appears to be some 2–3 mm thick, and as the walls of the pyramid slope inwards as they rise upwards, the clearance at the level of the top of the bar, over which any strap or lace must pass, is considerably reduced. There is no room for a straight metal tag to be passed through. The maximum gap (inaccessible for measurement) at the level of the top of the bar appears to be no greater in width than 1 cm, and is more likely to be 0·9 cm. This reduces steadily with height (fig. 228 *e*) so that the thicker the strap element or lace that passes over the bar, the narrower it must be; it must also be thin enough to have the necessary flexibility to pass into the interior of the pyramid and out again at the sharp angle called for. Thus, though the small gold strap-end, of uncertain attribution, Inv. 16, is only 1 cm in width and so can enter the slot, it is too wide to pass over the top of the transverse bar and, with a length of 1 cm, too rigid to turn the angle. The pyramids can only have been mounted on a cloth or leather strip some 5–6 mm wide or less, depending on the thickness. This could have been cut out of a wider strap.

[1] *Sutton Hoo,* Vol. I, pl. G.

a

b

c

d

e

f

g

FIGURE 227 The sword: (*a*)–(*f*) views of the pair of gold pyramids (Inv. 28 and 29) found to either side of the sword; (*g*) detail of the millefiori inlay in the top of one of them. (Scales: *a–f*, 2/1; *g*, 6/1). (Photo (*g*): British Museum Research Laboratory)

No metal fitments were found in association with the pyramids, to attach or adjust such a strip, so that the leather loops, if they were so mounted, must have been sewn down, giving the pyramids small possibility of movement; alternatively they could have been strung on the ends of a tape or lace.

The pyramids were found to either side of the sword exactly in line with the scabbard bosses at distances from them of 18 cm and 8 cm as a maximum. We do not know how they lay, whether the right way up or upside down, or both pointing downwards towards the tip of the sword. One of them it seems must have been the right way up as the under-surface preserved a carbonised layer of organic matter (p. 435) which had presumably been given physical protection by the pyramid above. Their exact alignment with the scabbard bosses may be fortuitous, but it suggests that they were attached to a strap which ran through the bosses transversely. Their role is considered in a later section dealing with the sword suspension and the function of the various mounts and assembly of the harness as a whole (p. 564 ff.). The layer of carbonised matter adhered to the whole area of the under-surface.[1] This could suggest equally that the pyramid had been mounted on leather or textile, or that it rested on an expanse of leather or textile of which only the small portion physically protected by the pyramid survives.

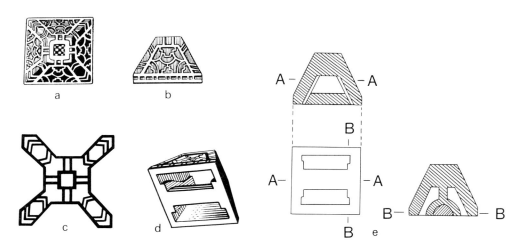

FIGURE 228 The sword: the gold pyramids. (*a*) from above; (*b*) side view; (*c*) plan of the cross element in the design drawn in two-dimensional form; (*d*) oblique view of the interior; (*e*) sections. (Scales: 1/1)

Minute signs of polish and abrasion on the edges of the slots and the sides of the transverse bar at the base of the pyramids are confined to the central areas, and suggest a degree of movement on a narrow cord or strap, possibly with a metal element.

[1] *Sutton Hoo*, Vol. I, 436.

3. *Cloisonné work in the sword-pommel, scabbard-bosses and pyramids*[1]

The cell shapes and larger patterns used in these three leading pieces of the gold jewellery are set out in figures 229, 231 and 233.

The pommel

Number of garnets 53

Foil underlays. The type of foil used is illustrated in figure 319 (type B2) and is discussed below.

Cell forms. The cell forms and characteristic patterns are shown in figure 229.

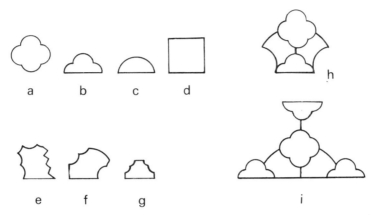

FIGURE 229   The Sutton Hoo sword: cell
forms in the pommel. (Scale: 3/2)

The cocked hat form gives rise to a series of curved fields, as indicated in figure 218. The designs on the two faces A (fig. 218*b*) and B (fig. 218*e*) differ, and twenty garnets are used in the design on A as against sixteen on B. As figure 218 shows, the design is based upon two types of cell that do not occur anywhere else in the Sutton Hoo jewellery, the quatrefoil cell and half-quatrefoil cell (fig. 229*a* and *b*). The third type of cell in primary use is the semicircle, a form which also occurs residually at the ends of the rectangular mounts, Inv. 6 and 7 (fig. 323*a*). The essential design on face B, has equilibrium and vitality. It may be reduced to the essentials shown in figure 229*i*. In its balance and simplicity it resembles a tableau of gymnasts; the curves give an impression of its concealed strength; even the supporting zig-zag step devices suggest springs. Face A has a slightly more complex design, having strong affinities with that of the cloisonné sword-pommel from Hög Edsten, Kville, Bohuslän, in Sweden, which could well be a late product of the Sutton Hoo workshop, the period when the purse-lid and pyramids were being produced there (fig. 230).

---

[1] A discussion of technical aspects of the garnet work, millefiori and blue glass inlays is included in ch. x (sect. 5, pp. 582-603). In this chapter also, the section on the sword suspension mechanism (pp. 564-82) discusses the parts played by the scabbard bosses and pyramids.

The elegance, clarity and relative simplicity of the cloisonné designs on the pommel, and the use of patterns and cell shapes that do not occur elsewhere in the Sutton Hoo jewellery, are compatible both with an earlier date and with origins outside East Anglia. Conversely, there is a complete absence of the mushroom cell and its variants and of the T-shaped and step-pattern cells, of plain rectangular cells used as bordering, and of other forms that are so characteristic of the Sutton Hoo workshop as defined by its leading pieces—the shoulder clasps, purse-lid and pyramids—which, from the inclusion of mille-fiori, we know to be local work.

FIGURE 230 Sword-pommel from Hög Edsten, Bohuslän, Sweden. (Scale: 1/1) (Photo: Statens Historiska Museum, Stockholm)

A further point distinguishes the pommel from all other items of jewellery in the Sutton Hoo treasure. As in the other pieces, there is patterned gold foil beneath the garnets. The regularity and continuity of the pattern suggests that it was impressed on the large sheets of foil mechanically by a rouletted wheel. The impressed pattern consists of squares of sixteen rectangular depressions with surrounding lines in relief. Except under the top central stone of the pommel the foil is set diagonally. This foil variant (with sixteen depressions in the square, instead of nine) occurs in no other item of the jewellery (fig. 319).

A notable technical feature of the pommel is the convex curvature of the faces and the concavity of the top panels, necessitating watch-glass curvature of the cut garnets. The faces of the larger sides are convex in two directions. The garnets were no doubt set and polished in position to fit the designed convexity. It has not been possible to remove any of the stones to see whether paste underlies the gold foil, and if so, to relate it to the pastes analysed and grouped by Dr Birgit Arrhenius.[1]

The scabbard-bosses

Number of garnets originally present. Inv. 26, 105; Inv. 27, 105.

Foil underlays. The foil backing used both for the cruciform design and for the spaces between the arms of the cross is the same. It is illustrated in figure 319 and referred to as type A1.

Cell forms. The cell forms and characteristic patterns are shown in figure 231.

These bosses are amazing *tours de force*, as are the pyramids. The cloisonné design has a petal-like appearance, derived from the twenty-four inward-pointing gold teeth that surround the base of the boss and the elegantly outward-pointing segments of garnet that fill the spaces between. Another notable feature is the effectiveness of the cross theme which seems unmistakably to represent the Christian symbol. The central area of the cross is picked out in stones of orange colour, whereas the segments between the arms have a deep lustrous purple tone. This colour variation is not

[1] Arrhenius 1971; see also App. B, p. 123 above.

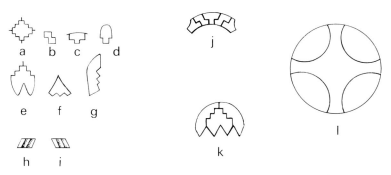

FIGURE 231 The sword: cell forms in the scabbard-bosses.
(Scale: 3/2)

effected by the use of shallow and deep cells, for the cells beneath the orange garnets are no deeper than those beneath the purple ones (cf. fig. 223). Nor is it the result of omitting patterned foil backings from behind the deeper coloured stones to reduce reflection of light as most of these have foil backings, though they are often very difficult to see. The colour changes are effected primarily by the thickness and shape of the stones, though there is evidence also that the garnets themselves vary in colour. This is best illustrated from an instance in the smaller boss, Inv. 27, where it can be seen that one of the four identically constructed mushroom cells has an orange-coloured stone, while the other three have stones of a deeper red; yet the four cells are of identical depths and the stones have identical foil backings. The use of orange-toned stones in contrast to the normal red in general use in the jewellery is particularly notable in the shoulder clasps (pls. 15 and 16 and p. 527 below). The convexity of the bosses adds lustre and effects of transmitted light to the stones. The sculptured stones round the edges of the bosses, in two tiers, divided by low inserted oblique gold walls, are held in place by patterned foil as elsewhere. These cells have a depth of 2 mm (figs. 222g, 223b).

A loose purplish garnet from one of the outer cells of Inv. 26 is illustrated in figure 232. It is convex, being 0·7 mm thick at the edges and 0·75 mm in the middle.

FIGURE 232 The Sutton Hoo sword: a garnet and its gold-foil underlay from one of the scabbard-bosses (Inv. 26). (Scale: 6/1) (Photo: British Museum Research Laboratory)

The pyramids

Number of garnets and other inlays. The number of inlays in both pyramids is the same, as follows:

	Garnets	Millefiori	Blue glass
Inv. 26	101	1	8
Inv. 27	101	1	8

Foil underlays. Type A1 throughout (fig. 319).
Cell forms. Cell forms are shown in figure 233.

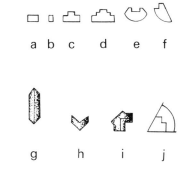

FIGURE 233 The sword: cell forms in the pyramids. (Scale: 3/2)

The identity of the two pyramids, not only in dimensions but in their cloisonné designs, which are exactly repeated on all four sides, is astonishing. The sloping faces of the pyramids show a panel surrounded by thick gold walls. Outside these panels the angles and upper corners of the pyramids are cut in solid garnet. The stones on the upper corner are faceted in three planes, recessed at the back to receive the corners of the thick gold frame that surrounds the central millefiori inset in the top of the pyramid, and further recessed below to admit the upward-pointing gold wall which retains the wedge-shaped blue glass inlay. The vertical bordering of long and short plain cells round the base should be noted. Plate 22 *e* shows the effect of one pyramid seen in transmitted light which bends through the prisms formed by the stones in the angles. These faceted stones represent perhaps the highest level in gem-cutting seen in all Germanic jewellery (p. 597 ff. below).

Gold analysis

Analyses have been carried out on all the gold jewellery from Sutton Hoo. The methods used and results obtained are given in chapter x, Appendix C. The results of analyses for items associated with the sword are shown in table 21.

TABLE 21   RESULT OF GOLD ANALYSES FOR ITEMS ASSOCIATED WITH SWORD

	Specific gravity	% Gold	% Silver	% Copper	% Lead	Sample weight (mg)
Pommel	—	97·0	2·46	2·38	—	4·62
Upper plate of the upper guard (Inv. 20)	—	93·5	3·75	2·28	0·40	1·84
Lower plate of the upper guard (Inv. 21)	—	91·7	3·72	3·65	0·92	1·02
Upper plate of the lower guard (Inv. 22)	—	90·1	8·33	1·38	0·17	0·72
Lower plate of the lower guard (Inv. 23)	—	93·6	4·15	2·19	0·04	1·78
Larger gold filigree clip (Inv. 24)	15·98	74·6	—	—	—	—
Smaller gold filigree clip (Inv. 25)	15·49	70·0	—	—	—	—
Larger scabbard-boss (Inv. 26)	—	86·5	10·5	4·30	—	3·49
Smaller scabbard-boss (Inv. 27)	—	89·0	10·6	2·70	—	4·80
Pyramid (Inv. 28)	—	76·8	20·8	2·50	—	3·21
Pyramid (Inv. 29)	—	77·8	20·2	2·94	—	5·50

A NOTE ON THE PATTERN-WELDING
OF THE SWORD-BLADE

by

ANGELA CARE EVANS

The condition of the iron sword-blade in the Sutton Hoo burial was indifferent when found (p. 273 and 282 ff.). It had corroded inside its scabbard and had been badly crushed during the collapse of the burial chamber and by the enormous downward pressures subsequently thrust upon it by the weight of sand in the mound. Grimes (p. 273 above) describes the sword-blade as being 'curiously brittle, cracked and fissured in many places' and notes that the excavators 'were obliged to take it up piecemeal'.[1]

The blade and its scabbard (p. 282) had corroded into one inseparable mass, but radiography has revealed that beneath the corrosion products the iron of the blade has survived sufficiently well in restricted areas for an interpretation of its structure to be possible. A pair of stereoradiographs was also taken and these, viewed on a special stereo-viewer,[2] contributed more confirmatory detail about the pattern-welded structure. Although the pattern survives clearly in patches over the length of the blade, it is frequently obscured by corrosion products (fig. 211), but taking the pattern overall, it seems reasonably clear that the blade of the Sutton Hoo sword is very close to that of the sword from the Ely Fields Farm cemetery in its basic construction.[3]

The radiographs suggest that it was built up of four bundles of seven rods twist-forged in an alternating pattern and lying back to back with four more bundles of seven rods.[4] The bundles of rods twist alternately to right and left, forming a double band of the characteristic herringbone pattern that is one of the most distinctive features of such blades.[5] The twisted bands alternate with straight bands along the length of the blade (fig. 211). A central core of plain metal does not seem to have been used as it apparently was in the Ely sword,[6] instead the bundles of rods were forged into a solid composite strip. In broad terms, and remembering that any interpretation of radiographic evidence may be misleading in one way or another,[7] the proportions of the pattern-welded blade appear to be as follows: the average length of both the twisted and straight areas is 5·3 cm, and the pattern repeats at least eleven times; the thickness of the composite rods varies from approximately 55 mm where the rods run straight to approximately 30 mm where the bundles are twisted. The cutting edges consist of two long strips of metal each running the length of the blade and forged onto the central pattern-welded core. The evidence of the radiographs suggests that the width of the cutting edge is approximately 1 cm wide towards the tip of the blade and is apparently of a similar width in the middle sections.

The sword-blade has been sliced in the British Museum Research Laboratory, but the cut section contributed no additional information about the physical composition of the blade, although it confirmed the existence of a skin- or fur-lined scabbard (p. 285, fig. 214).

[1] Grimes 1940, 72.
[2] We are grateful to Mr Leo Biek of the Inspectorate of Ancient Monuments Laboratory, for his assistance in interpreting the structure of the blade and for allowing us to make use of the stereo-viewer in the Department of the Environment, Fortress House, W1.
[3] Maryon 1948, 74 ff., and pl. XII.
[4] France-Lanord 1952, 413 and fig. 2.

[5] Cf. the pattern-welded blades from Nydam (Maryon 1960, fig. 1) and Arlon (Thomas-Goorieckx 1961, fig. 1), the blade from Hablainville, Lorraine (France-Lanord 1949, pl. III, 1) and the Carolingian blade with three bundles of rods now in the Strasbourg Museum (ibid. pl. V, 2).
[6] Maryon op. cit., 75.
[7] Anstee and Biek 1961, 89.

REPORTS RELATING TO THE SWORD AND SCABBARD SCIENTIFIC EXAMINATIONS CARRIED OUT IN THE BRITISH MUSEUM RESEARCH LABORATORY

by

W. A. ODDY and M. S. TITE

The backing material of the jewelled bosses on the Sutton Hoo sword scabbard

The positions of the two jewelled bosses on the scabbard of the Sutton Hoo sword are marked by round areas of whitish-brown material which is presumed to be the remains of the original settings for the bosses (p. 287).

The two circular areas have been examined under the binocular microscope. No meaningful structures are visible at low magnification, but at ×75 traces of an ordered structure are just visible in some areas. The crystal size is very small, and much of the whitish material from these patches was found to be amorphous when a sample was subjected to X-ray diffraction analysis.

A small sample of the material was analysed by X-ray fluorescence in the scanning electron microscope, and shown to contain iron and phosphorus as the main constituent elements with smaller amounts of aluminium, silicon and sulphur. Calcium was not detected by this technique, although an analysis by optical emission spectrography had indicated the presence of aluminium, iron, calcium and phosphorus with traces of copper, silver, manganese and silicon.

It must be remembered that neither technique is quantitative, and of the two the emission spectrograph is more sensitive to elements only present in trace amounts.

Interpretation and conclusions

The most likely explanation of the above results is that these areas of whitish/brown material behind the jewelled bosses now consist of iron phosphate and iron oxides, although it is unfortunate that the amorphous condition of much of the remains prevents the confirmation of this hypothesis by X-ray diffraction analysis. Scientifically it is impossible to determine whether the iron phosphate is a direct replacement product of bone or ivory, or whether it has been precipitated behind the studs to fill a void left by some other decaying material. The former is more likely because the direct replacement of calcium phosphate (from, for example, bone or ivory) by iron phosphate is known to have taken place in the Sutton Hoo ship-burial.[1]

2. *Report on corrosion products in the pommel and upper guard*

The pommel

Inside the pommel is a deposit consisting of green and reddish/black materials which have the appearance of the corrosion products of copper (pl. 22 *c*). X-ray diffraction analysis has shown that the green component is chiefly malachite ($CuCO_3 \, Cu(OH)_2$) and the reddish/black component is mainly amorphous but contains a small amount of cassiterite (SnO_2). From its appearance the reddish-black com-

ponent is probably cuprite (Cu_2O) which must be amorphous as it failed to give an X-ray diffraction pattern.

The deposit inside the pommel has been semi-quantitatively analysed by X-ray fluorescence analysis. The main elements detected were copper, tin and arsenic in the approximate ratio of 10:7:1.

It is thus clear that this deposit consists of the corrosion products of an arsenical bronze. However, the above ratio cannot be related to the original

[1] *Sutton Hoo*, Vol. I, 550–64.

composition of the alloy because of uncertainties in the semi-quantitative nature of the analysis, and because of possible segregation effects in the corrosion products.

The upper guard

The gold tray part of the guard contains an off-white deposit which has been shown by repeated X-ray diffaction analyses to consist chiefly of cassiterite (SnO_2). A semi-quantitative X-ray fluorescence analysis has now shown that the main elements present are copper, tin and arsenic in the approximate ratio 2:40:3. A microscopic examination has shown that the deposit consists of alternate dark and light-coloured layers in which a 'ghost' dendritic structure is visible. Although the reason for the different coloured bands is not clear, the segregation of corrosion products of a normal tin bronze into layers is a well-attested phenomenon. The presence of the dendritic pattern proves that the deposit was originally a cast metal and the analytical results show that it must have been a cast high tin alloy.[1]

Acknowledgement. Thanks are due to Mavis Bimson, M. C. Cowell and N. D. Meeks who carried out some of the experimental work.

3. *Fibres on the scabbard*

In various positions on the scabbard traces of fibres are visible which seem to be positioned between the wooden scabbard and the corroded iron sword blade. The cutting of a section of the blade with a wire saw[2] in an attempt to elucidate the structure of the pattern welding in the blade has enabled a closer examination to be made of one patch of these fibres which are in much better condition than elsewhere on the scabbard.

The cut section of the blade (fig. 212) shows the line of its original surface and clearly demonstrates that these fibres definitely form a layer enclosing it. These fibres have been examined under the microscope and figure 214 illustrates them at two different magnifications. The fibres are extremely even in diameter and uniformly round in cross-section. These features strongly suggest that they are of animal origin. On close examination at a high magnification they can be seen to be hollow, and to consist entirely of corrosion products of iron. It is quite common for animal hair to have a channel running down the centre of the fibre and what is now visible is probably the outer layers of fibres which have become fossilised by the iron corrosion products. Although it is not possible to identify the fibres in their present condition, they most probably represent a straight soft type of animal fur, rather than sheep's wool.

17 March 1976

[1] But see p. 111, n. 1.

[2] For the technique see R. Burleigh and M. A. Seeley, *Archaeometry*, 17 (1975), 116–19.

FIGURE 234   Enlargement of head A2; see also figure 238.

CHAPTER VII

THE SCEPTRE

1. *Introduction and primary accounts of discovery*

THE REMARKABLE STONE OBJECT now identified as a sceptre (Inv. 160 and 205) was first encountered on Sunday, 23 July 1939, during work on the area north of the nest of silver bowls (fig. 1). Phillips's diary for that day contains this passage:

'North of the iron-bound bucket, and partly passing under it, pointing a little west of north, with the north end higher than the south, was a long, square-sectioned stone object, tapering equally towards each end, and looking like a whetstone, which it probably was. Each end was decorated with four low relief bearded human heads, one on each face, the ultimate end in each case being shaped like a large melon bead. These ends had been coloured red and bound round with bronze claws which supported a cup-like final terminal of bronze at the south end, there being a strong suggestion that at one time, whether before the burial or after, an identical arrangement had been fixed at the north end.'[1]

Phillips's impression that an identical arrangement to that at the south end of the stone bar had been fixed at the north end seemed sound, was never questioned, and conditioned subsequent thinking. However, on the same day 'A pair of small bronze claws, probably connected with some rodding, perhaps a tripod, appeared emerging from the east side of the partition just above the iron-bound wooden bucket'. The stone object was removed the same day, when wood and gold-leaf-covered fittings of the shield were noted underneath. Three days later, on 26 July, the following entry appears:

'A beginning was made of dealing with the bucket, and this necessitated the investigation and removal of the small bronze claw like object which was projecting from the face of sand above the bucket [fig. 235]. This proved to be a bronze figure of a stag with its head looking north and lying on its right side. It had been mounted on an iron ring.'[2]

Figure 235 shows that, as found by the excavators, one end of the sceptre was sticking up at a higher level than the other, being completely exposed at this stage in the excavation while the other end remained deeply buried. The difference in condition of the two ends may be due to this position taken up by the stone in the

---

[1] *Sutton Hoo*, Vol. I, 738. [2] Ibid. 740.

FIGURE 235 The sceptre *in situ*: the antlers of the bronze stag can be seen projecting from the sand at the centre of the picture. Bucket no. 3 and part of the spears and angons complex are to the left. (Photo: S. Piggott)

grave following the collapse of the chamber, for the lower end remained in close contact with wood and iron in the dark wet sandy soil which enveloped the grave goods, while the damaged top projected into clean yellow sand (p. 343). As excavated the top of the stone bar was well above the level of the shield and situated between it and the iron stand. The lower end, buried deeper, lay under elements of iron-bound wooden bucket no. 3 (Inv. 119). It seems likely that the sceptre had been placed vertically in the chamber, and that its top was struck and damaged, and the stag, ring and pedestal broken off when something fell on it, either at the time of the general collapse of the chamber or earlier.

2. *General description*

Dimensions

Length of stone bar	58·3 cm
Overall length, including metal elements	82·0 cm
External diameter of iron ring	10·7 cm
Maximum width of bar	5·0 cm

Weight (in present condition) with stag and other metal fittings   3·25 kg

Estimated weight of stone alone   2·4 kg

Large stone bar, four-sided, of hard, very fine-grained grey stone shaped and carved at both ends in a similar manner (fig. 236*a* and pl. 11 *a, b*). At each end is a neck or constriction and beyond it a carved knob, roughly onion-shaped, originally painted red. Good traces of colour remain.

The stone bar carries at one end (which will be referred to as the top) a ring 10·7 cm

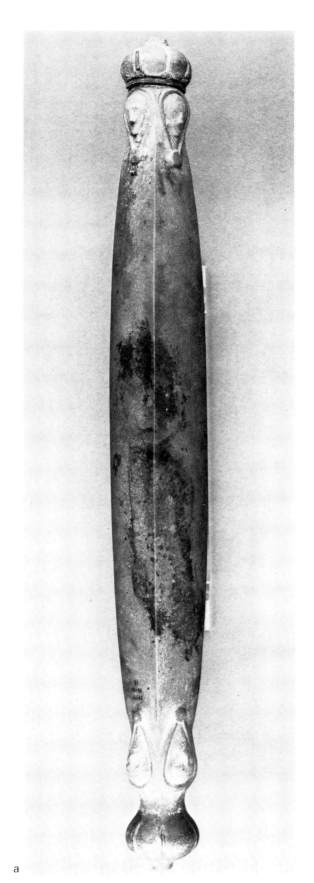

a

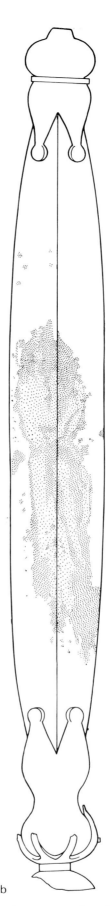

b

FIGURE 236 The sceptre: (a) the stone bar with the bronze saucer-fitting removed and (b) simplified drawing of the bar with the saucer-fitting in position; both showing areas of dark staining. (Scale: rather under 1/3)

in diameter, made up of two pairs of iron wires twisted individually in opposite directions, the four wires being held together at intervals by four bronze binding-clips. Two of these, to either side, are fluted, and two, those on which the fore and hind feet of the stag rest, at the top of the wire ring, appear to have been plain. The ends of the iron wire hoop or ring are fitted into the arms of a Y-shaped bronze pedestal. The fluted elements at each end of the Y-piece were cast with it and are not binding clips, as at first sight they appear to be (cf. fig. 274).

This pedestal in turn was attached to the knob at the top of the stone bar by eight flat and fluted (swaged) bronze strips. On top of the ring is mounted a finely modelled and stylised bronze stag (pls. 10 and 11c). At the other end of the stone (referred to as the bottom end) a shallow saucer of bronze 5 cm in diameter surmounts a circular bronze collar which in turn is attached to the corresponding painted knob by a cage of six carinated bronze claws. The whole of this terminal arrangement is cast in one piece and is held in place by two horizontal swaged strips.

The stone bar, seen in profile, tapers from the centre to each end, on each side reducing to a width of 3·2 cm and then expanding into a protruding carved human face or head. Each face is contained in and completely fills a pear-shaped frame. Below the ear-level of these faces the frames consist of a raised moulding of semicircular or rounded cross-section; above ear-level this merges at the lower end of the bar into a stone hood or cap. At the upper end of the bar the moulding line is continued by the decorated spandrels and horizontal moulding of the neck. These pear-shaped frames terminate at their pointed end in a raised oval pad which stands out to a slightly greater height than the border itself. The raised, sub-circular pads vary between 9 and 12 mm in maximum diameter. Beyond the projecting faces at either end and the hoods which surmount them, the stone contracts again into a cylindrical neck or constriction of circular cross-section (not square, as in the body of the stone) and then expands into the rounded onion-shaped knobs. Each knob is painted red and was grasped by a cage of bronze strips or claws. These followed closely the profile of the

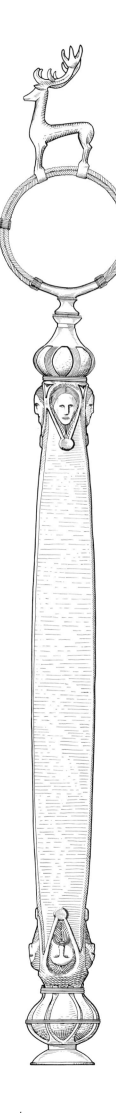

FIGURE 237　The sceptre reconstructed. (Scale: 1/3)

314

knob and joined the socketed fittings from which in turn the two finials of the sceptre developed, at one end the shallow dish, at the other the ring and the stag (fig. 237 and p. 339 ff.). The bronze elements attached to the knobs are damaged. At the lower end the cage of ribs is almost complete; at the top the strips are more than half missing.

The stone shows no traces of wear, beyond a slight polish of the angles, compatible with the stone being handled with some regularity. Apart from this it is in mint condition, and has certainly never been used to sharpen anything. It is very fine-grained and uniform in appearance and composition, and grey in colour. Fine glittering micaceous points can be seen all over, giving the stone a silky look. The stone has been examined by Mr S. E. Ellis of the Department of Mineralogy, British Museum (Natural History). Since it has not been thought desirable to remove a slice for analysis, his examination was visual. His report is printed as Appendix B (p. 383). Macrophotographs of the stone appear as figure 273 a, b. There is an extensive blackish area which can be seen chiefly on two adjacent faces. It appears as a continuous spread 23 cm in length (fig. 236 a, b). This is not an inclusion in the stone but is a superficial stain which was presumably caused by substances with which the stone came into contact under the wet conditions in the bottom of the burial chamber (p. 312).

Three of the human faces are conventionally bearded. Others at first sight seem beardless. The heads (figs. 238, 239) fall into two types, best distinguished as having either exposed chins (not bearded) or chins covered by a beard. At one end, that to which the stag and ring was attached, all four heads have exposed chins. At the other, one of the four heads has an exposed chin, the remaining three have covered chins. In these three the chin is neither visible nor indicated, except perhaps in one case (see face B3 below). A long beard covers and masks it. The beard extends to the bottom of the pear-shaped field and fills it out. Of the three faces with such beards covering their chins, two have also long moustaches. Of the five faces with exposed chins none has a moustache.

The five heads with exposed chins all show, beneath the jawline, patterns of carved grooves and raised lines closely resembling in treatment the beards of the three bearded faces. It is not clear whether these grooves and ridges, which are virtually identical in extent, pattern and general treatment with those of the beards, should be interpreted as off-the-chin beards, grown long and in no way different from the others except that they do not cover the chin. The heads with exposed chins differ in other ways from the three with covered chins and unambiguous beards to such an extent that it is possible to think that while the human heads with covered chins and, in two out of three instances, moustaches, were intended to represent men, or male deities, the five human heads with exposed chins, all moustacheless, may have been intended to represent women or female deities. The interpretation of these types is discussed at length below.

In figures 238 and 239 all eight masks or heads are shown together for comparison. Those in the lower row, B, are from the lower end, that with the saucer-fitting. The heads are arranged one above the other in pairs, numbered 1 to 4 for each face of the stone. In each vertical pair, heads A and B are thus at opposite ends of the same face of the stone.

The four A heads (those at the top of the stone, on which the stag is mounted) appear slightly more worn (pitted) and stained than the four B heads. This may reflect the greater degree of damage which this end of the stone has suffered generally, as may be inferred from the breaking off of the stag and its pedestal and the severely corroded condition of the fluted bronze strips which held it.

The sceptre is unique and shows every evidence of having been carefully designed, as might be expected for so significant an object. The chief enigma it presents lies in the human heads, their significance and treatment. These must be described in more detail.

3. The human heads: detailed description and discussion

I HEADS AT THE LOWER END OF THE SCEPTRE (B1–4)

The first heads in each group to be discussed will be described in full detail; since they show various characteristics that recur on the others these can then be dealt with more summarily.

Head B1 (fig. 238)

A male head, bearded and with a moustache. The long moustache, rendered as two raised lines, forms on the head's right side a re-entrant downward curve, on the left a steady convex curve: both are reflected in the beard below. The lower of the two mouldings representing the moustache hardly registers over the mouth, giving the effect of a plain space between moustache and mouth. The nose is thick, broad, straight and with a slight upward tilt at the point. The eyebrows project, forming distinct ridges. The mouth is a long straight split, with both lips standing out in a pout. The eyes are pointed; the left eye has a slightly moulded lower lid and looks more sunken than the right. The hair is not parted but is represented by a series of close-set mouldings radiating backwards and outwards from the firmly demarcated hair line.

There is no indication of ears but the hair stops at ear-level, just below the eyes. The cheeks are bare on both sides for a space of 1 cm before the moustache lines are reached. The beard falls away along its length on each side of a central ridge or arris.

The substance of hair and beard seems to be indicated by the thread-like raised lines thrown up between the incised grooves. Twenty-seven such lines form the hair, their ends lined up side by side along the hair line. Three of these raised lines (the eighth, tenth and eleventh from the left) bifurcate to fill the expanding field of the top of the head; at the top centre a V or inverted chevron, the point of which does not reach the hair line, is let in. It carries a central length of hair moulding.

The outline of the head is regular and follows exactly the line of the frame. The beard is depicted by seven raised lines descending from the lip. The central raised line bifurcates a little way below the lip, and in the space that opens up are inserted three inverted chevrons and finally, at the point of the beard, a raised triangle.

The face is full and rounded and projects 1 cm in front of the level of the upper surface of the frame. The stone stop or pad which marks the point of the frame is of roughly circular form, with irregularly bevelled edges. At its centre there appears a white spot, which is a slight hole or depression.

Head B2 (fig. 238)

This head alone at this end of the stone has an exposed chin, and it differs in other particulars also from the three heads with covered chins. It has a lopsided look. The right eye seems to be lower down than the left. The line of the chin on the right is slightly incurved, that on the left is straight. The chin is squared. The mouth is shorter by 1 mm than the mouths of the other three faces at this end and the eyes are more oblique. The nose is smaller and 2 mm shorter than the noses of the other B heads. The eyebrows are heavily modelled, as on face B1. The mouth has a slightly open look, not seen in the other B heads.

From the middle of the mouth to the extreme top of the head the length is 2 mm shorter than in the faces B1 and B4 and 1 mm shorter than in B3, the face with mouth somewhat higher. The maximum width of the head is the same in all four. However, the features proper, whether measured from the centre of the mouth to a point between the eyes, or from the centre of the mouth to a point between the tops of the eyebrows, are composed within a notably shorter length than in B1 and B4 and within a little shorter space than B3 (1·5 mm shorter). Between the centre point of the mouth and the point midway between the eyes, i.e. the space where the features are concentrated, the four B heads measure respectively: 1, 12·0 mm; 2, 9·5 mm; 3, 11·0 mm; 4, 13·0 mm. The corresponding measurements in mm for the four A heads at the other end of the stone are: 1, 10·5 mm; 2, 8·5 mm; 3, 10·0 mm; 4, 10·8 mm.

As in B1, 1 cm of bare cheek separates head hair and beard on each side of the face, the limits of hair and beard being clearly defined. The chin, though exposed, is not deeply undercut but the line of it is carried well up towards the ears, beyond the uppermost ridge of the hair-like patterns below it. Below the exposed chin the field is filled out by raised mouldings separated by grooves. The treatment of these (minutiae of style apart) is the same as for the mouldings on the four A heads. Five inverted chevrons, one inside the next, occupy the space between the pointed bottom of the pear-shaped field and the exposed chin. Seven converging strokes or mouldings maintain the angle of the chevrons, running obliquely inwards between the frame and the jaw line and continuing up to the level of the ends of the mouth.

The lowest element in the field is a chevron, not a solid triangle as in B1 or a straight stroke as in B4 (below). The raised pad at the point of the frame, which is shaped

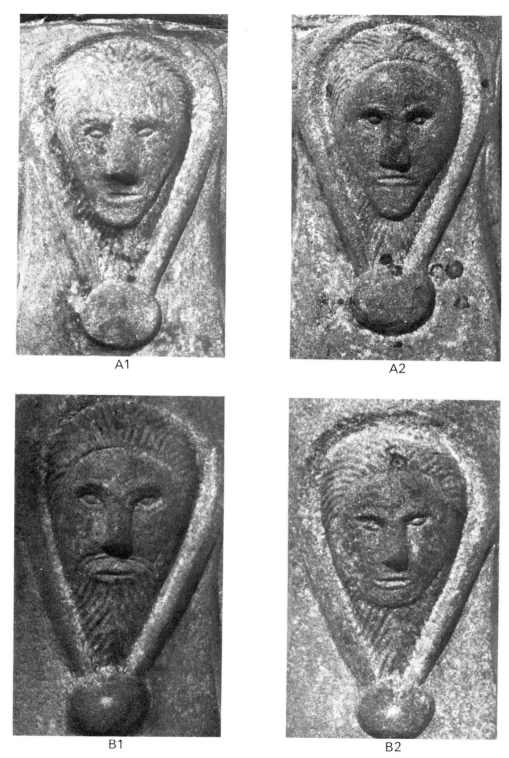

A1

A2

B1

B2

FIGURE 238　The sceptre: two pairs of carved faces from opposite
ends of the stone bar; heads A1 and B1, A2 and B2. (Scale: 7/4)

318

FIGURE 239   The sceptre: two pairs of carved faces from opposite
ends of the stone bar; heads A3 and B3, A4 and B4. (Scale: 7/4)

and bevelled round the edges as in B1, also has a white central mark, a depression deeper than in that of B1.

Head B3 (fig. 239)

A male head, with beard covering the chin; no moustache. The mouth is very slightly higher up in relation to the head than in the case of B1 and B4, and as a result the face looks slightly less long. This impression is reinforced by the sharp recessing of the beard below the mouth, suggesting a very short chin concealed beneath it. Eyebrows and eyelids stand out, being modelled with delicate deliberation. The eyes are deeper set than in any of the other heads except A2 (below); the mouth, however, is a lopsided gash (deeper on the left than on the right), with no modelling of the lips.

A feature that distinguishes B3 is that whereas in the other B heads the hair is swept back off the forehead and separated from the beard by bare cheek, here the hair is combed down straight off the sides of the temples, covering the cheeks and meeting the obliquely carved hair of the beard at either side along a sloping straight line. The slight carination down the centre of the beard is well defined. The lightly modelled eyebrows seem not to join centrally over the nose, as they do in B1 and B4, but to be separated. The eyes are deep-set and the eyeballs prominent.

The covering of the cheeks gives this head something of the look of a Norman knight in a mail hood. A further notable feature is the relative refinement of the carving. The individual threads of beard and head hair are thinner; the number of beard mouldings, for example, between the outer corners of the mouth and the point, is 13, as against 9 in B2 and 8 in B1. The lowest element at the point of the beard is a very small raised triangle. The stone pad below the pear-shaped frame has no central white mark or depression, such as has been noted in the case of heads B1 and 2. The tip of the nose is slightly damaged and there is a nick at the centre of the lower lip. Some indecisive marks around the upper lip suggest that a moustache may initially have been lightly scratched in and subsequently removed.

Head B4 (fig. 239)

A male head with beard and moustache, very similar to B1. There is a clear space or gap on the upper lip between the two halves of the moustache. The lips are not so deeply modelled as in B1 and eyebrows do not exist at all. The eyes are shown with the pupils accented, giving a staring expression. There is a suggestion of an eyelid under the left eye, but not under the right. Some 1 cm of bare cheek separates the head hair from the beard. On the left side of the head the beard is carried higher up the cheek by three mouldings, reducing the amount of bare space between hair and beard on this side of the face and giving the face a slightly unbalanced look. The head hair also descends lower on the right side, adding to the unbalanced look. The beard is terminated by a single vertical stroke. The circular pad below the pear-shaped field has a central spot as in B1 and 2.

General

The pear-shaped fields containing the heads at the upper end of the sceptre, from the top of the head to the circular pad at the lower end of the frame, are uniformly slightly shorter than those at the lower end of the sceptre.

Upper end	Length of head in mm	Lower end	Length of head in mm	Difference in mm
A1	38	B1	41	3
A2	38·5	B2	40	1·5
A3	37	B3	42	5
A4	38·5	B4	42	3·5

The difference averages about 3 mm. The maximum difference between any two is 5 mm; this is only slight but does represent a consistent difference between the two ends. It has an effect on the treatment of the mouldings or threads in the hair convention that fill up the lower end of the frame. In the case of the three obviously bearded heads at the lower end of the sceptre (B1, 3 and 4) the beards come to a point. In the slightly smaller frames at the top of the sceptre the lower end of the field is in general slightly broader and the strips or chevrons are not brought to a point (i.e. reduced in proportion to fill up the shorter space), but simply truncated. It is a broader, less shapely pattern. At the upper end of the stone the tops of the pear-shaped fields are slightly squared or flattened, less arched than at the lower end, the space being constricted by the short neck of the squat upper knob. The fields containing the heads at the lower end of the bar all measure internally, at their widest point, 23·5 mm. In the case of B3, with long hair down the cheeks, the head itself is fractionally narrower, its sides being more undercut or vertical, but the field is the same. The fields at the top average 22 mm in width. A4 is somewhat narrower, the sides of the head being cut steeper, but again the space within the frame remains the same as for the others.

The stone contracts to the same width at both ends on each side of the bar. Treatment of hair and of the space under the chin at the upper end of the stone is the same as at the lower end, apart from the truncation effect referred to above. All the heads at the top end of the stone have exposed chins. None of the circular pads at the points of the frames at the top of the stone bar show a central hole as seen in B1, 2 and 4.

Head A1 (fig. 238)

There is a slight modelling of the eyebrows but none of the eyelids. The eyebrows do not meet. The lower lip is slightly modelled, but not the upper. The eyeballs are pointed ovals. The chin is slightly hollowed between the lower lip and point. The outline of the jaw is sharply defined and cut at right angles to the plane of the carving, so that the chin juts well out from the patterned surfaces that may represent hair. The nose is big and square.

Head A2 (figs. 234 and 238)

The eyebrows are carefully modelled; they do not join. The nose, which is damaged, seems broad. The lower lip is slightly raised and the chin is long and pointed. The pattern of lines below the chin is carried up along the sides of the face to a point on the level of the middle of the nose. There is only a small gap between the head hair and the mouldings associated with the chin. The eyes are deep sunk and the pupils are mere pin-heads. The lower eyelids are lightly modelled. The hair line is more arched, less flattened, than, for example, in B3, and the forehead is larger in proportion than in the B heads.

Head A3 (fig. 239)

There is no modelling of eyebrows or lids on this face and the eyeballs are pointed ovals. The mouth is very large, with lower lip heavily raised, and chin hollowed between it and the point. As in A1 and 2 there is an expanse of bare cheek between the hair and lower patterning. The hair line is clearly but lightly marked, as in the other A heads. This is the heaviest-seeming of the A heads.

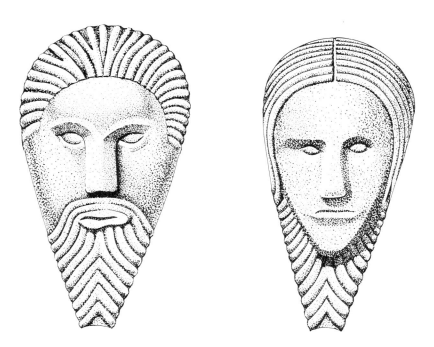

FIGURE 240 The sceptre: drawing of a head with bearded chin, B1, and of a head with exposed chin (i.e. no beard or perhaps with a throat, or off-the-chin beard), A4.
(Scale: 2/1)

322

Head A4 (figs. 239 and 240)

There is no modelling of eyebrows or eyelids. The eyes are at uneven heights and circular, more like pin-heads than almond-shaped, though not so completely so as in A2. This head alone of all eight has the hair centrally parted. It falls vertically to the level of the bottom of the nose and joins the patterning under the chin, leaving no bare cheek exposed between. The chin is narrow, pointed and thin, and is hollowed out between the lip and the point of the chin. The lower lip is slightly raised.

III DISCUSSION

It would be tempting to regard one end of the stone as representing male elements and the other as female. But are there any grounds for regarding the faces with exposed chins as female? Can they not be males, with an abnormal beard form?

There is no difficulty about identifying as male the three bearded faces, two of them moustached, at the lower end of the stone. In the case of the other five we have to consider the significance of the muffler or cravat-like patterning below and around the chins. As we have seen, there is no difference between the conventions and technique employed in rendering these below-the-chin patterns, and those used for the head hair throughout and for the beards and moustaches of those heads that have beard-covered chins. If the heads with exposed chins are to be considered as female we are bound to suppose that the hair so depicted, if hair it is intended to be, represents the hair of the head brought down under the chin. This would be possible in the case of A4, the one head with parted hair, where the head hair links with the patterning below the chin, and the latter could readily be interpreted as conventionalised plaits or ringlets. In all five heads with exposed chins, however, the moulded lines do not run parallel with the outline of the cheeks as hair descending from the top of the head would, but are cut at an angle running into the jaw line. The normal line of hair falling from the top of the head may be seen in faces A4 and B3 (figs. 239 and 240). The encounter of head and chin hair in B3, where they meet almost at right-angles, seems to rule out any possibility (except perhaps in the case of A4) of regarding the carved lines under the exposed chins as representing a continuation of the head hair. Apart from A4, there are clear expanses of bare cheek separating head hair and chin hair on four of the five heads with exposed chins. This seems to break any physical connection between the two. It does not seem plausible to suggest that these might be long locks thrown back off the head and then brought up on to the shoulders and under the chin from behind.

The treatment of the grooves and mouldings (hair convention) is the same in the heads with exposed chins as in the beards of the heads with covered chins. It is as though the five exposed chins had broken through a set of exactly similar beards, so that one is inclined to regard these linear patterns as representing off-the-chin beards, or throat beards, a style of male hair-dressing in which the lips and chin are shaved, but the beard allowed to grow under the chin and up towards the ears, as it will naturally. On this interpretation all eight heads would be male.

The interpretation of these phenomena as off-the-chin or throat beards is uncertain. Such a style of male hair-dressing has no documentation. Moreover there does seem to be a possible attempt at sex differentiation between the heads at the two ends, although the picture is complicated by B2, the one instance of an exposed chin at the lower end of the stone, for although the pear-shaped fields containing the heads are of approximately the same length at both ends, there is the slight but consistent difference in size already mentioned. It is possibly a consequence of this that the faces at the upper end are, as we have seen, slightly smaller. The feature which seems chiefly to distinguish the A heads from the B is the relative narrowness of the chins and their pointed undercut extremities. They may be compared with the chin and jaw of the head with uncovered chin at the lower end of the stone, B2 (fig. 238). This has a broad jaw and the chin is more rounded and not so deeply undercut as in the four at the other end. This head might, it seems, represent a young man with a throat beard, but the four at the other end seem, in comparison with the rest, to have the look of women, even if grim and perhaps elderly.

Short of parallels, one is inclined to ask whether these four heads at the top of the sceptre can represent matriarchs, or female deities or agents of the deity (priestesses, or seeresses) having a hermaphrodite character? The rôle sometimes played by old women in ceremonies connected with death is suggested by that of the 'Angel of Death' in Ibn Fadlan's account of the cremation of the Russ chieftain of the Volga, or that of the horrible old women of the German tribe, the Cimbri, who selected prisoners for sacrifice after battle and with their own hands cut their throats over a ceremonial cauldron:[1] although we have no reason to think that the heads of these sinister old women were bearded, either artificially or naturally.

4. *The two ends of the stone bar contrasted*

The stone tapers symmetrically to each end, and there is no difference in scale between the two ends. The knobs are of identical diameter. Nevertheless there are important and pronounced differences in the treatment of the two ends:

(1) At the lower end, with the three obviously male heads and the bronze saucer-fitting, the red-painted knob is uplifted (fig. 241 b and pl. 11 a). Its centre of gravity is high and it stands off from the end of the rectangular-sectioned part of the stone on a slender elongated neck with a long shallow curve. At the top, carrying stag and ring, the knob is depressed, its centre of gravity is low, and it sits directly on the rectangular-sectioned end of the stone without any neck, being separated from the body of the stone only by a deep groove in which the transition from square to circular cross-section is abruptly effected (fig. 241 a).

---

[1] Strabo, *Geography*, Book VII, 2.3; Glob 1965, 153 and 1969, 176.

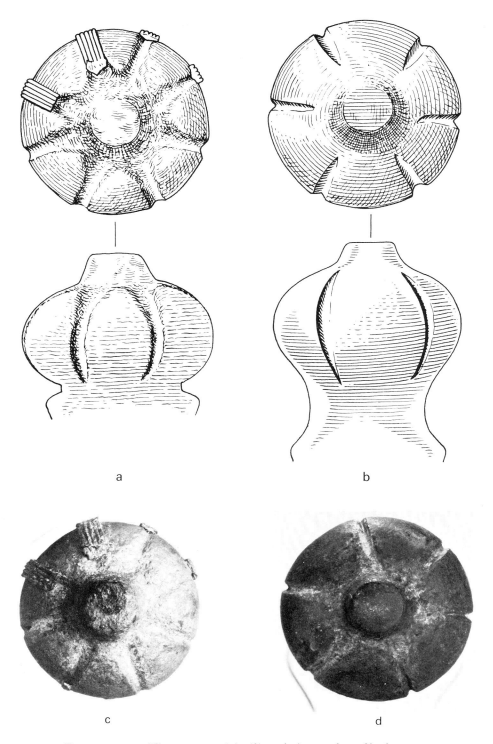

a

b

c

d

FIGURE 241 The sceptre: (*a*), (*b*) end view and profile drawings of the terminal knobs of the stone bar; (*c*), (*d*) photographs of the ends of the stone bar. Note the circular iron stain on the central conical projection in (*c*). (Scale: 1/1)

(2) The bronze cage at the lower end of the sceptre, which holds the saucer-fitting, was composed of six ribs; the bronze cage at the top, which held the pedestal carrying the ring and stag, had eight corresponding elements. This must be an original difference in number since the knob at the top is carved, under the eight elements, with a corresponding number of deep grooves, while the knob at the lower end is cut with six (fig. 241 c, d and pl. 11).

FIGURE 242   The sceptre: (a), (b) two views of the saucer-fitting and cage; (a) with portions of the two circumferential rings of fluted bronze strips attached. The carination of the 'claws', which echoes the similar carination of the stag's antlers and legs (p. 333), should be noted. (Scale: 1/1)

(3) The six ribs of the cage at the lower end are plain, thick and have a diamond-shaped cross-section (fig. 242 a, b). The rear carination of each rib fitted into a correspondingly V-shaped groove in the stone. They were intended to key the ribs into the stone, and prevent the fitting from rotating. In contrast, the eight bronze cage elements at the top were flat, wide, swaged strips with longitudinal flutings (five raised mouldings separated by four grooves, fig. 243 a).

(4) The ribs or strips were soldered to the inside of a narrow bronze ring which encircled the constriction below the knob and held them in, under the receding shape of the knob. At both ends of the stone bar this retaining ring is a flat strip with longitudinal flutings. At the lower end it is broader, having three flutings separating four raised mouldings; the narrower strip at the upper end has two raised mouldings and three flutings.

(5) The carinated claws of the cage at the lower end are hammered out into

PLATE 1   The Sutton Hoo shield. (Scale: 1/5)

PLATE 2   Bird's head and leg from the Sutton Hoo shield. Gilt-bronze with cloisonné garnet inlays. (Enlarged)

PLATE 3   Winged dragon from the Sutton Hoo shield. Gilt-bronze with garnets. (Slightly reduced)

PLATE 4 The iron shield boss with gilt-bronze decorative foils and cloisonné garnets. (Slightly reduced)

a

b

PLATE 5 Details from the Sutton Hoo shield: (*a*) a section of the flange showing a design of interlocked horses stamped in gilt-bronze foil; (*b*) disc with zoomorphic ornament from the top of the boss. The metal cell work in the centre, in which the original garnets are set, is modern. (Scales: *a*, slightly reduced, *b*, 1/1)

PLATE 6   Hand-grip extensions from the back of the shield. Iron with gilt-bronze covering and cast bronze terminals. (Scale: reduced)

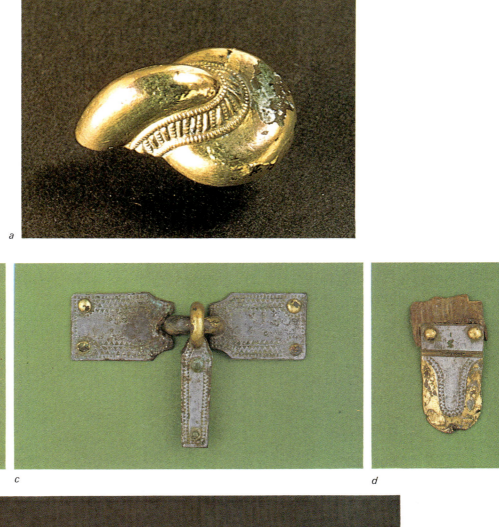

PLATE 7 Details from the Sutton Hoo shield: (*a*) cast gilt-bronze ring with band of imitation filigree; (*b*) and (*d*) gilt-bronze strap-ends from the strap used for hanging up the shield. Part of the leather strap, with tooled grooves, is seen in (*d*); (*c*) anchor fitment for the carrying-strap, tinned-bronze; (*e*) pyramidal studs in gilt-bronze from the back of the shield. These terminated the long rivets from the two uppermost small bosses on the front (pl. 1). (Scales: *a* and *e*, 2/1; *b–d*, 1/1)

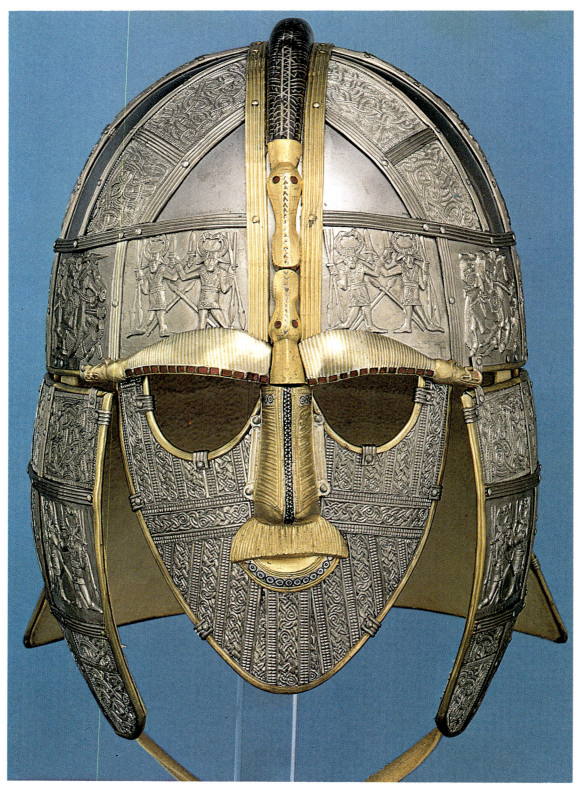

PLATE 8   The Sutton Hoo helmet, front view of the modern version made in the Royal Armouries in the Tower of London in collaboration with the British Museum.

PLATE 9   Left side of the reconstructed helmet showing rusted original fragments in a modern matrix. Iron and gilt-bronze with silver wire and garnet inlays.

PLATE 10   The Sutton Hoo sceptre (*a*), with (*b*) a detail showing the upper part of the stone-bar surmounted by a stag and ring. (Scale: reduced)

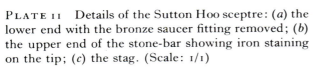

b

PLATE 11   Details of the Sutton Hoo sceptre: (a) the
lower end with the bronze saucer fitting removed; (b)
the upper end of the stone-bar showing iron staining
on the tip; (c) the stag. (Scale: 1/1)

c

PLATE 12 Oblique view of the upper part of the iron stand.

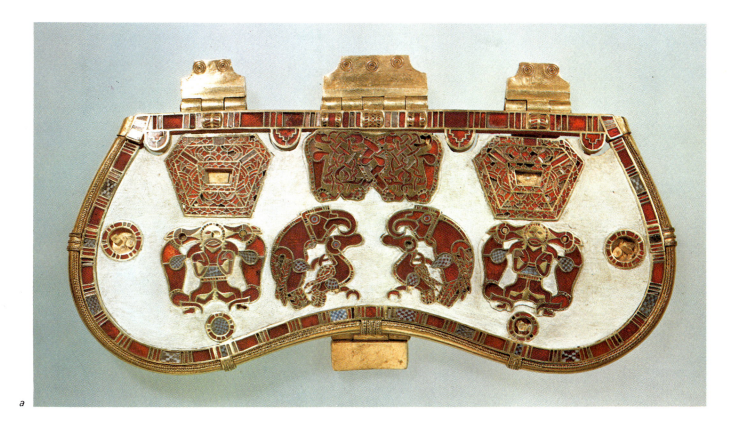

a

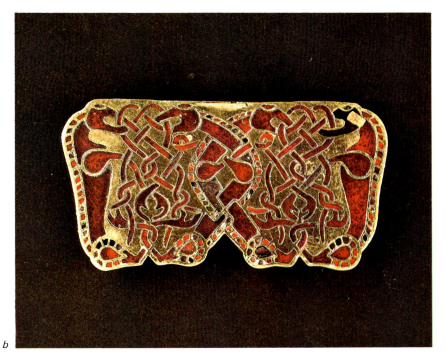

b

PLATE 13 The lid of the Sutton Hoo purse (*a*), with (*b*) a detail of the double plaque with animal interlace, made of gold and garnets. (Scales: *a*, slightly reduced; *b*, 2/1)

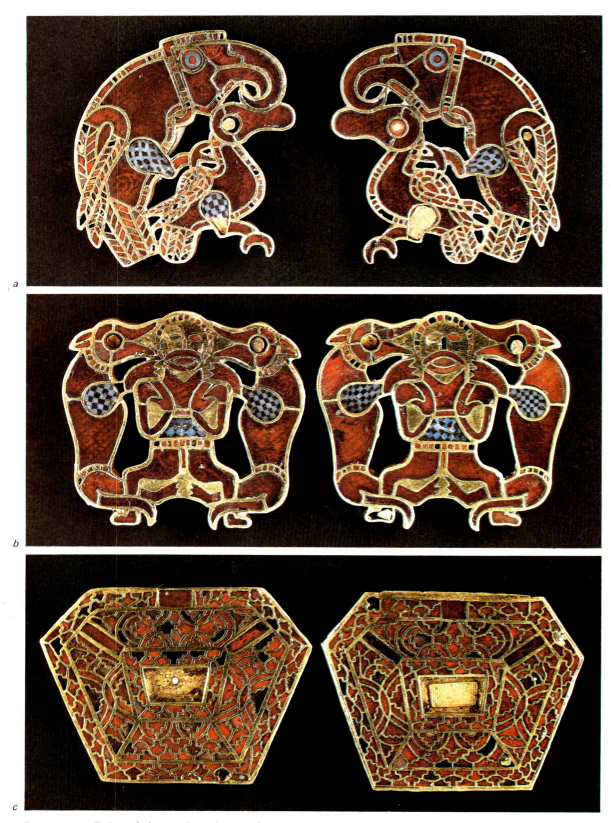

PLATE 14 Pairs of decorative plaques from the Sutton Hoo purse-lid: (*a*) bird of prey and duck; (*b*) man between beasts; (*c*) pair of hexagonal plaques with geometric designs. (Scale: 2/1)

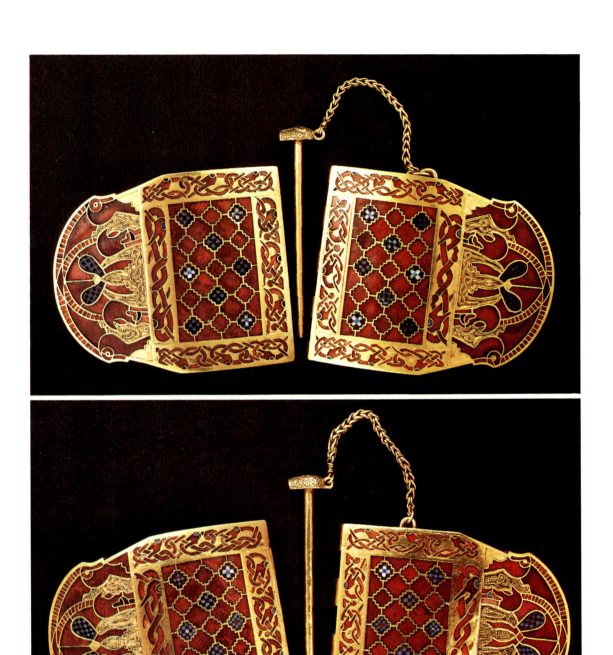

PLATE 15 Two hinged shoulder-clasps made of gold with inlays of garnet, millefiori and blue glass. (Scale: slightly under 1/1)

a

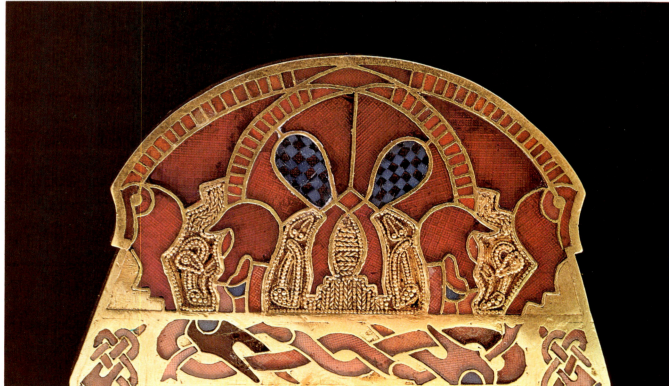

b

PLATE 16 Detail of one end of each of the two shoulder-clasps showing the intertwined boars and the gold filigree decoration; (a) Inv. 4a, (b) Inv. 5a. (Scale: enlarged)

PLATE 17   Panel of geometric design with garnet and millefiori inlays surrounded by animal interlace, from one of the Sutton Hoo shoulder-clasps (5a). (Scale: 3/1)

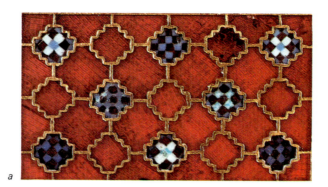

PLATE 18 The Sutton Hoo shoulder-clasps: details of the remaining three cloisonné panels; (a) and (b), 4a and b; (c) 5b. (Scale: 2/1)

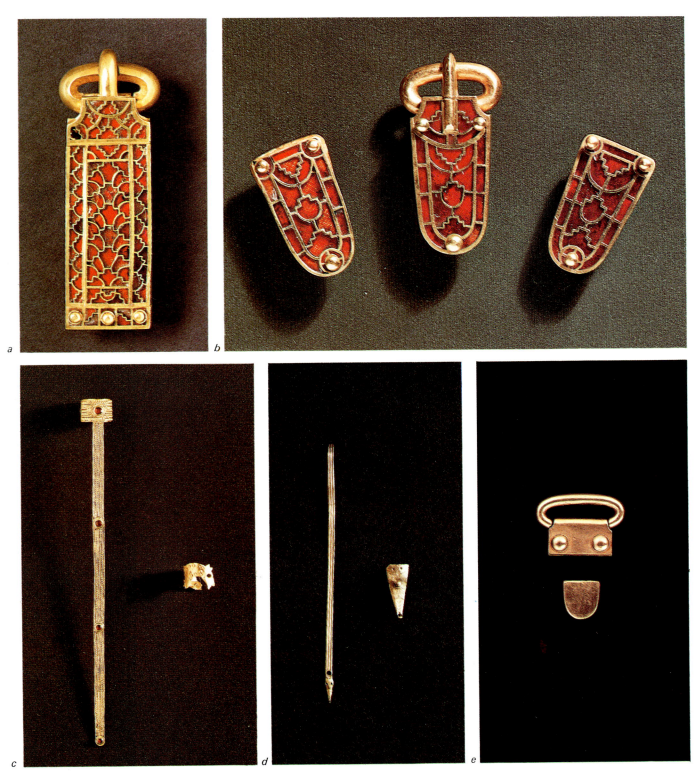

PLATE 19 Gold jewellery: (*a*) rectangular buckle; (*b*) buckle and pair of matching strap-mounts; (*c*) ring-headed filigree strip and gold-foil animal; (*d*) fluted strip with animal head and foil triangle with engraved animals; (*e*) gold loop and strap-end. (Scale: 1/1)

PLATE 20   The great gold buckle: (*a*), with (*b*) half of the loop with snake interlace; (*c*) disc with interlacing snakes from the base of the tongue; (*d*) shoulder with bird's head and boss; (*e*) the toe with crouched animal biting its leg. (Scales: *a*, 1/1; *b–e*, enlarged)

PLATE 21 Gold mounts associated with the sword; (*a*) the pommel seen from above; (*b*) the pyramids; (*c*) the scabbard-bosses and (*d*) mounts of the upper and lower guards. (Scale: 1/1)

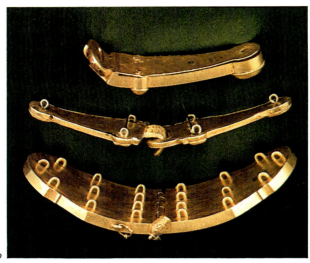

PLATE 22   The original elements of the Sutton Hoo sword mounted on perspex (*a*); (*b*) side view of the shoulder-clasps (below), the curved mount, Inv. 10 (top), and a pair of clasps from the Taplow burial (centre); (*c*) interior view of the Sutton Hoo sword-pommel and detail of the upper gold plate of the guard to which the pommel was attached; (*d*) gold filigree mounts from a purse, Beckum, Westphalia; (*e*) one of the gold and garnet pyramids from Sutton Hoo seen in transmitted light. (Scales: *a* and *b*, reduced; *c* and *e*, enlarged: *d*, 1/1.) (Photographs: *d*, by courtesy of the Westphälisches Landesmuseum für Vor- und Frühgeschichte, Münster, and *e*, Ian Yeomans)

PLATE 23 (*a*) Reconstruction of the Benty Grange helmet; (*b*) interior view of an assembly of Sutton Hoo helmet fragments showing the joins with the crest and the distinctive corrosion pattern; (*c*) a transparent red square from a millefiori inlay on one of the shoulder-clasps, showing gas bubbles; (*d*) foil, garnet and blue glass inlays from a bird's eye on the Sutton Hoo purse-lid (with modern dressmaker's pin); (*e*) a garnet on edge in one of the cells of the buckle, Inv. 11, showing the use of underlying foil to wedge the stone at the top of the cell (the space below is empty); (*f*) millefiori inlay from the purse frame showing a design of four T-shapes in red with stems pointing inwards. (Scales: *a* and *b*, reduced; *c–f*, much enlarged) (Photographs *c*, *e*, *f*, British Museum Research Laboratory, *d*, Ian Yeomans)

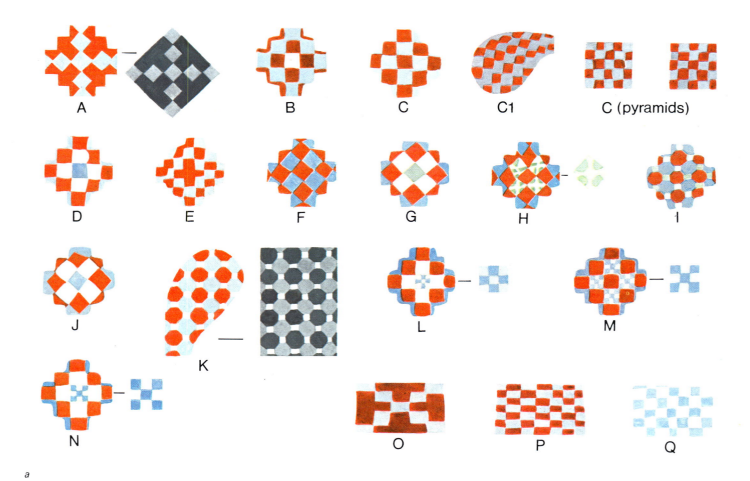

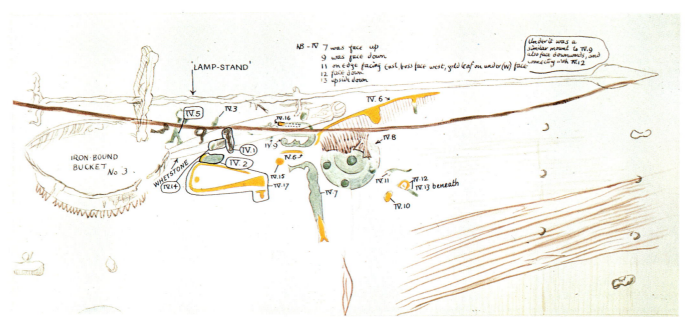

PLATE 24 (*a*) Millefiori inlays from the Sutton Hoo jewellery: A–Q the eighteen different patterns used. The monochrome drawings indicate the minimum areas required for the production of millefiori sheet for inlays A and K. (Scales: 4/1; details, 8/1.) (*b*) Detail of the west end of the burial deposit showing the shield remains *in situ*, based on a field plan by Stuart Piggott.

spatulate terminations. One of the terminations, 12·5 mm in length, survives complete (fig. 243 b). It passes behind the retaining collar and projects beyond it, its straight end resting on the shoulder of the rectangular part of the stone bar from which the neck at this end develops. There is no similar development of the flat swaged strips at the other end. They pass undifferentiated behind the retaining collar and are cut off flush with its lower edge (fig. 243 a).

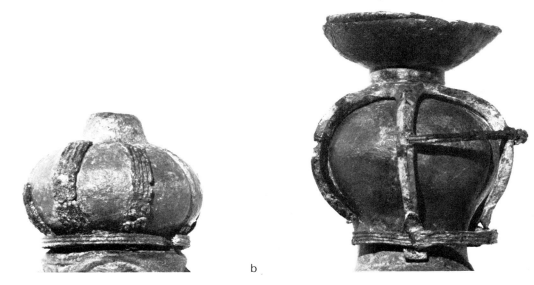

a   b

FIGURE 243   The sceptre: (a) the upper and (b) the lower end, showing constructional differences in the bronze cage mounts. (Scale: 1/1)

(6) The bronze cage of carinated ribs at the lower end is taller than that at the top, to suit the less flattened shape and more elevated carriage of the knob. A second lateral fluted strip or collar runs round the cage half way up it (fig. 243 b). The cage of flat strips at the upper end shows no trace of any such medial element, and would appear not to have had one. At the lower end, fragments of this narrow medial ring or collar are in position, and marks or erosions where it passed and adhered are still to be seen on those claws from which it is now missing. No such marks occur on the flat strips at the upper end, so far as they survive, and no fragments that might belong to such a ring survived from the original excavation, nor were any recovered in the 1967–8 excavation of the 1939 dumps.[1]

The medial ring on the cage at the lower end is narrow, showing three mouldings with two separating grooves. The retaining collar below the knob at the upper end is of the same design but cut from a somewhat broader strip of bronze.

(7) All the bearded and moustached heads are at the lower end. The four heads at the upper end all have exposed chins.

(8) The knob at the lower end develops, as has been said, from a long neck (pl.

[1] *Sutton Hoo*, Vol. I, 303–16.

11 *a*). The surface of the stone flows unbroken and plain from this neck round the four masks, dividing below the eye-level of the masks into the points of the frames converging in the circular pads at the bottom. At the upper end of the stone bar a horizontal angled shelf breaks the flow of the stone surface down from the constriction below the depressed knob, forming a definite shoulder. Below this shelf, in each of the four rounded triangular fields bridging the angled junctions between faces, is carved a bifid leaf motif (figs. 234 and 244). There is no such decoration at the lower end.

FIGURE 244 The sceptre: bifid motifs carved in the angles between the head-frames at the upper end of the stone bar. (Scale: 1/1)

At the upper end of the sceptre the pear-shaped fields are slightly flattened at the top, reflecting the angularity or squatness referred to (figs. 238–240). As they are also, as we have seen, slightly shorter than the fields at the lower end, they are broader in proportion.

(9) At the lower end, three of the roughly circular pads that terminate the pear-shaped frames round the human faces show central spots or shallow depressions. None of those at the top do.

There is thus a clear differentiation in design between the two ends of the stone, which must be significant.

5. *The pedestal, iron wire ring and stag assembly*

The iron wire ring and bronze pedestal which supported the stag measure together 14.8 cm in height (figs. 245 *a*, *b*). As stated on page 387, the four iron wires which make up the ring have their ends inserted into the ends of the Y-shaped bronze upper element of the pedestal. Drilling (fig. 275) and radiography (fig. 276) show the branching top of this Y-shaped element, which accommodates the ends of the wires, to be hollow throughout its length.

The pedestal is composed of three distinct parts, illustrated in figures 246 and 274. The wire ring is illustrated in figure 247.

Items 1(a) and 1(b) in figure 246 are cast as one piece, in spite of the fact that 1(a) is hollow and 1(b) solid. The whole pedestal assembly is held rigid by corrosion and cannot be taken apart, but radiography as well as visual examination have made the constructional details clear (App. C, p. 388). The tip of 1 (b), which just emerges into the hollow interior of the pedestal (3), is not splayed to retain a washer or other device

328

a   b

FIGURE 245   The sceptre: the bronze pedestal and iron ring that carried the stag;
(a) from the side and (b) from the front. (Scale: slightly under 1/1)

for keeping it in position; 1(b) is apparently a straight undifferentiated rod with its
tip slightly rounded. There appears to be nothing to lock 1(b) in place and it may
have been movable and capable of being withdrawn (pp. 347-9 below). It passes
through the collar (2). The function of this collar is not clear, but there must have
been some reason for its presence in the design; if the only purpose was to create a
fitting to hold 1(b), the vertical stem of the Y-shaped fitting, securely, it would have
sufficed to have 2 and 3 as a single casting. The exact shape of the bottom of the
intermediate component or collar 2 is not established. It rests loosely in the upper
basin of the pedestal-foot 3, somewhat like a ball and socket joint, although not
tight-fitting. It is difficult to see any purpose in this design unless the Y-shaped feature

329

1 (and hence the ring and stag above it) was intended to rotate, like the fish inside the large hanging bowl.[1]

The thick beaded bronze wire collar seen in plate 10, at the top of component 3 (the pedestal-foot), appears to have been soldered to its upper edge, presumably for decorative effect and to mask the junction of the two components. It was not attached to the loose collar, component 2, on the top of which rests a second collar, similarly beaded.

The bottom element of the assembly, the pedestal-foot, 3, is visualised as having been seated on and attached to the squat knob of the stone bar. The pedestal-foot and the cylindrical collar supporting the saucer-fitting at the other end of the stone bar would function in the same way. They would fit over the truncated conical

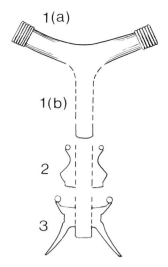

FIGURE 246 The sceptre: suggested construction of the elements comprising the pedestal assembly which carried the stag; a drawing partly in elevation and partly in section. The elements of the assembly cannot be separated and the inner surfaces are therefore shown by broken lines. (Scale: 1/1)

projections at each end of the stone bar (fig. 241) and be held to the knob by means of bronze extensions or attachments, 'claws' in one case, strips in the other. The six claws associated with the saucer-fitting at the lower end of the sceptre are cast in one piece with the saucer and its supporting collar. One would expect to find the same process for the eight swaged strips which held the bell-shaped pedestal-foot in position at the upper end but the difference in the gold content of the bronze of the pedestal and strips shows that this was not the case (p. 389). The pedestal-foot, however, from which these strips should have developed, now bears no trace of solder inside or out, nor does it show any rivet holes—the two methods by which the strips, if not cast in one piece with it, would have had to be attached to it. The method of manufacture of the claws at one end and strips at the other cannot be established but it would not seem practicable to cast them into their final form. A natural procedure would be to cast both the pedestal and the saucer-fitting with a skirt or surrounding sheet of metal from which the claws or strips could subsequently be cut and worked into shape by swaging or hammering or both.

The stag, the bronze clips which bind the wire ring, including those which held the stag in position, the different components of its pedestal, and the saucer-fitting at the other end of the stone bar, have been subjected to quantitative and qualitative chemical analysis, the important results of which are recorded in table 29, page 390, and discussed on pages 343–45 below and in the Research Laboratory report, Appendix C, pages 385–93.

[1] *Sutton Hoo*, Vol. I, pl. L (ii).

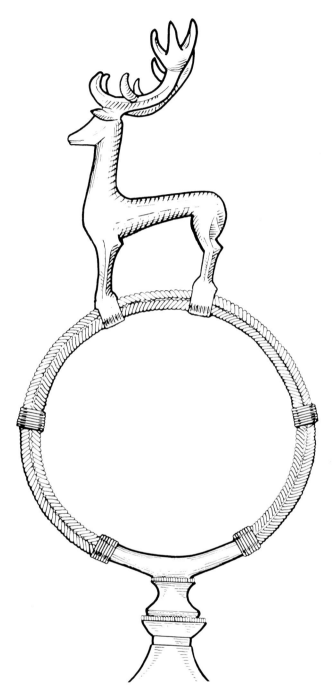

FIGURE 247 The sceptre: reconstruction
drawing of the stag, iron ring and pedestal.
(Scale: 3/4)

a

b

c

d

FIGURE 248 The sceptre: (*a*)–(*d*) four views of the bronze stag.
(Scale: 1/1)

6. *The stag*

The stag (fig. 248, pl. 11 *c*) is rendered in a highly distinctive style which in spite of its maturity and self-assurance is difficult to match. Its stylistic affinities are fully discussed by Dr Carola Hicks in Appendix A below (pp. 378–82). It is an extremely fine piece of naturalistic modelling, expressing grace, poise and energy. It carried a splendid head of antlers, now somewhat damaged in the collapse of the burial chamber and by corrosion; the brow tines are bent and the trez tines missing. The pose is lifelike. The legs are together in pairs, the back legs slightly bent, the forelegs straight and pointing forward, so that the stag is as though arrested, thrown slightly back on its haunches. Each pair of legs is amalgamated as one. In profile this gives a normal impression, but from the front the appearance is of a single leg and the idea that two legs are thought of is only minimally suggested by the carination or faceting of these unified limbs. As Dr Hicks suggests, the fusing of the front and back pairs of legs into single limbs may be a consequence of the intention to mount the stag on a narrow base—the wire ring. Almost every limb and part of the stag is carinated or faceted, as shown in figures 248, 249 and 250 (illustrating cross-sections of antlers, tines, front legs, back legs, ears, neck and body). All are to some extent shaped or stylized in this manner. There is a tendency to turn some of these diamond-shaped cross-sections into

FIGURE 249 The sceptre: (*a*)–(*c*) drawings of the stag in its present condition. (Scale: 1/1)

333

FIGURE 250   The sceptre: simplified cross-sections of the stag at
selected points. (Scale: 1/1)

hexagons by bevelling the corners. This is noticeable chiefly in the hind legs (figs.
249, 250). The bevelling is clearly seen on the hind legs when the stag is facing right,
and, less clearly, on both pairs of legs, with the stag facing left. Even the rump is
flattened into a triangle behind, as may just be detected immediately below the area
damaged by heavy corrosion. The belly is lightly carinated underneath, the tall neck
in front. The stag's back and the back of its abnormally long neck are rounded, not
carinated.

It is possible that this stylisation was adopted in order to simplify the casting
operation (the suggestion of Mr Denys Haynes, former Keeper of Greek and Roman
Antiquities, British Museum). The net result is to give the sculptured creature a
distinctive appearance and style. The stag is neither primitive nor provincial; on the
contrary, it is a work of sensitivity and sophistication and ranks as a small masterpiece.
It is almost unique as sculpture in the round in the context of Anglo-Saxon art of the
pagan period, although the Sutton Hoo ship-burial contains another rare example of

sculpture in the round—the fish in the large Celtic hanging-bowl.[1] The stag shows no trace of eyes[2] and, apart from the antlers, no indication of sex. There was apparently a small naturalistic tail or scut, the tip of which seems to survive among the corrosion on the flattened rump. The point of the sensitive muzzle is blunted. The mouth is a firmly cut, well-controlled straight slit of due proportion, not exaggerated or crudely cut; it tapers back down each side of the muzzle. The neck is almost as thick and bulky as the body. The antlers, particularly the crown tines, show staining with iron corrosion. The position of the stag in the ground (fig. 235) suggests that this derived from iron-bound wooden bucket no. 3.

The stag was damaged, presumably in the general collapse of the burial chamber or by the fall of some of its internal fitments. Its right antler is substantially intact, with three crown tines complete almost to the tips, but one of the crown tines of its left antler is fractured across halfway up, and the tip of another is broken off. Of the two tines that grow directly from the skull at the root of the antlers (the brow tines) the stag's left tine appears to be bent slightly outwards; its right tine is bent sharply over in the same direction.

In assessing some of the details of the stag, it is necessary to go back to photographs taken immediately after its excavation and before laboratory treatment (fig. 251). It was so heavily corroded that it was not possible to preserve every feature. The whole of the stag's right antler is slightly bent and its neck and head are very slightly bent over in the same direction, the left antler being now farther out from the body than the right one (fig. 248 c). A further indication of violent damage is given by figures 251 a and b. There was on each antler a single intermediate tine between the skull or brow tines and the crown tines. These had both been broken off. One was found in 1968 in relatively good condition.[3] The other probably suffered corrosion and disintegrated. The roots or stumps from which these two tines were broken can be seen in figures 251 b and c preserved in corrosion products. The traces of these two extra tines, clearly seen on the freshly excavated stag, were subsequently removed in the conservation process.

The picture derived from all these indications is consistent and indicates that the stag was struck a sharp blow from above. This would explain the detaching of the pedestal from whatever base it was attached to. The iron ring seems to have survived this episode intact, implying that it was still resilient, as the wires have little inherent strength and if corroded through would have shattered on impact. The ring later fractured, after being rusted through, as it lay flat in the ground detached from the object on which it had been mounted. Had the initial blow which separated the stag

[1] *Sutton Hoo*, Vol. I, pl. L (ii). To be published in detail in *Sutton Hoo*, Vol. III.

[2] Eyes could theoretically have been engraved and the engraved lines become filled with corrosion products and so rendered invisible. This state of affairs cannot be detected by radiography, but instances are known. Engraved animal designs have recently been recovered from several scramasax blades by the Laboratory of the Römisch-Germanisches Zentralmuseum, Mainz, by careful mechanical cleaning and the use of an air abrasive unit. The designs were not visible on radiographs. There is no apparent corrosion layer on the Sutton Hoo stag and it seems clear that no attempt was made to represent the eyes.

[3] *Sutton Hoo*, Vol. I, fig. 241.

a

b

c

FIGURE 251 The sceptre: the stag as excavated, before conservation. (a) three-quarters view from the front; (b) from above; (c) side view, with the ring and pedestal also before conservation. In (c) corrosion nodules can be seen in corresponding positions on both antlers, marking the position of the missing bez tines (intermediate between the brow and crown tines). (Scale: approx. 4/5)

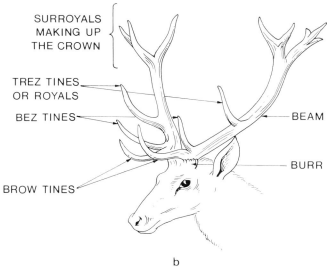

FIGURE 252   (a) Red deer stag in Richmond Park, Surrey. (Photo: Dr J. Jewell); (b) identification of red deer antlers.

from the object broken the ring, its fragments would have scattered, whereas they were found by the excavators still lying in a coherent ring-shape (fig. 1).

The stag was examined in 1972 at the British Museum (Natural History) by Dr Juliet Jewell, on whose report the following zoological observations are based. The stag is identified as a red deer (*Cervus elaphus*), a species known to have been widely distributed in the first millenium A.D., as it is at the present time, over Britain, Scandinavia, Europe, Asia Minor and elsewhere (fig. 252 a). This identification could only be made after the discovery in 1968 of the additional tine,[1] which in turn led to a rescrutiny of the earliest photographs, taken when the stag was unpacked after the war in the British Museum (fig. 251). As we have noted, the corroded stumps or roots of the additional tines can be seen occupying corresponding positions on both

---

[1] *Sutton Hoo*, Vol. I, 277–8, 335 and fig. 241.

antlers. These nodules of corrosion were cleaned off, and the stag when prepared for exhibition in 1945 and as copied in bronze in the British Museum Research Laboratory by Herbert Maryon was deficient in this respect. The stag, as it has hitherto been exhibited and published, appeared under its stylisations to be a perfect representation of a different species, *Cervus eldi*, the Siamese *thameng*, which has no intermediate tine on its long antlers between the brow and crown tines. This species is native to the Indian subcontinent and South East Asia. The extra pair of tines now recognised can be taken as trez tines, or 'royals', since there is a clear gap between them and the brow tines, even though they seem unduly low on the antler for trez tines. The normal positions of the various tines in the red deer can be seen in figure 252 *a* and *b*. The bez tines and brow tines alike spring from the burr. The bez, as is the case in the Sutton Hoo stag, is often missing in red deer antlers, but the trez, or 'royal', is invariably present. The Sutton Hoo stag has a particularly well-modelled cup-like crown of three points on each antler; it would be at least five years old and in spite of the absence of bez tines can probably be called a 'royal' because of this crown development. A 'royal' stag is normally one whose antlers carry twelve points (six on each antler, viz., brow tine, the bez and trez tines and a crown of three).

The damage suffered by the stag makes it difficult to reconstruct the details of the antlers with certainty. Brow tines are very variable in their positon and angle relative

FIGURE 253   The sceptre: reconstruction drawings of the stag in its original condition. (Scale: 1/1)

338

to the beam of the antler, but usually they face straight forward in the same plane as the beam, though they may be turned either outwards or inwards at a slight angle. We are probably justified in reconstructing the brow tines of the Sutton Hoo stag as originally going straight forward since the fracture of both of the trez tines and the obvious inward bend of the stag's right brow tine would indicate a blow from above and from one side, which could account for the present deflections. A drawing of the stag as it is thought to have originally appeared is given in figure 253.

Spectrographic analyses of samples from the surface of the stag have been carried out with the intention of establishing whether it had been tinned, silvered or gilded. No indication of plating was found (p. 387) and it must be regarded as unlikely that the stag ever appeared as other than the natural bronze colour, though if systematically kept burnished this could have maintained a bright golden appearance,[1] otherwise it would in due course acquire the green patina characteristic of early Anglo-Saxon bronzes.

7. *The evidence for connecting the stag assembly with the stone bar*

The assembly comprising the stag (Inv. 205), the iron wire ring to which it was affixed, and the bell-shaped pedestal with branching arms that held the ring, was originally mounted in the Research Laboratory on the top of the tall iron stand (Inv. 161), this conjunction being a decisive factor in the identification of that object as a standard (see p. 404 below). This restoration was published in 1947 and has been accepted for a quarter of a century. The stag on its mount was placed on the top of the iron stand for a variety of reasons. It was felt that the stand called for a finial of some sort, and the figure of the stag on its ring and pedestal seemed in proportion and well adapted to this purpose. The branching antlers with their crown tines seemed to echo the horns of the cattle at the corners of the openwork grid and at the extremities of the cruciform plate at the top of the stand. In the centre of this plate was a low circular convexity the diameter of which corresponded with that of the open bottom of the hollow bronze pedestal (fig. 277). Placed at this point the stag and its pedestal looked plausible; the fact that they were found beside the iron stand (fig. 1) lent support to the idea that they belonged together.

For purposes of final publication scientific study of the iron stand was carried out in 1970 using radiography. As a result a new shape for the stand, described in chapter IX and illustrated in figure 291, was arrived at. In the course of writing up these results, it was observed by Mrs V. H. Fenwick, F.S.A., then a special assistant working on the Sutton Hoo material, that there was no apparent means by which the bronze pedestal could be attached to the top of the stand. The pedestal has no rivet holes, shank, tang, or other feature by which it could be fixed, nor was there any effective projection from the top of the stand (above the cruciform plate) to which

---

[1] My suggestion long ago that the stag was silvered or tinned (Hodgkin 1952, 698 and 725, and Martin-Clarke 1950, 113, fol-lowing information from myself) has, I am afraid, misled some commentators (e.g. Hauck 1954*b*, 19 and 58).

the pedestal might have been soldered. It was possible that it could have been held by a low overlapping external collar or flange, but the upper surface of the plate (a thick layer of iron corrosion products) showed no indication of any such collar.

As a result of this observation the Research Laboratory was asked to analyse samples from the centre of the top of the stand with the object of finding traces of solder or residual bronze at the centre of the cruciform plate, where the slight circular swelling, assumed to have been the seating of the pedestal (fig. 277), was apparent. The lower edge of the pedestal is slightly nibbled or eaten away over virtually the whole of its circle (see figs. 245 and 254), so that traces or fragments of the missing bronze would certainly have remained buried in or beneath the corrosion at the top of the stand, had the pedestal been fixed there. Appendix C makes it clear that there is no evidence for the placing of the stag, its ring and its pedestal on top of the iron stand. Nine dispersed drillings were taken from the area of the central swelling (fig. 277). All gave identical analytical results, which in turn proved identical with a test analysis obtained from a drilling half way down the shaft of the stand. There is no suggestion of the presence at any time of bronze or solder. The negative evidence thus obtained against the positioning of the pedestal on top of the iron stand must be regarded as very strong. The lack of any means of effecting the connection mechanically has already been noted. The central raised circle on the top of the cruciform plate which surmounts the stand is, in fact, no more than the head of the vertical iron shaft which passes up through the plate and is burred over on to its top. Some other location for the stag, ring and pedestal had therefore to be found.

As soon as it was apparent that the stag and its supporting assembly did not belong to the stand, the absence of the finial from one end of the stone bar or ceremonial whetstone at once sprang to mind. The stag assembly lay in the burial deposit halfway between the stone bar and the iron stand, these being themselves close together (figs. 1 and 235). The connection was therefore *prima facie* possible.

Two other considerations favoured a connection of the stag assembly with the stone bar. First there is no surviving object in the burial deposit, other than the stone bar, that might have received it; and the lack at its base of rivet holes, tang, etc., make it impossible to regard the pedestal as possibly having come (for the sake of argument) from the end of a wood or bone staff which might itself, as an organic substance, have wholly disappeared. One could visualise the stag assembly as being held to a wooden seating solely by adhesives, but there is no wood trace in the bronze to suggest this, and such a joint would be unlikely to have stood up for any length of time to the natural stresses involved in the use of the object.

Secondly, the minute rescrutiny in 1967–8 of all the soil removed in 1939 from the burial chamber[1] failed to yield any trace of a second bronze saucer-fitting, or alternative termination, to match that still in position on one end of the stone bar, though the search did yield objects as small as a tine from the stag itself[2] and many fragments

[1] *Sutton Hoo*, Vol. I, 309–16.   [2] Ibid. fig. 241.

even smaller. The saucer-fitting with its claws is a substantial casting and the absence in the dumps of any trace of a second such fitting suggests that none existed, or at least that none was present in the burial chamber. Since some similar bronze fitment had evidently been part of the original design of the object—as implied both by the shaping of the stone at the vacant end into a projecting cone, matching that at the opposite end which fits into the collar below the bronze saucer, and by the remains of a cage of bronze strips running up the knob—the pedestal on which the stag and ring are mounted becomes the natural candidate for this position.

The missing finial must, like the pedestal-foot of the stag assembly, have had a hollow circular socket. This is implied by the shape of the projecting truncated cone at the end of the bar, which fits comfortably into the pedestal-foot. A tighter connection could have been effected by the use of adhesive or packing.

The means whereby the pedestal was attached to the stone knob is indicated by the presence on the knob of the eight fluted strips which follow its profile and converge to meet whatever fitting was present. These converging strips could have been joined to the pedestal in three ways: by being soldered on to its outer or inner edge, by being cast in one piece with it, or by being riveted to it. Unfortunately the pedestal had been cleaned out internally and cleaned up generally around the rim before the possible significance of any contained or adhering material was realised; thus if the strips were soldered to the pedestal no trace of this survives. A very small portion of the rim survives at one point, suggesting that the zone within which the decomposition or fracturing of the rim of the pedestal is confined is sufficiently shallow (fig. 254) to preclude riveting as a method of attachment, for the holes would have needed to be some distance in from the edge and would then show. There is no evidence to suggest that there were any projections from the base of the pedestal to which the strips might have been riveted. The neatest job would have been the casting of strips in one piece with the pedestal, as is the case with the claws of the saucer-fitting at the other end (see p. 330).

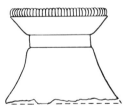

FIGURE 254 The sceptre: the stag-mount pedestal-foot showing the broken bottom edge with one small surviving length of original rim. (Scale: 1/1)

The pedestal, stag and ring together represent an extension of the object in length from the top of the knob of 26·75 cm, and the stag, which is a solid casting, weights this extension at its extremity. Would a connection of the kind envisaged, that is, an attachment of the stag assembly to the stone by means of eight flat strips cast in one piece with the pedestal, be strong enough to take the strain, especially if the stone bar were to be tipped on its side and moved about? A full-scale facsimile with bronze fittings was made to test the practicality of the arrangement (fig. 255).[1] This has served to demonstrate that a connection of this kind would have been mechanically sound.

[1] Made by Mr B. A. Nimmo, Senior Conservation Officer in the British Museum Research Laboratory.

The next step in the attempt to establish a connection between the stag assembly and the stone bar was to ascertain whether the bronze of the pedestal matched that of the eight fluted strips on the depressed knob from which the terminal was missing; if the strips had been cast in one piece with the pedestal the metal analyses should be more or less identical, allowing for impurities and possible effects of reworking the strips (swaging) after the metal was cast. It has proved possible, in spite of the high degree of corrosion which the metal had generally sustained, to obtain quantitative analyses of all the metal features of the sceptre: the results are presented in table 29 (p. 390), and the investigation is described and discussed by Research Laboratory staff in Appendix C.

It was hoped that these results would prove crucial and that they would provide clearcut answers to some of the points discussed, but in the event they are difficult to interpret. They seem generally to support the association of the stag assembly pedestal with the stone bar, not least by demonstrating the presence of a most unusual minor element, gold, in relatively high proportions, both in the pedestal-fitting at the top and in the saucer-fitting at the bottom. Meanwhile, there are other factors, no less significant, to connect the stag and its pedestal with the stone bar.

We have seen that the body, neck, legs, antlers and tines of the stag are all carinated or faceted (p. 333). This treatment seems to be reflected in the faceting of the bronze claws which hold the saucer-fitting at the opposite end of the stone bar, so that there seems to be an affinity of style connecting the stag with this fitting. There is a further indication of this: the profile of the cylindrical neck supporting the saucer at the lower end of the sceptre shows a recessed band (fig. 242); this is matched by a similar recession in the profile of the pedestal-fitting at the top of the sceptre (figs. 245, 246).

These observations suggest that the sceptre was designed as a whole. Either the bronze fittings were designed specifically to go with the stag, which could itself have been

FIGURE 255 The sceptre: replica made in the
British Museum Research Laboratory.

valued as an exotic piece, as an heirloom or antique, or as a work of art; or the stag, the sceptre and all its bronze fittings were made together at one time and place. As we shall see, chemical analysis seems clearly to disprove the latter possibility.

Another important piece of material evidence supports the association of the pedestal-fitting, and hence the stag mounted on it, with the stone bar. The interior of the pedestal-fitting when excavated was full of iron corrosion products, some appreciable quantity of which remained inside it (fig. 275 a). Where did this heavy iron corrosion come from? It could not have been derived from any part of the stone bar, in which no iron was used. It must therefore be derived from an outside source, need not have got into the socket after the stag assembly had been detached from its seating, whatever that was. The presence of the iron corrosion could be explained, as the open end of the detached pedestal lay in contact with the shaft of the iron stand in the ground (fig. 1). The end of the stone bar from which the terminal was missing, however, was through the centuries that followed the collapse of the burial chamber at a higher level and insulated from any contact with iron by clean sand (fig. 235). Yet an unmistakable nodule of rust is to be seen precisely on the top of the projecting cone at the end of the stone from which the metal terminal is missing (pl. 11 b). If the stag assembly had been mounted on this cone until some collapse within the chamber knocked it off, as is now suggested, how did this iron stain get there? A ready explanation is forthcoming. The cross-section through the pedestal-fitting (fig. 274) shows that, with the stone bar standing vertical, corrosion products from the ring of twisted iron wires could, in the wet conditions obtaining in the chamber, have trickled down the outside of the T-piece into the junction between it and the intermediate collar, and through this into the interior of the hollow pedestal, where it would come in contact with the tip of the stone bar, thus causing the iron stain.

All things considered, it cannot be doubted that the stag with its ring and pedestal were mounted on the end of the stone bar. They were certainly never mounted on the iron stand and no alternative use or place for the stag and its assembly amongst the grave goods preserved to us, or as may be inferred as originally present from any other indications, can be suggested.

8. *The implications of the analytical results from the metal fitments of the sceptre*

The results obtained by quantitative analysis of the various bronze fittings associated with the stone bar, and of the stag and its ring and pedestal, are evaluated by the staff of the British Museum Research Laboratory in Appendix C. The amount of analytical information hitherto published for bronzes or other metalwork of the Anglo-Saxon period is minute, so that the extensive coverage of a single important artefact by seventeen analyses is in itself a development of interest.[1]

The interpretation of analytical results is to be discussed by the British Museum

[1] Eight analyses from the bronzes of the Sutton Hoo shield are given in ch. 1, App. A, p. 116.

Research Laboratory in a later publication, in the light of experience from a very wide range of analytical and other work on the Sutton Hoo treasure as a whole. Meantime important archaeological inferences depend on the results and if we are to assess the significance of these in the archaeological discussion it is worth looking at the range of variation that can be expected in results obtained from different components associated with the same object.

Two analyses of the Y-shaped component were made which enable us to see the minor variations to be expected in two samples which could be from the same crucible melt (table 29, p. 390). If we accept this degree of variation we can see that the results obtained from the intermediate collar (table 29) is so similar to that obtained from the Y-shaped component that, though not cast in one piece with it, it could have come from the same pouring of metal. As the Research Laboratory points out (p. 388), this cannot be said of the collar and the pedestal-foot (fig. 246)—on the contrary, it is clearly indicated that they do not come from the same pouring. It is equally clear from the analyses that the swaged strips and the pedestal-foot were not cast in one piece and were not made from the same metal pouring.

If we compare the results obtained from the Y-piece and collar-fitting, parts 1 and 2 in figure 246, with those obtained from the saucer-fitting at the other end of the stone bar, we see that in the Y-piece and collar the tin content is high (about 9·5%) and the zinc content low (about 2·5%) (table 29). In the analysis of the saucer-fitting, the proportions of these two elements not only drop lower and rise higher, but they are exactly reversed, attaining 2% of tin and almost 10% of zinc. The lead value in the saucer terminal, almost 6%, is much higher than in the other bronzes; this casting too came from a different pouring of metal.

Apart from the attempt to establish whether components 1(a) and 1(b) were joined or were cast as one piece, the prime purpose of the analyses was to see if a connection could be demonstrated between the stag pedestal and the stone bar. If the swaged strips adhering to the vacant knob had proved identical in composition with the pedestal-foot (as should be the case if they were cast as a single piece of metal) this would constitute virtual proof of the attachment of the assembly to the stone bar.

If the analytical results for the socket of the pedestal at the base of the stag assembly and for the swaged strips on the depressed knob are compared it can be seen that they are not identical, but both are of the same general composition as the Y-piece and collar. The differences in the minor constituents may not seem of significance yet the percentages of iron, gold and silver are consistently different, and the figure which seems decisive is that for gold. The presence of gold in the analyses has already been referred to (p. 342) as a distinctive and significant feature of all the bronze fittings, values such as these (over 0·20%) being apparently unparalleled in published results from mediaeval bronzes; that the swaged strips only show 0·03% of gold establishes clearly that they cannot be from the same crucible melt as the base of the pedestal, an impression reinforced by the difference in the zinc content.

Although these two bronze fittings were evidently not a single casting, they are closer to each other than to the Y-piece, collar and saucer-terminal, and the results can consequently be held to provide some evidence for the connection of the pedestal assembly with the stone bar (pp. 339-43); as the differences imply that the pedestal-foot and bronze strips were not a single casting, they must, if they are to be connected, have been joined by some method such as soldering or riveting (p. 341).

Recently a quantitative analysis of the four well-known bronze helmet-dies from Öland (Sweden) was made in the British Museum by atomic absorption spectro-photometry and polarography.[1] Of these four dies, found together, two (A and B) were made by one craftsman on one and the same occasion, since they are not only identical and distinctive in style and condition, but fit together in a manner which shows that the impressions from them were intended to be employed on the helmet together one above the other. The analyses of the Torslunda plates (fig. 156) are included in table 30 (p. 391) and illustrate the differences in the alloy found in these four Swedish bronzes, of which A and B are the same age and made by the same craftsman, C is older, and D older still. It will be noted that the combined tin and zinc percentage in each case is much below that of the sceptre bronzes, that the gold content, though present, is infinitesimal and that the level of copper is higher. The variations in the percentage of zinc and iron between plates A and B (evidently made, as we have said, by the same man at the same time) (2·7% and 2·8% in A,[2] compared with 4·1% and 0·3% in B) are such as to make it appear reasonable to suppose that the swaged strips and the pedestal-foot, though evidently not cast in one piece nor made from the same crucible melt, might yet have been made at one time by the same craftsman using similar raw materials.

Table 30 (p. 391) in addition to the analyses of the Torslunda plates gives analyses of seven bronzes of the early Anglo-Saxon period (sixth–seventh century A.D.) specifi-cally undertaken so that the results might be compared with the figures obtained from the Sutton Hoo sceptre. All these differ markedly from the analysis of the stag. They also all show a general difference in the balance of the various elements from that seen in the sceptre mounts. This may be thought to lend support to the view that the sceptre mounts form a coherent group.

9. *The ceremonial status of the stone bar*

The sceptre, as reconstructed, is shown in figure 237.[3] The first and critically important point to emerge from the fitting of the stag and ring to the vacant end of the stone bar is that the object has a top and a bottom. Hitherto it had been thought

[1] For discussion of the Torslunda plates and two analyses obtained by different methods from the same set of samples and for a discussion of the relative ages of the dies, see Bruce-Mitford 1974, 214–22.

[2] In an earlier analysis (1967) of part of the same sample the result given for A was 4% zinc and 4% iron. Bruce-Mitford 1974, 217–18.

[3] The drawing shows the pedestal-foot of the stag assembly as being held to the knob of the stone bar by bronze strips cast in one piece with the pedestal-foot. Since chemical analysis has shown that the pedestal-foot and these bronze strips were not from the same pouring of metal it follows that the drawing is incorrect in this respect. They were not cast as one. Since we do not know what the actual method of attachment of the pedestal-foot to the strips was, however, the drawing has been allowed to stand.

of as a symmetrical object with similar ends. Its whole interpretation is affected by the new look.

The object, whatever its identity, was held in the hand. The gentle polish of its angles at the middle indicates this. Its design, with relatively fragile fittings at either end, makes it impracticable for use as a whetstone, and it has certainly never been used to sharpen anything. It is clearly an object of ceremonial and not functional import. The relatively delicate elaborations at each end would be in the way of its employment, for example, in sharpening swords, and inappropriate to any such purpose. Yet the stone is demonstrably of a type used for whetstones (App. B) and the whole object strongly suggests a giant whetstone mounted for ceremonial purposes.

Such an impressive, non-functional piece can only have been either an object of religious veneration or the expression of royal power and authority. The two are by no means mutually exclusive,[1] but in the secular context of this ship-burial it is difficult to see any other explanation for the object but that of sceptre. Its aspect and character, nevertheless, seem thoroughly barbaric, and there can be no doubt as to its pagan inspiration. The elaborately presented stag at the top must have been an emblem of special significance; but, if the sceptre identification is correct, what is the purpose of the strange bronze saucer fixed firmly to the stone bar at what is now seen to be its lower end?

Even without the knowledge that the stag and its pedestal and ring were mounted on it, the object, still being at the time referred to cautiously by the British Museum as a 'ceremonial whetstone', had been claimed by others as a sceptre, and with this in mind, the saucer-fitting was thought of as a receptacle for libations, or, as it was supposed that there were similar fittings at either end, as one of a pair symbolically representing sacrificial vessels, an idea which would harmonise with the painting red (the colour of blood) of the knobs at either end (pl. 11 a, b).[2] So the speculation proceeded. The newly effected transfer to the stone bar of the stag and ring naturally puts a new complexion on these studies. The saucer-fitting will not serve as a foot for the sceptre to stand on,[3] because although it will stand erect when balanced on the saucer, as the replica demonstrates (fig. 255), it is highly unstable. The saucer does, however, exactly fit the knee-cap, and it may be regarded as made to do so, and the sceptre as designed primarily to be held by the king when seated, with the lower end resting on his knee. The weight of the Sutton Hoo stone bar would indeed call for such an arrangement, since it is much too heavy to be held in the hand unsupported for any length of time.

---

[1] Cf. Gauert in Schramm 1954; Chaney 1970.

[2] A. Gauert, 'Das "Szepter" von Sutton Hoo', in Schramm 1954, 260–80, especially pp. 271–4.

[3] As suggested by the legal historian H. Baltl (1965) who observed the differences in design of the two ends and suggested some years ago, when the new reconstruction had not yet been arrived at, that the missing terminal might be different, and that the object might be a standing sceptre, similar to the judgement sceptres ('Gesetzszeptern') of the Middle Ages and later, which stood erect on the judgement-table before the judge (Baltl 1965, 14: 'Dann wäre der Stab also ein Standszepter gewesen, ähnlich den Gerichtsszeptern des Mittelalters und der späteren Zeit, die vielfach zum Stehen auf dem Gerichtstisch, vor dem Richter, vorgesehen waren').

If the burial is Raedwald's, as seems highly probable, the sceptre should probably be regarded as the symbol of his position as *bretwalda*, rather than as a dynastic sceptre symbolising his office as king of the East Angles.[1] His insignia of office as East Anglian king would not, we may suppose, be abandoned in the grave but would be passed on to his successors, whereas Raedwald alone of his dynasty held the position of *bretwalda*, and the insignia of his personal achievement could not properly be borne by anyone else once the *bretwalda*-ship had passed from the East Angles, as it did on Raedwald's death; it could therefore well have been buried with him.

The stag was made in a context different from that of the bronze fittings of the sceptre as a whole. The sharp difference in metallurgical composition of the bronze of the stag and of the two clips which fix it to the wire ring from that of the remaining fittings of the sceptre, make this clear. It may have been an exotic piece, perhaps an heirloom, which (undoubtedly for good reasons) was thought suitable to be installed as the crowning head-piece for the East Anglian *bretwalda*'s sceptre.

Analytical and stylistic evidence, on the other hand suggest that the remaining sceptre fittings, except for the swaged strips on the upper knob, though mostly cast from different crucible melts, were designed and made as one operation and for the purpose of carrying this stag and realising a pre-determined design. The coherence of the bronze fittings is indicated in particular by the abnormally high gold content in all the castings (except the swaged strips), which forms a rare technological link between them (p. 342); and by the match in style between the fittings at the bottom of the sceptre and the stag at the top, and between the terminals at both ends (p. 342).

It is perhaps worth noting also a visual correspondence between the fluted clips that hold together the iron wires of the ring supporting the stag and the fluted (swaged) strips on the knob below the pedestal, though these (p. 390 below) may be secondary and though the use of fluted bronze attachment or binding clips is common at this time.

We must refer again to a point of much interest even though its significance is not evident, and it may not affect our identification or appraisal of the object. It seems that the stag, its supporting wire ring and the Y-shaped bronze casting which holds the ends of the ring, may have been removable as a unit, and that this unit may also have been capable of rotation when in position. The intermediate collar beneath the Y-element (fig. 246, 2) would also be removable once the unit had been lifted, being unattached to the pedestal-foot and held in position only by the stem of the Y-element. It could have been soldered to the Y-element, in which case it would have come away with it. This collar accommodates about half the length of the stem of the Y-piece. The other half penetrates the pedestal-foot and projects only a short way into its hollow interior. There is no spreading at all to be seen at the lower extremity of the stem, where it is exposed in the interior of the pedestal, such as might have retained a washer

[1] For a detailed discussion of the historical background see *Sutton Hoo*, Vol. I, ch. x.

347

FIGURE 256 The sceptre: interior view of
the pedestal base with iron corrosion products
removed, showing the end of the stem of the
bronze Y-piece projecting into the interior of
the pedestal-foot. Hammer marks are seen in
the end of the stem. The hole visible in the
end of the stem is a drilling for bronze analysis.
(Scale: 2/1)

and locked the Y-shaped component in place; nor does any trace of a washer survive,
though theoretically such traces might have been removed when the iron corrosion
was cleaned out from the interior of the pedestal-foot.

Although the tip of the stem of the Y-shaped component is not spread, it can be
seen to have been hammered (fig. 256). This hammering was evidently undertaken
only to smooth or shape the end. It seems clear that there was no washer, or pin, or
any mechanical means of locking the vertical stem into position inside the pedestal-
foot.[1]

Though the stag with its ring and supporting Y-piece seem to us to have been free
to rotate and to be withdrawn, it is theoretically possible that the assembly might have
been packed with adhesives holding its component parts rigidly together, but no trace
of any adhesive or packing material can now be detected; furthermore, if the assembly
were intended to be held solid in this fashion it would surely have been constructed
differently from the outset.

The purpose of the intermediate collar (fig. 246, 2) should be considered in
connection with the possible rotation of the stag assembly. The movement of the

[1] It would not have been possible in any case to spread the
end of the bronze stem by hammering, since the transverse
elements of the Y-piece casting, which would have had to bear
the strain of any hammering on the point of the stem, is hollow;
and for this reason and because of its arched form would not
have been strong enough to stand the stress. There is no hole for
a pin in the tip of the stem, such as might have retained a washer,
and no room to insert a pin once the stem was in position inside
the pedestal-foot.

stag assembly, if it turned, did not bear on the top edge of this collar, since the beaded wire ring that surmounts its rim and makes contact with the underside of the transverse portion of the Y-piece above, shows no wear. If the stag assembly did rotate, the intermediate collar must, it seems, have turned with it. The large diameter of the concave top of the pedestal-foot, on the other hand, gives the intermediate collar ample space to turn in (fig. 246). The turning action here would not bear on the beaded wire ring which is soldered to the upper edge of the basin of the pedestal-foot, and which would serve to conceal the junction of the two parts and the movement within. It is difficult to conceive of a purpose for the intermediate collar, in what is as a whole a carefully conceived design, unless it is to make such movement easier, by transmitting the bearing of the rotation of the stag assembly to the ball and socket formation created by the lower surface of the collar fitting and the cup at the top of the pedestal-foot. Experience in handling the replica has shown that the branching antlers of the stag are particularly vulnerable and easily damaged. It may therefore be that the stag on its ring was made to be withdrawn to preserve it from damage when not in use.

One feature of the stone bar is still not explained. The eight deep longitudinal grooves cut in the depressed stone knob at its upper end (fig. 241 a, c) cannot have been designed merely to be covered by the flat swaged strips that now cover them. They match the longitudinal grooves on the knob at the lower end, and would seem to have been cut to key carinated claws like those that hold the saucer-fitting. If so, the present flat swaged strips are secondary.

In this connection we should note the pecking away of the stone around the projecting truncated cone at the top of the depressed knob (pl. 11 b and fig. 241 a, c), which seems to be related to the broad strips. There is no such pecking away at the lower end, under the saucer-fitting (figs. 241 b, d). This minor adaptation of the stone could also be a secondary development, associated with the replacement of original carinated strips by flat fluted ones, and with the fitting of the present pedestal-foot.

The existing arrangements at the top of the sceptre, then, may not be the original ones; if they are not, we can have no clear idea of what the original arrangements may have been. Whatever they were, it is clear that the essential difference we now observe in the two ends of the sceptre was built in from the start. There were always eight bronze holding strips at this end, as against six at the other; and the squat shaping of the knob, even without the pecking away which it seems is adapted to the present pedestal-foot, further indicates a basic differentiation and implies a terminal unit at the top of the sceptre, needing more support and firmer seating than the unit at the other end.

The harmony between the two finials as we now have them—the stylistic links between the saucer-fitting at the bottom and the stag and its pedestal at the top, and the metallurgical link between the saucer-fitting and the components of the pedestal on which the stag is mounted—remains unaffected. One may therefore think that the apparent changes, the possible secondary features, may have been connected with a repair; or perhaps with the design of a more elaborate mount for the self-same stag. A more interesting and effective support for the stag could perhaps at some stage have been substituted for a less adequate or less ambitious original one. This would explain the stylistic similarity that exists between what may be secondary features and features that are original.

10. *Contemporary sceptres and the Antique tradition*

The Sutton Hoo sceptre, as has been said (p. 346), has its barbaric aspect and features. Chief of these must be its manufacture from stone. The grim masks and red-painted knobs also have a thoroughly barbaric look. Yet the milieu in which it occurs, that, it seems, of a seventh-century Anglo-Saxon *bretwalda*,[1] is relatively civilised and sophisticated. The contents of the burial alone demonstrate this. Apart from all the majestic jewellery, the lyre and other superlative Germanic and Celtic pieces, the burial contains Byzantine silver, christening spoons with inscriptions in Greek, Merovingian gold coins. There are many reflections of the Late Antique in it. Even the helmet, of East Scandinavian type, is to be related both formally and technically to the products of the Imperial workshops (p. 220) and no doubt consciously reflects the silver-gilt and jewelled helmets of the Emperor and the Imperial guard. Professor Margaret Deanesly was perhaps the first to draw attention to the tendency for Anglo-Saxon kings and Celtic chieftains alike, not only in the sub-Roman period of the fifth century, but especially in the seventh, to reflect or simulate in their royal insignia the Roman symbols of authority. In the sub-Roman phase, the fourth-century Celtic *Gwledig*, Cunedda, is said to have worn a golden belt to signify a continuing authority as *Dux Brittaniarum* in the frontier zone between the Hadrianic and Antonine walls.[2] As Wallace-Hadrill has written of the Frankish and Anglo-Saxon kings of this period: 'The world of Liuvigild, Liutprand, Dagobert and of the kings known to Bede was a world of kings whose authority, however unsure we may be of its symbolism, had roots in the Roman as well as the Germanic past, and an active model, honoured if remote, in Byzantium.'[3] Bede describes the use of three varieties of standard by King Edwin of Northumbria, Raedwald's protégé and successor as *bretwalda*, citing their use as an expression of his royal dignity,[4] and in a number of passages in the *Historia Ecclesiastica* referring to royalty, he uses the word '*sceptrum*', though precisely what he meant by it is not clear. In no case need the use of an actual sceptre as we understand the term be implied. Colgrave considers it a sufficiently general term to be translated, in one context at least, as 'throne'.[5]

In connection with the royal power of the Merovingians, apart from one passage in Gregory of Tours, no unambiguous pre-Carolingian reference to sceptres can be found. We may recall, however, that Childeric I had close contacts with Byzantium,[6]

[1] Discussed in *Sutton Hoo*, Vol. I, ch. x.
[2] Deanesly 1943, 129–45, especially 135.
[3] Wallace-Hadrill 1975, 53.
[4] *Sutton Hoo*, Vol. I, 689–90.

[5] Colgrave and Mynors 1969. I am indebted to Mrs S. M. Youngs for the references in Bede and for her comments.
[6] Wallace-Hadrill 1962, 161–2.

which he may have visited; and that the Emperor Anastasius subsequently conferred on Childeric's son, Clovis (in St Martin's Church at Tours), consular rank, said to have been accompanied by the gift of a diploma, a purple robe and *chlamys* and a diadem.[1] His own authority may have been symbolized by a spear, as depicted on his signet ring, but he must, as a fifth century Frankish king, have been quite familiar with the use of sceptres.

It would not, then, be surprising if an Anglo-Saxon *bretwalda*, even so early as Raedwald, whose predecessor as *bretwalda*, Aethelberht of Kent, was under strong Frankish influence, looked to Late Antique or contemporary Byzantine examples for ideas to assist in the designing of a type of insignium (in this case a sceptre) that was traditionally used both in the Eastern and Western Empires. The Late Antique background, from which the Anglo-Saxons in the seventh century increasingly drew,[2] indeed provides in the consular diptychs of the first part of the sixth century types that have notable points in common with the Sutton Hoo sceptre. Figure 257 illustrates a selection of consular and Imperial sceptres, those associated with Boethius (A.D. 487), Areobindus (A.D. 506), Clementinus (A.D. 513), Anastasius (A.D. 517), Magnus (A.D. 518) and the Emperor (*c.* A.D. 500).[3]

a   b   c   d   e   f   g

FIGURE 257   Ceremonial staffs and sceptres depicted on late Roman ivory diptychs. (After Delbrueck 1929)

[1] *Historia Francorum* II, 38; cf. Wallace-Hadrill 1962, 175–6.
[2] Deanesly 1943; Bruce-Mitford 1961 in Bersu and Dehn, 150; Cramp 1973; Hunter 1974.

[3] After Delbrueck 1929, 7v, 9v, 11r, 16r, 20v, 22r and 51. For other examples see Taf. 14, 16, 29, 32, 33, 34 and 42.

In each case the sceptre is held in the hand. Two distinct types of sceptre (or ceremonial staff) can be identified, one longer than the other (fig. 257). The longer is a rod tipped with spherical knobs of equal weight at each end. The shorter type usually has a minor knob or finial below, while the top develops either into a larger spherical knob, or into a foliate shape resembling a capital, on which is seen mounted vertically a twisted ring (a laurel wreath). Within the ring, or surmounting the knob if there is no ring, an eagle is often depicted. In several examples one or more busts surmount the ring or knob. These represent the Emperor or Emperors from whom the Consul derived his authority.[1] In one instance where no bust surmounts the sceptre the diptych is that of an installed Consul before the formal receipt of Imperial confirmation (fig. 257a). Behind these consular sceptres is a long tradition of Imperial sceptres, most of them terminating in knobs.[2] Thus sceptres of the consular series show elements that are also found in the very different Sutton Hoo object: the human heads, the spherical knobs at one end or both, the ring set vertically at the top, and an animal associated with the top of the sceptre (in the consular sceptres, within the ring or crowning the knob, the Imperial eagle). The spherical knob is a constant feature of Roman sceptres, whether consular or Imperial.

There is little concrete evidence for continuity in the use of sceptres by Germanic or other barbarian kings between the Roman and Carolingian times, when both graphic representations and written references begin to occur. There can be little doubt, however, that some continuity of usage was maintained from the Roman period. Gregory of Tours has a reference to the royal sceptre which seems explicit, though he is using the word as a general synonym for royal power.[3]

The distinction between royal and other emblems of power must be borne in mind, for some objects that pass as sceptres may be rods of lesser office, or objects of religious use or domestic symbolism.[4]

Two possible examples of surviving sixth- and seventh-century sceptres, or at the least ceremonial staffs or rods, may be noted. They are very different from the Sutton Hoo stone bar, and though close to it in context and date were probably more akin in form to the sceptres or staffs of office of the antique tradition. The first is the 'miniature sceptre' found in 1958, with traces of a second and longer staff, now totally disintegrated, in the grave of the sixth century Germanic boy prince under Cologne Cathedral (fig. 258).[5] This is a lathe-turned wooden object, somewhat resembling the

[1] Delbrueck 1929, Text, 61–2.

[2] For a survey of sceptres in the ancient world see Daremberg et Saglio, *Dictionnaire des Antiquités Grecques et Romaines*, under *sceptrum*, also Delbrueck 1933, Taf. 96, 105, 108. The colossal bronze statue identified as (?) Marcianus (A.D. 450–7) at Barletta (Delbrueck 1933, Taf. 116) holds an orb in the left hand and evidently originally held a tall staff of the type seen held by Valentian II in the Missorum of Theodosius (A.D. 388) (Delbrueck 1933, Taf. 96). For Imperial sceptres on gems from Augustus onwards, see Richter 1971, Cat. 484–5, 495, 501, 502 (including a short knobbed type), notably that depicted as held by Honorius in the Rothschild cameo, Cat. 612.

[3] *Historia Francorum* IX, 9: 'ut ita dicam, ad ipsius regalis sceptri jactans gloriam.' The word here seems distinct from references to the official or royal use of spears, or *baculi, contus, virga, ornamenta*, etc. I am indebted to Professor J. M. Wallace-Hadrill for this reference and comment.

[4] These explanations might account for such discoveries as the cylindrical bar of tin fitted with bronze terminals from the Glastonbury Iron Age lake village excavations (Bulleid and Gray 1911, Vol. I, 245–6 and pl. XLV, L.50), or the Farley Heath 'sceptre' from an Iron Age temple site (Goodchild 1938, pls. LXXVII, LXXVIII, and 1947).

[5] Doppelfeld 1960b and 1964; for an account in English, Werner 1964.

lathe-turned elements of the plum or cherry wood cot and chair found in the same grave.[1] It is 56 cm in length and above a slim handle about 1·5 cm in diameter expands to a diameter of 3 cm and then contracts again. There is a flattened knob at the lower end. A series of finely incised circumferential lines and raised mouldings decorate the upper part. A damaged projection at the top may have held a finial, not preserved, and presumably therefore, as the grave was fully recorded, not of crystal or metal. No trace of attachment mechanism remains and the inferred finial could have been a glued-on head or other pictorial representation, or a sphere, in wood or bone, not capable of being fully turned on the lathe as the shaft was. This mysterious object lay beside the body of the six-year-old princeling. The identification as a sceptre put forward by Doppelfeld is accepted by Werner,[2] who refers to it as 'perhaps the most significant and interesting object in the entire burial-deposit', and says of it: 'This, considered in relation to the numerous weapons considered fitting to his rank [helmet, shield, sword, two spears, bow and arrow] can only be interpreted as a symbol of royal authority.' The formal characteristics of the staff, no less than its placing in the grave and its isolated nature, make this identification highly probable. The traces of a second staff of birch wood, some 74 cm in length, perhaps represent a second ceremonial rod of office.[3] Although we do not know the identity of this young prince, buried in special circumstances in the most important church in Cologne *intra muros*,[4] we may have here a prefiguration of the royal sceptre he would have inherited had he survived.

The other example, from Sutton Hoo, is the rod, probably of bone or ivory, which lay on the right side of the body-space; this is fully described in chapter VIII of this book. It is of

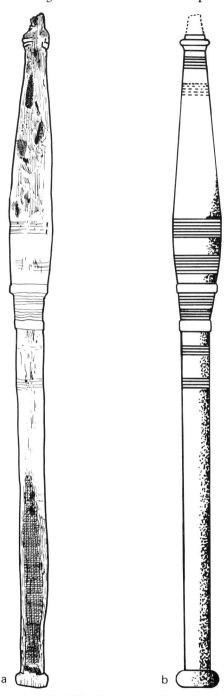

FIGURE 258   Wooden sceptre from the sixth-century grave of a boy prince in Cologne Cathedral. (*a*) after Doppelfeld and Pirling, 1966, 88; (*b*) in a restored version. (Scale: 1/3)

[1] Published illustrations give the stem of the object an oval cross-section, such as would rule out the possibility that it was lathe-turned. This appears not to be the true original section but due to distortion or crushing of the object (Doppelfeld and Pirling 1966, 88 caption).

[2] Werner 1964, 206–7.
[3] Cf. Doppelfeld and Pirling 1966, 88, caption text.
[4] Werner 1964, 207.

353

uncertain identification, since only the gold mounts survive, with no vestige of the object they were mounted on, but it comes from the Sutton Hoo ship-burial itself and is therefore local and contemporary. All we can say here is that the organic element, now perished, had a diameter of 1 cm and was of circular cross-section, and that the ring-topped gold strip with garnet and filigree decoration (Inv. 22), and the gold cut-out figure of an animal (Inv. 23, figs. 278, 281) were mounted on it, though in what relationship to each other we cannot say. It is probable that certain other minor gold fittings of similar weight and scale (figs. 283, 284) may have belonged to it (fig. 286). The object can only have been a light rod or wand, as different in aspect from the great stone sceptre as can well be imagined, but in dimensions perhaps not unlike that of the Cologne prince's burial. We cannot say anything more about this piece, but Hauck has been the first, following a general reference to it by myself, to take up and explore its possible importance.[1] Whether Hauck is correct in identifying the small gold cut-out animal which we have associated with it as a wolf is open to discussion. But the identification is possible (fig. 282). Greater naturalism in goldsmiths' work of the period is hardly to be expected.[2] Hauck's wolf identification is lent a measure of plausibility by the emphasis which the craftsman has placed on the teeth. Hauck relates it to a possible derivation of the family name of the Sutton Hoo dynasty, the Wuffingas, via Wuffa (Raedwald's grandfather, who Bede says gave his name to the family) from the root 'Wulf' (wolf).[3] This is a matter for philologists, but we should note that in the same burial deposit, on the purse-lid (pl. 14, fig. 377) in the 'man between beasts' scene, which occurs twice, the man is flanked by wolf-like animals (admittedly no teeth are here shown), and not by bears as in the analogous scene on one of the Torslunda helmet dies (fig. 156c),[4] which in spite of differences is so close to it iconographically as to be considered as indicating the general source of the purse-lid scene.[5] As the scenes on the purse (evidently a most important item of the regalia) are likely to be significant, this parallel may be thought to add plausibility to the reading of the cut-out animal on the staff or miniature sceptre as a wolf.

If the two objects just discussed are correctly identified, this would indicate familiarity of Germanic royalties and of the Anglo-Saxon *bretwaldas* or kings with staffs of office or sceptres in a variety of forms. The Sutton Hoo stone itself is the strongest evidence we have for the use of sceptres—in its case of an elaborate, particular and impressive kind, not necessarily typical—by seventh-century and hence presumably also by later Anglo-Saxon royalties, and so no doubt by other European royal houses

[1] Hauck 1954a, 50–1, after Bruce-Mitford in Hodgkin 1952, 699 ff.; and footnote 221 for a zoological comment on the identification of the animal represented by the little gold cut-out figure (fig. 281).

[2] In spite of the remarkable degree of it exemplified in the cast bronze stag and the cast bronze fish in the large Celtic hanging-bowl.

[3] Hauck's arguments on this are set out in the article cited above, pp. 50–1 and footnotes 223–7.

[4] See Bruce-Mitford 1974, ch. 10, for a discussion of these much-published bronze plates. The animals on the purse, perhaps because of the medium of gold and cloisonné garnets employed, and the small scale, are not depicted with teeth.

[5] For an iconographic analysis of the purse-lid scene and the equivalent Torslunda scene, see Bruce-Mitford 1974, 43–5.

of this period intermediate between the demonstrable Late Antique and the Carolingian usages.

From the Carolingian period onwards specific references to sceptres, or examples of them in illustrations and even in the archaeological record, occur with increasing frequency. Charlemagne is described by Notker as having had a golden sceptre made for his own ceremonial use as an emblem of his royal might,[1] and when his tomb at Aachen was opened in the year 1000 an account purporting to describe the scene says that the king's body was found seated, with crown and sceptre.[2] The use of a ceremonial staff as a symbol of territorial title and authority at this time is known from a contemporary document. In A.D. 787 Duke Tassilo III surrendered his Bavarian duchy by handing over to Charlemagne a staff of office or authority surmounted by a human effigy. He is assumed by most authorities to have received his duchy back by having the staff returned to him.[3]

Doubt may be thought to attach to Stollenmayer's attempt to recreate this sceptre of Duke Tassilo III from the pair of ancient candlesticks in the monastery at

FIGURE 259 Charles the Bald shown with crown and sceptre. (After a Carolingian psalter of before A.D. 869, Bibliothèque Nationale Lat. 1152. f. 3v)

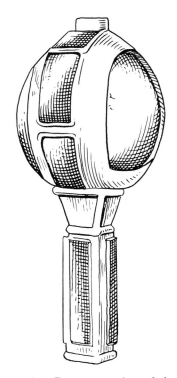

FIGURE 260 Reconstruction of the head of an Avar sceptre. (After Alföldi 1948)

[1] *De Karolo Magno* I, 17.

[2] *Chronicon Novalicense*, iii, 32, printed in translation in Grant 1907. I am indebted to Professor Wallace-Hadrill for the previous reference to the *Gesta Karoli Magni*, and to Mrs S. M. Youngs for the reference to Charlemagne's tomb.

[3] '...et rediit ei [Carolo] ipsam patriam cum baculo in cuius capite similitudo hominis erat sculptum', *Annales Guelferbytani*; and also *Annales Laurissenses minores*, anno 787 (*Monumenta*

Germaniae Historica, Scriptores, I, 43 and 119). For the handing back of the staff, Stollenmayer 1959, 56–7 and Aachen Catalogue, 367. See also discussions by K. Hauck in Schramm 1954, 209, and by A. Gauert, ibid. 266. For a reference to a connection with the Sutton Hoo sceptre, Chaney 1970, 147. The 'human effigy' strongly recalls the consular sceptres we have discussed (fig. 257).

Kremsmünster. The reconstruction is largely hypothetical[1] and even if it is accepted as physically feasible, the shafts from the candlesticks that form it have been held to be appreciably later than Tassilo's time.[2] A good graphic illustration of a Carolingian sceptre occurs in a portrait of Charles the Bald in the psalter B.N. Lat. 1152 f. 3v, written between 842 and 869 (fig. 259).

Alföldi reviewed the subject of early sceptres of eastern derivation in putting forward his entirely plausible reconstruction, out of the gold and enamelled mounts assimilated into the golden ewer in the monastic treasury of St Maurice d'Agaune, in Switzerland, of an Avar or Hunnish sceptre (fig. 260), which could well have been part of the great Hunnish treasure captured by Charlemagne in 790.[3] This continues the theme of the ball or disc-topped sceptre descended from Imperial tradition, seen again in the surviving tenth-century coronation sceptre of the Hungarian regalia.[4]

A further example of a barbarian sceptre, with a silver shaft or stem, surmounted by a capital-like development on which is a silver sphere, and with a depressed knob or moulding at its lower end may be cited, perhaps from the eighth or ninth century A.D. It is from the Taganča tumulus in the steppe lands of South Russia (Kiev); and serves to demonstrate the entrenchment at this early date, among royalty or chieftains in contact with the East Mediterranean and Byzantine worlds, of the use of sceptres as a symbol of power, and the persistence of formal characteristics derived from the late Roman Empire. An illustration of this sceptre is given in figure 261; another necked ball-top, in bone, attributed to a sceptre, from an Avar grave at Püspök-Szent-Erzsbét, in Hungary, is cited by László.[5]

The widespread use of sceptres is seen well established in representations of the eleventh century and onwards. The Anglo-Saxon usage is seen on coins and seals of Edward the Confessor (1043–66) and in depictions of both him and

FIGURE 261 A silver sceptre from Taganča, near Kiev. (After Alföldi 1948)

[1] The human faces at the top, put in to agree with the documentary reference already cited, are based on those of the Sutton Hoo stone. For a full discussion and for the sceptre reconstruction, Stollenmayer 1959; and the Catalogue of the Tenth Council of Europe Exhibition, *Karl der Grosse*, Werk und Wirkung, Aachen 1965, 367–8 (with bibliography).

[2] Schramm 1954, 286–7; Haseloff 1951; for a comment on date, Wilson 1964, 46.

[3] Alföldi 1948, who illustrates (Taf. 6) an earlier sceptre reconstruction by Emil Vogt. For a discussion of the Alföldi reconstruction, accepting the eighth-century Avar date, see K. Hauck, 'Kugelzepter der Awaren und der Ungarn', in Schramm 1954, 281–5.

[4] Alföldi 1948, Taf. 17.

[5] For these objects cited by Alföldi see G. László in *Szent István Emlékkönyv*, Budapest 1938, 519 ff., 532 ff., 534 ff. For the Taganča find, J. A. Khoinovski, Grabfund aus Taganča, *Kratkija archaeologičeskija svedenjija o predkach Slavjan i Rusi*, I, 1896, 118 ff. and Taf. VI–XI.

FIGURE 262 (*a*) Edward the Confessor (A.D. 1053–66) and (*b*) Harold Godwinson (A.D. 1066) depicted in the Bayeux tapestry, showing the use of sceptres (of two differing forms), as well as orb and crown, by late Anglo-Saxon Kings. (Photos: Victoria and Albert Museum)

Harold II in the Bayeux Tapestry (fig. 262), where Harold is also shown holding an orb, as on his silver pennies.[1]

11. *Sources, origin and significance*

If apparently based in some general aspects of its design on Late Antique models, in other respects the Sutton Hoo sceptre differs radically from any other known Late Antique sceptre-type. Its significance may have been less mundane than that of the consular sceptre, details of its design being more conditioned by the religion, myth and traditions of the pagan Germanic world. Those features that cannot be derived from sceptres in the Antique tradition should be especially studied:

(1) Its weight makes it impossible to hold for any length of time in the hand unsupported—a prime difference from all other known sceptres. This factor could explain the development, at the lower end, of the saucer-fitting—to rest on the knee.

(2) The substance is stone, again so far as we know unparalleled in the sceptres of the Late Antique world and those descended from them.

(3) The use of red paint on the knobs, and the treatment of the faces, have an authentically barbaric stamp.

(4) The number of faces (eight) and the fact that four of these occur above the

---

[1] See Twining 1960, pl. 44, nos. 3, 4, 6, 7, 8 and 9; for the Bayeux Tapestry instances, Stenton 1957, pls. I, V and 34. Cf. also for the English Regalia, Holmes and Sitwell 1972, pls. 5, 11 and 28.

saucer-fitting at the lower end (upside down when in use) is significant. The consular sceptres cited (fig. 257), apart from the long staffs showing spherical knobs of equal magnitude at both ends, have no significant elements at the lower end.

(5) Finally, there is the almost square cross-section of the object. The shafts of Antique and later sceptres, held in the hand, all appear to be of circular or at least rounded cross-section.

Analogies for these distinctive features of the Sutton Hoo sceptre, not found in possible Late Antique prototypes, should be sought in the Germanic or Celtic background, as should also the reason for the use of a stag to crown it.

I   THE HUMAN FACES AND THEIR STYLE

For throat-beards, or 'off the chin' beards, if these are what we are dealing with, I have not been able to find any parallel.[1] The possibility that the five heads which show this feature are intended to be female heads, or at least that the four at the top of the sceptre are, with perhaps a youth represented where one such head occurs at the lower end (face B2, p. 317), cannot be overlooked. But if this is so, why should the female heads be at the top of the sceptre, and the male heads at the bottom?

For the most striking of the heads, those with long beards and, in two out of three, moustaches, we have close at hand a number of analogies, and a strong tradition of faces, sometimes moustached and perhaps to be thought of as bearded, set in pointed fields. The most significant of these parallels occurs in the ship-burial itself—on the East Scandinavian shield (p. 59). The cloisonné face in the bird's thigh, allowing for the difference in medium, has strong affinity with the sceptre heads (figs. 63c and 234). The face, sharply pointed, resembles the full-bearded faces of the sceptre; the broad cloisonné border is visually detached from the face by its series of straight transverse cell walls, which run at right-angles to the outline of the face, whereas any lines meant to convey hair should run parallel to it. This detachment of the cloisonné border from the face within suggests an intention to simulate a frame, like those which surround the faces on the stone bar. Below the point of the chin in this cloisonné face is a single cell, differentiated by its transverse pointed oval shape and by its opaque inlay of deep orange. It lies outside the limits of the face and seems to correspond to the raised circles or pads that in each case terminate the borders round the faces on the stone, below the point of the chin. Other faces, of pointed oval form, occur repeatedly in the animal interlace decoration on the shield-boss, and on the bird's wing (figs. 39 and 49). The same face type occurs in the Vendel boat-graves material and at Valsgärde. The faces in animal-hips on two well-known rectangular mounts and on the shield-boss flanges in Vendel 12 and Valsgärde 8 (shield 1) may be cited.[2]

---

[1] Hauck's claim that such beards were worn in Anglo-Saxon England before the Norman conquest (Hauck 1954b, 55–66, note 250) lacks documentation. The beard types cited by him from Hayne 1903 do not appear to be of the Sutton Hoo 'off-the-chin' type, which Hauck refers to as 'fräseähnlich' (like a ruff).

[2] Stolpe and Arne 1927, pl. XXXIII, figs. 2 and 3; pls. XXXVIII, figs. 1, 2; Arwidsson 1954, Abb. 84, and also on the mount from Denmark illustrated by Salin 1935, fig. 546.

Such faces occur also more widely in Vendel-period material in Sweden. The tight-fitting contours round these heads strongly suggest that the broad cloisonné border round the face in the bird's hip on the Sutton Hoo shield stands for something extra—a frame. A further analogy to the moustached and bearded face in its frame, as seen in the sceptre, is provided by the pommel in the form of a crouched animal on the sword from Kirmukarmu, Finland. The faces in the hips of the animal have long moustaches.[1]

The Germanic and more particularly Scandinavian affinities of the Sutton Hoo sceptre faces is borne out by the treatment of the hair. Such fine and delicate control of the depiction of the hair in stone carving (figs. 238, 239 and 240) is unusual. It is paralleled by the equally fine treatment of the hair in stamped foil from the helmet-dies used on the Vendel helmets, and in the rider scene on the Sutton Hoo helmet (p. 193, figs. 143 and 145). The most significant Scandinavian parallel is provided by the wooden staff carrying a complete human figure and also a detached human mask found at Søholdt, Lolland, in Denmark, now in the National Museum, Copenhagen, cited by Hauck in this connection,[2] and a bronze head, with attachment rivets at the back, from the Vimose find, some centuries earlier than Sutton Hoo. This head is considered probably to have been attached to a staff and offers a particularly close parallel in its delineation of the features and in other respects (both heads are illustrated in fig. 263).

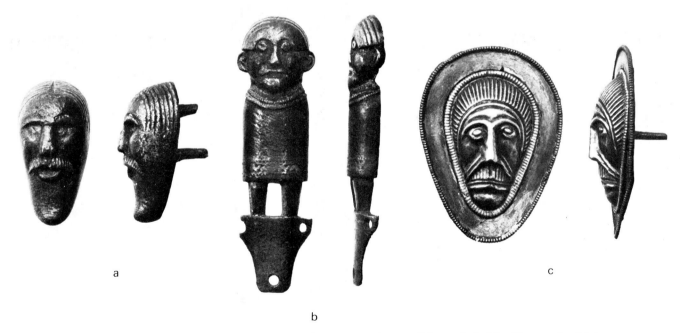

FIGURE 263   Bronze mask (a) and figure (b) from a wooden staff from Søholdt, Denmark; (c) bronze mount, thought to be from a wooden staff, from Vimose, Denmark. (Scale: 1/1)

[1] Kivikoski 1947, I, Taf. 55, 471. A local Suffolk parallel in pottery, for such faces (seventh–eighth century) in Ipswich ware, is published by Smedley and Owles 1967, 84–7.

[2] See Hauck 1954a, 201–3, for a full discussion; also Mackeprang 1935, *Acta Archaeologica* 6, 245–6.

The Søholdt staff was of wood, shod at the top with a bronze cylinder 6·2 cm long and 2·7 cm wide, into which a large staple holding a bronze ring 3·45 cm in diameter was driven from the end. To the sides of the staff, which disintegrated shortly after discovery, were affixed a bronze mask measuring 3·3 cm (held by cast shanks) and a human figure, tunic-clad and wearing a torc, 6·4 cm in height, both images evidently held to the wooden staff by nails. The larger head, especially in its hair treatment and treatment of the features, bears a strong resemblance to the Sutton Hoo bearded faces, except that the chin is long and beardless. The relationship with the bronze god figures, from Bregnebjerg (Fyn) and still more the wooden figure from Rude Eskilstrup (Seeland) suggest that this wooden staff was a religious emblem or staff of priestly office. It dates from the late Roman Iron Age.[1]

The similar bronze mask, also thought to be from a wooden staff, beaten up in the middle of a somewhat larger egg-shaped sheet of metal, found at Vimose (also in Copenhagen National Museum) is a still closer parallel to the Sutton Hoo faces, as the profile view in particular shows (pl. 10b and fig. 263c). The gaunt expression, the treatment of the hair, the absence of ears, the treatment of eyebrows and eyes, are particularly close. The face is without a beard, but it is tightly enclosed in a raised beaded border, and this again is within an outer border. There is no suggestion of any torc on this head.[2]

To summarise, these parallels indicate the presence in Denmark in the Roman Iron Age of wooden staffs bearing human masks or figures in bronze. The occurrence of the human face, brought to a point in a pear-shaped field, is common in East Scandinavia in Vendel art. The appearance of the same theme on the Sutton Hoo shield, notably in the cloisonné parallel on the bird's hip but also on the bird's wing and in patterns on the shield-boss (figs. 39, 49 and 63), the refinement of treatment given to the hair, and the treatment of features and the depicting of moustaches, suggest a strong general background in Scandinavian archaeology for the carved heads of the East Anglian sceptre. The presence of the East Scandinavian shield with its close parallel in the same burial as the sceptre, and the frequency with which such faces occur in Vendel art, make the general Scandinavian background more specifically relevant.

II   WHETSTONES AND THEIR POSSIBLE CEREMONIAL OR RELIGIOUS USE

The stone chosen for the substance of the Sutton Hoo sceptre is the fine-grained grit generally used for whetstones, a type of artefact which occurs very widely in northern archaeology. Ellis has published a detailed petrographical survey of Anglo-Saxon and mediaeval English honestones, with localisation of the stone sources in mind.[3] His published conclusions have in all cases been based on slices removed from the stone

---

[1] Schramm 1954, Taf. 78c, d.　　　　　　　　　　　　[3] Ellis 1969, 135–87.
[2] Schramm 1954, Taf. 8a, b; here figs. 263a and b.

for microscopic examination. It has not been thought desirable to do this with the Sutton Hoo sceptre at present, as it seems unjustified to mutilate an impressive and intact object when identification techniques may be developed in the future which will not entail slicing. Visual examination carried out by Ellis (see App. B, p. 383) indicates that the source of the stone is unlikely to be Scandinavian. He suggests a likely origin in the southern uplands of Scotland or the extreme north-west of England, or in local drift derived from these regions, with possible, but geologically less likely, sources in the Harz Mountains of central Germany, or the Rhineland (p. 384). Of these possible sources the most probable for the stone of the Sutton Hoo sceptre is the southern uplands of Scotland or north-west England, since the closest parallels to the stone (such as they are) come from this area; and whetstones with human heads and apparently ceremonial function seem to be characteristic of the Celtic background in the British Isles, and not to be found on the continent.

No comparison can be drawn between the elaborate and portentous object in the ship-burial and the plain, functional, and often well-worn workaday whetstones that occur with some frequency in Swedish boat-burials and other graves of the period; those, for instance, published from the boat-graves at Vendel, or the royal mounds at Old Uppsala.[1] None of these whetstones shows any trace of the elaboration or secondary significance of the Sutton Hoo piece. There is also a sharp difference in scale. The longest of the Vendel whetstones occurring in boat-graves 4 and 1, are 31·2 and 28 cm in length.[2] The Sutton Hoo stone, without the bronze fittings at the ends is 58·3 cm long and broad in proportion. It is not possible in all cases to tell the original length of the fragmentary whetstones found in the royal mounds at Old Uppsala, but the thickness of the largest fragment is approximately 3·3 cm.[3] That from Sutton Hoo reaches 5 cm. In sheer bulk the Sutton Hoo object greatly exceeds any whetstone known from the Scandinavia of its era.

More significant, perhaps, are two very small unstratified whetstones from the town site at Birka (the *svarta jorden*) presumably of Viking date (figs. 264 a–d) which have been called miniature sceptres.[4] They are of greyish-black slate. The longer is no more than about 5 cm in length, the smaller about 2·5 cm. The longer is of a thickish rectangular section and is shaped and modified at what must be regarded as its top. Its sides begin to taper in towards the top, where a V-shaped rebate occurs on each face (fig. 264 b). A hole is drilled in the point of the V-shaped rebate on the broad face seen in figure 264 a. This hole runs through to the opposite face. The projecting top of the stone, which evidently carried a finial or mount, is thinned by the rebates on all four faces so that it projects like a tenon and continues the taper; its top is stepped down in the middle (fig. 264 a). The smaller of the stones (fig. 264 c, d) is flatter and thinner in its proportions than the larger one. Its bottom edges and corners are bevelled and the two narrow sides of the stone curve inwards towards the

[1] Nerman 1948, 71–3; Lindqvist 1936 b, figs. 96, 97 (No. 14), 105; Stolpe and Arne 1927, pl. VII, fig. 9 (and pls. XI, fig. 5 and XV, fig. 10, for whetstones in Viking period graves).

[2] Nerman 1948, 72.
[3] Lindqvist 1936 b, fig. 96 (East Mound).
[4] Arrhenius 1973 b, 59–60 and fig. 1.

upper end where, at about a quarter of the stone's length from the top, they turn out again sharply at an angle similar to that of the bevelling of the two outer corners at the bottom. The sides then continue straight to the top, forming a head to the stone of approximately the same width as the lower end. It could be said that these two stones, if not merely functional, are more suggestive of idols than sceptres. They seem to provide nevertheless, in an East Scandinavian setting, at a later date than Sutton Hoo (probably tenth-century A.D.), a possible instance of ritual use of whetstones or similar objects, in which the tops of the stones are differentiated either by shaping or by a finial. The two stones show little or no sign of wear, though the smaller of the two shows several scratches (fig. 264c), possibly, as Dr Agneta Lundström suggests, caused by the sharpening of needles.[1]

Only in the British Isles are true parallels to the Sutton Hoo stone bar to be found (figs. 265b, 266–269) though none is very close. There are bars of fine-grained stone, large and small, some close to the Sutton Hoo stone petrographically. Some of these are more or less featureless, while others have been carved into human heads or faces. Some are undoubted whetstones and show signs of use as such. Others do not appear to be functional, or else show traces of use not as a whetstone but as a hammerstone. Others again of whetstone substance, appear, like the Sutton Hoo stone, to have a symbolic or ritual purpose.

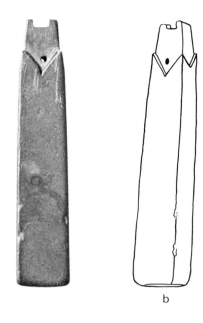

a

b

c

d

FIGURE 264 Photographs and drawings of two miniature whetstones from Birka, Sweden. (Scale: 1/1)

Most are fragmentary, and few have been found in a reliably datable context, but one which has, a stone bar found in association with a group of Anglo-Saxon graves at Uncleby, in Yorkshire, is datable to the late sixth or early seventh century A.D. and is of particular relevance and importance.[2] It is genuinely massive, a plain flat-sided stone bar of rectangular (almost square) cross-section, slightly thicker in one direction than the other, tapering only rather inconspicuously at either end (fig. 265b), and lacking perforations or mouldings of any sort. The maximum width (5·1 cm) is fractionally greater than the maximum width of the Sutton Hoo bar (5 cm, p. 312

[1] Verbal communication.   [2] Yorkshire Museum 330–47.

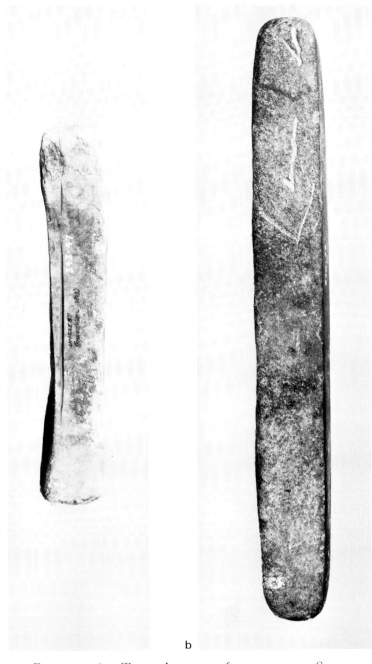

a   b

FIGURE 265 Two whetstones from a pagan Saxon
burial place at Uncleby, Yorkshire: (a) found with the
contents of grave 11; (b) set upright in the chalk at the
foot of grave 11. (Scale: 1/3)

above, measured between points of maximum convexity on opposite faces), but since
the faces are flat and do not fall away from the point of maximum thickness, as in
the Sutton Hoo stone, the mass is even greater. Although its length is 46·2 cm as
against the 58·3 cm of the Sutton Hoo stone, it is the heavier of the two, weighing
2774 g against the approximate 2400 g of the Sutton Hoo stone. When the two are

placed side by side, the Uncleby stone bar makes the Sutton Hoo sceptre look delicate and slim.

The Uncleby stone shows no signs of use as a sharpener, but some battering is apparent on the exposed points at either end. The end of one broad face is marked with three crudely gouged grooves (fig. 265 b).[1] Microscopic examination shows calcareous deposits on the unmarked half of the stone, confirming Canon Greenwell's account of its discovery in 1868 standing upright in the surface of a chalk barrow containing a group of Anglo-Saxon interments. The markings were therefore on the exposed part of the stone, and Miss Evison has further observed a darkened, polished area on the undamaged surfaces of the bar consistent with its having been held in the hand with the three marks facing away from the bearer. These observations suggest that this great stone with its crude carving had a special significance. It stood upright at the foot of a burial containing grave-goods of the seventh century, the date of other interments in the barrow cemetery. The furnishings of the grave (no. 11) are not rich but include a second whetstone of different stone and showing signs of intensive use as a sharpener (fig. 265 a).[2] Unlike many of the comparative pieces, the large Uncleby stone is from an Anglo-Saxon context, of known provenance and dated by association to the seventh century. Petrographically it is close to the Sutton Hoo stone but 'lacks its large micas' (App. B below, pp. 383-4, and Ellis 1969).[3]

Two other fragments of stones closely resembling the Sutton Hoo sceptre petrographically, both unfortunately undated, are specially relevant. They also are of fairly massive proportions and carved with human faces (figs. 267 and 268).[4] One comes from Hough-on-the-Hill, Lincolnshire, a stray find, not from the site of the Saxon cemetery and so of uncertain date, though likely to be Iron Age or Saxon;[5] the other, a relatively unknown example, from Lochar Moss, Dumfriesshire, South Scotland. The Hough-on-the-Hill example is one end of a stone bar showing a constriction for the neck and above this a round ball-like head (fig. 267); the bar is of a rounded, slightly flattened rectangular cross-section. The fragment is interesting and different from other examples in three respects: the body (breast, shoulders and back) is covered with a decoration of shallow concentric pairs of circles, and drilled down into the top of the head is a circular shaft 4 mm in diameter and 2 cm deep. This evidently carried some sort of terminal fitting, but there is nothing to indicate whether this was of metal or some other substance. The petrological characteristics of this hone are closer to that of the Sutton Hoo stone than to others of the known whetstones. The face is primitive, the features rudimentary, and the eyes expressionless drilled holes; there

---

[1] There are also scattered patches of a thick red substance like sealing-wax at the ends, but this colouring has been analysed and found to contain a mixture of pigments only available in modern times; it would therefore appear to be a recent accidental accretion.

[2] Yorkshire Museum 343-7, of sandy limestone, 29·4 cm in length. Ellis 1969, 173.

[3] The Uncleby stones are published in detail in Evison 1975, 79-83, where reference is made to other Anglo-Saxon whetstones

with possible ritual use. Earlier publications of Uncleby are Meaney 1964, 302-3, who follows Reginald Smith's editing, in the *Victoria County History of Yorkshire*, of Canon Greenwell's notes; Baldwin Brown 1915, 415 and 805, who mentions twelve whetstones at Uncleby although only two are now known to the authorities of the Yorkshire Museum where the Uncleby finds are housed; and Ellis 1969, 158-9.

[4] Ellis 1969, 161 and 173.

[5] Petch 1957, pl. II, fig. 4 and pp. 17-19.

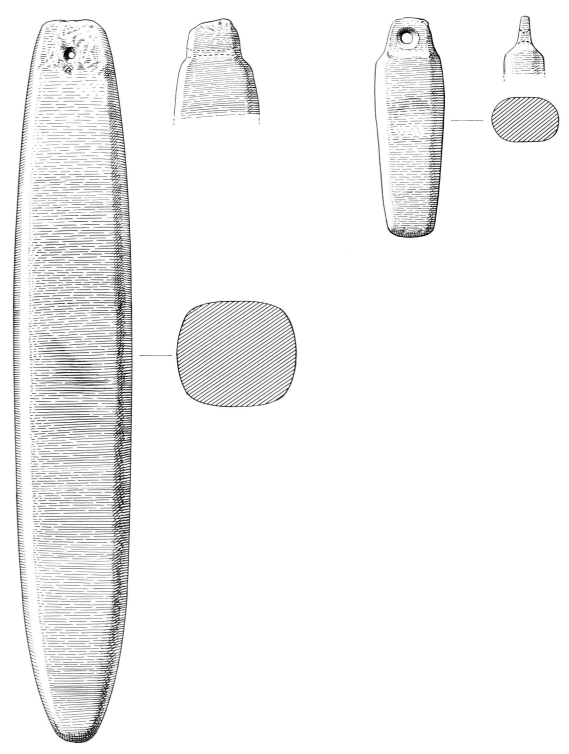

FIGURE 266　Two stone bars or whetstones from a rath at Coleraine, Northern Ireland, with modified tops for metal mounts, perhaps for suspension, now in the British Museum. These two stones are illustrated for comparative purposes and are not discussed in the text.

FIGURE 267   Carved stone figure from Hough-on-the-Hill, Lincolnshire. (Scale: slightly over 1/1)

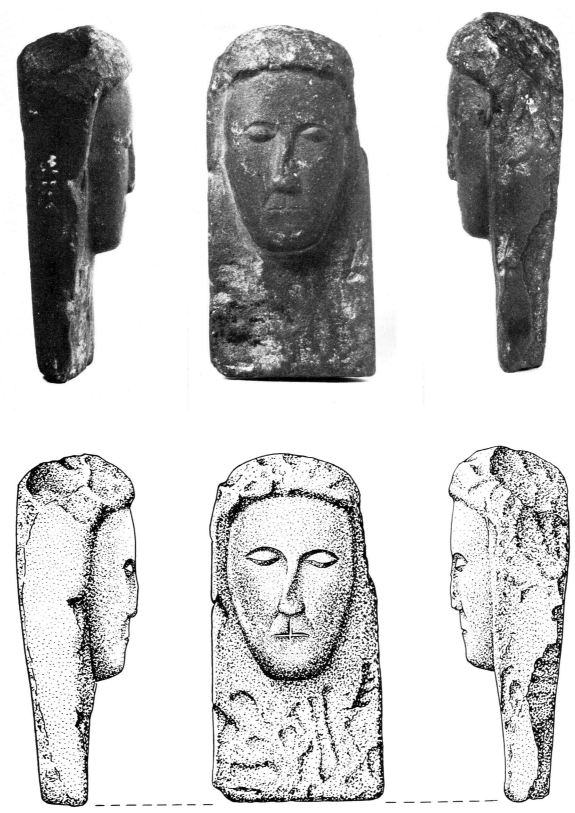

FIGURE 268   Photographs and drawings of a carved face, apparently part of a stone
bar, from Lochar Moss, Dumfriesshire. (Scale: 1/1)

367

a   b   c   d

e   f   g   h

FIGURE 269 Examples of fine-grained stone bars or hone-stones with carved or incised heads or faces and other motifs: (*a*)–(*d*) basalt hone from Llandudno, North Wales; (*e*), Portsoy, Banffshire; (*f*) the Broch of Main, Shetland, and (*g*), (*h*) Church Island, Lough Currane, Northern Ireland. (Scales: *a–d, f–h*, 1/1; *e*, 7/8)

368

is a long chin, and a groove cut in the stone represents the end of the hair line at the back of the neck; wavy incised lines represent the hair itself.

The Lochar Moss stone (fig. 268) is a fragment split off from its seating, but the shape and proportions suggest that it probably came from a large stone bar. The human face is of a different order from that of the Hough-on-the-Hill stone; the features are better represented, the eyes not drilled but bulging in a tradition that seems to be Celtic, but finds a counterpart in the faces of the Sutton Hoo sceptre. As a stray bog find there is no evidence apart from style and analogy for the date of this piece.

Other stones showing human heads or faces are recorded from (1) Portsoy, Banffshire, (2) Llandudno, North Wales, (3) the Broch of Main, Shetland and (4) Church Island, Lough Currane, Ireland (fig. 269).[1]

In spite of the general parallel (whetstones with faces) we must observe that in none of these instances do the faces show beards or moustaches, or any of the stylistic traits of the faces on the Sutton Hoo sceptre. The Welsh and Irish examples are regarded as 'of Dark Age date'; the Dumfries stone from Lochar Moss again seems to belong to this context. They appear to show in the Celtic west and north a tradition of whetstone-type objects with human heads.

To summarise, it seems that there is a context for the Sutton Hoo stone bar in the British Isles, though no real parallel to it. The geological background and the habit of carving stone bars with faces seem to point to Celtic tradition. On the other hand the face *types* on the sceptre and their *style* are paralleled only in the Germanic background, and chiefly in Scandinavia.

A notable example of such stylistic traits in an Anglo-Saxon context, from Dorchester in Oxfordshire, and dating probably from the sixth century, is illustrated in figure 270.[2] It is a beautifully patinated bronze casting of very fine quality depicting two human faces of identical size and form, with long hair executed in fine lines, even longer moustaches, and long pointed chins. The moustaches are carried down to the point of the chin to either side. The two faces form the front of a single hollow casting with a back plate, and the profile faces which form the front angles are set back to back. They come from an early Anglo-Saxon object of uncommon type, a padlock.[3] They offer an interesting parallel to the Sutton Hoo faces, both in style and in the juxtaposition of two virtually identical faces facing outwards.

In the light of the above survey it seems likely that the sceptre was created in England, no doubt in East Anglia, in the royal workshops of its owner. This apparent

[1] (1) Smith 1923, fig. 163: Thomas 1963, 3–5, pl. II.

(2) Kendrick 1941, pl. XVII: Bruce-Mitford 1974, 7 and pl. 7.

(3) *Proceedings of the Society of Antiquaries of Scotland*, LVIII (1923–4), fig. 5. This was unstratified and can probably be disregarded as from a later period.

(4) Bruce-Mitford 1974, 7 and pl. 7.

[2] The object was found in the upper filling of a ditch with pottery of a fourth-century A.D. attribution but containing also a Saxon sherd. I am greatly indebted to Mr Jeffrey May, F.S.A.,

for allowing me to illustrate this piece from his excavations in advance of his own publication of it, and for placing at my disposal the drawings by Miss Marion Cox (fig. 270).

[3] Over eighty padlocks have been found in the excavations, still in progress, at Helgö, near Stockholm. Many of them are published in Volumes I and II of the Helgö publications (Holmqvist and Arrhenius 1961 and 1964). A much fuller account and analysis of the group is given by Jan-Erik Tomtlund in *Fornvännen* 1970 (Hänglåsen på Helgö, pp. 238–47).

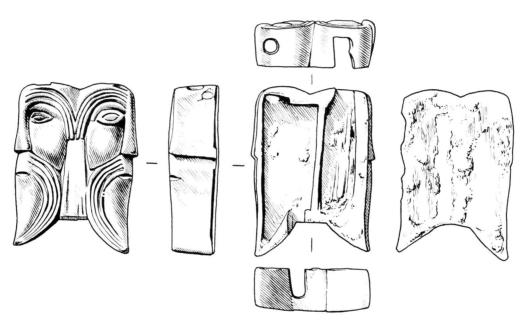

FIGURE 270 Human face profiles on a bronze padlock from Dorchester-
on-Thames, Oxfordshire. (Scale: 2/1) (Drawings by Miss Marion Cox)

blend of Celtic and continental Germanic features, and the strong Scandinavian links,
seen in the sceptre's affinities with the shield (the human faces in the bird's hip
and elsewhere), may seem to show a degree of fusion of three traditions similar to
that reflected at Sutton Hoo in the appearance of Celtic millefiori and Scandinavian subject matter[1] in the Germanic gold jewellery.

III   THE SCEPTRE'S SIGNIFICANCE

It must surely be accepted as beyond all reasonable doubt that in this strange and
singularly impressive object in the Sutton Hoo ship-burial we have a sceptre, a
massive staff of stone crowned with a ring and stag, held in the king's hand to signify

[1] For example, the man between beasts plaques and the double plaque with animal interlace on the purse-lid,
pp. 512, 503 and pls. 14b and 13b.

his royal title, power and majesty. But this does not fully explain its form or details, nor exhaust its interest.

The Sutton Hoo sceptre has already engendered a considerable literature. In this, a central role in future discussions must be taken by the contributions of Berges, Gauert and Hauck,[1] in spite of the fact that their essays were written before the transference of the stag assembly from the iron stand to the stone bar had taken place. A further important article by Hauck (1954*b*), full of ideas, may also be cited. Subsequent writers, each finding what he wants to find, have drawn upon these primary discussions, in some cases uncritically.[2]

But scholarly essays in interpretation, however speculative, do at least seek to reveal the object's essence, and as our understanding of the essence of one major piece in the ship-burial may well affect our vision of other elements in it, these and other theories (including some suggestions of my own) should be taken into account, with due recognition of the lack of any objective means of judging their validity. Three observations from different sources, taken together, could, it seems to me, throw light on the special significance that the sceptre may have had to those who used and beheld it. In an important work William A. Chaney has written: 'The most fundamental concept in Germanic kingship is the indissolubility of its religious and political functions.'[3] To this we may add, as the second observation, that with the exception of the East-Saxon kings, all the early Anglo-Saxon royal houses, including the Wuffingas, traced their descent from Woden (in the case of the Wuffingas, from Caesar also).[4] Thirdly, there is the passage (though it refers to an Anglo-Saxon kingdom other than East Anglia) from Alcuin's letter of A.D. 797 to the people of Kent: 'Scarcely any of the royal kindred remains; and *by as much as their origin is uncertain, by so much is their power less*' (my italics).[5]

Can such concepts throw light on the details of the sceptre's design? Can they help to explain the eight faces, of which we can say that they are not merely conventional, since no two are the same, and there seems to be a reaching out for individuality? Why, also, are there so many heads? And why eight? None of the other whetstones cited, so far as we are able to tell, had more than two.[6] It is true that the Sutton Hoo stone bar has four sides and two similar ends; but this of itself does not require that all the available positions must be so used. We could have had two faces at each end only, on opposite sides of the stone; or four at the top and none at the bottom. And what do the two differing hair-styles convey?[7] Are the heads all those of men, or may some be women?

---

[1] 'Das eiserne "Standarte" und das steinerne "Szepter" aus dem Grab eines angel-sächsisches Königs bei Sutton Hoo' in Schramm 1954, 238–80.

[2] For some unrestrained speculation see Sidney L. Cohen, 'The Sutton Hoo whetstone', *Speculum* 1966, 466–70.

[3] Chaney 1970, 11.

[4] *Sutton Hoo*, Vol. I, 693 ff. and fig. 434; Sisam 1953, 32; Chaney 1970, ch. 1, The Woden-sprung kings.

[5] From *Monumenta Germaniae Historica: Epistolae*, IV, Ep. 129, p. 192 (Chaney 1970, 17).

[6] That from Portsoy, Banffshire, has a face at each end (fig. 269 *e*).

[7] Cf. P. E. Schramm, 'Zur Haar- und Barttracht als Kennzeichen im germanischen Altertum und im Mittelalter', in Schramm 1954, 118–27.

The three concepts cited above, it should be said at the outset, may seem more relevant to the object's interpretation if it is the sceptre of the Wuffinga royal line than if it is that of the *bretwalda*. Hauck suggests that the sceptre is a staff on which are depicted the ancestors of the royal house: Woden himself, founding fathers, traditional leaders of the land-taking and so on. Hauck's arguments for the existence of such staffs, which he calls *Ahnenstäbe* (staffs depicting ancestors)[1] perhaps amount to little more than speculation, but some such theory is needed to account for the eight faces. In the light of the quotation from Alcuin and the known importance attached by the Wuffingas and other Anglo-Saxon royal houses to their line of descent, Hauck's suggestion that the heads on the sceptre form a kind of visible genealogy is very attractive.

Hauck assumes, as do Berges and Gauert, that the sceptre is the dynastic symbol of the Wuffingas, and the whole trend of his thinking is to stress the preoccupation of that dynasty with Woden.[2] Against this should be set the view, expressed above (p. 347), that the sceptre is perhaps unlikely to be that of the East Anglian kings as such, and more probably a sceptre used, and presumably devised, by Raedwald to express his greater power, non-dynastic in essence, as *bretwalda*.

A key factor in Hauck's argument for the religious nature of the sceptre (whether it is that of the Wuffinga dynasty or not), and for the incorporation in it of Woden as a prime ancestor and emphasis in all the eight heads on descent from Woden, is his supposed identification on the sceptre, consistently employed, of the torc motif, a symbol associated with Woden. The raised pear-shaped frames which surround the faces and terminate in circular pads below (fig. 239), Hauck claims, represent torcs. The twisted wire ring on which the stag stands is also, he suggests, symbolic of the torc (fig. 247).[3] In spite of the analogies he cites of the torc-bearing Germanic officers of Justinian's bodyguard in the mosaic in the chancel of San Vitale, Ravenna, and on the great silver dish known as the Missorium of Theodosius, in Madrid, these identifications seem doubtful. In particular, the perspective treatment, which shows the supposed torc clinging to the profile of the head and running round its top, is contrary to the consistent convention seen in all unambiguous depictions, including those cited by Hauck.[4] On the other hand, Hauck quotes representations of deities in which the collar or torc is shown, halter-like, surrounding the whole head. Were it not for this one would dismiss the torc analogy for the frames as baseless. Torcs are normally depicted, as on the Gundestrup cauldron, the Justinian and Theodora mosaic at Ravenna and the Missorium alike, to show both terminals. The raised frames

[1] Hauck in Schramm 1954, 208–9, and n. 288.

[2] Hauck 1954 b.

[3] For convenient references to torcs in the Scandinavian Roman Iron Age and in the milieu represented by the Gundestrup cauldron see Glob 1965 and 1969, pls. 2, 60, 61, 66–9, and text (see index, under rings).

[4] Hauck 1954 b. For convenient reference to the torc and its significance in Germanic and Celtic life and its appearance in the archaeological record, see Glob 1965 and 1969 (English edition of Glob 1965), pls. 66–75. The Gundestrup cauldron (illustrations of which appear in Glob's book) provides a series of important depictions. As against Hauck's theory it may be argued that, although twisted neck-rings without terminal or pendants are common enough, torcs proper are provided with two ring-terminals. The Sutton Hoo frames might have been expected to show some indication of twisting if the torc imagery had been intended.

round the faces of the Sutton Hoo sceptre, with pad or disc below, are, if anything, more suggestive of a medallion on a ribbon or chain.

When Hauck and Berges and Gauert discussed the sceptre's status and meaning, a number of aspects (apart from the association with it of the stag and ring, which was not then known) do not seem to have been taken into consideration. These include the number of faces (eight); whether any of these are female; the use of the saucer-fitting; the possible nature of the finial (then missing, but assumed to be similar to the saucer-fitting) at the vacant end; the built-in difference in the design of the two ends of the object; formal and stylistic parallels to the stone and the heads; and finally, the sceptre's age and possible place of origin.

As we have seen, apart from the distinction between faces with chins covered by beards and those with exposed chins, the sculptor evidently sought to differentiate all the faces in some degree. No two are exactly the same in detail or expression. The variations in depth of eye and shape of eyeball, the insertion or omission of eyelids and eyebrows, the more delicate treatment of the heads with 'off-the-chin beards' and their possible female aspect, show this. This differentiation on individual heads could support the idea that the staff sought to represent a series of different identities, favouring the *Ahnenstab* theory.

All the faces are uncompromisingly grim. They are severe and in some cases (figs. 238 and 239) even murderous in expression. If there were substance in Hauck's identification of the pear-shaped borders with circular stop beneath with a torc or neck ring with circular medallion or pendant, this might relate these grim images to Iron Age representations of deities, such as those on the Gundestrup cauldron; and bearded heads[1] and phallic images also belong to this sphere of religion. The red (blood-coloured) knobs and the saucer-fitting which has been thought to evoke receptacles in which sacrificial blood was collected, might be thought to support this in some degree.

Stone must have been chosen as the substance of the sceptre for important reasons. It could have been chosen because of its identity with, or resemblance to, the stone habitually used for whetstones; or for some virtue or quality held to reside in stone as such. It may indeed *be* a whetstone, an object, as is indicated below (p. 374), which could have a specific significance in Germanic myth and religion; or again, on a more mundane level, the material could have been chosen because this fine-grain type of stone lends itself to mounting and refinement of carving.

If the stone was intended to represent a whetstone it could, as a sharpening instrument, as Sir Thomas Kendrick said of it at an early stage, very well symbolise the mastery of a king over the weapons of his followers. 'Nothing like this monstrous stone exists anywhere else. It is a unique, savage thing; and inexplicable, except perhaps as a symbol, proper to the King himself, of the divinity and mystery which surrounded the smith and his tools in the northern world.'[2] This reading of its

---

[1] Cf. the Broddenbjerg god, Glob 1969, pls. 74, 75.　　　[2] Kendrick 1939, 128.

symbolical significance would be unaffected by the presence of the stag or by the sceptre identification.

The notion of male and female heads could possibly meet in some way with the ideas expressed on the meaning of the stone bar by Magoun,[1] particularly if the off-the-chin beards and facial differentiation in the doubtful heads may be thought to contain an element of sexual ambiguity:

'That indescribably fearsome-looking object, probably a sceptre or mace, counted among the regalia and often compared to a whetstone (which it is not really like and which it cannot possibly be) remains "inexplicable". It is dangerous, if not frivolous, for non-archaeologists to tread on such uncertain ground as may here be involved, but it is difficult for me at least not to entertain the notion that this dynastic symbol, if that is what it is, may not be a greatly stylized phallic symbol of vigour and fertility; from an earlier time in central Sweden, including Uppland, literal phallic symbols of stone have been found in graves. There would be every reason, of course, to assume that Christian East Anglians of the mid-seventh century would not have been conscious of such a background of the object, if such was the background.'[2]

Half a dozen or so relevent larger monuments from the Iron Age still stand in the fields of Sweden,[3] but these are merely painted stones, of vaguely phallic aspect, not whetstones with bronze attachments.

There is no doubt that the use of stone in the sceptre's design is of paramount significance; even if the stone bar with human faces, and indeed the whetstone with human faces (figs. 267–269), is in the Celtic tradition, its possible significance in the world of Germanic, particularly Scandinavian, religion and mythology (which already enter into the regalia, it seems, in the figural scenes of the purse and which dominate the imagery of figural scenes on the helmet) must also rank high in our consideration of what is, after all, the symbol of an Anglo-Saxon king, whose royal line may have Scandinavian origins.

Saga evidence perhaps allows us a glimpse of an early phase of religious symbolism where in Germanic myth the whetstone was the equivalent of the thunderbolt of Zeus, and wielded by the supreme sky-god in his capacity as ruler of all and guardian of justice. It is possible to think, as Miss Simpson suggests, that early Germanic kings may have had sceptres made from whetstones because their functions as rulers and guardians of justice descended from, or were parallel to, those of the sky-god; the faces on the Sutton Hoo stone could then represent, in a barbaric idiom, power, knowledge, all-seeing justice.[4] The significance of the whetstone, its connection with

[1] Magoun 1954, 125–6.
[2] Magoun cites Eugen Mogk, in Hoops 1915–16, 414–16 (Phallusdienst).
[3] One, visited by me in 1967 with Ulf Erik Hagberg, was painted red, a colour traditionally renewed by the people of the district.
[4] I am indebted to Jacqueline Simpson for a penetrating analysis of the passages in Snorri's Edda, Skáldskaparmál, chs. 6 and 24 and in Gautrek's Saga, ch. 9, to which she has drawn

my attention, and hope that Miss Simpson's ideas will shortly be available in extended form in print. Professor Wallace-Hadrill has also kindly drawn my attention to the reference in Snorri, Skáldskaparmál, 6. I am much indebted to Professor Wallace-Hadrill for his kindness in reading the whole of my text on the interpretation of the sceptre, and for supplying a number of references in connection with the use of sceptres by Merovingian or Carolingian kings. He should not, however, be assumed to agree with all or any of the ideas here put forward.

the cult of Thor and its possible symbolic identity with a thunderbolt, have been referred to by other writers.[1]

12. *Conclusions*

This study of the sceptre has been lengthy, as it was necessary to satisfy students that the stag and its ring and pedestal really came from the end of the stone bar, and to define the sceptre's precise characteristics. My preferred view is that in it we have the sceptre of Raedwald as *bretwalda*. The significance of this title has been discussed in *Sutton Hoo*, Volume I (p. 699). It means 'ruler of Britain'—not ruler of the British, still less of the Anglo-Saxons—and has been thought to carry with it some claim to the inheritance of power over the Roman province. The title thus makes a claim which most of the Celtic island would not have accepted; yet a substantial Celtic population in Northumbria, Elmet and the western borders, and Celtic elements elsewhere, came under the authority of an Anglo-Saxon High King. Raedwald was the first of these to extend his authority to the lands with major Celtic populations north of the Humber. The substance of the sceptre was a whetstone, to Germanic minds the emblem of Thor, perhaps also seen as the sharpener of the swords of the king's war band and companions. Yet whetstones, or whetstone-like staffs or stone orthostats, were a familiar manifestation of religion or power to the Celts also, and the stone of the Sutton Hoo sceptre seems to have come from the Celtic lands in the north. Crowning the sceptre was a stag, which, after an exhaustive search in time and space, seems most likely to be Celtic (pp. 378-82). Though the evidence is slight and largely negative, I concur with Dr Hicks's view on this point and would support also her allusion to another distinguished piece of Celtic bronze sculpture in the round found in the self-same context: the fish in the large hanging-bowl. The fish,[2] like the stag, is naturalistic and yet elegantly stylised; it demonstrates, as does the exceptional calibre of the hanging-bowl with the otter or seal heads of the eschutcheon-hooks round its rim, that in workshops somewhere in the Celtic west or north semi-naturalistic bronze sculptures in the full round of the highest quality were being made. Yet, in spite of what may be a Celtic finial, the general concept of the sceptre and some of the main features of the design also seem to reflect the Late Roman insignia of the Eastern Empire. How statesmanlike and inherently probable would be the conception that the Germanic *bretwalda* from East Anglia, less affected than his predecessor Aethelbert by Frankish example, proudly and closely connected, as it may seem, with pagan Scandinavia, and now extending the authority of Saxon *bretwalda* over the Celtic north, should devise as emblem of this new role a sceptre which combined with an Imperial aura and similitude elements recognisable as of both Germanic and Celtic significance. The same apparent blending of Celtic, Anglo-Saxon and Scandinavian is to be found in the Sutton Hoo gold jewellery, also to be regarded as regalia.

[1] Gamber 1966, 272, 285; Cohen 1966; Wallace-Hadrill 1975, 55.

[2] Identified at the British Museum, Natural History, as belonging in the salmonoid group.

If the reading of the sceptre as Raedwald's as *bretwalda* is correct, it could have been made some time before A.D. 616, the date of the death of Aethelberht of Kent, since Bede states that Raedwald acquired the *imperium* before Aethelberht's death. The sceptre's making could however be associated with the height of Raedwald's power, after Aethelberht's death, when in 617 he extended his authority over Northumbria, killing the Northumbrian king Aethelfrith at the Battle of the Idle, and establishing his protégé Edwin on the Deiran throne. The stag, as a particular component of the sceptre, could be older, a pre-existing object chosen to crown it. If the stag is to be connected with a Celtic metalwork school, it need be no older than the fish in the hanging-bowl and could be contemporary with the making of the sceptre.

The essence of this formidable sceptre must be the stone bar or whetstone. It forms the sceptre's substance, mounted functionally at the bottom in the saucer-fitting, at the top surmounted by a stag, which, as the crowning theme of the sceptre, must be of more than decorative significance. Like the eagle of Consular and Imperial sceptres, it must have been an understood symbol of the rank and authority of the wielder of the sceptre.

Two possible reasons, which are mutually compatible, for the choice of a stone bar, and perhaps more specifically a whetstone, as the essential core of the sceptre, present themselves. The first is that the object fits broadly with a Celtic background, since, as we have seen, whetstones with human faces occur uniquely in Celtic contexts, utilizing a raw material that was conveniently to hand, but no doubt having social or religious import (figs. 267–269). The second, and this must have primacy, is that the whetstone may have been of major significance in the mythology or sacral basis or social funcion of Germanic kingship. If the saga references to whetstones cited (p. 374) are to be given any weight, the ceremonial whetstone could well be a recognised symbol of power and the dispensing of justice. The Celtic and the Germanic elements could very properly meet in a *bretwalda*'s regalia.

Perhaps we have in the Sutton Hoo sceptre an object of greater complexity than we suppose. Can this mounted stone stand, in terms of ancient Germanic mythology, for a thunderbolt, symbolically thrown, as the saga stories would indicate; the red knobs suggesting blood shed or fire struck; with which are perhaps ritually associated faces differing sufficiently from one another to indicate ancestors, or predecessors in power, under the protection of the sky-god? This is speculation, and all such suggestions must be so; but it seems possible that, at what we can now see as the end of an era in East Anglian history, the last pagan king sought to fuse in his *bretwalda*-ship the Roman legacy and the sacral power of Germanic kingship, with the role of suzerain over Celts and Celtic lands, in a new, imaginatively conceived, expertly designed and executed symbol—a sceptre that expressed a freshly achieved political vision.

Christianity, a new concept of authority, and the ritual of consecration, was about to supervene and to render the pagan associations and authority behind the sceptre

376

obsolete. There could, then, have been two reasons why the Sutton Hoo sceptre was buried. First, that it was not the sceptre of the East Anglian royal house and so did not require to be handed on, but was personal to Raedwald; and second, if it was the East Anglian dynastic sceptre, that, in spite of Roman formal reminiscences, it was an object in its essence thoroughly pagan, and therefore unacceptable in terms of continuing use as a symbol of royal power in a Christian kingdom.

A NOTE ON THE PROVENANCE OF
THE SUTTON HOO STAG

by

CAROLA HICKS

At first sight the stag contrasts in startling fashion with the rest of the animal ornament encountered in the burial chamber. The latter for the most part shows a purely decorative treatment characteristic of Style II in the mainstream of Germanic animal art. The naturalism and full-round modelling of the stag makes assignment to a definite style difficult because it can be compared superficially to many figurines of differing origin. Bronze animals in the round, used as pendants, terminals, other ornamental attachments and on their own, occur in earlier periods in the art of Asia Minor, Luristan, the Koban and Ordos, as well as in Hallstatt, Scythian and Celtic art. They were also common in the art of Roman Gaul and Britain. Detailed study of the stag suggests that it is in this local Romano-Celtic background that the closest parallels should be sought, and that it is less likely to be an exotic import belonging to a remote time or place.

The treatment of the stag is in general simple and naturalistic, but there are certain features which depart from total realism. The large antlers, length of the neck and slenderness of the body give a sense of balance to the figure but are not true to nature. The rounded modelling is tempered by the distinct carination of parts of the body, already described (pp. 333-4); this is particularly marked in the case of the legs and antlers, giving them a hexagonal rather than diamond-shaped cross-section (fig. 250). This is probably a deliberate stylisation, not merely a by-product of the method of bronze casting used. The body has a slightly leaning-back attitude with the line formed by the neck and front leg at an acute angle to the line of the back. If the body is held horizontally, the hind legs end at a higher point than the front (fig. 248 a). It is significant that despite the otherwise fully three-dimensional treatment only two legs are shown, one at each end of the body. This stands in contrast with the pair of widespread antlers and suggests that the legs were depicted in this way so that the stag could be placed on a narrow base, such as the ring on which it now stands.

Naturalistic depiction of animals has always been a popular form of art and one which could exist as an integral part of styles where figures were also treated purely ornamentally. This dualism is to be found in Eurasiatic, in Celtic and in Germanic art. The simpler animals, often shown on media such as pottery, wood and textiles, as well as on the display metalwork of chieftains, represent an important and constant expression of local taste and form an underlying element of continuity from the Iron Age onwards.[1] Naturalistic representations were common in Roman art and in the post-Roman period animals continued to be shown in this straightforward way alongside the fragmented or ribbon-like creatures of Salin's Styles I and II; the animals on the Hildersham and Lullingstone bowls are examples of this other style, and creatures with plain outlines also occur on some Anglo-Saxon pottery.[2] There is also the question of the naturalistic style seen on the quoit brooches and a wider range of sub-Roman metalwork.[3]

An animal figure modelled in the round is not, by nature of its form, capable of such extremes of treatment as two-dimensional animal ornament, but small figurines can be a recurrent part of such more abstract styles. Bronze animals in the round are typical of Celtic art, both on the continent and in Britain, and a wide range of creatures including stags, boars, horses and birds are known. Such figures continued to be made during the Roman period where a delicate and fluctuating balance was reached between the meticulous detail and staid

[1] Cf. Thomas 1963, discussing the ancestry of Pictish stones.
[2] Hanging-bowls: Lethbridge 1951 a; Henry 1936, pl. xxx.3; pottery: Myres and Green 1973, 59–61; Lethbridge 1951 b.

[3] Hawkes and Dunning 1961.

realism of classical art and the sometimes exaggerated and stylised nature of a Celtic animal. The terms 'Romano-British' and 'Gallo-Roman' can be used to describe this compromise between two widely differing styles where a strong local tradition could modify provincial Roman art, with the result that native bronze workers could maintain an ultimately Celtic style right on into the early Anglo-Saxon period.[1]

Examples of stag figurines of the Roman period include the bronze stag from Richborough,[2] associated with late third to fourth century finds, which has a stocky well-modelled body but delicately stressed muzzle; two holes behind the ears suggest that there had been detachable antlers. From Roman Gaul there are stags from Erquy, Crotet, Saumur and Montmaurin;[3] these are shown with a varying degree of realism which can include detailed treatment of the eyes, depiction of all four legs and a roughening of the body surface to indicate the hide; but the large pricked ears and bent hind leg of the Sutton Hoo stag are also characteristic features. The

antlers of these statuettes are generally incomplete. A stag from south of the Limes in the Netherlands[4] has antlers with abbreviated tines and a realistically depicted coat.

A most interesting but enigmatic figure is the stag said to come from Gateholm Island, Pembrokeshire. (fig. 271) which is now unfortunately untraceable and appears to be of doubtful provenance.[5] As can be seen from the only photograph available it has, like the Sutton Hoo stag, only one leg element at each end of the body, slight faceting of the limbs and a head with distinctly marked muzzle but no indication of eyes; the antlers are broken. The island appears to have been occupied from the Iron Age to the post-Roman period, and if the stag did come from Gateholm it would provide a significant parallel to the Sutton Hoo example as being of native origin and probably pre-seventh-century date.

Animal figures in the round are also known in the Anglo-Saxon period, an important factor in this survival being the hanging-bowls which continued the traditions of Celtic craftsmanship beyond the period of Roman occupation. The cast suspension hooks were modelled in the form of the heads or bodies of animals and birds. This is seen in the escutcheons on the earliest bowls, such as those from Silchester, Barton and Sarre,[6] and remained a typical feature of the later bowls, their naturalism, lack of decorative detail and occasional faceted treatment contrasting with the linear patterns and, uniquely in the case of the Benty Grange escutcheon,[7] the zoomorphic interlace of the flat enamelled escutcheons. This simplicity of outline can be seen on two creatures associated with hanging-bowls, the solid bronze fish set inside the large Sutton Hoo bowl (whose body decoration of champlevé enamel spots can be compared to that of the Roman animal brooches made in Britain and the other northern provinces, again suggesting a continuity in animal ornament) and the quadruped with a long neck and tail looped through its legs set inside the lost Witham bowl.[8]

The Benty Grange boar is not cast but has been carefully constructed from hollow tubes to give the outward appearance of a solid figure in the round.[9]

FIGURE 271   The bronze figure of a stag from Gateholm Island, Pembrokeshire. The base is modern. (Scale: approx. 1/1) (By courtesy of Archaeologia Cambrensis)

[1] As has been demonstrated by Hawkes (1951) through the study of bucket animals, although he stresses that some degree of Romanisation must also be recognised.

[2] Bushe-Fox 1932, fig. 1, no. 30.

[3] Richard 1971a, 22–3 and Fouet 1969, pl. XLIX.

[4] Zadoks-Josephus Jitta, Peters and van Es 1969, no. 78.

[5] Gordon Williams 1926, 191. I am grateful to W. G. Thomas

and J. L. Davies for their helpful correspondence about the Gateholm stag.

[6] Henry 1936, pl. XX, 2 and 3; pl. XXI, 3.

[7] Bruce-Mitford 1974, fig. 37.

[8] Wilson 1964, 114.

[9] Bruce-Mitford 1974, ch. XI.

Boar-crested helmets are worn by the warriors on the Gundestrup cauldron, on one of the Torslunda dies and on the panels of the Vendel 1 helmet. Whatever the place of manufacture of the cauldron it apparently depicts scenes of Celtic religion and mythology; the helmet stamps, more specifically Germanic, also inherit the common vocabulary of North European art of the late Iron Age. The Benty Grange example shows that such animal-crested helmets were still being made in the Anglo-Saxon period and provides another example of continuity from the Celtic Iron Age.

The Sutton Hoo stag can be associated with this range of small animals in the round. It is a particularly attractive, lively and well made figure and it may be these special qualities which brought it into association with the other exceptional objects in the burial. As there are precedents for bronze stags in Celtic and provincial Roman art, it is with this tradition of figures in the round that the Sutton Hoo stag may be associated; examination of individual stylistic features confirms that its place may be found in this cultural horizon.

An important element is the faceting of the various parts of the body. This technique is first seen in Scythian metalwork both on relief plaques and figures in the round. It is characteristic of Scythian animal ornament and can probably be regarded as the skeuomorphic survival of a carving technique, the metalwork retaining the smooth planes and sharp ridges of wood and bone-carving, the media in which the Eurasiatic animal style may have originated. Even after the adoption of metalworking, this element continued to be used as an ornamental detail in Scythian art and was later among the features of the animal style which were adopted into Celtic art. The faceting of the legs, neck or body in a manner resembling that of the Sutton Hoo stag can be seen on a number of Celtic bronze animals.[1] The Bulbury ox, described as a chariot-fitting, even has legs of hexagonal section, like those of the stag. The Gateholm stag appears to have a slight faceting of the legs, although it is not as distinct as on the Sutton Hoo stag. This technique could be caused by the use of a hard wax original, which would have had to be carved in the manner of wood; the effect

undoubtedly points to a Celtic (and ultimately Scythian) strain in the stag's ancestry.

Another feature of the stag is that its fore and hind legs are cast as conjoint pairs. While this is a logical simplification for two-dimensional animals it appears out of character on this three-dimensional creature. If this is for the purpose of mounting it on the iron ring, precedents include two-legged Scythian animals in the round decorating rattle and pole tops,[2] and various Hallstatt and Celtic animals used as mounts and handles.[3] Scythian relief animals are almost invariably shown with all four legs, although this leads to ornamental distortion and confusion; and it is not until the Sarmatian aspect of the Eurasiatic style that the convention of using two legs to represent four becomes acceptable for animals seen in profile. This can be seen on the metalwork found in northern Europe reflecting Sarmatian influence, such as the Gallehus horns, Herpaly boss and Roermond disc, where two and four-legged creatures are shown side by side.

Associated with this feature is the leaning-back posture caused by the slightly bent hind leg and the sloping line of neck and front leg. This attitude is characteristic of the range of Sarmatian-inspired animal ornament on the Baltic–Black Sea metalwork types. Its origin perhaps lies in the legs being bent to suggest motion and liveliness with the natural result that if only two legs are shown the animal does appear to lean back and the motif thus becomes a stylised posture used as an ornamental device. This position is also seen on some of the animal brooches of the Roman period which combine Celtic and Sarmatian influences, and on the Benty Grange boar.

The extremely large antlers are treated with a degree of naturalism which does not compare with anything in Scythian art, where antlers, though large and important, are treated in a purely ornamental manner with the tines appearing as rows of symmetrical curls, and often terminating in birds' heads. Celtic antlers often have a herringbone shape, and are generally conventionalised. On the Roman stag figurines, the antlers are usually short and stumpy, probably for the practical reason that large ones are all too easily broken; the exceptionally good con-

---

[1] For example a deer from the Taunus (Jacobsthal 1944, pl. 175), a boar from Bata, Hungary (Piggott 1970, no. 90), a horse from Freisen (Jacobsthal 1944, pl. 174), an ox from Bulbury, Dorset (Fox 1958, pl. 50).

[2] László 1970, pls. 12 and 13.
[3] Jacobsthal 1944, pls. 190, 194.

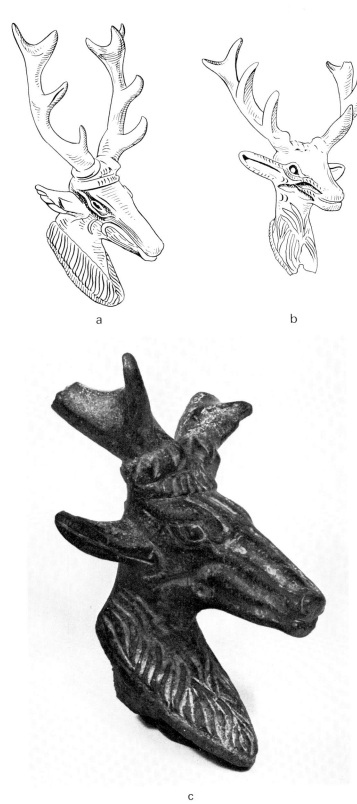

dition of the Sutton Hoo antlers could imply that unusual care was taken of this figure. However, an extremely close resemblance to the treatment of the antlers can be seen on another type of Roman bronze, the stag's-head escutcheons of Lloseta (Mallorca) and Rennes (fig. 272 a, b); an almost identical head, from which the antlers are missing, was found at Brampton, in Norfolk (fig. 272 c).[1]

On the first two examples the antlers are shown with brow tine, trez tine and three-pointed crown—an accurate depiction of the antlers of the red deer, and seen also on the Sutton Hoo stag. Although the three heads cannot be accurately dated, they appear to be of the Roman period: the Brampton head was a surface find, other finds from the site suggesting occupation from the first to fourth centuries A.D.; the Rennes head was said to have been found with Hadrianic coins and the Lloseta head is without provenance. Their close similarity demonstrates the uniformity of provincial Roman art, and at the back of the Brampton and Lloseta heads is a square hole and a series of engraved dots, possibly workshop marks, as if they were designed to be suspended from behind.

The head of the Sutton Hoo stag is considerably simplified in comparison with these other heads (which have large eyes, surface patterning, and are also of greater dimension), but the similarity of the antlers is striking and suggests that the Sutton Hoo stag was influenced by this provincial Roman convention.

Another interesting parallel, and one providing evidence of the general fragility of antlers, is the 'iron' antler which was found on Traprain Law, in a possibly second-century context.[2] The proportions are like those of the Sutton Hoo antlers with a distinct trez tine and a two-pointed crown. The basal tip is flattened and thinner than the rest as if it had been made to fit into a socket. The concept of detachable antlers, apart from being practical, recalls the antler cult which originated in the east, with manifestations in Eurasiatic and Celtic art, and survived into the early mediaeval period.[3] Further evidence for separate antlers is provided by the small bronze stag from Richborough which has sockets for antlers behind each ear. Another example of antlers made separately and of a different material from the

FIGURE 272 Three bronze stag-head terminals of the Roman period: (a) from Lloseta, Mallorca; (b) from Rennes, France, and (c) from Brampton, Norfolk. (Scale: 2/3) (Photo: Norwich Museums)

[1] Lloseta: Obrador 1963, 214; Rennes: Richard 1971 b, 259; Brampton: Wilson 1969, 223.
[2] Curle 1915, fig. 44, no. 1.
[3] Salmony 1954.

rest of the body are those of the Pazyryk reindeer;[1] the bodies are carved in wood but the enormous antlers, which are larger than the rest of the animals, are of leather. The abnormal survival of organic materials in these tombs shows how limited an impression is usually obtained from excavations; and it is not possible to dismiss the influence of hypothetical wood carvings on bronze animal figures such as the Sutton Hoo stag. The Pazyryk carvings also demonstrate the lively existence of the Eurasiatic animal style in the very wood and bone prototypes which the metalwork technique of Scythian animal art suggests.

The significance of the stag itself should be considered. The deer, and particularly the reindeer, was the creature most frequently depicted in Scythian art; it was also popular in Celtic art and survives for a long time in the art of the British Iron Age and into the Saxon period, particularly as pottery decoration.[2] The cult significance of the stag was still recognised in the Merovingian period with the rite of stag burial in the sixth-century cemetery of Bernerring, Switzerland.[3] The metal analysis of the Sutton Hoo stag suggests that it is not of the same origin as the bronze elements attaching it to the sceptre. If, as has been suggested, it was already regarded as a valuable possession and heirloom, it may have been deliberately mounted upon the similarly remarkable stone bar to serve as a totemic symbol of the ruling house. The name 'Heorot' for Hrothgar's hall also implies that the animal was then regarded as a symbol associated with royalty.

Although it is impossible to give a firm date to the stag, its stylistic features and the fact that it is a small bronze animal in the round suggest that it is strongly influenced by the Romano-British tradition discussed above. The slender, attenuated proportions and delicate head show the undoubted survival of Celtic elements in this style; yet the realistic details of treatment in the lifelike observation of the antlers, large pricked ears and muzzle together with a general simplicity of outline imply that Roman influence is also present. A fifth- or even sixth-century date would not be impossible if continuity in native bronze working is accepted, as indeed the hanging-bowls demonstrate that it was, and the Benty Grange boar and Sutton Hoo fish also show that this lively semi-naturalistic style survived into the early Anglo-Saxon period.

[1] Rudenko 1970, pl. 137 g and h.
[2] Thomas 1963, 36.

[3] Deonna 1957, 6.

PETROGRAPHY AND PROVENANCE OF THE SUTTON HOO STONE BAR

by

S. E. ELLIS

(British Museum, Natural History)

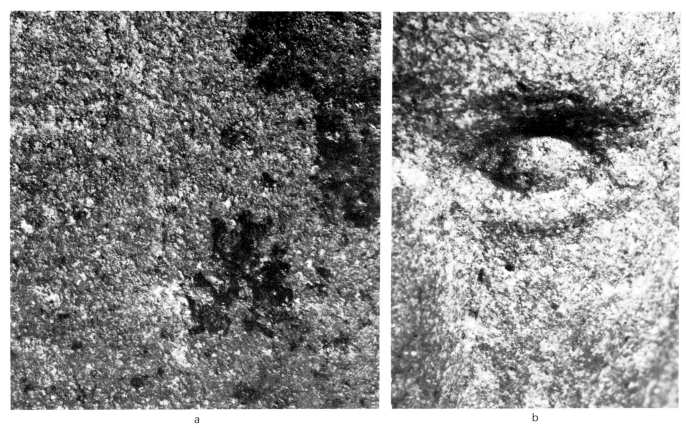

a   b

FIGURE 273   The Sutton Hoo sceptre: enlarged photographs of the surface of the stone bar of the sceptre. Part of a black stain (p. 315) is seen in (*a*); (*b*) detail of one of the faces.

Without a thin section, a detailed petrographic study of the stone is not possible, but an examination with a low-powered binocular microscope reveals its general character (fig. 273*a* and *b*). It is an arkosic greywacké-grit of grain-size mainly between 100 μ and 300 μ, composed of quartz with abundant feldspar and scattered opaque mineral and rock fragments, some of which appear to be of basic lavas. Some of the latter, and the abundant unoriented white mica flakes, are up to 1 mm in diameter. There

seems to be some interstitial calcite, irregularly distributed.

This description puts the stone into sub-group IIb(a) of my review of Saxon and medieval honestones,[1] all four types of which are based on hones from early Saxon sites in eastern England (Uncleby, Hough-on-the-Hill, Harrold, Fonaby and Mucking). As these types are based on detailed mineralogical characters, the sceptre cannot confidently be assigned to any one of them, but in terms

[1] Ellis 1969, 156 ff.

of general similarity the closest match is with type (2) from Hough-on-the-Hill, which differs from it in being finer-grained. The large, possibly ceremonial hone from Uncleby, type (1), resembles the sceptre in grain-size but lacks its large micas; it may be worth noting that it also resembles it in shape (rectangular section, tapering towards the ends). These honestones are closely comparable with greywackés of types common in the Lower Palaeozoic (Ordovician and Silurian) of the southern uplands of Scotland and extreme north-west England, which also occur as erratics in the glacial drifts of eastern England, although rarely in unflawed blocks large enough to furnish the raw material for the sceptre or the Uncleby hone. Somewhat similar rocks also occur on the Continent, certainly in the Palaeozoic (mainly Devonian) of central Germany (Harz Mountains, Upper Saxony) and possibly also in the Rhineland, where greywackés superficially resembling the sceptre are not uncommon. A Scandinavian source seems unlikely; although the stone superficially somewhat resembles some rocks in the greywacké facies of the Ringerike sandstone of the Oslo district, these are petrographically unlike those of my subgroup II B(a).

To sum up: so far as an opinion based on a superficial examination is justified, there are three likely provenances—(1) south Scotland or north-west England; (2) local drift, derived from (1); (3) central Germany. It is not possible to decide between them on petrographic grounds without, perhaps even with, thin-section study.

SCIENTIFIC EXAMINATION OF THE STAG ASSEMBLY AND THE BRONZE FITMENTS OF THE STONE BAR

by

M. J. HUGHES, W. A. ODDY and A. E. WERNER

1. *Introduction*

Reappraisal and research on the iron stand and sceptre led to the suggestion, now accepted, that the bronze stag and its supporting ring were originally mounted at one end of the whetstone and not on top of the iron stand (pp. 339-43). This appendix presents the scientific evidence which is relevant to this problem.

2. *Examination and analyses of the sceptre components*

THE STAG ASSEMBLY

The stag assembly consists of five main component parts, shown in figures 274 and 275 *b*. They are: bronze stag, ring of twisted iron wires, bronze Y-piece, collar, and pedestal-foot. Each of these separate pieces of bronze has been analysed quantitatively; the positions from which samples were taken are shown in figure 275 and the results are presented in table 29.

The quantitative analyses have been carried out by two different techniques; atomic absorption spectrophotometry and polarography. These methods of analysis have already been described together with a discussion on the likely accuracy of the results.[1] The usual weight of the samples was between 1 and 10 mg (0·001 to 0·010 g), and they were obtained by drilling in all cases except one (pp. 386-7 below). Using this method of sampling, the first portion of the drillings from the surface are rejected and the analysis is only carried out on uncorroded body metal.

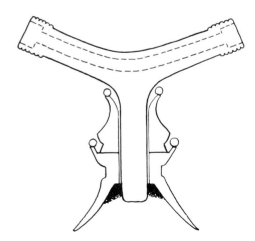

FIGURE 274   The sceptre: presumed section of the bronze pedestal from the stag assembly. (Scale: 1/1)

TABLE 22   RESULT OF ANALYSIS OF A SAMPLE FROM THE STAG

	%
Copper	83·3
Tin	15·2
Lead	0·25
Zinc	0·25
Iron	0·29
Silver	0·04
Antimony	0·01
Gold	Not detected
TOTAL	99·34

[1] M. J. Hughes, M. R. Cowell and P. T. Craddock, 'Atomic Absorption Techniques in Archaeology', *Archaeometry* 18 (1) 1976, 19-37.

FIGURE 275   The sceptre: (a)–(e) the stag and enlarged details of the bronze pedestal-fitting and saucer-terminal, showing the positions of drillings taken for analysis. In (c) the drill-bit is shown in position through the junction of the arms and stem of the Y-piece. (Scales: various)

The bronze stag

The small stag figure is cast in bronze; under the microscope dendrites are clearly visible, especially under the chin. A sample was drilled from the flank (see fig. 275 d) and analysed, with the results shown in table 22 above.

The absence of gold and the relatively low concentrations of lead and zinc are regarded as significant. The analysis corresponds approximately to a 15 % tin bronze, which is quite a hard alloy, although it has a lower melting point than a bronze containing less tin, and would thus be easier to cast.

The stag is now separated from the twisted iron ring, but there are loops of bronze around the iron ring at the positions where its feet must originally have been fixed. These bronze loops or clips are extensively corroded and are not sufficiently thick to enable a sample to be removed by the normal drilling procedure. It was however possible to obtain a sample for quantitative analysis by first mechanically cleaning an area of the surface free of corrosion products and then scraping off a sample of metal. The results are shown in table 23.

TABLE 23 RESULT OF ANALYSES OF A SAMPLE FROM THE PLAIN BRONZE LOOPS ON THE IRON RING

	%
Copper	77·6
Tin	13·4
Lead	0·01
Zinc	0·01
Iron	0·44
Silver	0·08
Antimony	0·18
Gold	Not detected
TOTAL	91·72

The low figure for the total analysis is due to the almost inevitable presence of some corrosion products in a sample obtained by scraping, rather than drilling, from a corroded object, even after the surface has been cleaned.

The concentrations of elements in these bronze loops are very similar to those in the stag, but the differences in the analytical results for lead, zinc and antimony seem to preclude the possibility that they were cast as one. Qualitative emission spectrography of samples from the broken surfaces between the feet of the stag and the bronze loops failed to reveal traces of solder and it seems likely that the loops were cast on to the iron ring and the stag's legs at the same time. This suggestion is strengthened by the fact that these loops are not decorated with grooves like the other bronze clips which hold the iron ring together (below). Furthermore the manner in which the stag has broken away from these loops at its feet, and not at the thinnest part of its legs, suggests that there was a potential point of weakness at the feet.

Qualitative analysis by emission spectrography of samples from the surface of the stag revealed only traces of lead and silver and the absence of gold. Hence it is unlikely that the stag was plated with any of these metals. The bronze stag was radiographed in order to look for any traces of inlay in the eyes, as none could be detected under the microscope, but nothing was revealed.

The iron wire ring or loop

This consists of four strands of square-sectioned iron wire which have been twisted in pairs in opposite directions. The free ends of the loop are tucked into the open ends of the Y-piece to form a ring, probably after having had the separate strands of wire at each end hammer welded together. The four twisted wires are held together by the two bronze loops below the stag's feet and by two clips of bronze ribbon placed at either side of the ring. As the two clips are fluted, probably by swaging, it is presumed that they were made by wrapping swaged bronze ribbon round the iron wire, but because of the advanced state of corrosion it is impossible to locate any joins with certainty.

The fact that the ring of twisted wires is not a complete circle but a loop with its ends tucked into the bronze Y-fitting was demonstrated in the course of taking a sample by drilling through the tube of the Y-piece, when it was found to be only loosely filled with iron corrosion products and not tightly packed as it would be if this section had originally contained metallic iron.

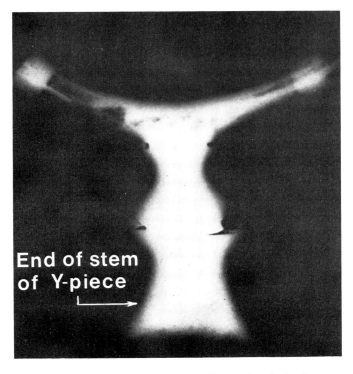

End of stem of Y-piece

FIGURE 276 The sceptre: radiograph of the bronze pedestal of the stag-assembly showing the hollow construction of the curved arm of the bronze Y-piece, and the presence in it of iron corrosion products. (Scale: approx. 1/1)

The bronze Y-piece

The free ends of the wrought-iron ring were pushed into a curved bronze tube. This is part of a Y-shaped component whose vertical section is solid, as shown in figure 274. In order to establish whether the vertical rod, whose end is visible in the interior of the pedestal-foot, is part of the same component as the bronze tube, the assembly was radiographed (fig. 276). Unfortunately the metal is so dense that it is not possible to prove the connection of these two components by this method. However samples for analysis were taken by drilling from both these pieces of bronze from the positions shown in figure 275 a and b.

TABLE 24   RESULTS OF ANALYSIS OF BRONZE SAMPLES FROM THE Y-PIECE

	Bronze tube %	Vertical rod %
Copper	84·5	82·0
Tin	9·38	9·22
Lead	2·00	2·24
Zinc	2·64	2·72
Iron	0·66	1·22
Silver	0·18	0·15
Gold	0·24	0·22
TOTAL	99·60	97·77

These analytical results are sufficiently similar for it to be postulated, neglecting the possibility of coincidence, that these two components were made from the same pouring of metal. The observed differences are due to (1) imperfect samples possibly containing very small amounts of extraneous matter, (2) the error factor in the analyses which could be as much as $\pm 1\%$ for the copper results, and (3) inhomogeneity in the casting itself which is particularly relevant to components which segregate, such as lead, or remain undissolved, such as iron. In order to determine whether the hollow tube and solid vertical rod were cast in one piece or soldered together a drilling was made through the area of the junction, as shown in figure 275 c. This starts at the junction, proceeds downwards into the vertical rod and emerges from the whole assembly through the side of the collar. This drilling was carried out in ten successive steps, each of about 1 mm, and the ten samples were analysed individually with the results shown in table 25.

TABLE 25   RESULTS OF ANALYSES OF BRONZE SAMPLES WITHIN THE Y-PIECE

Sample number	Depth of drilling	Copper %	Lead %	Tin %	Iron %
1	Surface drilling	85·7	2·12	10·4	0·93
2	1 mm	88·6	2·09	*	0·45
3	3 mm	84·5	2·34	9·44	0·45
4	4 mm	84·3	1·91	9·44	0·41
5	5 mm	81·4	2·06	9·42	0·55
6	6·5 mm	82·3	2·08	9·16	0·40
7	8 mm	83·1	1·56	11·4	0·68
8	10 mm	83·0	1·78	11·7	0·35
9	10·5 mm	Corrosion products of iron			
10	Surface drilling	Corrosion products of iron			

* Tin present but not analysed.

These results are all very similar. If there had been a soldered joint between the bronze tube and vertical rod the analytical results for the first two or three samples which were taken from the junction should be different from the rest. The observed variations in the amounts of lead, tin and iron are to be expected because of the small size of the samples. It is thus concluded that the bronze tube and vertical rod which make up the Y-piece were cast as one. Microscopic examination of the surface of the tube reveals traces of a dendritic pattern, proving that the metal was cast.

At the point where the sample was drilled from the bronze tube (see fig. 275 b) the walls of the tube are about 3 mm thick and the interior diameter is about 3 mm. The tube is loosely filled with material which was identified by X-ray diffraction analysis as iron corrosion products, and there are cavities which appear as black spots on the radiograph (fig. 276).

The collar and pedestal-foot

The collar and the pedestal-foot surround the vertical rod of the Y-piece. Samples were taken by drilling for quantitative analysis from the positions shown in figure 275 b.

The difference in the amounts of tin and zinc shows that the collar and the pedestal-foot were not made from the same pouring of metal, but the similarity of the analysis of the collar to that of the Y-piece admits the possibility that these were made from the same crucible of alloy. The observed differences, particularly in the lead content, could be due to the factors mentioned above. A residual dendritic pattern on the surface of both the collar and the pedestal-foot proves that they were cast to shape.

TABLE 26 RESULTS OF ANALYSES OF BRONZE SAMPLES FROM THE COLLAR AND PEDESTAL-FOOT

	Collar %	Pedestal-foot %
Copper	82·4	83·2
Tin	9·64	6·00
Lead	3·42	2·81
Zinc	2·24	7·29
Iron	0·90	0·70
Silver	0·19	0·20
Gold	0·32	0·39
TOTAL	99·11	100·59

The Y-piece, collar and pedestal-foot are now corroded together (fig. 275). The bottom of the Y-piece is surrounded by rust which appears to have been deposited in a free space. In order to determine whether the free end of the Y-piece had originally been held by solder poured into the pedestal-foot, several samples from the area surrounding the end of the vertical rod within the pedestal were taken for qualitative analysis and all were found to contain iron, copper, lead, tin and traces of several other metals. Since the body metal of the collar, pedestal-foot and Y-piece contain all these elements it is not possible to be certain whether solder was originally present, but it seems unlikely.

The terminals of the stone bar

When the stone bar was excavated in 1939, one end was decorated with an almost complete bronze fitting, known as the saucer-fitting, but the other end had only a few swaged bronze strips. Both these metal terminals are attached around knobs at the ends of the stone bar. These knobs are coloured red, and the pigment has been identified by X-ray diffraction analysis as hæmatite (iron oxide). The impression gained upon sampling the pigment was that wax may have been used as a binder.

The saucer-fitting

A sample was obtained for quantitative analysis by drilling in the centre of the saucer-fitting, the exact position of the drilling being shown in figure 275 e. The results obtained are given in table 27.

Qualitative analysis by emission spectrography of samples from both the surface and the body of the

TABLE 27 RESULT OF ANALYSIS OF A SAMPLE FROM THE SAUCER-FITTING

	%
Copper	81·9
Tin	2·06
Lead	5·92
Zinc	9·73
Iron	0·72
Silver	0·21
Gold	0·34
TOTAL	100·88

saucer-fitting gave very similar results, and there was no evidence for the surface plating of the bronze with another metal. The saucer-fitting was made by casting, and a residual dendrite pattern is visible in some parts of the surface.

The swaged strips

The swaged strips which are attached to the opposite end of the stone bar from the saucer terminal are fragmentary and appear to be extensively corroded. However it was possible to obtain sufficient sound metal from the centre of a small fragment of one of the bronze strips to enable a quantitative analysis to be carried out, with the results shown in table 28.

TABLE 28 RESULT OF ANALYSIS OF A SAMPLE FROM THE SWAGED BRONZE STRIPS

	%
Copper	82·5
Tin	7·20
Lead	2·98
Zinc	4·33
Iron	0·17
Silver	0·06
Gold	0·03
TOTAL	97·27

This has a different composition from the alloy used to cast the saucer-fitting, but is generally similar to the composition of the pedestal-foot. The main differences are in the zinc and gold contents which preclude the possibility of their being from the same melt and the strips cannot therefore have been cast in one piece with the pedestal-foot.

3. *Discussion of the analytical results*

All the quantitative analytical results on the bronze fitments of the stag assembly and the stone bar are collected together in table 29. In addition seven objects of the early Anglo-Saxon period (two Celtic hanging-bowl escutcheons and five Anglo-Saxon items) have been quantitatively analysed for comparative purposes, and the results are given in table 30. This table also contains the results on several other bronze objects of a similar date but not of Anglo-Saxon origin, and includes the four Torslunda plates and four other dies.

other analyses in tables 29 and 30, a 15% tin bronze is unusual. The alloy is fairly hard, and would be a slightly different colour from the other components of the sceptre.

These other components all have tin, zinc and lead contents which total between 14 and 18%, but the relative proportions of these three elements are variable. However in all cases the rather yellowish colour of the alloy would be very similar. It seems probable that these three elements were deliberately added to a level of approximately 16%, but that they

TABLE 29   ANALYSES OF BRONZE COMPONENTS FROM THE SCEPTRE
(RESULTS EXPRESSED IN PERCENTAGES)

	Y-piece		Collar (c)	Pedestal-foot (d)	Swaged bronze strips (e)	Saucer-fitting (f)	Stag	Bronze clips from top of iron ring
	Tube (a)	Rod (b)						
Copper	84·5	82·0	82·4	83·2	82·5	81·9	83·3	77·6
Tin	9·38	9·22	9·64	6·00	7·20	2·06	15·2	13·4
Lead	2·00	2·24	3·42	2·81	2·98	5·92	0·25	0·01
Zinc	2·64	2·72	2·24	7·29	4·33	9·73	0·25	0·01
Iron	0·66	1·22	0·90	0·70	0·17	0·72	0·29	0·44
Silver	0·18	0·15	0·19	0·20	0·06	0·21	0·04	0·08
Gold	0·24	0·22	0·32	0·39	0·03	0·34	Not detected	Not detected
Antimony	—	—	—	—	—	Trace	Trace	0·18
Total	99·60	97·77	99·11	100·59	97·27	100·88	99·33	91·72
Weight of the sample (mg)	2·07	3·41	2·70	1·67	5·72	2·87	8·58	1·53

It should be noted that traces of several other metals, particularly arsenic and bismuth, were detected by qualitative emission spectrography in some cases. An analytical result is given for antimony in only one of the columns in table 29, because the facilities for the quantitative determination of antimony were not available when the other analyses were carried out. It is likely that traces of antimony are present in some or all of the other bronze fitments of the stone bar.

The results show that the stag and the bronze loops on which it stood at the top of the iron ring are approximately 15% tin bronzes containing no gold, whereas all the other fitments of the sceptre are more complex alloys in which zinc and lead play a significant part in addition to the copper and tin, and in which (with one exception) a significant amount of gold is present. In comparison with the

were mixed indiscriminately to give this amount. The Y-piece and collar have similar overall analyses, as have the pedestal-foot and the swaged bronze strips, but only in the former case (the Y-piece and the collar) can the analytical evidence be said to support the suggestion that either of these pairs of components could have been made from the same melt.

The feature which distinguishes the bronze fitments of the stone bar, with the exception of the stag and apparently the swaged strips, from other bronzes of the period is the significant amount of gold in the alloy. This, together with the general similarity of the analyses of the pedestal-foot with that of the swaged strips are the two positive facts which may be said to connect the stag assembly with the stone bar. Traces of gold are only rarely reported in bronze analyses. Of the 438 bronze objects of the

TABLE 30 ANALYSES OF BRONZE OBJECTS OF THE DARK AGES
(RESULTS EXPRESSED IN PERCENTAGES)

	Buckle	Hanging-bowl escutcheon	Hanging-bowl escutcheon	Bridle ring	Bridle ring	Buckle	Brooch	Torslunda Plates[1]				Dies			
Object								A	B	C	D	(fig. 12, 1)	(fig. 8, 6)	(fig. 14, 1)	(fig. 10, 1)[2]
Provenance	Brooke, Norfolk	Barlaston, Staffs.	Barlaston, Staffs.	Brooke, Norfolk	Faversham, Kent	Breach Down, Kent	Kenninghall, Norfolk	Öland, Sweden				Barton on Humber	Unknown	Suffolk	Suffolk
Registration number	Brit. Mus. 1870 11-5 18	Brit. Mus. 1913 7-17 8	Brit. Mus. 1913 7-17 9	Brit. Mus. 1870 11-5 22	Brit. Mus. — OA	Brit. Mus. 1879 5-24 55	Brit. Mus. 1883 7-2 7	Statens Historiska Museum				Hull Museum, Grave 1	Brit. Mus. 1906 7-10 3	Moyses Hall Museum Bury St Edmunds K.32	Moyses Hall Museum Bury St Edmunds K.32
Copper	80·5	89·5	95·5	74·0	66·5	81·5	88·0	88	89	88	88	78·0	76·2	84·3	78·9
Tin	11·2	7·0	2·1	8·0	8·4	5·3	6·3	3·4	3·6	1·4	7·6	5·1	0·6	4·1	9·8
Lead	7·0	1·2	1·5	17·0	21·0	5·6	3·2	2·1	1·9	0·9	3·2	10·1	5·4	4·3	6·5
Zinc	0·43	0·26	0·04	1·25	4·4	8·0	1·95	2·7	4·1	8·8	0·8	2·6	12·5	4·4	0·3
Iron	0·03	0·03	0·02	0·19	0·55	0·14	0·33	2·8	0·3	0·5	0·1	0·13	0·17	0·21	0·13
Silver	0·05	0·10	0·06	0·06	0·06	0·05	0·04	0·7	0·8	0·4	0·1	0·13	0·09	0·10	0·20
Gold	Trace	Not detected	Not detected	Not detected	Not detected	Not detected	Trace	0·09	0·09	0·16	0·03	0·04	Not detected	Not detected	Not detected
Antimony	Trace	Trace	Trace	0·15	0·1	0·1	0·1	0·14	0·10	0·10	0·11	Trace	Trace	Trace	Trace
Nickel	0·05	0·11	0·15	0·02	0·03	0·05	0·04	0·04	0·04	0·05	0·04	0·06	0·05	0·05	0·07
TOTAL	99·26	98·20	99·37	100·67	101·04	100·74	99·96	99·97	99·93	100·31	99·98	96·16	95·01	97·46	95·90
Sample weight (mg)	0·0108	0·0099	0·0106	0·0103	0·0110	0·0108	0·0105	0·011	0·010	0·011	0·012	0·010	0·010	0·010	0·010

[1] Lettered according to Bruce-Mitford 1974, ch. 9.

[2] Capelle and Vierck 1971.

Middle and Late Bronze Age which were analysed by Smith and Blin-Stoyle[1] very few had any trace of gold, and in those that had, the level was apparently below 0·01%. A small amount of gold is present in the Torslunda plates, and gold was detected in the cloison walls of the Leighton Buzzard brooch and in some of the small buckles and strap fittings from Sutton Hoo, but as far as can be ascertained, bronze with an 'accidental' gold content of 0·2 to 0·4% has no precedent.

It has been suggested in the past that the stag is not of Anglo-Saxon origin and that it was already old when mounted on top of the stone bar. Certainly its analysis is sufficiently different from all the other objects whose results are reported in table 30, but there is the inescapable fact that it was almost certainly secured in position by castings (the loops round the iron ring) made of a very similar alloy. If the stag is old it must have been broken off a larger object, part of which was melted down to cast the loops at the feet.

4. *Analysis of the top of the iron stand*

This examination was carried out to see whether any scientific evidence existed to connect the stag and its pedestal-fitting with the iron stand (p. 339 ff.).

Samples were drilled from nine positions on the top of the iron stand and from one position near the bottom of its stem for qualitative analysis by emission spectrography. The sample from the stem was to act as a control. The sample positions are indicated in figure 277. Some of them were chosen to correspond with the diameter of the base of the pedestal-foot, supposing that it had been placed over the central circular elevation on the top of the stand. Any unusual features within this general area were sampled. The corroded iron was extremely hard, but

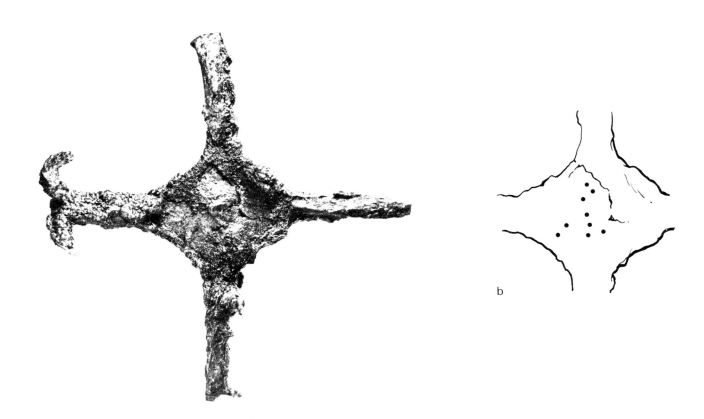

a

b

FIGURE 277   The iron stand: (*a*) the upper plate of the iron stand, (*b*) drawing showing sample positions.

[1] Smith and Blin-Stoyle 1959.

in each case a drilling about 1 to 2 mm deep was made.

The ten samples had identical analyses, which revealed the presence of traces of silicon, aluminium, manganese and copper in the iron. As the control sample from the iron staff contained the same elements as the drillings from the top of the stand, there is no evidence for either the presence of solder, or of traces of copper, in this position. Hence it is unlikely that the stag assembly was ever placed on top of the iron stand in antiquity.

5. *Conclusions*

(1) The bronze alloy used to cast the stag is very different from that used to make the other bronze components of the sceptre assembly.

(2) With the exception of the swaged strips and the stag, the bronze fitments of the stone bar all contain an unusually high amount of gold. This is in the region of 0·2 to 0·4% and cannot at present be paralleled in other bronze analyses. This factor connects the saucer terminal with the Y-piece, the collar and the pedestal-foot.

(3) The complex alloy which was used to cast the Y-piece, collar, pedestal-foot and the saucer-fitting and to make the swaged strips is a further factor connecting the components definitely associated with the stone bar with those associated with the stag. In this alloy, lead, tin and zinc all play a significant part together with the copper, although their relative proportions vary from piece to piece. Although the swaged strips contain virtually no gold, their general composition is otherwise similar to that of the pedestal-foot and forms a tenuous link between the stone bar and the stag assembly.

(4) No trace could be found on top of the iron stand of either soft or hard solder or of fragments of copper. As the bottom edge of the pedestal-foot is broken all round, some traces of it would almost certainly have remained on top of the iron stand if the stag assembly had ever been permanently positioned there.

Acknowledgements. Many members of the staff of the Research Laboratory have contributed to this work, particularly Mavis Bimpson, P. T. Craddock, R. Cowell and B. A. F. Nimmo.

CHAPTER VIII

THE WOOD, BONE OR IVORY ROD

———————

1. *Introduction and primary account of discovery*

THE EVIDENCE relating to the wood, bone or ivory rod, perhaps a ceremonial staff (Inv. 30–33, 302; figs. 278, 284-5, 281, 283, 279 c and 286) discussed in this chapter, and for its features and possible appearance, is entirely circumstantial. The basis for it is the gold filigree and garnet mount described in the first of the following extracts from C. W. Phillips's excavation diary.[1]

Thursday 27 July 1939   'Progressive cleaning [of the area between the iron stand and the drinking-horn/maplewood bottle complex] revealed. . . . 3. A rod of filigree with a small circlet of filigree attached (III.7) to the end. This was set with three small garnets *en cabochon* and equally spaced, one at each end of the object and one in the middle. This was slightly across the middle line of the sword later found. Free from the filigree rod there was a tiny garnet set *en cabochon* in filigree. It was just to the south of the west end of the filigree rod (III.7).'

Monday 31 July 1939   'The sand, etc., remaining in the floor of the burial area was carefully sifted and a number of small objects was found. . . . 2. A small piece of gold-plate binding for a cylindrical object in the form of an openwork animal. The three gold pins which secured it to the object of which it was part survived in place. This came from the sword area.'

The strip (figs. 278, 279 and 280) is 96 mm in length and the ring at the top has an internal diameter of 7 mm. There was no trace associated with it of the substance on which this gold and garnet strip had been mounted. However, a patch of reddish soil remained adhering to the back of the straight gold strip after its arrival in the British Museum. When analysed this gave a phosphate reading of 8%, the second highest value recorded from the area of the sword surface.[2] In almost the same position on the sword, but from the underside of the blade (no. 14 of table 25 in Vol. I) came the highest reading—9·8%. A further high result, 4·4%, came from a sample (no. 44) taken close to the gold strip (Inv. 30). The phosphate values from the scabbard tend to fall away from this group of high readings on each side. As the rod itself has wholly disappeared, this is the sole basis for the suggestion that the gold fitting had been mounted on bone or ivory, rather than wood.

Relatively high readings are also obtained from elsewhere on the scabbard, e.g.

[1] *Sutton Hoo*, Vol. I, 740-1, 743.   [2] Ibid. 535 ff., fig 402, table 25.

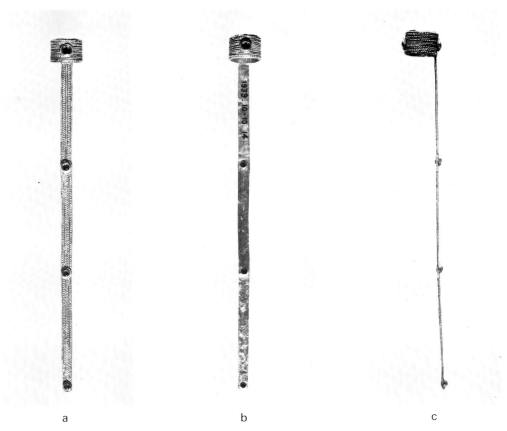

a   b   c

FIGURE 278   Gold ring and attached filigree strip (Inv. 30): (*a*) front view showing plaited filigree and garnets set *en cabochon*: (*b*) back view showing single *en cabochon* garnet and holes pierced through the strip from the front behind the garnet settings; (*c*) profile view of the strip showing the relief cabochon settings. (Scale: 1/1)

7·9% and 5·3% near the two scabbard-bosses, and 3·3% some 25 cm below the gold strip, nearer the point of the scabbard. The evidence for bone or ivory as the substance of the rod is by no means clear, in view of the general extent of impregnation of the scabbard by phosphate, and the upsetting of the balance of truly comparable readings, resulting from the cleaning of the scabbard, described previously.[1] It remains equally possible that the substance on which the gold strip was mounted was wood. On the other hand it would be possible for both the two highest phosphate values which occur close together on the scabbard, 8% and 9·8%, to have been caused by a bone or ivory rod which had fractured as it lay across the iron sword, one of the broken parts having been partly driven under the blade. At all events, the gold strip and ring had evidently been fitted on to a straight shaft of circular cross-section having a diameter of 7 mm.

The decorative features of the staff did not stop with the ring-headed strip. The detached setting with a garnet (Inv. 302; fig. 279 *c*) identical with those on the strip, is an additional item, since all five of the garnet settings carried on the strip are present

---

[1] Ibid. 537.

and correct (fig. 278). From the position in which Inv. 302 was found it had been mounted on the shaft above the ring-head, towards the end opposite to that towards which the long strip developed. It was drawn or marked in the ground by Piggott, in his plan of Areas III and IV.[1] The curved gold-foil animal (Inv. 32; figs. 281 and 282) is an important piece which, it seems, was also mounted on the wood, bone or ivory rod. It has sprung slightly open, but when closed up it appears to take up an internal diameter exactly the same as that of the ring (7 mm). The animal mount does not appear on any plan, being a late find that came to light in the final sifting of the soil in the area of the main jewellery concentrations; but the diary clearly identifies it and states that it came 'from the sword area' (p. 394). We can therefore feel confident that it also was mounted on the cylindrical shaft, to which it must have been fastened by the three gold pins, 3 mm long, that project inwards from its inner surface (fig. 282).

Consideration should also be given to two other items which do not readily relate to the heavier strap-mounts, buckles, etc., that belong to the sword-belt or to the waistbelt on which the great gold buckle was presumably mounted. The two objects (Inv. 31 and 33; figs. 283–285) are a gold-foil triangle 17 mm long and 5 mm wide, and a thin plain gold strip, 74 mm long, with tiny zoomorphic head. There is no evidence at all to associate this latter piece with the rod or staff, and there is no identifiable record by the excavators of the plain foil triangular mount.[2] The thin strip (figs. 284 and 285) may be said to come from the sword area, since it is shown on the burial deposit plan (fig. 314) close to the cloisonné triangular zoomorphic strap-mount, Inv. 18, which is described by Phillips as 'from the sword area'. It seems likely that the triangular mount may have come from the object represented by the wood, bone or ivory rod, since it has a gold pin of the same sort as those of the foil animal, Inv. 32, and the engraved animals it carries are very similar to the foil animal (figs. 282 and 283). Furthermore, although the mount has been somewhat flattened, it was curved (fig. 283 b) and the curvature agreed approximately with that of the ring-head on the strip and the foil animal.

All the objects described above must be regarded as disassociated from the textile or leather strap-work of the harness on which the main body of solid buckles, mounts and strap-ends belonged. The straightness and fragility of the two strips are hardly compatible with the flexibility of straps, and the circular form of the ring and cut-out foil animal is equally exclusive. The surviving gold pin of the triangular mount is not clenched over at the end, as it must have been if set into leather, and seems more

[1] Plan 3, *Sutton Hoo*, Vol. I, 140.

[2] On Piggott's composite plan on tracing paper (Plan 8, *Sutton Hoo*, Vol. I, 141–2) and on no other plan, a gold object of roughly triangular shape marked 'II.2' is shown near the large pad of textiles at the west end of the drinking-horn complex. It is not shown on Piggott's field plan of the area (Plan 2, Vol. I, 140). It has been included in the burial deposit plan (fig. 1) on the evidence of Plan 8, but it has there been given too specific a shape. It could, to judge by Plan 8, be the plain strap-end, Inv. 16, or even, though it would not be to scale, the missing strap-end, Inv. 13 or 14, found in sifting (p. 445), put in retrospectively by hearsay; or from scale and shape it could be the foil triangle, Inv. 31. Its status and identification in Plan 8 must remain uncertain, though on p. 580 it is tentatively accepted as Inv. 16 and assigned to a place on the shoulder support for the main waistbelt.

likely to have been inserted, as were the pins of the foil cut-out animal, into a hole drilled into something hard.

All five items mentioned, four of which may be held to have been mounted on the inferred cylindrical shaft, are described in this chapter, and not with the remainder of the gold jewellery in chapter x.

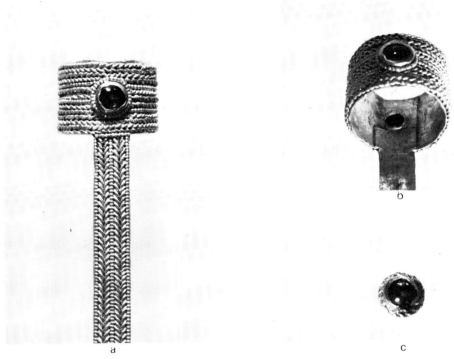

FIGURE 279 The ring and filigree strip: (*a*) detail of the ring with cabochon garnet setting and part of the flat strip, showing the filigree work; (*b*) the inside of the ring showing the back of the cabochon setting in (*a*) and the junction of the ring and strip; (*c*) the detached cabochon garnet setting (Inv. 302). (Scales: *a*, *b*, 3/1: *c*, 4/1)

Detailed description

Filigree strip and ring (Inv. 30) *and detached setting* (Inv. 302; figs. 278–280)

Dimensions

Length	96 mm
Width of long strip	3 mm
Diameter of ring	18 mm
Height of ring	6 mm

Thin gold strip decorated on one face with filigree work of fine quality and three convex garnets in spaced circular settings (fig. 278). On to the top of the strip is soldered, with gold solder, a ring made from a flat strip of gold twice the width of the long gold strip. This broader ring is also set with two externally mounted convex garnets in circular settings, one being in line and equally spaced with the three settings on the filigree strip, the other opposite it.

Each circular gold setting carries a beaded wire collar, mounted on the shelf surrounding the setting. The cabochon garnets of the settings have plain pointillé gold-foil backings which can be seen in some cases exposed from the back, there being a hole in the gold strip under each cabochon setting.

The filigree on the strip (figs. 279 and 280) comprises a simple beaded wire border on each side, inside which run two twisted wires each built up from a pair of wires twisted together. A third beaded wire runs down the centre of the strip separating the pairs of twisted wires, which are so set in relation to each other as to appear to form running downward-pointing chevrons. The horizontal ring shows a more irregular filigree design built up from the same components.

The strip shows no surviving nails, but behind each garnet setting is a perfectly circular hole with a low upstanding flange (fig. 278 b). Two of these show fillings of a substance resembling iron corrosion, the nature of which is not clear. If these holes did not accommodate (iron?) nails, their upstanding flanges might perhaps have been sprung over small (bone, ivory or wood) studs projecting from the rod.

The ring is taken to be the top of the object. The gold strip appears to taper slightly at the bottom or opposite end.

The small detached gold setting, Inv. 302 (fig. 279 c), is identical with those on the strip; it preserves its beaded wire collar.

Figure 279 b shows, in an interior view of the ring at the end of the strip, the splaying-out and flattening of the end of the gold strip where it enters the transversely set ring.

FIGURE 280   The gold filigree strip: drawing showing a detail of the filigree design. (Scales: strip, 1/1, filigree detail, 3/1)

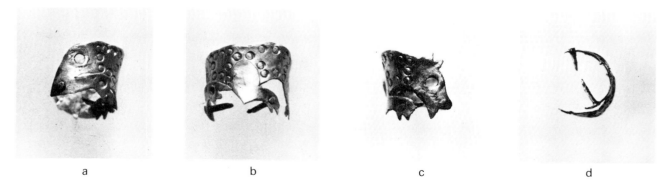

| a | b | c | d |

FIGURE 281   Mount in the form of a gold-foil animal (Inv. 32). (Scale: 2/1)

Gold-foil animal (Inv. 32; figs. 281 and 282)
Dimensions

Diameter in its present relaxed state	10 mm
Height	8 mm
Length of projection of rivets	3 mm and 4 mm

Cut-out animal in gold-foil. The main part of the animal's body is decorated with punched circles (fig. 282), but hips, legs and head are left plain and free from punched decoration. Each foot has a circular mark in its centre and three toes or claws, cut as pointed triangles. On the rear foot the central mark is a punched circle, but on the front foot it is the head of a gold nail. Another nail is fixed near the hock of the hind leg. In addition there is a clean hole, larger than the punched circles, on the rear hip. The animal's eye is also a hole. The two surviving nails are complete (fig. 281 *d*).

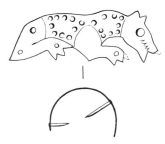

FIGURE 282 The gold-foil animal: detailed drawing. Gold nails survive in the front paw and in the hock, the body is distinguished from the head and legs by an incised line and a decoration of punched circles; the stylised zig-zag of the teeth is incised. (Scale: 2/1)

Triangular gold-foil mount with engraved animals (Inv. 33; fig. 283)
Dimensions

Length	16 mm
Width	6 mm
Length of projecting nail or pin	4 mm

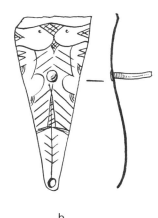

a   b   c

FIGURE 283 Triangular gold-foil mount (Inv. 33): (*a*) front view with incised addorsed animals in part resembling the gold-foil animal (Inv. 32); the remains of a nail survive in the centre of the triangle, and there is a hole for a second nail; (*b*) drawing of the mount showing the incised design of animals and the sinuous profile; (*c*) back view of the mount. (Scale: 3/1)

399

The mount consists of a flattened gold-foil fragment cut into a triangle. The upper edge shows that it was originally uniformly curved. At its central point is a gold nail, by means of which it was attached. At the extreme point of the triangle is a hole, apparently for another attachment nail now lost. The back of the mount is plain (fig. 283c). At first sight the front also appears to be undecorated but closer examination reveals an incised zoomorphic design scratched lightly on to the surface (fig. 283b). The mount is intended to be seen with the point of the triangle downwards.

The outlines of two small animals back to back and facing outwards are incised to the left and right of the central nail. Their front hip-joints converge at the nail. The bodies are extended down to the point of the triangle and are decorated with hachures. The back legs are omitted. The front hips and paws are left undecorated and have three toes or claws similar to those of the animal on the curved foil mount. The heads are simple outlines with V-shaped cut-outs for mouths and punched dots for eyes. Separating the two heads is a pattern of cross-hatching.

Seen frontally the faint decoration of engraved animals does not register, but the triangular cut-out shape, with the two punched eyes and the tip of the nose accentuated by the nail head, gives the effect of an animal head from the front. The faintly engraved animals and the fragility and slight dimensions of the mount seem to reflect the great delicacy that characterises the other pieces discussed in this chapter and, if they are correctly attributed, characterises the rod itself.

Fluted strip with animal head (Inv. 31; figs. 284 and 285)
Dimensions

Length	c. 75 mm (the end of the strip is bent)
Width	2 mm

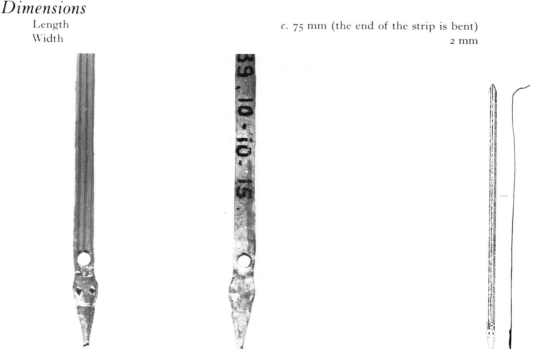

FIGURE 284 Fluted gold strip with animal-head terminal (Inv. 31): details (Scale: 3/1)

FIGURE 285 Fluted gold strip (Inv. 31) (Scale: 1/1)

400

The strip has a plain undecorated back and the front is decorated by two flutings between three slightly angular ridges along its length. The end away from the terminal animal head is now bent over into an irregular kink, but this may not be an original feature. The bent end is cut to a finished rounded point and the flutings are carefully terminated before the end is reached (fig. 285); this end may have been held beneath another mount as a method of attachment. The bottom end is modelled into a simple animal head, with two punched eyes made with light blows of the triangular corner of a punch or graving tool. The snout of the animal is sensitive, lightly modelled, long and tapered. Immediately at the base of the animal head is a single nail hole. No nail remains. This nail hole is the only apparent means of attachment on the strip. The strip does not relate to any of the gold objects which lay close to it in the ground, all of which are much more substantial, with heavy nails and back-plates for fastening to leather straps. Like the heavier filigree strip, the thin fluted strip would be much too fragile to be mounted on anything pliant, and the single nail hole would not of itself be sufficient to attach it safely to a belt. If originally mounted on the rod this piece could have been thrown somewhat out of position (fig. 314) when perhaps the suspended harness fell (p. 439).

Figure 286 provides a speculative impression of what such a ceremonial rod might have looked like, and offers a basis for discussion. It has the diameter indicated by the three mounts that show curvature, and the rod as a whole is light and reflects their delicacy. The length is uncertain. The sequence in which the mounts appear relates to the rough locations in

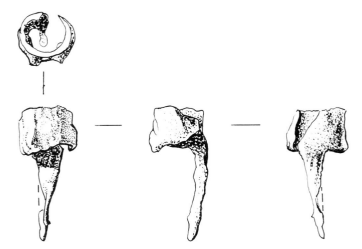

FIGURE 287 Iron clip-like fitting from Hawnby, Yorkshire. (Scale: 1/1)

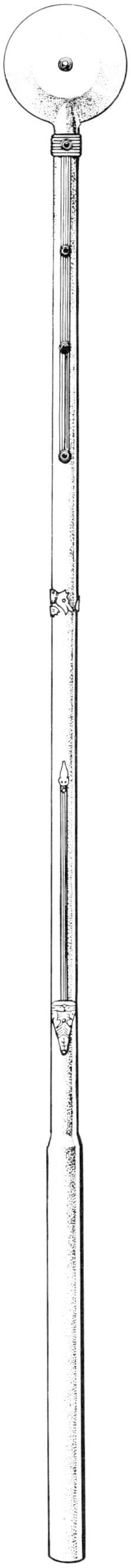

FIGURE 286 The wood, bone or ivory rod: suggested reconstruction. (Scale: 1/2)

which they may have been found, except in the case of Inv. 30, 31 and 302, which are drawn on plan and for which the sequence is clear. For the role which such a rod could have played see chapter VII (p. 354) where it is related to the supposed sceptre found in the young prince's grave under Cologne Cathedral.[1] An unusual iron fitting comparable in shape to Inv. 30 was found at Hawnby, Yorkshire (B.M. 82, 3–23, 36), in a male grave containing *inter alia* a Celtic hanging-bowl, and is illustrated in figure 287.

[1] Doppelfeld 1964.

CHAPTER IX

THE IRON STAND

I. Introduction and primary accounts of discovery

THE STAND (Inv. 161; figs. 290, 291) was first encountered, but only one corner of it, on 23 July 1939.[1] It was further investigated and removed on 27 July, as described by Phillips in his diary:[2]

FIGURE 288   The iron stand *in situ*: the spanner-like object (Inv. 210) is seen lying against the shaft of the stand, slightly to the left of the end of the rule. (Photo: O. G. S. Crawford)

[1] I am much indebted to Mrs V. H. Fenwick, F.S.A., for her assistance with the iron stand, and for comments on the construction of the main grid as seen in the radiographs. Her crucial observation leading to the removal of the bronze stag from the top of the stand, where it had originally been placed, is described in the sceptre chapter (p. 339). It has of course a vital bearing on the nature and possible use of the iron stand.

A full account of the excavation of the iron stand (Inv. 161) is given in *Sutton Hoo*, Vol. I, 183, and it is shown in the ground in ibid. figs. 116 and 117; it is just visible in fig. 118 of Vol. I

(the statement in the caption that the iron stand had been removed when the photograph was taken is incorrect: it is still concealed, as are the shield remains; the upper corner of the grid is just visible, projecting from the unexcavated soil above the bucket—see Phillips's diary, Vol. I, 738, n. 1). Its relationship to the other grave-goods at the west end of the chamber and to the various phenomena observed at this point in the excavation may be studied in the burial deposit plan (fig. 1) and in the archaeological plan (Vol. I, fig. 112).

[2] *Sutton Hoo*, Vol. I, 740.

'The morning was begun by investigating and removing a long iron object which lay across the boat at the foot of the west end of the burial chamber. It was about five feet in length and consisted of a long iron bar with a heavy pointed end to the north. Fixed at a point about one foot from the south end was a square grill frame of iron with horned animal heads at the corners. The south end carried a small equal-armed cross of iron at right angles to the line of the bar, and this appears to have been decorated with similar horned animal heads at the ends of the cross arms.

About eight inches to the north of the position of the frame there was a further iron projection from the rod. This was of uncertain purpose, but would in any case have prevented the travel of the frame any further down the rod in the event of the frame having been free to move. The condition of the whole was fair. The rod was in quite good condition, also the frame, but the animal heads were in most cases represented by little more than the horns.

Attached to one corner of the frame (sweated on by corrosion) was an iron or bronze (?) object terminating at its north end in a round plate with a large incision which made it in effect a clumsy fork [Inv. 210]. The iron rod and its attachments were successfully removed intact.'

In his first published account of the object Phillips made the following suggestion as to its purpose: 'It seems to have been a portable flambeau which could be stuck in the ground where required. Its head would be wound round with tow soaked in oil, the bull heads playing their part in helping to retain the combustible materials in place.' This interpretation was tentatively followed by Kendrick in his Inventory of the finds included in the same article: 'xlvii ?Flambeau with grid and branching terminals, and pointed end for driving into ground. L. 5½ ft.' And, again in the same account, Phillips refers to the stag:

'Near the frame part of the flambeau a small bronze figure of a stag with large antlers and mounted on an iron ring was found lying on its side. It appeared to have no relation to the surrounding objects, and will probably prove to be the crest of an elaborate helmet, crushed remains of which were found some 3 ft. to the east.'[1]

The stag on its ring and pedestal were thus adjacent to the iron stand in the ground, a circumstance consistent with their subsequent association by the Research Laboratory (p. 339), and to judge from the precise position of the stand as indicated on Piggott's plan (pl. 24 b), sufficient to account both for the iron corrosion deposits inside the hollow bell-shaped pedestal, which could have been in direct contact with the frame or stem of the stand, and for the green staining (p. 415, pl. 12) on the surviving strut of the four which supported the grid.

The stand (pl. 12 and figs. 290, 291) lay along the line of the west end wall of the burial chamber (figs. 1 and 288). It must have been close against the wall. It was the most westerly element in the deposit, except for the projecting points of the angons, further south. Nothing occurred west of it. The stand seems to have been driven inwards into the burial-chamber in a horizontal position, pushing all before it, as can be inferred from the positions of the sceptre and the shield in relation to it (cf. fig. 30, which indicates the consequential movement that took place in the ground).

[1] Phillips 1940 a, 162–3, 195, 163.

404

FIGURE 289   The iron stand: Detail of the upper plate;
in the middle a circular projection represents the burred
over end of the shaft. In the foreground the iron bands
of bucket no. 3 can be seen. (Photo: O. G. S. Crawford)

As figure 290 shows, the long iron shaft was bent downwards, presumably by the
weight of overburden that fell on it when the chamber collapsed. The stand was not
centred on the keel-line, which passes a little below the large transverse grid on the
shaft (fig. 1). The pointed foot of the stand projected northwards as far as the fourth
strake on the port side, lying slightly higher than the top of the stand. The stand is
calculated to have been, in its original state, unbent and with its slightly defective
point (p. 411) complete, 1·70 m in height. It could have stood erect at this point, just
clearing the sloping roof of the chamber as we have reconstructed it.[1] It might,
equally, have stood a foot or so closer in towards the central axis of the deposit,
leaning against the wall. The pointed foot could have moved upwards and outwards
when the stand fell. It is much more likely that the stand was placed erect in the burial
chamber, in one or other of these positions, than that it was left by the burial party
lying horizontally. Apart from general considerations, the direct evidence for this is
that the lower of the lateral iron plates on the shaft had dropped some 30 cm from

[1] *Sutton Hoo*, Vol. 1, fig. 230.

the point at which it was originally held (p. 414). This could not have occurred with the stand lying horizontal.

The falling sideways of the erect stand could have been responsible for some of the chaos at the west end of the chamber, though this may have been caused in other ways of which we have no indication. The grille of the stand seems to have broken through the rim and wall of bucket no. 3 (fig. 289); the stand could have been the agent which, when it fell, struck the sceptre, detaching the stag terminal, and knocked the large hanging-bowl from the wall to which it had been nailed. It might also have brought down the lyre on top of the hanging-bowl.[1]

2. *General description*

The iron stand is in a bent and defective condition and badly corroded (pl. 12, fig. 290). A reconstruction drawing of the complete object, showing details of construction and ornamentation, is seen in figure 291 *a* and a modern replica in figure 291 *b*.

Original dimensions calculated as

Height	170·2 cm
Measurements of open work grid, with projections	28·5 × 30·5 cm
Measurements of openwork grid without projections	22 × 25·5 cm
Depth of cage supporting the openwork grid	20·5 cm

Weight of modern replica

5·3 kg

The main constituent was a straight shaft, the original length of which may be given as 170 cm. The cross-section of the shaft is square at the top but slightly rectangular at the lower end (fig. 291 *a*). It tapers from bottom to top. The shaft is pointed at the bottom. Thirteen centimetres above the point as it survives, on opposite sides of the shaft, are two wrought-iron openwork scrolls, now clogged by corrosion but clearly

FIGURE 290   The iron stand in its present condition after consolidation and conservation treatment.
(Scale: slightly under 1/10)

[1] Ibid. pp. 188–9 and fig. 121.

a

b

FIGURE 291   The iron stand: (*a*) drawing; (*b*) the modern replica made by F. Landon of Jarvis Brook, Crowborough, Sussex. (Scale: approx. 1/8)

407

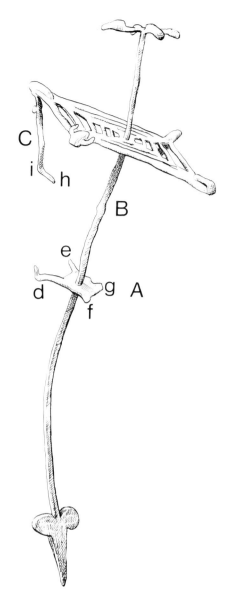

FIGURE 292   The Sutton Hoo iron
stand: lettered sketch.

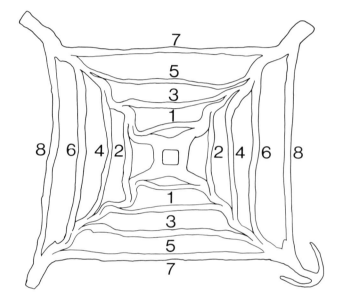

FIGURE 293   The iron stand: drawing of
grid showing the sequence of construction.
(Scale: 1/4)

seen in the radiograph (fig. 294 b). The scrolls project just sufficiently to take the weight of the human foot. They project 4·5 cm from the shaft (fig. 291 a). Immediately above the scrolls the shaft measures 20×16 mm, the slightly longer dimension being in the same plane as the scrolls. From this point the shaft tapers to the top where, immediately below the transverse plate (fig. 291 a), it is square and measures 9×9 mm. The point of the stand is twisted through 45 degrees and the bend has carried it 20 cm out of line from the vertical axis of the shaft.

Three separately made wrought-iron elements were added to the shaft over the upper third of its length. On the top is a small horizontally set cruciform plate (fig. 289). This consists of a square of metal the corners of which are drawn out into projecting arms folded back on themselves in an upward direction and shaped into the likeness of simplified animal heads furnished with horns (fig. 303 a). These have now largely disintegrated, and are best seen in the 1939 excavation photographs (e.g. fig. 289 above) in the condition they were in when first exposed; a good general impression of their appearance is conveyed by the modern replica (fig. 291 b). The top of the shaft passes through this small cruciform plate, which is presumably held on a slight rebate to prevent its sliding down the shaft. The protruding top of the shaft was burred over on to the upper surface of the plate to hold it against the rebate. The burred-over end of the shaft appears in the corrosion layer of the upper surface of the plate as a regular swelling of circular shape 25 mm in diameter (figs. 289 and 303 a).

Twenty-three-and-a-half centimetres below the cruciform plate the shaft passes through a large wrought-iron grid, skilfully constructed. This grid, originally at right-angles to the shaft, is now distorted from the horizontal, one side being appreciably higher than the other (fig. 290). Twenty centimetres below this grid, as calculated below (p. 412) and shown in the reconstruction (fig. 291 b), the shaft passed through the third element, another small cruciform plate (fig. 303 b). From the corners of this plate four iron struts or bars ran upwards to join the corners of the large grid and to support it.

These projections of the grid are folded back on themselves in an upward direction, roughly hammered into the semblance of animal heads and furnished with horns, as in the case of the top plate (figs. 301 and 302). The grid is a lightly oblong rectangle (fig. 293). It measured overall (including the corner projections) 30·5×28·5 cm but the rectangularity is more apparent in the grid itself (25·5×22 cm), ignoring the projections. The longer axis of the grid is in the same plane as the projecting scrolls and the slightly broader face of the shaft at its lower end. The difference in the length of the sides is slight but definite and would seem to give the object a front and sides, the broader face being presumably presented to the onlookers. It is possible that the difference is accidental, as the overall projection of the corners does something to counterbalance the greater difference between the sides of the grid itself, and the grid is in any case not very regularly made. But it is equally possible that the operative part of this feature may have been the grid edges (from which features of a non-durable kind might have been displayed), and the fact that the larger dimension is in the same plane as the projecting volutes and slightly broader face of the shaft lower down suggests that the difference, though small, is intentional.

The type of animal represented in the zoomorphic treatment of the corners of the top plate and of the openwork grid is not clear. The projections did not extend much, if at all, beyond the point where the horns develop, so that there is no projecting face or muzzle. The backward-moving horns would be zoologically impossible for outward-facing heads. It seems clear that in both the top plate and the grid the animal heads at the corners are turned inwards. Seen in this way the pointed heads appear long and slender and certainly do not represent bulls. They might be thought to depict sheep or rams, but the straightness of the horns is against this. The likelihood is that they are meant to represent cattle heads (*bos longifrons*). The heads at the corners of the grid were slightly larger than those on the small plate at the top, but otherwise similar. In both cases the horns taper and, after their initial backward bend, run straight.

Only one of the four iron bars or struts which joined the corners of the grid with those of the small plate below survives (fig. 290). At its top is a small well-executed, outward-turned scroll (fig. 297 *a* and *b*). If these scrolls, of which there may have been four (one on each strut), are related to the animal heads they would represent curls on the back of the neck. They are more probably decorative features unconnected with the heads. This would be evident if it could be shown that there were scrolls lower down the struts, where no animal heads occur, a point to be discussed later. Part of a second strut, attached to an adjacent corner of the grid, survives to a length of 5·5 cm (fig. 290).

Because of its poor surface condition the stand was subjected to an exhaustive survey by radiography, with a view to establishing or confirming its constructional and decorative details. This intensive survey, involving the making of some forty exposures of various parts of the stand, enabled the detail shown in the drawing (fig. 291 *a*) to be recovered and the replica (fig. 291 *b*) to be made. In addition to radiography, analytical tests were carried out on the top of the stand and (for comparison) on the lower part of the shaft; these demonstrated that the bronze stag on its ring and pedestal had not been mounted on the top of the stand, as had earlier been supposed.[1] The analytical results are incorporated in the Appendix to chapter VII (p. 392-3). The scientific study of the stand was carried out by the British Museum Research Laboratory, the radiographs being taken by Miss Mavis Bimson, and a joint report on the deductions from the radiographic work was prepared by W. A. Oddy, Miss Bimson and Dr A. E. A. Werner. The conclusions of this report are incorporated in the following account, with a selection of the radiographs and a number of fine black and white photographs specially taken in the Laboratory (figs. 294 *b*, 295, 297 *b*, 299, 300).

The radiographic survey was directed to answering a series of specific questions designed to throw light on:

(1) the structure and the decorative characteristics of the open-work grid;

(2) the original position, on the shaft, of the lower plate that supported the four struts that joined the corners of the grid; and, hence, the depth of the cage formed by the struts and the plate, and the design and proportions of the object as a whole;

(3) the structure of the foot, including the projecting scrolls;

(4) the structure of the projecting animals heads;

(5) the decorative treatment of the other elements of the stand, namely the four struts which support the grid and the length of shaft between the grid and the top

---

[1] All reproductions of the stand before 1972 show the stag on its ring and pedestal so mounted.

410

plate, which all appeared to show decorative treatment, and of other parts of the stand which did not.

The various parts of the iron stand are discussed here in turn, from the bottom upwards.

The foot (fig. 294 a and b)

The projecting elements on each side of the foot were openwork scrolls made from separate strips of metal and forged on to the main shaft (figs. 291 a and b, 294 a and b). Their lateral projection was only 4·5 cm, sufficient to enable the weight of the foot to be brought to bear to drive the point into the ground, but allowing them no more than the minimum size, so that no unnecessary weight should be added to the object. The point of the stand is broken off (fig. 294 b). It may be thought to have been at least 2·5 cm longer.

The shaft

The radiographs show no decorative treatment of the shaft.

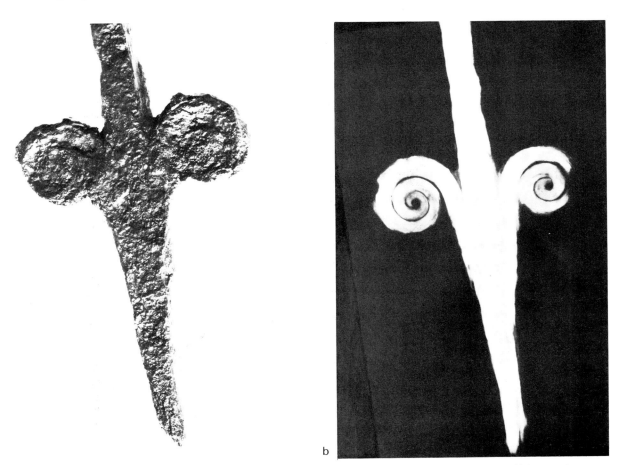

a   b

FIGURE 294   The iron stand: (a) detail photograph of the foot showing present condition and impression of volutes; (b) radiograph showing construction of volutes. (Scale: 1/2)

The lower plate and the cage of four struts supporting the grid

Figure 290 shows the stand in its present condition and figure 292 is a simplified drawing based on it. In the following discussion certain features are referred to by the letters shown in figure 292.

The lower plate. The present condition of the lower plate is seen in figure 303*b* and indicated in figure 292, where its relationship to the large grid above and to the one surviving strut, C, can also be seen.

Lengths of iron strut (figs. 295*b*, 303*b*) protrude from two adjacent corners of this plate, which lies at an angle across the vertical line of the shaft. This is not the result of its being bent or deformed, but suggests that it was not originally fixed at the position it now occupies (point A) but may have dropped down the shaft from higher up. In this connection it may be noted that at a point 20 cm below the grid there is a swelling on the main shaft (figs. 292 B, 295 *a*) and that this swelling is roughly in line with the inward-bent lower end (h, fig. 292) of the one strut (C) that still survives,

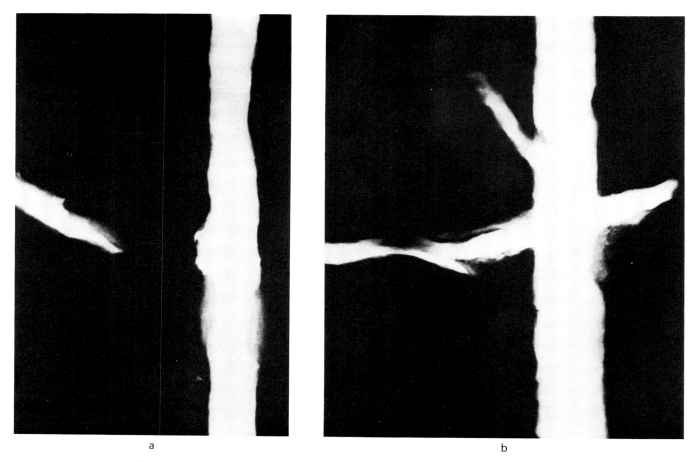

a b

FIGURE 295 The iron stand: radiographs of (*a*) point B (fig. 292) and the tip of strut C showing the relationship between them; (*b*) the strut d, showing the welded join between it and the lower plate. (Scale: 1/1)

attached to a corner of the grid. The lower half of strut C can be seen to be bent outwards to a corner (figs. 292, i, 297). If this bend were straightened the effect of this would be to bring the lower extremity inwards and close to the vertical shaft, in the vicinity of the swelling at point B (fig. 292).

If the strut C had originally extended as far as point A before joining the lower plate, in the position (fig. 292, A) which it now occupies, one would expect to find it fractured or disintegrated at its lowest surviving point, without any special change of character. This is not the case. The strut changes shape at its lower end, losing its square cross-section and becoming progressively broader and flatter (figs. 295 *a* and 297).

A radiograph (fig. 295 *b*) of the side view of the lower plate and of its iron projection, d, shows what appears to be a forged join between the corner of the plate and the end of a second piece of iron. This second piece of iron, which is of flat form, is evidently the end of one of the struts. Although the same region of the projecting piece of iron, e, is well preserved, radiographs show no such join. This suggests, as was indicated by the Research Laboratory, that the lower plate was constructed from a single

FIGURE 296   The iron stand: detail of the cage of the replica showing the double twisting of the struts and the reverse twists of the double border to the top of the cage.

long rod of iron, without joins (fig. 298), the lengths e and f then being bent up to join the corners of the grid, and that the other two struts were forged on as separate lengths of metal.

Radiographs of the shaft at point B, where there is an apparent swelling, show that this swelling represents what the Research Laboratory describe as 'an abnormality in the structure' and an 'ambiguous feature'. Figure 295 a indicates that it is not corrosion but solid metal, projecting further than the general line of the vertical shaft.

The combination of all these factors makes it certain that the lower plate was originally situated at point B. That it should have been free to fall suggests that it was a relatively loose-fitting at B; if its function was to support the grid above, it must nevertheless have itself been held in some way, but no pin, collar or other structural feature can be detected, any more than in the case of the grid itself.

The struts. The 'cage' beneath and apparently supporting the grid was formed by the four struts. These consisted of a square-sectioned rod (fig. 297) which had been twisted as shown in figure 296, the twisting being in two lengths of 6·5 cm each, twisted in opposite directions, with a plain section in between some 5 cm in length.

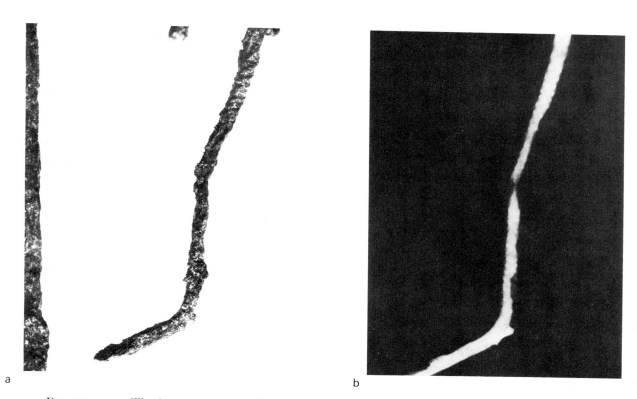

a   b

FIGURE 297   The iron stand, strut C (fig. 293): (*a*) the strut in its present condition showing the curl at the top, the twist of the strut and the spur of a possible second curl at the elbow of the strut; (*b*) radiograph. (Scale: approx. 1/2)

414

Two-and-a-half centimetres below the upper end of the complete, or nearly complete, strut is a small outward-turned curl in wrought iron (figs. 296 and 297). Although some 5 to 6 cm of the top of the second of the struts remains, there is no sign of a similar curl having been present on it. At the lower angle or elbow of the preserved strut, where it bends in towards the shaft (i, fig. 292) there is again an ambiguous feature. It is a slight projection which appears in the radiograph as dense and separated from the main body of the strut by a faint line. Its nature is uncertain but it could be the remains of an outward-turned curl similar to that at the upper end of the strut. As figure 297a shows, it appears on the original as a small spur or excrescence, lacking the flatness and breadth of the curl at the other end of the strut. It could nevertheless be the vestige of such a curl. The radiograph (fig. 297b) seems to show the added metal merging with the strut at its lower end, and emerging from it at its upper end, suggesting that the feature developed in an upward direction. If so it would appear to counterbalance the curl at the top. The point at which twisting of the strut begins would be approximately at the same distance from the upper and lower curls. These factors may suggest that the irregularity seen in the radiograph does represent a curl, but the evidence is insufficient to justify its inclusion in the replica (fig. 296) or the reconstruction drawing (fig. 291 a).

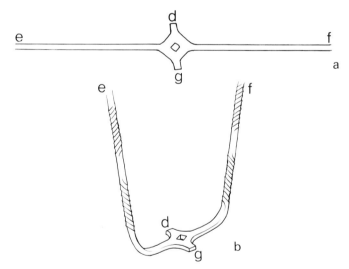

FIGURE 298   The iron stand: sketch of the lower plate, (a) with arms extended; (b) with arms bent upwards to form part of cage. (cf. fig. 291 a)

The whole length of the surviving strut, from above the upper curls to below the elbow with this slight abnormality, is stained with green (pl. 12). This staining is almost certainly derived from the bronze stag and its pedestal (fig. 1), the only bronze object known to have been in the vicinity. The stag evidently lay at a slightly higher level than the iron strut (fig. 235), and its corrosion products could have diffused down on to the iron beneath. This raised the possibility that the small amorphous projection, which is strongly green in colour, could be bronze, and perhaps a part of the stag figure or its pedestal incorporated with the corroding iron. Analysis shows, however, that the green is superficial and that the added piece of metal is iron. In figure 288 the strut is not visible; the whitish lump on the upper near corner of the grid can be identified as representing the corner in which the horns are now preserved; the position of the lower plate can be clearly seen.

Finally, it is apparent from the radiograph (fig. 297 b) that the preserved strut was one of the two separate rods of metal forged to the lower plate, and must therefore have joined the plate at a point opposite d (g, fig. 292). As it can be seen from figure 288 that the preserved strut and the projection with the remains of a forged join are on the same side of the stand, instead of on opposite sides, this suggests that the lower plate, in addition to having dropped down the shaft, must have rotated through about 120 degrees.

FIGURE 299   The iron stand: radiographs of the grid (Scale: 1/2)

416

The large grid

The peculiar structure of this is evident from superficial examination, but more clearly seen in the radiographs (figs. 299 and 300), on which the drawing (fig. 293) is based. The grid seems to have originated with a small metal plate like those on the shaft above and below it, with a square central hole and with its four corners elongated. On to these extended corners, working outwards, additional iron bars were successively forged and the corners elongated again to take the next sequence of bars. This method of construction is responsible for both the thickness and undulations of the diagonal elements which run from the central plate to the four corners of the grid. These strong diagonals were not independent bars of metal but were created by degrees as each fresh strip of iron was added to the growing grid. The method also explains the irregularity of the grid and the unevenness of its interior spaces. The struts that make up the interior were hammered to produce a grid that is uniformly flat on both faces; all are plain single struts of square cross-section. Each of the four outer edges of the grid is composed of two struts set one above the other. These can be seen, in oblique light, to have been continuously twisted over almost their whole length, the two elements being twisted in opposite directions (fig. 296). The twisting is confirmed and clarified by radiography (fig. 300). The pairs of struts which form the outer edges of the grid were not contiguous. There was a gap between them, certainly 3 mm and perhaps as much as 8 mm wide (fig. 300). The depth of the two edges of the grid together was some 18 mm. The plain bars forming the central part of the grid are little more than 8 mm thick. The level of the whole interior of the grid was thus, on the upper and lower faces, slightly recessed from its edges.

FIGURE 300 The iron stand: radiograph of the edge of the grid showing double twisted bars (cf. fig. 296). (Scale: 1/1)

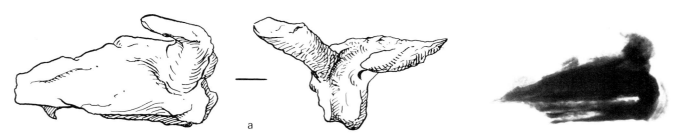

FIGURE 301   The iron stand: (*a*) drawing, and (*b*) radiograph of one of the stylised animal heads from the corners of the grid. The radiograph shows clearly how the head of the animal curves over the upper surface of the grid to face inwards. (Scale: 1/1)

The animal heads and the construction of the corners of the frame

Radiography (fig. 301 *b*) has failed to show how the animal heads and the corners of the grid at which they are developed were constructed. Close examination of the original suggests that the method of construction may have been as shown in figure 302. The projecting corners of the frame, which possessed an extra thickness (being the point of junction of the four bars that form adjacent edges of the frame), were hammered over upwards and then inwards and downwards, that is, folded back on themselves. The horns may have been made by cutting into the upper angles of the inward-folded bar from its extremity and then hammering out and shaping the cut pieces. There is no indication that an extra strip of metal was added to the upper surface of the folded-over corner projections, and subsequently split to form the horns. Cutting away of the two upper angles of the folded-over bar could have contributed to the tapering

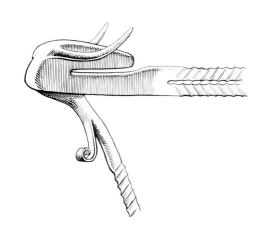

FIGURE 302   The iron stand: reconstruction drawing based on radiographs of a corner of the grid, showing the construction of an animal head and a curl at the top of one of the struts. (Scale: 1/2)

effect of the muzzles of the animals. The struts that supported the four corners of the grid from below were, it seems, not wrapped round the corner projections to form the animal heads, as is suggested in the general drawing of the stand (fig. 291 *a*). It seems clear that the upper ends of the struts were partly butted against the underside of the corner projections and partly forged into them. The technique apparently employed here of splitting the rod of metal and working separately on the split-away portion is illustrated by the curl at the top of the surviving strut (figs. 297 *a*, 302).

The upper plate

This small plate (fig. 303 *a*) clearly shows a folding over upwards and backwards of elongated corners to form animal heads, reinforcing the belief that this was

418

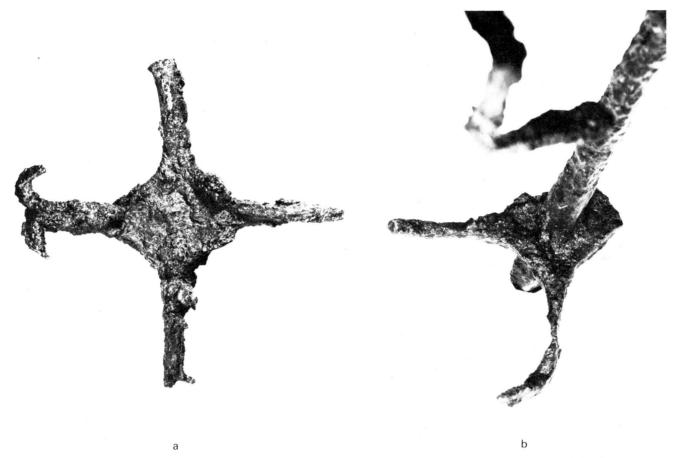

a   b

FIGURE 303   The iron stand: (*a*) the upper plate in its present condition. The remains of the horns of one of the stylised animal heads that decorated this plate as well as the grid appear at the left of the picture; (*b*) the lower plate seen from above; fragmentary remains of two struts survive. (Scale: 1/2)

probably the method employed also on the grid, where the animal heads were larger in proportion but apparently of the same construction. The central swelling seen in plate 12 and figures 289 and 303 *a* must represent the projecting tip of the vertical shaft hammered over to retain the plate.

3. *An iron object (Inv. 210) possibly connected with the stand*

Dimensions

Length (when flattened)	16 cm
Width of round terminal plates	6 cm

The object is illustrated in figure 304 and radiographs revealing its structure are shown in figure 305. Its discovery is recorded in Phillips' diary in the passage dealing with the iron stand (p. 404 above). Like the stand, it lacks decorative treatment. Its form does not lend itself to twisting, as parts of the stand do. It may not be connected with the iron stand, but was found in contact with it. Its character is unique. It does not appear to be complete in its own right, and must have had a specific function.

a   b

FIGURE 304 The spanner-like iron object of uncertain use (Inv. 210) found adhering to the stem of the
stand (cf. fig. 288): analysis of the white encrustations seen on the surface of the iron has shown that the
object has been in association with a high phosphatic source during burial (p. 422). (Scale: 1/1)

The only other object of iron construction in the neighbourhood is bucket no. 3, at
a small distance away (fig. 1). There is no precedent for the association of such an
object with an iron-bound wooden bucket, although buckets are a relatively common
type of find. It is tempting to associate this unique object with the stand (also unique):
the use and purpose of each is equally obscure. The only other possibility seems to
be that the object is in some way connected with the construction or fitments of the
burial chamber; but for this it seems too insubstantial.

420

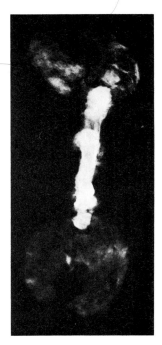 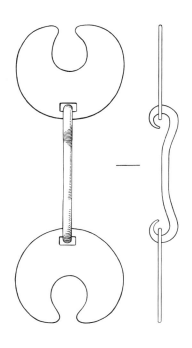 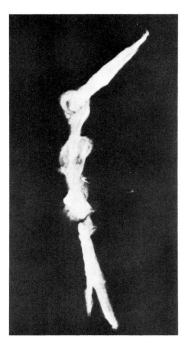

FIGURE 305 The iron object (Inv. 210): radiographs and reconstruction drawing. The profile view clearly shows the method of attachment of the central bar to the circular terminals. (Scale: 1/2)

As the radiographs (fig. 305) demonstrate, the object consists of a central straight element, apparently an iron bar, connected at each end to two roughly circular plates, each of which has a deep, rounded bite taken out of its further side. The two plates hinge, the ends of the bar being formed into flattened loops which pass through a slot at the back of each plate. Neither of the plates show rivets or holes or any obvious method of attachment to any other object. The plates appear to be flat, not dished. In figure 288, Inv. 210 can be identified with the iron agglomeration against the shaft of the stand seen immediately below the tip of the white ruler in the background. It is not recorded on any plan. The evidence for the identification is in the first place visual, though this is not decisive. Experience in reading photographs of the burial deposit has taught us that appearances can be deceptive. The resemblance of figure 288 to the object, Inv. 210, is, however, supported by a close analysis of Phillips's account. 'Attached to one corner of the frame (sweated on by corrosion) was an iron or bronze (?) object terminating at its north end in a round plate with a large incision which made it in effect a clumsy fork.'[1]

Evidently the 'round plate with a large incision', which seems to correspond with appearance on the photograph, was not itself sweated on to the corner of the frame by corrosion but was the terminal of the object recorded, at its north end. No object can be seen attached to the two corners of the grid that are uppermost in figure 288. The only object known to be attached to the corner of the frame is strut C (fig. 292).

[1] *Sutton Hoo*, Vol. I, 740.

In figure 288 strut C is not visible but it can be shown from the position both of the grid and of the plate and its projections lower down, to be attached at the lower corner nearest to the camera. The object that seems to be Inv. 210 lies in contact with the shaft of the stand at exactly the point where the lower end of strut C emerges. It would seem clear that at this stage, with no trace of similar struts running from the exposed corners of the grid, Phillips took the strut to be an extraneous piece of metal attached to the corner of the grid by corrosion. His account makes it clear that he was uncertain whether the object so attached was of iron or of bronze. We have seen that strut C shows traces of green stain over its whole length even after cleaning and conservation, and the appearance must have been more marked in its uncleaned state. The fact that the notched terminal belonged to something which might have been of bronze, and was attached to the corner of the frame, making 'in effect a clumsy fork' indicates that the 'object' was in the nature of a stem or handle. It may be taken as certain that the appearance in figure 288 is Inv. 210, and this makes clear its precise relationship in the ground to the stand.[1]

The surfaces of the object show no trace of textile or leather. This is true of the stand also. It should nevertheless be borne in mind that there may have been features of an organic nature, such as leather straps or cloth, associated with the stand, and that the explanation of Inv. 210, if it was connected with the stand, may be found in this. The closest formal parallels to this object in the burial deposit are the silver handles of the silver bowl with classical head (Inv. 77). It will be recalled that these were found detached under the Anastasius dish and were thought by the excavators to have been handles of a leather bag.[2]

At three points on Inv. 210, the two extremities and the middle, are white encrustations which have proved to be highly phosphatic, giving values respectively of 14·5, 20 and 26·5% P_2O_5. The material appears to be identical with similar phosphatic material found on the top of the Anastasius dish where it is thought to have been derived from burnt bone.[3]

4. The function of the stand

The iron stand has as yet no parallel in Germanic archaeology, although certain pieces come to mind as showing similarity to one or other feature of it. It is included in this volume in the belief that it is possibly a standard of some kind and if so properly classed under regalia.

There are certain facts about the stand which are basic to its interpretation. The first is its position in the burial deposit (fig. 1). At the west end of the chamber, where the stand was placed, were items for recreation (gaming-pieces and the lyre); armour and weapons (the shield, the helmet, spears and angons, and the sword); the royal

---

[1] It has been accordingly drawn in this position in the Archaeological Plan, *Sutton Hoo*, Vol. I, fig. 112, no. 30.

[2] Ibid. figs. 145 and 148.

[3] Ibid. 533, fig. 384; see also 538, n. 1 and particularly 542, n. 1.

sceptre, perhaps the most significant object in the burial; and the rare imported bronze bowls—the finest of Coptic bowls and hanging-bowls. Domestic gear was at the other end of the chamber and these pieces, of imposing quality even if of domestic use, included a lamp (Inv. 166). This was an elaborate iron object 18·9 cm high, with three short legs and a deep bowl, filled with beeswax.[1] If, therefore, the stand is a lighting device, it would seem likely to have a more than domestic significance, being used perhaps on special occasions or royal progresses.

Other factors about the stand that are basic to its interpretation are that it is portable (the estimated original weight of 11 lb 10 oz (5·3 kg) makes it little heavier than the standard army rifle used at the beginning of the 1939–45 war) and that it was intended to be stuck in the ground, or fitted into a prepared socket. Compatible with this is the fact that with the stag-fitting removed it is not unduly topheavy and is capable of standing erect without extra support. As has been said, the projecting volutes at the bottom, above the point, are narrow, but they are just big enough to take the weight of the human foot; this may support the idea that their purpose was to enable the point to be driven into the ground, but they could also be compatible with its being set into a prepared socket. No accessory such as a block or socket survived in the burial chamber, so that any fitment of this kind for the reception of the stand may have been a permanency, perhaps set in front of the hall door, or of the high seat in the hall, or in some such well-understood position. It is also possible, as has been suggested by Professor Sune Lindqvist,[2] that the point might have engaged in a leather frog, to enable the stand to be carried by a leather strap slung over the shoulder, in the manner of modern regimental colours. None of these possibilities excludes any of the others, and all may have applied.

Other features of the stand to which attention may be drawn are that the edges of the large horizontal grid are open, there being on each face a gap between pairs of iron rods which twist in opposite directions (fig. 296); and that the cattle heads, on both the openwork grid and the top plate, face inwards. Another distinctive feature is the cage of ribs below the grid. This may have been no more than a device for holding the grid rigid, but it could also have played a special part in the employment of the stand as a whole. The grid may have been merely a device to reduce weight by openwork structure in what was intended to be no more than an elevated platform. On the other hand this openwork construction may be essential to the use or significance of the object.

The idea that the stand is some kind of lighting device is very persistent. There is no more evidence for this than there is for any other suggested explanation. It has been thought of as possibly an elevated platform for the holding of pottery lamps, but such lamps are not known in Migration period or Merovingian period archaeology, although they occur in late Anglo-Saxon contexts. One example of such pottery lamps found on the Anglo-Saxon town site at Thetford in Norfolk, is shown in figure 306.

---

[1] Ibid. Vol. I, fig. 364.   [2] Verbal communication.

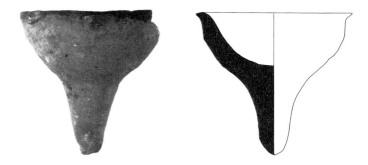

FIGURE 306 Pottery lamp with spike from Thetford, twelfth century. It is possible that lamps similar to this could have been mounted on the grid of the iron stand. (Scale: 1/2)

Medieval analogies exist for wrought iron splinter-holders, iron stands with various devices for the sticking in or gripping of resinous splinters, which burnt readily. It has been suggested[1] that the gaps between the iron rods, twisted in opposite directions, which form the sides of the grid, served this purpose, but no trace of wood is to be found in these crevices. It seems clear that the sixteen cattle horns that embellish the top of the stand were never vertical enough, long enough or sharp enough to act as pricket candle-holders, nor is there any device for trapping melted wax, a precious commodity, nor any evidence that candles were used before the era of Alfred the Great, whose time-keeping candles of beeswax are described by Asser. If the iron stand must be seen as a lighting device, then Phillips's original suggestion, a flambeau, is the one which seems best to fit its design and could account for all its features. The cage below the grid could have held a container (of wood or leather, since no trace survived) for oil or wax. Wicks or ropes might have been led up from this, twisted round the horned heads at the corners of the grid and fed through the gaps between the horns and muzzles of the cattle heads at the top, at which level they would be lit. All this is pure speculation. No trace of any substance, such as wax, or tow ropes, or even carbonisation, was detected when in 1945–6 the stand was subjected to cleaning and initial conservation, although there was much curiosity and speculation at the time as to its possible uses. The beeswax cake in the iron lamp (Inv. 166) is perfectly preserved, and throughout the deposit textile impressions (such as might have survived from wicks) register readily in corroding iron. The stand has shown no indication of either.

The problem of the use and purpose of the stand is not to be solved at present. Fresh discoveries on the Sutton Hoo site or elsewhere may provide the answer. Nevertheless analogies to individual features of the stand do exist, and it may be briefly considered against the general background of craftmanship and ideas.

[1] Verbally by Professor Sune Lindqvist, and by F. W. Robins (1953).

424

FIGURE 307   Iron trivet from Lilleberre, Norway
now in the British Museum, (Scale: 1/5)

FIGURE 308 Iron grid from Veszprem,
Hungary, now in the Bakony Museum. The
grid is similar in construction to that of the
Sutton Hoo stand and has a central circular
hole, presumably for a vertical shaft to pass
through. (Scale: approx. 1/4) (photo: by
courtesy of the Bakony Museum)

425

Openwork wrought-iron grids or pot-stands occur as domestic appliances, and such pieces as the tripod from Krefeld-Gellep grave 1782 (with a bronze vessel in position on it) and those from Weimar, grave 21, and Biebrich may be cited.[1] Not much different from these is the type of flat grill or pot-stand not unlike the grid of the Sutton Hoo object, but more open in construction, on three short legs. An example from Lilleberre in Norway, now in the British Museum, is illustrated in figure 307. The analogy in construction, so far as the grid is concerned, is evident. Even more relevant is the iron grid from Veszprem, Hungary (fig. 308),[2] thought to be of Roman date. This carries us a stage further, since the method of construction by a series of lengths of iron rod added in sequence is identical with that of the Sutton Hoo grid. It has the same small central plate, with a square hole in it, and no legs, indicating that the grid was mounted on a vertical shaft. The method of construction, in wavy irregular lines, is the same, and the corners project.

The majority of these grids are apparently simple domestic furniture in aristocratic use. All lack animal heads, although these are to be found in wrought iron in fire-dogs from the Valsgärde boat graves 5 and 6 in Sweden (fig. 309).[3] The horns of the firedog from Valsgärde 6 (fig. 309 a) are cut back from the solid in the manner suggested for those of the Sutton Hoo grid, and the ears are delicately split off from the neck, like leaves, in exactly the manner in which the curl is formed at the top of strut C (fig. 302).

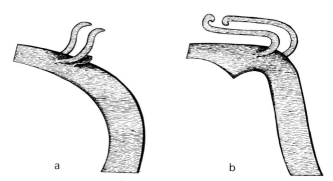

FIGURE 309   Firedogs in iron with stylised heads; (a) from Valsgärde 6, and (b) from Valsgärde 5.

Apart from such grids, only one of which, Veszprem, was mounted on a vertical shaft, a number of iron shafts are known. The contemporary example which stood erect in the sixth-century A.D. Krefeld-Gellep princely grave, and led directly to its discovery (fig. 310 b), is incomplete.[4] The surviving 78 cm length is a twisted iron rod of basically square cross-section with an iron ring at the top and at the bottom a

[1] Pirling 1964, pl. 58, Götze 1912, pl. XIV, no. 6; Kutch 1921, pl. 2, no. 19.
[2] Thomas and Szentleleky 1959, pl. XVII. I am grateful to Professor Greta Arwidsson for drawing my attention to this piece.

[3] Arwidsson 1942 a (Valsgärde 6), pl. 32 and pp. 77–8; and Valsgärde 5 (unpublished).
[4] Pirling 1964, 201–2 and Abb. 4, 4.

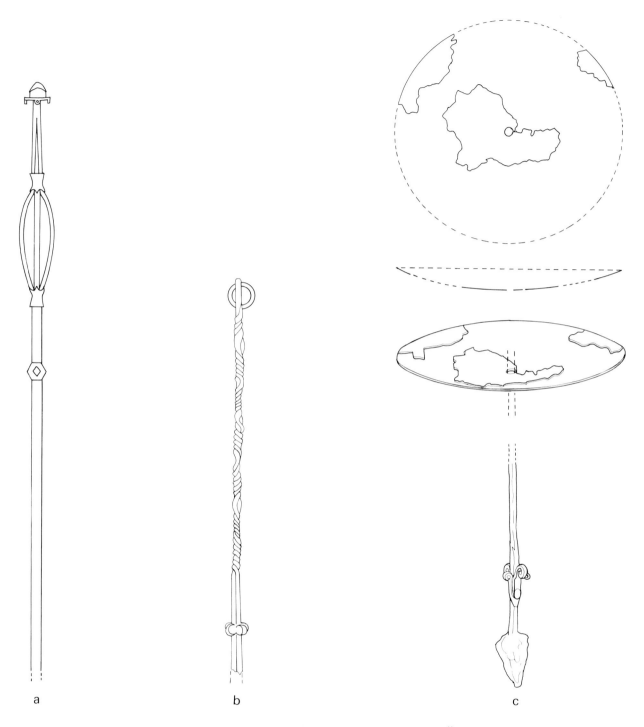

a   b   c

FIGURE 310 Iron stands from continental contexts: (*a*) Klinta, Öland, iron stand with bronze fittings, surmounted by a model of a house; (*b*) upper part of the iron spit found in grave 1782, Krefeld Gellep: four volutes project from the shaft which is twisted in a manner similar to the struts on the Sutton Hoo stand; (*c*) Vallstenarum, Gotland, iron stand with volutes, associated with a bronze saucer-like fitting. (Scales: *a* and *c*, 1/4; *b* approx. 1/7) (After Pirling 1974 and Petersson 1958 and Nerman 1972 respectively)

427

flattened spatulate foot, forged on as a separate piece of metal, and above this four small horizontal spiral projections one on each face. The bottom edge of the spatulate lower end is broken, but it must be held, on the analogy of an identical but complete find from Worms, to be restorable as a long slender point and the object to belong, with the Worms parallel and analogous examples from Weimar and Biebrich,[1] to a well-defined group of spits.

Two objects of Viking date may be noted. Projecting volutes, separately forged on to the stem, above a point resembling that of the Sutton Hoo stand, characterise an incomplete iron object (fig. 310c) from Vallstenarum on Gotland, unfortunately unstratified, cited by Nerman.[2] If Nerman's association of the bowl fragments with the vertical shaft is correct, this would be no doubt some kind of lighting device, since the shallow elevated bowl could contain oil, or catch drips. The whole must have been a good deal smaller than the Sutton Hoo stand, and it is riveted together and of crude construction. It may be a lighting device, but the resemblance to the Sutton Hoo stand is entirely superficial. A remarkable piece also from the Viking period (c. A.D. 950) found by K. G. Petersson in a boat-cremation at Klinta, Köpingsvik, on Öland, could perhaps be taken to be of ceremonial or religious rather than domestic significance (fig. 310a).[3] This consists of an incomplete shaft of iron of square cross-section, with bronze fittings, with a surviving length of 74 cm. At the top, on a small platform, is a bronze model of a boat-shaped or hogback house of Trelleborg type, with a door flanked by posts and with small figures of cattle originally standing on the platform outside the house; some centimetres below this, between bronze sockets, a pointed-oval cage, 16 cm long, of four elements which may have been twisted, develops vertically round the continuing shaft. This openwork feature is defined top and bottom by bronze collars. Some inches below this on the iron shaft is a bronze faceted polyhedral knob or collar. The bottom end of the shaft is broken off and missing.[4] Here again, the object is not isolated but belongs to a distinctive class. Three parallels, but lacking the elaborate top of the Klinta example, found at Birka, the Viking town in Lake Mälar, in graves 760, 834 and 845, are referred to by Arbman, without discussion, as measuring rods.[5]

The Sutton Hoo stand is, in fact, without any convincing parallel. Its significance, in spite of the loss of the stag as a finial, may perhaps be sought, as I have suggested elsewhere, in its historical setting. This would seem to favour identification as a standard, indeed, as a standard of a particular sort. In making this interpretation we should allow for the augmentation or dressing of the stand by elements of a perishable kind, whether foliage or cloth, or of some other sort.

We know from Bede that Raedwald's successor as *bretwalda*, Edwin of Northumbria, used standards of three different types as emblems of his royal power and dignity.

[1] Kutsch 1921, 30, Abb. 2 and 3.
[2] Nerman 1970, 340–1.
[3] Petersson 1958, who refers to the Sutton Hoo stand in this connection.
[4] The top of the stand is well illustrated by Capelle, who refers to it as a spit in a paper dealing with house-types (Capelle 1969, Taf. XIV, 37, 38).
[5] Arbman 1940, Taf. 125; 1943, 278, 305, 320.

Edwin spent at any rate the latter part of his exile at Raedwald's court in East Anglia, and it was Raedwald who restored him to the Deiran throne in 617, following the battle on the River Idle in Yorkshire. Since Edwin was the first Northumbrian *bretwalda*, while Raedwald held his *bretwalda*-ship in succession from Aethelberht of Kent, who in turn had come under the influences of the Roman mission, it seems more than likely that Edwin derived his ideas of a *bretwalda*'s regalia, badges of office, or insignia, and indeed of his way of conducting himself generally as *bretwalda*, from Raedwald. If so, it is likely that Raedwald himself used some form of standard. Such an object might then *prima facie* be expected in a *bretwalda*'s burial. The object found lying beside the iron stand is interpreted as a *bretwalda*'s sceptre (p. 375). We thus have at Sutton Hoo a specific historical context documented to lend some support to such a suggestion. We do not know what Anglo-Saxon standards were like, but we know that there was a tendency amongst Anglo-Saxon kings to adopt Roman usages.[1]

Bede's account of Edwin's kingship should be given in full:

'It is related that there was so great a peace in Britain, wherever the dominion of King Edwin reached, that, as the proverb still runs, a woman with a new-born child could walk throughout the island from sea to sea and take no harm. The king cared so much for the good of the people that, in various places where he had noticed clear springs near the highway, he caused stakes to be set up and bronze drinking cups to be hung on them for the refreshment of travellers. No one dared to lay hands on them except for their proper purpose because they feared the king greatly nor did they wish to, because they loved him dearly. So great was his majesty in his realm that not only were banners carried before him in battle, but even in time of peace, as he rode about among his cities, estates, and kingdoms with his thegns, he always used to be preceded by a standard-bearer. Further, when he walked anywhere along the roads, there used to be carried before him the type of standard where the Romans call a *tufa* and the English call a *thuf*.[2]

FIGURE 311 Sketch based on an illumination in the St Gall Psalter, f. 163v., showing a rider holding a *vexillum* in the form of a fire-breathing dragon. (After Poulsen)

The possible nature of Edwin's standards is discussed elsewhere.[3] The *vexillum*, as used in the Roman Army, was a light tactical banner employed in battle. A kind

[1] *Sutton Hoo*, Vol. I, 690, n. 2; Bruce-Mitford 1974, 13; Cramp 1973; Hunter 1974.

[2] Colgrave and Mynors 1969, 192–3: 'Tanta autem eo tempore pax in Brittania, quaquauersum imperium regis Eduini peruenerat, fuisse perhibetur ut, sicut usque hodie in prouerbio dicitur, etiam si mulier una cum recens nato paruulo uellet totam perambulare insulam a mari ad mare, nullo se ledente ualeret. Tantum rex idem utilitati suae gentis consuluit, ut plerisque in locis, ubi fontes lucidos iuxta publicos uiarum transitus conspexit, ibi ob refrigerium uiantium erectis stipitibus aereos caucos suspendi iuberet, neque hos quisquam, nisi ad usum necessarium, contingere prae magnitudine uel timoris eius auderet uel amoris uellet. Tantum uero in regno excellentiae habuit, ut non solum in pugna ante illum uexilla gestarentur, sed et tempore pacis equitantem inter ciuitates siue uillas aut prouincias suas cum ministris semper antecedere signifer consuesset, necnon et incedente illo ubilibet per plateas illud genus uexilli, quod Romani tufam, Angli appellant thuff, ante eum ferri solebat?'

[3] Bruce-Mitford 1974, 7–17.

FIGURE 312 Bronze dragon head of a Roman *vexillum* found at
Niederbieber, Kreis Neuwied, West Germany. (Scale: 1/2)

of cloth streamer or windsock was attached to an open metal mouth in the form of
a dragon's or basilisk's head, the whole arrangement being carried on a light rod. An
illustration in the St Gall Psalterium Aureum (f. 163v) of the ninth century (fig. 311),
shows that a similar device was used in the Carolingian army and a classic find of
a hollow sheet metal dragon head from a *vexillum* of this kind has recently been made
in the Roman fort at Niederbieber, Kreis Neuwied (fig. 312).[1] Edwin's *vexillum*,
carried before him in battle, may have been of this tactical genus, if less elaborate.
What of the two other types of standard that Edwin regularly used, as described by
Bede? The standard-bearer who led his mounted cavalcades on horseback on official
visitations may have carried some devolved Saxon version of the legionary *signum*, in
which, in a common variant, a man-sized shaft, with a spike at the bottom and carrying
a transverse bar loaded with pendant battle honours, was crowned by an animal or
bird effigy, or a laurel wreath (cf. fig. 313). The Sutton Hoo object might be such
a piece, carried on a leather shoulder-strap when riding, with its point held in a leather
frog. Interest should perhaps be concentrated on the third variety of standard, *tufa*,
even if Bede's use for it of the general term *vexillum* (*illud genus vexilli*, but perhaps
using *vexillum* no longer in the strict Roman sense) might suggest something lighter.
The Anglo-Saxon *tuuf* or *tuf* conveys a definite sense of foliage or feathers (Latin
equivalent *frondosus*, according to Ducange). The fittings of the upper part of the Sutton
Hoo stand—the 'basket' below (within the cage described by the four struts), the grid

[1] As yet unpublished; I am most grateful to Dr H. Eiden for permission to publish this photograph
prior to his own publication.

a   b

FIGURE 313   Fourth-century gold Roman coin and barbarian copy showing examples of different
standards. (Scale: 1/1)

with inward-pointing retaining horns at its corners, and others brought closer in together higher up at the corners of the small top plate—could seem well adapted to the carriage, ordering and display of foliage, bracken, or holly branches, or, for all we know, peacock's feathers.[1]

This identification must remain speculative; but that this object, both in the historical context of the royal ship-burial and seen in relation to the other grave goods, was a standard, and in particular a *thuuf* (crowned by foliage or feathers and not by an effigy), seems a reasonable suggestion. A lamp or torch carrier, perhaps placed before the high seat, is another suggestion compatible with the ceremonial rather than domestic use which its location in the burial deposit may be thought to support.[2]

[1] A peacock's bones were found in the Gokstad ship (Brøgger and Shetelig 1951, 86) and the bird is also represented amongst the mass of bones recovered from the Viking maritime trading town of Hedeby (Müller 1972 a, b).

[2] Wallace-Hadrill 1960, 188–9, reprinted with a fresh commentary in Wallace-Hadrill 1975, 48–9, where scepticism as to the standard identification is expressed, wonders whether the object could not be a portable rack for the holding or suspending of heads or scalps, such as may be seen dangling from saddle-bows on the golden vase from Nagyszentmiklòs, and as reported by Ammianus (*Rer. Gest.* Lib. XXXI, 2, 21). Such a usage would scarcely be compatible with the ethos of a settled seventh-century Anglo-Saxon royal court on the eve of the conversion.

For some support for the standard explanation see Bertram Colgrave in Colgrave and Mynors 1969, 192, note: 'An object was found at Sutton Hoo in the burial ship which is supposed by some to be a royal standard of this kind. It is quite possible that Edwin learned this practice at Raedwald's court, though doubtless the royal standard was a Roman borrowing. Bede probably got the word 'tufa' from Vegetius. The Old English word *thuf* (tuft of feathers or foliage) with which he equated it, suggests that the standard was bushy or covered with foliage, as the Sutton Hoo object may well have been, judging by its shape and form. It may even have been the mark of the *Bretwalda*.'

431

CHAPTER X

THE GOLD JEWELLERY

⟨⟩✦⟨⟩

Introduction and list

NO EUROPEAN JEWELLERY of its era excels the Sutton Hoo jewellery in technique
or originality or can compare with it in elaboration, ambition and accomplishment.
It is the finest and most significant assembly of gold cloisonné work to survive from
the Germanic era, and a major archaeological and art historical document.

Excluding the coins, blank flans and ingots, and counting separately the individual
plaques and studs of the purse-lid, there are forty-five individual pieces of gold
jewellery from the burial deposit. They include not only a number of generally familiar
forms—buckles, strap-ends and mounts, all of the highest quality—but also *chefs
d'œuvre* such as the purse and shoulder-clasps, which are in many respects or entirely
unique. Nearly all the pieces are designed to be mounted on cloth or leather. The
shoulder-clasps, each provided with twenty strong gold staple-like loops at the back,
were evidently designed to be sewn very firmly on to a garment. Eleven of the mounts
were components of the purse-lid, the purse as a whole being carried on (?) cloth
suspension straps attached to hinged gold strap-ends on the frame of the lid. Most
of the remaining jewellery is probably from the harness from which the sword was
suspended.

The gold objects are catalogued under the inventory numbers 1–75 and 302.[1] The
coins, blanks and ingots contained in the purse are given separate individual inventory
numbers (Inv. 34–75). They seem to have been a royal equivalent of Charon's obol
and so to have a specifically funerary character.[2] It seems that the remainder of the
gold items should be regarded not as personal but as ceremonial ornament,[3] hence
their inclusion in this volume under the general heading of regalia.

The individual pieces of gold jewellery are here listed in Inventory order. Most
of the pieces have cloisonné garnet decoration. Those that do not are asterisked.

---

[1] *Sutton Hoo*, Vol. I, 438–40 and 457; Inv. 302 (here fig. 279 c) is the small cabochon garnet in a gold setting associated with the bone, wood or ivory rod (p. 395).

[2] *Sutton Hoo*, Vol. I, 586–7, following Grierson 1970.

[3] The absence of jewellery of a personal kind is discussed in *Sutton Hoo*, Vol. I, ch. VIII, 512–17.

Items of gold jewellery

Inv. no.

1   * Great gold buckle with niello inlays. Carved with Style II interlace

2, 3   Fittings of the purse-lid and bag

4, 5   Pair of hinged and curved shoulder-clasps

6, 7   Matching pair of rectangular strap-mounts with depressed mushroom-cell design

8, 9   Matching pair of rectangular strap-mounts with step-pattern cells and cable-twist borders

10   Curved mount in the form of a dummy buckle

11   Rectangular buckle

12–14   Matching set of buckle and two strap-mounts each with a rounded end

15   * Runner of plain gold resembling a small tongueless buckle

16   * Plain gold strap-end

17   T-shaped strap-distributor comprising a rectangular mount of the same dimensions as Inv. 6–9 but with a hinged and swivelling development at one side ending in a strap-holder

18   Triangular strap-mount with zoomorphic details

Items directly associated with the sword and scabbard

19   Pommel

20, 21   * Upper and lower plates of the upper guard, attached to the pommel

22, 23   * Upper and lower plates of the lower guard

24, 25   * Two filigree clips from the grip

26, 27   Two scabbard-bosses

28, 29   Two slotted mounts in the form of truncated pyramids

Other items

30   Ring with attached strip decorated with filigree and small cabochon garnets.

31   * Thin fluted strip, plain, with animal head

32   * Circular mount of foil in the shape of a cut-out animal, with attachment pins

33   * Triangular foil mount with attachment pin at the back, incised with design of two erect animals back to back

302   A small circular setting with a cabochon garnet exactly matching the five still in position on Inv. 30, but not from Inv. 30.

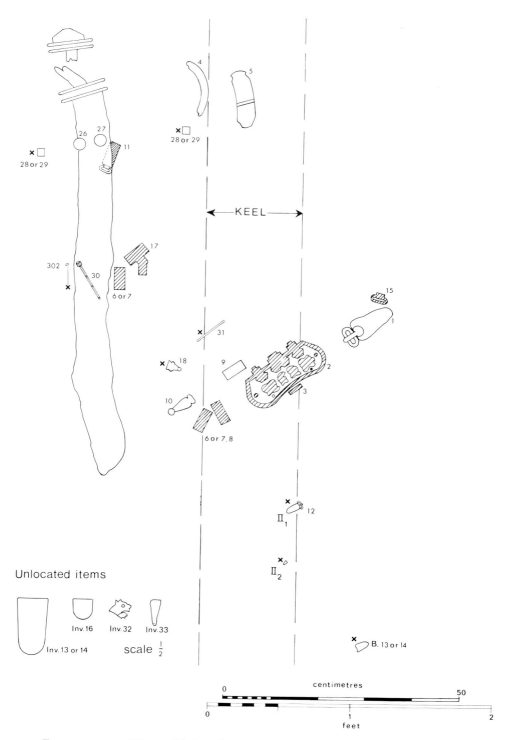

Unlocated items

Inv. 16   Inv. 32   Inv. 33

Inv. 13 or 14   scale ½

F I G U R E 314   The gold jewellery: plan showing the positions of the various pieces (identified by inventory numbers) as they lay in the ground. Pieces shown shaded were found upside down; it is not known whether the pieces marked with a cross were upside down or the right way up. Four items for which no positions are recorded are shown in an inset sketch. The identifications II₁, II₂, and B are associated with outlying gold objects (p. 439).

434

1. *The finding of the jewellery and primary account of discovery*

The first items of gold jewellery were seen by the excavators on Friday 21 July 1939, when both pyramids came to light in quick succession. Finds which included the purse complex and great gold buckle were made on the following day, and on Thursday 27 July the shoulder-clasps and sword and scabbard fittings were amongst objects revealed during cleaning around the sword and in the area between it and the drinking-horn and maplewood bottle complex. Finally, ten days after the first discovery of jewellery, three small items were found during sifting of sand on the floor of the burial chamber. The following extracts from C. W. Phillips's diary describe the finding of the jewellery.[1]

Friday 21 July 1939
'A careful investigation of the presumed area of the burial deposit west of the shield[2] was now carried out by Mrs Piggott. A further indefinite mass of wood was found directly west of the shield and on this traces of textile were observed before the end of the day. Carrying further west from this the sand was cleared off an area where a small piece of sheet iron[3] had been disturbed on 19 July. This had been found to have distinct traces of glass adherent to its underside. While this area was being cleaned a splendid piece of jewellery was found consisting of a small pyramid of solid gold cast with a small internal hollow crossed by a bar at the base leaving two long rectangular slots. This pyramid, the top of which was flattened, was wonderfully decorated with cloisonné work of shaped and inset glass and possibly lapis lazuli. Behind this was placed *pointillé* gold leaf which enhanced the effect of the whole. In the middle of the flat top was a beautiful square inset of blue and white chequered millefiori work. Adherent to the whole of the back of this piece was a thin layer of smooth black carbonised matter.

Shortly after this a second object identical with this was found close by. This was also in wonderful condition but had a few small masses of sand concretion. These objects were handed to Mrs Pretty when she visited the site at 5.30 p.m.

Saturday 22 July 1939
After lunch the careful sweeping-off of superficial sand from the surface of the central mass of the deposit west of the shield and east of the find spot of the little pyramids was begun. Almost at once traces of gold objects were revealed to the north of the sword blade.[4]

These had been covered with a thin layer of wood, but were showing through it. In view of their obvious richness and importance it was plainly unwise to leave the objects *in situ*, so the slight layer of rotten wood was cleared from them and they were planned and photographed. Upon removal they were found to consist of the following objects:

1. Gold strap-end loop.[5]
2. Great gold belt-buckle.
3. Purse complex:
   (*a*) Frame.

[1] *Sutton Hoo*, Vol. I, 736–7, 740–1, 742, 743.
[2] Not the shield; this object, not yet fully exposed and referred to throughout this part of the diary as the shield, was later identified as the great silver dish.
[3] Later found to be a piece of the sword.

[4] Area A on Piggott's field plan (*Sutton Hoo*, Vol. I, 141) and later re-drawn in an enlarged version (here fig. 315).
[5] This item was incorrectly rendered in *Sutton Hoo*, Vol. I, 737 as 'Gold strap-end and loop.'

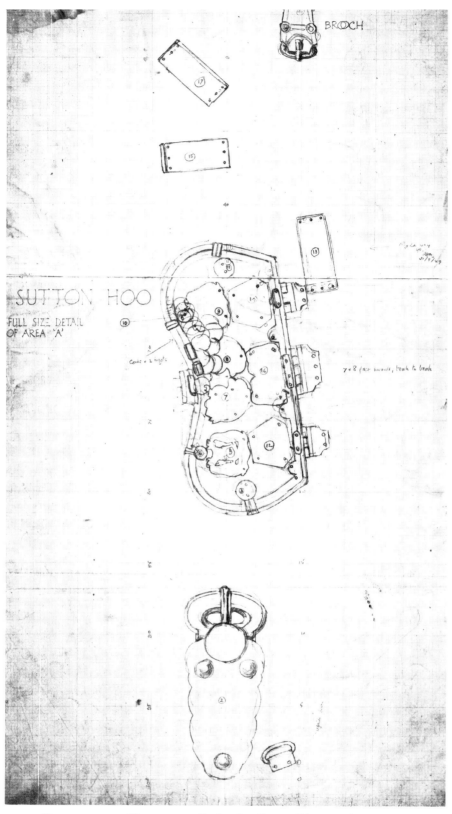

FIGURE 315   Plan 4, pencil plan by Stuart Piggott of 'Area A'.
(The damaged top of the plan is not shown.)

436

(*b*) Eleven cloisonné gold plaques, all in the field of the frame, and, in common with it, face downwards . . .

(*c*) Thirty-nine gold coins in mint condition, apparently barbarous copies of Byzantine coinage.

(*d*) Two small gold ingots.

4. Three rectangular cloisonné plaques, that nearest the purse face upwards, the others face downwards, and lying on the tilt.

5. Gold cloisonné strap-end buckle.[1]

All these objects after they had been removed, boxed, and labelled, were placed in the custody of Mrs Pretty.

East of Area A and towards the shield [see p. 435, n. 2] another gold object appeared during the brushing, a gold strap-end, cloisonné with garnet.

Thursday 27 July 1939

The next work was to begin the examination of the area between this iron object[2] and the hump of wood amidships. Progressive cleaning revealed:

1. Two large gold cloisonné armlets(?) hinged in the middle and fitted with a hinge-pin capped with a small animal head in filigree secured to the object by a fine gold chain (III.3 and 4).[3]

2. A gold and garnet cloisonné T-piece with a swivel joint in the shank of the T (III.5).

3. A rod of filigree with a small circlet of filigree attached (III.7) to the end. This was set with three small garnets *en cabochon* and equally spaced, one at each end of the object, and one in the middle. This was slightly across the middle line of the sword later found.

   Free from the filigree rod there was a tiny garnet set *en cabochon* in filigree. It was just to the south of the west end of the filigree rod (III.7).

4. Another rectangular gold and garnet cloisonné plaque (III.6) identical with the rectangular plaques in Group A was found just east of the T-piece (III.5).

5. Fragments of a gold-fitted wooden box(?) (IV.2).[4]

6. An iron sword with gold mounts laid with hilt to the west along the middle line of the boat . . . Beneath the blade at the point where the studs were found was a gold and garnet cloisonné buckle face downwards which had been slightly bent by pressure (III.8).

Saturday 29 July 1939

In clearing up the sword area a triangular piece of gold and garnet cloisonné work was found, obviously belonging to rest of set already found.

Monday 31 July 1939

The sand, etc., remaining in the floor of the burial area was carefully sifted and a number of small objects was found.

1. Small hollow gold tongue-piece, probably part of the purse.

2. A small piece of gold plate binding for a cylindrical object in the form of an openwork animal. The three gold pins which secured it to the object of which it was part survived in place. This came from the sword area.

3. A Merovingian gold coin, fairly certainly fallen out of the purse, bringing the number found to 40.'

[1] Inv. 10, the 'dummy buckle' (fig. 317).
[2] Inv. 210, the spanner-like object attached to the iron stand, fig. 304.
[3] These are packing list numbers, not individual numbers for objects on the plan.
[4] Probably a piece of the shield.

437

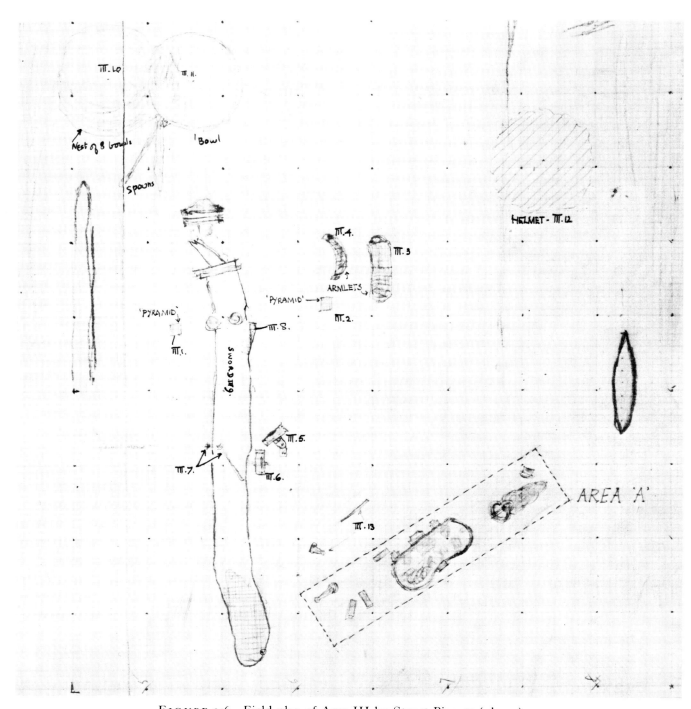

FIGURE 316   Field plan of Area III by Stuart Piggott (plan 3).

438

2. *The positions of the individual pieces in the ground*

The pyramids (Inv. 28, 29, pl. 21 *c*), the first pieces of gold jewellery seen by the excavators, are drawn on Piggott's plan of Area III (fig. 316). They are there numbered III.1 and III.2 and are seen positioned to either side of the sword in line with the two bosses on the scabbard. One pyramid (III.2) lay twice as far away as its partner from the sword and close to the pair of shoulder clasps discovered soon afterwards.

It is not known whether the pyramids were the right side up when found. The fact that they lay in straight alignment with the scabbard-bosses but to either side of the sword suggests that they may have been mounted on a strap which passed through the bosses. They could however have been mounted on separate straps, tapes or cords attached in some way to the hilt or scabbard-mouth, perhaps as terminal embellishments for the sword-knot (*friðbond*).

The bulk of the jewellery was essentially confined to Area III with a few outlying pieces (fig. 314). In general the highest concentrations of jewellery were in two areas; on, near or beneath the sword and adjacent to the purse-lid (largely the material in Area A, fig. 315). The shoulder-clasps, which although near the sword cannot have been connected with it, stand apart from these groupings, as do the pieces east of the purse group towards the horns and maplewood bottles complex, a small buckle, a piece of uncertain identification, and one strap-end (these are numbered II.1, II.2 and B on fig. 314, following Piggott's Plan 8). Even with these outliers, however, the jewellery lay in a small and localised area within the burial deposit as a whole, towards the west end of the chamber, centred on the keel line, within the 'body space'[1] and at the centre of the most significant of the other objects in the deposit. On 22 July the region of the purse-lid and adjacent pieces was completely excavated and drawn by Piggott at full scale on a plan designated as Area A (fig. 315).[2] Phillips noted that the objects in Area A 'had been covered by a thin layer of wood but were showing through it' (presumably the remains of the fallen burial chamber roof). The items of jewellery found on that day are listed as the plain gold looped strap-mount (Inv. 15) the great gold buckle, the purse and its contents, three rectangular strap-mounts (Inv. 6 or 7, 8 and 9) and the curved dummy buckle (Inv. 10). They are shown in figure 317 with inventory numbers attached. On the same day, to the east of Area A, was found the object marked 'B', 'a gold strap-end, cloisonné'.

The positions of the various items of jewellery as found in the ground (figs. 314 and 316) seem to bear no rational or consistent relationship to a possible body in this area, whether extended or seated or in any other posture.[3] Their lie in the ground seems to derive from some internal energy of their own. This, and the fact that so many pieces were found upside down (fig. 314) suggests that the bulk of the jewellery, mounted on a leather harness, had been suspended from the roof of the chamber and

---

[1] *Sutton Hoo*, Vol. I, 489 and fig. 384.
[2] Plan 4, *Sutton Hoo*, Vol. I, 141 and fig. 129; this is a redrawn version, of the plan with inventory identifications, some of which have now been modified (cf. here fig. 317).
[3] *Sutton Hoo*, Vol. I, ch. VIII.

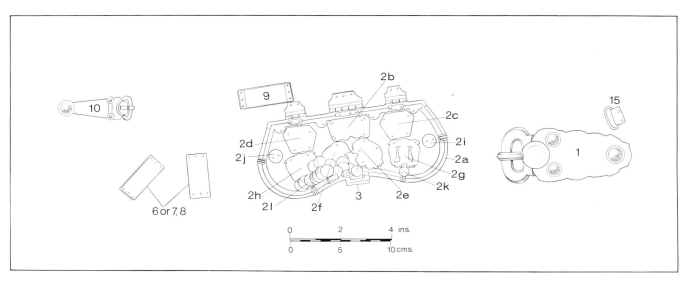

FIGURE 317   Redrawn version of the field plan of Area A (fig. 315) showing inventory numbers.

had fallen while the leather remained supple. In particular, it is difficult to visualise in any other way why the purse was upside down while the adjacent great gold buckle, probably mounted on the same belt (p. 565) remained the right way up.

It is not easy, even using the diary and plans together, to work out in all cases which mount is which. The larger pieces (purse, great gold buckle, shoulder-clasps, etc.) are readily identified from the plans and descriptions, but some of the smaller pieces are not. The following comments relating to the position or identification of some of the pieces may be made.

(1) The small plain mount in buckle form, but tongueless (Inv. 15, pl. 19*e*, fig. 353), lay upside down close to the tip of the great buckle, with its attachment plate, like that of the buckle, facing away from the rest of the jewellery in Area A. The strap which could be accommodated by the plates of this fitment would be 1·7 cm wide× 2 mm thick. The loop could accommodate a strap of 1·8 cm in width and up to 4 mm in thickness.

(2) The gold buckle (Inv. 1, pl. 20) lay right side up and lengthways in relation to the purse-lid next to it, with its loop nearest to the purse, its plate pointing in the same direction as the small plain looped mount beside it.

(3) The purse-lid (Inv. 2, pl. 13) lay face down in the ground. The frame was warped and bent: it was straightened in the Museum in the early stages of conservation (fig. 357*a*, *b*). Piggott's full-scale plan of Area A shows the position of each of the plaques and studs, etc., individually numbered, as they were found within the frame (figs. 360 and 317, b–l). The sliding gold clasp or catch (Inv. 3) which had been attached to the bag of the purse is shown lying loose and also upside down just below the central point of the re-entrant curve of the purse-frame. On the lower edge of the frame may be seen some of the coins (Inv. 34–70) and the two ingots (Inv. 74–75), as described in the diary. The three flans or blanks (Inv. 71–73) were not specifically mentioned

but were presumably amongst the coins. No sign of leather or of any other substance such as bone is mentioned by the excavators in connection with the purse-lid, and it seems clear that the substance which occupied the space inside the frame and on which the gold cloisonné plaques were mounted had wholly disappeared, as well as the substance of the bag. The bag, as distinct from the rich lid, must have been present in the burial since its contents, namely the coins, blanks and ingots, were found in a group within the purse frame. It is possible that a faint outline discernible in certain photographs (figs. 355, 356) may represent the limits of the bag.

(4) Three rectangular strap-mounts set with garnets were found in Area A, numbered 13, 15 and 17 on Piggott's plan (fig. 315). Numbers 15 and 17 were found upside down and 13 was right side up; number 13 is Inv. 9 (a mount with cable-twist and step pattern), and is the only one of the four similar rectangular mounts which can be positively identified *in situ*, the remaining three being each found face downwards. There is only one photograph of numbers 15 and 17 *in situ* (fig. 355). A photograph showing the fourth rectangular mount, numbered III.6 on the plan, reveals it lying at a slant in the ground near the sword, so that it is possible to get a glimpse of the garnet panel along its side. In the photographs the backs of the three upside-down mounts are indistinguishable from each other, and this photographic view is the only evidence we have for establishing which is which. Unfortunately the photograph is at a small scale and the mounts are seen to be slightly out of focus when enlarged. The garnet design looks more like the wavy pattern used on the sides of Inv. 6 and 7 (fig. 328) than like the angular cells of Inv. 8 and 9 (fig. 327), but the photograph may be misleading. If the piece marked III.6 on the plan is either Inv. 6 or 7, then the pieces numbered 15 and 17 in Area A must be Inv. 6 or 7 and 8; that is, one each of the two differing designs represented, but which is which (and so the sequence of the designs) cannot be established. The position close together of three of these four very similar mounts must be significant. They and the fourth similar mount were carried on a strap of uniform width. This being so, it looks very much as if III.6 and the T-shaped mount (Inv. 17; III.5) have become artificially separated from their fellows in the ground. It is possible that the strap may have broken, separating mounts that were adjacent to each other on the harness as worn. Another object listed as found on 22 July was the curved 'dummy buckle' (Inv. 10, figs. 317 and 341). It lay in line with strap-mount Inv. 9, and, like it, was right side up.

(5) The final find of gold on 22 July was 'to the east of Area A' where object B, 'a gold strap-end, cloisonné', was found. This is marked on Piggott's composite tracing[1] and on his field plan of Area II (showing the Anastasius dish complex), but not on the field plans of Areas III and IV. It must be Inv. 13 or 14, one of the pair of strap-mounts (they are not strap-ends) set with garnets which match the similarly designed buckle, Inv. 12 (Area II.1), the finding of which is not mentioned in any account. This strap-mount (Inv. 13 or 14) lay just north of the large pad of textile

[1] Plan 8, *Sutton Hoo*, Vol. I, 141.

which survived in the drinking horn region on the keel-line area. It appears to have been the most far-flung piece of the jewellery.

For the next few days the excavators turned to other areas of the burial deposit. No more jewellery was uncovered until 27 July, when the two shoulder-clasps, the T-shaped strap-distributor, the filigree strip with cabochon settings, a detached cabochon setting (Inv. 302) and the fourth rectangular mount were found, together with the pommel, upper and lower guard-plates, scabbard-bosses and filigree clips (Inv. 24 and 25, not mentioned in the diary) associated with the sword, and finally the rectangular buckle (Inv. 11), which lay largely under the sword, face downwards. These were found in the sequence in which they have been mentioned.

(6) The pair of massive curved gold shoulder-clasps (Inv. 4 and 5) lay face up in the ground to the right of the sword-hilt (fig. 207). They were given the numbers III.3 and III.4 on Piggott's plans. They were very close together and not positioned as if worn on a body, where they would have been kept apart by the neck and even further spaced, halfway down the slope of the shoulders.[1] As figure 207 shows, the pin-heads both lay in the same direction, to the south. As worn on the shoulders, the pins should be pointing in opposite directions, the heads presumably to the inside to counter the tendency of the pins to work out with the movement of the body. The shoulder-clasps give no indication of having fallen, as do the scattered and inverted harness-mounts. On the contrary, they strongly suggest that they were placed in the burial chamber as found, having been removed from the garment to which they had been attached.[2] They are in first-class condition and lay right side up; heavy curved objects would tend to fall upside down.

(7) The T-shaped strap-distributor, Inv. 17, was found beside the scabbard, close to the rectangular mount identified as III.6 (fig. 316), and was allotted the number III.5 on Piggott's field plan. It was lying face downwards. As it evidently came from the same strap as the four rectangular mounts, Inv. 6-9 (p. 441), it is not surprising to find it near III.6. The separation of these two mounts from the three rectangular mounts in Area A has already been discussed (above). Their position adjacent to and halfway along the scabbard may be of significance. Of this set of five matching mounts, found in two separate groups, only one was the right way up (fig. 314).

(8) The small gold filigree strip (Inv. 30) with ring-head and set with cabochon garnets (figs. 278 and 279) lay obliquely across the scabbard at about its central point. It was given the number III.7 on Piggott's drawing and it lay parallel to the T-mount and rectangular buckle (III.5 and III.6) which were in the ground alongside the sword. The strip was at the same angle as the T-mount (III.5, Inv. 17). In the ground 'just to the south of the west end of the filigree rod', alongside the left side of the scabbard and at the circlet end of the strip, was found a loose cabochon garnet setting (Inv. 302) exactly matching those on the filigree strip (diary, 27 July). The strip and its relationship with the loose cabochon setting is discussed in chapter VIII.

[1] See also the discussion of the clasps in *Sutton Hoo*, Vol. I, 517-21.

[2] *Pace* Gamber 1966, 270, his proposed layout of the leather cuirass is based upon the presumed absence of a body.

(9) The sword fittings (chapter VI) were all in position when the sword was excavated. The pommel and upper guard-plates, with a section of the tang, were broken from the rest of the hilt and the tang was fractured at its junction with the blade. The blade in the region of the scabbard-bosses was badly damaged (fig. 209). The jewelled elements fortunately did not suffer from whatever impact or pressure the other parts failed to withstand. The two filigree hilt-clips were found in position (p. 277 and fig. 209) but are not marked on any plan. The pair of hemispherical garnet mounts on the scabbard remained embedded in the remnants of the white substance in which their long staple-like gold attachment loops had been set.

(10) Underneath the sword and below the right-hand scabbard-boss as it lay in the ground was the rectangular buckle, Inv. 11, marked III.8 (fig. 316). It lay face downwards and had been slightly bent by pressure. Some of the garnets are broken or loose in their cells. The buckle is in worse condition than any of the other pieces of jewellery. A glassy imprint of its back remained on the underside of the scabbard (fig. 318), but this was largely removed in 1945 in an attempt to expose the surface of the scabbard. It is not clear how this buckle came to be upside down and

FIGURE 318   Detail of the under side of the sword-scabbard, showing the impression of the back of the buckle which impinges on the lid of the wooden box (Inv. 300). (Scale: 2/1)

underneath the sword. Its relationship to the other cloisonné strap-mounts is discussed below (p. 568). If the buckle fell, as we suppose the rectangular strap-mounts did (p. 440), it was subsequently driven into the space under the sword at this point. The possibilities are best judged from figure 209, which shows the sword hereabout raised by material under it. This included the wooden box on the lid of which the rolls of tape were placed. The edge of the buckle evidently drove in one side of this lid.[1]

(11) The remaining gold pieces were found later. On Saturday 29 July, 'in clearing the sword area, a triangular piece of gold and garnet cloisonné work was found obviously belonging to the rest of the set already found'. This was a most interesting triangular zoomorphic strap-mount (Inv. 18, fig. 350).[2] It was fortunately included on the field plan despite its late appearance and was numbered III.13 by Piggott. It was located near the edge of Area A, and near the curved clasp or dummy buckle, Inv. 10 (fig. 314), but we do not know which way up it lay in the ground. It is shown as outside the confines of Area A (p. 439), the only part of the deposit to be planned at full scale, where details of the individual pieces can be recognised, and it does not appear in any photographs. It is said to have come from 'the sword area'. Its placing on the plan (fig. 316) gives an indication of what the expression 'sword area' as used by the excavators may be taken to mean.

On Monday 31 July the sand remaining in the floor of the burial area was carefully sifted and several small objects were found. The position in the ground of the following pieces which were found at this time cannot be pinpointed.

(i) A small hollow gold tongue-piece, referred to by the excavators, but with no evidence for the statement, as 'probably part of the purse'. It may perhaps have come from the general area in which the purse was found (but see 12(i) below). This must be the small plain gold strap-end, Inv. 16. In view of its dimensions it is most unlikely to be related to the plain gold runner (Inv. 15, pl. 19e) which was found near the purse and beside the great gold buckle (fig. 317). It is tempting to associate the two, since both alone among the strap-mounts are plain and undecorated, but the dimensions of the runner, Inv. 15, are too great for a strap of the width and thickness indicated by Inv. 16 (internal loop clearance 18×4 mm, whereas the small plain strap-end is $10\times1\cdot1$ mm).

(ii) A gold Merovingian coin, presumably derived from the purse and bringing the number of coins and blanks up to forty.

(iii) 'A small piece of gold plate binding for a cylindrical object in the form of an openwork animal. The three gold pins which secured it to the object of which it was part survived in place.' This came 'from siftings in the area of the sword'. Only two of the three gold attachment-pins survive. This is the little cut-out foil mount in the shape of an animal (Inv. 32) bent round in a curve which when closed has the same diameter as the ring at one end of the filigree strip (Inv. 30) found lying across the scabbard. It was evidently mounted on the same object, and is dealt with in chapter VIII.

[1] See also *Sutton Hoo*, Vol. I, fig. 357b.   [2] *Sutton Hoo*, Vol. I, pl. F(ii).

444

(12) Items of jewellery inserted by Piggott on Plans 2 or 8[1] but either not mentioned or not identifiable in the diary (fig. 314, II.1, II.2 and B).

(i) 'II.2' coloured yellow on Plan 8, could from its size and shape represent the small plain gold strap-end (Inv. 16), described in the diary as a small hollow gold tongue-piece, and said to have come from 'the burial area'; if so it would be from the east end of the area and not to be associated with the purse by virtue of its location. It is marked only on the composite traced Plan 8 and is there shown near the textiles associated with the drinking-horn complex and not far from the small cloisonné buckle, Inv. 12. No date of discovery is shown. Its appearance on this 'fair copy' composite tracing but not on any of the field plans could indicate that it was one of the items found at a late stage when planning had been completed, and was put in by Piggott on his composite plan on the basis of information received.

(ii) 'III.13' is a narrow fluted gold strip with animal head terminal (Inv. 31). This is discussed in chapter VIII. It is shown on the crayoned field plan of Areas III and IV (Plan 3) but is outside Area A. It lay parallel to the top edge of the purse-lid in the ground and is shown close to the added triangular zoomorphic mount, Inv. 18. The two after lifting were packed in the same container under the common number 'III.13'. No date of discovery is known, but the fact that both this strip and the triangular mount, Inv. 18, appear on Piggott's field plan of Areas III and IV, from which figure 316 is an extract, and are drawn in in the same manner as the rest, suggests that this positioning for both these pieces is reliable.

(iii) Marked on Piggott's composite tracing Plan 8 and also on his field plan of Area II (Plan 2), where it is called II.1 (cf. fig. 314), is the garnet-inlaid buckle, Inv. 12, which goes with the two matching strap-mounts, Inv. 13 and 14, one of which we have discussed in (5) above, as having been found on 22 July and planned on two field drawings as 'B', near the textile pad at the west end of the drinking vessel complex. The buckle, Inv. 12, lay some 22 cm east of the purse. No date for its discovery is known. East of it, of the gold items, were only II.2, a piece of uncertain identification ((i) above) and one of the garnet-inlaid strap-mounts (Inv. 13 or 14). The two pieces of the suite, Inv. 12–14, whose locations are known are in the same area away from the bulk of the jewellery, though themselves some 33 cm apart. The second garnet strap-mount which matched that identified as 'B' (either Inv. 13 or 14) is not marked on any plan or mentioned in the diary. It was not seen *in situ* but was recovered in sifting spoil at the side of the trench (p. 454, n. 2).

(iv) Finally, the small triangular foil mount with incised animal design, Inv. 33, discussed in chapter VIII. This is not recognisably marked on any plan (although it could be the piece II.2 on Plan 8 discussed above), nor is it mentioned in the diary or any other account. One must therefore assume that it was found during further sifting of the sand remaining in the burial area. The lack of mention is all the more to be regretted since internal evidence suggests that this piece is probably to be

[1] *Sutton Hoo*, Vol. I, 140–2.

445

associated with the 'bone or ivory rod' (p. 396). The other small gold objects listed above as 'found in sifting' were found five days after the last previously recorded find of jewellery. The sifting in which they came to light certainly included the area of the purse and sword, as the diary references make clear. If Inv. 33, the triangular foil mount, had been found in this process it would be reasonable to assume that it came from this area too, but the absence of any reference to it in the list of items so found suggests that it may have been found only in sifting the spoil at the side of the trench, as in the case of the unprovenanced Inv. 13 or 14.

The mutual relationship of the mounts, purse and great buckle in and around Area A is not clear. The fall of the leather harness from the burial chamber roof, as we envisage it, must have happened before the collapse of the chamber and when the leather was still supple. The heavy mounts would have fallen with some degree of force on to the floor of the chamber, or on to the body if one were present, the force depending upon the height from which they fell—perhaps not more than one to two metres, since we may suppose the jewelled harness to have been 'in contact' with the rest of the deposit, that is, not too far removed from it in height. If the purse with its contents and the great buckle were attached to the straps which held the smaller mounts as well, the weight of these heavier pieces could tend on falling to pull towards them most of the rest of the harness. A few pieces of jewellery may have broken away and been scattered nearer the sword or further afield. It is at all events plain that none of the jewellery, except those pieces actually mounted on the scabbard and sword hilt, is in any sense in its original position and that the whole is not laid out as it would have been if worn on a body, or attached to the sword, or laid in an orderly arrangement on the chamber floor. Yet there must be some logic in the physical relationship of the pieces. They show some sequence and were not found merely piled up in a heap.

It is perhaps significant that the heaviest pieces (except the shoulder-clasps, p. 442) are concentrated in one small area whereas the smallest and lightest mounts are in general the outliers. No serious damage, such as a fall might have caused, is to be seen on the various mounts, apart from the chipping or breakage here and there of a garnet, which might have happened before burial.[1] We should remember the evidence suggesting that the floor of the burial chamber was covered by a carpet or coarse rug; this and other textiles or cushions,[2] or for that matter the remains of a clothed body which could have occupied this apparently empty space, would have reduced the effects of the fall. However, the twisting of the frame of the purse-lid, which is not strong, could have occurred in such a fall. The lack of damage to the ornamental plaques, the undisturbed state of the mounts and of the heaped contents of the purse, and the absence of scars or cuts on the gold are against the warping of the purse frame having

[1] The buckle, Inv. 11, which lay upside down partly trapped under the sword (ch. VI, fig. 209) alone shows considerable damage (p. 443).

[2] Cf. *Sutton Hoo*, Vol. I, ch. VII and fig. 363.

446

been caused by a blow as it lay flat. The upside-down position of the purse-lid, its twisting, and the accumulation of its contents at one end, would all be compatible with its having fallen, not long after the burial, on an end or corner before toppling over, the plaques at that time being kept in position by the intact state of the substance of the lid.

As gold does not corrode, there are no remains of leather or textile associated with the jewellery, or from the area in which it lay, as there might have been in the case of bronze or iron. There is thus no evidence from organic remains to help in any attempt to reconstruct the strap-work or dress on which the gold items were mounted. This can only be done on the basis of the dimensions and features of the individual pieces and their positions in the soil, discussed in this section. The process of reconstruction is carried further in section 4.[1]

3. *Description of the individual pieces of jewellery*

The pieces of gold directly associated with the sword (Inv. 19–29) are described in chapter VI. Those that have been associated with the inferred 'bone, wood or ivory rod' (Inv. 30–33 and 302) are described in chapter VIII. These pieces apart, the Sutton Hoo gold jewellery may be subdivided on grounds of style or design into the following groups or distinct pieces.

I   Two strap-mounts and a buckle, all rounded at one end, matching in style and workmanship.

II   Four rectangular plaques in matching pairs, a T-shaped strap-distributor and a rectangular buckle.

III   An elegant curved mount designed to look like a buckle but tongueless.

IV   A distinctive triangular strap-mount of zoomorphic character.

V   A plain gold buckle-shaped mount (tongueless buckle) and a small plain gold strap-end.

VI   A purse.

VII   Two shoulder-clasps.

VIII   A great gold buckle decorated with animal interlace.

They are dealt with in this section in these categories and in the above sequence. In the descriptions that follow all weights refer to the present condition of the object; that is, less that of any garnets or other elements that happen to be missing.

---

[1] Only one scrap remains of leather or textile in connection with any of the jewellery. When the curved mount, Inv. 10, was taken to pieces in the Laboratory in 1945, a small piece of leather was found inside the separate circular element which held the convex cloisonné boss at the toe of the buckle. It was penetrated by a central hole and may have served as a washer over which to hammer the end of the rivet that held this capsule to the main body of the buckle. It was unconnected with the belt or strap to which the mount had been fixed, and does not imply a leather strap. Another suggestion of leather or textile, which unfortunately does not survive, is contained in a passage in the diary (p. 435) referring to one of the gold pyramids when first found. Phillips says of them: 'Adherent to the whole of the back of this piece was a thin layer of smooth black carbonised matter.'

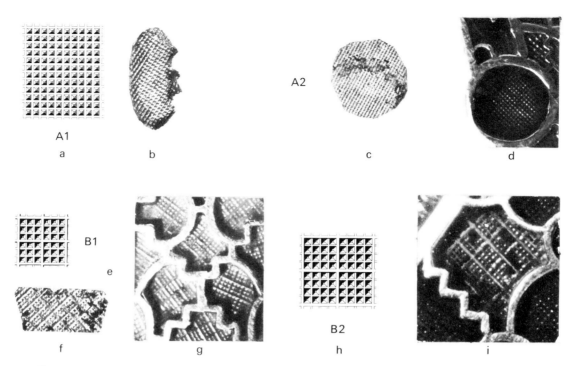

FIGURE 319 Gold foil: drawings and photographs, enlarged, showing the different types of gold foil used in the jewellery. (*a*) drawing and (*b*) photograph of plain pointillé pattern A1; (*c*) (*d*) photographs of A2; (*e*) drawing and (*f*) (*g*) photographs of B1; (*h*) drawing and (*i*) photograph of B2. The foil used to illustrate A1 is from the curved mount (Inv. 10) (*d*) is from the zoomorphic mount (Inv. 18). The foil in (*f*) is from a hexagonal mount of the purse, and (*g*) is from the curved mount (Inv. 10); (*i*) is from the sword pommel. (Scales: drawings, 8/1; photographs, approx. 4/1)

In those pieces that are decorated with garnets the stones, with very rare exceptions, are mounted on backings of gold foil. Four different varieties of this can be recognised: two types of plain pointillé patterning, referred to as A1 and A2, and two varieties of waffled pattern (a grid subdivided into smaller squares) referred to as B1 and B2. To avoid verbal repetition in the descriptions of individual pieces, these varieties of gold foil are defined here at the outset (fig. 319). The difference between the two varieties of A is one of fineness. A1 is the standard form; the finer variety A2 occurs in one piece only, Inv. 18. The standard grid pattern generally used, B1, is one in which the grid squares each contain nine smaller squares. In the foil type B2 there are sixteen contained squares; it occurs only on the sword-pommel. The foil type A1 is from time to time found upside-down in the cells. There seems to be no consistency in this, no deliberation in the reversal of the foils; the effect under close inspection is that of a rather finer scale pointillé pattern than that seen when the foils are the right way up. This effect is illusory.

448

(Inv. 12–14)

Dimensions

	Buckle (Inv. 12) cm	Strap-mount (Inv. 13) cm	Strap-mount (Inv. 14) cm
Length	4·6	3·1	3·1
Length of cloisonné-bearing plate	3·6	3·1	3·1
Width of cloisonné-bearing plate	1·8	1·6	1·6
Thickness of cloisonné-bearing plate	0·3	0·25	0·25
Length of back-plate	3·0	3·1	3·2
Width of back-plate	1·7	1·6	1·7
Thickness of back-plate	c. 0·03	0·03	0·03
Overall length of rivets	0·8	0·7	0·65
Gap between buckle-plate and back-plate (i.e. thickness of strap accommodated)	0·35	0·3	0·3
Overall length of tongue	1·7		
Projection of tongue	1·0		
Length across loop	2·3		
Thickness of loop	0·4		
Inner dimensions of loop (i.e. width and thickness of strap accommodated)	1·5×0·4 (max.)		

Weight	21·115 g	9·242 g	9·961 g
Number of garnets	24	24	24

Foil underlays. Types A1 and B1. A1 is used in the outer borders, B1 in the main field. Certain cells of Inv. 12 have no underlays.

Cell forms. Cell shapes and characteristic patterns are shown in figure 320.

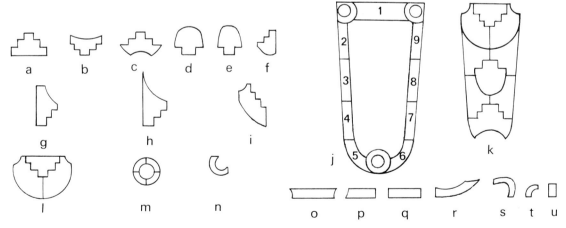

FIGURE 320 Cell forms and characteristic cell patterns from the cloisonné buckle and two matching strap-mounts (Inv. 12–14): (a)–(f) basic cell shapes; (g)–(i) residual shapes; (j) the border cells of a strap-mount numbered; (k) the central field of a strap-mount; (l) pattern from the central field; (m), (n) rivet surrounds from a strap-mount; (o)–(u) border cells. (Scale: 3/2)

449

The strap-mounts and buckle (fig. 321) are a matching set from the same hand. The strap-mounts are identical in size, the front plate that carries the cloisonné work being in each case 3·1 cm in length; and the plate of the buckle, Inv. 12, from its point to the upper corners where the shape contracts to fit the saddle or collar cut in the buckle-loop to receive it, is also 3·1 cm. Both strap-mounts are 1·6 cm in maximum diameter. The buckle-plate is only fractionally wider at 1·8 cm. The cloisonné designs are the same, and differ in certain respects from those of any other piece among the jewellery. The design of the buckle differs from that of the two strap-mounts only in that a tongue-plate is simulated in the cloisonné work at the base of the tongue. This simulated tongue-plate, which carries its own design, encroaches on the field of the buckle-plate, slightly compressing the design of the plate as compared with that of the two strap-mounts, otherwise virtually identical with that of the buckle. The buckle-tongue is rigid, in one piece with the plate, and the hinged loop falls away from it.

The designs of the three pieces differ also in the treatment of the rivets. In each case the cloisonné-bearing front plate is joined to a plain gold back plate by three gold rivets with deep hemispherical heads, one at the point and two at the shoulders. In the mounts these rivets are set within garnet rings of segmental cells; the rivet at the rounded end passes through a gold tube at the centre of a ring containing four stones which form a circle, each stone making a quarter-circle (fig. 320 *m*). The rivets in the corners are similarly set into a garnet quarter-circle (fig. 320 *n*). The buckle has no such surrounds for its rivets, and the rivet-head at its rounded end is bigger than the two at its shoulders and those of the strap-mounts. As its function demands, the buckle is a rather more complex piece than the mounts and has a more complex and effective overall design.

The cloisonné design of these three matching pieces includes the cell-forms shown in figure 320. In all three pieces a central field contains the main cloisonné design of cells of varying shapes and a continuous outer border of long narrow garnets encloses the central field.

The borders

In the two strap-mounts (Inv. 13 and 14) cells 1–9 have garnets of varying lengths as follows (mm):

Inv. 13			*Inv. 14*	
(1)	8·0	(Maximum between points)	(1)	7·0
(2)	5·0		(2)	5·0
(3)	5·5		(3)	7·0
(4)	5·5		(4)	6·0
(5)	8·0	(Maximum length in straight line)	(5)	6·5
(6)	8·0	(Maximum length in straight line)	(6)	7·5
(7)	6·5		(7)	6·0
(8)	5·5		(8)	6·5
(9)	6·0		(9)	6·0

On Inv. 13 stones 1–9 have each a width of 2 mm; on Inv. 14 the width is 2·5 mm.

450

It would appear that all the straight stones of the border of Inv. 13 were cut to a unit size of 2×8 mm, and that the ends of 1, 2 and 9 were subsequently ground back against a rounded wheel to fit the curve of the cloison-surrounds of the two shoulder rivets. We have thus the situation illustrated in figure 320 (*j* and *o–r*) where the stones in cells 3, 4, 7, 8 are of shape *q*, those in cells 2 and 9 are of shape *p*, and that in cell 1 of shape *o*, the curves in each one matching those of the gold rivet-cloisons.

The stones of the border of Inv. 14 could also have been cut to a unit length of 8 mm, and similarly cut back to suit the cell shapes that had been constructed. They were however uniformly 0·5 mm wider than those in Inv. 13. The border stones of the plate of the buckle, Inv. 12, correspond in width, size and treatment (with minor adaptations to suit the idiosyncrasies of the buckle design) with those of Inv. 13. The two bordering cells above the transverse lower curve of the dummy plate (fig. 321) appear wider than the other bordering cells on the buckle.

The central panel

The main element on the centre plates of all three pieces is a solitary mushroom cell, of ample, perfect shape, which dominates the object, supported on four stems, in a conspicuous central position. The device of suspending or supporting single complete cells on stems is not new and can be found much earlier, for example, on a fifth-century rectangular mount from Vienna[1] where a step pattern cell is so treated; but at Sutton Hoo it is in regular use and at the beginning of an important development. The device gives special prominence to the chosen cell shape and creates clarity and boldness of effect in the design. The second theme to register is step-pattern—single T-shaped cells at top and bottom of the field pointing inwards and balancing each other. The cell shapes here are modified by the fact that the step-pattern cells at both ends of the buckle and at the rounded end of each mount are combined with the curve of the border. Only the two cells at the straight end of each strap-mount rise from a flat surface and are wholly rectilinear. At the straight end of the strap-mounts, and the tongue end of the buckle, the simple two-step cells are set in an arched field (figs. 321 and 320*l*) and joined to the arch by a short straight cell-wall. This theme—a stepped cell within an arched or semicircular field—is popular *inter alia* in Kentish cloisonné work (cf. the Kingston brooch, fig. 431).

The buckle shows the same design as the mounts except that a dummy tongue-plate, outlined by a thick gold border, is depicted around the base of the tongue. This compresses the cloisonné design of the rest of the buckle-plate area into a length of 1·8 cm. The dummy tongue-plate is divided in two longitudinally. The root of the tongue, a raised plain gold moulding, divides it down the centre for a distance of some 7 mm, and the line of this division is continued, to meet the thick gold wall which defines the lower edge of the dummy tongue-plate, by two parallel gold walls containing a single rectangular garnet. The fields on each side contain the shoulder rivet-heads,

[1] Arrhenius 1971, fig. 80.

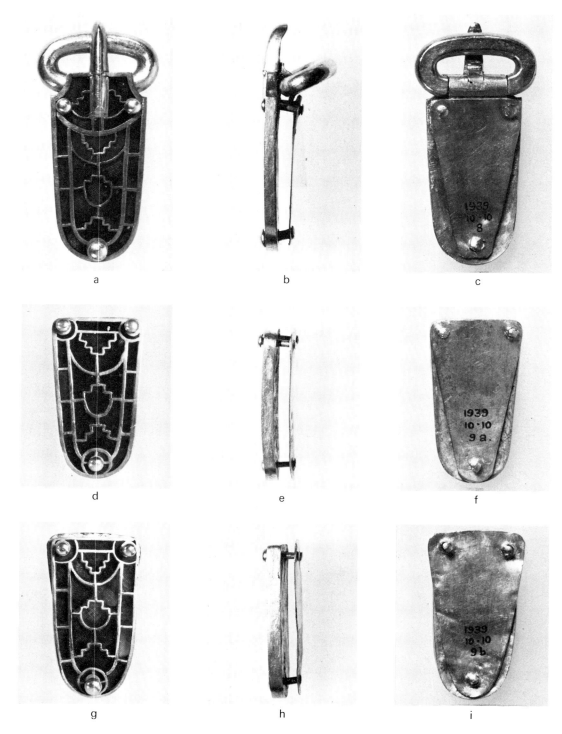

FIGURE 321 The cloisonné buckle (Inv. 12) and two matching strap-mounts
(Inv. 13 and 14). (a)–(c) Inv. 12; (d)–(f) Inv. 13; (g)–(i) Inv. 14. (Scale: 3/2)

both passing through circular gold tubes. Between these tubes and the tongue are additional stepped cell-walls which create two half-mushrooms on each side of the tongue (fig. 320*f*). The base of the tongue-plate continues the effect of the borders round the main plate: three garnet-filled cells, two curved and one transverse, here complete the border round the central field, fulfilling the function performed on the strap-mounts by the single long cell along the straight end.

The achievement of a simple design of step-pattern and mushroom cells supported on ligatures brings, as by-products of the main design, a residue of secondary incidental background shapes. From the point of view of gem-cutting, such cells often present more complexity than the primary cells and call equally for professional tools and skill.

The buckle shows slight variations in design as compared with the strap-mounts. Presumably because of the more restricted field available as a result of the encroachment of the dummy tongue-plate, the cell-walls used in the central panel are notably thinner than in the strap-mounts. The rivet at the point of the buckle-plate is larger than the six rivets of the strap-mounts but is not provided with the garnet collar seen in these (p. 450). The two rivets on the dummy tongue-plate not only also lack the garnet collars provided for the corresponding rivets of the strap-mounts, but the heads themselves are smaller, and the cloison-walls are thinner than those of the strap-mounts.

In contrast with all other items of jewellery in the Sutton Hoo deposit in which rivet-heads are exposed (they are concealed on the purse-lid and on the triangular mount, Inv. 18) the rivet-heads on this suite of pieces are not surrounded by beaded wire collars. The tubes in which the rivets are set, however, are themselves strongly constructed and prominent.

The back-plate on Inv. 14 may be a replacement. It is larger than the cloisonné part of the mount and lacks the crisp triangular form of the back plates of the buckle and the other strap-mount. Its tip is rounded, not squared off as in the buckle and, to a lesser extent, in Inv. 13, and its sides are curved, not straight as in Inv. 12 and 13. It has a battered look, perhaps suggesting that this strap-mount was more exposed in use than the buckle and its fellow. This appearance, however, may have another cause (see below).

The two types of foil have been allotted to different elements in the design with deliberation. In the employment of B1 an attempt has been made to line up the foils in Inv. 12–14 so that the angles at which the main lines of waffle-pattern run are the same in all cells, but the effect is not consistently achieved. The absence of any foil backing for the small cells directly at the base of the buckle-tongue should be noted. Since these cells are no narrower or deeper than the other bordering cells the intention may have been to achieve another variant visual effect.

General comments

This suite of matching pieces comprises two virtually identical strap-mounts with one matching buckle. We can be sure, from the extremely careful re-examination of the 1939 spoil heaps by Ashbee,[1] that there was no second buckle that might possibly have gone astray.[2]

Although the strap-mounts match the buckle neither is capable of passing through its loop. They are not strap-ends.

The cell repertoire (fig. 320) of this set of buckle and two strap-mounts comprises: the classic mushroom cell used alone in its most explicit and developed form; the half-mushroom cell with an extra step, like a two-step mushroom cell split in half (this occurs only on the buckle where the half-cells are set on either side of the tongue); and step-pattern cells with two or three steps, which occur at the ends of the central fields. At the curved ends of the three mounts the open end of the step-pattern cell is subtended not by a straight line but by a curve, convex in relation to the step-pattern cell. At the top of the buckle-plate the step-pattern cell is closed by a curve concave in relation to the cell. The cells with convex arcs closing them at the rounded ends of the objects, although bitten into at the point (particularly in the two strap-mounts) by the circular settings for the garnet collars of the terminal rivets, can be read as mushroom cells with two steps, but not made explicit—that is, as latent or crypto-mushroom themes. Other cells in the repertoire are long straight rectangular cells, sometimes lopsidedly curved and pointed at one end, sometimes strictly rectangular, used for bordering; small curved cells which are segments of circles; background or residual cells which are of irregular shape which tend to be large and to be a combination of curves and straight sides, or step-pattern and straight sides, or step-pattern with a straight side and a curved side (fig. 320 *g–i*).

The strap-mount, Inv. 14 (fig. 321 *g–i*), appears to be slightly warped or twisted. The back-plate is a little battered-looking, as has been noted (above); some of the garnets seem loose, while gaps have opened up between the stones and the cell-walls. Also the garnets show slight damage (one cracked and one chipped) at the upper right hand corner. On the other hand the strap-mount, Inv. 13, has a slight but regular curve; the point curves backwards, making the cloisonné front slightly convex (fig. 321 *e*). In this strap-mount the garnets are firmly in position and the surface is regular. There are no signs of external damage or pressure. Since it is undamaged it is unlikely that the curvature could have occurred in the ground. The objects lay in sand and there was nothing resistant against which they could have bent. Inv. 14 on the other hand may have been subjected to pressure, or trodden on and flattened, if it is the one of the pair which was recovered from the spoil heap later. We should therefore regard

---

[1] *Sutton Hoo*, Vol. I, ch. IV, especially 303–16 and 331–43.

[2] One of the two strap-mounts, we do not know which, was recovered from a dump in 1939 (p. 441), during a sifting process designed to bring to light anything that had been missed. This was stated to me verbally by Jacobs, one of the two workmen employed on the excavations by Mrs Pretty. Jacobs remained in the service of the Pretty family after the war. He stated that he had himself found the piece in sifting.

454

the strap-mounts as slightly curved. The buckle itself also seems to have a very slight curvature (fig. 321 b).

The garnets appear identical in colour and other respects with those on the purse (e.g. in the bird and the man-and-beast plaques on the purse-lid).

The buckle-tongue is thick and is rounded on its upper surface, its under surface being flat. It is rigid, the loop only having a limited movement. The point of the tongue curves downwards (fig. 321 b). The line of the tongue is continued backwards on to the dummy tongue-plate as a midrib. This midrib continuation of the line of the tongue is about 1·5 mm wide (less than the maximum width of the tongue) but corresponding with its narrowed upper part; the midrib rests on a wider gold base from which it stands up. The width of the gold base is 3 mm. Where the tongue crosses the outer line of the buckle (i.e. of the notional tongue-plate), it is itself crossed by a lateral moulding of the same width as the frame of the buckle-plate (fig. 321 a).

It will be noted that the three pieces are not all of exactly the same shape: Inv. 14 is less pointed that Inv. 13 and the buckle-plate of Inv. 12 is still fuller than that of Inv. 14. These are the sort of variations that can be expected in craft work and have no other significance.

The interior width of the loop of the buckle, Inv. 12, is 15 mm. The width of the strap on which Inv. 13 and 14 were mounted should be the same as that of the mounts themselves and of matching Inv. 12, i.e. 16–17 mm. The strap on which the buckle was mounted must therefore have been reduced in width in order to pass through its own loop, if it had to do so.

The width of the buckle-loop (15 mm) could accommodate a strap from the swivelling element (b) of the T-shaped strap-distributor (Inv. 17). The curved clasp (Inv. 10) has a loop aperture 1·6 cm wide and 2 mm across. A strap of 15 mm width could pass through the loop, but the small buckle (Inv. 12) would be carried on a 3 mm thick strap, thicker than that for either the T-shaped mount or the curved clasp, in which the gaps between the mount and the back plate are 2 mm and 1 mm respectively.

It should be noted that in all this gold jewellery only one strap-end, the small plain gold one, Inv. 16 (the position of which in the ground is not known) is capable of passing through the loop of Inv. 12. This small strap-end matches the plain gold tongue-less mount or runner (Inv. 15) in appearance, and indeed is the only gold item capable of passing through its loop. It is however very much smaller than the aperture of the loop of Inv. 15, and I do not think it could have been used in conjunction with Inv. 15 (p. 444 above).

*Pair of identical rectangular strap-mounts with pattern of depressed
mushroom-type cells* (Inv. 6, 7; fig. 324)

Dimensions

All dimensions are the same for each mount.

Length	5·2 cm
Width	2·0 cm
Length of central cloisonné-bearing section	3·5 cm
Width of central cloisonné-bearing section	1·7 cm
Thickness of central cloisonné-bearing section	0·5 cm
Length of back-plate	5·1 cm
Width of back-plate	1·9 cm
Thickness of back-plate	0·05 cm
Overall projecting length of rivets	0·6 cm
Gap between cloisonné plate and back-plate (i.e. thickness of strap accommodated)	0·2 mm
Thickness of rivet-bearing shelves	0·25 cm at inner edge sloping to 0·15 cm

Weight

Inv. 6	36·121 g
Inv. 7	36·028 g

Number of garnets originally present

	Central panel	Each long side	Each end shelf	Total
Inv. 6	66	19	28*	160
Inv. 7	66	19	28*	160

* Or 16, if the cells forming the narrow circles round the rivets did not originally hold garnets. There are twelve of these cells on each shelf and they are now empty except for two in which there are shiny black residues which may be the remains of original stones (see below).

Foil underlays. Type A1, throughout.
Cell forms. Cell forms and characteristic patterns are shown in figure 322.

The two mounts are identical in design and dimensions (fig. 324). Each carries the same number of garnets (160) in an identical cell-pattern; the only variation is in small differences, particularly in the sizes of corresponding cells on the two plaques, such as can be expected in any handcraft. On each mount the raised central cloisonné field, measuring 3·5 cm × 1·7 cm contains sixty-six garnets; each of the sloping end shelves which accommodate the rivets has a principal design of sixteen garnets; and there is a collar of four very narrow cells round each of the three rivets, making in all twenty-eight cells per shelf. When the rivet-heads and their filigree collars are held in place, the tiny rings of cells are not wholly covered; half the cell width and the outer ends of the four transverse walls in each ring are visible (fig. 323 a). In Inv. 7 these small cells

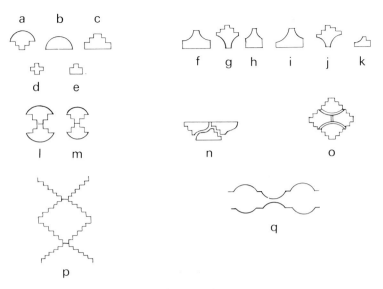

FIGURE 322 Cell forms and characteristic cell patterns of the rectangular mounts (Inv. 6 and 7): (a)–(e) basic cell shapes; (f)–(k) residual shapes; (l)–(q) patterns. (Scale: 3/2)

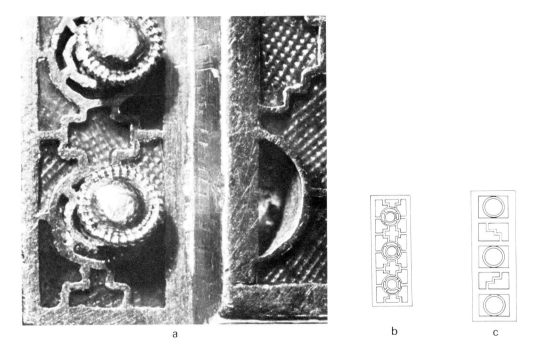

FIGURE 323 (*a*) Rectangular mount (Inv. 7); enlarged detail of a terminal rivet-shelf showing the circular shafts which enclose the rivet shanks and portions of the rings of narrow segmental cells which surround them (p. 456); with (*b*) a drawing. (*c*) Cell work of the rivet shelf at the end of the rectangular buckle (Inv. 11). (Scales: *a*, 6/1; *b*, *c*, 3/2) (Photo: British Museum Research Laboratory)

457

are all empty, but in Inv. 6 traces of (?) garnets appear to remain in two. As the cells are narrow and deep, and not provided with foil underlays, the (?) garnets are almost black in appearance.[1] The long vertical sides of the mounts are also set with garnets, each containing nineteen stones. The identity of the two mounts in all respects is remarkable.

The cell forms (fig. 322) in the main elevated central fields comprise a depressed two-step mushroom-type cell; a step-pattern cell of three steps, spaced round the outsides of the central field, the steps developing inwards, the initial step being higher than the others; simple semicircular cells, two at each end of the central field; residual cells, stepped and unstepped, of various forms (fig. 322 *f–k*). The depressed mushroom cells are joined in pairs stem to stem creating an overall form like a double-headed axe, the pairs, and also the individual mushroom cells of each pair, being held in suspension by straight cell-walls from the sides of the panel. The mushroom cell pairs of the 'axe-heads' down the central axis of the mount are slightly larger than those

a   b   c   d

e   f

FIGURE 324   Rectangular mounts: (*a*), (*c*), (*e*), Inv. 6; (*b*), (*d*), (*f*), Inv. 7. (Scale: 3/2)

[1] In the corresponding twenty-four cells on the similar pair of mounts, Inv. 8 and 9, no trace of inlay remains.

458

to either side (fig. 322 *l–m*). The strong rhythms of the panels and the generally ambivalent effect of the design are notable (fig. 324); they seem to stretch the resources of the cloisonné technique to its limits and to be reaching for a freer medium.

The end shelves show between the rivets two simple equal-armed cruciform cells and, again, each is suspended by straight stems from the sides of the panel. In the space separating each outer rivet from the ends of the shelf is a half-cross or T-shaped cell. The rivet shafts run through gold tubes, each surrounded by a narrow ring or collar of four cells (fig. 324 *a*, *b*), combining to form a circle. The residual cells (fig. 322 *k*) are a half-version of figure 322 *g*, in simplified form.

The sides of the plaques carry identical panels of a running cloisonné design of steps and S-curves (fig. 322 *n*). The design is quite different from the themes of the main panels or the end-shelves. It reverses about a central feature and consists of four S-curves on the left-hand side of the central motif, leaning to the left, and four S-curves on the right-hand side, leaning to the right; each of the swaying segments into which the field is thus divided is bisected by a gold wall in step-pattern into identical but reversed upper and lower shapes. The result is a running curvilinear pattern of elegant S-curves regularly supported by delicate step-pattern springs. In the middle of the panel the two adjacent curves which lean away from each other are bridged by an inverted step-pattern theme (fig. 328 *a*).

In the design of the main decorative panel, which covers the front of the mount, there is complex movement with a subtle play of reversed curves. As the side panels can be read as a series of swinging S-curves, so the basic design of the main panels can be read as a trellis of ten long lines of steps, five leaning to the left and five to the right, crossing nearly at right-angles (fig. 322 *p*). The rhythm of the curvilinear motifs (fig. 322 *q*), the repetition of pairs of staggered mushroom cells joined stem to stem and, running through them, the large-scale reticulation of step-pattern ladders, give the panels an abnormal vitality and seem to seek rhythmic effects transcending the normal limitations of the medium. The static effect of the cell pattern on the shelves to either side may be contrasted with the swinging movement of the main panels between. The gold foil backings, as has been said, are throughout of type A1. The garnets seem shallow and the effect is to make the centre panel at any rate seem brick-red or pinkish in tone. The design is not only very delicately and perfectly executed but sophisticated and original in conception.

In both Inv. 6 and Inv. 7, the underside of the cloisonné-bearing portion of the mount, over an

FIGURE 325 Rectangular mount (Inv. 6 or 7): early photograph of the mount dismantled to show the back of the upper cloisonné-bearing plate; a countersunk area corresponding with that of the cloisonné panel can be seen. (Scale: 1/1) (Photo: British Museum Research Laboratory)

area corresponding with but slightly smaller than the central raised cloisonné panel, is recessed (fig. 325). The back-plates are solid sheets of plain gold.

On the inner surface of the back-plate of Inv. 6 two parallel lines are scratched across its width. In the same position on the inner surface of the back plate of Inv. 7 is an incised cross. On one end of Inv. 7 two small 'V' incisions can be seen. Similar marks occur in the same position on Inv. 8 and 9. On Inv. 8 they take the form of two diagonal cuts.

Pair of identical rectangular strap-mounts with step-pattern cells within cable-twist borders (Inv. 8 and 9, fig. 327)

Dimensions (the same for each mount except where shown)

Length	5·2 cm
Width	2·0 cm
Length of central cloisonné-bearing section	3·6 cm
Width of central cloisonné-bearing section	1·7 cm
Thickness of central cloisonné-bearing section	0·5 cm
Length of back-plate	5·1 cm
Width of back-plate	1·9 cm (Inv. 8); 1·8 cm (Inv. 9)
Overall length of rivets	0·5 m
Gap between cloisonné plate and back-plate (i.e. thickness of strap accommodated)	0·2 cm

Weight   42·336 g (Inv. 8); 40·822 g (Inv. 9)

Number of garnets originally present

	Central panel	Each long side	Each end shelf	Total
Inv. 8	118	19	28*	212
Inv. 9	116	19	28*	210

* Sixteen if the cells of the narrow circles round the rivets were originally empty.

Foil underlays. A1 and B1. There is a difference in the employment of the foils in the two mounts. On both Inv. 8 and Inv. 9 the simple pointillé pattern (A1) is used in the cable-twist interlace themes. But whereas B1 in Inv. 9 is confined to the stilted cruciform step-pattern cells at the centre of each of the eight broadly rectangular shapes

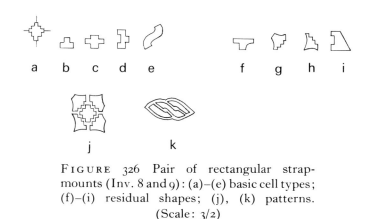

FIGURE 326 Pair of rectangular strap-mounts (Inv. 8 and 9): (a)–(e) basic cell types; (f)–(i) residual shapes; (j), (k) patterns. (Scale: 3/2)

460

confined within the interlace, in Inv. 8 it is used not only in these central cells but also in the background cells of irregular shape which surround them.

Cell forms. Cell forms and characteristic patterns are shown in figure 326.

This pair of mounts is of the same size and form as Inv. 6 and 7. The only difference lies in the designs of the cloisonné of the edge panels and of the main raised panel; the design of the end shelf is identical with that of Inv. 6 and 7.

Each of the edge panels, as in Inv. 6 and 7, has a running design which reverses about a central theme, but in Inv. 8 and 9 the theme is a simple equal-armed cross of the type seen on the end shelves; the reversing design consists of two opposed series of simple one-step vertically set cell-walls, reverberating outwards from the shape of the cross. As in Inv. 6 and 7, each edge panel contains nineteen garnets.

The design on the main panel consists of eight evenly spaced step-pattern cells of full cruciform shape, with three steps a side. Each of these cells occupies the centre of a broadly rectangular field and is supported on four straight elements. The sides of the eight roughly rectangular fields which contain the individual step-pattern cells

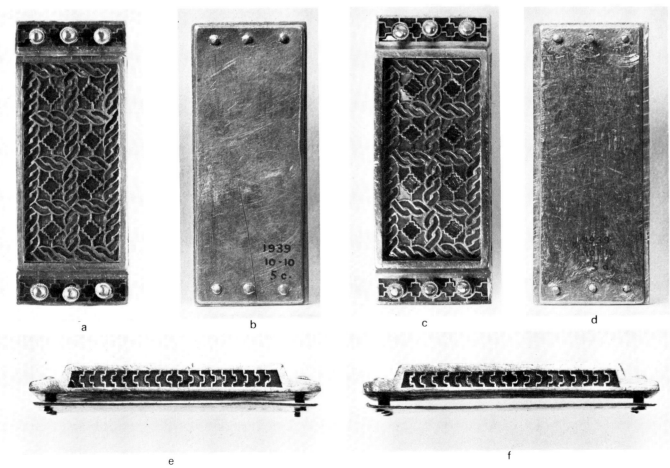

FIGURE 327 Pair of rectangular strap-mounts: (*a*), (*b*) and (*e*) Inv. 8; (*c*), (*d*), (*f*) Inv. 9. (Scales: 3/2)

461

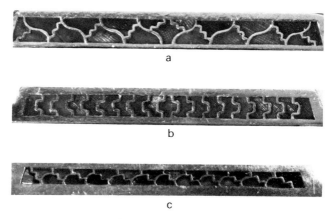

FIGURE 328 Strap-mounts: cloisonné designs of the edge panels of (*a*) Inv. 6, (*b*) Inv. 8 and (*c*) Inv. 17, for comparison. (Scale: 2/1)

are formed by a running *guilloche* or cable-pattern interlace, executed in cloisonné work, which is a unique *tour de force* (fig. 329 *d*). Once again the artist-designer-craftsman transcends the pre-existing limitations of his medium, achieving a liberation in expression akin to that found in pen-work.

The fluency of the cloisonné interlace is remarkable. What impresses is not only the achievement of smooth twist-motif but its build-up into continuous running lengths in which smooth transitions and changes of direction are effected between one element of interlace and those adjoining it. Allowing for the difficulty of the medium, the interlace is as coherently designed and smoothly executed as that, of Late Antique descent, seen in contemporary or later Insular illuminated manuscripts (fig. 329 *a* and *b*).

The twist is effected by a rare technical device first recognised in the Sutton Hoo

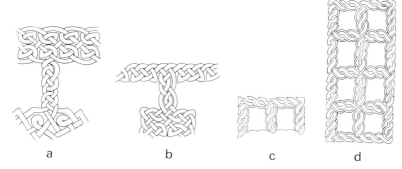

FIGURE 329 Details of running interlace from panel-work in (*a*) the Book of Durrow (Trinity College Dublin, f. 117 *v*); (*b*) the Echternach Gospels (Paris Bibl. Nat. Lat. 9389, f. 18 *v*), with (*c*) a detail from the Sutton Hoo strap-mount, Inv. 8, and (*d*) panelled design of continuous running interlace in cloisonné work from Inv. 9. (Scales: *a*, *b*, reduced; *c*, *d*, 1/1)

462

FIGURE 330 Strap-mount (Inv. 9): enlarged detail showing the use of beaded or sealed cells to bring out the interlace theme. The use of two types of foil can be noted, A1 in general use but B1 in the cruciform step pattern cells. (Scale: 4/1)

jewellery.[1] This is the use of the 'beaded cell', created by the overlap of the ends of two consecutive S-elements, and sealed with a gold lid, which serves as a pivot for each twist of the cloisonné 'rope'. This device makes for fluency and avoids both angularity and incoherence. The fluency is enhanced by a similar sealing with plain gold lids of the small spaces between the loops of the outermost interlace and the walls of the frame, best seen at the left-hand end of Inv. 9 in figure 330.

Close inspection suggests that the design in Inv. 9 is more successful than in Inv. 8. The interlace at the four corners is more rounded, less angular. The junction between the central long interlace element in figure 329d and the end element at the top is much more smoothly executed, the interlace in general clearer and better managed (figs. 327a, c, 329c–d). It is almost as if in Inv. 8 the goldsmith was attempting a novel and tricky 'paper' design for the first time, and that by the time he came to make Inv. 9, he had solved the technical difficulties. In Inv. 8 and 9 the cloisonné work of the central panel, with the interlace design, is abnormally shallow and is built up on a separate tray which was then inserted into the mount (fig. 331). This device is not resorted to in the matching pieces Inv. 6 and 7, or in any other piece of the Sutton Hoo jewellery.

The tray has been removed from the mount Inv. 9, in which it was loose, in order to examine its construction and establish how it was held in position, and photographs

[1] Kendrick 1939; Bruce-Mitford 1974.

463

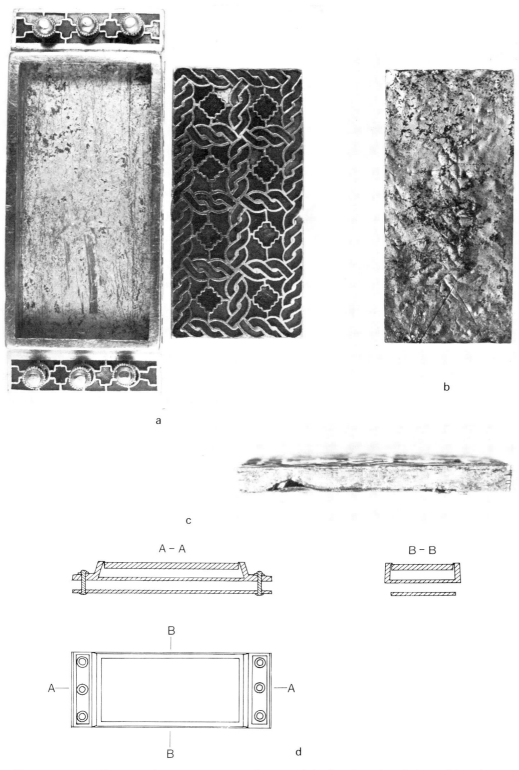

FIGURE 331 Rectangular strap-mount, Inv. 9: (*a*) showing the cloisonné-bearing tray removed; (*b*) rear view of the cloisonné tray with the cable twist design showing through; (*c*) end view of the tray with a cell wall exposed; (*d*) sectional drawings. (Scales: *a*, *b*, 2/1; *c*, 4/1; *d*, 1/1)

have been taken (fig. 331). The tray is 1·7 cm wide, 3·6 cm long and minimally under 2 mm thick. Figure 331 c shows an enlarged view of an end. The tray consists of a base plate on which the lower edges of all the cell walls rest, and to which they appear to have been individually soldered, since the cable-twist pattern and panelled layout of the cloisonnage are visible on its outer surface in light relief (fig. 331 b), suggesting a degree of integration between them. The side walls of the tray then seem to have been soldered to the exposed edges of the cloisonné grid so formed. In places the outer surfaces of these side walls reflect the resistance or recession of the cell walls inside, in much the same way that the cell patterns register through the base-plate. One of the cell walls can be seen edge-on through a small hole at one end of the tray (fig. 331 c). The associated cells appear quite empty, with no trace of any contained paste. At one end there is a V-shaped cut on the base-plate (fig. 331), perhaps an assembly mark. The cells appear to be about 1·5 mm deep.

The edges of the box of the main mount in which the tray is contained overhang sharply inwards all round. A clean zone some 1 mm in depth along the tops of the inner side faces of the mount must mark where the cloisonné tray was wedged in position right at the top of the box, with empty space beneath it. Although externally the whole mount, apart from the cloisonné tray, appears as one solid casting, cracks can be detected along the bottom side angles internally which show that the base plate was once detached. The parts must have been very skilfully assembled. Since the base-plate was evidently once detached, the gold cloisonné tray could have been, and assuredly was, inserted from the back and wedged by pressure from behind into the mouth of the mount. Measurement and construction must have been extraordinarily exact to provide the perfect fit achieved. The tray was held in position by pressure alone. The effectiveness of this method of construction may be judged by the fact that the tray in the identical mount Inv. 8 still remains in position as when made. Cross sections of the mount are given in figure 331 d.

Rectangular strap-mount with hinged terminal for a second strap attached
(Inv. 17, fig. 334)

Dimensions

Length of main mount (a in fig. 333)	5·3 cm
Width of main mount	2·0 cm
Thickness of main mount	0·5 cm
Length of central cloisonné-bearing section of element a	3·7 cm
Width of central cloisonné-bearing section	1·55 cm
Length of back-plate	5·3 cm
Width of back-plate	1·9 cm
Thickness of back-plate	0·05 cm
Thickness of strap accommodated by element a	0·2 cm
Overall length of rivets	0·6 cm
Length of hinge	1·8 cm
Length of element b (fig. 333) excluding the hinge-bar	2·1 cm
Width of element b	1·8 cm

465

Length of moving strap-end terminal c (including the circular element which dovetails into element b and is partly concealed by it)   2·5 cm approx.
Width of moving strap-end terminal c   1·3 cm
Thickness of b and c where they overlap   0·6 cm
Length of strap-end accommodated within c   1·1 cm
Width of strap accommodated in c   1·4–1·5 cm
Thickness of strap accommodated in c   0·15–0·2 cm

Weight   73·243 g

Number of garnets

Central panel	Each end shelf	Long side	Long side adjacent to hinge	Hinge	Element b attached to hinge	Moving strap-end terminal c	End shelf of c	Total
44	16	24	8	22*	17	9	0	156

* All honeycomb cell type.

Foil underlays. A1 throughout.

Cell forms. Cell forms and patterns are shown in figure 332.

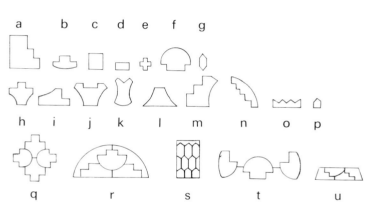

FIGURE 332   The hinged T-shaped mount (Inv. 17): cell forms and patterns. (a)–(g) basic shapes; (h)–(p) residual shapes; (q)–(u) patterns. (Scale: 3/2)

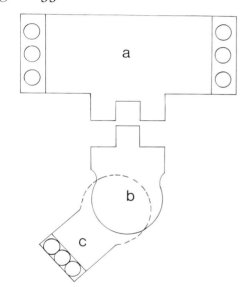

FIGURE 333   The T-shaped mount: sketch with letters to distinguish the parts.

The T-mount or strap-distributor, Inv. 17 (fig. 334), has as its main element a rectangular mount intended to be fitted to a strap of the same width and thickness as that associated with the four rectangular mounts Inv. 6–9. Part of a hinge mechanism is soldered to one side. The mount itself is of the same size and general character as Inv. 6–9, and the cloisonné designs of the end shelves which carry the rivets and of the side panels are closely similar or identical. Thus all these mounts are related.

The long edges of the mount carry a running cloisonné pattern (fig. 328 c) similar to that of Inv. 6 and 7, but slightly different. Read vertically it can be seen as a line of half-mushroom cells emerging from the left-hand edge of the field, each one joined to the right-hand edge of the field by a straight ligature (fig. 332 u). Read sideways it can be seen as a succession of steep curves breaking down into a step-pattern.

466

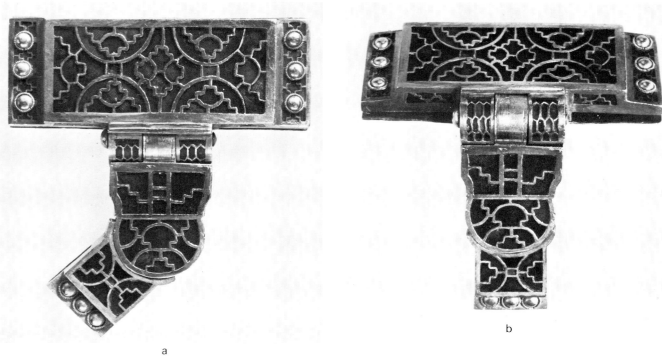

a

b

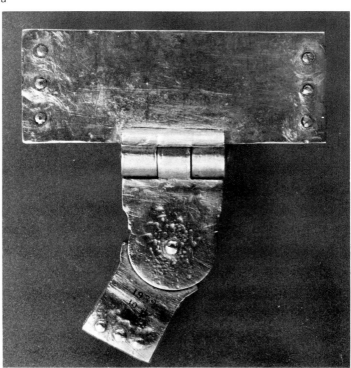

c

FIGURE 334   The T-shaped mount: Three views in which the hinge and
swivel mechanisms are well seen. (Scale: 3/2)

467

The main panel and the two side elements attached by the hinge have a design dominated by the mushroom cell and the mushroom and step-pattern combination. A favourite theme is to enclose the mushroom cell and step-pattern element within a large semicircle (fig. 332 r); this in turn leads in certain parts of the pattern to the suspension of mushroom cells by oblique ligatures, giving a distinctive visual effect.

In spite of its essential similarity to the rectangular mounts, Inv. 6–9, the T-mount, Inv. 17, differs in certain important respects.[1] The cloisonné design of the main panel and of the side pieces is on a larger scale and less delicate than those of Inv. 6–9; the cell walls are much thicker and more prominent, the cells deeper and the garnets thicker. There is also a strong resemblance between the cloisonné designs of the T-shaped distributor and those of the buckle and strap-ends, Inv. 12–14 (fig. 321). A notable common element (apart from the sharing of thicker cell-walls, deeper cells and thicker garnets) is the use of still thicker walls to divide fields: compare the inner gold frame separating the borders from the central fields in Inv. 12–14 (fig. 321 a, d, g) with the two straight walls below the hinge in element b of the T-shaped mount (fig. 334 a, b). The element and its broad borders may be compared with the imitation tongue-plate with cut-away shoulders of the small buckle, Inv. 12. Certain cell shapes and cloisonné themes also correspond (cf. figs. 320 d, g, i and 332 f, m, n). Cell patterns also link Inv. 17 with the curved mount Inv. 10 and less obviously with Inv. 11 (figs. 332, 339 and 336).

If we compare strap-widths, we find that the strap which emerged from the swivelling element, c, is 1·4 cm wide and had a thickness of about 2 mm. This would fit the buckle-loop of Inv. 12 (internal length 1·5 cm and internal width 4 mm). As there are also close affinities in the cloisonné work it might *prima facie* appear that the T-mount or strap-distributor, Inv. 17, and the suite, Inv. 12–14, were directly connected, but closer examination does not support this view (see pp. 568/80 and figs. 423–5).

The hinge mechanism and use of 'honeycomb cell' garnets

The 'honeycomb' cell, in the flattened form used in Anglo-Saxon cloisonné work, where it is uncommon,[2] occurs in the Sutton Hoo jewellery only in the hinge of this piece. The cells are aligned so that their long axes are in the direction of the movement of the hinge, which thus operates as it were with the grain of the cloisonné work and not across it. The hinge mechanism is illustrated in figure 335 a and b. The raised ridge immediately above the hinge acts as a stop to forward movement of the b–c elements. The arc through which b–c can move backwards and forwards is some 110 degrees, and the arc of movement from side to side of element c is 40 degrees, the field of movement being limited by small projections on each side of the upper part

---

[1] I am indebted to my wife, formerly Miss Marilyn Luscombe, for a number of these points, made by her in joint discussions of the jewellery.

[2] Cf. the composite brooches from Milton, near Abingdon, Berkshire, and Faversham, Kent (Kendrick 1933, 431 and pl. IV, 2, 3; Jessup 1950, pl. XXV; Avent 1975, pls. 71, 73, 74).

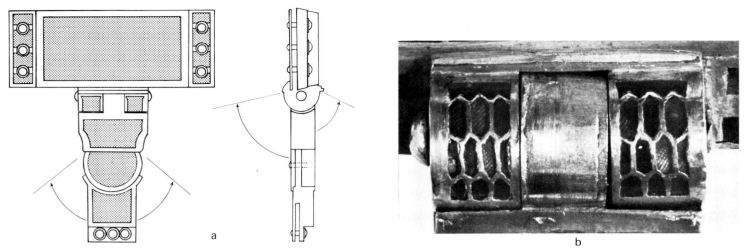

FIGURE 335 The T-shaped mount: (*a*) drawing to illustrate the movement of the hinged and swivelling parts; (*b*) detail of the hinge showing a version of the 'honeycomb' cell used on the hinge. (Scales: *a*, 1/1; *b*, 4/1)

of element b, which act as stops. Like all the moving parts of the gold jewellery, the mechanism operates with perfect smoothness.

Rectangular buckle (Inv. 11; pl. 19*a*, fig. 337)
Dimensions

Length	7·3 cm
Width of rectangular buckle-plate	2·2 cm
Length of buckle-loop (external)	2·7 cm
Length of tongue projection	1·3 cm
Width of tongue	0·4 cm
Gap between buckle-plate and back-plate (strap thickness accommodated)	0·25 cm
Dimensions of buckle opening	1·6×0·3 cm

Weight
64·926 g
Number of garnets originally present
103, as below

		Main plate			
Tongue plate	Central panel	Each long border	End borders	Rivet shelf	Total
16	30	18	5 and 6	10	103

Foil underlays. Type A1 throughout; one cell (a half-mushroom), the third down on the right-hand side of the central panel, has no foil underlay.

Cell forms. Cell forms and patterns are shown in figure 336.

The buckle has a rectangular plate and cut-away shoulder. The end of the plate at the buckle end is slightly stepped up and has the form of a tongue-plate simulated in the cloisonnage, the cut-away shoulders of the buckle forming its upper corners. The tongue is rigid. The buckle is constructed on several levels. It comprises a loop, tongue and dummy buckle-plate in cloisonné work, a narrowed central rectangular

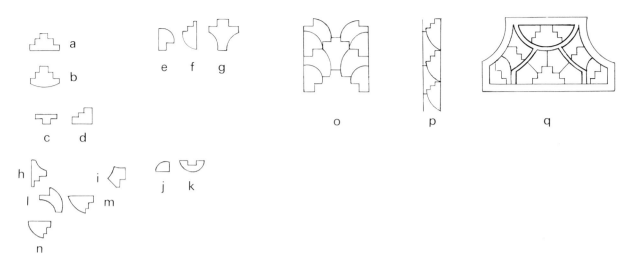

FIGURE 336   Rectangular buckle (Inv. 11): cell forms and characteristic cell patterns. (a)–(g) basic shapes; (h)–(n) residual shapes; (o)–(q) patterns. (Scale: 3/2)

cloisonné field with separately designed end panels all set at a level slightly lower than the tongue plate; long cloisonné borders again at a lower level flanking the central field, and finally a still lower end shelf, carrying three rivets. The edges of the buckle are plain; it is as though two cloisonné panels from the edges had moved up on to the face of the buckle, constricting its main decorative panel. The terminal rivet-shelf does not slope emphatically as it does in the rectangular mounts, Inv. 6–9 (figs. 331 d, 338), and the T-shaped strap-distributor, Inv. 17, though a very slight tapering in its thickness can be detected.

The three rivets in the end shelf have largish domed circular heads surrounded by beaded wire collars. They hold a plain gold back plate to the main front plate of the buckle which carries the cloisonné work. The back plate is held by two more rivets at the upper end in the two lower corners of the tongue-plate just below the point at which the shoulders are cut away. These two rivets do not show on the front of the buckle; inserted from the back, they are given prominence there by domed circular heads and filigree collars identical with those of the three rivets on the shelf on the front (fig. 337 c). These two rivet-heads are slightly larger than those on the front, the rivets themselves being thicker and stronger, which is appropriate since here two rivets perform the function shared by three at the other end of the buckle-plate.

The loop is attached to the buckle-plate in a manner similar to that seen in the small cloisonné buckle, Inv. 12. A separate broad sheet of gold is inserted to act as a hinge (fig. 337 c). It is welded to the underside of the dummy tongue-plate where this narrows and projects to meet the tongue. It is then bent and tucked loosely inside the back plate, the cut end fitting in between the two rivet-shanks (fig. 338 b).

The buckle is interesting formally in that the different fields which make up the total design are not only clearly demarcated in plan by dividing walls, but are also set at different levels, as figure 338 shows.

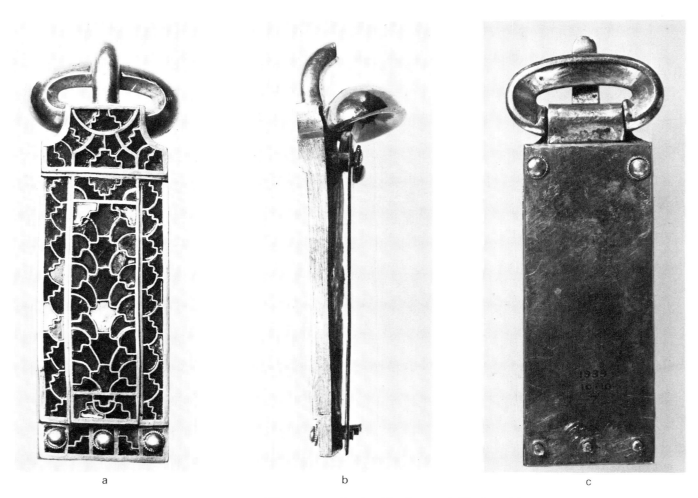

a   b   c

FIGURE 337   The rectangular buckle (Inv. 11) (Scale: 3/2)

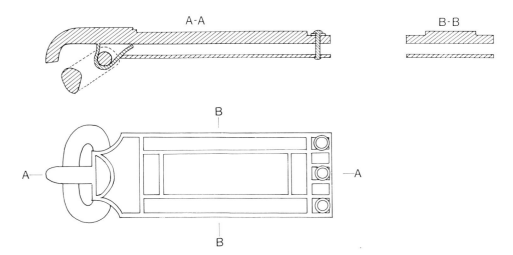

FIGURE 338   The rectangular buckle (Inv. 11): simplified
longitudinal and transverse sectional drawings. (Scale: 1/1)

The cloisonné design may be said to have two orthodox basic cell types only, step-pattern and half-mushroom cells. No complete mushroom cell appears on the buckle. While the dummy tongue-plate, the rivet-shelf and the end panels of the raised central field have designs consisting almost entirely of step-pattern cells and themes, the panels bordering the central field have a running pattern of half-mushroom cells. These have two steps to their stems, and run away from the loop end. They are supported from the outer edge of the buckle by straight ligatures giving rise to a corresponding line of a subsidiary cell form (fig. 336 *p*).

The central panel has curious elements which, with the subtle use of half-mushrooms, suggests considerable freedom and familiarity with the use of the mushroom theme in design. When mushroom cells are combined in various patterns residual shapes are incidentally formed: such residual shapes on the curved mount (dummy buckle), Inv. 10, are illustrated in figure 339 *m* and *n* and on Inv. 17 in figure 332 *h*. In this buckle, Inv. 11, however, the typical incidental shape (fig. 336 *g*) is elevated to the status of a central theme, while the half-mushrooms are pushed out to the sides, the interspaces being filled with curious mushroom segments to give what seems at first sight and even on long familiarity, an incoherent design (fig. 336 *o*). There seems to be some tension between the downward-flowing movement of the borders (downwards if the buckle-loop is regarded as the top), with their series of half-mushrooms and outward tending lines of steps, and what may be seen as an upward tendency in the central panel with its central column of vase-shaped cells and its two sequences of half-mushrooms moving upwards. The upward tendencies of the design of the central panel, however, are neutralised by its slumping residual shapes.

Many of the favourite themes seen on other pieces, such as complete cruciform step-pattern cells or complete mushrooms, or the step-pattern cells inside semicircles, or mushroom cells inside large cruciform or half-cruciform cells (e.g. figs. 320, 326 *a*, 332 *q* and 340 *h*) do not appear on this buckle.

The width of the buckle is greater by 2 mm than the rectangular mounts, Inv. 6–9 and 17 (22 mm as against 20 mm), and less than the back plate width of the curved mount, Inv. 10 (25 mm).

The buckle-tongue curves downwards and its tip is cut off flat. It is of a D-shaped cross-section, flat underneath (fig. 337 *b*). The buckle-loop is of plain gold and carefully shaped. From the front it appears relatively massive and heavy, with a steep-sided interior. Seen from behind, however, the loop is concave (fig. 337 *c*). It moves through an arc of 90 degrees and, as in the case of the great gold buckle, has a small oblong notch cut in its upper surface to accommodate the flat under-surface of the tongue. The curve of the tip of the tongue is congruent with the curve of the front edge of the loop.

The buckle is in relatively poor condition. Many of the garnets are cracked or broken and sunk into their cells; five are missing. The buckle is warped and the loop end of it seems to be twisted or bent upwards. It was found lying upside down half underneath the sword scabbard at a point where this is badly shattered (fig. 318). It is the only piece in the jewellery to have sustained obvious damage.[1]

III   CURVED MOUNT (DUMMY BUCKLE)

Inv. 10 (figs. 341, 343)

Dimensions

Length (in a straight line between extremities)	7·6 cm
Width	2·6 cm
Length of back-plate	5·9 cm
Width of back-plate	2·5 cm
Thickness of back-plate	0·025 cm
Length of loop aperture	1·6 cm
Width of loop aperture	0·2 cm
Thickness of mount	0·45–0·5 cm (at shoulders, 0·6 mm)
Gap between mount and back-plate	0·1 cm

Weight   70·718 g
Number of garnets

Curved plate	Loop	Total
109	32	141

Foil underlays. Types A1 and B1. All the stones, including the two small cabochons, are backed by foil, except in certain instances on the shoulders of the loop. It is very difficult to see the foils under some of these curved stones on the loop, which are of cloudy appearance, but foil seems to be genuinely absent in two or three instances. There is a tendency to align the pattern of foil of type B1 in the same manner in corresponding cells, but this is not so systematic or remarkable as it is in the shoulder clasps (p. 523). Type B1 is used exclusively in the main triangular cloisonné field. Type A1 is employed everywhere else.

Cell forms. Cell forms and patterns are shown in figures 339 and 340.

This mount is among the finest pieces in the treasure. It is unusual in type in the corpus of Anglo-Saxon material, of exceptional interest and brilliantly designed. It takes the form of a curved buckle of narrow triangular shape, with a strong ornamental elaboration of the three rivets which hold the back-plate to the strap or belt on which the piece was mounted. The concealed rivet-heads are covered by bosses, two of small size, each holding a cabochon garnet, and a large boss at the toe of the mount set with four garnets in a more elaborate convex construction. These bosses stand out from the surface in sharp relief. There are other subtler indications of a feeling for relief in the design. The tongue (figs. 341 *a* and 342 *a*) stands out like a hogsback of plain gold from the surrounding cloisonné surface; the dummy buckle-plate is slightly elevated at its inner end, as though tilted forwards (fig. 342 *a*). The three bosses are

---

[1] Damage to Inv. 14 is discussed on p. 443 and that to the purse frame, since made good, is to be seen in fig. 357 *a*.

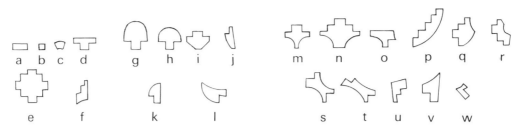

FIGURE 339   The curved dummy buckle (Inv. 10): cell forms and patterns. (a)–(l) basic shapes; (m)–(w) residual shapes. (Scale: 3/2)

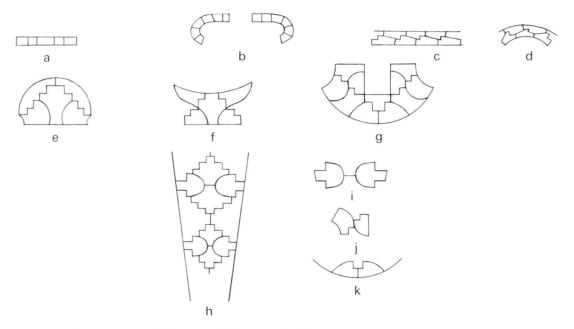

FIGURE 340   The curved dummy buckle: patterns and themes in the cell work: (a)–(d) borders; (e)–(h) patterns; (i)–(k) themes using mushroom cells or half mushrooms as seen in (g) and (h). (Scale: 3/2)

the more strongly emphasised by the fact that their cylindrical substructures break the triangular outline and project to give the mount a deliberate zoomorphic (horse's head) look. The body of the mount is of the same thickness as those of other mounts (e.g. Inv. 6–9, 17) but its sides, like those of the rectangular buckle, Inv. 11, are plain, without cloisonné decoration. As in Inv. 11, the central field carries narrow borders with a running cloisonné design. The back-plate is abnormally thin and frail-looking, in surprising contrast to the solidity of the mount itself and to the more substantial back-plates of Inv. 6–9 and 17 (0·5 mm).

The gap of only 1 mm between the back-plate and the body of the mount contrasts markedly with the 2–3 mm gaps of the mounts and buckles hitherto considered. The narrowness of the gap and the frailty of the back-plate suggest that, in contradistinction to the other mounts the accommodated strap in this case may have been textile

474

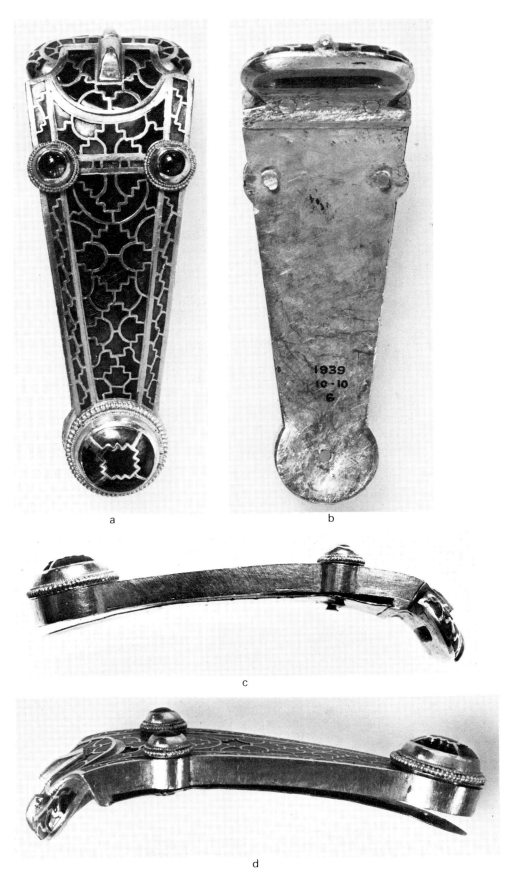

a   b

c

d

FIGURE 341   The curved dummy buckle (Inv. 10): (*a*)–(*d*) front, back and two profile views. (Scale: 3/2)

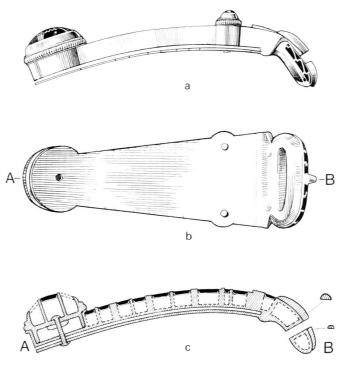

FIGURE 342 The dummy buckle: (*a*)–(*c*) drawings, including a suggested sectional view. The depths of the cells and exact garnet thicknesses are not known except in the case of the cells of the large boss. (Scale: 1/1)

(probably linen) rather than leather. The width of the strap on which the curved mount was fastened, indicated by the maximum breadth of the back-plate (2·5 cm), is broader than the 2 cm strap width associated with Inv. 6–9 and Inv. 17. The loop of Inv. 10, however, has an internal length of only 1·55 cm, with a width of 2 mm.

The resemblance in design to that of a buckle extends to the provision of a tongue-plate (figs. 341 *a*, 346) which, in addition to the canting-up of its back edge already noted, is marked off from the main cloisonné fields by a thick curve of plain gold frame.

The mount, though faithfully reproducing the appearance of a buckle, is a dummy. As figure 342 *a* shows, the tongue is cut away where it would cross the loop and reappears, at smaller scale, on the far side of the loop. The two portions of the tongue do not taper, there is merely a reduction in scale of the tip. The loop of the mount must have either engaged a hook (as in the pair of curved clasps from the Taplow barrow, fig. 343, pl. 22 *b*) or served as a runner through which a detached strap or belt was drawn: the latter seems the more likely function, as comparative evidence strongly suggests that the 'dummy buckle' was mounted on the sword-scabbard (p. 572 below).

The mount has a continuous shallow curve which intensifies as the shoulders are reached; the loop curves back still more sharply (fig. 342).

476

FIGURE 343   Curved clasps from the Taplow barrow, Buckinghamshire (pl. 22*b*, centre).
(Scale: 3/2)

The cloisonné work

The garnets appear thick, and have a lustrous dark red colour. The cell walls as seen in the face of the design are even and solid, and where seen in depth, strongly constructed (fig. 347). One garnet detached from the large boss at the toe of the mount is illustrated in figure 344. It is of plano-convex form, 1 mm thick at the edge but deeper where the stone becomes convex in the middle. Its foil backing is a classic illustration of the plain pointillé pattern A1; the edges of the foil are turned up, giving a tray-like appearance.

The main decorated surface of the mount has a central field of sub-triangular form with substantial frames and outer cloisonné borders; the frames show affinity with the designs of Inv. 12–14 and 17 (the small buckle with two matching mounts and the T-shaped strap-distributor). The repertoire of cell shapes and patterns, although much more restricted in Inv. 12–14, is markedly similar, mushroom and half-mushroom cells in combination with step-patterns being dominant (fig. 339). The edges of the curved mount are left plain. The running step-pattern cloisonné borders which flank the main field of the curved mount (fig. 341 *a*) are an angular version of the same theme as seen on the sides of Inv. 17 (fig. 328 *c*). As with Inv. 11, it is as though the cloisonné side-panels had crept up on to the front of the mount.

The dummy tongue-plate (fig. 341 *a*) and the cloisonné panel immediately below on which it impinges, strike a new note, not to my knowledge paralleled in any other Anglo-Saxon cloisonné work, but encountered in a pair of disc brooches from the grave of Queen

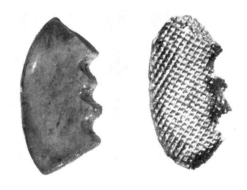

FIGURE 344   The dummy buckle: garnet with curved and stepped sides, and associated foil tray (type A1) from the large boss at the toe of Inv. 10. Garnet thickness 0·7 mm.
(Scale: 6/1)

477

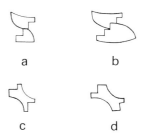

a   b

c   d

FIGURE 345   The dummy buckle: (*a*) theme of interlocked half-mushroom cells, giving the effect of an S-curve crossed by a line of steps, with (*c*) the residual cell form associated with this theme, (*b*), (*d*) the corresponding mushroom cell theme (using the two-step mushroom cell) and residual cell from a pair of disc brooches from the burial of Queen Arnegunde at St Denis. (Scale: 3/2)

Arnegunde at St Denis.[1] This is the rhythmic crossing of S-curves with straight ladders of step-pattern. This new and distinctive theme is brought about by a subtle juxtaposition of partial mushroom cells (half, or more than half, mushrooms) set upside down or back to back in relation to each other (figs. 340*j*, 345).[2]

Comparison of formal characteristics with the small cloisonné buckle Inv. 12 is instructive. This also has a dummy tongue-plate in the cloisonné work, defined below by a thick curved gold wall. The shoulders of the buckle-plate are cut away as in the curved mount. As in the mount, the root of the buckle-tongue extends over halfway down the dummy tongue-plate; the tongue itself stands out in relief and has a similar cross-section (figs. 321*a*, 341*a*). A prominent feature in the design, serving to close the main cloisonné field at the top and linking the two small bosses, is a narrow cloisonné-bearing bar. This consists of two solid-looking walls separated by a narrow line of plain rectangular stones, three oblong and two square, separated by light cell-walls. The two square garnets are no more than 1 mm square. There is an analogy with the curved zone in the cloisonné of the dummy tongue-plate of Inv. 12.

A notable feature of the mount, reminiscent in its exuberance of the packing of the curved hinge of Inv. 17 with garnets (fig. 335*b*), is the setting of continuous inlays of stones all the way round the curve of the loop (fig. 346). The use of the running step-pattern in the borders of the main field is continued here in deeper form, and the use of plain rectangular cells in the lateral bar between the two small bosses on the front of the mount is echoed. The upper surface of the loop is set with small plain cells of rectangular or keystone shape, with the running step-pattern below. The setting of this running step-pattern in garnets round the loop displays notable virtuosity on the part of the gem-cutter. While in the side-panels of Inv. 17 and Inv. 6 and 7 (fig. 328), and in the borders flanking the main cloisonné field of the rectangular buckle (fig. 337) and in the curved mount itself, the running step-pattern design is flat, here it is set out round a curve. Every stone is plano-convex and each is curved in two directions.

The back-plate

Down the edges of the back-plate small nicks occur, eight on one side, seven on the other, spaced at more or less regular intervals (figs. 341*b* and 342); their significance is not clear. The back-plate is a separate thin sheet of gold. The curved

[1] Arrhenius 1971, figures 124, 126. For Arnegunde's grave see Doppelfeld and Pirling 1966; France-Lanord and Fleury 1962.
[2] Somewhat similar rhythms built from step-pattern and curvilinear themes occur on the Heidenheim disc-brooch (Arrhenius 1971, fig. 126).

478

FIGURE 346   The dummy buckle: detail of the shoulders and loop (Inv. 10).
(Scale: approximately 5/1)

body of the mount and the loop are also separate pieces of metal, apparently joined with gold solder or a light weld (fig. 341 *b*). Two rivets which strengthened the join can be seen, their heads filed flat.

Construction of the bosses

The three bosses appear to be of similar construction, though the small bosses are less complex than the large one. All three are surrounded by double filigree collars, a thicker wire below and a thinner one above (fig. 432 *f*, *g*). The wires are beaded, not twisted. Inside the beaded wire collars, which rest on the projecting flange of a base plate on which the boss is constructed, an inward-curving circular gold wall rises to hold, for the two small bosses the single cabochon stone, and for the large boss a cloisonné garnet design of a central cruciform step-pattern cell of three steps a side surrounded by four supporting garnets.

The structure of the large cloisonné boss at the toe of the buckle is shown in figure 347, an enlarged oblique view into the interior structure where a garnet is missing, and in the section drawing figure 342. As in the two scabbard-bosses (p. 296) the central cruciform step-pattern garnet is supported on strong walls which run all the way up

479

FIGURE 347 The dummy buckle (Inv. 10): the toe, showing the empty cell from which the garnets and foil illustrated in figure 344 were removed. (Scale: 4/1)

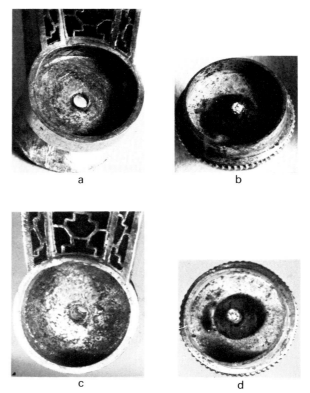

a

b

c

d

FIGURE 348 The dummy buckle: (a)–(d) details of the toe, showing (a) and (c) oblique and vertical views of the interior of the hollow cylinder into which the socket of the cloisonné and filigree bearing stud was inserted; (b), (d) views of the interior of the socket showing the shank of a large central rivet surrounded by remains of leather. (Scale: 2/1) (Photos: British Museum Research Laboratory)

from the base-plate. The cells beneath are empty. There is no record of any filling substance in the laboratory notes of 1945, and though this is not conclusive, the use of empty cells is characteristic of the gold jewellery as a whole (pp. 599–601). As in the scabbard-bosses the tall and very substantial cell-walls, which held the four peripheral stones, do not extend to the base at the edge of the setting: a gap runs all round the outer wall. The cells, except for that holding the central stone, are thus all interconnected internally. Had the cells from which the garnets were removed contained packing, this would not have been removed by the Research Laboratory in 1939 or 1945, without record; even had the now empty cells been cleaned out, the packing in the other cells where the garnets were not removable would not have been disturbed. Any filling in the cells whose tops remain sealed by garnets would show in the open spaces between the cells, but there is nothing to be seen. As in the scabbard-bosses (p. 285) we have a deep and elaborate construction in which the garnets are supported solely by pressure at the tops of empty cells (section 6, pp. 599–601 below).

480

As figures 342 and 348*b*, *d* show, a disc of leather survives inside the drum of the large boss immediately below the flat base-plate on which the cloisonné work is built. This is unconnected with the space available at the back of the mount to receive a strap, and since no washer is called for here it would seem to be the vestige of a substantial leather plug which filled the empty drum at the base of the setting.

Condition

The curved mount shows no sign of wear, and apart from a certain amount of scratching appears to be in virtually mint condition. The use of the mount in relation to the sword is discussed on pages 572-74.

IV TRIANGULAR ZOOMORPHIC STRAP-MOUNT OR COUNTER-PLATE
Inv. 18 (fig. 350)

Dimensions

Length	2·9 cm
Width	2·2 cm
Thickness of cloisonné-bearing main element	0·4 cm
Overall thickness of mount	0·9 cm
Length of back-plate	2·5 cm
Width of back-plate	2·1 cm
Thickness of back-plate	0·05 cm
Thickness of strap accommodated	0·4 cm

Weight	12·326 g
Number of garnets	56

Foil underlays. Types A1 and A2. The foil behind the three flat stones in the large circular settings is much more finely patterned than that used elsewhere on the mount, even in much smaller cells; it does not occur anywhere else in the Sutton Hoo material. The foil used in the other cells is of type A1.

Cell forms. Cell forms and patterns (including zoomorphic themes) are shown in figure 349.

The triangular mount differs from the other items of gold jewellery, both in shape and decorative treatment. It is a relatively small piece but solidly constructed. Its width corresponds exactly with that of the plate of the rectangular buckle Inv. 11, though the thickness of strap that could be accommodated, is greater. The triangular shape of the mount is distinctive, but its function as a mount is not clear. It is not a strap-end, since it is open on all sides and is far too thick to pass through any buckle-loop, even that of the great gold buckle. It might have served as a strap-distributor (p. 577 below), perhaps accommodating two thicknesses of 2 mm strap, one such strap probably being 2 cm wide (the width of the top end of the zoomorphic design), the other, at an angle to this, perhaps 2·5 cm wide to fit the length of the back-plate (fig. 350*b*) which is

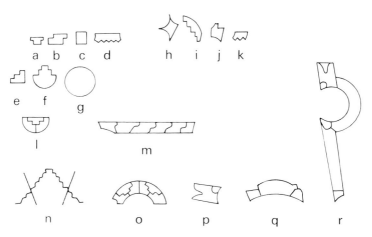

FIGURE 349 The triangular zoomorphic mount (Inv. 18): cell forms and patterns (a)–(g) basic cell types; (h)–(k) residual shapes; (l)–(o) themes and patterns; (p)–(r) zoomorphic and crypto-zoomorphic themes. (Scale: 3/2)

considerably shorter than the mount itself. It must have performed a specific function, since it is a solitary piece differing both formally and decoratively from the other mounts.[1] It could possibly have served as a counter-plate to the rectangular buckle, Inv. 11, but it does not match it in style. It is not decorated *en suite* with the buckle as counter-plates should be, nor does it seem to be a piece of equal quality.

The back-plate, for reasons not apparent, does not cover the whole area of the cloisonné-bearing part of the mount. It falls 4 mm short of the mount in length (fig. 351). Nevertheless the back-plate is wider than the main portion of the mount, and when the mount is viewed from the front the back-plate shows round the edges like a projecting ledge, suggesting that the cloisonné-bearing part of the mount was perhaps fitted to a strap or belt broader than itself. The mount shares its zoomorphic character, and triangular form, with the curved mount, Inv. 10. Apart from this, the two are worlds apart (p. 473). In both, the circular settings which project beyond the general outline mark the positions of the three rivets that hold the mount and its back plate together. At the back of the curved mount the rivet ends are flattened, a point of consequence (p. 574). In the triangular mount the rivet-heads at the back, although without the beaded collars seen on the two rivet-heads at the back of the rectangular buckle, Inv. 11, are domed and have a decorative effect.

In the triangular mount the three circular cells give the effect of the eyes and nostrils of an animal head, and this effect is exploited in the cloisonné design. The eyes are reinforced on the inside by a curved setting of cells with a thick outer cell-wall. Above the eyes the two cells at the upper corners of the mount give a suggestion of upstanding ears. They are also complete animal heads in themselves, each with its

---

[1] Strap-mounts, such as the rectangular mounts, Inv. 6–9, apart from embellishment, had the function of preventing the strap on which they were mounted from becoming twisted.

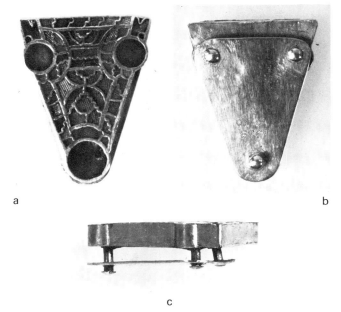

FIGURE 350 The triangular zoomorphic mount
(Inv. 18): (Scale: 3/2)

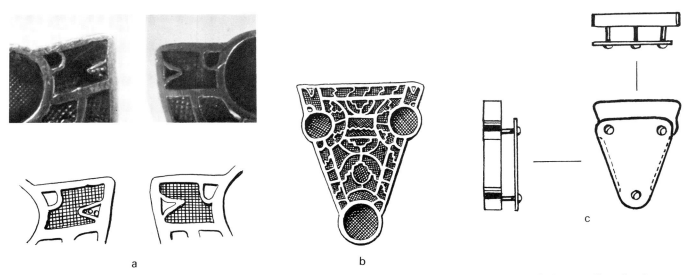

FIGURE 351 The zoomorphic mount (Inv. 18): (*a*) photographs and drawings of the small animal
heads in the cloisonné work; (*b*)–(*c*) drawings of the front, sides and back of the mount. (Scales: *a*, 4/1;
b, 3/2; *c*, 1/1)

contained eye and mouth and with a suggestion, even, in filigree granulation, of teeth
or tongue (figs. 351). These small animal heads are ingeniously constructed. Within
a single sub-rectangular cell two minor cells are built, one a simple curve cutting off
the corner to form the eye, and the other an acute-angled triangular cell, apparently
Plugged with a gold lid carrying three detached granules of filigree, which forms a mouth
(figs. 349*p*, 351*a*).[1]

---

[1] The granules and their metal base are missing from the mouth of one of the heads, but can be supposed
to have been present originally.

The mount follows the general fashion of thicker cell-walls dividing the surface into panelled fields. The mushroom cell occurs once only, in two-step form and upside down in relation to the zoomorphic design of the whole, in the lower centre of the mount, housed in step-pattern (fig. 351 b). Small T-shaped cells occur, and straight ligatures and plain rectangular cells. Some of the characteristics of the other jewelled pieces thus appear. The really surprising thing about this mount, however, in this context, is the apparent feebleness and incompetence of its workmanship. The design is muddled, uninspired and badly executed. This can be seen in the enlargement (fig. 350 a) and drawing (fig. 351). The step-pattern themes have lost all their crispness, the stepped angled cell-walls in the border at the top, for example, look like a line of tadpoles. Cells that should balance do not; well-known themes such as the stilted T-shaped cell within a semicircle (at the centre of the mount) are flattened; the T-cell alone in the panel above this is off-centre; and other such infelicities are easily found. Yet the patternwork in the eye surrounds and elsewhere, with T-shaped cells and straight walls in a narrow curved space bears some resemblance to that of the superior design and workmanship in similarly shaped fields on the scabbard-bosses (fig. 352).

Certain irregularities in the cloisonné design call for comment. The strong lines of the borders that divide the surface of the mount up into field and panels appear to break down at four points. This can be seen best in the panels that surround the eyes. At the top the thick outer wall of the panel round the eye joins a straight wall which, as well as serving as the underjaw of the little animal head, represents, above the eye, the inner

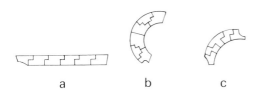

FIGURE 352   Cell-work details from (a), (b) the zoomorphic mount (Inv. 18) and (c) a scabbard-boss (Inv. 26). (Scale: 3/2)

border of the mount's side panel. At the lower end of the panel round the eye the thick outer border does not meet a similar transverse wall but joins on to the end of the thick wall which defines the side panel to form a right-angled corner. From this corner a thin straight cell-wall runs out to meet a small pear-shaped cell, fitted into the angle between the circular eye cell and the outer border of the mount. The same occurs on the opposite side of the mount in the corresponding position. At the foot of the mount a curved cell just above the large circular cell is similarly terminated by thin straight cell-walls forming pear-shaped cells in the two angles formed by the outside walls of the mount and the large circular cell.

This curious element in the design must be significant. It does not recur at the top of the mount, where the two animal heads occur. I suggest that we have here an example of a further if cryptic suggestion of the animal theme (fig. 349 q). The pear-shaped cells recall the treatment of animal hips, and the configuration at the toe of the mount, above the large circular cell, recalls strongly the crouched animal on the toe of the great buckle. The occurrence of cryptozoomorphic themes in cloisonné jewellery has recently been stressed by several authorities.[1] This

[1] Werner 1971; Arrhenius 1970, figs. 8–16; Arrhenius 1971, figs. 124–132; Speake 1970, figs. 4b, 3c, and 1975.

could well be the explanation of the treatment of the cell work on the triangular mount (fig. 349 p–r). Granular filigree occurs minimally on this mount, in the jaws of the two small animal heads. It is the only occurrence of granulation in the Sutton Hoo jewellery except for the shoulder-clasps (p. 607, figs. 434–436). It appears, as has been said above, to be associated with the use of a gold lid over the cell, but the purpose of the gold lid could be different here from that seen elsewhere in the jewellery. Its purpose seems to have been rather to act as a base for granulation to fill the diminutive animal mouth, rather than to neutralise a background space.

PLAIN STRAP-RUNNER IN THE FORM OF A TONGUELESS BUCKLE AND PLAIN STRAP-END

Plain strap-runner (Inv. 15; fig. 353)

Dimensions

Length of plate	1·1 cm
Width of plate	1·7 cm
Diameter of ornamental rivet-heads	0·5 cm
Length of loop	2·45 cm
Width of loop	1·1 cm
Maximum width of loop aperture	0·4 cm
Length of loop aperture	1·8 cm
Thickness of loop	0·4 cm
Gap between front and back plates of mount (i.e. thickness of strap accommodated)	0·2 cm

Weight
9·7 g

FIGURE 353 The plain gold strap-mount (Inv. 15): (a)–(b) front and rear views; (c) end view. (Scale: 3/2)

The loop and plate are plain. The short plate is cut away very slightly at the corners through which the loop passes. The plate consists of a single comparatively thick sheet of gold folded over on itself. The buckle-loop passes through the folded edge. Two rivets hold the folded plate together and would retain the strap (fig. 353 c). The rivet-heads are large and ornamental, with massive domed heads and minute filigree collars encircling them. This is a piece of very high quality and fine workmanship. The mechanism operates fluently and the loop swings freely through an arc of some

485

330 degrees. The loop is smooth and rounded, of uniform circular section except where it narrows to pass through the plate. In this respect it differs from the loops of the buckles, Inv. 10, 11 and 12, which are all flattened on their undersides. The two rivets are 3·5 mm in length overall and their ends are burred over. The width of the plate (1·7 cm) is approximately equal to the overall width of the pyramids, Inv. 26 and 27 (1·8 cm), but broader than the interior space designed to accommodate the strap-element that passed through the pyramids. The plate width of Inv. 15 also equals that of the two cloisonné strap-mounts, Inv. 13 and 14.

Small plain gold strap-end (Inv. 16; fig. 354)

Dimensions

Length	1·1 cm
Width	1·0 cm
Width of strap accommodated	0·9 cm
Thickness of strap accommodated	0·125 cm

Weight

1·570 g

a   b   c

FIGURE 354 (a)–(c) The small plain gold
strap-end (Inv. 16). (Scale: 2/1)

This diminutive plain gold strap-end is finely made. The strap was held by two rivets at the open end; the heads and spread ends of the rivets have been filed away on both outer faces flush with the surfaces of the strap-end. Although the strap width is appreciably narrower than the opening at the back of the two pyramids, Inv. 26 and 27, measured at the base level, this opening contracts with the tapering of the pyramids, and at the level of the top of the internal bar crossing the back of the pyramids the strap-end could not be accommodated; thus the pyramids could not have been carried on the strap associated with this strap-end.

1. *The purse-lid (frame and contained plaques and studs)*
(pls. 13, 14; figs. 358, 367)

Dimensions

Length	19·0 cm
Width (without the hinges)	8·3 cm

Number of garnets — 1,526
Number of millefiori inlays — 33
Number of blue glass inlays — 4
Number of lidded cells — 101

Foil underlays (fig. 319). Type B1 only is used in the purse-frame. A1 is used on the studs and both A1 and B1 in the plaques.

Cell forms. The cell forms used on the purse-frame are summarised in figure 359. Those of the individual plaques and studs are illustrated in the text along with the descriptions of the plaques and studs (figs. 368, 370, 371, 374, 376, 378).

1. *The frame and lid*

The remains of the purse-lid consist of the curved gold outer frame with three hinged gold plates at the top to which were attached the straps by which the purse was suspended, and various gold plaques and studs that decorated the lid within the frame. No trace remained of the substance of the purse or its lid.

FIGURE 355   The purse (Inv. 2) *in situ*: with other pieces from Area A (p. 440). (Photo: M. Guido)

487

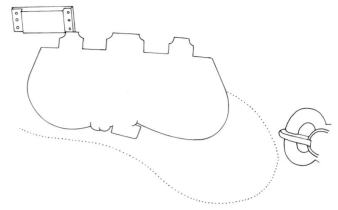

FIGURE 356 The purse: drawing based on figure 355 indicating the possible outline of the bag of the purse.

The frame and its plaques and studs are embellished all over with continuous spreads of unbroken cloisonné work of garnets with some polychrome inlays (in general millefiori, but in certain instances blue glass). A separate gold clasp or sliding catch (Inv. 3) was attached to the mouth of the bag. The catch mechanism is described on page 516.

The gold frame consists of a straight bar at the top and a curved portion below. The sides of the frame swell outwards and downwards from the ends of the straight bar and are then brought inwards and upwards to meet in a central re-entrant curve. At the centre of this curve a hinged tongue projects (fig. 380d). This was designed to engage and lock into the sliding catch that had been sewn into the lip of the bag.

Though no trace is recorded of the material of which the bag of the purse was made, a curving line discernible in photographs may represent its outline (figs. 355 and 356). It is not supported by any note or comment by the excavators. This line could possibly represent the loop of the belt on which the great gold buckle was mounted, and from which the purse seems also to have been suspended (p. 565), but it seems more likely to represent the outline of the bag.

The purse-lid as excavated lay upside down and at an angle oblique to the central longitudinal axis of the burial deposit, the keel-line (fig. 314). Its three hinged strap-terminations pointed to the south-west. Figure 360 shows the purse-lid and the contents of the purse (coins, blanks and ingots) as drawn at full scale in the ground by Stuart Piggott; figure 355 shows the purse in the ground in relation to nearby items of jewellery.

When found the frame was distorted; it was subsequently straightened (figs. 357a, b). The coins and ingots had accumulated on what was in the soil the lower end of the distorted lid (fig. 360).

The frame enclosed seven decorative plaques—three matching pairs and one double plaque were arranged in two rows (pl. 13a, fig. 358a). At each end of the upper row is a plaque of hexagonal form, the display surface of which is completely covered with

488

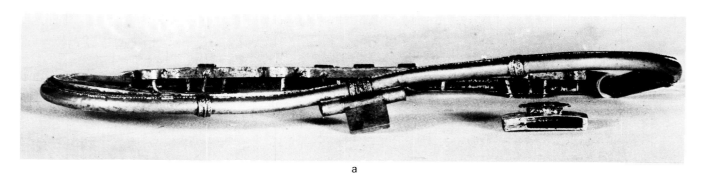

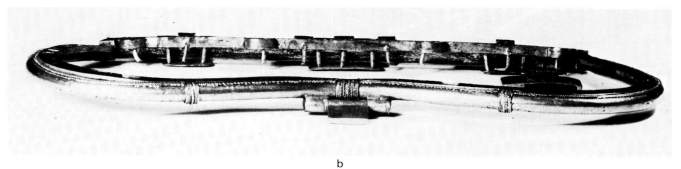

FIGURE 357 The purse: oblique view of the frame of the purse-lid (*a*) as excavated; (*b*) after straightening. The sliding catch from the bag is on the right. (Scale: slightly under 1/1)

a small-scale geometric cloisonné design round a large central cell that contained a millefiori inlay. Between the two hexagonal plaques is a larger double plaque which, since the purse-lid narrows towards the top, gives the impression of a pair of similar plaques that have been amalgamated to save space. The design of the double plaque is wholly zoomorphic. It depicts four erect animals in facing pairs with interlacing limbs and jaws. The bodies of the two animals appearing back to back in the middle of the plaque are bent sharply outwards and interlocked, thus amalgamating the two designs. The distinction between the two plaques is maintained by a re-entrant triangular space at the bottom of the plaque between the pairs of animals. In the lower row the outer plaques are an identical pair, depicting, in outline and internal detail, a man between two erect animals identical in form and size. The two inner plaques are also a pair but reversed, facing inwards. Each represents a bird of prey stooping on and in the act of grasping a smaller broad-billed bird, presumably a duck. Also within the frame of the purse-lid are four circular studs, two large, placed at each end of the lid on a median line corresponding to the maximum length of the lid; and two small, further in, each placed centrally below one of the two man-between-beasts plaques.

The field within the frame is entered by four round-ended inward projections from the straight bar that forms the top element of the frame. These four projections each carry in cloisonné work a clear, simple theme of a T-shaped cell supported on a stem. The projections are in the form of stilted semicircles, the sides being slightly prolonged. Two of the projections are of smaller size, two larger, but their arrangement is the

489

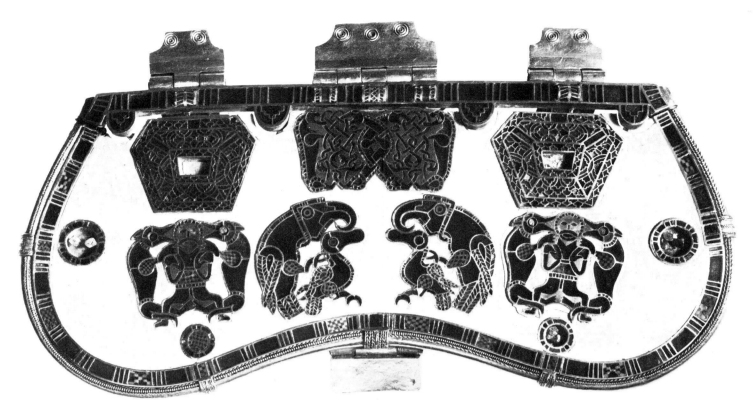

a

b

FIGURE 358 The purse: (*a*) the purse-lid, as reconstructed in 1945; (*b*) rear view of the reconstruction. (Scale: 1/1)

490

reverse of that in the case of the studs; the outside projections are the smaller, the inner ones the larger, creating a subtle balance with the disposition of the studs. The small projections occur at the extreme ends of the bar. The large, in the middle, separate the central double plaque from the hexagonal plaques to either side of it. The smaller cells show a simple one-step T-shaped cell. In the larger projections the T-shaped cell is correspondingly larger and has two steps (fig. 359 k). The placing of the plaques and studs, given above, is not in doubt, since they were recorded undisturbed *in situ* (fig. 355).

The frame (Inv. 2 (a); figs. 357, 358)

Dimensions

Length	19·0 cm
Width	8·3 cm

Weight	172·5 g
Number of garnets	241
Number of millefiori inlays	13

Foil underlays. B 1 only.

Cell forms. The four semicircular inward projections from the purse-bar (the straight top element of the frame) contain single T-shaped cells, with one and two steps. The cells in the frame otherwise consist of regular rectangular forms, with very small parallelograms and diamond or half-diamond cells in the dummy hinges (below).

The purse-frame, of gold throughout, is made in two main parts which join: a straight bar at the top, with the three hinged strap-holders on the outside and the four inward projections into the field; and the curved element which fits round the rest of the lid and encloses the plaques and studs. The straight bar is of heavier, thicker and stronger construction than the curved portion of the frame.

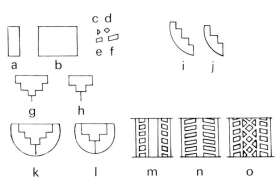

The straight bar is the only part of the frame to have features in relief. On it are five non-functional barrel-shaped projections. These projections occur only opposite the hinges by which

FIGURE 359 The purse: cell forms and patterns used in the frame (a)–(h) basic forms; (i), (j) residual shapes; (k)–(o) themes of patterns. (Scale: 3/2)

the strap-terminators are attached—one projection opposite each of the two outer hinges and three opposite the central one. The projections are set with garnets. Some of these, in the three projections opposite the central hinge, are of minute size.[1] In the case of the two outer hinges, the single barrel-like projections coincide

---

[1] The setting of garnets in a hinge (in this case a pseudo-hinge and not part of the moving mechanism) recalls their analogous use in the hinge of the T-shaped strap-distributor, Inv. 17 (fig. 335 b).

with and pick out the tubular portion of the mechanism which is cast in one piece with the strap-terminator; but in the central hinge the barrel-shaped projections coincide with the three tubular portions of the hinge mechanism that are attached to the purse-bar.

The straight bar has no filigree edge-binding and no polychrome inlays, both of which are prominent features of the curved portion of the frame.

The curved portion of the frame defines the swelling and re-entrant shape of the lid. At the centre of the bottom a projecting tongue is hinged, to engage a sliding catch attached to the bag, thus closing the lid. The frame is made up of two components: an inner shallow flat tray with cloisonné decoration which, in several sections (fig. 365), runs its whole length; and a strong outer tube of uninterrupted construction, which has a U-shaped cross-section opening on the inside (fig. 363 *a, d*). The substance of the lid (ivory, bone, wood or leather), to which were riveted the cloisonné tray on the inside of the frame, and all the contained plaques and studs, ran under the tray and into the hollow outer rim all the way round. It was held to the outer rim

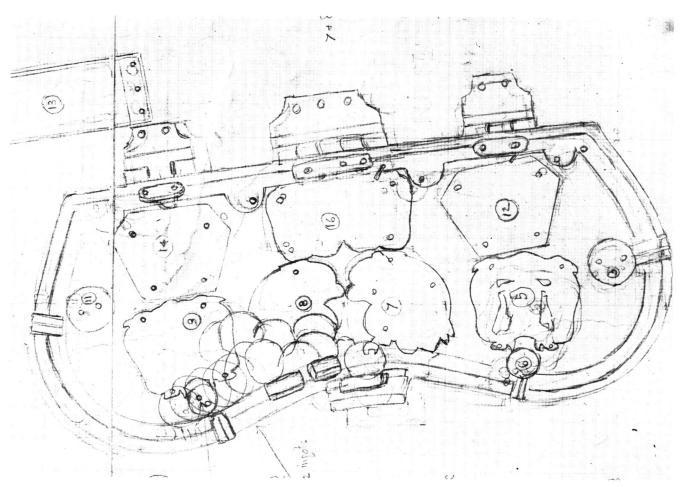

FIGURE 360   The purse-lid upside down in the ground, as drawn by Stuart Piggott.
(Scale: slightly reduced)

a

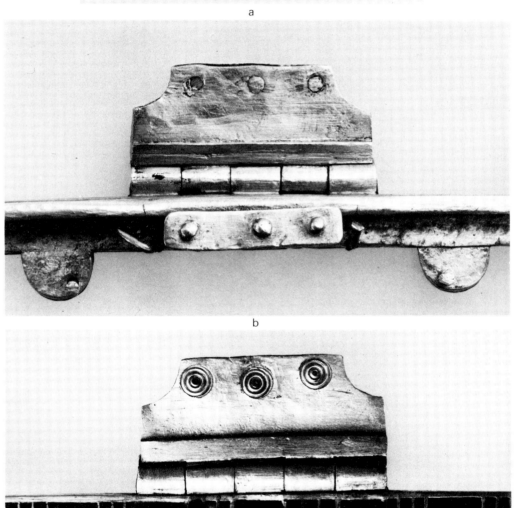

b

c

FIGURE 361   The purse: enlarged details of the central hinge and
adjacent bar. (Scale: 2/1)

493

and to its cloisonné lining tray by five filigree clips, three broad and two narrow. At the back of the lid the ends of the filigree clips are held by gold rivets inserted from below through the substance of the lid and clenched inside the gold back-plate of the tray (figs. 363c, 365 and 380e). Two rivets were used for each of the broad clips as against one rivet for each of the narrow clips (fig. 358b). The ends of the filigree clips which appear at the front of the lid show two different methods of attachment. The three at the bottom are soldered to the inner edge of the tube (figs. 358 and 380d). The two upper clips are tucked in between the tube and the lining tray.

The hinges and hinged tongue on the purse frame. The two outer hinges accommodate a 12 mm leather or cloth strap. The central hinge accommodates one with a width of 22 mm. The thickness for all three straps is only 1 mm, suggesting cloth rather than leather. The hinges move freely. Each of the smaller hinges has two decorative devices in the form of dot and double circle ornaments; the longer hinge has three. These are really rivet-heads which have been flattened by application of the same drill that was used to cut the circles in the eyes of the birds of prey in the two bird plaques.

The frame and evidence for the assembly of the lid, plaques and studs

Although the relative positions of the plaques and studs within the frame are known (fig. 355), the exact assembly of the lid, in default of any of the original substance on which the gold elements were mounted, is only to be worked out from internal evidence. The lid was restored in the Research Laboratory in 1945, and this restoration was on exhibition until 1972 and has appeared in all illustrations of the purse so far published (fig. 358). White-painted plywood, intended to represent an original sheet supposedly of bone or ivory, was used for the substance of the lid; into this the plaques and studs were countersunk so that their garnet decoration lay flush with the surface of the plywood. The plywood was fitted into the purse-frame with its upper surface flush with the upper surface of the lining tray, not passing under it.

At the time it was thought that the lid had been composed of two layers: an upper one (h in fig. 263b) of the same thickness as the plaques and studs, into which the latter were countersunk so that their faces were flush with its surface; and a slightly more extensive lower layer (d) which projected all round, to run under the marginal cloisoneé lining tray and fit into the open tubular outer element of the frame. The plaques and studs, sunk through the upper layer, were thought to have rested on the lower one, with the rivets which project from their backs penetrating through the lower layer and clamped on its underside (fig. 363).

There is, however, no evidence for the existence of the upper layer then envisaged. The 1945 reconstruction, its plaques and studs countersunk flush with the surface of the lid, led its authors into something of a *reductio ad absurdum*. This arises from the openwork design of the four plaques in the lower row (fig. 358a, b). Since these were visualised as countersunk the restorers felt that the holes of their openwork designs

494

a

b

FIGURE 362 The purse: enlarged detail of (*a*) the side
hinge and the right-hand upper corner of the frame, showing
the junction of the straight and curved parts; (*b*) back view
of the corresponding left-hand corner. (Scale: 2/1)

must be filled up, since otherwise they would show as awkward narrow irregular and
very small holes, 3 mm deep, in the flush surface of the lid. They solved this difficulty
by filling the holes with plaster painted to match the surrounding lid, as may be seen
in the back view of the lid (fig. 358*b*) in which its lower layer is omitted.[1] If in the
original these holes had been filled in, irregular pieces of the material of the lid (? bone
or ivory?) would have been needed to fill them, producing the effect achieved with
plaster in the reconstruction. It would not have been easy to fit such plugs of bone

---

[1] In this reconstruction as much as possible of the back of
the purse mounts was left exposed for purposes of access and
study. The supposed lower layer of the lid was omitted. The
new reconstruction, with the plaques free standing, is also left
partly exposed at the back.

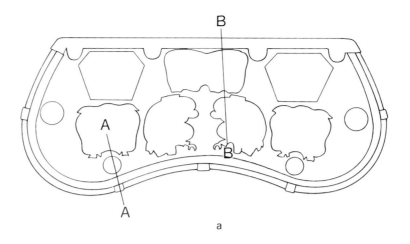

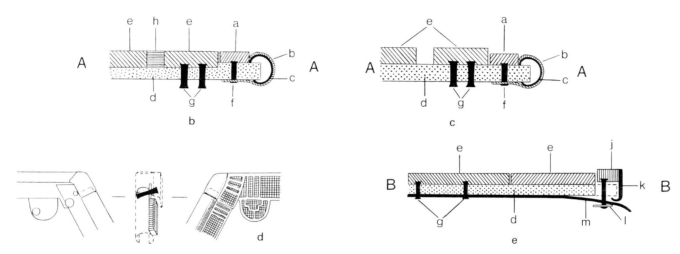

FIGURE 363   The purse: (*a*) sketch of the purse showing the location of the sections; (*b*) (*c*) cross-sections of the purse lid (A–A) as reconstructed (*b*) in 1945 and (*c*) in 1972; (*d*) drawing illustrating the method of attachment of the straight and curved parts of the frame (compare fig. 362); (*e*) sectional drawing through the purse-bar and lid (B–B) showing the method of attachment of the (?) leather of the bag and its suggested extension to line the back of the lid. (Scales: *b*, *c*, 3/2; *d*, *e*, 1/1)

or ivory, twenty-four in number, securely into these holes. It could have been done if desired by a craftsman as skilled as this master-jeweller, but if he had intended that these parts of his design were merely to be blocked off, why did he not extend to them the lidded-cell technique (p. 598) devised for that express purpose and so effectively used in the two outer plaques of the lower register and, supremely well, in the double plaque above? Conversely, if the master-goldsmith intended these spaces to be filled by the same substance as the lid, why did he not supply the individual mounts with a continuous base-plate, so that the inlays could be cut and inserted into the residual cells as if they were garnets? It seems clear that the master-goldsmith intended the openwork design to register as such. The sides of the plaques, external and internal, are fully finished, as though intended to be seen; this applies also to the sides of the remaining three plaques and to the four studs (figs. 364 and 367). Appliqués normally stand out on the surface to which they are applied. Countersinking of inlays or enamels, giving the champlevé effect seen in the 1945 reconstruction, would be characteristic of the Celtic background rather than of Germanic goldsmiths' work. The effect of the free-standing plaques and studs in the purse-lid is illustrated in figure 367. A similar effect must have been achieved in the Beckum purse (pl. 22 d).

The construction of the purse-lid (figs. 357, 358 and 363)

The straight bar which constitutes the top of the purse frame is a relatively complex structure (figs. 358 a, b, 366). It is thicker and more solidly built than the curved part of the frame. The general thickness of the straight bar (excluding the projecting barrel-like mouldings) varies between 8 and 9 mm; the thickness of the curved section varies between 5 and 6 mm. In addition, standing off at three points at the back of the bar are long and narrow gold washers, held by rivets thicker and longer than the others, projecting for a further 1·5–2 mm below the under-surface of the bar. The bar is also thickened and strengthened by the barrel-shaped projections already mentioned.

The decorative plaques and studs within the frame have a uniform thickness of 3 mm. This is the same as the general thickness (excluding the barrel-like projections) of the solid part of the straight bar, which carries its cloisonné decoration. The rivets projecting from the backs of the plaques and studs were the means whereby they were fixed to the purse-lid (fig. 364); they vary in effective length between 3·5 and 4·5 mm, indicating that the substance of the lid was not of uniform thickness. The average thickness may be taken as 4 mm.

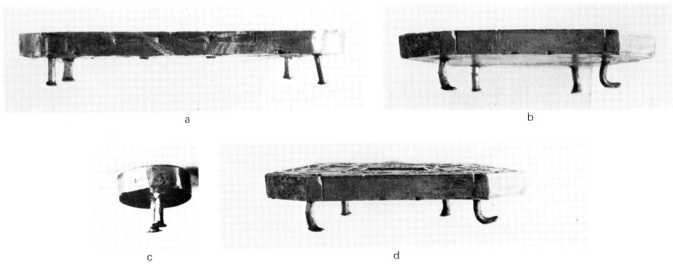

a

b

c

d

FIGURE 364   The purse: side views of two decorative plaques, (*a*) Inv. 2(b); (*b*), (*d*) two views of Inv. 2(d); and (*c*) of one of the small circular studs. (Scale: 2/1) (Photo: *c* British Museum Research Laboratory)

The construction of the curved frame in relation to the plaques and to its own inner lining tray is as shown in figure 363. In the new, post-1972 reconstruction (fig. 363 c), the plaques have been raised one millimetre in relation to the frame. There is otherwise no difference from their positioning in the previous reconstruction. The chief difference is that the postulated upper layer of (?)bone or ivory in which the plaques and studs were supposedly set has been removed, leaving them free-standing on the lid surface.

In the old reconstruction the plaques were set with their faces flush with the top of the cloisonné tray (shown as 'a' in fig. 363). Since this tray is 2 mm thick, whereas the plaques are 3 mm thick, the backs of the latter would have projected 1 mm below the level of the bottom of the tray (the plaques and the white substance housing them can be seen so projecting in fig. 358 b). This being so, the 4 mm attachment rivets (g) which emerge from their backs would have projected at least 2 mm below the level of the bottom of the tray, as demonstrated in figure 363 b.

In raising the plaques so that they rest on the substance of the lid their surfaces have been lifted to a level 1 mm higher than the cloisonné surface of the lining tray. This in turn reduces the projection of the rivet-heads below the supposed lower surface of the lid from 2 to 1 mm (fig. 363 c). It is possible that this apparent gap between the rivet-heads and the (?)bone or ivory lid (which must have fluctuated, since the lengths of rivets projecting from the backs of the plaques only averages 4 mm, but in fact vary between 3·5 and 4·5 mm) is due to unevennesses in the thickness of the lid substance. It is perhaps more likely that the material of the purse bag may have been brought up through the back of the purse-bar and extended to line the underside of the lid, covering the (?)bone, ivory or wood in a 1 mm thick layer. The gold heads of the rivets holding the plaques and studs would be visible against the material.

It will be noted that in figure 363 the outer element of the rim, c, is not shown attached to the lid. Rim and lid may have been held fast together by adhesives inside the rim, but if so no trace of such adhesives has survived. The tubular rim seems to have been held to the lid only by any clamping effect which may have been imparted to it and by the five filigree-covered clips fixed at intervals round the frame (pl. 13 a, figs. 358 a and 365). The rim itself is held in place at either end by a dovetail joint with the straight bar which forms the top of the frame. The tube proper of the rim projects beyond the limits of its surface filigree and dovetails into two plain gold sockets soldered on to the extreme ends of the purse-bar (figs. 362 and 363 d).

One might suppose that the thickness of the (?)bone or ivory lid generally exceeded the uniform 3 mm of the opening in the inside of the curved frame intended to receive it, and that its under-surface was stepped down to arrive at the reduced 3 mm thickness that would slot into the frame. This does not seem to have been so. The five clips that bind the frame (fig. 358 b) after adhering tightly to the curving outer surface of the tube, flatten out uniformly on to what must have been the under-surface of the lid. To this they were held by rivets which ran upwards through the substance of the lid into the underside of the cloisonné tray, where they were clenched (fig. 365). The distance between the inner surface of the flattened-out lower ends of the clips and the under-surface of the tray must give the true thickness of the lid substance at these points. This measurement (3 mm) is the same in the case of each of the five clips. It seems unlikely that the clips would have been countersunk into a lid of extra thickness stepped down to 3 mm only where it entered the frame: there would be little need for such refinements of work on the inside of the lid. We can perhaps reasonably assume that the 3 mm thickness given both by the opening on the inside of the frame and by the spacing, a little further in from the frame, between the ends of the flattened-off clips and the underside of the lining tray, extended uniformly over the whole area of the lid. If so (that is, if the lid substance was essentially 3 mm thick over its whole extent), when the seven plaques were super-imposed on it the rivets extending from their backs would project between 0·5 and 1·5 mm clear of its under-surface. This seems to indicate that the lid was lined with, or that it was itself composed of, a substance either of markedly varying thickness, or capable of com-pression, such as leather.

FIGURE 365 The purse: enlarged detail of the back of the frame, showing a join between two sections of the cloisonné lining-tray, and rivets connecting the tray with a filigree binding clip. The photograph is taken at the central point of the curved portion of the frame and shows the back of the hinged tongue that engages the sliding catch on the purse bag (cf. fig. 363). (Scale: 2/1)

The question whether the lid was lined is related to the question, how was it attached to the bag?—for the lining substance would most probably have been the material of the bag introduced onto the back of the lid. The method by which the bag was attached to the lid is illustrated in figure 363 e, a section through the purse-bar at its centre point, and is best understood by examining the construction of the purse-bar along its length. Figure 357 b provides a low-angle view looking directly into the interior of the empty purse-bar from the inside. This photograph, taken after the bar had been straightened in the Research Laboratory in 1939, is shown in figure 366, with various components lettered. Fifteen rivet or rivet-like shanks or projections (a–o) can be seen. Of these, seven (a–g) can be accounted for as attaching three long gold washers (w) to the cloisonné-bearing top element of the bar. The three long washers are centred on the hinge positions. They vary in length; the central washer, of rectangular form, is the longest, matching the greater length of the central hinge as compared with the two outer hinges; it is held by three rivets (fig. 366 c, d, e). The

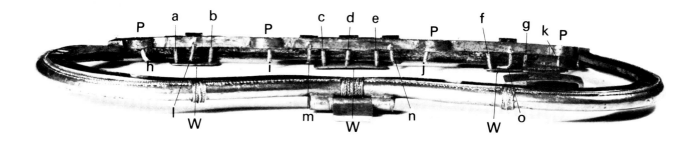

FIGURE 366 The purse: oblique view of the empty frame. The five raised cloisonné mouldings can be clearly seen in profile above the level of the bar; the four cloisonné-decorated inward projections are marked P and the three gold washers W; fifteen rivet-like shanks are lettered a–o.

two outer washers are shorter, in agreement with the shorter length of the two outer hinges; they are of oval form, or, at least, rectangles with rounded ends; each is held by two rivets. The seven rivets all have rounded heads (fig. 361). In each case the clearance between the inner surface of the washer and the under-surface of the cloisonné-bearing upper element of the bar is 6 mm.

Four other rivets (h–k) are attached one each to the four deeper-than-semicircular inward projections (p) from the frame-bar; these rivets are thick and appreciably shorter than the seven that hold the washers. They have a 4 mm clearance. They held the main substance of the lid to the straight bar. The seven longer rivets also held the lid substance, but served in addition to fasten to the back of the lid something else, an additional element not held by the shorter rivets. This additional element had a thickness of 2 mm less the washer-thickness (about 1 mm); in other words, the additional element was a layer of a millimetre or slightly over in thickness. This was presumably the leather or cloth of the purse-bag, which would have been drawn into the lid under the straight bar, to pass over the washers and to be fastened by them to the back edge of the lid substance. In addition, adhesive might have been used to hold this cloth or leather to the lid. It remains uncertain whether this leather or textile covered the back of the lid.

In figure 366 four other shanks (l–o) remain to be accounted for. These are driven in at an oblique angle, calculated to miss the long washers referred to above. They occur under four of the five raised barrel-shaped cloisonné mouldings on the frame. Two of them (fig. 366n and o) are not rivets but long nails, the ends of which have been hammered over. They have been driven in from the front. These four obliquely-running nails or rivets were evidently intended, like the stout rivets through the deeper-than-semicircular projections, to penetrate and hold the substance of the lid. Their obliqueness—each can be seen to disrupt the vertical edge of the cloisonné tray

500

to some degree (fig. 361, n)—is a puzzling feature. As their clearance, allowing for their obliqueness, is not as great as that of the rivets holding the long washers, it may be that they were inserted before the cloth or leather of the bag was introduced, and were not intended to hold it. If the substance of the lid was bone, ivory or even wood, the gold nails must have been driven into prepared holes. The fact that these were oblique would not present any special difficulty. Their function is not clear, but it is possible that the five convex drum-like elements are separate settings inserted into the cloisonné tray, in lieu of individual cell-walls for these tiny stones, and that the oblique nails or rivets were intended to hold these complete settings in place without fouling the long washers that were to be fitted, or had been fitted, directly below them.

If this is so the central drum-shaped setting of the five, which does not coincide with an oblique nail as the others do, must have been riveted so that in this instance only the rivet served to hold both the drum-shaped setting and the long washer. This is probably the true explanation, as here alone the functions could be combined; the drum-settings elsewhere do not coincide, as they do here, with the positions mechanically necessary for the balanced holding of the long washers at the back of the frame.

The curved portion of the frame is joined to the straight bar by a weak joint at each end. It will be seen that the top of the curved portion of the frame is set at a slightly lower level than that of the straight element (fig. 362 a). The upper surface of the lining tray of the curved part of the frame is set down in relation to the cloisonné upper surface of the bar, so that an extension of its base-plate can pass under the bottom of the cloisonné-bearing element of the bar (fig. 363 d). Similarly, an extension of the tubular part of the frame passes inside the socket built to receive it at each end of the bar. The join is weak and lacks rigidity. Apart from the dovetailing of the outer extensions of the curved frame with the sockets, only two rivets at each end, passing through an extension of the floor of the lining tray, useful it would seem for little more than preventing lateral movement, hold the two parts of the frame together. The weakness of these joints suggests that it was the substance of the lid that supplied rigidity and held the lid together, which in turn seems to indicate that the substance was not leather, but bone, ivory or wood.

The material of the purse-lid

There is no evidence of the nature of the substance of the lid on to which the gold plaques, studs and frame were mounted. In the literature hitherto it has been said to be of 'bone or ivory'.[1] This claim was based on the opinion expressed in 1939–40 by the Research Laboratory that the condition of the (gold) rivets was such as to indicate that they had been fastened through something 'harder than wood', and hence, presumably, bone or ivory. The justification for this view is not now apparent. Whatever it was, the substance of the lid must have been strong enough to supply

---

[1] Cf. the British Museum *Handbook* in its various editions.

501

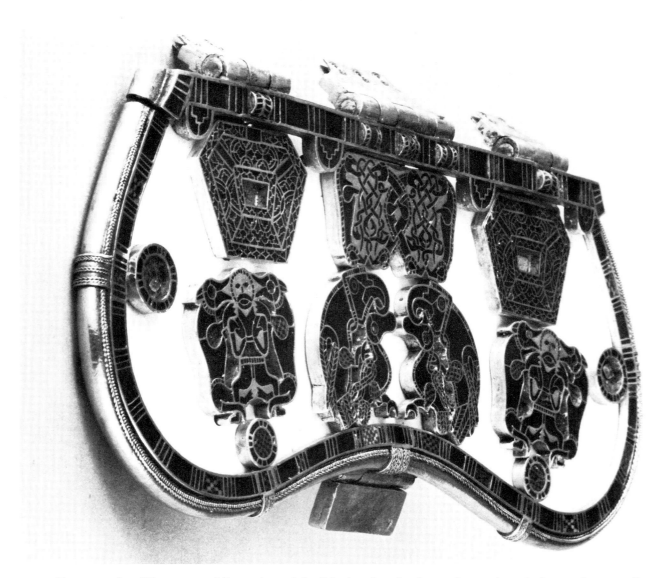

FIGURE 367   The purse: oblique view of the lid, showing the decorative studs and plaques free-standing on the surface in accordance with the 1972 reconstruction. (Scale: enlarged)

rigidity at the weak joins between the tubular frame and the straight bar (above). For this reason it seems unlikely that leather could have been used, but it is possible, as the thickness would be 3 or 3·5 mm, that the substance might have been hide. It may also seem likely that the substance of the lid was not leather because the lid itself, as distinct from a possible lining attached to its back, cannot have been a natural extension of the substance of the purse-bag, which could well have been of leather, as in the Krefeld-Gellep purse (fig. 383) and that from the Beckum *Fürstengrab*.[1] The lid substance of the Sutton Hoo purse was a separate entity completely enclosed by its frame.

Attachment of the lid to the bag occurred only at the back of the straight bar at

[1] Winkelmann 1962.

the top of the frame, where the substance of the bag was clamped by the three long gold washers. It is possible that the leather of the bag (1 mm or a little more in thickness) thus introduced to attach the bag to the lid, may also have been used to cover the back of the lid, being anchored to it by the four circular studs, which have extra long shanks and which could thus be seen to have had a structural as well as a decorative purpose. Wood, bone or ivory seem more probable substances than leather, and of these bone or ivory (either elephant or walrus ivory) would be the less likely to warp.

2. *The cloisonné plaques and studs contained within the purse frame*

Double plaque with zoomorphic interlace (Inv. 2(b); pl. 13b; fig. 369)

Dimensions

Height	2·3 cm
Length	4·3 cm
Thickness	0·4 cm

Weight   18·454 g

Number of garnets and lidded cells. Garnets 203, lidded cells 72 (estimated, because of ambiguity in certain cases).

Foil underlays. Type A1 in small or narrow cells (e.g. bordering cells and jaw and leg interlaces); B1 in all the larger cells (body, head, etc.).

Cell forms. These are in general unique shapes dictated by animal anatomy. Lines of minute rectangular cell forms are used as bordering (fig. 368 a–b). Residual or background cell shapes, and the garnet-cutting needed to fill them, are eliminated by use of a 'lidded cell' technique (see below, p. 598), by which plain gold lids are used instead of garnet inlays to seal off background shapes.

Two otherwise separate pairs of facing erect animals, with elongated jaws and legs

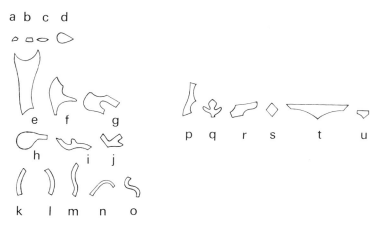

FIGURE 368 The purse: cell shapes used in the zoomorphic double plaque, Inv. 2(b): (a)–(o) standard bordering cells and unique forms devised in executing the animal design; (p)–(u) select background cells sealed by gold lids. (Scale: 3/2)

503

a

b

c

FIGURE 369 The zoomorphic double plaque, Inv. 2(b): (a),
(b) front and back; (c) radiograph print enlarged to the same
scale. (Scale: 2/1)

interlacing in the space between them, are linked by the interlocking back to back
of the two inside animals on each pair. The resulting effect of two similar but separate
plaques merging is reinforced by the re-entrant triangle at the bottom of the plaque
in the centre, which tends to separate the pairs of animals from each other.

Lines of very small rectangular garnets are used for bordering. The backbones of

504

the animals are lined with small cells, as in the case of the boars on the shoulder-clasps (fig. 390). The hips or hindquarters of the animals are also outlined in small garnets (cf. the treatment of human heads and animal haunches in the man-between-beasts plaques, fig. 377). It should be noted that while in the four plaques, Inv. 2c–f, animal and bird eyes are circles set in the middle of the head, in the double plaque the eyes are of narrow pointed oval or lozenge shape and set in the top of the head. Apart from the achievement of fluent interlace in the cloisonné medium, in itself a *tour de force* also seen in the shoulder-clasps and the two rectangular mounts Inv. 8 and 9, the plaque offers a good and early example of 'penetration' where, above the triangular re-entrant in the profile of the plaque at bottom centre, the bodies of the two central animals intersect, the backbone of the animal on the left (fig. 369 a) being clearly seen to pass through the body of the other animal involved. Several examples of penetration occur in the zoomorphic interlace of the gold buckle (p. 550, figs. 396 and 406 a, b).

The openwork technique in the four representational plaques in the lower ornamental register on the lid clarifies the pictorial subject matter and gives it meaning and visual impact. In the double plaque 2(b) the openwork method is replaced by an extensive use of lidded cells (cells sealed with plain gold lids, instead of being set with stones) which effectively block out the background areas. The number of concealed cells in this plaque is estimated to be seventy-two. The fragile nature of the central interlace elements would have made any attempts to reproduce the design in openwork impracticable, hence the use throughout of lidded cells. A large garnet is missing from the head of the animal on the right.

The design as a whole appears to be a version in gold and cut stones of the subject of interlinked horses more naturalistically rendered in stamped gilt-bronze foil on the flange of the shield-boss (pl. 5 a; figs. 39, 384 c).

The back of the plaque (fig. 369 b) shows four rivets in the four corners, and eleven holes, some of rivet size and one containing a broken-off rivet-shank. The remainder are apparently to be connected with the reconditioning or repair of the plaque (p. 600 below).

Hexagonal plaques (Inv. 2(c) and (d); pl. 14 c; fig. 372)
Dimensions of both plaques

Height	2·8 cm
Width	3·3 cm
Thickness	0·3 cm

	2(c)	2(d)
Weight	13·539 g	16·872 g
Number of garnets used	223	230

Foil underlays. Type A1. No foil is used behind the three large plain cells of each plaque (fig. 370 d, e). Type B1 occurred in the central trapezoidal cell beneath the millefiori inlay in 2(c).

Cell forms. Cell forms and themes are illustrated in figures 370 and 371.

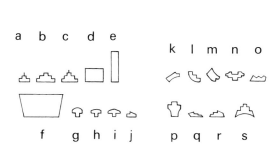

FIGURE 370 The hexagonal mounts, Inv.
2(c), 2(d): (a)–(j) basic and (k)–(s) residual
cell shapes. (Scale: 3/2)

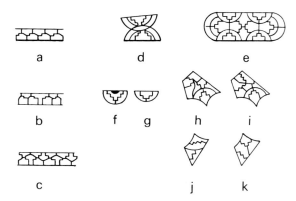

FIGURE 371 The hexagonal mounts: (a)–(k)
Cloisonné themes and patterns; (a), (b) and
(f)–(k) show differing passages from corresponding fields in the two mounts. (Scale: 3/2)

Inv. 2(c) (fig. 372 a–c). The whole surface of the mount, except for the central cell, is covered with garnet inlays in small-scale geometric shapes and arrangements. The decorative design is built up on the central cell which contained a single expanse of millefiori. This was set on a foil rectangle of type B1, smaller in size than the cell. The remains of the millefiori inlay and the foil have not been remounted on the purse. They are shown in figure 373. At the centre of this empty central cell is a small round hole. The millefiori rod used is that seen in the purse frame (pl. 13 a), showing four dark T-shaped elements in red, with stems pointing inwards, on a dull white background (pp. 591 and 593, pl. 23 f). This large central inlay must have had a striking bullseye effect. The rest of the cloisonné design seems conceived to protect the inlay and to focus and comment on it. The inlay, in a thick-walled trapezoidal cell, is surrounded by a cloisonné border which follows its shape and carries a running step-pattern theme (fig. 371 b). Four strongly-marked lines radiate from the corners of this surrounding border. Strong dividing walls of the same thickness as those of the outer border of the central setting join its lower corners to the equally thick frame of the outer border of the plaque. A stronger radial emphasis is supplied at the upper corners by long cells each containing a single dark garnet and having thick walls again of the same weight as those of the inner frame round the central setting. These long cells do not join the central feature to a corner of the hexagon but to the middle of the two shortest sides (fig. 372 a). Four irregularly-shaped panels fill the spaces between these radii, the whole decorative zone so completed being contained within the cloisonné outer border of the plaque, which again is defined by thick inner and outer frames, and contains a running design of depressed mushroom cells (fig. 371 c).

Inv. 2(d) (fig. 372 d–f). A foil underlay is present in the central trapezoidal cell but no trace of the presumed millefiori inlay remains. The plaque is closely similar to 2(c), but there are minor and in some instances deliberate differences. The plaque appears to have been repaired since the outer gold wall at the top seems to have been

506

FIGURE 372 The hexagonal plaques: views of the fronts and backs, with radiograph prints enlarged to the same scale. (a)–(c), Inv. 2(c); (d)–(f) Inv. 2(d). The angled black shape visible in the central cell of the upper border in (c) is the shank of a bent rivet projecting from the purse-bar, all the plaques except 2(b) having been radiographed in position of the purse. (Scale: 2/1)

reinforced or replaced. A separate strip of gold, almost the full length of the side, has been fitted; overlapping joints at either end can be seen and this top edge of the plaque is of double thickness (figs. 372 d, 364 b). The radiographs of the two panels, which one would expect to be virtually identical, are in fact radically different, that of 2(d) appearing much denser over the central area (fig. 372 c and f). This seems to indicate that in addition to the repair to the top edge of the plaque the back of

2(d) is reinforced internally by an additional gold sheet. There is no sign of damage to the back-plate. The impression of an extra plate is confirmed by the presence, revealed on the radiograph, of a small central hole in the central cell (fig. 372*f*). The hole does not penetrate the back-plate, and must therefore exist in a concealed plate.

The geometric character of the two plaques Inv. 2(c) and (d), their uncompromising shapes, panelled style and small-scale abstract ornament, stand in strong contrast with the other plaques with representational designs.

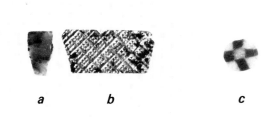

a   *b*   *c*

F I G U R E 373 Hexagonal plaques, Inv. 2(c): (*a*), (*b*) fragment of millefiori, inlay O, found in the trapezoidal cell at the centre of Inv. 2(c) with the foil underlay from the cell; (*c*), millefiori eye in blue and white (inlay Q) from the eye of one of the wolves in either plaque 2(g) or 2(h). (Scale: 4/1)

The colour effect of these hexagonal plaques is more brick red and less dark plum-coloured than that of the rest of the work on the purse in general. This derives from the fact that thin garnets have been used. As elsewhere in this jewellery colour distinctions are deliberately sought. The three large plain rectangular cells (of types *d, e* in fig. 370) at the upper corners of the frame round the central setting and at the top centre of the outer borders of the plaques have no foil backing and thicker garnets, and as a result have a much darker colour, used with punctuating effect in the design.

Some variations in the cell patterns of 2(c) and 2(d) are illustrated in figure 371*a, b*, and *f–k*. Step-pattern and depressed mushroom themes are dominant in the cell work. The lidded cells are used in plaques 2(d) (figs. 371*f*, 372*d*).

Bird plaques (Inv. 2(e), (f); pl. 14*a*, fig. 375)

Dimensions

	2(e)	2(f)
Height	3·3 cm	3·1 cm
Width	2·8 cm	2·8 cm
Thickness	0·3 cm	0·3 cm

Weight

	11·313 g	12·872 g

Garnets and other inlays

	Garnets	Millefiori	Blue glass	Lidded cells
Inv. 2(e)	197	2	2	0
Inv. 2(f)	192	2	2	1

Foil underlays. A1 behind small cells, B1 in larger cells.

Cell forms. Cell forms and themes are illustrated in figure 374.

Both plaques show an almost identical rendering of a hawk or bird of prey catching a broad-billed bird, presumably a duck. In 2(e) the birds face right, and in 2(f) they face left. The claws of the hawk, in the guise of triangular cells in the border of the duck's body, can be seen to enter the duck's body. Whereas the hawks have talons

508

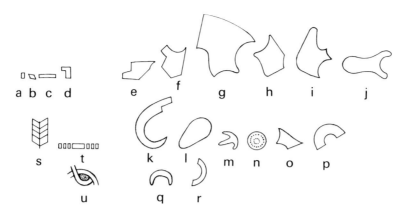

FIGURE 374 The bird plaques, Inv. 2(e) and 2(f); cell
forms and themes: (a)–(d) basic shapes; (e)–(r), unique
forms devised in realising the birds; (s), (t) geometric
themes; (u), use of the lidded cell, occurring only in 2(f).
(Scale: 3/2)

and squared tails, the broad-billed birds have a foot form suggestive of webbing, and
rounded tails.

Apart from small rectangular parallelograms or triangular-shaped cells used in
bordering and for wing and tail feathers, the cell shapes are unique, devised to meet
the requirements of a unique representational design. No conventional cell forms are
used except for the minute rectangular or triangular oblong or slightly curved cells
(fig. 374 *a–d*). The feathers of wings and tail are similarly rendered in small plain cells,
sometimes parallelograms (figs. 374 *b, s*) and arranged in chevron form, at other times
strung out in lines with groups of three minute stones separated by larger rectangular
stones (fig. 374 *t*). The remaining cells are shaped to suit the design of the birds' bodies.
There is only one instance of a step-pattern theme in the entire plaque, in the top
element of the bird of prey's bill. The plaques thus show a combination of very large
cells of unique form with minute cells, some of which contain stones less than 1 mm
square. As the plaques are reversed in relation to each other some cell shapes appear
to be duplicated in mirror image.

Figural scenes. The naturalistic effect is achieved partly by the cut-out profile and
clearcut shapes of the plaques and the attitudes of the birds, and partly by the relative
naturalism of internal details such as the wing and tail shapes and feathered treatment.
Such effects have not before been encountered in Germanic cloisonné work. It is a
development far beyond that seen in simple bird brooches such as that from Rome[1]
where the outline shape only, with a conventional circular eye in the middle of a
circular head, gives the bird brooch verisimilitude; or the eagle from Apahida II[2]
where, as in the Rome bird brooch, it is the profile which makes the bird, the interior
cell work being no more than a conventional framework to carry the inlays. In the

[1] Arrhenius 1971, fig. 76.   [2] Horedt in Hoops 1971, Taf. 49, 50.

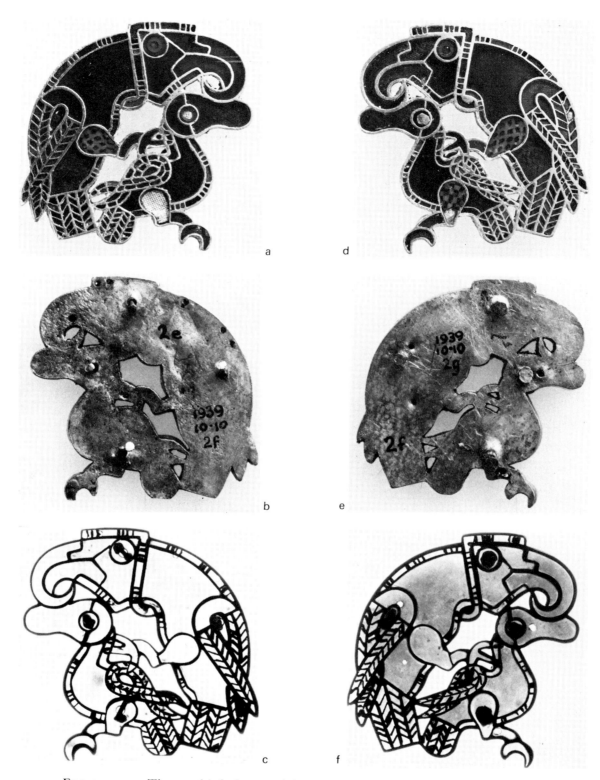

a
d

b
e

c
f

FIGURE 375 The two bird plaques: (a)–(f) front and rear views, with radiograph prints enlarged to the same scale: (a)–(c), Inv. 2(e): (d)–(f), Inv. 2(f). (Scale: 2/1)

Apahida eagle, however, the large garnets in the beak have their shape conditioned by that of the beak itself, and the longitudinally serrated garnets in the feet bear some resemblance to claws or talons. The naturalism of the Sutton Hoo plaques is of a different order, both as regards the drawing of the subject in all its detail and in the subordination of the cell design to the naturalistic rendering of the subject. Other bird representations in cloisonné work are by comparison heraldic and conventional.

The four birds' eyes introduce engraved garnets—an uncommon element in Anglo-Saxon jewellery. In both birds the eyes are circular stones engraved with a ring filled with opaque blue glass (pl. 23 d).

Differences between 2(e) and 2(f). The back of 2(e) (fig. 375 b) shows four attachment rivets and ten or eleven holes or punctures made from the back, probably made in reconditioning the plaques (p. 600). Inv. 2(f) shows four such holes. In both plaques the rivets have been driven in from the front, whereas the other holes are made from the back. Seven small irregular openings separate the two bird bodies in 2(e), as distinct from eight in 2(f).

Plaque 2(f) is very slightly shorter than 2(e). There are minor differences in design, notably in the cloisonné treatment of the tail of the bird of prey, where in 2(f) the small-cell chevron pattern is carried further up the body coming to a triangular point, and slight variations in the wing shape of the ducks or smaller birds: in 2(e) the duck's wing tips curve inwards, in 2(f) they are straight; the inner wing and tip of the outer wing of the bird of prey in 2(f) are thinner and more elegantly twisted than in 2(e).

In 2(e) a garnet is inserted at the centre of the rounded junction of the two wings of the smaller bird, as in both birds of prey. In 2(f) sufficient room has not been left for the insertion of a garnet and the space is imperfectly sealed with gold. In 2(e) an opening occurs immediately above the top curve of the pair of wings of the duck, between its body and the claws of the bird of prey; in 2(f) part of the bird's body (another garnet-filled cell) shows here. In 2(f) the bird of prey shows a sealed cell just behind the point of the bird's chin, between the curve back of the angled eye surround or lappet and the bird's neck; in 2(e) less space was left between lappet and chin and the smoothed-over junction can hardly be described as a lidded cell. Inv. 2(e) has five more garnets than 2(f).

In both plaques the large cells appear relatively deep and have thicker garnets, as their size renders necessary. They display the grid foil pattern B1, and their stones are plum-coloured. The curved semicircular cells at the top of the wings, the birds' hips and all the small cells, which have pointillé foil backings, appear much shallower. This may be no more than an impression conveyed by the thinness of the garnets, as a result of which the foil is set shallower in relation to the surface. The construction of such minute cells would be easier if the cloisonnage were shallower. The radiographs, however, show no distinction between the small and large cells, such as would indicate the presence of an extra gold floor here between the areas of small inlays and the base plate of the plaque as a whole. The stones in the small cells have a brick-red or pinkish colour, presumably due to their thinness.

The man-between-beasts plaques (Inv. 2(g), 2(h); pl. 14*b*, fig. 377)
Dimensions

	2(g)	2(h)
Height	3·0 cm	3·0 cm
Width	3·3 cm	3·2 cm
Thickness	0·4 cm	0·4 cm

Weight 15·562 g 15·278 g
Number of garnets and other inlays and of lidded cells (identical in both plaques)

Inlays of all kinds	95
Garnets	90
Millefiori	5
Lidded cells	13

Foil underlays. Types A1 and B1, as in the previous pair of plaques.
Cell forms are shown in figure 376.

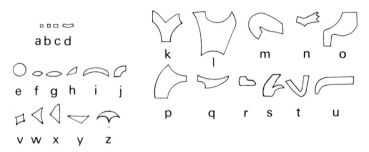

FIGURE 376 (a)–(z) Cell shapes in the plaques depicting a man between beasts, 2(g) and 2(h): (a)–(d) basic shapes; (e)–(u), shapes devised in realising the design; (v)–(z), selected residual cells covered by gold lids. (Scale: 3/2)

Each of these plaques renders in cut-out silhouette a scene of a man spread eagled between two erect wolf-like animals. The man, seen frontally, is passive, with legs turned outwards and arms bent upwards at the elbow; his hands, with thumb and fingers separated and thumb turned outwards, grasp his own shoulders. He is moustached and perhaps bearded; the nose is represented by a single thin vertically set garnet, the eyes by pointed ovals, apparently sunk into solid gold, but in fact set in individual cells, surrounded by lidded cells. The moustache is very big; the hair is rendered by a ring of small shaped and graded stones. The sex of the figure is deliberately indicated.

The middle part of the man's body is ambiguously treated; a line of small square garnets in cells across the lower part is too high to represent a skirt hem and too low to be a waistbelt; a single transverse cell higher up, between the raised wrists, also

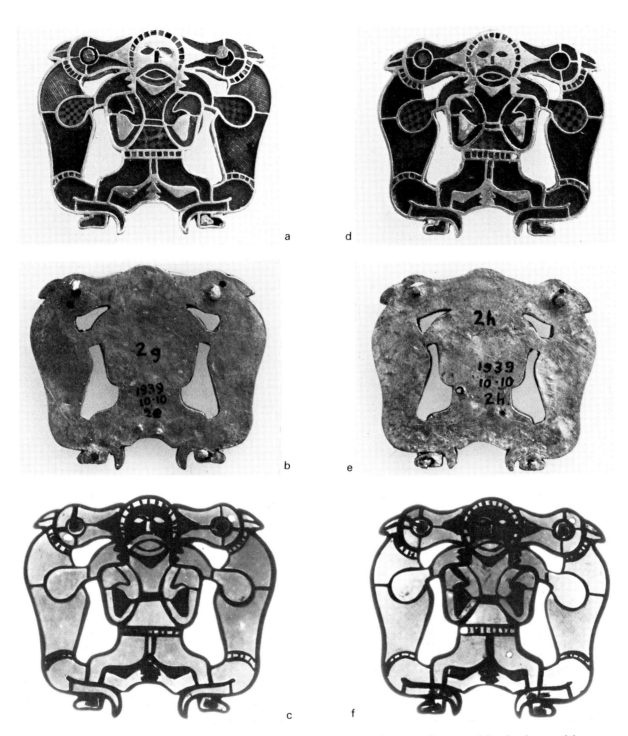

FIGURE 377 (a)–(f) The two man-between-beasts plaques; front and back views with radiograph prints enlarged to the same scale: (a)–(c), Inv. 2(g); (d)–(f), Inv. 2(h). (Scale: 2/1)

seems too high to be a waistbelt. The area between, which resembles an apron, is filled with a single large inlay of millefiori glass of a chessboard type pattern but set obliquely and with the unit squares larger than in any other instance of such patterns in the jewellery (p. 593).

The animals are erect with open mouths pressed against the sides of the man's head as though whispering in his ears. Their tails and hind legs interlace with his; their front paws rest on his shoulders. The scene is tightly composed. Four open spaces occur between the bodies of the man and the two animals. The man's shape is further thrown up by an extensive use of lidded cells; his head is completely surrounded by them, and itself contains three. The crook of each armpit contains one large lidded cell, and the animals' hind legs are separated from the man's body by the same device.

The same considerations and comments apply to 2(g) and 2(h) as to 2(e) and 2(f). There is the same use of two kinds of foil, of thin and thick, small and big, dark and light-seeming garnets. There are similar small variations in details of the craftsmanship between the two plaques. In 2(g) the animals' tails protrude slightly more below the level of the man's feet than in 2(h). The man's legs are more widely spread (41 mm as against 37 mm) and the animals' hind legs consequently are bigger; his fingers are slightly larger than in 2(h). The number of garnets representing the hair (beautifully graded) is one fewer in 2(g) than in 2(h) (16 instead of 17).

The use of small cells is more limited in these two plaques than in 2(b), 2(e) and 2(f). The bodies of men and beasts are not outlined with long and narrow or small square cells, the use of minute stones in rows being instead confined to the picking out of belts, collars, hair and hips, that is, to internal features. The stones which delineate the hair or top of the man's head in 2(g) are very subtly graded.

Both plaques, besides being in openwork, show extensive use of the lidded cell technique. The animal and human figures are outlined with thick walls, the human figures more strongly outlined than those of the animals.

Circular studs (Inv. 2(i)–2(l); fig. 379)

Dimensions	*Inv.* (i) (j)	*Inv.* (k) (l)
Diameter	12 mm	8–9 mm
Diameter of internal field	8 mm	5 mm
Thickness	4 mm	4 mm
Length of rivet-shank projecting from back of stud	5 mm	5 mm

Weights	Inv. 2(i)	Inv. 2(j)	Inv. 2(k)	Inv. 2(l)
	2·899 g	2·660 g	1·792 g	1·788 g (including inlay)

514

Number of garnets and other inlays

	Inv. 2(i) and 2(j)	*Inv.* 2(k) and 2(l)
	18 garnets	12 garnets
	1 millefiori	1 millefiori

Foil underlays. Pointillé foil used for central millefiori cell as well as for peripheral cells.

Cell forms. Plain rectangular or trapezoidal.

All four studs have their edges slightly faceted or flattened at one point, probably indicating that they were set in contact with the frame (figs. 358*a*, 367 and 379).

The studs were placed one opposite each of the four filigree clips holding the rim of the purse-lid. Each was held by two strong rivets (fig. 364*c*). The studs are solidly built. The central circular millefiori inlay which occupies the whole of the interior is surrounded by a thick gold cell-wall. Between this and the thick outer wall of the stud is a circular field set with long trapezoid or

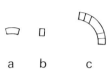

a   b   c

FIGURE 378   The purse-lid: cell shapes and theme from the border of a stud. (Scale: 3/2)

keystone-shaped garnets separated by pairs of small garnets. Figure 379*e* shows the backs of the plaques at enlarged scale. The rivet ends are well spread and not just bent over, and must have been hammered against a hard substance. This may support the view that the original lid substance was bone or ivory.

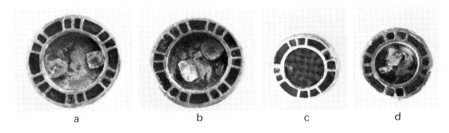

a   b   c   d

e

FIGURE 379   The purse-lid. The four circular studs, Inv. 2(i)–2(l) originally with millefiori inlays, one of which remains in position: (*a*)–(*d*), front views, (*e*) oblique view. (Scale: 2/1) (Photo: *e*, British Museum Research Laboratory)

3. *Clasp from purse-bag and the locking mechanism* (Inv. 3; fig. 380)

Dimensions

Length	24 mm
Width	10 mm
Overall projection of tang from back of clasp	2·7 mm
Length of tang	15 mm
Thickness of leather or cloth to which the clasp was attached	2 mm
Depth of aperture to receive the tongue from the frame of the lid	3 mm
Length of aperture	16 mm
Depth of step in aperture	1·5 mm

Weight
9·489 g

The catch, of solid gold, is undecorated. It must have been fixed to the bag with the opening to engage the tongue uppermost. Its outer surface, so placed, is slightly concave, showing that the bag reflected in its shape the re-entrant curve of the frame

a

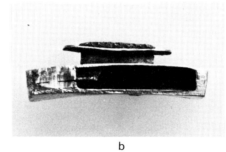
b

c

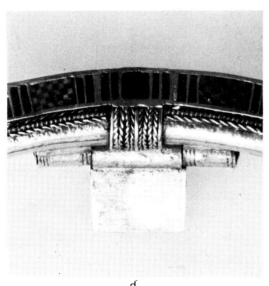
d

e

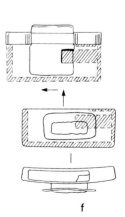
f

FIGURE 380 The purse: the fastening mechanism with drawings to illustrate its operation: (*a*)–(*c*) the sliding catch (Inv. 3); (*d*), (*e*) the hinged tongue attached to the lower edge of the purse frame, which locked into the sliding catch; (*f*) explanatory drawing. (Scale: *a–e*, 2/1; *f*, 1/1)

of the lid. The edge of the bag may have been stiffened or reinforced to hold a mouth shape congruent with that of the lid. The minimum clearance given by the tang (i.e. the distance between the main part of the catch and the washer over which the end of the tang is burred) is 2 mm. At the outer ends of the washer it has risen to 2·6 mm. A natural thickness of 2·5 mm for the material at this point (where it would have been compressed by the hammering of the tang), seems indicated. Alternatively, if the bag was fastened when fairly full the pull of the material of the bag might have bent the ends of the washer slightly outwards, the basic 2 mm of clearance giving the true thickness. This does not necessarily give us the thickness of the bag itself as the material may have been reinforced at the catch.

The catch mechanism is illustrated in figure 380 *f*. Within the cavity shown in figure 380 *b* and *f*, an internal projection can be seen (on the left in fig. 380 *b*). When the tongue is inserted and the clasp is then moved sideways, this projection engages in the slot cut in the tongue and effectively locks the purse-lid in the closed position.

4. *General observations on the purse*

The purse, with its large size, its extraordinary richness of polychromy and profusion of shapes, both in individual cells and of the plaques, and the astonishing efficacy and impact of its representational scenes in the gold and garnet medium, is one of the most surprising and intriguing elements in the burial. In spite of its apparent novelty, however, it ranks as the supreme representative of an established class: the purse with large ornamental lid. Parallels are illustrated in figures 381 and 382 *a* and *b*; the closest to the Sutton Hoo purse in impact, as it is of gold with complete all-over encrustation of garnets, is that from the second princely grave, dated to the second half of the fifth century, found at Apahida, Romania in 1968,[1] and now in the Museum at Cluj (fig. 381). This lid, 18·5 cm in length, is only 5 mm shorter than the Sutton Hoo purse-lid. A curious feature of its design is the depiction in the cloisonnage of a buckle, with green inlays as well as garnets. The form of this buckle is close to that of one found in the cemetery at München-Aubing, in a man's partially robbed grave, no. 812, in which was another purse-lid of much humbler character but even larger size than those from Apahida and Sutton Hoo (fig. 382 *a*).[2] This has a simple iron rim, held by fluted bronze clips at intervals, and with it were traces of leather; its shape is almost exactly that of the Sutton Hoo lid, with a straight bar at the top and re-entrant curved frame below; its length, 26·5 cm, is considerably greater and its depth is 11·5 cm compared with the 8 cm of the Sutton Hoo lid. The München-Aubing purse, which from its general context is attributed to the early sixth century, suggests that the large size and precise form of the Sutton Hoo purse were already very well established by the date of its burial.

[1] Horedt and Protase 1970; Hoops 1971, 366–7 and Taf. 27.

[2] Unpublished. I am grateful to Dr H. Dannheimer of the Prähistorische Staatssamlung, Museum für Vor- und Frühgeschichte, Munich, for providing me with details and with the drawing used in fig. 382 *a*.

FIGURE 381 Gold purse-lid inlaid with garnets and coloured glass, of the second half of the fifth century A.D., from Apahida, near Cluj, Romania (now in Cluj Museum). (Scale: 1/1) (By courtesy of Professor K. Horedt)

518

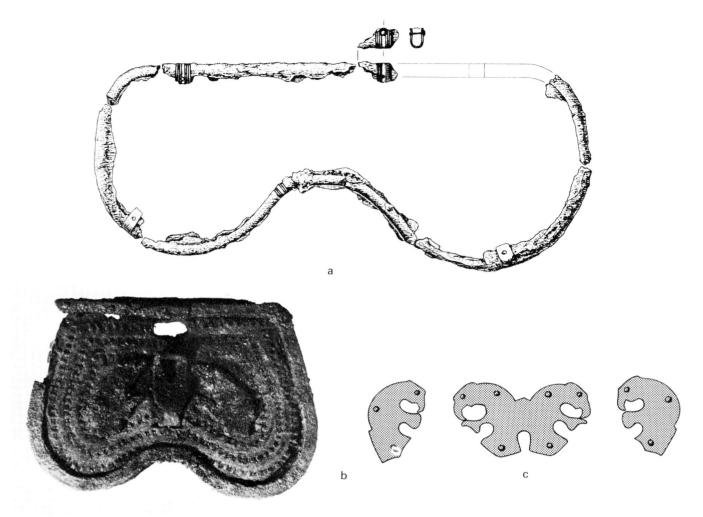

FIGURE 382 Purses and purse mounts: (*a*) purse-frame from München-Aubing, grave 812; (*b*) leather purse with bird mounts from Köln-Mungersdorf, grave 10; (*c*) mounts from Harquency-Mülheim, after Coutil and Werner. (Scales: *a*, 1/2, *b*, 1/1, *c*, not known). (*a*, by courtesy of Dr. H. Dannheimer, Munich; *b*, photo: Rheinisches Bildarchiv, Kölnisches Stadt Museum)

Another purse-lid relevant to the Sutton Hoo discovery was found, associated with leather remains of a pouch, in grave no. 10 in the Rhineland cemetery of Köln-Mungersdorf.[1] It is relatively small, but relevant because of its shape and the appearance on it of representational subjects in the form of two cut-out bronze birds. The birds are identical images reversed and show square-tailed birds of prey facing inwards, with drawn-up leg and curled talons, resembling those on the Sutton Hoo lid. Some twelve of the male graves in the Köln-Mungersdorf cemetery contained purses, all designed to be worn on the left side near the waist.

Of different type but revealing in intimate detail the character of the purse is the example excavated by Dr Renate Pirling at grave no. 2268 at Krefeld-Gellep, and subsequently reproduced on the basis of the surviving metal and leather remains and the excavation records, under the direction of the workshops of the Römisch-

---

[1] Fremersdorf 1955, 93 and elsewhere. I am indebted to Dr Hayo Vierck, Münster, for drawing my attention to this piece.

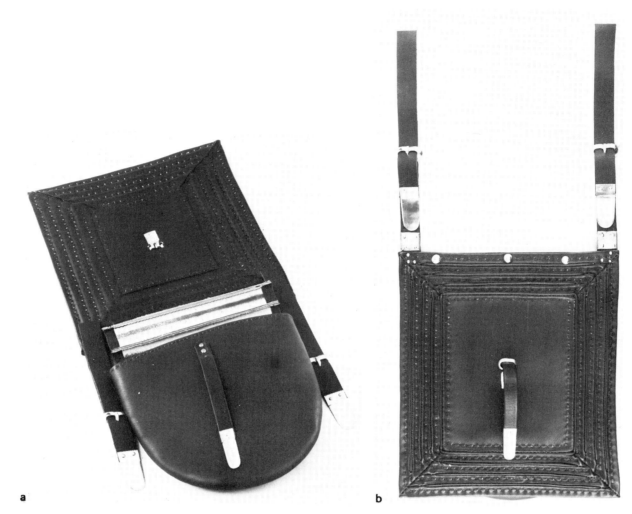

FIGURE 383   Reconstruction of the leather purse from Krefeld-Gellep, grave 2268, after
Pirling and Stande; (*a*) open (*b*) closed. (Scale: 1/4)

Germanisches Zentralmuseum, Mainz (fig. 383).[1] In this the lid is big enough to
conceal the pouch completely, and the suspension of the purse on longish straps from
the ends of the iron purse-bar (fig. 383, front view) is relevant for relating the Sutton
Hoo purse to the belt on which it was evidently carried (p. 565). The purse-lid from
the *Fürstengrab* at Beckum, Westphalia[2] was furnished with applied gold fitments (pl.
22 *d*). They are hollow, box-like upstanding mounts, some 5 mm in height, with
finished sides and embellished with scraps of filigree in a curious style.[3] They are of
interest not only in providing a parallel for rich gold ornaments applied to the surface
of a purse-lid, but also because they must have been free-standing on the surface of
the lid in the manner deduced for the Sutton Hoo plaques. This same grave has a
singular relevance to the Sutton Hoo purse in another context, that of the horse
burials associated with it (fig. 384 *a*, *b* and p. 522 below). The Merovingian bronze purse

[1] Pirling 1973, 81–7.
[2] Winkelmann 1962, colour plate, fig. 3; *Sutton Hoo*, Vol. I,
fig. 383.

[3] Closely paralleled on the composite disc brooch with cloisonné garnet and other inlays from Rosmeer (Roosens 1969,
66, fig. 1).

520

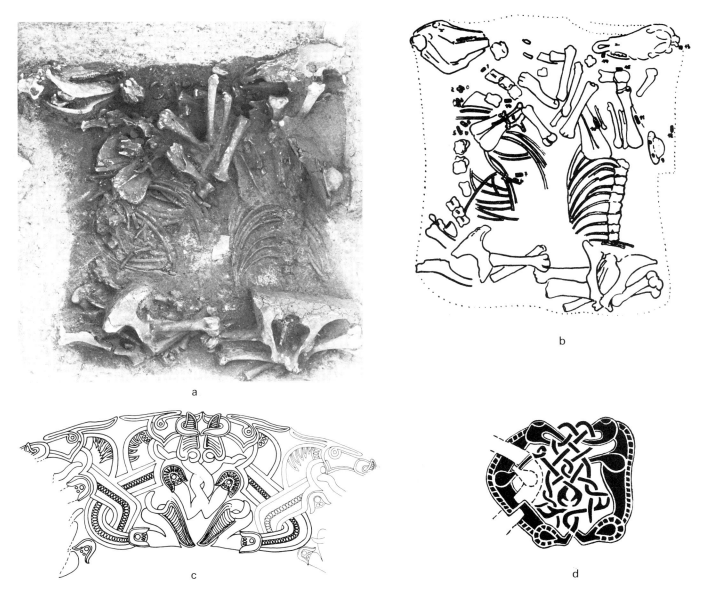

FIGURE 384 (*a*) One of the burials of horses in pairs associated with the *Fürstengrab* at Beckum, Westphalia; (*b*) plan of the grave shown in (*a*); (*c*) detail of facing horses with interlacing limbs from the flange of the Sutton Hoo shield-boss: (*d*) design of facing inter-linked animals from the zoomorphic double plaque on the Sutton Hoo purse. (Scales: *c*, 1/1, *d*, 3/2) (Photo and plan: *a*, *b*, W. Winkelmann, Westfälisches Landesmuseum für Vor- und Frühgeschichte, Münster)

mounts found at Harquency-Mulheim (Dep. Eure) show a group of representational mounts in bird form (fig. 382*c*).[1] These are two reversed plaques showing single birds facing in opposite directions and a double plaque, two birds back to back, an analogy to the double plaque on the Sutton Hoo purse-lid.

The figural scenes on the Sutton Hoo purse-lid,[2] because they appear as part of the design of an important item of regalia, may be thought to have had a special

[1] L. Coutil 1895, 37 where the mounts are referred to as from a casket. See however Werner 1950*a*, 52–7, with a valuable discussion of purses.

[2] Cf. Haseloff 1952.

521

significance, known to those who commissioned them and those who saw the purse. The subject is too complex for discussion here, but the relationship of the design of the double plaque on the purse to that of the horses on the flange of the shield-boss (figs. 36, 384*c*) should be stressed. Allowing for the difference in media (cloisonné garnet work, as compared with a design stamped from a die prepared from a wax model, allowing refinement of detail and naturalism) and taking into account the fact that the two are found in the same royal burial, one with strong East Scandinavian associations, this may be thought to be more than coincidence. A clue to the deeper significance of the design may be found in a remarkable parallel in a ritual context, associated with the *Fürstengrab* at Beckum, the purse from which is discussed above. Horses, arranged in facing pairs with their legs intertwined, were found buried in relation to the prince's grave (fig. 384*a*).[1]

FIGURE 385   The man-between-beasts motif as seen on a die from Torslunda, Öland (fig. 156) and on the Sutton Hoo purse-lid. (Scale: 1/1)

The man-between-beasts scene has been related to a similar scene depicted on East Scandinavian helmets of the group to which the Sutton Hoo helmet belongs, the parallel occurring on a Torslunda die (figs. 156*d*, 385). The Valsgärde 7 helmet provides another version of the Torslunda scene (fig. 164).[2] In spite of the differences between the two helmet versions, in both of which the man is evidently engaged in combat, and the static, formalised version of the cloisonné rendering on the Sutton Hoo purse, the compositional parallel of the purse scene with the Torslunda die is very striking,[3] and the context must be thought to favour a relationship with Vendel art rather than with the various cycles of Mediterranean scenes, which do not offer convincing alternatives.[4] No close parallel to the scene depicting the bird of prey and the duck can be cited.

---

[1] I am indebted to Dr Winkelmann, the excavator of the Beckum site, for drawing my attention to this parallel: see Winkelmann 1962, 9 and abb. 2 and 9; see also Jankuhn in Hoops 1971, 126–9 and Müller-Wille 1970–71, 206, no. 95.

[2] Bruce-Mitford 1972*b*; 1974, ch. 10.
[3] Bruce-Mitford 1974, 43–5.
[4] *Pace* Haseloff 1952.

Inv. 4 and 5 (pls. 15–18, figs. 386, 392)

Note. In each clasp the half to which the chain and pin are attached is referred to as 'a', the other half as 'b'.

Dimensions

	Inv. 4	*Inv. 5*
Length, fully extended, assembled, with pin in position	11·3 cm	11·8 cm
Width	5·4 cm	5·4 cm
Thickness	0·5 cm	0·5 cm
Length of staples projecting from the backs of the clasps	0·4 cm	0·4 cm
Length of chain	6·0 cm	6·0 cm
Length of pin-head with projecting loop for chain attachment	1·2 cm	1·2 cm
Width of pin head	0·55 cm	0·55 cm

Weight

4a: 95·960 g ⎱ 183·803 g
4b: 87·843 g ⎰

5a: 106·130 g ⎱ 201·570 g
5b: 95·440 g ⎰

Inlays in the intact design

Garnets	452	468
Millefiori	20	20
Blue glass	26	26

(See also table 34, p. 617).

Foil underlays. Types A1 and B1 are used consistently throughout, generally B1 for larger cells, A1 for smaller. There is also a consistent use of A1 underlays for all borders, including the zoomorphic interlaces round the central panels, although some cells in these interlace borders are almost as large as the smallest of those carrying the grid pattern B1. The distinction is carried through in the naturalistic animal figures: in the boars' heads in Inv. 4b for example, the pointillé backing A1 is used in cells 2–6 (fig. 387) and in the hindquarters in cells 2–4 (fig. 387) but in both cases the grid pattern B1 is used in cell 1; in the boars' heads of Inv. 4a and A1 foil type is used in the corresponding cells 2–5 but not in cell 6.

A variant arrangement occurs in Inv. 5. In 5a the boars' mouths, eyes and upper jaws have the A1 backing foil, but the lower jaws carry strips of B1. In 5b, only the boars' eyes have A1 foil backings, all the remaining cells of the boars' heads having strips of B1.

In the large cells of the boars' bodies where the foil registers with particular effect the major grid-lines of pattern are set at different angles (pl. 16). In every case it will be seen that in the corresponding cells on each side of the symmetrical design the foil is set at the corresponding but opposite angle so that the direction of the grid-lines balances.

The care and consistency with which this has been done recalls the refinement in

FIGURE 386   The shoulder-clasps, separated into halves. Above, Inv. 4, below, Inv. 5. (Scale: 1/1)

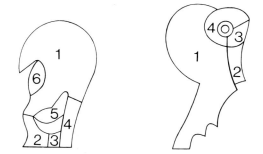

FIGURE 387   Shoulder-clasp, Inv. 4a: cells of boar's head and leg numbered to show distribution of foil-types A1 and B1 (see text). (Scale: 5/2)

the finish of the Sutton Hoo ship remarked by Ole Crumlin-Pedersen when visiting its re-excavation in 1967. He noted that the long axes of the roves were uniformly aligned along the length of the ship, something which was not to be found in any early ship then known, including the famous Viking ships in Oslo.

Cell forms. Both clasps show the same range of cell forms, as illustrated in figures 388 and 389. They comprise:

(1) Irregular cells of special shapes and sizes dictated by the unique requirements of the zoomorphic garnet interlaces and by the naturalistic figure subjects (boars) depicted.

(2) Small rectangular bordering cells and terminal border shapes.

(3) Stilted cruciform step-pattern cells, that is, cruciform step-pattern cells that are supported away from the edges of the field containing them and from adjacent cells (in this case all similar) by straight gold walls or ligatures. These occur in two sizes, 7 mm and 5 mm across (fig. 388 *f, e*), with bordering step-pattern cells of two types (fig. 388 *g, h*). In category 1 *ad hoc* cell shapes required by the zoomorphic themes, most of which are illustrated, indicate the size and complexity of the gem-cutting. The incidental formation of residual cells is neutralised, and the time and expense of cutting garnets to fill them is avoided, by use of the lidded cell technique already described (pp. 463, 505) and by the employment of panels of filigree work. Some of these concealed shapes are illustrated in figure 389 *r–w*. It could be said that in the rectangular cloisonné panels the smaller stilted cells which carry millefiori insets or garnets embody the main design, and that the larger step-pattern cells and border step-pattern cells are residual. As perfect cells of orthodox shape, dovetailed regularly with the smaller stilted cells, they are of equal weight in the design and can be considered leading cell types in their own right.

The shoulder-clasps are identical in their general design and size, but there are minor variations of detail. They are solidly made and each consists of two virtually identical halves which join to form a hinge, the halves being held together by long well-made gold pins on which the hinges pivot; these can be easily withdrawn, allowing the halves of the clasp to come apart (fig. 386). Each pin has a large ornamental head in the form

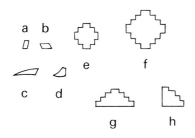

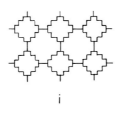

FIGURE 388 The pair of shoulder-clasps (Inv. 4 and 5): cell forms and patterns. (a)–(h) basic shapes; (i) geometric theme. (Scale: 3/2)

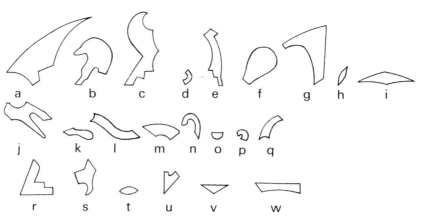

FIGURE 389 The pair of shoulder-clasps: cell forms and patterns. (a)–(i) unique forms devised to achieve the design of interlocked boars (fig. 390); (j)–(q) unique forms used for the zoomorphic interlace (fig. 391); (r)–(w) selection of background cells sealed by gold lids. (Scale: 3/2)

of an animal's head, rounded above but flat underneath, and with flattened snout, which is in turn secured to one of the halves of the clasp by a gold chain attached to a stout staple projecting from the side of the clasp. The mechanism of the hinge is virtually identical to that of the great gold buckle (p. 536).

Each half-clasp consists of a rectangular portion, the outer corners of which are tapered off to provide transition to a rounded end of slightly reduced width. The rectangular portions have a central rectangular field of geometric cloisonné work framed on all four sides by panels containing zoomorphic interlace executed in garnets, brought out clearly and sharply by use of the lidded cell technique. The curved ends of the clasps each contain a design of pairs of naturalistically rendered overlapping boars, facing inwards and with their bodies intersecting. The spaces between the legs and heads of the boars are filled by gold panels carrying filigree ornament. On the back of each clasp are twenty solid staples, 3 mm in length, by means of which the clasps were presumably fixed to a base of cloth or leather, or both (pl. 22 b, fig. 392).[1]

FIGURE 390 The shoulder-clasps: design of two intersecting boars from the ends (Scale: 3/2)

[1] For the backs of the clasps see also *Sutton Hoo*, Vol. I, fig. 387.

The staples have an internal opening of 2 mm. If the staples penetrated, for the sake of argument, through a 2 mm thickness of leather or other material, they could have been held by split pins or pegs, in the manner of a cap badge. No trace of any such pins has survived and it would in any case be tedious to have to insert forty such devices. The clasps, objects of the highest value, were presumably sewn firmly by means of the staples. The 3 mm staples could have passed through a 2 mm supporting pad of leather, to be sewn on to the cloth of the garment proper below. This must have been a two-piece affair, the halves of the clasp being attached to separate parts of the garment, to be assembled on the body.

Polychromy. There is much colour variation in the garnet inlays of the backbones of the boars, and also in certain other parts of the design (pl. 16a, b): in Inv. 5a the inner elements of the boars' backbones are uniformly a bright red, and the outer lines of cells are all orange; in Inv. 5b, on the other hand (pl. 16b), ruby, orange and yellow stones are mixed up more or less at random in both zones. The changes appear to be effected in part by selection of stones and partly by variation of thickness. This point is further discussed in section 6 (p. 603).

Filigree. The clasps have a special importance in showing the decorative use of filigree. It is used between the legs and heads of the boars at the ends of the clasps and on the animal heads of the hinge-pins; it differs from the range of filigree elsewhere in the Sutton Hoo material in rendering zoomorphic themes and in the use both of granulation and of annular filigree (figs. 386 and 393). Further illustrations and comments are provided in figures 434–6 and on pages 603–7 below.

Detailed description

Inv. 4

Central panels. The central panels of Inv. 4, as in the sister clasp, Inv. 5, contain classic examples of step-pattern design. The step-cells are of two sizes and four varieties (fig. 388e–h). The main pattern seems to reside in the smaller stilted cells, some with polychrome inlays. These cells are uniformly cruciform with three steps on each side (fig. 388e). The steps are precise and sharply angular. Each cell is suspended on four short straight ligatures or stems, giving it an isolation which serves to accentuate its form. These stems are not only straight in themselves but are set in perfectly straight alignment across the panels, in whatever direction they are read. This neatness and accuracy is characteristic of the products of the Sutton Hoo goldsmith's workshop. The impact of these cloisonné step-pattern panels derives largely from the perfect control and regularity with which they are executed.

Of the fifteen step-cells suspended on stems in this way to form the main pattern, eight contain inlays of millefiori glass, fully described in section 5 (pp. 587–90). The patterns vary (pls. 17, 18). The background cruciform step-pattern cells are larger than the cells in which the main design is executed and in them the four extremities of the cross shape are longer, being formed by the stems that support the stilted cells. That the main pattern resides in the smaller suspended cells and the grid they present is made clear not only by the four-point suspension which picks them out but also by the fact that they carry the conspicuous polychrome inlays, distributed evenly throughout the grid. The foils behind the garnets in both panels are of type B1. The foil sheets are carefully set so that the pattern always runs the same way and the muddled effect which carelessness in this respect can produce is avoided. The millefiori work is remarkable, indeed unique, in containing transparent red squares or elements, behind which are foil underlays of the type A1.

Zoomorphic borders. Around the central panels are unique borders of zoomorphic interlace in garnet cloisonné work, executed with perfect fluency (pl. 17, fig. 386). In the two halves of Inv. 4 the zoomorphic interlace borders are identical in design. The border above the panel (fig. 386) has a design of two animals each consisting of a head, a ribbon body and one rear leg (fig. 391 *a*). The heads are returned inwards and the jaws of each animal bite across its own body. The leg is articulated by a hip joint and an angular 'elbow', and the foot appears as a slight expansion of the limb towards the end, which is cut concave with a point to each side. The eye is a semicircular cell at the top of the head and contains an inlay of opaque pale or chalky blue glass. In 4b the design of this panel seems more perfunctory than in the others. The animals' legs lack the pointed elbow seen in the others, the foot is not expanded and the Style II chins on the animal heads are less pointed.

The bottom border (fig. 391 *b*) consists in each case of three detached animals each rolled into a knot. The three are close together, each facing the same way. Again, each animal consists of a head and ribbon body with one hind leg only. The jaws, especially the upper jaw, are more elongated than in the animals of the border above the panel. The hind leg is not demarcated by a hip joint and a heel or elbow, but appears to begin as a straightening-out of a garnet against the frame, accompanied by a slight thickening. The rear leg does perhaps have an elbow or sharp angle at the extremity of the pattern; it then takes a twist and re-enters the centre of the design to end over the head and just in front of the eye. The foot is again expanded and crescent-shaped with one toe now longer than the other. The eyes are semicircles set in the upper part of the head (fig. 391 *b*). The animals appear the right way up when seen from the direction of the curved end of the half-clasp.

F I G U R E 391 The shoulder-clasps. Animal interlace designs from the border round the cloisonné panel of half-clasp Inv. 4a, figure 386: (*a*) the upper border; (*b*) the lower border; (*c*) a side border. (Scale: 3/2)

528

The side panels in both halves of the clasp contain designs also made up of three animals but in this case with no hind leg, having only a head and a ribbon body. The jaws are again elongated and interlaced (fig. 391 c) the upper jaw of animal 2 (the middle animal) being exceptionally long-drawn-out. The front animal is self-contained, but the tail of the second animal's ribbon body takes a turn round the front one's neck and its upper jaw extends backwards to interlace with the third animal, the end of whose ribbon body also takes a turn round the neck of the middle one. The designs in the two side panels are identical (though the execution varies slightly), except that the pattern is reversed. The sequence of animals faces the same way but the heads are to the outside in both cases, as is uniform throughout these panels.

FIGURE 392   The shoulder-clasps: side view, showing attachment staples. (Scale: 1/1)

The ends of the clasps. The boars of Inv. 4 are virtually identical, though the hind quarters in 4b are perhaps a little less fat, allowing more space for the filigree-bearing plates between hind legs and heads. The boars are naturalistically rendered in a very effective way. The eyes are small lentoid garnets set in the top of the head. The only significant differences between the two intersecting boar representations is that in the case of Inv. 4a the tiny circular cell which provides the pivot round which the tails rotate is sealed, whereas in 4b it is not. In 4a additional cells are included in the tails, three garnets being used as against the greater virtuosity displayed in one of the boars in 4b which creates this eloquent feature with only two.

The filigree animals, which occupy the spaces between the legs and the heads of the boars, are snake-like creatures with no limbs and with heads like tulips (figs. 434,

436a, b). Their bodies consist of a thicker central beaded wire flanked by contour lines in a finer beaded wire. The heads are seen in profile with open mouths; in 4a a single gold granule in a fine wire ring forms the eye in each case. The heads here are drawn in the fine gold wire that has been used for contouring the body. These creatures are of the same sort as the snakes which form the central element in the interlace of the great gold buckle and which occupy the fields on each side of its buckle loop. (For other examples of the snake theme see figure 408.) In Inv. 4b where a little more space has resulted between the hind legs and the heads of the boars, the snakes' bodies are knotted (pl. 16a, fig. 436b) and in the constricted extension of the field above are four minute gold granules. The heads are of coarser construction than in 4a, with the inner beaded wire of the body continuing into the jaws, and the finer contouring wire continuing round the thicker wire. In these heads no room is left for eyes.

The boars' shoulders are set with identical large expanses of millefiori glass in a complex pattern, and characterised by the appearance of white spots at the junctions between the red and blue elements (pl. 16a, fig. 434). The inlay is fully analysed in plate 24a and figure 428. As we have seen (p. 523, fig. 387), the foil backing for the boars' tails, crests and jaws is of the pointillé type. As elsewhere in the jewellery, the smaller cells contain thinner garnets, giving a brick-red colour and producing a different effect from that of the dark plum colours with more lively foil patterns of the large cells in the bodies of the boars.

The lower outer corners of the curved ends of the clasps, behind the boars' hind legs, are single cells sealed with gold lids. This has the important effect of throwing up the boar figures in a clear silhouette so that they seem to balance very precisely on the upper edge of the rectangular portion.

The nature of the pin-heads for both pairs of clasps may be seen in figure 393, with details of the fine chain. This repeats exactly the method of construction of elements 18 and 19 of the great iron suspension chain for the largest cauldron.[1] The animal heads are flat underneath, to lie against the side of the clasp (fig. 393c), and are snub-nosed. They originally contained lentoid garnet eyes in settings high up on the top of the head. The decoration consists of inset panels covered all over with small beaded filigree annulets. The panels, which accentuate the structure of the head, are defined by beaded mouldings.

Inv. 5

On this clasp the loop which holds the security chain is positioned opposite the middle of the central step-pattern panel, whereas in Inv. 4 the loop occurs at the top of this portion of the clasp. This clasp is closely similar to Inv. 4, but the following differences of detail or points of interest should be noted:

(1) In 5b the cells behind the boars' hind legs are not lidded but contain garnets.

(2) In 5b the eyes of the animals in the upper border panel are concentric semi-circles. The outer ring contains a garnet, the inner one opaque blue glass.

[1] *Sutton Hoo*, Vol. III.

530

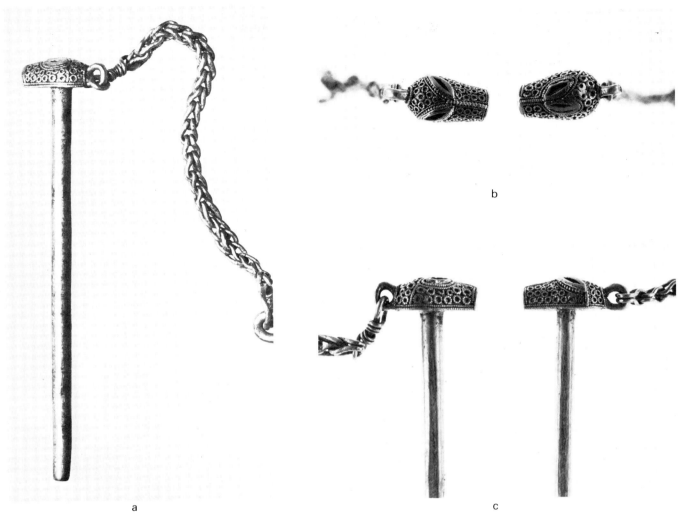

FIGURE 393   The shoulder-clasps: (*a*) fastening-pin showing the full length of the chain and its attachment staple; (*b*), (*c*) two pin-heads, seen from above and from the side. (Scale: 2/1)

(3)   In 5a the small diamond-shaped space above the knees of the boars' front legs contains a garnet. In the other three designs this is a lidded cell.

(4)   The millefiori sheets used in the boars' shoulders are from a different stick or sheet from that used in Inv. 4.

(5)   In 5b a small cell is inserted just above the tusk in the left-hand boar's head; this has a thick, spread upper wall and may represent a repair to a broken stone or a special accommodation for a single stone prepared for the position which broke and had to be put in in two pieces. In 5a the inlay in the left hand animal head in the upper zoomorphic interlace border, as seen in figure 386, is glass, in poor condition, presumably a replacement for a lost garnet.

(6)   The tusks of the two boars in 5a are in opaque blue glass. The inlays of the six remaining boars' tusks on the clasps are missing.

(7)   In 5a the boars' heads and front legs are slightly smaller than in 5b and 4, and

the diamond-shape above the knees of the front legs is a little lower; this affects the shape of the spaces available for filigree fillings and so their design.

(8) In both 5a and 5b the boars' tails are similarly composed using two garnets only; the garnet shapes, however, differ from those in the two-garnet tail of the boar in Inv. 4b.

(9) Details from the filigree devices on the clasp-ends and on the pin-heads are shown in figures 432 b, c and 434–6. Two clasp-ends are also shown in plate 16. In Inv. 5 the zoomorphic subjects are animals and not snakes. The design in the outer fields (outside the boars' heads) is that of an animal looking back over its shoulder (fig. 436 c). The creatures in the inner fields are of the same kind but elongated to fit the different shape of field (fig. 435 a, b). They are the same animals as those which form the interlacing borders round the rectangular panels, creatures with head, body and one hind leg with accentuated hip, in the case of the filigree versions filled with granulation.

It is not clear what, if anything, the filigree fill-ups in the central space between the boar figures in Inv. 5 may represent.

Discussion

The clasps are unique in Germanic archaeology. As no satisfactory analogies can be found to suggest otherwise, they may be taken as being shoulder clasps.[1] They are a pair, and the only other function which it seems they might possibly perform is that of wrist-clasps. This may seem plausible, since wrist-clasps are a recognised item of Anglian costume and familiar in Anglian burials in England, but Anglian wrist-clasps are normally flat, or only very slightly curved, and light; they are fastened together by hooks and never hinged. The Sutton Hoo clasps are very heavy and could only have been mounted on thick strong cloth or leather. If they were used as wrist-clasps and the wrists were raised much above shoulder level the pins would tend to fall out; the weight of the clasps, if the sleeves were lifted above the head, would also tend to pull down the material which, if substantial, must have been relatively open and loose because of the size and flat curvature of the clasps as assembled and properly displayed (the hinge mechanism should not be exposed in use). In a garment with loose sleeves, moreover, there would be no point in having wrist clasps, since their function in Anglian dress was to draw the sleeves in to the wrist. Lastly, wrist-clasps appear to be found only in women's graves.

In the case of the Sutton Hoo ship-burial we are dealing with a male grave of abnormal character, and the gold jewellery in it is thought of as comprising items of regalia. Wrist-clasps of a special kind might theoretically be part of royal ceremonial robes. The curvature of the clasps, however, must be regarded as too flat and long to suit the wrist position, where the halves of the clasps would find themselves

---

[1] Similar interlocking plates held by a hinge-pin and chain are to be seen in a context of relevance, namely, in the helmet from boat-grave Vendel 14, where this device is used to join together the two cheek-pieces in front of the point of the chin. Lindqvist 1950a, fig. 2; Stolpe and Arne 1927, pl. XLI, fig. 5.

FIGURE 394 The breastplate of the muscle-cuirass from the statue of the Emperor Augustus at Prima Porta (Vatican Museum) illustrating the use of shoulder-clasps on Imperial armour.

533

frequently at an angle to one another, with the interior of the hinge exposed. If the clasps were extended to their fullest, concealing the hinge, as the design would seem to envisage, then the curvature is too flat for any normal sleeve. On the other hand the clasps fit very comfortably to the curve of the shoulder, where they sit naturally: it may be regarded as virtually certain that they were worn in this position. If this is so, they must have been used to join the front and back of a two-piece garment or surcoat, assembled on the body. Such shoulder-clasps are worn as part of Imperial costume and of cavalry dress, the Imperial versions being associated with the ornate embossed *cuir-bouilli* muscle cuirass. This is seen on an Imperial statue in the Museum of Vaison-la-Romaine in Provence; on that of the Emperor Augustus from Prima Porta, in the Vatican (fig. 394), and on the colossal bronze figure at Barletta, commemorating perhaps Theodosius the Great (379–385) or Valentinian I (364–375). This last wears the leather cuirass with parade armour, but the shoulder-clasps presumed present are obscured by a cloak.[1] It has been possible to trace close links between the Sutton Hoo helmet and helmets produced in the Constantinian Imperial workshops (p. 220), and to suggest links between the Sutton Hoo sceptre and Consular and Imperial sceptres of the fifth and sixth centuries A.D., and an equivalent relationship between a feature of a *Bretwalda*'s ceremonial dress and Roman Imperial body armour is not unlikely.

It has been said that the Sutton Hoo clasps are unique. So they are, in almost all respects. Some other clasps, other than the Anglian wrist clasp group, however, may be briefly considered in relation to them. An important curved pair was found in the Taplow barrow in 1883. One of them is illustrated in figure 343 and plate 22b. Contemporary plans of the Taplow burial deposit, the richest Anglo-Saxon burial known until Sutton Hoo came to light, differ in many respects and are not reliable, but they all agree in showing the clasps together as a pair side by side, on the left side at the waist. This position would be compatible with their curvature, which is too great to allow of their being worn at the front of the body. The curvature could match the shoulders, but the agreement of all the plans in showing the pair at the waist is against this. Each of the half clasps has three loops at the back; they were joined by a hook on one which engaged a loop on the other. They are of bronze overlaid with gold sheeting stamped with fluent Style II interlace. The latest view taken is that they were worn at the ends of a double belt, perhaps of two brocaded bands fastened together, and from this I see no reason to differ.[2] The belt would not have been adjustable by means of the clasps, but may have been adjustable by means of a slide of organic material such as bone. There is no parallel for such clasps worn at the side of the waist, let alone for a pair used together.

A further analogy may be mentioned, though it is remote. Two curved clasps (SHM 14392) were ploughed up at Grumpan, Sävare, Västergötland, Sweden, with three

---

[1] The Vaison-la-Romaine figure is illustrated in the Museum Guide (British Museum 1964). For convenient reference to the figure of Augustus, Gamber 1966, plate LIVb, and Robinson 1975, plate 433. For the Barletta colossus (referred to again in connection with the great gold buckle, p. 557), see Gamber 1966, where the shoulder-clasp identification for the Sutton Hoo pieces is accepted without hesitation.

[2] Crowfoot and Hawkes 1967, 47.

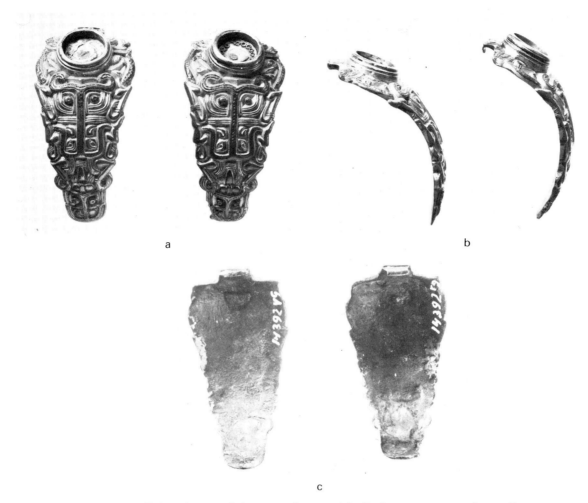

a

b

c

FIGURE 395   Pair of curved bronze clasps with Style 1 ornament from Grumpan, Västergötland: (*a*) front view; (*b*) side view; (*c*) rear view. (Scale: 1/1) (Photos: Statens Historiska Museum, Stockholm)

C-bracteates.[1] They have rich Style I cast decoration (fig. 395 *a–c*). They are too sharply curved and too small to play the role of shoulder-clasps and their use is unknown though they could perhaps have been worn on arm or ankle. They seem to be unparalleled. Though to all intents and purposes identical, they do not seem to be a pair, since both appear to have had hooks (one with the downward-bent point broken off) and neither seems to have had a loop to engage a hook. Their hooks might have engaged a loop of cloth or other organic material, but the two pieces could not have operated together as a paired clasp.

[1] Mackeprang 1952, 168, no. 267 and pl. 24; I am indebted to Dr Agneta Lundström for this reference.

VIII THE GREAT GOLD BUCKLE
Inv. 1 (pl. 20, figs. 396, 397)

Dimensions

Length	13·2 cm
Width	5·8 cm
Thickness of buckle (not including domed rivet heads or sliding catches on back-plate	1·1 cm
Thickness of back-plate	0·2 cm
Interior dimensions of buckle loop	3·0 ×0·7 cm
Gap between back-plate and main portion of buckle when the back-plate is straightened and the buckle is fully locked (i.e. thickness of strap or belt)	0·1 cm

Weight

Whole buckle	412·7 g
Loop alone	86·78 g

Large gold buckle of complex construction, the upper surface covered all over with carved zoomorphic ornament. The buckle is heavy and thick in appearance but is hollow, the back-plate opening on a seven-sectioned hinge held by a long gold pin. The hinge is almost identical in construction with those of the shoulder-clasps. Three spaced tubes, 7–8 mm in length, are soldered to the top edge of the main and moving portion of the back-plate. They interlock with four similar tubes soldered to the remaining smaller rigid portion of the back-plate, which forms part of the solidly built shoulders of the buckle to which the heavy gold loop is attached (figs. 401 *a*, *c* and 397 *a*, *b*). The back-plate of the buckle opens out to an angle of approximately 95 degrees (fig. 402) when it is stopped by the edge of the solid shoulder. The gold rod on which the hinge-mechanism operates is slightly spread at one end but not at the other, and can only be extracted by drawing out from the expanded end. The hinge-pin on which the back-plate moves is little more than a third of the thickness of the shorter, stouter bar, also of gold, on which the heavy buckle-loop hinges (fig. 400 *a*).

The buckle-tongue has a circular basal shield 30 mm in diameter and 5 mm thick (fig. 403 *d–f*) from which it projects for a distance of 25 mm, being made in one piece with it. The tongue tapers slightly to the tip which turns downwards and is flattened off below (fig. 403 *f*). A raised midrib reinforces the tongue, continues round its downward-curving tip and is flattened off congruently with the flat under-surface of the tip. The tongue with its circular base-plate is hinged and moves independently of the buckle-loop. On the underside of the circular tongue-plate is a neat attachment-loop, made from a broad flattened strip of gold, situated at the point of balance of the tongue and its plate. Through this loop, providing a hinge for the tongue, runs the bar on which, by means of rearward projections to either end, the buckle-loop also hinges. The mechanism is illustrated in figures 397 *c* and 401 *b*. A flange stops the tongue from moving downwards more than a certain distance, while the flat circular

FIGURE 396   The great buckle (Inv. 1). (Scale: 3/2)

a

b   c

FIGURE 397   The great gold buckle: (*a*) profile, (*b*) rear view and (*c*) side view, showing the hinged back-plate in a partly opened position. (Scale: 1/1)

plate prevents any movement of the tongue above the horizontal plane of the surface of the buckle. The buckle-loop can move downwards more freely, but is finally stopped against the shoulders of the buckle and the top of the back-plate which projects to dovetail with the two rearward projections from the ends of the loop (fig. 402).

The walls of the buckle are in general 1·5 mm thick, but thicken slightly at the upper end or shoulders of the buckle, where there is much more weight to be supported.

The opening and locking mechanism

The hinged back-plate is opened or locked by means of three sliding catches, two situated in line near the shoulders of the buckle and one near the point (figs. 397b and 400). This mechanism for opening or locking seems to have been the least satisfactory feature of the buckle, being evidently vulnerable and having had to be reinforced.

On the inside of the back-plate are three small oval upstanding sockets set with their long axes transversely to that of the buckle (figs. 400e, 401f). These sockets are positioned in relation to the three circular sliding catch-plates on the outside of the back-plate (figs. 397b, 398, 400b, c, 401e). The sliding catch-plate near the point of the buckle is larger than the pair situated towards its shoulders, and the corresponding socket on the inside is also thicker and larger than those associated with the other two plates. This reflects the sight difference in the sizes of the three plain bosses with beaded collars on the front of the buckle. That at the tip has a diameter of 15 mm as against the 13 mm of the other two. The increased size of the boss at the toe of the buckle and of the corresponding sliding catch mechanism reflects its greater mechanical role, its function being shared between the two bosses for which there is room at the broader upper end of the buckle. Each catch-plate has a short shank which projects at right-angles from its back, passes through a slot cut in the back-plate and is soldered to a small gold plate lying flat on the inside of the back-plate, with a projecting pin

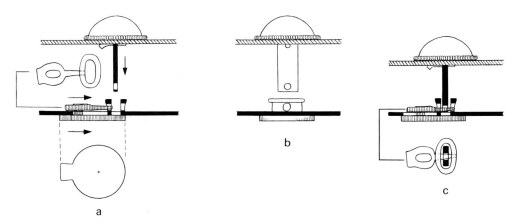

FIGURE 398 The great gold buckle: technical details of the locking mechanism. (a) side view and (b) frontal view of one of the catches, open, (c) side view showing the catch shut. (Scale: 1/1)

539

(figs. 398, 400 *d* and 401 *f*). The external catches can be moved backwards and forwards along the slots cut in the back-plate and the small plates with projecting pins on the inside of the back-plate move with them. When the catches are as far inwards as possible the pins just engage the inner edges of the corresponding sockets, which are drilled with holes to receive them. When the catches are moved in an outward direction as far as they will go, the pins (in effect small bolts) are driven through the projecting sockets. The three long shanks which project from the backs of the bosses have two holes in them (fig. 399 *a*). One, at the top, is separated from the underside of the boss only by the thickness of the front plate of the buckle. Wedge-shaped gold pins (figs. 400 *d*, 398) driven through these hold the bosses tightly to the front plate. The second hole is at the tip of the shank. The shank passes across the open interior of the hollow buckle and its tip, containing the hole, enters the corresponding upstanding socket on the back-plate. When the three sliding catches are moved outwards the pins which serve as little gold bolts transfix the holes in the ends of the shanks and project from the far side of the socket, locking the buckle. The short stems or shanks attached to the circular sliding catch-plates are not all of the same design: the one attached to the catch on the toe of the buckle is oblong in section; those attached to the other two catches are circular in section. The small flat plate which carries the locking-pin associated with the sliding catch at the toe of the buckle is also of different size and shape from the two others (fig. 401 *f*).[1] There is thus a consistent if minor variation in the design of all parts of the fastening mechanism at the toe of the buckle from that of the mechanisms associated with the other two bosses.

The smooth working of this locking mechanism must have depended upon the rigidity and exact performance of all the parts involved. If one of the long tangs descending from the bosses on the front, or one of the locking-pins, is bent; or if one of the vertically set sockets is pushed out of the vertical; or if one of the locking-pin plates works loose, then the whole mechanism is liable to be rendered inoperative and the buckle will not shut or lock. The system of gold walls constructed inside the back-plate at the upper end of the buckle (fig. 401 *f*) must, it seems, have been devised to hold the vertical sockets rigid and may be a secondary feature. These reinforcing walls, however, are low and would not seem very effective. It is not possible to say definitely that they are secondary, but the relative crudity of the device suggests that this was not part of the original design, which in other respects was skilful and efficient. The reinforcing walls seem to concede the inadequacy of the original design for the special rôle that the buckle must have been intended to fulfil, which evidently required that it should be easily opened and closed (p. 588 ff. below).

From figures 401 *f* and 398 it will be seen that the oval sockets which received the ends of the long shanks from the bosses on the front are set up round the edges of holes cut in the back-plate. These holes are oblong and of the same size as the interior

---

[1] One of the two small plates carrying locking-pins in the upper part of the buckle is missing. It was present when the buckle was first received in the Museum and its absence cannot therefore indicate that the buckle was defective when buried.

a

b

c

FIGURE 399   The great gold buckle: (a)–(c) three views of the
bosses from the front of the buckle with their shanks. (Scale: 3/2)

openings of the sockets, permitting the tips of the shanks that descend from the bosses
on the front of the buckle to be accommodated in the 2 mm thickness of the back-plate.
By this device the holes in the shanks through which the locking-bolts pass, and which
are slightly set back from the ends of the tangs (fig. 400e), come exactly opposite the
bolts. The oblong holes in the back-plate over which the upstanding sockets are
mounted lie transversely, as do the sockets. The larger slots in which the shanks of
the sliding catches on the back-plate move backwards and forwards run at right angles

541

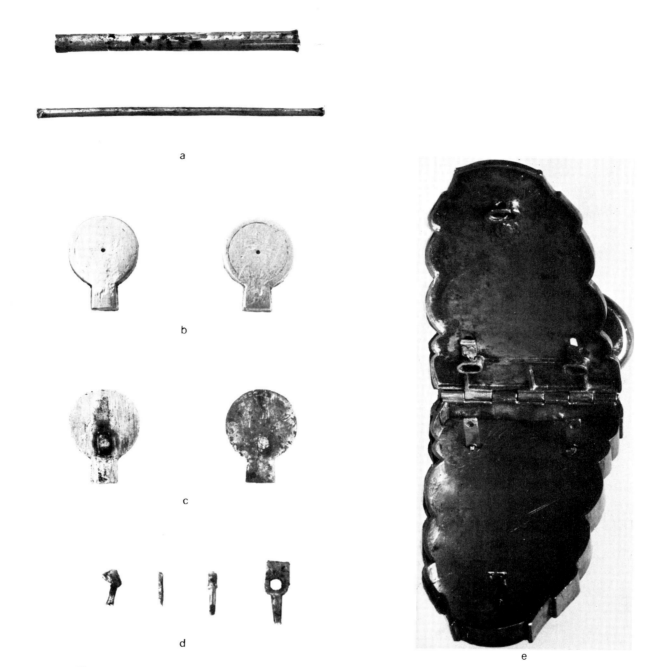

a

b

c

d

e

FIGURE 400 The great gold buckle: (*a*) hinge rods from the buckle loop (above) and the back-plate hinges; (*b*), (*c*) front and back views of two sliding catches from the outside of the back-plate; (*d*) the three fixing-pins which held the bosses on the front of the buckle in position with (right) a plate with projecting pin: the short shank from the sliding catch (as seen in (*c*) above right) enters the plate with projecting pin by means of the hole, the end of the shank being burred over on its outer surface (see (*e*)); (*e*) view of the buckle fully opened showing the mechanism for opening and closing. (Scales: *a–d*, 3/2; *e*, reduced)

542

to them, together forming a T-shaped cut-out in the back-plate. As a result of this the upstanding sockets, placed on the edges of these holes and only attached to the back-plate with gold solder, had evidently a precarious purchase. The two long tangs which descend from the pair of bosses near the shoulders of the buckle, as they engage their corresponding sockets, come in at a slight angle, and now exert some pressure on the edges of the socket. They may from the outset have tended to dislodge them or put them out of alignment. Where the inner socket wall passes across the junction of the lateral and upright elements of the cut-out area they are not supported from beneath at all. Examination of all three sockets at this point with a binocular microscope shows that the small thickness of socket wall forming the lower part of the hole through which the bolt passes has in each case been worn and bulges into the space below, and in the case of the upper right-hand socket (fig. 400 f) is actually fractured. As a result the sockets would have become more vulnerable to pressure that might push them out of alignment. As we have seen, the two sockets in the upper part of the buckle are subject to such pressure because the tangs that descend from the bosses on the front of the buckle, being close to the hinge of the back-plate, approach them at an angle. The socket at the point of the buckle is not subject to such pressures, the corresponding tang can enter it vertically from above without touching the edges of the socket. This, and its stronger construction with reinforced rim, seems to explain why it has not been bolstered up with inserted supporting walls as have the two other sockets: it seems clear that the low gold walls that support and hold the sockets at the upper end of the buckle were inserted after experience of use had shown the weakness of the original construction.

Other structural features

The chest of the buckle under the hinge can be seen in figure 401 a and c to be reinforced by a separate vertical wall of gold, the ends of which are returned towards the point of the buckle and tapered off slightly. The returned ends fit into recesses on each side which correspond with the outward projection from the profile of the buckle taken by the angular eyebrows of the two birds' heads which occupy the shoulders of the buckle. The vertical wall seems to shore up the hinge from below, and its presence implies that behind it the head of the buckle is not solid but continues hollow for a certain distance. This wall in the chest of the buckle could have been inserted merely to provide an end to the open interior space, which must have had a specific use (p. 556 below). It could also have been intended to strengthen the buckle at a point of stress or weakness, or to hold the hinge steady. There is no indication that the buckle was ever damaged at this point. The inserted wall coincides with and would seem to be keyed by two rivets, the filed down heads of which can be seen in figure 401 b, above the two bosses in the undecorated curved field. Another pair of rivets with filed-down heads can be seen above these at the base of the two projections which flank the tongue-loop. These are probably for the better attachment

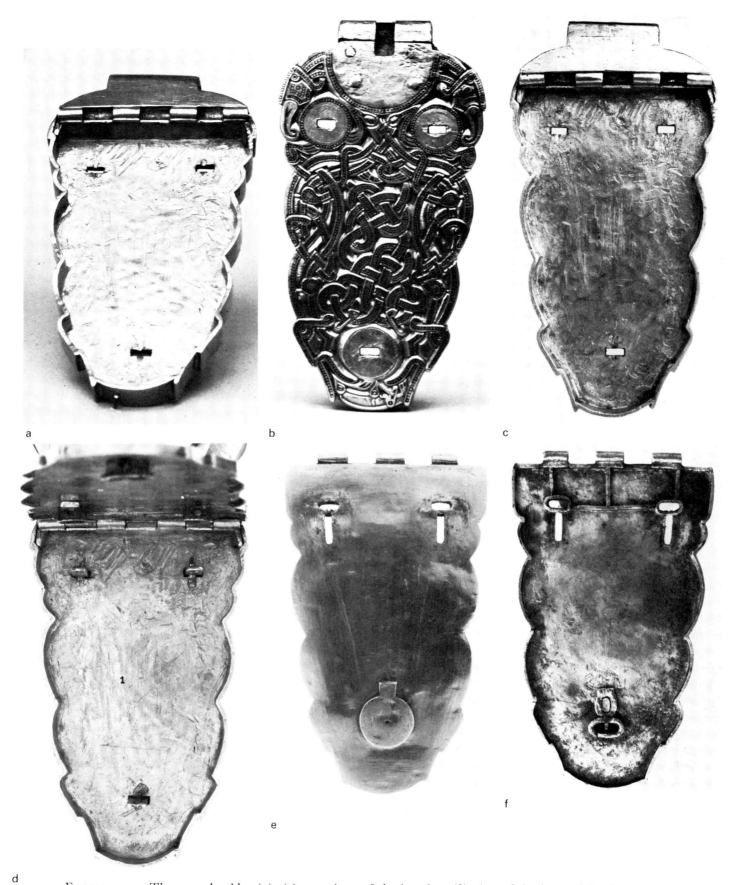

a

b

c

d

e

f

FIGURE 401   The great buckle: (*a*), (*c*) two views of the interior; (*b*) view of the front of the deep upper plate of the buckle, with the bosses and their fixing-pins removed; (*d*) interior of the upper plate showing the shanks of the bosses on the front of the buckle entering the interior and held by fixing-pins; (*e*) (*f*) exterior and interior views of the back-plate with one sliding catch (at the toe) in position. (Scale: slightly under 1/1)

544

of the two projections which seem to have been made separately and partly welded, partly riveted in position.

The alloys of various parts of the buckle have been analysed with a view to seeing whether any significant difference could be detected which might indicate whether reinforcements or individual elements of the buckle (the loop, for example) were more likely to be replacements or repairs, or part of the buckle as originally made. The results are included in the Appendix by the Research Laboratory (p. 618 ff.) giving the results of the gold analysis programme for the jewellery in general. They may be repeated here for convenience (for the positions from which samples were taken see fig. 443).

TABLE 31   RESULTS OF GOLD ANALYSIS FROM THE BUCKLE (INV. 1)

	Gold %	Silver %	Copper %
The wall of the main part of the buckle	89·2	8·9	1·8
The loop	82·4	15·1	2·4
The tongue-plate	80·2	16·8	2·4
The low reinforcing walls associated with the locking-sockets at the upper end of the buckle	85·4	10·2	4·2
The wall supporting the chest of the buckle	77·7	15·0	3·2

The analyses of tongue and loop within the limits of the analytical technique are very similar (as compared with the markedly different result from the body of the buckle), and they could have been cast from the same melt of metal. The relatively low gold figure for the supporting wall in the chest of the buckle could be thought to suggest that it may have been a later insertion. On the whole the results are not archaeologically significant, except in demonstrating a strong probability that the loop belongs to the buckle as an entity, and on metallurgical grounds is not likely either to have been made later or taken over from an earlier buckle, a possibility suggested to me by Professor Sune Lindqvist[1] because of the different aspect of the interlace and the absence of niello of the loop.

The loop

The buckle-loop (fig. 403 a–c) is massive and beautifully made. Its surface and edges are finely shaped and rounded. Its inner side is cut away to receive the projections from the top of the buckle-plate which hold the hinge-pin that engages the loop of the tongue and the two projecting outer elements of the loop (figs. 401 b, 403). The shoulders of the buckle are hollowed

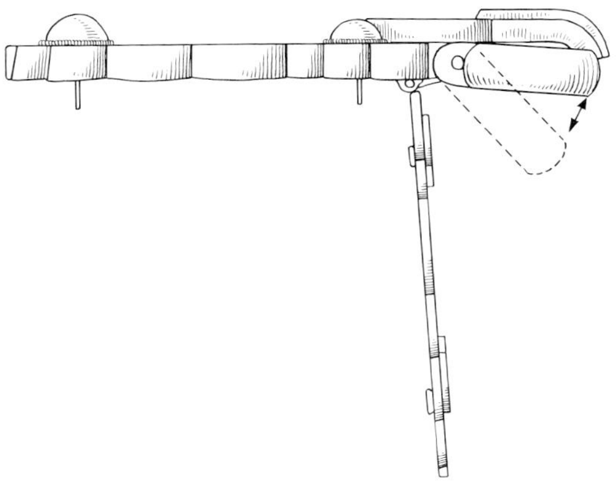

[1] Verbal communication.

FIGURE 402   The great gold buckle: shown with the back plate fully opened; the angle of drop of the buckle-loop is also indicated. (Scale: 1/2)

at the top while the projecting side pieces from the loop are convex; the two surfaces fit into each other to yield a unified design while still preserving free movement (figs. 397 b, 402). There is no gap between the shoulders and loop of the buckle. The upper surface of the loop is cut across transversely to receive both the flat under-surface of the tongue and, to a greater depth, the downward-turned but flat-cut point. Clear of the tongue to either side are panels of interlace, discussed in more detail below. We have seen that the evident difference in its style and treatment as compared with the ornament on the plate and tongue-plate have given rise to the suggestion that the loop may be either a later replacement or else taken over in the first instance from an earlier buckle. There is no physical evidence to suggest this, and we have seen that on the contrary analysis of the gold alloy suggests that the tongue and loop could have been cast from the same pouring of metal. Yet the ornament on the tongue-plate exactly matches in weight, style and technique that of the buckle-plate, sharing its differences from the ornamentation of the loop. Metallurgically the tongue forms a link between the two. We may be the more confident that the loop was made for this buckle, since they make a perfect formal match. If, in spite of the close similarity in metallic composition, it were a replacement, it is most unlikely, because of this exact formal match, that it could have been taken over from any other buckle. It must have been made specifically as a replacement for this one.

Figure 403 a–c shows the buckle-loop detached. The two widely spaced projections from the rear edge of the loop have transverse holes which carry the hinge-pin (fig. 400 a) on which the loop moves. The rear edges of these projections slope away to an increased depth at the outside (fig. 403 a, b). This slope follows the receding curve of the shoulders of the buckle, the projections fitting into two concealed recesses in the shoulders (fig. 404). These recesses find an outward formal expression in the design of the birds' heads on each side. The projection upwards from the necks of the birds of the angled membrane at the back of the eye continues across the thickness of the buckle and forms an end wall to the recesses into which the two projecting pieces of the loop fit (fig. 404 b).

A substantial circular washer in dark metal, 1 mm thick, with a central hole through which the hinge-pin passes, is visible in figure 403 c (right) and is seen enlarged in figure 403 g. This metal is silver. The washer is neatly and solidly bedded in the surrounding gold, as befits a working part of the loop mechanism. It is gripped to either side by gold flanges worked round its edges and carried slightly inwards over its top edge to retain it. It appears to rest on a ledge of unburnished metal, with the characteristic roughish finish of the rest of the concavity at the back of the loop between the two projections. The central hole in the washer is 3 mm in diameter, just sufficient to take the gold hinge-pin. No corresponding washer seems to have been used on the other side of the loop, although an initial allowance for one seems to have been made. The elements from the buckle-plate which engage with the loop (fig. 404) fit exactly into the space between the silver washer and the opposing projection. A

a

b

c

d

e

f

g

FIGURE 403   The great gold buckle: (a)–(c) loop; (d)–(f) tongue; (g) detail
of the loop showing a silver washer. (Scale: a–f, 1/1; g, slightly under 2/1)

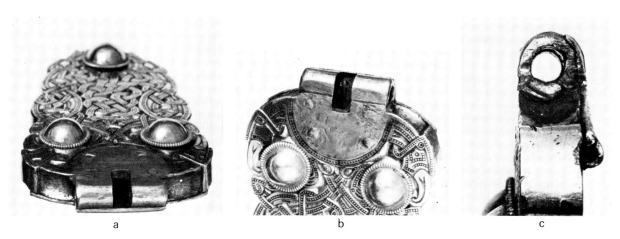

FIGURE 404 Three views of the shoulders of the great gold buckle with the loop and tongue removed showing concealed recesses in which the loop pivots. (Scales: *a*, *b*, 1/1; *c*, 2/1)

small pad of silver, however, has been inserted at the inner end of the concealed recess low down against the base of the element from the buckle-plate where it meets the washerless projection from the loop (fig. 404 *c*). This seems to have acted as a filling to take up any looseness in the fitting of the loop and ensure that it moved with perfect smoothness.

The loop looks solid but in fact is hollow. The interior cavity may not be large but it is continuous, and air can be blown through it. Access to the interior cavity is through two small, virtually inaccessible openings which emerge into the projections which house the hinge-pin.

The decoration

The buckle has an undulating symmetrical profile (fig. 396) which at first sight might appear to have been determined primarily by the logic of the animal design it carries, within the desired long, subtriangular form called for in such a buckle. The point raised above that the necks and angular backs of the heads of the birds conceal recesses for the loop mechanism, together with a further factor discussed below (pp. 557-8), indicate that the form of the buckle was primarily functional.

Apart from the three plain collared bosses the entire upper surface of the buckle is covered with a continuous uninterrupted spread of carved zoomorphic interlace. There are no internal or external borders, no defined fields and no panelling or framing of individual parts of the design. The ornament spreads continuously and without restraint over the whole surface of the buckle. This rich prodigality or ornamental overloading matches that seen on the garnet cloisonné jewellery, although the sides of the great gold buckle and of its loop are plain, whereas in the cloisonné jewellery the all-over garnet inlays invade the sides of mounts, a hinge, the loop of the curved mount, end shelves holding rivets in the rectangular mounts, and other parts not normally decorated.

548

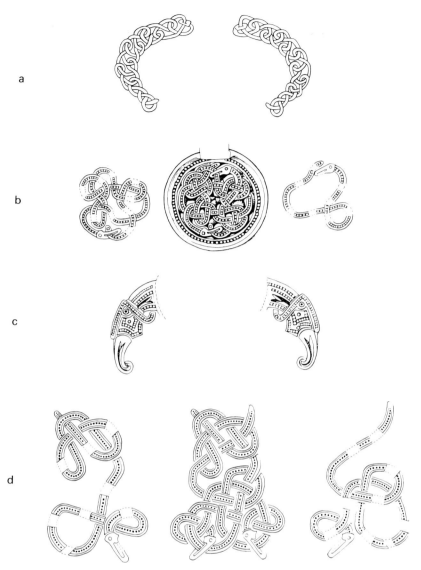

a

b

c

d

FIGURE 405   The great gold buckle: (a), (b), (d)
details of zoomorphic designs of snakes; (c) bird heads
from the shoulders of the buckle. (Scale: 1/1)

The space at the top of the front plate of the great gold buckle normally covered by the circular tongue-plate when the buckle is worn or lying flat, but exposed to view when the tongue is tilted forwards, is undecorated and only relatively roughly finished (fig. 401 b). It is marked off by bordering which separates it from the pendent animal heads at the shoulders of the buckle and from the animal interlace covering the rest of the plate. This bordering consists of two curving, parallel engraved lines, filled with niello, concentric with the tongue-plate, with, between them, a line of small square punch holes also filled with niello. The punch used is identical with that employed for the similar decoration on the unit of interlace in the middle of the buckle-plate (two interwoven snakes). The border remains visible outside the circumference of the tongue-plate when this lies flat on the surface of the buckle-plate.

From the sides of the niello bordering which encircles the tongue-plate, as if developing from the tongue-plate, the necks and heads of two birds in typical Germanic Style II with angular eyebrows and sharply pointed chins thrust outwards to form the shoulders of the buckle. Their chins and the tips of their beaks rest against the outsides of the two circular plain hemispherical bosses. From each of these bosses, their feet pushing against opposite sides of the boss, two animals with rear and front legs develop; the animal whose hindquarters rest on the inner circumference of a boss crosses over to the opposite side of the buckle and appears to be hunting or pursuing the second animal which lies primarily along the edge of the buckle. The animal bodies undulate down either side of the buckle-plate, the undulations making its profile. The chins and lower jaws of the two leading animals in the zoomorphic procession rest against the boss at the toe of the buckle. The jaws of these last creatures open, and between them, on a slight curve which forms the toe of the buckle and reflects the curve of the large terminal boss, crouches a small complete quadruped, seen upside down in figure 396. The central space of the buckle-plate between the surging animals and the circular tongue plate is filled with a pair of snakes locked together in a tight interlace. All the animal ornament of the buckle is drawn in figures 405 and 406.

The three plain bosses on the front of the buckle are mounted on circular platforms, in the middle of which rectangles are cut out (fig. 401 b). The flat rectangular shanks of the bosses pass through these holes into the interior of the buckle. The two circular platforms that accommodate the bosses at the top of the buckle-plate are surrounded by niello ribbons containing a line of circular gold spots (invisible in frontal views of the buckle, being concealed by the thick beaded wire collars that surround the bosses). The platform of the large single boss in the toe of the buckle has no such surrounding ribbon of niello and gold spots (fig. 401 b).

The small animal hindquarters between two upper bosses, seen upside down when the buckle is viewed with its loop to the top, have pear-shaped hips pointing outwards, from which develop very short hind legs, out of proportion to the animals as a whole, and feet furnished with four spread and clearly marked toes. These legs and toes rest against the inside edges of the bosses. The pear-shaped hips were filled with niello (figs. 406-7). Immediately below these two hindquarters the bodies of the animals develop and cross over each other, their split contours immediately intersecting to provide an instance of 'penetration': the bodies move outwards to penetrate and interlace with those of the second pair of animals that occupy the greater part of the outer edges of the buckle, which they appear to be pursuing. The hind legs of the outer animals rest on the outside edges of the two bosses. These legs have four toes whereas the front feet of the same animals have only three. The small crouching animal across the toe of the buckle has three toes on each foot.

The interlacing snakes and animals are for the most part flat, reserved in a flat surface with the background cut away. The snakes in the tongue-plate and the pairs of surging animals are in ribbon style, and the ribbons carry down their centres a

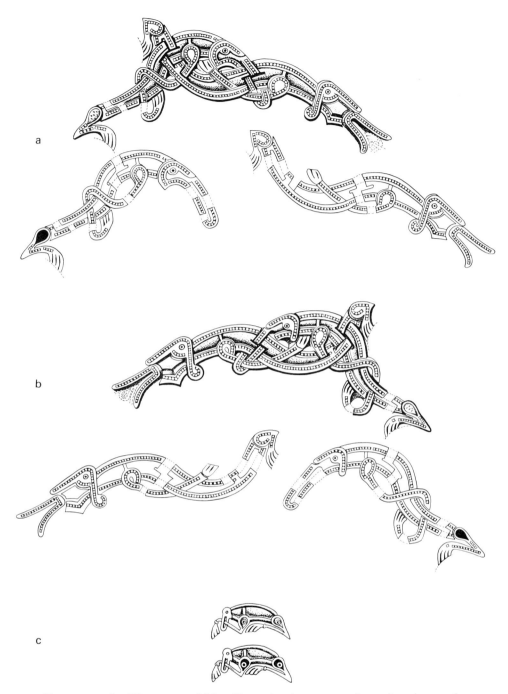

a

b

c

FIGURE 406 The great gold buckle: animal ornament from the edges and toe of the buckle: (*a*) right side (with the loop regarded as the top); (*b*) left side; (*c*) crouched animal at the toe, in two versions, one showing niello inlays in the shoulder and hip. (Scale: 1/1)

pattern of small, close-set reserved gold circles set in a ribbon of niello. The technique is discussed below (p. 536). The snakes in the centre field carry a pattern, exactly matching that used to border the area concealed by the tongue-plate, of parallel engraved lines picked out with niello inlay and a line of small detached punched squares, also filled with niello, running between them.

All the animals have stylised and emphasised pear-shaped hips. In the quadruped across the toe of the buckle the hips are hollowed out and a ring of metal is left standing up in the middle. In the animals with hips lying against the tongue-plate the hip is hollowed out like a basin, the bottom of which appears as a low convex mound stabbed with holes like a pin-cushion—seven stabs in each mound—apparently made with the triangular point of the graving tool; these sunken fields were filled with niello (fig. 407 *i*) as probably occurred also in the animal on the toe of the buckle. In the other six hips the shape is merely outlined in the flat by a border of circles in niello which follows the contour of the hip. All the animal feet on the buckle are short and stubby and not of the feathered and elongated type seen, for example, throughout the zoomorphic ornament of the shield.

The animals which primarily occupy the edges of the buckle have plain lightly convex bodies between the nielloed borders. A raised bar runs transversely across the body opposite each hip; a similar bar can be seen in the same position on the small crouched animal, which also has raised collars across each ankle. The front feet of the surging animals are demarcated by a transverse raised curve. The treatment of animal feet, heads and legs on the buckle is illustrated in figure 407.

The zoomorphic interlace on the buckle-loop (fig. 405 *a*) is of smaller scale and seems to have a lighter, more intricate rhythm than the interlace on the rest of the buckle. It is too narrow to carry inlays and there is no indication that the background was ever filled with niello. Small snake's heads near the tongue to either side give it its zoomorphic character.

The ornament on the buckle is almost equally divided between animals and snakes. Designs consisting wholly of snakes occupy exclusively the buckle-loop, the circular tongue-plate and the central field (symmetrical in shape though its contained interlace is asymmetric) in the middle of the buckle-plate; animal designs occupy the peripheral areas.

The snake heads on the tongue-plate and the buckle-plate bear a formal resemblance to the animal heads with long closed jaws and no crest or lappet in the middle of each side of the buckle (fig. 407 *a* and *d*) and the crouching beast on the toe of the buckle has exactly the same form of head as the snakes. In the front hips of the two animals whose heads appear at each side of the toe of the buckle, a faintly engraved or scratched inner contour in the field of the hip gives the effect of a twist. The scratched line is visually not unlike the fine cracks which can show round the edges of lidded cells on the cloisonné jewellery (figs. 377 *d* and 386).

The large predatory bird heads which thrust down from the shoulders have the typical Style II angled eye-surround, sharply pointed jaw and curved beak. The other animals are in pairs. The two rear animals which seem to be in pursuit and to be springing on the front animal from behind and below, have long narrow closed crocodile-like jaws which end in a rounded muzzle, locked through the bodies of the front animals and on to their front legs. The two rear animals have no lappets or forelocks or crest, and no line of ornamental demarcation between eye and face. They have a rounded back to the head which comes to a slight point well back below the eye. The heads of the front animals also have rounded backs but the border outlining the back forms a crest or straight forelock on top of the head and a twist below. The eye is marked off with a surround of gold circles in niello (fig. 407b). The mouth is shorter than that of the pursuing animal and is open as if in a cry of pain; the tips of the jaws or lips curl outwards and between two open mouths, across the toe of the buckle, is the small crouched animal. The eyes of the two pairs are of the dot and circle variety, formed apparently with the same ring-punch and subsequently filled with niello (fig. 409a).

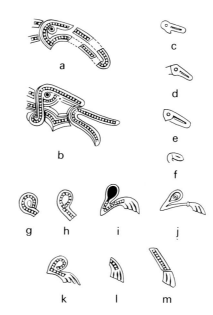

FIGURE 407 The great gold buckle: details of animal heads, feet and hips (Scale: 1/1)

The only decorated surfaces of the buckle which do not have niello inlays are those on the loop. The difference in appearance is striking, accentuated as it is by the smaller scale and lighter rhythm of the interlace. The rather tumultuous irregular character of the interlace, however, resembles that of the rest of the buckle, particularly the central snake design. There is every reason to suppose that the loop is an original part of the buckle; the fact that no niello was used on it and that the snake heads are simpler in form than the other snake heads on the buckle is probably due to lack of space—the constriction of the ornamental field and the resultant thinness of the snakes' bodies.

It is difficult to find any analogy for the buckle or its ornament. Formally, it is not unlike a number of Frisian buckles. Its all-over zoomorphic ornament finds an analogy in the large damascened Frankish iron buckles of the later seventh century. The ornament offers some points of resemblance.

The closest parallel to the rambling interlace of the loop, with its snake theme evidenced only by a simplified head biting its own body at one end and a pointed extremity at the other, is that from Farthing Down (fig. 408a) to which attention was drawn long ago by E. T. Leeds.[1] The interlace is open and large. The small scale and quick rhythm of that on the Sutton Hoo buckle-loop are paralleled on a Vendel I mount (fig. 408b), in a design which also includes running knot-work; this boat-grave contained examples of similarly light but non-zoomorphic interlace[2] and others belonging to the full East Scandinavian Style C; they are more organised and seem to reflect the geometric basis of Insular interlaces of the Hiberno-Saxon phase of the end

[1] Leeds 1936, fig. 15.   [2] Stolpe and Arne 1927, pl. VIII, figs. 6, 8.

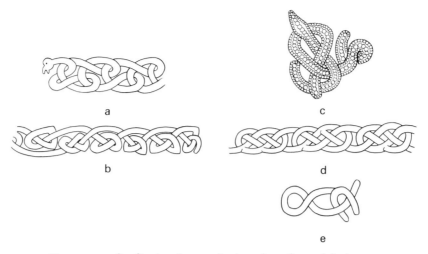

FIGURE 408 Snake themes in interlace from (*a*) the cup from Farthing Down, Surrey; (*b*) bronze mount from Vendel 1; (*c*) pyramid of pale gold, from Selsey, Sussex; (*d*) and (*e*) interlace details from the sword hilt and the upper edge of the pommel from Crundale Down, Kent. (Scales: *a*, 1/2, *b–e*, 2/1)

of the seventh century.[1] The snakes on the Crundale Down buckle (fig. 414 *b*) are also of a later period than Sutton Hoo, belonging to a phase shared by the Selsey gold pyramids (fig. 408 *c*) in which the snake or animal head is seen from above, splayed out with both eyes showing. The plain interlace on the silver-gilt mount associated with the sword pommel, with Book of Durrow type animals, from the same grave at Crundale Down (fig. 408 *d*) is also presumably of this later period, but is closer to the Sutton Hoo buckle-loop in its rhythm and rambling character. These examples probably date from the second half of the century. The broad, open bodies of the animals on the Sutton Hoo buckle recall the treatment of the horse figures on the flange of the shield-boss. The procession of animal heads, though the heads in this case are individually different, is matched in East Scandinavian Style II (cf. fig. 53). The animal heads with open mouths on both sides of the toe of the buckle are not unlike those of the four animals in the tail of the bird on the Sutton Hoo shield (fig. 49). The combination of snakes with animals, though they are segregated on the Sutton Hoo buckle, is characteristic of Vendel Styles A and B in East Scandinavia. The slightly wandering lines of circular punch marks are reminiscent of the similar linear assemblies of punched circles on the animal heads on the Sutton Hoo helmet and in the bear figures in relief flanking the Vendel 12 spear-head (fig. 152). The buckle is of broadly West European form, not found in East Scandinavia, with an ornamental repertoire and treatment that has a strongly East Scandinavian look.

[1] Cf. Olsén 1945, 92, 93, 96; Abb. 83, 342, 343 and others.

554

FIGURE 409 The great gold buckle: enlarged details of punch-work. (*a*) ring punch (circle of gold in ring of niello) and double ring punch (niello inner circle and outer ring); (*b*) square punch yielding gold circle in niello square; (*c*) rectangular punch (left); (*d*) further example of the ring-punch seen in (*a*) and a square punch (gold square in a niello square); (*e*) detail of square punch in (*d*) seen in isolation without niello filling. In (*b*) bottom left, can be seen the examples of punch impressions cut through by the engraving tool. Individual punch impressions, broken apart on a curve, are seen on the right. An isolated punch impression and others lacking niello fillings, are seen top left. In (*c*) on the right, overlapping impressions of the punch, cutting through the central gold circle, can be seen.

(Scale: 6/1)

Technique

The intricate zoomorphic interlace of the front of the buckle is in a chip-carving technique. The surfaces that form the animal bodies and carry the decorative themes are reserved, while the background is cut away in deep grooves and angular depressions. The patterns may have been cast in broad outline, but it is clear that much of the surface has been carved, often at the final stage in the completion of the ornament, after the niello inlays had been filled in. Such details as the gaps between the toes of the animals and the niello-filled bordering lines to either side of the central line of niello squares in the snakes' bodies and round the perimeter of the tongue-plate are cut with a graving tool. The niello inlays on the buckle-plate and the tongue-plate take the form either of a ribbon of niello in which there appears a continuous line of gold circles, or of niello rectangles set in gold ribbons bordered with niello-filled engraved lines.

The niello work is largely based on the use of two punches, one with a small rectangular head and a larger square one, with a central circular hole which, when the punch is struck, leaves a column of gold standing up in a sunken square. The individual punch is well seen in figure 409 *b*—a detail of the hips associated with the animal feet that rest against the right-hand upper boss. The lines of gold circles are built up by repeated applications of this punch in which its impressions often overlap —in not a few instances an application of the punch has cut in half the preceding circular gold column, or taken a slice off it (fig. 409 *c*). Not until after this ornament was executed was the engraving tool used to cut through the ribbons, create breaks in the interlace and give clarity and definition to the design. Figures 409 *b* and *c* show enlarged details of interlace in which it can be seen that the graving tool in forming the breaks in the interlace, has cut through niello fill and the reserved gold columns.

The animal eyes are made with a double ring-head (dot and circle) punch, the impression left by which is filled with niello (fig. 409 *a*).

The use of the buckle

The gold buckle gives rise to several unprecedented problems. The possibility that it is a reliquary is discussed below. Theoretically it might be considered as a buckle-reliquary, an object in its own right, not intended for functional use on the dress, but its position in the burial is against this. It lay very close to the purse on an alignment which would agree with both objects being carried on the same belt; this is further indicated by the fact that the purse-lid was suspended from straps no more than 1 mm thick, and this is also the thickness of the belt that could be accommodated by the closed buckle. It is difficult to see it as anything other than a buckle for the waist-belt. A suggestion that it decorated a sash of the kind that was tied round the chest of a moulded leather cuirass of Roman imperial type, the presence of which in the ship-burial has been thought to be implied by the pair of shoulder-

556

clasps,[1] is impracticable, since the great weight of the buckle could not be supported in such a position.

It is not clear how the Sutton Hoo gold buckle was attached to a belt. There is no question in this case of riveting the cloth or leather between two close-set plates. The buckle has no rivets or detached back-plate and is, as we have seen, hollow, with a large interior space. The substance of any belt must have entered the narrow gap between the hinged back and the deep front portion of the buckle-plate. That a gold buckle with a uniform general thickness of 11 mm should be carried on a belt only 1 mm thick, however fastened, also seems incongruous: sheer weight would seem to call for some more substantial mount. The thinness of the belt suggests that it was of cloth as a woven material of this thickness would be stronger than leather. It is difficult to see how the end of a belt, once admitted, was retained. When the buckle is shut, as figure 398 c shows, three flat tangs, set transversely across the pull of the belt, cross the interior space of the buckle. The belt, unless it bifurcated, must at least have been penetrated, perhaps through a prepared eyelet, by the centrally placed tang situated near the toe of the buckle. Perhaps all three tangs passed through prepared eyelets in the (presumed) cloth of the belt in this way. But this cannot, it seems, have been the sole means by which the cloth was held, or the means by which the strain on the belt was taken. The tangs are vulnerable, because the thinness of the metal is presented to the drag of the belt; they could easily be bent, and as we have seen (p. 540) any small deflection would be liable to render the locking mechanism inoperative. How then was the drag of the belt countered? It seems likely that the interior of the buckle held a block of wood or bone to which the cloth of the belt was fastened. Since no metal rivets or tacks were found inside the excavated buckle the cloth must have been held with an adhesive or with wooden dowels that would not survive, or else

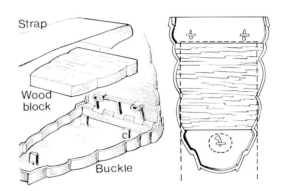

FIGURE 410 The great gold buckle: impression of the interior, showing a possible method of attachment of a belt to a (wooden or bone) block. If the buckle were a relic-holder the relic could have been contained in a cavity in the block. (Scale: 1/2)

stitched or sewn round the postulated block. Such a block could hardly have filled the whole of the interior space of the buckle, having three holes cut through it to admit the tangs and sockets of the locking mechanism, since it would then have interfered with the low reinforcement walls on the upper part of the buckle's interior on the back-plate (fig. 401 f). More probably the postulated block was confined to the centre space between the three tangs. This central space is further restricted by the sliding catches which move inwards, but the block of bone or wood envisaged could have been carved out to accommodate the small slides of the catch plates. If the outer edges

[1] Gamber 1966. The colossal bronze imperial figure wearing a moulded leather muscle-cuirass, at Barletta (cited by Gamber), shows a simple sash tied with a knot, and no buckle.

557

of the block were cut to fit exactly into the corresponding undulations of the buckle-walls this would keep the block immovable and remove all strain from the locking devices. The undulating profile of the buckle could be functionally explained in this way. The idea is illustrated in figure 410.

There can, it seems, be only two possible reasons for designing a buckle like this, of precious metal and hollow, with a back plate that opens and shuts. One would be to enable the belt to be freely removed or replaced, enabling the superb buckle to be worn with a succession of cloth belts, perhaps of silk, linen or gold braid, appropriate to different settings or occasions.

The second reason would be to have ready access to something else in the interior of the buckle, for which it acted as a resplendent container. At this point the idea that the belt-buckle was a relic holder may be considered. The idea of a belt-shrine is familiar to Insular archaeology since the discovery of the eighth century Moylough belt-reliquary, now in the National Museum in Dublin.[1] In this the leather belt itself was the relic, encased in sheet metal embellished with enamelled plaques and furnished with non-functioning 'buckle'. The Sutton Hoo buckle, however, from its elaborate moving parts and its place in the deposit, would seem to have been functional.

A class of functional relic-holding belt buckles mostly from the Swiss region is now well identified.[2] R. Moosbrugger-Leu discusses four examples, three in bone and one in bronze (fig. 411); one from grave 108 of the cemetery associated with the Late Roman fortress of Kaiseraugst; a second and similar piece occurred in the cemetery of Basel-Aeschenvorstadt.[3] A third is from grave 33 in the Wahlern-Elisried gravefield. This is furnished, behind the openwork figural scene on the front of the buckle, with a mica inspection window.[4] The fourth example, in bronze, which carries an inscription with the name of Willimer and includes a Christian cross and a chalice in its design, is from the environs of Yverdon. In all these cases the relic chamber is a cavity slotted into an edge of the buckle. The cavity is accessible in the case of the Kaiseraugst and Basel-Aeschenvorstadt buckles by removing the buckle-loop, not readily accomplished; in the Wahlern-Elisried example by removing a separate bone bar or billet which seals the cavity; in the Yverdon buckle by the pivoting of a bronze strip in the edge of the buckle (fig. 411 c). These and other examples demonstrate the existence in this region of Switzerland and the Rhone valley of a class of relic-containing apotropaic buckles and belts, which Moosbrugger-Leu attributes in their initial phase to the Late Roman or sub-Roman fifth–sixth century Christian community,[5] a period earlier than that of the Sutton Hoo buckle. Many examples may, on the other hand, date from around A.D. 600 or later (i.e. contemporary with the Sutton Hoo buckle) and are of the Burgundian type.[6] Several of the buckles show explicitly Christian

[1] Duignan 1947; O'Kelly 1965.
[2] France-Lanord 1961, *Die Gürtelgarnitur von Saint Quentin*, where a very late date is suggested.
[3] Moosbrugger-Leu 1967, 148 ff.
[4] Ibid. 149. References to further examples are given by Moosbrugger-Leu in his footnotes.

[5] Ibid. 148.
[6] For the later dating of this group of buckles, and discussion of their ethnic and historical context, see M. Martin 1971, 36 ff., esp. 42 ff. I am indebted to Professor Joachim Werner for this reference.

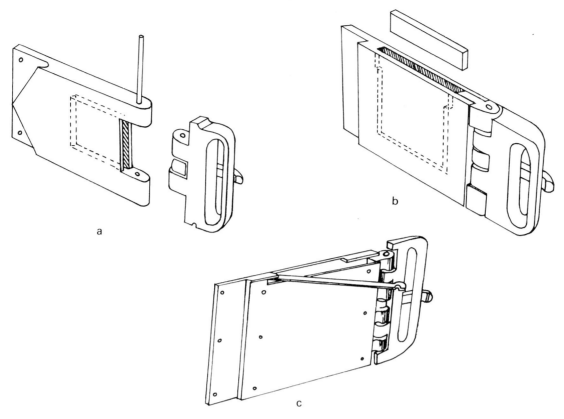

FIGURE 411   Sketches of reliquary buckles from (*a*) Kaiseraugst, (*b*) Wahlern-Elisried and (*c*) Yverdon, showing different methods of access to relic-containing cavities. (Scale: 1/2) (After Moosbrugger-Leu)

iconography (Daniel in the Lions' Den, the Soldiers at the Tomb, peacocks flanking a vase for example). The Kaiseraugst buckle, however, is plain, with no external sign of Christianity. A buckle with relic cavity, similar to those discussed by Moosbrugger-Leu, has recently come to light in excavations near Augsburg, from a burial associated with a church. The cavity contained traces of plants, cotton and beeswax,[1] and includes a Christian cross prominently in its decorative scheme. The Wittislingen brooch, with Christian inscription, and the Soest brooch, may also be considered as possible, though more doubtful, instances of relic containers.[2] The knobs at the feet of these two brooches, cast in very high relief and sealed at the back with a silver plate, apart from saving metal while achieving very high relief, provide a small chamber which could have contained a relic or amulet, though in the Wittislingen brooch the cover-plate is lost and the chamber empty, and in the Soest brooch, where the cover-plate

[1] Information from Professor Werner, who is to join in the publication of the find. In the Augsburg buckle (St Ulrich, grave 8), which was found with substantial parts of its broad leather belt, access to the interior space is provided, as in the Yverdon buckle (fig. 411 *c*) by a pivoting bronze strip. I am indebted to M. France-Lanord for allowing me to see photographs of this piece, together with a proof of the text he is contributing. The find is expected to be published in *Münchener*

Beiträge zur For- und Frühgeschichte for 1976. Other buckles that rank as relic containers of which M. France-Lanord has informed me are from Monnet la Ville and Einville-au-Jard.

[2] Werner 1950 *a*, Taf. 1 and 2, Soest, Taf. 3; on the hollow-cast high relief foot-knob of the Soest and Wittislingen brooches, p. 20, and on the inscription on the Wittislingen brooch (by Bernhard Bischoff and Werner Betz), pp. 65–72.

559

survives, the chamber appears not yet to have been opened. The minute gold pendent capsule in codex form found with the Hög Edsten pommel (fig. 232) most recently discussed by Arrhenius, is also held to have been a reliquary.[1] Reference may finally be made to the late Merovingian bronze strap-end with concealed cavities from Walda (Swabia) discussed by Dannheimer and regarded as an object of Christian amuletic significance.[2] The Sutton Hoo buckle exhibits no overt sign of Christianity, and its ornament is that of the Germanic north: any reliquary explanation of its peculiar form and construction must remain speculative.

The only analogy to the Sutton Hoo buckle in design and form known to me, though differing in some of its constructional features, is the large silver belt buckle from Crundale Down in Kent, from the same grave that contained the sword with the well-known pommel with its Book of Durrow-style animals.[3] This is in some ways very relevant. It is 15·2 cm long (as compared with the 13·2 cm of the Sutton Hoo buckle), is in silver and has on its upper surface applied decorative panels of pale gold with filigree and garnet-work. The centre of the plate carries an applied fish in high relief. The buckle is 1 cm thick, excluding the protrusion from its upper surface of fish and bosses. Its construction, with independently moving tongue and loop, and three large plain gilt bosses with beaded wire collars on the front, is similar to that of the Sutton Hoo buckle. The Crundale Down buckle is damaged, particularly in the region of the right-hand boss of the pair in the upper part of the buckle, as seen in figure 412, and in the area between it and the adjacent boss. The back-plate is detached. Nevertheless the shape can be restored as shown in figure 413. The distance between the main part of the buckle and its back-plate when the buckle was in use was 1·5 mm, not much greater than in the case of the Sutton Hoo gold buckle, and small in relation to overall size.

The Crundale buckle had a mechanism similar to that of the Sutton Hoo gold buckle in that the bosses had projecting from their backs long tangs with holes at their ends (fig. 413 a, c), which can only have been designed to enter and lock into sockets, now missing, on the inside of the back-plate. Solder patches on the back-plate show where these sockets were fixed. They were not associated with sliding catches, however, since there was no catch-plate mechanism on the outside of the back-plate, as there is in the Sutton Hoo buckle. The tang-ends were presumably locked in the sockets by pins capable of extraction through the gap between the back-plate and the main buckle-plate. Though the tangs lie lengthways inside the buckle, not transversely, and could therefore have stood up better to the strain from the pull of a belt than those in the Sutton Hoo buckle, this particular mechanism would not seem to have any point unless the buckle could open. If the buckle were not meant to be capable of opening, simple

[1] Arrhenius 1971, 156 and fig. 142; see also Arbman 1949–50, 141, 143 and figs. 4 and 5. A ninth-century version of the miniature book reliquary occurs amongst the finds from the early Slavonic town site of Mikulčice in Czechoslovakia excavated by Poulik (Bruce-Mitford 1975 b, pl. IV.2).

[2] Dannheimer 1966, especially 349 ff. and Taf. 27.
[3] Salin 1935, 329, fig. 709.

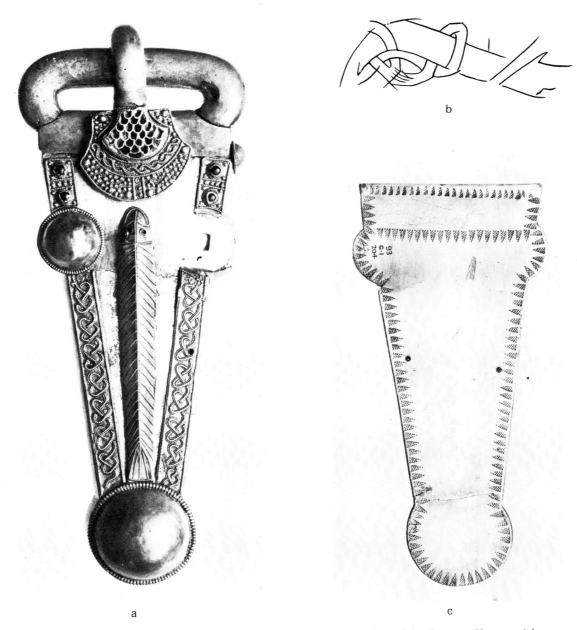

FIGURE 412 (*a*) (*c*) Silver and silver-gilt buckle from Crundale Down, Kent, with detached back plate; (*b*) drawing of engraved zoomorphic sketch from the panel at the top of the back-plate. (Scales: *a, c,* 1/1; *b,* 2/1)

riveting would have sufficed. There seems to be a gap between the upper end of the back-plate and the transverse element over the main hinge, from which the buckle-loop is hung (fig. 413*c*). The presence of a small hole some half-centimetre further down the buckle from the bar of this hinge on each side suggests a further hinge at these points, corresponding with that in the equivalent position in the gold buckle. The hinge device could have been a pivot at both ends as distinct from a hinge-bar extending all the way across the buckle. There is no sign of hinge components having

561

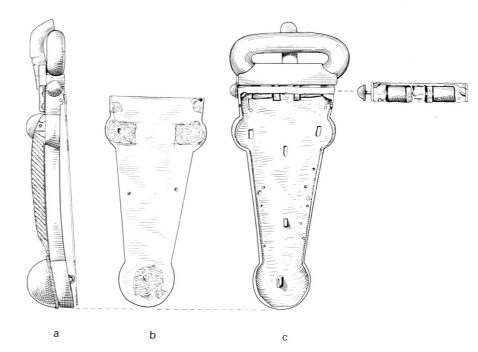

a   b   c

FIGURE 413   Drawings of the Crundale Down buckle (Kent).
(Scale: 1/2)

been attached to the lateral element above the main hinge at the back of the buckle
or to the detached back-plate (fig. 413 b, c). The gap which opens between them when
the back-plate is correctly fitted suggests either a certain freedom of movement,
sufficient to give access to the interor of the buckle, or some missing element. The
two solder-marks in the upper corners of the back-plate (fig. 413) show where loops
or sockets to engage the pivots might have been attached.

The Crundale Down buckle is a piece of relatively late date, perhaps around A.D.
650 or later, and comes from near Canterbury; with its prominent and unique fish device it may confidently be regarded as a Christian object. There is therefore less difficulty in accepting it as a relic container. If the Sutton Hoo buckle with its hollow interior and more readily operated opening mechanism is to be explained in the same way, this would be compatible with the more overt signs of Christianity in the ship-burial. Although the evidence cited below indicates that the gold buckle was locally made in the East Anglian royal workshops before 625, the analogy for such reliquaries which seems to be provided by the Kentish buckle seems relevant, especially in the light of

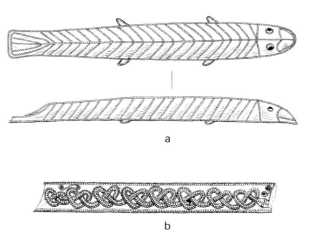

a

b

FIGURE 414   (a) Relief appliqué in the form
of a fish, with filigree details, and (b) zoomorphic interlace, from the Crundale Down
buckle (Kent). (Scale: 1/1)

562

Raedwald's conversion to Christianity in Kent, shortlived though this may have been.

A buckle which bears a notable resemblance in some respects to the Sutton Hoo buckle, though different stylistically, was found in 1957 in coffin no. 11 at St Denis, the corner of which rested upon that of Arnegunde, indicating that it was deposited after the Queen's burial.[1] The buckle, of which a description is to be published by Michael Fleury and Albert France-Lanord, is silver gilt, 11·8 cm in length as against the 13·2 cm of the Sutton Hoo buckle, with an undulating profile and three collared bosses. It is covered with a generally related though stylistically dissimilar zoomorphic ornament and there is in addition a restrained use of pieces of inlaid garnet. The buckle has a rectangular counterplate decorated *en suite*.[2] However, it has thick front- and back-plates; it is not a container and does not open, the belt end being riveted between the two plates. It is not a candidate as a possible reliquary buckle.

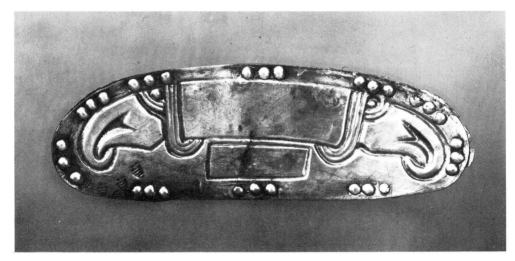

FIGURE 415   The silver patch on the large hanging bowl. (Scale: 1/1)

Origins of the Sutton Hoo buckle

The buckle fits satisfactorily into the East Anglian milieu, where the East Scandinavian affinities noted in its ornamentation (pp. 553-4) would be at home, and where we know from Sutton Hoo and other finds (the Wilton cross, for example)[3] that goldsmith's work of the highest calibre was being produced. A single point tends to confirm this; the beaks of the Style II birds' heads on the buckle have a deep central groove running from the tip to the base of the beak, where it divides into two short pointed arms separated by a V-shaped promontory of metal. The Style II birds' heads on the silver patch on the largest of the three hanging-bowls in the ship-burial (fig.

[1] France-Lanord and Fleury 1962, 342. Grave 11 can be dated with some precision to the last quarter of the sixth century, according to M. France-Lanord (verbal communication).

[2] I am most grateful to Messrs Fleury and France-Lanord for

supplying me with photographs and particulars of this piece and of the accompanying gold-mounted scramasax sheath.

[3] Also the Ixworth cross. See *Sutton Hoo*, Vol. I, fig. 439.

415) provides a unique parallel for this idiosyncrasy,[1] and gives further confirmation that the goldsmith who made at least the finest pieces of the jewellery and the great buckle turned his personal attention to the hanging-bowl—a point also suggested by the replacement of the lost enamel eyes of the cast boars' heads below the circular escutcheons by garnets in beaded wire collars, and compatible with his adoption of millefiori themes in the most important items of the regalia.

4. *The design of the harness and the functions of the various pieces of jewellery*

The assemblage of gold jewellery represents a royal harness, such as a king might wear on occasions of state. How was it put together and what was its appearance when worn? The positions of the various pieces in the ground have been commented on in pages 439-47. Apart from the purse-lid and clasp, those pieces which have been assigned to the bone, wood or ivory rod (ch. VIII), those physically attached to the sword or scabbard, and the two shoulder-clasps, there are sixteen other individual mounts. Most of these should belong to the harness associated with the sword, presenting an unparalleled richness of fitments.

The various mounts, buckles and special forms associated with the wearing of the long sword (*spatha*) have been much discussed in the archaeological literature over the last three decades, and especially recently.[2] Since no Germanic burial of the Merovingian age has produced as comprehensive or rich a set of harness mounts as those of the Sutton Hoo ship-burial, it is all the more to be regretted that the disorder in which the pieces were found makes impossible any definitive demonstration of the function of the different mounts or the exact type of sword suspension harness involved. Practical experiment with leather straps and replicas, which it has not been possible to undertake at present, may in due course yield an accepted answer. For the time being some comments and suggestions may be put forward.

The picture of the sword-belt is complicated by the presence of the purse, the great gold buckle and the shoulder-clasps. Were these outstanding pieces, and the sword and its harness, worn at one and the same time, combining to create an overwhelming and resplendent gold and garnet regalia, as is assumed by Gamber?[3] The presence of a large purse on the left side could interfere with the sword suspension, unless the sword was slung high up under the armpit, as shown in figure 416b. Is the wearing of a broad waist-belt, carrying the great gold buckle and purse, compatible with the simultaneous wearing of another belt round the waist or hips, from which the sword is hung?[4]

[1] This point has been independently observed and stressed by Dr George Speake in his doctoral thesis submitted to the University of Oxford in 1975 (at present unpublished) entitled 'The beginnings and development of Salin's Style II in England'. Dr Speake stresses the uniqueness of this treatment of the birds' heads in the corpus of Style II ornament. I am much indebted to him for allowing me to read his thesis in advance of publication.

[2] For a comprehensive survey, with many references to earlier literature, see Menghin 1973a and b; also Ament 1974.

[3] Gamber 1966, especially pl. LVII.

[4] Cf. Menghin 1973a, fig. 38; Gamber *loc. cit.*

It has been suggested[1] that the great gold buckle was non-functional, being a form of capsule, a reliquary in buckle form, not intended for use as a working buckle. My impression is that, even if it contained a relic, it was a functional buckle as well. Not only are all the normally operational parts in full working order, but the apparent damage and reinforcement to its interior mechanisms suggest strain. Chiefly, however, its position in the ground strongly suggests a working association with the purse, an item normally worn on the waist-belt, and perhaps also with the plain gold strap-loop or runner, Inv. 15, found close beside it. The thickness of the belt that carried the great gold buckle would be only 1 mm or fractionally over, suggesting cloth rather than leather (p. 557). The purse was suspended on straps of the same thickness (1 mm). This, and their relative positions in the ground, surely indicate that these two outstanding pieces were worn on the same belt, which must have been a waist-belt. The maximum width of this belt would be 5·0 cm, but if it was affixed to an internal block of bone or wood (p. 557) it may have been some 1 cm less (figure 410, a hypothetical drawing, shows it as only 4 cm wide). The buckle must have been worn at the centre front. Purses are normally found on the left side, as in the princely burials at Krefeld Gellep 1782 and Beckum,[2] or all twelve purses recorded from male graves in the Köln-Mungersdorf cemetery (p. 519). At Sutton Hoo the purse in the ground (fig. 314) lay to the *right* of the great buckle from the point of view of a recumbent body; but it was upside down, and the buckle itself well away from a central position. The relative positions could have been reversed in the fall of a suspended harness. On the other hand it is quite likely that the Sutton Hoo purse was carried on the right. This would no doubt have been necessary if the sword belt was to be worn simultaneously with the three major items of regalia (purse, shoulder-clasps and great gold buckle); and there was furthermore no dagger (cf. fig. 156*d*) or scramasax to be accommodated on the right. We cannot positively infer more from the relative positions of these two pieces as uncovered than that they were mounted not far apart on the same belt, but there seems a strong suggestion that the purse was carried on the right. In the ground (fig. 314) the buckle is the right way up while the purse is upside down but with its strap-holders correctly pointing upwards as worn. If the belt were undone, it would be easy for the purse and the buckle to be adjacent and yet reversed in relation to each other in this way (fig. 424). This broad (?cloth) belt would need to be carried no lower than the waist, if the purse was suspended on straps from it, even if these were short.

Close to the great gold buckle lay (upside down) the plain gold looped mount, Inv. 15, a solidly and finely made piece, with exceptionally handsome rivet heads with filigree collars on the front (fig. 353). It does not match any of the other mounts in its decorative character or proportions. It is a simple loop which never had a tongue (p. 485).[3] The strap width accommodated by the loop is larger than the width of

---

[1] By Professor J. Werner, in correspondence.
[2] Cf. *Sutton Hoo*, Vol. I, figs. 379 and 383.

[3] *Pace* Gamber 1966, pl. LIII (here fig. 422) and p. 267.

the plate (18 mm as against 17 mm). As has been said (p. 444), the only other plain gold strap-fitting in the assemblage is the very small strap-end, Inv. 16. Its plainness might seem to match that of the looped mount, Inv. 15. However, the disproportion between its dimensions and those of the loop (the loop measures internally 18 mm×4 mm; the strap-end only 10 mm×1·1 mm) would seem to preclude their having been designed to go together.

The location in the ground and character of the plain gold looped strap-mount with a broad but relatively shallow plate (unlike the buckles, which run to length) combine to suggest that it may have been fitted on the upper edge of the belt, close to the great buckle, to support the abnormal weight represented by the buckle and the purse. There is a precedent in some of the massive late Roman belts with heavy chip-carved mounts, as reconstructed by Bullinger.[1] Examples from Rhenen grave 846, Spontin, Rhenen 829, Weinheim, Dorchester and Leibenau grave 1/1957, show such a supporting strap associated with a loop fixed to the upper edge of the belt. If the Sutton Hoo gold runner was so positioned, the strap attached to it could have been tailored to the wearer and, as seems to have been the case with the late Roman belts cited, non-adjustable. If it were to be adjustable it would require a buckle. If the supporting strap were of cloth of the same kind and thickness as the belt (1 mm), the

a   b   c

FIGURE 416 Three methods of sword suspension in use in the late Roman and early mediaeval periods: (*a*) the Iranian or Eastern method; (*b*) the baldric or shoulder-belt (*balteus*); (*c*) two-point suspension system represented in Continental graves of the Merovingian period.

[1] Bullinger 1969, Tafeln, Abb. 34, 39–1, 42–1, 44–1, 45–1 and Abb. 50 and 51–1.

only available buckle (Inv. 12) which accommodates a 3 mm thickness, would hardly be suitable, although the strap on which it was mounted would be of appropriate width (17 mm). The supporting strap, however, could have been thicker and of leather. At first sight the cloisonné decoration of the small buckle, Inv. 12, which closely resembles that of Inv. 17 and also its intimate relationship with the two virtually identical strap-mounts, Inv. 13 and 14 (pp. 450, 468), seem to be against its use in conjunction with the plain looped mount, Inv. 15: this point will be discussed later.

The rôle of the shoulder-clasps has been touched on in pages 532-35. They may well be the equivalent of the shoulder-clasps seen on imperial armour in use with the muscle cuirass (fig. 394).

To turn to the one obviously remaining element, the sword and its belt, three different methods of wearing the sword come into consideration. One, the baldric, derived from the Roman shoulder-belt (*balteus*), is seen pictorially in contemporary use in East Scandinavian contexts, in one of the Torslunda plates, and on the Vendel 14 helmet, and is concretely illustrated by the complete baldric found in position attached to sword 1 in the Uppland boat-grave, Valsgärde 7 (figs. 416b, c). It is depicted on a plaque attributed to the end of the seventh century from a Frankish grave.[1] Another method of wearing the sword, of ultimately eastern (Iranian) derivation, is illustrated by Ortwin Gamber, in his discussion of the Sutton Hoo sword fittings, from the cameo in the Louvre depicting the capture of the Emperor Valerian at Edessa by King Schapur (A.D. 260). King Schapur's sword is suspended by the Iranian method, while Valerian is seen wearing the contrasting Roman shoulder-belt.[2]

This Iranian or eastern method is also classically illustrated on the ivory diptych portraying Stilicho, in the cathedral treasury at Monza (fig. 416a).[3] In this Iranian-derived suspension system the sword is carried on a low-slung subsidiary strap itself suspended from a belt worn round the hips. The sword hangs vertically and is held at one point only, where the subsidiary belt passes under a bridge positioned vertically on the display surface of the sword, towards the upper end of the scabbard. A third method is described and illustrated by Menghin; in this the sword is carried not on a subsidiary belt but on the hip-belt itself; it is supported, and its angle of tilt controlled, by an additional strap connecting a point at the rear of the main belt to a special form of mount placed fairly low down on the scabbard (fig. 416c).

In trying to determine the type of sword-belt represented in the ship-burial we have to consider the dimensions of the various eligible pieces, their relative positions in the ground, the strap width and thickness they accommodate, their style and, with due reservations as to the conclusions that one may legitimately draw from such evidence, the alloy from which they are made.

The strap widths and thicknesses accommodated are summarised in table 32.

[1] From Grésin, Puy de Dôme, France, on a large barbaric pottery plaque thought to depict Christ, because of the alpha and omega depicted to either side of the hood. Salin 1950-59, Vol. IV, pl. XI, 1. For its later use see fig. 426.

[2] Gamber 1966, pl. LIII A.
[3] Cf. Menghin 1973a, fig. 1.

TABLE 32   STRAP WIDTHS AND THICKNESSES ACCOMMODATED BY THE PLATES AND
LOOPS OF THE VARIOUS GOLD MOUNTS AND BUCKLES IN THE SUTTON HOO SHIP-BURIAL

		Strap width	Strap thickness	Loop capacity
Item		mm	mm	mm
Inv. 1	(great gold buckle)	40–50	1	30×7
		(see p. 565)		
Inv. 6	(rectangular mount, mushroom design)	20	2	
Inv. 7	(rectangular mount, mushroom design)	20	2	
Inv. 8	(rectangular mount, cable-twist)	20	2	
Inv. 9	(rectangular mount, cable twist)	20	2	
Inv. 10	(curved strap-runner with loop, *Schlaufenbeslag*)	26	1	15·5×2
Inv. 11	(rectangular buckle)	22	2·5	16×3
Inv. 12	(small buckle with rounded end)	17	3	15×4
Inv. 13	(strap-mount with rounded end)	16	3	
Inv. 14	(strap-mount with rounded end)	17	3	
Inv. 15	(plain gold strap-mount with loop)	17	2	18×3·5 (×4 maximum)
Inv. 16	(small strap-end)	9	1·25	
Inv. 17	(T-shaped strap distributor) main mount	20	2	
	swivelling element C	13–14	1·5–2	
Inv. 18	(triangular zoomorphic mount)	22	4	

We may start with five mounts clearly from the same strap, Inv. 6–9, and the hinged T-mount, Inv. 17: all were mounted on a strap exactly 2 cm wide and 2 mm thick. Gold analysis (p. 625) suggests the possibility that Inv. 6–9 may even have been cast from the same melt (p. 613). There are two relevant buckles, Inv. 11 and 12. Neither exactly matches the five mounts in width or strap thickness carried, or in design. From its proportions and long rectangular shape, Inv. 11 would be a better match for the five mounts than the too small and delicate seeming Inv. 12. The buckle, Inv. 11, is 2 mm wider than the mounts, Inv. 6–9 and 17, and accommodates a 2·5 mm thickness of strap.[1] If it terminated the belt on which the five mounts were mounted, the strap will have widened very slightly at the front between the terminal buckle and the mount next to it. This precise type of buckle, moreover, has been specifically associated with sword belts.[2] It remains an open question whether the belt on which these six pieces were mounted was a shoulder-belt or a hip- or waist-belt.

The East Scandinavian link at Sutton Hoo must not be overstressed, but it certainly exists, and the analogy with the well-documented Valsgärde 7 sword 1 baldric should be considered (fig. 417). This shoulder-belt or baldric has no fewer than ten decorated rectangular mounts of tinned bronze in addition to six or seven mounts associated with

[1] The thickness of strap held by the various mounts and buckles is in many instances difficult to establish because some rivets are bent, others not fully extractable. Every effort has been made to arrive at correct dimensions. The same strap may of course itself vary slightly in thickness as between one part of the strap and another.

[2] Ament 1974, 160, where the type is defined, though here Ament is apparently influenced by his reading of the Sutton Hoo buckle, Inv. 11, as that of the sword belt, and where Kentish examples are cited.

568

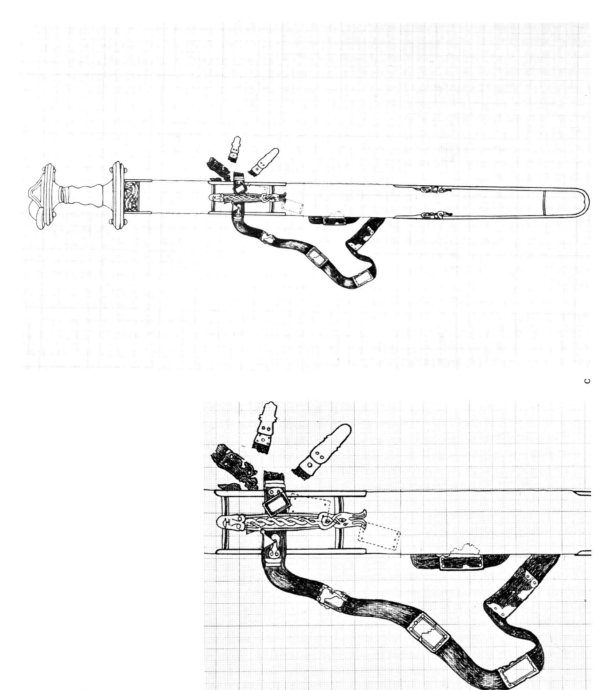

FIGURE 417 (a) the sword and scabbard, Valsgärde 7; (b) the baldric and mounts drawn as found; (c) the whole sword and scabbard shown with its suspension mechanism. (Scales: a, 1/2, b, 1/3; c, 1/6) (Photos: Uppsala Universitets museum för nordiska fornsaker, by courtesy of Professor Greta Arwidsson)

c

b

a

569

the sword suspension in some way.[1] The baldric mounts vary both in length and width, the smallest mounts occurring at the ends of the strap near the scabbard, and the largest and broadest in the middle, so that the baldric must have narrowed systematically to each end. The additional mounts referred to include a pair of matching strap-mounts, not attached to the scabbard, which, though quite different in material and style, recall the pair of cloisonné mounts from Sutton Hoo, Inv. 13 and 14; and two pyramids (fig. 426 c), tall and thin and differing in design from the many pyramidal mounts known from Anglo-Saxon and Continental sites, but hollow pyramidal mounts none the less. As at Sutton Hoo these pyramids can have no direct connection with the attachment of the scabbard to the suspension belt (cf. the examples cited by Menghin where pyramids perform this function[2]). There are no buckles associated with the Valsgärde 7 baldric.

The Sutton Hoo sword shows a method of attachment of the scabbard to the strap on which it is carried, by means of the two scabbard-bosses, which is unique among surviving archaeological material. Their setting and suggested method of functioning is illustrated in figure 224. They are not situated at the edges of the scabbard as envisaged by Ament and Menghin,[3] but are mounted on its display surface. The bosses act as buttons. The effect is exactly matched visually on the Vendel 14 helmet panel (fig. 416 b). There is no trace of metal fitments or clips of any sort at the edges of the Sutton Hoo scabbard, or of any bridge, such as there is in both the Valsgärde 7 swords (fig. 417 a) and in the Vendel 1 and Vallstenarum swords and, so far as the bridge is concerned, that depicted on the Torslunda plate.[4] But in spite of this, there

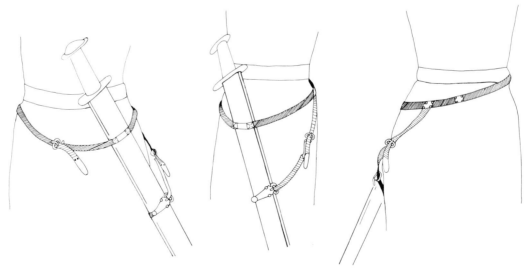

FIGURE 418   Reconstruction of a two point suspension system on a human figure, front, side and rear views. (After Menghin)

[1] Although not allowing positive identification, the spaced longitudinal markings on the baldrics worn by the walking warriors of the Vendel 14 helmet scene (fig. 416 b) may be thought to represent a series of mounts of this sort; it is difficult to see any other reason for them.
[2] Menghin 1973 a, figs. 27–33.

[3] Ament 1974, Abb. 2, 1: Menghin 1973 a, 25.
[4] Menghin 1973 a, figs. 19, 2 and 4, and 20, 1 and 2. The nature of the superficial tapering wood feature on the upper part of the Sutton Hoo scabbard is not clear, but it is nothing to do with any bridge of this type. For the Torslunda plate scabbard with a bridge see our figs. 156 and 416 b.

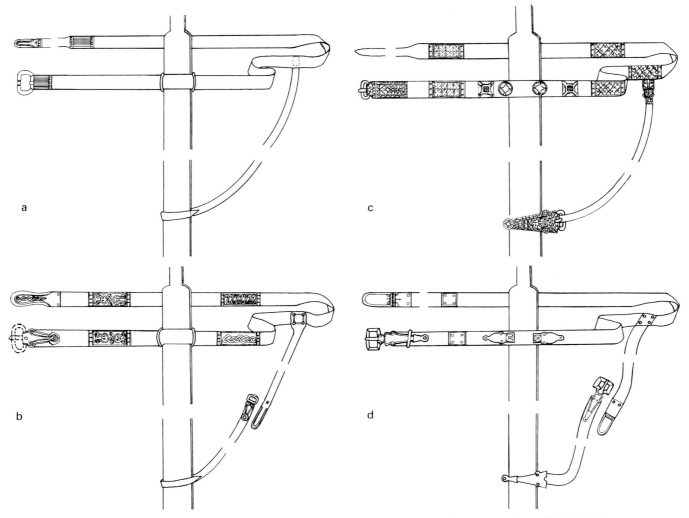

FIGURE 419   Reconstruction of the sword-belts from (*a*) Altenerding, grave 674; (*b*) St-Sulpice, grave 168; (*c*) Sutton Hoo and (*d*) Lauterhofen, grave 29. (Scale: 1/6) (After Ament)

is none the less a *prima facie* case for relating the Sutton Hoo sword harness to the baldric group familiar from East Scandinavian examples.[1] We must however bear in mind that Sidonius Apollinaris (d. 481)[2] refers to a Frankish delegation at the Burgundian court as wearing their swords on shoulder-belts, so that this method is not to be thought of as exclusively Scandinavian.[3] As Menghin stresses, in most groups of mounts associated with swords found in Continental graves it cannot be said whether they are from baldrics or waist-belts; many compromises and mixtures of method evidently occurred.

Following Menghin's analysis of the evidence from Continental and Anglo-Saxon graves, Ament has put forward a reconstruction of the Sutton Hoo sword-belt (fig.

[1] The Valsgärde 7 sword 1, while illustrating the baldric, or shoulder belt for sword suspension, has a quite different method of attachment of belt to scabbard from that of the Sutton Hoo sword (fig. 417*b*). At Sutton Hoo there is no trace of such fittings. The attachment method is more like the Vendel 14 helmet die version.

[2] Cited by Menghin 1973*a*, 8.
[3] The instance from Puy de Dôme has already been cited (p. 567, n. 1). Salin (*op. cit.*, 105, n. 4) discussing the importance attached to sword belts, refers to the apparently almost indiscriminate use of both the terms *cingulum* and *balteus* by Gregory of Tours.

419c). This shows it essentially as a belt of the Dirlewang grave 27 type illustrated by Menghin (here figs. 421, 418) following R. Christlein's reconstruction.[1] In Ament's version (fig. 419c) the buckle, Inv. 11, is shown, on a slightly broadened strap, as terminating a waist-belt on which are mounted the two rectangular matching pairs, Inv. 6–7 and 8–9, and the strap-distributor, Inv. 17. This last is placed at the rear centre of the belt, dividing evenly the four rectangular mounts. A narrow strap runs downwards from element C of the strap-distributor and is attached well down on the scabbard by the curved mount or dummy buckle, Inv. 10, thus providing a two-point suspension, which should allow the sword to be set at a trailing angle. With his reconstruction of the Sutton Hoo sword-belt, Ament illustrates reconstructions of three others, from Altenerding grave 674, Lauterhofen grave 29 and St-Sulpice grave 168, all of which are compatible with a similar suspension arrangement, but employ varying numbers of mounts (figs. 419a, b, d). The first of these is dated by Ament to the sixth century, the second to around A.D. 600, the third to an advanced seventh-century date, with the Sutton Hoo harness occupying an intermediate position between the two later examples.

Some minor comments on Ament's version may be made. The Sutton Hoo pyramids are shown as the same width as the other mounts: they are in fact slightly smaller (18 mm square as against 20 mm wide) with an effective aperture of less than 1 cm (fig. 228) and the scabbard-bosses are in fact mounted, as has been said already, on the display surface of scabbard and not at its edges. The sequence of mounts in the ground (fig. 314) would suggest that the T-shaped strap-distributor, Inv. 17, was probably not central between the pairs of rectangular mounts, but, as Gamber shows it on his much less satisfactory attempt to reconstruct the harness, had three mounts to the right of it and one between it and the belt-buckle (fig. 422).[2] A more fundamental criticism of Ament's reconstruction will be offered below.

A decisive factor in the reconstruction of the Sutton Hoo harness, and one which must be regarded as fully established, is the recognition of the role of the curved mount or dummy buckle, Inv. 10. This is a curved runner (*Schlaufenbeschlag*) (fig. 420) of

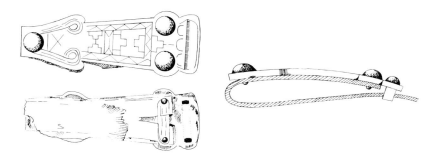

FIGURE 420 Curved scabbard-mount from Donzdorf,
grave 66. (Scale: 2/3) (After Menghin)

[1] Christlein 1971, 22–26 and Abb. 7.
[2] Gamber 1966, pl. LIII B. His reconstruction is unworkable for a variety of reasons: this is discussed in the caption to fig. 422.

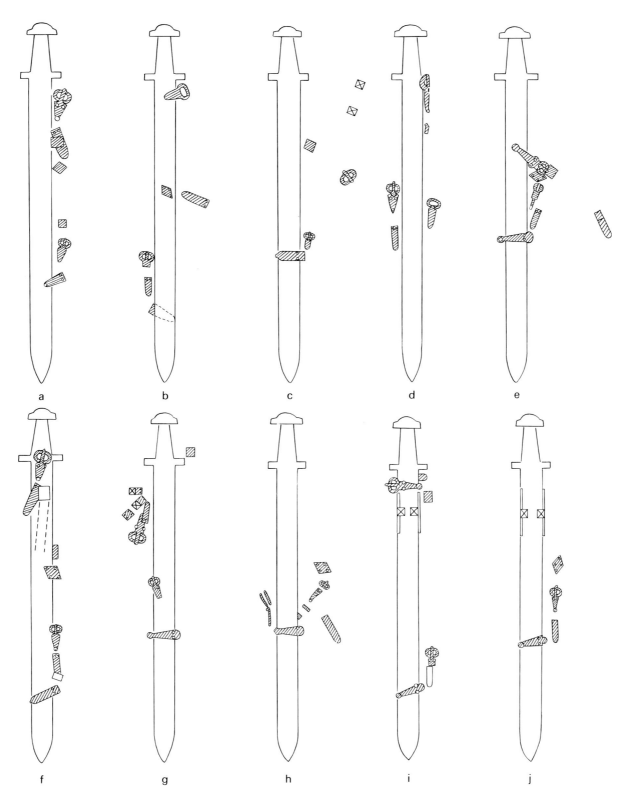

FIGURE 421 Ten swords from Continental graves showing fittings of the scabbard and sword belt as excavated. All show curved scabbard mounts (especially (e)–(j), the lowest mount) and rectangular or trapezoidal mounts serving as strap-distributors. (a) and (e) Mindelheim, graves 34 and 11; (b) and (c) Marktoberdorf, graves 197 and 196; (d) Beggingen, grave 78; (f) Dirlewang, grave 27; (g)–(j) Donzdorf, graves 36, 48, 65, 75. (After Menghin)

a type recognised in many examples from Continental graves, mostly around A.D. 600 or of the seventh century (fig. 421 *a–f*).[1] The Sutton Hoo curved mount fits perfectly the width and curve of the scabbard, and the loop is turned downwards with sufficient sharpness to engage effortlessly the under-part of the strap which is drawn round the back of the scabbard. The filing off at the back of the ends of the two rivets at the shoulders of the mount (fig. 341 *b*) must have been effected to enable the mount to lie flat against the edge of the sword, and may be taken as another indication of the special use to which the mount was put. Such mounts were evidently not permanently attached to the scabbard but could be removed simply by loosening the strap which they terminated. There is no mark on the damaged surfaces of the Sutton Hoo scabbard to indicate the position occupied by Inv. 10. The identification of the dummy buckle in this way makes it clear that the Sutton Hoo sword was held on a two-point suspension type of belt.

In the case of the St-Sulpice and Lauterhofen grave 29 swords (fig. 419*b* and *d*) Ament's reconstructions show as adjustable the strap that runs between the strap-distributor on the belt (a lozenge-shaped or rectangular plate that performs the function of the more sophisticated hinged mount of the Sutton Hoo belt) and the curved mount on the lower part of the scabbard. The strap is in two parts and a buckle and strap-end are introduced to enable adjustment to take place.

Ament shows no such buckle and strap-end in his proposed reconstruction of the Sutton Hoo belt. It is to be considered whether Inv. 12, the small buckle from the set of three matching mounts, Inv. 12–14 (fig. 321 *a*), and the minute strap-end, Inv. 16 (fig. 354), can have performed this role. The buckle is carried on a strap of 17 mm width which is not far from the right strap-width to match that emerging from the loop of the curved scabbard mount, Inv. 10, the 'dummy buckle' (maximum 16 mm). But this latter strap was only 1 mm thick, so that the strap-carrying capacity of the buckle (3 mm) is too great for it to have been mounted on this strap, even allowing for doubling the strap within the buckle as reinforcement. The small strap-end carried a 1·2 mm thickness of strap and so would agree with the 1 mm thick strap on which the curved scabbard mount, Inv. 10, was mounted, but it would be necessary to assume that the strap was reduced substantially in width to its strap-end (from some 16 mm to 9 mm). The buckle, Inv. 12, could more plausibly have been carried on the strap emerging from the moving element C of the T-shaped strap-distributor, Inv. 17 (fig. 333). This had a width of 13–14 mm, and might have broadened slightly to the buckle, as the main belt seems to have broadened to its rectangular buckle, Inv. 11. The strap emerging from element C of Inv. 17 had a thickness of approximately 1·5 mm, and if doubled would just fit the buckle, Inv. 12 (strap thickness capacity 3 mm). The cloisonné style of Inv. 12 (p. 468) also matches that of the C-element of the T-shaped distributor, Inv. 17 (figs. 321 *a*, 334). This solution might thus seem

[1] The mounts, often of the same zoomorphic form as Inv. 10, are in all cases positioned low down on the scabbard with the loop to the right, as shown in figure 421.

a possibility, but it does not account for the two strap-mounts, Inv. 13 and 14, which match Inv. 12 in all respects and the prime objection would seem to be the position in which Inv. 12 was found in the ground. Had it been mounted on the strap which joined Inv. 17 and Inv. 10, it might have been expected to be found much closer to Inv. 17. If the two parts of the strap were fastened, as implied by the allocation of a buckle to this position, the buckle should have been found somewhere between Inv. 17 and Inv. 10. If the two parts of the strap were unfastened it might still have been expected to be found within a foot or so of it in one direction or another. There seems no explanation of how it could have reached the position in which it was in fact found (fig. 314), in view of the positions of Inv. 10 and 17.

The main defect in Ament's proposed reconstruction of the Sutton Hoo sword-belt, however, is that it seems impossible to reconcile the idea that the pyramids were on the same belt as the other mounts with their positions in the ground. The positions of the other mounts show that the scabbard, if mounted on the belt as Ament suggests, had been unbuttoned from it, and that the belt was not fastened to the sword. We have already considered evidence which suggests that the harness in general had been suspended above the 'body space' (p. 439). Had the pyramids been mounted on this belt they should have been found lying scattered amongst the other mounts: they must have been mounted on a separate strap. The removal of the pyramids from the sword belt would tend to assign to them a different role, perhaps that of decorative buttons associated with a sword-knot, or tag-ends associated in some way with the sword or its harness, as must have been the case with the Valsgärde 7 (sword 1) pyramids (fig. 426 c). The traces of black substance recorded by the excavators as seen 'all over' the back of one of the pyramids, may be thought to suggest a strap, but we do not know the nature of this material. It could have been underlying cloth which had no essential connection with the pyramid but had been preserved by the physical protection afforded by it.[1]

If the pyramids were mounted on a subsidiary belt, following the Iranian mode of suspension, this could provide an explanation for the position of pyramids and scabbard bosses in relation to the main sword-belt.

In the Iranian type of suspension the main sword-belt was worn on the hips with the sword attached by a subsidiary belt hanging from it (fig. 416 a). Though Ortwin Gamber has claimed this method of suspension for the Sutton Hoo sword (fig. 422), it does not seem to be represented in the archaeological material that survives from Germanic graves. On such an Iranian-type belt the sword hangs vertically on a looser subsidiary belt which permits the sword to be freely tilted under pressure from the hand; it does not provide for the sword to be held or adjusted to an oblique angle as a permanent carrying position, a requirement provided for by two-point suspension systems such as those reconstructed from the mounts in Germanic graves by Christlein, Menghin and Ament. If this extra facility were desired, it seems possible that the

[1] It suggests that this pyramid at least was the right way up when found.

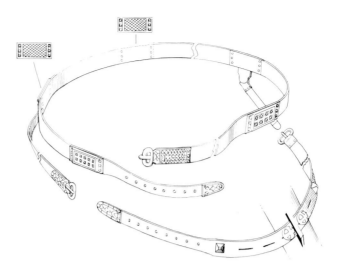

FIGURE 422 Suggested reconstruction of the Sutton Hoo sword belt by Ortwin Gamber (after Gamber 1966, pl. LIII, B). This is unsatisfactory for several reasons. The mounts with rounded ends, Inv. 13 and 14, shown as strap-ends, will not pass through the buckles to which they are opposed, and must be omitted. There is no vertical 'bridge' on the Sutton Hoo scabbard, as here shown between the scabbard-bosses. The plain gold loop, Inv. 15, (right) is not a buckle. The opposing strap-end, Inv. 16, shown terminating a strap from the T-shaped hinged mount is in any case too small to be associated with it. The curved mount, Inv. 10, is not accounted for. The positions of, for example Inv. 12 (buckle) and Inv. 15 (plain strap-end) as found cannot be reconciled with the places allotted to them in the harness.

two-point suspension system and the Iranian type of suspension could be combined to provide it. Can the Sutton Hoo mounts be accounted for in this way? We would have to suppose, because of the lie of the pieces in the ground, that the subsidiary belt (in position attached to the scabbard buttons and with the pyramids to either side) had been wholly detached from its main belt: but it can only have been detached if it was provided with buckles (fig. 422). Only one buckle (Inv. 12) is available for this role. If we suppose that this buckle was attached to the part of the strap which ran into the main belt (as in fig. 422, on the left) this might be compatible with the position in which the buckle was found, but since there is no second buckle the other end of the subsidiary belt must have been permanently stitched to the main belt, if not held by the hinged C element of the T-mount, Inv. 17. If so this seems once more, with the main belt where it is, to be quite irreconcilable with the positions of the pyramids as found. This solution also, apart from being apparently unevidenced in the archaeological material, does not conform to the picture that has emerged from those burials, studied by Christlein, Menghin, Ament and others, in which the curved scabbard mount (*Schlaufenbeslag*) represented by Inv. 10 in the Sutton Hoo jewellery, is present (cf. fig. 419). The Sutton Hoo burial is of course abnormal in many respects. The harness may be ceremonial (we are treating it as part of the regalia) and need not necessarily conform in all respects to what seems the predominantly South German or alpine pattern. This solution would also leave still unaccounted for the two round-ended strap-mounts, Inv. 13 and 14, which match Inv. 12, and which, to

576

judge by the known location of the one recorded, would be even more out of place as found had they been carried on the subsidiary belt.

Ament's version leaves unaccounted for not only the mounts, Inv. 12–14 (the small cloisonné buckle and two matching strap-mounts), but also Inv. 18 (the triangular zoomorphic mount), and Inv. 15 (the plain gold runner, which we have placed on the main belt with the great gold buckle, fig. 423) and the small plain strap-end, Inv. 16. These cannot be related to the separate attachment of a scramasax, since, as we now know, there was no scramasax (p. 241). A possible, but not I think plausible, use for two of these, Inv. 12 and 16, has been suggested, in allowing for adjustment of the strap connecting the curved mount, Inv. 10, and the strap-distributor, Inv. 17 (p. 574). The thinness of the suspension straps of the purse, which matches that of the main belt carrying the gold buckle, and the fact that there were three such straps and not two, preclude the idea that the purse might have been worn on a shoulder belt. Nor would such a shoulder belt for the purse account satisfactorily for the various mounts for whose use no suggestion has yet been offered.

The Valsgärde 7 baldric, found attached to its sword and with its mounts in sequence, has, as we have said, no buckles. The fact that the Sutton Hoo mounts include two buckles and a curved scabbard-slide of recognised type as well as a strap-distributor (Inv. 17, corresponding in function to the lozenge-shaped or rect-angular metal plates of the belts illustrated by Menghin and Ament), one of the buckles being of a type otherwise associated with sword-belts (p. 568), seems to tip the scales against a shoulder-belt for the Sutton Hoo harness, and in favour of a hip-belt. It seems most probable that the sword was carried on some version of the hip-belt with a two-point suspension.

In the light of the above discussion, and from my reading of all the available evidence from the burial, I put forward the following suggestions, as my provisional solution to the problem of how the harness was constituted (my conclusions are summarised in figures 423 and 425).

The triangular zoomorphic mount, Inv. 18, I explain as a counterplate used in conjunction with the buckle, Inv. 11, on the main sword-belt, this belt being in general of the type illustrated by Menghin and Ament (figs. 418, 419). Inv. 18 is not decorated *en suite* with Inv. 11, and was not designed to go with it: it may have been taken over from another belt. It has the same width (22 mm) so that one can visualise the belt expanding slightly in width at the front of the body symmetrically to either side of the buckle and counterplate. The extra strap-carrying capacity of Inv. 18 would have to be explained by the doubling of the strap thickness here to suit and reinforce this particular mount which it was desired to use; or to attach a separate tapering end-piece which would pass through the loop of Inv. 11 (maximum interior loop width 16 mm). The only other possible use for the triangular zoomorphic mount would be elsewhere on the belt as a strap-distributor. Its 4 mm strap holding capacity would be equal to that of two straps having the thickness of the sword belt (2 mm). It would

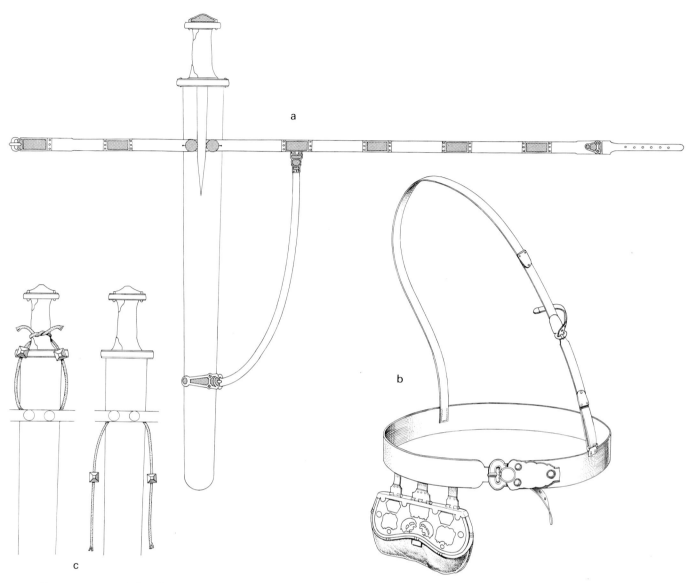

FIGURE 423 The Sutton Hoo harness: suggested reconstruction. (a) sword-belt; (b) broad waist-belt holding the great gold buckle and the purse, with supporting shoulder-strap; (c) tapes carrying the pyramids forming a sword-knot.

be the counterpart of the diamond-shaped or square mounts seen in this role in figure 421. But we already have a strap-distributor, Inv. 17, elaborately designed for this role: we should have to relate the triangular mount to a second belt, and to the combination of the two-point suspension system with the Iranian type of harness which has been hinted at above. Even in this role, the triangular mount seems unsuitable. Its length is 2·9 cm and it can only have been set vertically on the 20 mm wide belt if one assumes that the belt was specially enlarged at this point to take it. If set sideways it is still fractionally too wide if away from the area of slight expansion at the front of the belt, as its role would require it to be. The rivet spacing would indicate a minimum strap-width for a subsidiary strap of 2·6 cm, and this does not suit any of

578

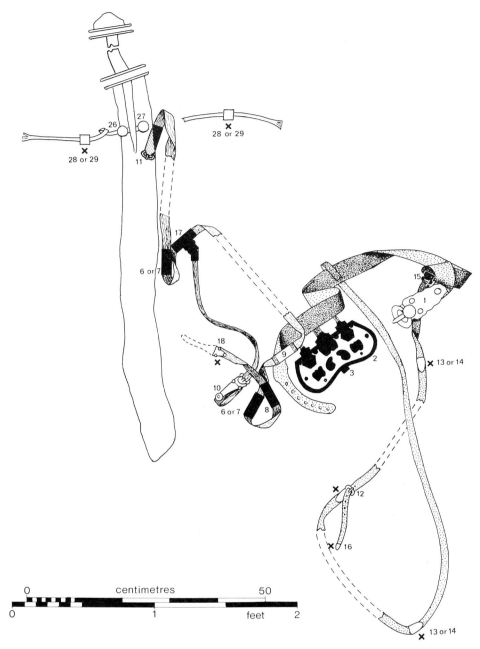

FIGURE 424 The strap-mounts, buckles and other fittings as found in the ground, linked up to show how they relate to the reconstructions in figure 423.

the remaining mounts. The solution seems altogether too far-fetched. I therefore return to the role I have assigned to this piece as a counter-plate to the buckle, Inv. 11. The triangular mount would thus mark one end of the belt, with Inv. 11 as the other. The intervening mounts and Inv. 10, the dummy buckle, would fall into place as shown in figure 423.

The shoulder-clasps (Inv. 4 and 5) lay separately, detached from whatever garment they had been mounted on.

I suggest that the purse was worn on the right, attached to the broad main (? cloth) waist-belt by three short cloth straps. The shoulder-strap which supported the heavy waist-belt was, I suggest, 1·5 mm thick and was looped through the plain gold runner, Inv. 15. The three matching pieces, Inv. 12–14, were all mounted on this strap. Their 3 mm strap holding capacity makes them suitable for holding the double thickness of strap which the loop, Inv. 15, implies for the front end at least. The width of these mounts, carrying straps of 16–17 mm, matches the internal width and capacity of the loop of Inv. 15 (18 mm). The shoulder-strap would be adjusted by the buckle, Inv. 12. The double thickness accommodated by the buckle-plate (3 mm capacity) would be extended to accommodate the second of the cloisonné mounts (Inv. 13 or 14) in a position which balanced with its fellow mount. The shoulder-strap could be sewn to the main belt at the back.

The advantage of this proposed allocation of Inv. 12–14 is that these obviously matching mounts, designed *en suite*, can be kept together, and their positions in the ground can be more readily accounted for. They do not seem to fit happily into any other role in connection with the sword-belt.

The minute plain gold strap-end, Inv. 16, I have assumed to be a decorative finial for the strap which, emanating from the loop of Inv. 15, passed through the loop of Inv. 12, and I would propose to equate it with the unidentifiable small gold item II$_2$, seen on the plan between Inv. 12 and Inv. 13 or 14 (see p. 445 above for a discussion of the identity of this element on the plan). It is true that the strap-end does not match the buckle in size or decoration but it matches the other buckles still less. Its use here would imply not only a narrowing of the strap to pass through its buckle-loop, which is normal enough, but a thinning of the strap to a 1 mm thickness. It would be a kind of special styling for the shoulder-belt which is perhaps feasible at a key point in so elaborate and rich an assembly. The strap-end though small is meticulously finished; the rivet-heads and ends have been carefully filed flush with the surface. There seems indeed no other role which this strap-end might play, unless it can be thought to have been loose amongst the coins and ingots of the purse; it will not pass through the pyramids. It will be recalled that one of the coins from the purse escaped the original excavation and was found only in the same late sifting process that brought to light the gold strap-end. It would, however, be extraneous in the purse, not fitting in with what has been conceived of as the ideology of the coins and ingots, which otherwise formed the sole contents.

The small cloisonné buckle and matching strap-mounts seem to be outliers, so far as the rest of the jewellery is concerned. The two whose locations we know were not far from the drinking-horns (fig. 314) and we should consider the possibility that they had decorated a baldric associated with one of the horns. There is however no loop or other metal fitting necessary for the attachment of such a baldric associated with the drinking-horn remains, and the gold cloisonné mounts are quite out of keeping in style with the silver-gilt zoomorphic mounts of the horns whereas they match the cloisonné work of the regalia.

580

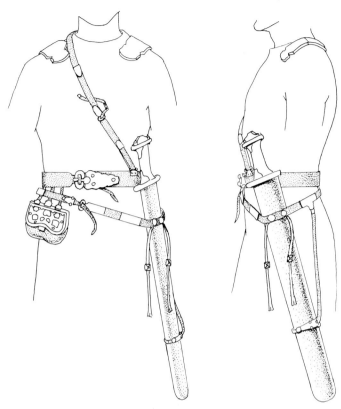

FIGURE 425 The gold regalia as it may
have been worn.

The pyramids, I suggest, were sword-knot embellishments, perhaps attached to tapes which passed under the scabbard-bosses, since to perform their function, that of tying the blade into the scabbard, they must have been firmly attached to the scabbard at some point. No other means of attachment is evident. The pyramids need not have terminated the strap or tapes of the sword-knot (fig. 423).[1] They must have been mounted on something thin, pliable and narrow, the thinness being necessary if the mount underlay the scabbard bosses, so that these latter could have a stable base. The drawing (fig. 423c) shows the inferred tapes as continuing beyond the pyramids. In this way one could have avoided their hanging downwards in a position where the undersides were exposed or where the millefiori insets and decorated faces would not be fully effective when the sword-knot was tied. Figure 425 shows the sword harness and the waist-belt as they might have been worn together.

[1] The triangular expansions at the end of the sword-knot tapes in BM Cotton MS Tiberius C VI (fig. 426 b) are not pyramids—if they were they should be seen hanging upside down. This expansion of the ends of tapes is a matter of fashion, as may be seen from the drawing from folio 9 r of the same MS (fig. 426 a), where a similar appearance is associated with the neck of the shirt; the ends of stole and maniple are similarly expanded on fol. 71 v.

FIGURE 426 (*a*) (*b*) Details from a Late Saxon manuscript (BM Cotton Tiberius C VI). (*a*) fol. 9 *recto*: Goliath, showing tapes with expanded triangular ends, used to draw up the neck opening of a shirt, and a baldric; (*b*) fol. 10 *verso*: detail from a scene of Christ tempted by the devil, showing a sword with sword knot. The swords are of late Saxon type, A.D. 1000, with 'brazil nut' pommels; (*c*) bronze pyramidal mounts associated with sword 1 in the Valsgärde 7 grave. (Scale: *c*, 1/1) (*c*, by courtesy of Professor G. Arwidsson)

5. *Millefiori and blue glass inlays*

I INTRODUCTION

Millefiori and plain blue glass insets occur in three items only of the Sutton Hoo jewellery: the pair of shoulder-clasps, the purse-lid, and the pair of pyramids. The purse-lid incorporates seven individual plaques, each an outstanding piece of craftwork, and four studs; all these have millefiori inlays, except for the zoomorphic double-plaque. The purse frame also carried millefiori insets. Table 34, page 617, shows the distribution of inlays of all kinds in the jewellery as a whole.

The total number of millefiori insets, in seventeen main varieties of pattern, is seventy-five.[1] The size of individual inlays attains as much as 7×5 mm and $8 \cdot 5 \times 4$ mm in the pear-shaped inlays of the boars' hips on the shoulder-clasps; and circles of millefiori 8 mm in diameter and trapezoid pieces measuring 7×4 mm on the purse.

[1] Of these, one (in the purse-frame, p. 592, cell 13) is a modern replacement.

The different millefiori patterns represented are shown in plate 24 *a*. The distribution of the different designs in the items so ornamented is shown in figure 429.

As is well recognised, the manufacture of millefiori in the immediate post-Roman centuries is confined to the British Isles. Re-used pieces of sheets of Roman millefiori occur in certain Anglo-Saxon jewels, but until the Sutton Hoo discovery freshly created millefiori has been found only in metalwork of Celtic origin, notably in the hanging-bowl and penannular brooch series.[1] A further point distinguishes enamelling and millefiori at Sutton Hoo. Hitherto all enamelling found in Celtic contexts had been opaque. At Sutton Hoo we encounter for the first time transparent elements, both on the large Celtic hanging-bowl where blue translucent glass looking like jelly is used to trace large pelta-shapes in the enamel, and in the gold jewellery, in the millefiori insets, in which all the red elements are transparent. No opaque red occurs in the millefiori on the jewellery, although the red enamels of the hanging-bowls are opaque. The red transparent elements in the Sutton Hoo millefiori inlays, moreover, can be seen in every case except the two inlays in the pyramids to be backed by pointillé gold foil, which reflects light and glitter exactly as in the garnet cloisonné work. The elements in the Sutton Hoo millefiori, minute though they are, thus have both the appearance and the treatment of garnets. In the inlays in the boars' hips (Inv. 4) the edges of the red elements show concavities alternating with projecting points which look like the working on the edge of a stone and this could suggest that these transparent elements are minute garnets. They are small enough (little more than 1 mm) to be by-products of the grozing or trimming undergone by larger stones. It is clear from the purse-lid that the gem-cutter who worked with the master goldsmith could cut garnets of this size. For example, those in the convex drums inserted in the purse-bar opposite the central hinge, and those used in the backbones of the erect animals in the zoomorphic double plaque, to represent the hair of the men-between-beasts and in the borderings and wing and tail feathers of the birds, are of this order, and in some instances less than 1 mm square. If these red elements in the millefiori were garnets, the inlays must of necessity be in the nature of miniature mosaics. One could envisage that to make these the small stones were set out in rows and the enamel powder filled into the spaces, the whole being fired at low temperature and subsequently polished, a process which could initially blur over the joins between the '*tesserae*', though here and there such joins between squares can be seen.

As there was no possibility of telling by ordinary visual inspection or low-power magnification whether these transparent red elements were in fact glass or garnet, the problem was referred to the British Museum Research Laboratory. That these elements are glass is established by several remarkable photomicrographs, one of which is reproduced in plate 23 *c*, taken by the Laboratory staff. In these, skeins of gas bubbles

[1] The occurrence of millefiori beads, which became common in Viking period contexts (cf. Arbman 1940, vol. I, e.g. Taf. 120, 1l, v, u; 2a, b, d; Taf. 121, 3a, 5f, 9a, 11a, 13; Taf. 122, 15, 17g) is a separate problem. Their introduction may be due to Insular or Eastern contacts. For a classic study of the use of millefiori at the end of the Roman period, see Françoise Henry's paper 'Émailleurs d'Occident', *Préhistoire* 1933, 65–146.

can be seen in the depth of the small red cubes, rising like bubbles from the escape hatch of a submarine, and completely different in appearance and character from the rutile inclusions sometimes found in garnet (fig. 427). In one instance a large bubble is shared between a red element and an adjacent blue element.

The occurrence of millefiori inlays in the Sutton Hoo regalia is of outstanding art-historical importance because in this context they seem to demonstrate the introduction of Celtic craft traditions and techniques, by whatever agency, into a Germanic, Anglo-Saxon workshop of higher calibre than any other yet known in Europe. Their presence constitutes proof that the superb jewellery so adorned is of English and not Scandinavian or Continental manufacture. This and other elements, the development of lidded cells (yielding a champlevé effect) for example, suggest a creative fusion of Celtic and Germanic ideas which could, particularly in so dynamic a context, be seen as one of the more significant beginnings of the process of fusion of two different art and craft traditions which leads, fifty or more years later, to the masterpieces of Hiberno-Saxon art and the Northumbrian renaissance.

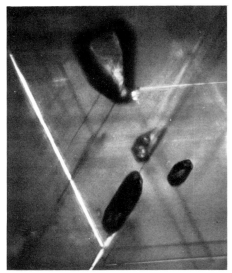

FIGURE 427 A stone from St Cuthbert's Cross: microphotograph showing inclusions in garnet, for comparison with gas bubbles seen in plate 23(c). (Photo: British Museum Research Laboratory)

The Sutton Hoo millefiori referred to above will now be described in detail, beginning with the shoulder-clasp, Inv. 5, in which the millefiori are less complex than in the companion piece, Inv. 4.

II   THE SHOULDER CLASPS
(Inv. 4, 5; pls. 15, 24 a and fig. 429 a)

The boars' hips

Inv. 5. In this clasp all four millefiori fillings in the boars' hips are the same, with only such minor variations as are inherent in the technique. They show a pattern of regular chessboard type, opaque blue and translucent red squares alternating. (Two of the inlays can be seen in pl. 16 b.) This pattern, which occurs also in certain cells in the rectangular panels, is referred to as inlay C. Through the translucent red squares a backing of gold foil with simple type A 1 pattern can be seen. In 5 a (the half of the clasp to which the pin is attached) the individual red squares in field 9 (fig. 429) are slightly larger than those in field 10. The number of red squares represented in field 9, whether complete or in part, is eighteen, as against nineteen in field 10. In each of the corresponding inlays of 5 b the number of red squares

584

represented is also eighteen but more of them are complete; this is the consequence of a slightly more ample cell shape. Fields 9 and 10 in 5b are not identical with the corresponding fields in 5a, being broader at the base and fractionally longer. These four inlays were all derived from the same rod. The regularity of the squares, as seen by the naked eye, is remarkable, although distortions can be seen under magnification. This must rank as millefiori work of the highest quality.

Inv. 4. The millefiori inlay in the boars' hips in Inv. 4a is illustrated in plate 24a and is identified as inlay K. This inlay is particularly elaborate and remarkable and is difficult to analyse (fig. 428). The colours used are blue, red and white. The red elements are transparent, revealing pointillé gold-foil backings. In the enlargement (fig. 434) the red elements can be seen to be anything but regular or rectangular in shape. They are roughly shaped irregular pieces with one common factor: all are polygonal, with straight or incurved sides; quite sharp projecting points can be seen on either side of the more striking concavities.

A pattern built up from rods of polygonal cross-section is readily conceivable in ordinary millefiori technique, and the shapes of individual components of the rod could be pulled or distorted in the drawing-out process, but it is difficult to see how the strange variety of unique shapes presented by these red elements in the millefiori of the boars' hips of Inv. 4 could be arrived at. They do not seem to reflect any regular stress pattern recognisable in the behaviour of the other elements. The stretching of a millefiori rod should impose some regularity of distortion on its component parts. The predominant colour of these inlays is the opaque chalky blue, which appears identical with the opaque blue glass fillings of the eyes of the animals in the zoomorphic interlace borders round the rectangular panels. Each red element in the millefiori sheet is surrounded by four white spots which, in visual effect, appear to be carried in or contained by the predominant blue flux. Figure 428 illustrates the basic pattern of rods from which these inlays, and also those of the boars' hips of 4b, which are similar, must be derived. The blue appears dominant because the white elements are in any case smaller, rather drab and tonally not far removed from the blue. The impression given is of the blue elements swamping and sweeping through the red. But the white spots are really intended, as figure 428 indicates, to be small squares which should block off all the red elements from each other, rather as cruciform step-pattern cells forms are isolated on stilts in the main cloisonné panels. The ambitious design seems to have

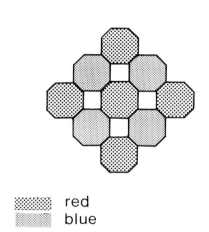

red
blue

FIGURE 428 Apparent shapes and arrangement of glass rods used for millefiori inlays in the boars' hips of shoulder-clasp Inv. 4 (inlay K).

585

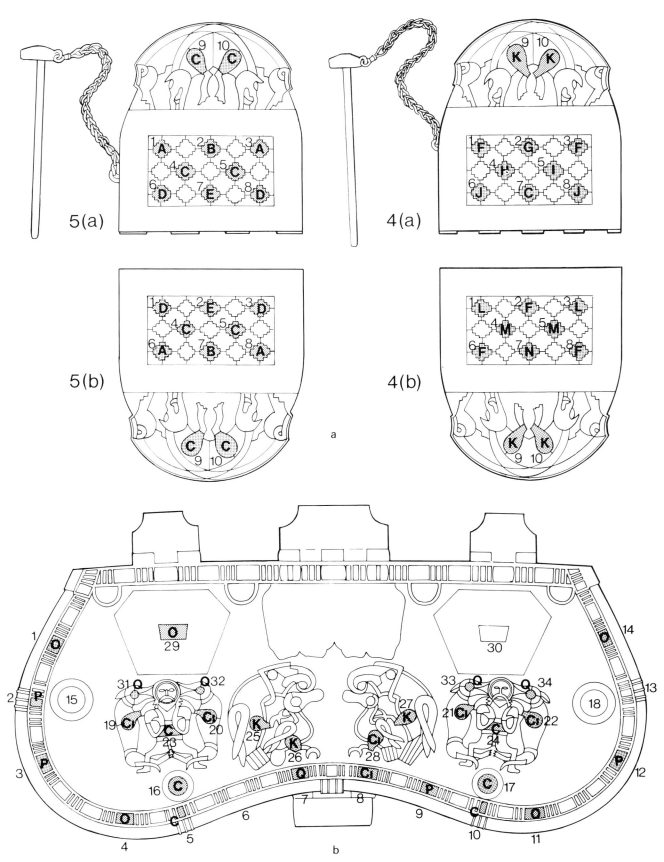

FIGURE 429 Key to the millefiori inlays in (a) the shoulder-clasps and (b) the purse-lid, showing the distribution of the different inlays (p. 582).

gone astray in the execution. It is perhaps on too small a scale to register effectively, and the irregularity of the red elements is met by a corresponding loss of the octagonal and square shapes intended for the blue and white elements. The blue seems to fill up the irregularities and concavities seen in the red elements and this causes the blue colour to seem to flow, and to resemble a continuous trellis that incorporates the white squares and dominates the red. The white elements tend to retain their shapes; in some instances their edges and their polygonal shape, usually square, is quite sharp, at others the edges or a corner are slightly smudged or blurred and lose their shape. This may have taken place in the final process of polishing or smoothing down the cut inlay, or may simply be the result of a manufacturing technique in which some inter-reaction of adjacent rods is inevitable.

Although close study of the inlays in the boars' hips in 4a and b in the past convinced several qualified observers (including Dr Françoise Henry and myself) that the irregularly shaped red elements must be garnets, two of them have now yielded the classic photographs (e.g. pl. 23c) which prove them to be glass. We seem to have in inlay K a particularly ambitious millefiori design which has not proved entirely reproducible in the manufacturing (fig. 428).

The rectangular panels

Each of the four rectangular panels carries, in its pattern of smaller, stilted cruciform step-patterns cells, eight millefiori inlays. Figure 429a provides a key in which the four half-clasps are drawn schematically and the cells bearing millefiori are individually numbered. Plate 24a depicts in colour the different designs represented. Each rod or assembly of rods is designated by a letter. The inlays have all been trimmed down from larger expanses of millefiori and for inlay A this is drawn in to show the full range of the millefiori sheet detectable in the cell, and not merely the complete pattern seen in the middle. The inlays in clasp Inv. 4 are much more complex and varied than those in Inv. 5. The latter clasp will again be described first because its millefiori inlays are simpler.

Inv. 5a. Cell 1. A regular pattern of transparent red and opaque dark blue squares comprising a design of four T-shaped motifs with their stems pointing inwards and resting against a central dark blue square. The pattern is set obliquely so that the blue squares appear as diamond shapes. The effect of the design is largely neutralised by the fact that the transverse elements of the T's are cut into by the stepping of the cell's walls. The inlay, as it is, is shown in plate 24a, A, which also shows the design as a completed square made up of twenty-five lesser individual square rods, nine of them blue and sixteen red. *Inlay A.*

Cell 2. Chequer pattern of translucent red and opaque dark blue squares, in which the red elements appear smaller than the blue, perhaps an optical effect. At the centre

587

of the design is one opaque white square. The individual squares are smaller than those in the cell 1 inlay and the whole squares are more numerous as a result. *Inlay B.*

Cell 3. The same as cell 1 (Inlay A).

Cells 4 and 5. Chessboard pattern of transparent red and opaque dark blue squares, shown in plate 24 a, C (drawn from cell 5). The pattern appears identical with that used in larger sheets in the boar's hips, in cells 9 and 10 in both halves of the clasp. The inlays could all have been cut from the same prepared sheets. The same design occurs also in cells 4 and 5 in the other half of the clasp, Inv. 5b and on Inv. 4 (see below). *Inlay C.*

Cell 6. Chequer pattern of transparent red and dark blue cells having at its centre a cross made up of four white squares with a more vivid blue square at the centre. The white squares of the cross are flanked on all sides by transparent red squares. This has the effect of bringing out the cruciform central theme both by the contrast in colour and by the transparency of the surrounding squares in comparison with the solid-looking squares that make up the cross. This inlay occurs again in cell 8, and in cells 1 and 3 of Inv. 5b. *Inlay D.*

Cell 7. Chequer pattern of transparent red and opaque dark blue squares, of smaller scale than in the other inlays so far described except for that of cell 2. In the design a red rod has been substituted for the blue rod which in a regular pattern would be due to appear at the centre. By this device a cross theme in transparent red, made up of five red squares, has been achieved at the centre of the cell. *Inlay E.*

Cell 8. The same as cell 6 (inlay D).

Inv. 5b. Cell 1. The same as cells 6 and 8 of 5a and as cell 3 in 5b (inlay D). The extra vividness of the central blue square is maintained in all four pieces of this inlay.

Cell 2. The same as 5a, cell 7 (inlay E).

Cell 3. The same as cell 1 (inlay D).

Cells 4 and 5. The same as cells 4 and 5 of 5a and the boars' hip inlays in cells 9 and 10 of both halves of the clasp (inlay C).

Cell 6. The same as cells 1 and 3 of 5a (inlay A).

Cell 7. The same as cell 2 in 5a, but slightly larger in scale, which implies that it is from a different portion of the rod (inlay B).

Cell 8. The same as cell 6 (inlay A).

Inv. 4a. Cell 1. Chessboard pattern of transparent red and opaque extra dark blue squares of very regular shape, similar to the inlay C of Inv. 5a. It is used also in this clasp in cell 3. The inlay is set obliquely, so that the squares are seen as diamond shapes. The extra darkness of the blue component makes it clear that the inlay cannot be derived from the same sheet or bundle of rods as inlay C. The colour distinction is quite clear to the naked eye. This inlay appears also on this clasp in cells 4a, 3 and 4b, 2, 6 and 8. *Inlay F.*

Cell 2. This inlay closely resembles the inlay D seen in Inv. 5, cell 6 (pl. 24a, D). It shows a central cross of white opaque squares, surrounded by transparent red squares, with dark blue squares filling up the pattern, but instead of the vivid blue square used for the centre of the cross in inlay D, the central square is here bright green. *Inlay G.*

Cell 3. The same as cell 1 (inlay F).

Cell 4. Chequer pattern of transparent red and opaque white and dark blue squares, set obliquely. A central transparent red square is surrounded by the four apparently white squares, forming a not particularly explicit cross theme; the angles between the arms of the cross are filled with transparent red squares. The design was continued in dark blue and red squares. The four predominantly white squares forming the arms of the centre cross are themselves composed of nine minute rods, four of which are green (pl. 24a, H, detail, where the design of one of the 'white' squares is shown enlarged). The shapes of the minute individual rods, not unnaturally, are not well preserved. *Inlay H.*

Cell 5. Complex design of transparent red and opaque dark blue octagonal rods separated by smaller white and green squares. The scheme is similar to that in the hips of the boars on both halves of the clasp (Inv. 4a and b, cells 9 and 10) with the introduction of the extra colour, green. *Inlay I.*

Cell 6. Chequer pattern of transparent red and opaque dark blue and white squares; a white cross with a pale blue central square and red squares between the arms. The inlay set obliquely as in cell 2. The only difference from inlay D, which occurs for example in cells 6 and 8 of Inv. 5a and 1 and 3 of Inv. 5b (pl. 24a, D), lies in the paler blue of the central square. The colour is slightly lighter than the other blue squares of the inlay, but not the vivid blue maintained in the four occurrences of inlay D. *Inlay J*.

Cell 7. A regular pattern of translucent red and opaque dark blue squares, identical with that seen on clasp 5 in cells 4 and 5 in both halves (inlay C).

Cell 8. The same as cell 6 (inlay J), also set obliquely.

Inv. 4b. Cell 1. Chequer pattern with central cross of white squares, with a central square built up of nine lesser squares, five white and four blue, all of which have retained their shapes. The central cross is surrounded by red squares with dark blue squares outside them. *Inlay L*.

Cell 2. The same as cells 1 and 3 in 4a (inlay F).

Cell 3. The same as cell 1 (inlay L).

Cells 4 and 5. Chessboard pattern of translucent red squares and opaque dark blue squares, with four blue and white squares in the middle surrounding a central transparent red square (pl. 24a, M). The four blue and white squares are made up of nine minute squares, five dark blue and four white. *Inlay M*.

Cell 6. The same as 4a, cells 1 and 3, and 4b, cells 2 and 8 (inlay F).

Cell 7. Cruciform design identical with 4b, 1 and 3, except that in the central square, which is subdivided into nine, there are five blue and four white lesser squares, not five white and four blue as in cells 1 and 3. The centre and corner squares are the blue ones, so that this colour predominates. The central squares containing the nine blue and white lesser squares is itself scarcely 0·5 mm in width. *Inlay N*.

Cell 8. The same as in cells 4b 2 and 6, and 4a 1 and 3 (inlay F).

III   MILLEFIORI INLAYS IN THE PURSE-LID

Figure 429b is a sketch-plan of the purse-lid in which individual numbers are allotted to the cells bearing millefiori. This numbering will be used in the discussion which follows. Designs not already identified in the inlays of the shoulder-clasps are allotted individual identifying letters, beginning with O, following on from the inlays A–N already described. The inlays showing new designs are illustrated in plate 24a, O–Q.

Millefiori inlays occur in the purse-lid along the curved portion of the frame, in the four circular studs in the interior field and apparently on six out of the seven

590

ornamental plaques. They were not used in the straight bar which carries the hinges at the top of the lid, nor in the zoomorphic double plaque. Plain opaque blue glass rings were inlaid in the circular garnets which form the eyes of the four birds, but the eyes of the wolf-like animals flanking the man in the man-and-beasts plaques contained millefiori (fig. 429).

The inlays which occupied the large trapezoidal cell at the centre of each of the hexagonal plaques in the upper register are missing, but the patterned foil from the bottom of the cell in Inv. 2(c) (the right-hand one in plate 14c) is preserved, and to it adhered a small portion of a millefiori plaque of red and pale opaque blue squares. This indicates the nature of the filling of one, and by inference both, of these trapezoidal settings: the fillings were millefiori, not garnet. These particular inlays are given great prominence and the hexagonal plaques could be regarded as built round the centre pieces, setting them off as a cobra's hood sets off the intense head at its centre; on the figural plaques of the lower ornamental register of the lid the distribution of polychrome inlays is extended up towards the top of the lid by eight eyes. Otherwise the coloured glass inlays are confined to the hips of the wolves' front legs, the legs of the birds, and the midriffs of the spread-eagled men. The sense of symmetry and balance shown in the distribution of the millefiori inlays, seen throughout the jewellery, is maintained in the frame.

The frame

This now carries twelve millefiori insets, but originally probably held fourteen. The garnet occupying cell 6 probably replaces a lost inlay, and the inlay in cell 13 is modern; the distribution of inlays is otherwise almost symmetrical. The inlay of cell 6 should correspond with that of cell 9. The inlays in the frame will be dealt with in numerical order. All measure 3 mm in one dimension (the width of the cloisonné lining tray that contains them) and all are in cells of rectangular form.

Cell 1. Inlay 5 mm×3 mm, of transparent red and whitish opaque elements. The red elements, which are of very dark colour, are T-shapes with the stems pointing inwards to rest against a central pale blue square, in the manner of inlay A (pl. 24a, A). The inlays are cut from a different rod, however, for the T-themes, resembling the T-shaped cells of early Germanic metalwork, are of varying shapes, fitted to an oblong and not a square. The whitish elements, which have a slightly blue tint, are much paler than in inlay A. The T-elements, moreover, are not here obviously built up of four equal squares, as in inlay A, but are apparently each a single piece of glass. The T-elements at each end of the rectangle have thin stems, while those in the long sides of the panel have very broad stems. In cell 1 the T-element at the left-hand end of the design is larger than that at the right-hand end (pl. 13a). *Inlay O* (see also pl. 23f).

This inlay is repeated in Cells 4, 11 and 14, the inlay being reversed in cell 11.

Cells 2 and 3 have the same inlay, the inlay in cell 3 being larger and providing a clearer view of the design of the sheet as a whole (cell 2 is 2×3 mm, cell 3, 6×3 mm). This is a pattern of transparent red and opaque pure blue rectilinear elements; the individual elements are rectangular rather than square, their long axes running along the length of the inlay. The scale of units or individual elements is smaller than that of the inlays of type inlay C seen in the same illustration (pl. 24a, P). *Inlay P.*

The red elements seem slightly narrower than the blue. The same inlay occurs in cell 9 and by inference occurred in cell 6 (now occupied by a garnet) and cell 13, these cells being symmetrically disposed.[1] It appears also to occur in cell 12, though here the pattern is seen at slightly larger scale, as if cut from a less attenuated portion of the same rod.

Cells 5, 8 and 10. These cells each carry the same pattern, seen to better advantage in cell 8 (6×3 mm) than in cells 5 and 10 (2×3 mm). This is inlay C, seen also in the boars' hips and in the rectangular panels of shoulder-clasp, Inv. 5 (pl. 24a, C).

The inlay in cell 8, however, is not cut from the same set of rods as 5 and 10, since the blue squares have a pinkish tone not seen in 5 and 10. The inlay in cell 5 of the frame matches that of cell 10 exactly, and agrees in colour with the similar inlay of cell 17 (the circular stud immediately above it). The cell 8 inlay seems to share its different pinkish-blue with the inlay in cell 28 (the duck's hip) just above it, and in the hip joints of the other animals. The inlay of cell 8 may be referred to as *inlay C 1*, a variant of C, having the same general design but with a colour difference in the blue (pl. 24a, C1).

Cell 7. Chessboard pattern of bright opaque white and vivid blue squares, very regularly executed (pl. 24a, Q). Presumably a replacement for a lost inlay of type C1 as seen in cell 10, as the two cells should correspond. *Inlay Q.*

The plaques and studs (Cells 15–34)
Cells 16 and 17 (Circular studs). Chessboard pattern of transparent red and opaque dark blue squares of type inlay C, but on a reduced scale. The outer elements of the pattern appear to radiate outwards, being elongated consistently in a direction away from the centre. Blue squares identical in colour with the similar inlay in cells 5 and 10 (inlay C; pl. 24a, C). It may be supposed that the inlays now missing from cells 15 and 18, the other circular studs, were the same.[2]

---

[1] The inlay of similar type but of red and green squares now occupying cell 13 is an experimental inlay made in 1945 out of transparent celluloid toothbrush handles in an attempt to work out mosaic techniques thought at the time to have been used in creating these chequer-pattern inlays. Such a mosaic technique, especially had garnets been employed, as was then thought to be the case for the transparent red elements, would have indicated Germanic imitation of the Celtic millefiori, and not the employment of a Celtic specialist.

[2] The inlay of cell 17 had not been replaced when the colour photograph (pl. 13a) was taken. It can be seen restored to its position in fig. 367.

Cells 19, 20, 21 and 22 (the hips of the wolf-like animals in the man-between-beasts plaques). Chessboard inlays of transparent red and opaque blue units, all probably of type inlay C 1, as in cell 8 (pl. 24 *a*, C). They share the same blue glass with pinkish tone. Though in the four inlays the units vary somewhat in size and shape, the four inlays could it seems be cut from the same rod, the variant elements depending on the position in the drawn-out rod from which they were cut.

In cell 22 the units are regular and square, lacking the elongation seen in cell 8. In cell 19 the phenomenon of the elongation of the outer units in the inlay (already noted in the cell 16 inlay) occurs. It appears as if a central rod comprising sixteen square units has been surrounded by individual rods of identical glass which have become more elongated or distorted.

Cells 23, 24 (midriffs of the men in the man-between-beasts plaques). Chessboard pattern of transparent red and opaque blue squares, set obliquely, apparently as seen in cells 5, 10 and 16 (inlay C). The squares of this chequer board pattern are larger than in any other instance of chequer-patterns used in this jewellery. This need not imply the use of a different rod but only the cutting of the inlay from a different part of the rod where the scale was less reduced.

Cells 25–27 (hips of the birds). Complex inlays of the type used in the boars' hips in shoulder-clasp, Inv. 4 (inlay K). The octagonal blue and red elements are badly distorted, the blue seeming to flow round the red, as seen in cells 9 and 10, Inv. 4 a and b. Small drab white elements separating facets of the octagons can be seen faintly but unmistakably in all three inlays.

Cell 28 (bird's hip). Similar to the inlay of the adjacent cell 8 and to the inlay of cell 22 (inlay C1).

Cells 29, 30 (hexagonal plaques, see p. 506). The fragment of inlay surviving from cell 29 is clearly a piece of inlay O, with four T-shaped dark red elements, and a greyish (sugar icing) white for the other squares. The fragment appears to show the narrow stem of one of the T-elements at the ends of the inlay. These cells, 29 and 30, are of trapezoid shape; this is also true of cells 4 and 11 carrying this inlay on the frame.

Cells 31–34 (eyes of the four animals in the man-between-beasts plaque). Small circular chequer inlay of opaque bright blue and white squares, showing a white square at the centre surrounded by four blue squares, with white squares in the corners. Though the colours seem a little duller and the squares a little more distorted, this could be from the same rod as the inlay in cell 7, inlay Q (fig. 373 *c*).

Inv. 28 and 29

Each pyramid has one millefiori inlay (3×3 mm) set in its flat top. The two inlays are cut from the same rod or sheet, although they do not quite coincide. The pattern is a regular chessboard type of transparent red and opaque dark blue squares. It is the same as that used in the boars' hips and in cells 4 and 5 in both halves of Inv. 5. Both the inlays are shown in plate 24 *a* as variants of inlay C. The running together of the two red cells in the upper right corner, and a distorted cell seen below it and to the left in plate 24 *a*, can be seen in both inlays (pl. 21 *c*). Uniquely in the jewellery these two millefiori inlays do not have patterned gold-foil underlays. Inlay C.

V INLAYS OF BLUE GLASS IN SHOULDER-CLASPS, PURSE-LID AND PYRAMIDS

In the three major items that contain millefiori insets, inlays of darkish opaque blue glass, the surface having sometimes a rather soapy look, also appear. These inlays occur only in those items that have millefiori and were evidently intended to enhance the effect of polychromy sought in those pieces. Seventy-two such inlays were probably used in all, the glass used apparently being the same throughout.

In the shoulder-clasps these blue inlays are used for the tusks of the boars on Inv. 5 a, the inlays of the tusks are missing in 5 b, but were presumably also of blue glass, as such details correspond in the two halves. In Inv. 4 the fillings are missing in all four tusks. It cannot be stated that these inlays were also of blue glass, though it seems probable. In addition in both clasps these inlays were used in the eyes of the twenty-two interlacing animals in the borders round the panels of each clasp. Assuming that all the tusk inlays were of blue glass, this gives a total of fifty-two such inlays used in the clasps.

In the purse the use of plain blue glass is confined to the eyes of the four birds in the bird of prey and duck plaques, where blue glass rings were inserted in engraved circles in the circular garnets.

Each pyramid has eight blue glass inlays, slabs set in pairs chevron-wise in the angles (pl. 22 *e*, fig. 233).

VI GENERAL DISCUSSION

A proper appraisal of the phenomenon of the millefiori at Sutton Hoo and the cultural significance of it appearing so decisively and distinctively in the finest pieces of the royal ceremonial harness, must await future discussion. The millefiori in the gold jewellery must be measured against the practice of the craft as we have it in the Celtic background, particularly in the penannular brooch and hanging-bowl series, and must also be related to the millefiori of the large Sutton Hoo hanging-bowl, which shows unusual characteristics (including the use of transparent glass) and was repaired by the Sutton Hoo goldsmith.[1] A few summarising points and preliminary comments may be tentatively offered here.

As a result of the microscopic examination carried out in the British Museum Research Laboratory by Miss Mavis Bimson and Mr W. A. Oddy, there is no doubt that the inlays under discussion are genuine millefiori, and not in any essential different from the tradition of millefiori work already rooted in Ireland and the Celtic west and north. Yet there are novel elements which make it difficult to say whether this is the work of a Celtic specialist, or of a Saxon craftsman trained in a Celtic workshop, or a Saxon craftsman imitating Celtic work in a spirit of rediscovery—having been informed generally as to the technique—after being fascinated by the large hanging-bowl, in which Celtic millefiori finds its finest expression, and which the Sutton Hoo goldsmith himself repaired.[2]

It is perhaps simplest to explain the phenomenon as resulting from the employment in the East Anglian royal workshop, alongside the gem-cutter and in close association with the goldsmith, of a Celtic specialist in the craft or, if such a thing were historically acceptable at this date, a Saxon craftsman returning to East Anglia fully trained from a Celtic metalworking school. Such a man must have been given the assignment of making millefiori to fit into the design drawn up for purse, shoulder-clasps and pyramids. It seems that the uniform appearance of transparent red elements may be the logical, unsought for but happy consequence of the task thus uniquely set, for on the gold jewellery the millefiori inlays required only to be set cold, like garnets. Since no paste or similar backing substance seems to have been used to fill the cells under the garnets anywhere in the Sutton Hoo jewellery, the millefiori inlays would need to be held in position in their cells, as are the garnets, by gold-foil sheets, turned up tray-like round their edges (pl. 23 d, fig. 344) and wedged in the tops of the cells; hence the use of patterned gold foil behind the millefiori. Also as no firing was called for (as is the case with Celtic enamelling) the red elements would stay transparent and hence their garnet-like appearance.[3]

If we have here a Celtic, or Celtic-trained, craftsman working alongside the Germanic goldsmith it is all the more plausible to think that his inlay A on the purse-frame (essentially a grouping of four typical Germanic cloisonné T-shaped cells, as seen in the two outermost semicircular projections from the purse-bar into the interior field) and also in the shoulder-clasps (pl. 18) shows his adoption of a Germanic jewellery theme into his own repertoire. The theme, and developments of it, becomes

[1] For a survey of Celtic enamels and the Roman millefiori factories, see the works of Dr Françoise Henry, particularly Henry 1933, 1936, 1956 and 1965.

[2] For a discussion of this point see the hanging-bowl chapter in *Sutton Hoo*, Vol. III. Apart from the substitution of garnets with foil underlays and beaded wire collars for the original enamel fillings of the eyes of the cast bronze boars' heads on the bowl, the large silver patch shows Style II bird heads sharing uniquely a stylistic idiosyncrasy with the great gold buckle (see p. 563 above).

[3] See Henry 1956, 82, n. 45. Dr Henry explains the translucency of the red elements of the Sutton Hoo pieces in this way, although unaware of the functional nature of the gold foil, which indicates that the goldsmith and millefiori maker need not have been setting out to imitate garnets, this use of gold-foil backing being in practice the only way in which the goldsmith could get the millefiori inlays to stay at the tops of their cells. A deliberate Saxon imitation of the millefiori effect, though in two shades of red, not in a second colour, is provided by the Kingston brooch (Bruce-Mitford 1966, pl. 1, here fig. 431).

established in Hiberno-Saxon metalwork.[1] It is found also on the Roundway Down necklace, another early seventh-century instance of fusion of Celtic with Germanic traditions in metalwork (fig. 430).

The size of some of the millefiori inlays, up to 8×5 mm as inserted into the cloisons, but here implying a millefiori sheet of at least 10×8 mm from which they have been cut down, makes it the more difficult to visualise these as produced in the normal way from bundles of rods. Yet it is clear that these major inlays are of a single make, and not built up from lesser units. Certain insets like nos. 2, 6 and 8 of the shoulder-clasp panel of Inv. 4a, where the minute central square, less than 1 mm across, of the white cross of the inlay is itself subdivided into nine lesser squares (pl. 24a, H), can only have been produced by the orthodox millefiori technique.

In the Sutton Hoo jewellery all the millefiori designs are rectilinear. Where, as in Inv. 4 (inlay K), they are not built up from square-sectioned rods, the rods are octagonal mixed with square. The colours used are blue in various shades, white, red and, inconspicuously, green. These restrictions in the pattern and colour range seem to show a desire to respect the red and gold colour scheme of the jewellery and to reinforce the rectilinearity of the step-pattern cells and conspicuous grid foil

FIGURE 430 Cell pattern on a glass inlay from the linked pins found at Roundway Down, Wiltshire (fig. 441 k). (Scale: 3/2)

FIGURE 431 Detail from the Kingston (Kent) brooch, showing imitation millefiori and zoomorphic filigree. (Scale: 4/1) (Photo: Merseyside County Museum)

[1] Henry 1956, fig. 18, d, h, i, l–o.

backings, without introducing distracting and discordant elements. There is no technical difficulty about producing curvilinear star-shaped and other elaborate patterns, or colouring the millefiori green and orange, so that it seems that the specialist employed here is tailoring his normal millefiori range to suit a particular task.

In the shoulder-clasps, as the survey on pages 484 to 590 shows, fourteen different millefiori designs are employed (inlays A–N). Figure 429a, showing the distribution of different inlays in the cell pattern, indicates the attempts to balance the inlays in the panels on the two halves of each clasp. The distribution was evidently carefully thought out. The work on the clasps is of very high quality and under sure technical control throughout, apart from some lack of success in retaining the shape of the components in the patterns using the octagonal rods (inlay K). The balanced use of the same inlays in corresponding parts of the design is equally observed in the purse.

It seems possible that the adoption of this Celtic theme *par excellence* into what we have suggested may be a Saxon *bretwalda*'s regalia (p. 534) may have a more than decorative significance. It appears to parallel the use of the bronze Celtic stag, cast in the round, to surmount the Germanic sceptre. Can the use of Celtic devices in the Sutton Hoo regalia be the mark of an *imperium*, whatever its real nature may have been, which included a claim to some sort of suzerainty or title over the former Roman province as a whole? Or an affirmation of the *bretwalda*'s role, more particularly after A.D. 617, when Raedwald slew Aethelfrith and settled Edwin on the throne of Northumbria, as overlord of substantial Celtic elements in the population? If the live millefiori were found in a different Germanic context one would not dream of making such a claim, but here it occurs, uniquely, in what may reasonably be claimed as a *bretwalda*'s regalia. It may be no more than the adoption of a decorative element of a highly distinctive and novel form; yet that element is exclusively and distinctively Celtic, and surely in this context a more than merely decorative significance may be read into it.

6. *Style and technique*

It is no exaggeration to refer to the Sutton Hoo master goldsmith, assisted by a gem-cutter or lapidary of altogether exceptional gifts, as the most brilliant of his age. In saying this one is paying tribute to more than an outstanding technical skill. That perhaps is to be matched by the makers of such masterpieces as the Kingston brooch and the sword and scramasax mounts of Childeric I. One is paying tribute in particular to his unique imagination, inventiveness and flexibility of mind. He seems to us, from our knowledge of the surviving material, to be a pioneer, a breaker of technical and imaginative barriers. His work also shows an exceptional refinement, matched by the extraordinary skill of his lapidary, and suggests abnormal boldness and independence.

We should first define what we understand the work of the master goldsmith to be. The jewellery covers a diversity of pieces showing variation, it may be thought, in hand and date. Full analysis must await a later opportunity to go in greater detail into the interconnections of the pieces and the relationship of the Sutton Hoo jewellery with Continental material. We are, however, fortunate in being able to single out three of the most remarkable items in the assemblage which show all the signs of being the work of the same team of master goldsmith and lapidary, and which we can also say with complete assurance are locally made—that is, made in the East Anglian royal workshops. These are the purse, the shoulder-clasps and the pyramids. These items, alone in the assemblage, have the tell-tale insular millefiori inlays, and two of them— the purse and shoulder-clasps—have the novel device of the lidded cell technique, fully developed and confidently deployed; this with the use of millefiori and some openwork design is the key to the unusual impact of these pieces. These features, and with them the effective realisation of figural scenes, are all encountered for the first time in the Sutton Hoo jewellery.[1] Continental jewellery appears completely innocent of these technical devices and their decorative exploitation, except for what seems to be the use of a beaded or sealed cell to effect a twist in the burnt remains of a cloisonné panel apparently from a pyramid, from Odenshög (the west mound) at Gamla Uppsala; the Tongres mount, a Continental-found piece which must be a product of the Sutton Hoo workshop;[2] and perhaps another fragmentary item of zoomorphic character from Gamla Uppsala also from the west mound.

It is the use of the lidded cell, combined in the case of the man-between-beasts and the bird plaques with openwork design, which allows the figural themes achieved in cloisonné work on the purse-lid to be made explicit, clear and uniquely effective. The situation without the use of these devices can be seen from the obscure effect of such rare pictorial cloisonné pieces as the Reinstrup brooch[3] and the upper portion, with a skilful but hardly legible animal interlace, of the Wynaldum brooch.[4] The effect of using the lidded cell on animal ornament representation in cloisonné can be judged again in the Tongres mount.

Important use of the lidded cell is also found in the pair of rectangular mounts, Inv. 8 and 9, with the cable-twist interlace (figs. 327 and 330). Here the technique is used to seal the loops round which the interlace rotates, and the small residual triangular spaces between the re-entrants of the interlace and the straight frame, with the fluent result seen in figures 327 and 330. An unobtrusive use of the technique is also to be seen on the purse-lid, where it occurs twice in one of the hexagonal mounts, which are purely geometric in design, in the inner elements of the two semicircular themes below the border surrounding the central millefiori setting in Inv. 2 (d) (figs.

[1] The use of pieces of Roman millefiori in Anglo-Saxon settings, as for example in the necklace found with the Sarre brooch, is a different matter. Here it is a question of freshly made millefiori, the living craft.

[2] Cf. Bruce-Mitford 1974, pl. 10 d for the Gamla Uppsala pyramid fragment, pls. 90 a–c and 91 for the Tongres mount. For the second zoomorphic piece which may show the lidded cell device used at Gamla Uppsala see Lindqvist 1936 b, 179,

para. (c) and fig. 100; also Arrhenius 1971, fig. 141 a. The pyramid panel referred to above is described and illustrated by Lindqvist op. cit., 179, para. (a) and fig. 101.

[3] Bruce-Mitford 1974, pl. 15 c and fig. 6 j; Arrhenius 1971, fig. 153 a.

[4] Bruce-Mitford 1974, pl. 88 a and fig. 46 c, where the piece is incorrectly described as a buckle.

371 *f*, 358 *a*, left). I would regard the two cable-twist mounts without hesitation as the work of the same master goldsmith as the purse plaques. These mounts in turn are evidently by the same hand as the matching pair Inv. 6 and 7 and the T-shaped mount from the same strap. The majority of the minor cloisonné mounts—major pieces in any other context—can be closely related to these and to the purse-lid, shoulder-clasps and pyramids on grounds of technique, cell repertoire and decorative themes. I would regard the minor mounts, apparently designed as a set for the sword-harness, at least as products of the same workshop as the purse-lid, clasps and pyramids; though not necessarily all by the same hand, most of them probably were.

Two pieces only seem to stand apart from the rest: the triangular zoomorphic mount, Inv. 18 (pp. 481–85), and the sword-pommel. The mount shows peculiar features, already described, among them the use of granulation on a minor mount, the use of a foil underlay (A2) of a fineness not encountered in the rest of the jewellery; the use of flat stones for eyes and nostrils, instead of cabochon settings; a subdued use of the mushroom cell theme, which occurs only once (p. 484); and a feebleness or at any rate lack of exactitude and conviction, in the execution of the cloisonné design. These divergences make it clear that it is not the work of the hand that can be recognised in the rest of the jewellery. It does not have the same personal style. Yet it shows certain affinities with the scabbard-bosses discussed above (p. 484) and some features found in others of the mounts. The triangular mount may be a product of the Sutton Hoo workshop or its milieu, though it does not show the hand of the master; on the other hand it could have been made elsewhere, on the Continent or in the North. The sword pommel has a distinct style and cell repertoire and, as has been said, is almost certainly of foreign workmanship and may be anything up to three-quarters of a century earlier than the bulk of the jewellery (p. 304).

A systematic attempt has been made to establish the technique employed in all the pieces of cloisonné jewellery for the setting of the garnets and other inlays, in the light of the recent analytical work by Dr. Arrhenius on the substances used to support the stones of the inlays and the technique of cloisonné frames not soldered to base-plates but carried in a continuous bed of paste.[1] It has not been practicable to examine all the jewellery in this way as the perfect condition of some pieces, including the sword-pommel, the pyramids and the shoulder-clasps, has made it impossible to get at the interiors of the cells without damage. This is particularly to be regretted in the case of the sword-pommel, which shows every indication of being an early piece of Continental origin, in my view, more likely to be East Scandinavian than Rhenish. Examination of a number of pieces has been possible, however, notably the damaged buckle (Inv. 11), where several stones are missing or fallen at an angle in the cell, and the purse-lid. The scabbard-bosses and the curved mount (dummy buckle), from which certain stones are missing or removable, and one of the rectangular mounts with

[1] Arrhenius 1971, *passim*.

interlace (Inv. 9) have also been examined. In all these the cells have been found completely empty. The technique followed by the goldsmith throughout has been to set stones on foil cut-outs of the same shape but slightly larger, which have then been wedged in the tops of the cells, to be held there by pressure alone.[1] The subsequent polishing of the surface has tended to spread the tops of the cell walls, but the overhang is so delicate as to be scarcely noticeable. Plate 23 e is a Research Laboratory photograph showing a stone on edge in Inv. 11, with the foil still wedged against its edges; beneath the foil is an empty cell. Perhaps the most perfectly preserved example of a foil tray is that from one of the bird's eyes on the purse (pl. 23 d). The complete mastery of gem-cutting and assembly and the evident close collaboration of goldsmith and lapidary are astonishing. The fact that so many of the pieces remain in perfect condition is proof of the soundness of this setting technique in really skilled hands.

An observation of a wholly different nature tends to support the conclusion that no pastes were used in the cells to support the garnets from below, or to carry the cloisonnage. Figures 369, 372, 375 and 377 show the backs of the seven decorative plaques that were mounted on the purse-lid. Holes can be seen in six of them. Some are situated close to existing rivets (figs. 369 b, 375 b and e, 377 b and e), and might be thought to indicate the positions of earlier rivets that have been replaced. Two (figs. 372 b, 377 e) are not near existing rivets, but are nevertheless so positioned as to suggest that there must once have been rivets at these points. These latter two holes and some of the others have raised ridges around them so clean and conspicuous as to show that the holes were driven through from the inside; the remainder (seen in figs. 369 b, 375 b and e and 377 e) seem to have a random distribution: they are not associated with rivets or in positions where rivets could have been readily inserted or would have been necessary. Some of these holes (e.g. fig. 375 b and e) are clearly made from the outside; in others the slight external ridges are compatible with their having been thrown up by the working to either side of a probe or drill brought to bear from the outside. All these latter holes must have been made, it seems, in connection with a programme of repair or reconditioning of the seven mounts: their purpose can only have been to push back into place, or extrude for resetting, garnets that had sunk in their cells and could not otherwise be extracted. This is particularly clearly indicated by five holes along the upper right-hand edge of the back of the bird mount 2e (fig. 375 b). The holes can be related to the small stones in the outer borders of the birds in 2e and also occur behind the outer border in the double plaque. Theoretically this could have proved necessary in the finishing stage before the plaques were first mounted on the lid, but the fact that many of the rivets were evidently replaced indicates that the programme was carried out later, when removal of all the affected plaques from the lid would have been a necessary preliminary. This

[1] Occasionally the inlays seem to have been held by pressure alone without the use of overlapping foil to assist in the wedging process. Examples may be seen in the hexagonal plaques of the purse-lid where the foils under the central millefiori inlays are smaller than the cells, and certain cells have no foil (p. 594).

would have entailed the cutting off or filing away of the splayed ends of the rivets on the under-surface of the lid so that the mounts and the cut rivet-shanks could be withdrawn. The rivets could then be replaced and the plaques remounted by removing the garnets that covered the rivet positions, inserting new rivets (figs. 369 *b*, 375 *b* and *e*), mounting the plaques and finally replacing the garnets. The same holes must have been used in many instances, but in others it seems to have been thought desirable to pierce fresh holes, perhaps rather because of the condition (? looseness) of the holes pierced in the substance of the lid than because of the state of the holes in the base plates of the mount. If this interpretation of the holes associated not with riveting but with randomly distributed garnets is correct, it suggests that the cells beneath the garnets were empty. Had they been filled with paste or cement of some kind to hold the garnets up the garnets could not have sunk, and there would have been no need for such steps to have been taken to restore them.

In general the cell-walls are soldered on to the base plate of the mount and are often of considerable depth (cf. figs. 223, 347). Only two pieces show a variation: in the two rectangular mounts with cable-twist pattern (Inv. 8 and 9) the cloisons are built up on a separate tray or plate, which has been inserted into the mount. As this technique is not followed in the other pair of similar mounts (Inv. 6 and 7), the variation may have been adopted because of the difficulty of execution of the Inv. 8 and 9 design.

The early organisation of the garnet trade, where the pre-cut stones might be mass-produced in centres such as Alabanda in Asia Minor (whence the term *alman-dine*), using templates for predetermined sizes and shapes, cannot have applied to the Sutton Hoo jewellery. Here the stones were evidently cut and polished on the spot. Many of the shapes are quite unparalleled, the consequence of the unique interlace and figural designs which the designer sought to achieve. Such shapes as figures 368 *e–o*, 374 *k*, *m*, *q* and 376 *q–u* are fragile and vulnerable, and would not lend themselves to mass production.

The gem-cutting is of a particularly high order. The reactions of a delegation of modern gem-cutters and goldsmiths from the Goldsmiths' and Silversmiths' Company who examined the jewellery, give an indication of the quality of work and of what may be involved in terms of raw material and man hours. The modern lapidaries thought that the flat step-pattern stones in rectangular panels on the shoulder-clasps would each take the best part of a day to produce, with primitive equipment (fig. 388 *e–h*). The exceptionally shaped set of garnets from the boars' heads and bodies were considered even more difficult: with modern aids and equipment, and allowing for no wastage, it was estimated that each such stone would take the best part of a day, and because of the brittleness of garnet it was thought that the wastage would in fact be considerable; the cutting of these very fine points would require patience, great care, and plenty of time. In antique conditions and not allowing for wastage, it was considered that each would take two days to cut and polish. The faceted stones, as on the pyramid angles, were thought 'astounding', and it was felt that the complex stones, faceted in three planes and recessed on the upper corners (in fact garnets) must be of glass. If garnets, they would take at least three days each to cut and polish, allowing no wastage. It was held that the gem-cutting in general showed 'wonderful skill and patience' and could not be bettered today, whatever technical aids might be employed. The fact that over four thousand individual garnets are used in the Sutton Hoo jewellery must carry implication of much interest for the extent of the gem trade, the length of time taken to make such an assemblage of high grade jewellery, and the workshop organisation required.

A further distinctive element in the Sutton Hoo jewellery is the use of carved garnets and faceted garnets. Relief-carved garnets occur round the basal edges of the scabbard-bosses, on the angles and upper corners of the two pyramids and, in the form of rings engraved in flat stones, in the four eyes of the birds on the purse-lid (pl. 23 d).

Relief cutting of garnets is extremely rare in Anglo-Saxon cloisonné work; the small circular necklace-pendant with single rosette-shaped stone, from Preshaw, Hampshire (British Museum 1937, 5–7, 2) is a fine but almost solitary example. It could be a garnet of early date remounted in a seventh-century setting, and according to Arrhenius, could be of Sassanian origin.[1] A new find, a remarkable pendant containing one very large cabochon stone, 32 mm in length, carved into a bearded and moustached profile male head wearing a Phrygian cap, comes from Epsom in Surrey (British Museum 1970, 3–1, 1).[2] This again is an imported stone carved in the Middle East and remounted in a seventh-century Anglo-Saxon setting. The continuous double ring of carved stones round the base of the Sutton Hoo scabbard-bosses, made up of small lengths of garnet resembling twisted sticks of barley sugar, is paralleled in the Petrossa treasure and on the Tressan (Herault) buckle,[3] both of fifth-century date. This recrudescence of elements characteristic of fifth-century work is evidenced in several other features of the Sutton Hoo jewellery. The relief-cutting of garnets is comprehensively reviewed by Arrhenius;[4] its highly skilful application at Sutton Hoo illustrates a continuity of early traits and technology, and their adoption in the seventh century by the pre-eminent goldsmith and lapidary of their day.

Garnets engraved with rings inlaid with gold occur in a number of Anglo-Saxon finds, notably from Kent. Examples are two square-headed brooches from Howletts, an unusual rectangular ornament from Faversham (BM 1918, 7–11, 1, 2 and 1091.70) and a very fine finger-ring set with a single garnet, recently found in excavations in Dover (Canterbury Museum). In all Continental examples where the inlay survives this is gold.[5] The use of opaque blue glass instead of gold in the four engraved circles

[1] *Antiquaries Journal* XVII, 1937, 322–4; Arrhenius 1971, fig. 10 and p. 13.
[2] Henig 1974, no. 734; p. 96 and pl. XLVI.
[3] Arbman 1947–48, fig. 29 (p. 136); Arrhenius 1971, fig. 7; and (Petrossa) figs. 5 and 6.
[4] Arrhenius 1971, ch. II, 11–18.
[5] In the case of the Hög Edsten, Bohuslän, pommel (fig. 232)

the inlay is missing from the circle that is engraved in the single stone that crowns the pommel. The circles engraved in all the twenty-four of the thick (1·5 cm) garnets in the remarkable fifth-century pendant capsule in the treasure found at Hesselager, in south east Fyn, Denmark (Voss 1951, figs. 1 and 2) are empty. If they originally held fittings these must have been of gold.

that occur in garnets on the Sutton Hoo purse-lid is unique. Visually the blue glass is indistinguishable from the inlays used for the eyes of animals on the shoulder-clasps and in the angles of the pyramids. Similar opaque blue glass inlays occur fairly widely in Anglo-Saxon jewellery of around A.D. 600 or somewhat later.[1] Its use instead of gold in engraved garnets, may, like the appearance of millefiori inlays, be taken as a sign of the Sutton Hoo workshop, or at least as a further indication of Celtic influence and so of Insular origin.

Polychrome effects in the jewellery achieved not by the use of eye-catching millefiori or blue glass inlays but by the subtler deployment of garnets of different natural shades of red, and of different thicknesses, has been referred to in the description of individual pieces. It is found in Ostrogothic pieces of the fifth and sixth centuries[2] and in works of the Childeric school. A particular and distinctive instance may be singled out here. In the pair of cable-twist mounts, Inv. 8 and 9, there is a deliberate alternation between pink and darker red tones, more readily seen in some light conditions than in others, but definite. The individual cruciform step-pattern cells in the middle of each of the sub-square spaces left within the interlacing elements are all of a darker red than the four immediately surrounding residual cells, and much of the cable-twist interlace has a pink tone. This has been achieved, it seems, by a deliberate use of carefully selected stones of cloudy appearance.[3]

7. *Filigree work*

Filigree work is not a prominent feature of the Sutton Hoo jewellery, but where it does appear it shows an appropriately high level of technical skill and artistic range. It is characteristic of the florid cloisonné style of the Sutton Hoo workshop to cover the whole available surface with garnets or millefiori, leaving little or no scope for filigree. Any use of it on such pieces is in general relegated to inconspicuous but neatly executed collars round rivets or bosses (figs. 432 *f–i*). Of the cloisonné-decorated pieces, only the shoulder-clasps and the purse make any substantial use of filigree, and on the purse-lid it is confined to the five binding-clips and the outer edge of the curved portion of the frame, where the distinction between twisted and beaded wire is well seen (fig. 433 *e–g*). The predominant use of filigree occurs on pieces where garnets occur minimally or not at all: the filigree strip with ring head, with its five small spaced cabochons, the two clips on the sword-grip and the heads of the pins that fasten the shoulder-clasps. In these latter a balance is struck between garnet work and filigree similar to that seen on the filigree strip. Each pin-head had two small cabochon eyes and the rest of the surface is entirely covered with filigree (fig. 432 *b, c*).

Much of the filigree is orthodox work in the sense that it consists of simple beaded

---

[1] It has been claimed that lapis lazuli is a substance used in Anglo-Saxon gold cloisonné jewellery, but I know of no established instance of this, on either English or Continental Germanic jewellery.

[2] Cf. the Çesena treasure.

[3] Cloudy stones occur even on the finest pieces, such as the pyramids, Inv. 28 and 29, but not used with the deliberate seeking for a consistent effect seen on the cable-twist mounts.

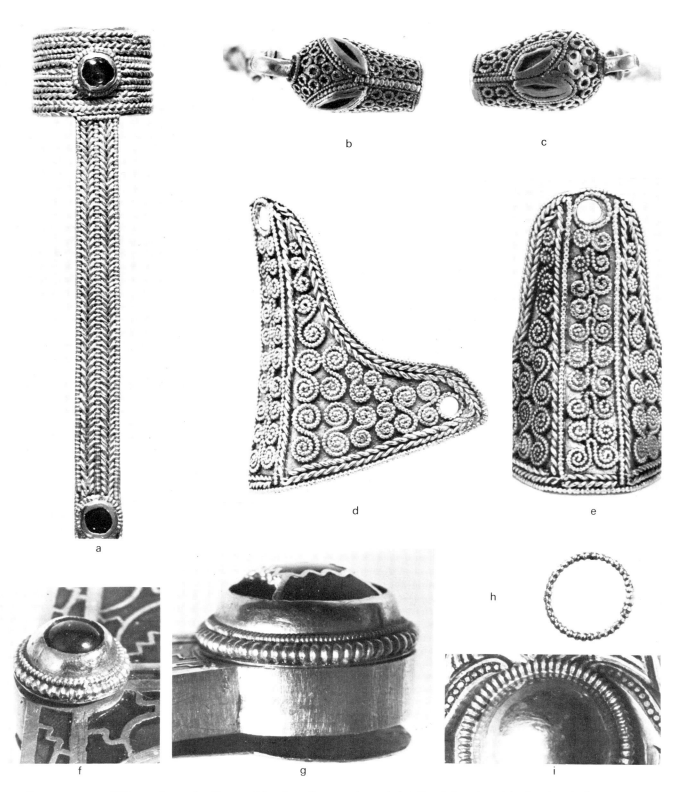

FIGURE 432 Filigree from the Sutton Hoo jewellery: enlarged details. (*a*) strip with ring head, Inv. 30; (*b*) (*c*) heads of the fastening pins from the shoulder-clasps; (*d*), (*e*) filigree clip from the sword-hilt; (*f*) and (*g*) collars round small and large bosses on the curved mount, Inv. 10; (*h*) filigree collar from a rivet on the sword-pommel; (*i*) collar round the large boss on the toe of the great gold buckle. (Scale: *i*, 3/1; the rest, 4/1)

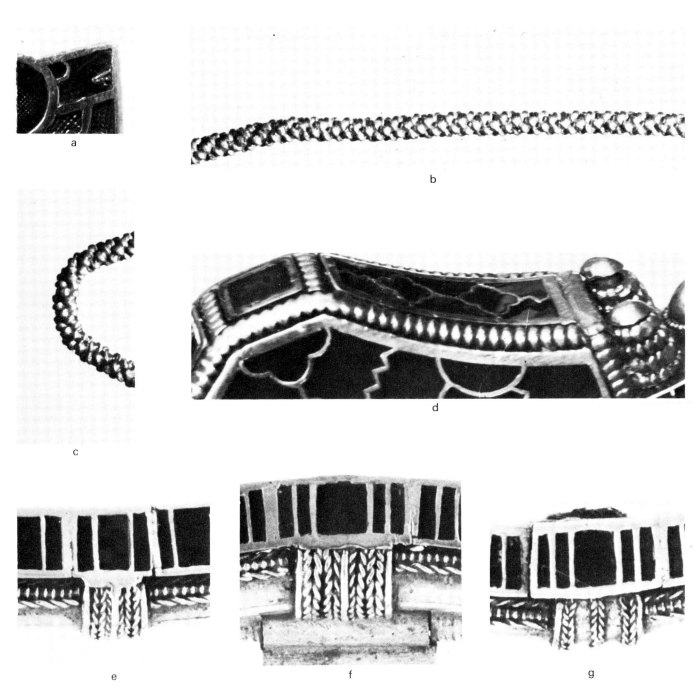

FIGURE 433 Filigree from the Sutton Hoo jewellery: enlarged details. (*a*) animal head from a corner of the triangular zoomorphic mount, Inv. 18; (*b*), (*c*) details of a filigree rope from the lower guard of the sword hilt; (*d*) thick beaded wire and rivet collars on the sword pommel; (*e*)–(*g*) three filigree clips of different design from the frame of the purse lid. (Scale: 4/1)

or twisted wires, the latter regularly combined side by side in pairs with the twists in the opposite direction, producing a running chevron effect (figs. 432*a* and 433*e–g*). Beaded wires are usually smaller in gauge than the twisted wires when they are used in association (figs. 432*a, e* and 433*e–g*). The coarsest beaded wire is that used to outline the panels of the sword-pommel (fig. 433*d*). It shows considerable wear. A

FIGURE 434   Shoulder-clasps: detail from the half-clasp Inv. 4a. (Scale: approx. 10/1)

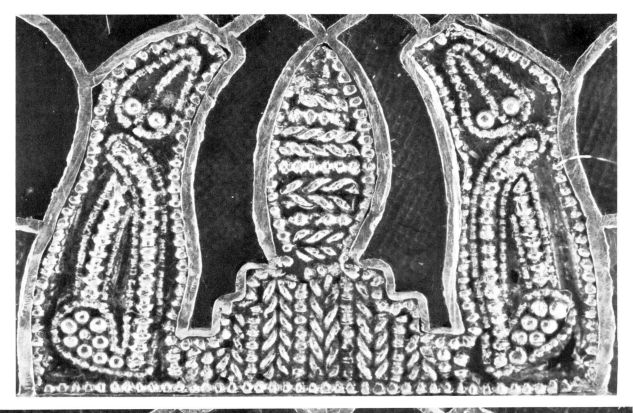

FIGURE 435　Shoulder-clasp: filigree details from Inv. 5a and b. (Scale: approx. 8/1)

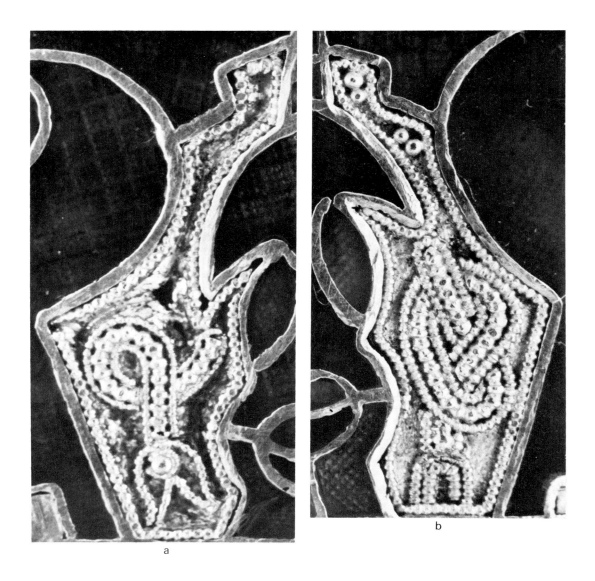

a

b

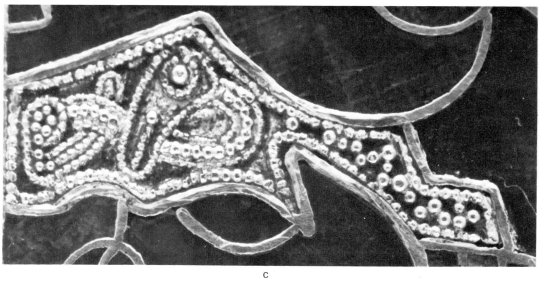

c

FIGURE 436   The shoulder clasps: details of filigree: (*a*) Inv. 4a; (*b*) Inv. 4b;
(*c*) Inv. 5b. (Scale: approx. 8/1)

FIGURE 437 Enlarged detail of the gold buckle from the Taplow barrow, Buckinghamshire.
(Scale: slightly under 4/1)

remarkable filigree element in the sword, which can be paralleled elsewhere (e.g. fig. 437), is the use of thick ropes made up apparently of tightly twisted wires closely bound round a core of indeterminate nature (fig. 433 b and c).

The most varied and ingenious use of filigree occurs in the shoulder-clasps (figs. 434, 435 and 436). Here annular filigree occurs, uniquely in the Sutton Hoo material, on the pin-heads (fig. 432 b, c); zoomorphic ornament in the form of snakes (figs. 434, 436 a, b) and small animals, recognised by hips and feet, is executed in filigree. Granulation is used in animal hips, to represent eyes, and as fill-ups for confined spaces. Spreads of braiding, using beaded and twisted wires in combination, occur (pl. 16 b, fig. 435 a, b). In the zoomorphic ornament, snake or animal bodies are 'contoured', a thick inner beaded wire being flanked by beaded wires of smaller gauge.

A distinctive note is struck by the clips from the sword-hilt. Their low gold content

609

FIGURE 438 Enlarged details illustrating gold filigree: (*a*) ring from Snape, Suffolk; (*b*) bird-buckle from Faversham, Kent; (*c*) brooch from Dover, Kent; (*d*) silver-gilt buckle from Crundale Down. (Scale: 4/1)

(70 and 74·6%) as compared with the high values from the other elements of the sword (table 35, p. 625) suggests that they are a late and local addition to the hilt. They show a very proficient use of two filigree devices that do not occur elsewhere in the Sutton Hoo material, S-scrolls, neatly executed in beaded wire, and, along the flat spikes or central panels of the clips, what has been referred to as the 'hook and eye' motif (fig. 432 e). The only use of granulation on any piece of the Sutton Hoo jewellery apart from the shoulder-clasps, is in the small animal heads (fig. 433 a) on the zoomorphic mount (Inv. 18).

The filigree work in the Sutton Hoo jewellery may be compared with a small selection of other leading Anglo-Saxon pieces, mostly from Kent, illustrated in figure 438. The Taplow barrow buckle shows filigree delineating animal ornament applied to the crests of an underlying zoomorphic design in repoussé work, an established technique not used on the Sutton Hoo clasps, perhaps because of the confined spaces available which are wholly subsidiary to the main design. This buckle also provides an example of the rope theme of twisted wires bound round a core of indeterminate nature seen on the sword-hilt (p. 277).

8. *Gold analysis*

Figure 439 shows Dr J. P. C. Kent's classic time-fineness graphs relating to the Merovingian gold tremissis series. The fineness figures for the individual coins were obtained not by direct analysis but by a reorganised and refined specific gravity technique, an account of which, by W. A. Oddy and M. J. Hughes, appears in Volume I.[1] The usefulness of their results rests on the prior analysis of a number of similar coins, including the Sutton Hoo coins, by neutron activation analysis of the whole coin, a non-destructive method, which showed that the Merovingian gold tremisses may be treated as binary alloys of gold and silver for the purposes of the specific gravity analysis, the copper constituent being of the order of up to 3%.

Table 35, Appendix C, gives the results of forty-nine direct analyses of all those items of the Sutton Hoo jewellery that have garnet decoration, and also of the great gold buckle, these pieces having been subjected to sampling. Five analyses were made from different parts of the great gold buckle and all the component elements of the purse-lid were individually analysed. As in the case of the coins, the copper constituent is in general up to 3%, with a result of above 4%, up to a highest value of 4·83%, in five cases only. No result yielded over 5% of copper. This means that the pieces of gold jewellery can be effectively regarded as binary alloys, like the coins.[2]

In eight pieces of the Sutton Hoo jewellery, where there were no garnet settings,

[1] *Sutton Hoo*, Vol. I, ch. IX, sec. 4, 648–53; and in greater detail in Oddy and Hughes 1972.
[2] As noted also by Brown in his analysis of the results of all the sixth and seventh-century Anglo-Saxon gold objects in the Ashmolean Museum, thirty in number (Brown and Schweizer 1973), with an equal consistency of results. The variation in copper content was between 0·5% and 3%, with one item only above this, which was 6·5% from each of two samples (AM.10, the Bucklington pendant).

the improved specific gravity technique was employed for the analysis. As the results from the direct analyses of the other pieces indicate that the items of gold jewellery may be treated as binary alloys of gold and silver, the gold percentages obtained by the specific gravity method for these eight pieces may be expected to be as accurate as in the case of the coins, and fully comparable in accuracy with those of the directly analysed pieces.

It should be remembered that coins of the Merovingian series were not circulating in any quantity in the Anglo-Saxon kingdoms, and certainly not in East Anglia, at the time when the Sutton Hoo jewellery was being made, before A.D. 625. The jewellery was therefore probably made from the melting down of earlier jewellery, or even from Byzantine solidi acquired for the purpose, with the addition of the substantial silver constituent at this stage. The fineness of the gold of the jewellery was not a matter of critical interest as it was in the coinage. We are better able to date the Sutton Hoo jewellery from internal evidence in relation to the *terminus ante quem* supplied by the date accepted for the burial than by gold content. We can think of the Sutton Hoo jewellery analyses rather as a possible means of testing the hypothesis that before A.D. 625 Anglo-Saxon jewellery may be dated by statistics obtained from Continental coins. In the case of Sutton Hoo, at any rate, it does not follow from the equation between jewellery and coins, as both being effectively binary alloys, that the jewellery was made from coins,[1] nor should we look primarily to the time-fineness graphs to date the jewellery. Yet the general 'flight from the gold standard', if we may so put it, may be broadly reflected within the jewellery.

Some comments should be offered here on the results of the analyses, with due reservations as to the conclusions that can be legitimately drawn from this kind of evidence. The results show a range of gold content from 97 to 70%. This compares closely with the range found in the coins, blanks and ingots in the purse, 96·9 to 69·2%.[2]

The highest result, 97%, is provided by the sword-pommel, one of the highest results yet obtained from any piece of gold jewellery found in an Anglo-Saxon context.[3] The gold mountings of the upper and lower guards, which are integrally associated with the construction of the sword, all show a gold content of above 90%. The two filigree clips from the grip have the lowest gold content (70 and 74·6%). They can probably be regarded as late additions to the sword-hilt. If the hilt is of foreign manufacture, as presumably the blade is, the two clips were certainly made in East Anglia and at an appreciably later date. The pommel could theoretically have been taken from an earlier sword, though the perfectly congruent construction and workmanship of pommel and hilt would indicate otherwise. If the blade is Rhenish, as most pattern-welded blades are held to be, the hilt could have been made for the imported

---

[1] In any case there would be variation depending on the type of coins used. The Sutton Hoo hoard itself shows in contemporary association a wide range of gold content in its constituent coins. If a mixed bag of coins were used for melting down, intermediate results would be obtained.

[2] Sutton Hoo, Vol. I, 652.

[3] See Hawkes, Merrick and Metcalf 1966 and Brown and Schweizer 1973, where rectification of the shortcomings of the milliprobe technique as employed for Hawkes *et al.* in 1966 has been effected; the results provided by Hawkes *et al.* must be treated with some reservation.

blade in England or East Scandinavia.[1] The gold embellishments associated with the scabbard show a gold content of 86·5 and 89% for the two scabbard-bosses, an essential part of the scabbard suspension system, and of 76·8 and 77·8% for the outlying pyramids.

The results from the thirteen constituents of the purse-lid and the gold clasp from the purse-bag are, as might be expected, homogeneous, the range of the gold content being between 79·5% (from an abnormally small sample) to 85·5%, and of silver from 11·3 to 16·4%—a variation in both gold and silver content of about 6%. The gold buckle shows a range of 77·7 to 89·2% of gold, the sharpest difference being between the main part of the buckle, which has a relatively low silver content, and its loop and tongue with tongue-plate. The analyses of the two shoulder-clasps are almost identical, with very high gold content (93·5 and 94%). The four matching rectangular mounts, Inv. 6–9, which seem to have been made at one time and by the same hand, show closely similar analyses and uniformly high gold value (91·5, 92·3, 90·3 and 93·7%). The small buckle and two matching strap-mounts, Inv. 12–14, which again must be the work

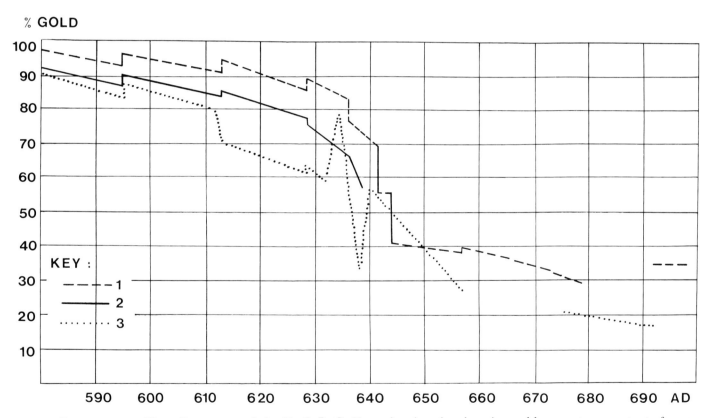

FIGURE 439 Time-fineness graph by Dr J. P. C. Kent showing the changing gold percentage content of Merovingian tremisses by decades from A.D. 580–700. Key: (1) Provençal high standard, based on coins minted at Marseilles, Arles and Uzès; (2) Provençal low standard, based on coins minted elsewhere in Provence; (3) extra-Provençal standard. The latter is the relevant graph from the point of view of any gold-content/date equation in Germanic jewellery. (After Kent in Hall and Metcalf 1972)

[1] See p. 303 for scepticism as to the Rhineland origin for e.g. the Hog Edsten pommel, Bohuslän, Sweden; cf. fig. 230, claimed by Arrhenius, on the basis of analysis of the substance underlying the garnets.

of one hand and made as a matching set, show virtual identity of composition for Inv. 12 and 13, with a variation between the gold and copper elements in Inv. 14. As said above, it is not clear what deductions may be made, if any useful conclusions can be drawn at all, from these and other results.

In addition to analyses of the Sutton Hoo pieces, twenty-eight analyses of leading pieces of Anglo-Saxon gold jewellery in the British Museum and seven from two items outside the British Museum—the Kingston Brooch (Liverpool Museum) and objects from Roundway Down (Devizes Museum)—were carried out for comparison. These results are given in Appendix C, table 36, and the pieces are illustrated in figures 441 and 443. In general, the lateness of those pieces which are normally attributed to later dates in the seventh century because of the paleness of their gold and their type or style is consistently supported by relating their percentage gold content to Kent's time-fineness graphs.

The Sutton Hoo find demonstrates, in the filigree clips from the sword-hilt, that jewellery with a gold content as low as 70% could be made as early as A.D. 625, just as it shows that Merovingian tremisses with values as low as 69.2% could be in circulation by the same date.

WEIGHTS OF THE GOLD JEWELLERY ITEMS IN THE SUTTON HOO SHIP-BURIAL

The gold items (other than the coins, blanks and billets) were weighed in the Research Laboratory in September 1972, with the exception of the four studs from the purse lid and the cabochon garnet (Inv. 302), which were weighed later. The weights are those of the objects in the condition in which they were at that time. In some pieces (e.g. the hexagonal plaques and two of the studs on the purse-lid, and the rectangular cloisonné buckle, Inv. 11) certain inlays of garnet or millefiori have been missing since the time of discovery. A few inlays that had fallen out had not been restored to the pieces from which they had been derived, either because the settings were damaged or because they were being retained

for examination. Scrapings for gold analysis had been removed from certain pieces in 1945 (App. C). These reductions of weight are not likely to be significant but should be noted.

The Research Laboratory state that during the weighing in 1972 each object was weighed twice by two members of staff, each using a different microbalance, one a Stanton 'Unimatic' balance, the other a Torbal torsion microbalance. This ensured accuracy in the results and eliminated errors in their recording. The results as given in table 33 are the mean of the two individual weighings, which were found to agree to within ± one unit in the last significant figure.

TABLE 33 WEIGHTS OF THE GOLD ITEMS IN THE SHIP-BURIAL (OTHER THAN COINS, BLANKS AND INGOTS)

Inventory number		Description	Actual weight (grams) to nearest significant figure
1		Great gold buckle	412·7
2		Purse-lid:	
	(a)	Frame	172·50
	(b)	Double plaque with zoomorphic interlace	18·454
	(c)	Hexagonal plaque	13·539
	(d)	Hexagonal plaque	16·872
	(e)	Openwork plaque (birds)	11·313
	(f)	Openwork plaque (birds)	12·872
	(g)	Openwork plaque (man and beasts)	15·562
	(h)	Openwork plaque (man and beasts)	15·278
	(i)	Circular stud	2·899
	(j)	Circular stud	2·660
	(k)	Circular stud	1·792
	(l)	Circular stud	1·788
3		Sliding-clasp from the purse bag	9·489
4		Shoulder-clasp	
	(4a)	Clasp 4a	95·960
	(4b)	Clasp 4b	87·843
5		Shoulder-clasp	
	(5a)	Clasp 5a	106·13
	(5b)	Clasp 5b	95·440
6		Rectangular strap-mount	36·121
7		Rectangular strap-mount	36·028
8		Rectangular strap-mount	42·336

9	Rectangular strap-mount	40·822
10	Curved mount (dummy buckle)	70·718
11	Rectangular buckle	64·926
12	Small cloisonné buckle with round end	21·115
13	Cloisonné strap-mount, matching 12	9·242
14	Cloisonné strap-mount, matching 12 and 13	9·961
15	Plain strap-mount in form of tongueless buckle	9·702
16	Strap-end, plain	1·570
17	T-shaped strap-distributor	73·243
18	Strap-mount, triangular, zoomorphic	12·326
19, 20, 21	Sword-pommel with attached guard-plates	51·287
22, 23	Two guard-plates, with attached filigree ropes, from lower end of grip	20·905
24	Filigree clip from hilt	2·035
25	Filigree clip from hilt	1·133
26	Scabbard-boss	17·725
27	Scabbard-boss	14·886
28	Pyramid	14·253
29	Pyramid	14·121
30	Ring and attached filigree strip set with five garnets	2·988
31	Strip, fluted, zoomorphic	0·5173
32	Mount, circular, in the form of an animal	0·2607
33	Mount, triangular, foil, with engraved animals	0·1372
302	Detached cabochon setting	0·0614

TYPES AND DISTRIBUTION OF INLAYS

TABLE 34 ANALYSIS OF INLAYS IN THE GOLD JEWELLERY, WITH NUMBERS OF COVERED CELLS

Inventory no.	Description	No. of garnets	No. of millefiori insets	Plain blue glass	Total inlays	Lidded cells†
2	Purse-lid	1,526	33	4*	1,563	101
2(a)	(i) Frame, straight bar element (ii) Frame, curved portion	241	13	—	254	—
2(b)	Zoomorphic double plaque	203	—	—	203	72
2(c)	Hexagonal plaque	223	1	—	224	—
2(d)	Hexagonal plaque	230	1	—	231	2
2(e)	Birds	197	2	2	201	—
2(f)	Birds	192	2	2	196	1
2(g)	Man between beasts	90	5	—	95	13
2(h)	Man between beasts	90	5	—	95	13
2(i) (j)	Two circular studs, large (total)	36	2	—	38	—
2(k) (l)	Two circular studs, small (total)	24	2	—	26	—
4	Shoulder clasp					
4a	Half with pin and chain	227 }452	10 }20	13 }26	498	131 }262
4b		225	10	13		131
5	Shoulder clasp					
5a	Half with pin and chain	233 }468	10 }20	13 }26	514	122 }249
5b		235	10	13		127
6	Mushroom cell mount	160	—	—	160	—
7	Mushroom cell mount	160	—	—	160	—
8	Cable-twist mount	212	—	—	212	—
9	Cable-twist mount	210	—	—	210	—
10	Curved mount (dummy buckle)	141	—	—	141	—
11	Rectangular buckle	103	—	—	103	—
12	Small buckle	23	—	—	23	—
13	Strap-mount with rounded end	24	—	—	24	—
14	Strap-mount with rounded end	24	—	—	24	—
17	T-shaped strap distributor	156	—	—	156	—
18	Triangular zoomorphic mount	56	—	—	56	2
19	Sword-pommel	53	—	—	53	—
26	Scabbard-boss (larger)	105	—	—	105	—
27	Scabbard-boss (smaller)	105	—	—	105	—
28	Pyramid	101	1	8	110	—
29	Pyramid	101	1	8	110	—
30	Filigree strip with ring head	5	—	—	5	—
302	Detached garnet in circular setting	1	—	—	1	—
TOTALS		4,186	75	72	4,333	614

* Inlaid in garnets in the birds' eyes.

† Approximate numbers and excluding sealed overlaps and edge cells in cable twist mounts.

REPORT ON THE ANALYSIS OF THE GOLD OF THE SUTTON HOO JEWELLERY AND SOME COMPARATIVE MATERIAL

by

M. J. HUGHES, M. R. COWELL, W. A. ODDY and A. E. A. WERNER

1. *Introduction*

Analysis of the gold jewellery from Sutton Hoo was first carried out by A. A. Moss using the well-established method of fire assay and also chemical gravimetric methods. The purpose of Moss's work was to establish a general view of the composition of the jewellery by analysing some key items. Since the technique involved the removal of samples weighing 0·5 gm or so from the objects, only a few of the larger items could be analysed by these methods. Analyses of precious metals by fire-assay[1] have a good analytical precision, although clearly the size of sample required for accurate work precluded analysis of many of the jewellery items.

With the introduction of polarographic and atomic absorption analysis techniques into the Research Laboratory it became possible to undertake a systematic programme of analysis of all the Sutton Hoo jewellery, and to provide comprehensive analyses not only for the gold content but also for the two minor alloying elements, silver and copper. The development of a reliable specific gravity technique for application to gold alloys also made possible the analysis of some of the very small non-jewelled gold items, including the gold coins.

These two techniques were therefore applied to all the gold jewellery from Sutton Hoo and to a selected group of about forty other items of Anglo-Saxon gold jewellery for comparison purposes.

The methods of analysis used are described below followed by discussion of their degrees of precision. The tables with which the report concludes list all the results obtained for the Sutton Hoo pieces (table 35) and the comparative pieces of Anglo-Saxon jewellery (table 36).

2. *Methods of analysis*

The majority of the analyses here presented were carried out by atomic absorption spectrometry: this enables the concentration of gold, silver and copper in the metals to be estimated. It is necessary to remove small samples from the objects in order to carry out the analyses.

For the sampling technique it was decided against drilling the objects because many of them are finely worked and the more inconspicuous parts of them which might seem to provide suitable areas for sampling (for example, the back plates) are of thin sheet gold which would suffer unacceptable damage if drilled. The alternative method of sampling by surface scraping also presents problems. Previous work by the Research Laboratory has shown that where small (1–2 mg) samples are removed from gold antiquities without first preparing the surface, erroneous results are obtained because the 'surface-enriched' layer becomes incorporated in the sample.[2] However, experiments indicated that if the area from which the sample was to be taken was first lightly scraped with the sampling tool (a triangular-bladed steel knife of the type used by gold and silversmiths) to remove the surface layer, then 2–5 mg of gold could be removed at that point and the results would not be affected by surface enrichment. The amount of sample taken had to be judged individually for each object depending on the part of the object and its size, so that no aesthetic damage to the jewellery was caused.

The samples were then weighed and dissolved in *aqua regia*, and for most items the concentrations of

[1] Forbes 1971; E. A. Smith 1947.

[2] Hughes and Oddy 1970.

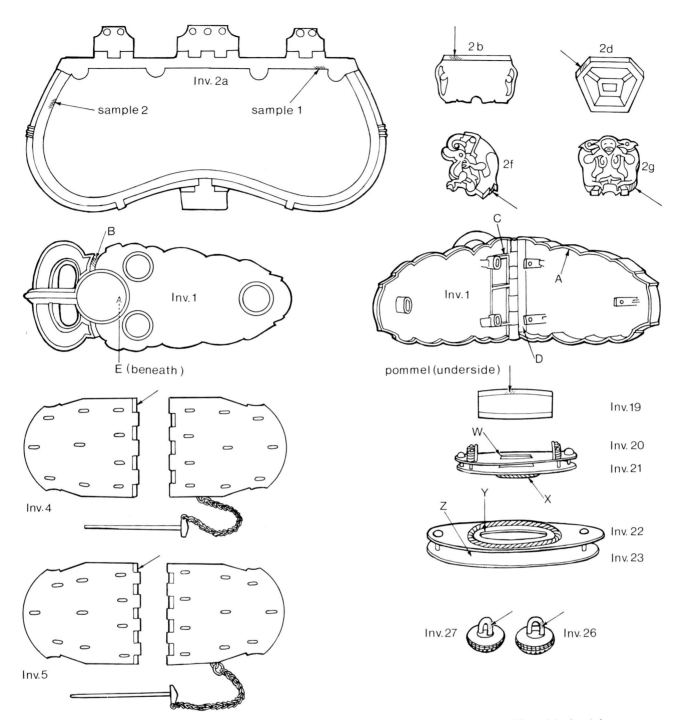

FIGURE 440 Sampling points for gold analyses of objects from the Sutton Hoo ship-burial.

gold, silver and copper were estimated quantitatively by atomic absorption spectrometry. However, in the earlier stages of the analytical programme before atomic absorption spectrometry was in such widespread use in the Research Laboratory, copper concentrations were measured instead by polarographic analysis; also in a few cases gold was not directly measured, and in these the result presented in table 35 (obtained by difference) is marked with an asterisk.

The items which do not contain any garnets, but which were too small to sample for the above methods of analysis, were analysed by the specific gravity method.[1] This technique involves weighing the gold when it is suspended in a suitable dense liquid, and is completely non-destructive.

[1] Hughes and Oddy 1970; Oddy and Hughes 1972 and 1975.

FIGURE 441 Anglo-Saxon jewellery analysed for gold content, for comparison with the results from the Sutton Hoo jewellery: (*a*) two clasps and buckle from the Taplow barrow, Buckinghamshire; (*b*) pendant and six coin pendants from Faversham, Kent; (*c*) buckle from Crundale Down, Kent; (*d*) two pendants from Wye Down, Kent; (*e*) pendant from Wrotham, Kent; (*f*) ring from Snape, Suffolk; (*g*) pyramidal mount from Selsey, Sussex; (*h*) pendant from Wingham, Kent; (*i*) sword pommel from Crundale Down, Kent; (*j*) bird-buckle from Faversham, Kent; (*k*) linked pins from Roundway Down, Wiltshire. (Scales: *a*, *c*, 1/2: the rest 1/1) (Photo: *k*, Devizes Museum)

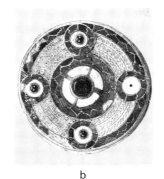

a   b   c

FIGURE 442 Anglo-Saxon brooches from Kent analysed for gold content: (*a*) Kingston, (*b*) Sarre, (*c*) Dover. (Scale: 1/2) (Photo: *a*, Merseyside County Museums)

3. *Discussion of analysis errors*

ATOMIC ABSORPTION

While atomic absorption can generally be regarded as an analysis technique which can yield results with good precision, a number of factors need to be considered in interpreting the significance of the gold analytical results.

First, each of the three measured elements, copper, silver and gold, is determined separately, hence each produces an independent error which may result in analytical results totalling slightly more or slightly less than 100%. Secondly, the precision with which the determination of each element can be made depends directly upon the weight of sample available for analysis. The relationship between the analytical precision and sample weight is not one of simple proportion, but it is generally true that as the sample weight is reduced the errors increase. In this situation it is possible to assign some sort of analytical precision for most of the samples which have sample weights between 3 and 5 mg, but where the samples weigh, for example, less than 3 mg, errors become increasingly large. Thirdly, in order to give strictly accurate figures for analytical precision, it would be necessary to quote individual estimates of precision for each element for each sample of gold, and this would clearly be of little practical value for the interpretation of the results. The situation is akin to the error terms quoted for individual radiocarbon dates, where the errors need to be estimated individually for each sample and depend upon several factors.

Estimated analytical precision for samples weighing more than 3 mg

The majority of the gold jewellery which was analysed by atomic absorption spectrometry was of sufficient size to allow the removal of more than *c.* 3 mg of its metal for analysis, and this weight forms a convenient dividing line as regards estimates of the analytical precision. A general estimate can therefore be given of the analytical precision for samples weighing over 3 mg (very few weighed more than 10 mg), provided that this estimate is regarded as a general figure and distinctions between samples of closely similar weights are not pressed too far.

An estimate of the analytical precision for this group of samples is as follows:

Gold $\pm 2\%$ of the gold percentage itself
Silver $\pm 2\%$ of the silver percentage itself
Copper $\pm 5\%$ of the copper percentage itself

It should be stressed that these estimates of precision apply strictly to the type of gold alloys being analysed in this programme. For example, the precision for copper $\pm 5\%$ has been arrived at by taking into consideration the fact that the gold alloys here analysed never contain more than 5% copper by weight. It is a general rule applied to atomic absorption determinations that the smaller the quantity of the element present in the sample, the larger the errors

621

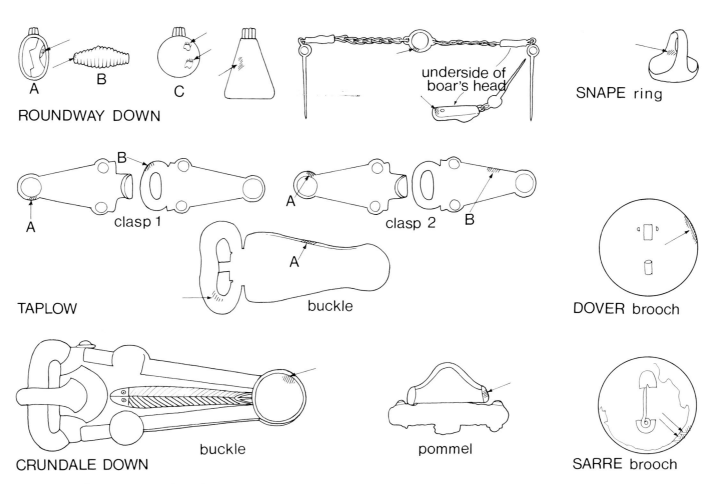

ROUNDWAY DOWN

underside of boar's head

SNAPE ring

clasp 1

clasp 2

TAPLOW

buckle

DOVER brooch

CRUNDALE DOWN

buckle

pommel

SARRE brooch

FIGURE 443   Sampling points for gold analyses of some of the pieces of Anglo-Saxon jewellery illustrated in figures 441 and 442.

in actually estimating it, because of the physical limitations of the analysis instruments.

The significance of these listed figures for precision can best be explained with the aid of an example:

> *Purse-frame, sample 2 (table 35)*
> Quoted analysis (sample weight 3·05 mg):
> gold 80·5%; silver 16·4%; copper 1·72%

The analysis result together with an estimated analytical precision is therefore approximately:

Gold   80·5±1·6%   (i.e. ±2% of 80·5% by weight)
Silver   16·4±0·3%   (i.e. ±2% of 16·4% by weight)
Copper 1·72±0·09% (i.e. ±5% of 1·72% by weight)

98·62%±2%

When the actual analytical results are considered for the Sutton Hoo jewellery and the comparative pieces, of the fifty-one samples of gold analysed, only five of the samples with weights greater than 3 mg gave results with analysis totals which fell outside the range 98–102% (i.e. in accordance with the above estimate of precision). This indicates that the estimated precision is approximately correct.

Estimated analytical precision for samples weighing less than 3 mg

Because of the delicacy of some of the jewellery it was not possible to remove as much as 3 mg of gold from every item. In these cases most sample weights fell in the range 3 mg–1 mg and only a few samples weighed less than 1 mg However, the analytical precision worsens as the sample weight decreases, so that it is very probable that for samples weighing about 1 mg the accuracy will have decreased to about ±4% of the gold percentage itself, ±4% of the silver percentage and ±10% of the copper percentage. Thus for the above example of the purse frame, if the sample of the same metal had weighed only 1 mg the result and analytical precision would then have been as follows:

Gold	80·5	±3·2%
Silver	16·4	±0·6%
Copper	1·72	±0·2%

SPECIFIC GRAVITY

The maximum likely error in the measurement of specific gravity of gold objects weighing about 1·5 gm is ±0·06 and the standard deviation and the 'most probable' error are each ±0·02.[1] This means that the error in the estimated gold content of objects containing only gold and silver varies from ±0·5% for gold-rich alloys to ±1% for silver-rich alloys. However as early mediaeval gold always contains a little copper, the measured gold content is usually slightly too low.

The problem of the discrepancy between different methods of analysis has been discussed extensively[2] and the outcome is that it is safe to say that the true gold content of a mediaeval gold object will almost certainly lie between the figure obtained by the specific gravity method and a value about 3% higher: in the majority of cases it will be much nearer to the specific gravity figure.

4. Results of analysis

The results of the quantitative analyses show that silver is the major alloying element in the gold jewellery. The copper level is never above 5% by weight and many of the objects contain no more than 2% copper. Thus one may conclude that copper was not used deliberately to debase the gold even where the gold percentage is quite low. This conclusion is relevant to the use of the specific gravity method for the determination of the gold content of Sutton Hoo objects since, in applying the method, the assumption was made that the copper was always less than 5% by weight, so that the jewellery could be considered as essentially a binary alloy of gold and silver.

The results of the analyses are shown in tables 35 and 36. Objects for which analyses are quoted for gold, silver and copper were determined by atomic absorption. Where the gold has been estimated by difference the gold percentage is marked with an asterisk. In some cases, very small amounts of lead were detected by qualitative emission spectroscopy and subsequently measured by atomic absorption spectrometry. The results for lead are reported in footnotes to table 35.

The positions from which samples were taken for atomic absorption analysis are shown in figures 440–443.

Acknowledgement. We are grateful to Mrs Susan Blackshaw for carrying out some of the specific gravity measurements.

---

[1] Hughes and Oddy 1970.
[2] Oddy, Schweizer *et al.* 1972; Oddy 1972; Schweizer 1973; Oddy and Blackshaw 1974.

Inv. no.	Description of object	% Gold	% Silver	% Copper	Sample weight (mg)	Specific gravity
1	Belt buckle					
	inside main body of buckle, sample A	89·2*	8·92	1·80	4.09[1]	—
	loop, at side, sample B	82·4*	15·10	2·40	3·02[2]	—
	reinforcement, sample C	85·4*	10·20	4·22	5·12[3]	—
	inside buckle (? repair), sample D	77·7	15·20	3·25	15·70	—
	under side of pin, sample E	80·2	16·80	2·40	13·98	—
2	Purse					
2(a)	frame, sample 1	82·0	14·50	2·66	4·51	—
2(a)	frame, sample 2	80·5	16·40	1·72	3·05	—
2(b)	double plaque with zoomorphic interlace	82·5	16·10	2·06	3·10	—
2(c)	hexagonal plaque	80·5	15·00	2·30	4·53	—
2(d)	hexagonal plaque	82·0	15·20	2·56	2·66	—
2(e)	plaque of two birds facing right	80·0	15·60	1·90	4·90	—
2(f)	plaque of two birds facing left	83·0	16·30	2·08	3·47	—
2(g)	plaque of man-between-beasts	79·5	15·80	2·58	2·09	—
2(h)	plaque of man-between-beasts	81·0	15·60	1·70	4·05	—
2(i)	circular stud	85·5	11·60	1·50	3·42	—
2(j)	circular stud	85·5	11·90	1·66	3·50	—
2(k)	circular stud	84·5	11·30	2·40	3·92	—
2(l)	circular stud	84·5	11·40	2·80	3·49	—
3	Clasp of purse (by atomic absorption analysis)	82·5	13·60	3·00	4·41	—
3	Clasp of purse (by specific gravity)	79·5	—	—	—	16·53
4	Pair of hinged shoulder-clasps	94·0*	1·77	4·47	7·88[4]	—
5	Pair of hinged shoulder-clasps	93·5*	1·86	4·47	6·15[5]	—
6	Strap-mount with mushroom-type cells	91·5	4·14	1·17	6·27	—
7	Strap-mount with mushroom-type cells	92·3	4·94	1·14	7·28	—
8	Strap-mount with step-pattern cells	90·3	7·78	1·21	5·62	—
9	Strap-mount with step-pattern cells	93·7	4·01	1·16	6·53	—
10	Curved clasp	83·2	15·80	2·42	3·06	—
11	Rectangular buckle	83·8	13·60	3·90	3·18	—
12	Small cloisonné buckle	77·2	18·80	3·74	3·45	—
13	Strap-mount	76·9	19·40	4·83	4·18	—
14	Strap-mount	80·5	19·80	0·81	2·10	—
15	Plain gold strap-runner	84·6	—	—	—	17·15
16	Strap-end	76·7	—	—	—	16·20
17	T-shaped strap-distributor	83·0	13·90	1·50	5·14	—
18	Triangular strap-mount	79·5	16·50	2·15	1·91	—
19	Sword-pommel	97·0	2·46	2·38	4·62	—
	Upper guard-plates					
20	upper plate, sample W	93·5*	3·75	2·28	1·84[6]	—
21	lower plate, sample X	91·7*	3·72	3·65	1·02[7]	—
	Lower guard-plates					
22	upper plate, sample Y	90·1*	8·33	1·38	0·72[8]	—
23	lower plate, sample Z	93·6*	4·15	2·19	1·78[9]	—
24	Filigree clip from sword-grip	74·6	—	—	—	15·98
25	Filigree clip from sword-grip	70·0	—	—	—	15·49
26	Scabbard-boss, loop at back	86·5	10·50	4·30	3·49	—
27	Scabbard-boss, loop at back	89·0	10·60	2·70	4·80	—
28	Pyramid	76·8	20·80	2·50	3·21	—
29	Pyramid	77·8	20·20	2·94	5·50	—
31	Fluted strip	86·0	—	—	—	17·31
32	Curved mount	87·9	—	—	—	17·58
33	Thin gold triangular mount	75·7	—	—	—	16·07

* Result obtained by difference.

[1] Lead 0·06%.   [4] Lead < 0·02%.   [7] Lead 0·92%.
[2] Lead 0·04%.   [5] Lead 0·15%.   [8] Lead 0·17%.
[3] Lead 0·13%.   [6] Lead 0·02%.   [9] Lead < 0·04%.

TABLE 36   RESULTS OF ANALYSES OF EARLY ANGLO-SAXON GOLD JEWELLERY FROM OTHER SITES (IN PERCENTAGES BY WEIGHT)

British Museum registration no.	Description of object	% Gold	% Silver	% Copper	Sample weight (mg)	Specific gravity
On loan from	Selsey, pyramid					
Miss M. B.	one half pyramid	56·1	—	—	—	14·13
Lawrence	other half pyramid	59·2	—	—	—	14·41
1094.70	Faversham, bird buckle	84·2	—	—	—	17·09
1094.A.70	Faversham, bird buckle	81·3	—	—	—	16·73
1138.70	Faversham, pendant	81·3	—	—	—	16·72
79, 5-24, 32	Wingham, pendant	71·0	—	—	—	15·56
79, 5-24, 33	Wingham, pendant	78·5	—	—	—	16·39
1927, 5-12, 1	Wrotham, pendant	68·9	—	—	—	15·34
1884, 12-21, 7	Faversham, coin pendant	95·5	—	—	—	18·66
1884, 12-21, 8	Faversham, coin pendant	95·9	—	—	—	18·72
1884, 12-21, 9	Faversham, coin pendant	95·1	—	—	—	18·60
1884, 12-21, 10	Faversham, coin pendant	83·0	—	—	—	16·93
1884, 12-21, 11	Faversham, coin pendant	87·6	—	—	—	17·53
1884, 12-21, 12	Faversham, coin pendant	89·5	—	—	—	17·79
93, 6-1, 187	Wye Down, pendant	26·6	—	—	—	11·96
93, 6-1, 188	Wye Down, pendant	52·7	—	—	—	13·84
60, 10-24, 1	Sarre, brooch	69·0	29·8	3·05	2·90	—
1950, 12-6, 1	Snape, ring	86·5	10·7	1·97	3·98	—
79, 10-13, 1	Dover, composite brooch	81·0	18·4	1·41	2·34	—
83, 12-14, 17	Taplow, gold thread	88·5	9·6	1·4	2·13	—
83, 12-14, 1	Taplow, buckle, loop	78·5	15·0	2·48	3·36	—
83, 12-14, 1	Taplow, buckle, sample A	79·0	15·2	1·98	3·71	—
83, 12-14, 2	Taplow, clasp, sample 2A	79·0	18·4	2·79	1·79	—
83, 12-14, 2	Taplow, clasp, sample 2B	78·0	18·7	1·86	3·20	—
83, 12-14, 2	Taplow, clasp, sample 1B	78·0	21·1	1·55	2·13	—
83, 12-14, 2	Taplow, clasp, sample 1A	82·0	18·5	1·82	2·97	—
93, 11-3, 1	Crundale Down, sword-pommel	68·5	31·3	2·58	3·83	—
93, 6-1, 204	Crundale Down, large buckle	61·0	39·0	2·54	3·35	—
Liverpool Museum	Kingston brooch[1]					
	sample from back	83·5	11·3	2·35	2·13	—
	sample from edge	83·5	11·3	2·15	2·44	—
Devizes Museum	Roundway Down[2]					
	pendant A	48·5	46·0	3·52	1·49	—
	pendant C	64·5	29·2	3·40	0·84	—
	triangular pendant	77·0	18·3	1·80	1·86	—
	coiled head B	65·0	29·9	3·10	0·87	—
	ornament with pins (mixed sample, two positions)	56·5	42·8	2·52	2·08	—

[1] We would like to thank Mr Geoffrey Lewis, Director of the Liverpool Museum, and Dr Dorothy Downes, Keeper of Antiquities, for kindly allowing us to take samples for analysis from the Kingston brooch.

[2] We would like to thank Mr F. K. Annable, Curator of the Devizes Museum, for kindly allowing us to take samples from objects in the Roundway Down group.

BIBLIOGRAPHY

Compiled by Susan M. Youngs

ÅBERG 1923   N. Åberg, *Die Goten und Langobarden in Italien*, Arbeten utgifna med understod af Vilhelm Ekmans Universitetsfond, Uppsala 29, Uppsala, 1923

ÅBERG 1926   N. Åberg, *The Anglo-Saxons in England*, Uppsala, 1926

AGATHIAS   Agathias, *Historiae*, Bk 5, ed. R. Keydell, *Corpus Fontium Historiae Byzantinae*, II, Berlin, 1967

ALFÖLDI 1934   A. Alföldi, Eine spätrömische Helmform und ihre Schicksale im Germanisch-Romanischen Mittelalter. Mit einem Exkurs über den Fund von Brangstrup, Funen, *Acta Archaeologica*, 5 (Copenhagen, 1934), 99–144

ALFÖLDI 1948   A. Alföldi, Die Goldkanne von St Maurice d'Agaune, *Zeitschrift für schweizerische Archäologie und Kunstgeschichte*, 10 (Basel, 1948), 1–28

ALMGREN 1948   B. Almgren, Romerska drag i Nordisk figurkonst från folkvandringstiden, 1948 *Tor* (Uppsala, 1948), 81–103

ALMGREN AND NERMAN 1923   O. Almgren and B. Nerman, *Die ältere Eisenzeit Gotlands*, 2 vols., Stockholm, 1923

AMENT 1974   H. Ament, Merowingische Schwertgurte vom Typ Weihmörting, *Germania*, 52 (Berlin, 1974), 153–61

ANSTEE AND BIEK 1961   J. W. Anstee and L. Biek, A study in pattern-welding, *Medieval Archaeology*, 5 for 1961 (London, 1962), 71–93

ARBMAN 1940, 1943   H. Arbman, *Birka, I. Die Gräber*, 2 vols., Stockholm, 1940, 1943

ARBMAN 1947–48   H. Arbman, Les epées du tombeau de Childéric, *Meddelanden från Lunds universitets, historiska museum, 1947–48* (Lund, 1948), 97–137

ARBMAN 1949–50   H. Arbman, Verroterie cloisonnée et filigrane, *Meddelanden från Lunds universitets historiska museum, 1949–50* (Lund, 1950), 136–72

ARENDT 1932   W. Arendt, Beiträge zur Entstehung des Spangenharnisches. Ein alttürkischer Waffenfund aus Kertsch, *Zeitschrift für historische Waffen- und Kostümkunde*, new series 4 (Berlin, 1932), 49–55

ARRHENIUS 1970   B. Arrhenius, Svärdsknappen från Vallstenarum på Gotland, *Fornvännen*, 65 (Stockholm, 1970), 193–209

ARRHENIUS 1971   B. Arrhenius, *Granatschmuck und Gemmen aus nordischen Funden des frühen Mittelalters*, Acta Universitatis Stockholmiensis, Studies in North European Archaeology, Series B, Stockholm, 1971

ARRHENIUS 1973*a*   B. Arrhenius, East Scandinavian Style I—a review, *Medieval Archaeology*, 17 for 1973 (London, 1974), 26–42

ARRHENIUS 1973*b*   B. Arrhenius, review of *Sutton Hoo Ship-burial, handbook*, 2nd ed., *Fornvännen*, 68 (Stockholm, 1973), 59–60

ARRHENIUS AND HOLMQVIST 1964   B. Arrhenius and W. Holmqvist, *Golden Age and Viking Art in Sweden*, Stockholm, 1964

ARWIDSSON 1934   G. Arwidsson, A new Scandinavian form of helmet from the Vendel-time, *Acta Archaeologica*, 5 (Copenhagen, 1934), 243–57

ARWIDSSON 1935   G. Arwidsson, Den sjunde båtgraven vid Valsgärde, *Fornvännen*, 30 (Stockholm, 1935), 49–52

626

Arwidsson 1942*a*   G. Arwidsson, *Die Gräberfunde von Valsgärde, I, Valsgärde 6*, Acta Musei Antiquitatum Septentrionalium Regiae Universitatis Upsaliensis i, Uppsala, 1942

Arwidsson 1942*b*   G. Arwidsson, *Vendelstile Email und Glas im 7.-8. Jahrhundert*, Acta Musei Antiquitatum Septentrionalium Regiae Universitatis Upsaliensis ii, Valsgärdestudien i, Uppsala, 1942

Arwidsson 1954   G. Arwidsson, *Die Gräberfunde von Valsgärde, II, Valsgärde 8*, Acta Musei Antiquitatum Septentrionalium Regiae Universitatis Upsaliensis iv, Uppsala, 1954

Asser   Asser, *Life of King Alfred*, ed. W. H. Stevenson; reissue Oxford, 1959

Avent 1975   R. Avent, *Anglo-Saxon Disc and Composite Brooches*, 2 parts, British Archaeological Reports, 11 (i), (ii), Oxford 1975

Baagøe 1969   J. H. Baagøe, Lyspind, taellelys og bondestage, *Arv og Eje 1969. Årbog for Dansk Kultur-historisk Museumsforening 1969, Danske Museer*, 18 (Copenhagen, 1969), 19–82

Baldwin Brown 1915   G. Baldwin Brown, *The Arts in Early England*, vol. iii, London, 1915

Baltl 1965   H. Baltl, Der vierkopfige Stein, in F. Elsener and W. H. Ruoff, eds., *Festschrift Karl Siegfried Bader*, Zürich, 1965, 1–24

Battiscombe 1956   C. F. Battiscombe, ed., *The Relics of St Cuthbert*, Durham, 1956

De Baye 1889   J. de Baye, *Les Bijoux francs et la fibule anglo-saxonne de Marilles, Brabant*, Caen, 1889

Beck 1964   H. Beck, *Einige vendelzeitliche Bilddenkmäler und die literarische Überlieferung*, Bayerischen Akademie der Wissenschaften Phil.-hist. Klasse Sitzungsberichte, 1964, vol. vi, Munich, 1964

Behm-Blancke 1973   G. Behm-Blancke, *Gesellschaft und Kunst der Germanen, Die Thüringen und ihre Welt*, Dresden, 1973

Behmer 1939   E. H. Behmer, *Das zweischneidige Schwert der germanischen Völkerwanderungszeit*, Stockholm, 1939

Behrens 1953/55   H. Behrens, Germanische Bilddarstellungen im Gebiet der unteren Elbe und unteren Weser, *Hammaburg*, 4 (Hamburg, 1956), 83–90

Beninger 1934   E. Beninger, *Die Germanenzeit in Niederösterreich*, Vienna, 1934

Berges and Gauert 1954   W. Berges and A. Gauert, Die eiserne 'Standarte' und das steinerne 'Szepter' aus dem Grabe eines angelsächsischen Königs bei Sutton Hoo (um 650–660), in P. E. Schramm and others, *Herrschaftszeichen und Staatssymbolik*, Schriften der Monumenta Germaniae historica, 13/1, Stuttgart, 1954, 238–80

Beinaimé   J. Bienaimé, *Le Trésor de Pouain au Musée de Troyes* (guide, undated)

Böhner 1948   K. Böhner, Das Langschwert des Frankenkönigs Childeric, *Bonner Jahrbücher*, 148 (Kevelaer, 1948), 218–48

Böhner 1949   K. Böhner, Die fränkischen Gräber von Orsoy, Kreis Mörs, *Bonner Jahrbücher*, 149 (Kevelaer, 1949), 146–96

Böhner 1959   K. Böhner, *Das Grab eines fränkischen Herren aus Morken im Rheinland*, Kunst und Altertum am Rhein, Führer des Rheinischen Landes-museums in Bonn Nr. 4, Bonn, 1959

Böhner 1976   K. Böhner, ed., *Les Relations entre l'empire roman tardif, l'empire franc et ses voisins*, Union internationale des Sciences préhistoriques et protohistoriques, XXX, Nice, 1976

Borovka 1928   G. I. Borovka, *Scythian Art*, trans. V. G. Childe, London, 1928

Bouffard 1948/49   P. Bouffard, Le Casque à bandeaux du lac Léman au Musée national suisse, *Zeitschrift für schweizerische Archäologie und Kunstgeschichte*, 10 (Basel, 1949), 121–30

Brailsford 1964   J. W. Brailsford, *British Museum Guide to the Antiquities of Roman Britain*, 3rd ed., London, 1964

British Museum 1923   *British Museum. A Guide to the Anglo-Saxon and Foreign Teutonic Antiquities*, by R. A. Smith, London, 1923

British Museum 1964   *British Museum. Guide to the Antiquities of Roman Britain*, by J. W. Brailsford, 3rd ed., London, 1964

Brøgger and Shetelig 1951   A. W. Brøgger and H. Shetelig, *The Viking Ships, their Ancestry and Evolution*, Oslo, 1951

Brown and Schweizer 1973   P. D. C. Brown and F. Schweizer, X-ray fluorescent analysis of Anglo Saxon jewellery, *Archaeometry*, 15 (Oxford, 1973), 175–92

BRUCE-MITFORD 1961   R. L. S. Bruce-Mitford, Revival of Roman influences in the 7th and 8th centuries in Anglo-Saxon archaeology, in G. Bersu and W. Dehn, eds., *Bericht über den V. Internationalen Kongress für Vor- und Frühgeschichte Hamburg vom 24. bis 30. August 1958*, Berlin, 1961, 158

BRUCE-MITFORD 1966   R. L. S. Bruce-Mitford, The reception by the Anglo-Saxons of Mediterranean art following their conversion from Ireland and Rome, *Settimane di Studio del Centro italiano di Studi sull'alto Medioevo*, 14 for 1966 (Spoleto, 1967), 797–825

BRUCE-MITFORD 1972a   R. L. S. Bruce-Mitford, *The Sutton Hoo Ship-Burial: a handbook*, 2nd ed., London, 1972

BRUCE-MITFORD 1972b   R. L. S. Bruce-Mitford, The Sutton Hoo helmet—a new reconstruction, *British Museum Quarterly*, 25 (London, 1972), 120–30

BRUCE-MITFORD 1974   R. L. S. Bruce-Mitford, *Aspects of Anglo-Saxon Archaeology*, London, 1974

BRUCE-MITFORD 1975a   R. L. S. Bruce-Mitford, *The Sutton Hoo Ship-Burial*, vol. I, London, 1975

BRUCE-MITFORD 1975b   R. L. S. Bruce-Mitford, ed., *Recent Archaeological Excavations in Europe*, London, 1975

BULLEID AND GRAY 1911   A. Bulleid and H. St G. Gray, *The Glastonbury Lake Village*, vol. 1, Glastonbury, 1911

BULLINGER 1969   H. Bullinger, *Spätantike Gürtelbeschläge*, Dissertationes Archaeologicae Gandenenses, XII, 2 vols., Bruges, 1969

BURLEIGH AND SEELEY 1975   R. Burleigh and M. A. Seeley, Use of a wire saw for slicing certain sample materials for thermoluminescent dating, *Archaeometry*, 17 (Oxford, 1975), 116–19

BURLEY 1955–56   E. Burley, A catalogue and survey of the metal-work from Traprain Law, *Proceedings of the Society of Antiquaries of Scotland*, 89 (Edinburgh, 1955–56), 118–226

BUSHE-FOX 1914   J. P. Bushe-Fox, *Excavations on the Site of the Roman Town at Wroxeter, Shropshire in 1913*, Reports of the Research Committee of the Society of Antiquaries of London, 2, Oxford, 1914

BUSHE-FOX 1932   J. P. Bushe-Fox, *Third Report on the Excavation of the Roman Fort at Richborough*, Reports of the Research Committee of the Society of Antiquaries of London, 10, Oxford, 1932

CAPELLE 1969   T. Capelle, 'Schiffsförmige' Hausgrundrisse in frühgeschichtlicher Zeit, *Frühmittelalterliche Studien*, 3 (Berlin, 1969), 244–56

CAPELLE AND VIERCK 1971   T. Cappelle and H. Vierck, Modeln der Merovinger-und Wikingerzeit, *Frühmittelalterliche Studien*, 5 (Berlin, 1971), 42–100

CEDERLÖF 1955   O. Cederlöf, The Sutton Hoo ship-burial and armour during the Vendel period, *Journal of the Arms and Armour Society*, 1 (London, 1955), 153–64

CHADWICK 1926   H. M. Chadwick, *The Heroic Age*, Cambridge, 1926

CHADWICK 1958   S. E. Chadwick, The Anglo-Saxon cemetery at Finglesham, Kent: a reconsideration, *Medieval Archaeology*, 2 for 1958 (London, 1959), 1–71

CHAMBERS 1959   R. W. Chambers, *Beowulf and the Heroic Age in England*, 3rd ed., Cambridge, 1959

CHANEY 1970   W. A. Chaney, *The Cult of Kingship in Anglo-Saxon England: the transition from paganism to Christianity*, Manchester, 1970

CHIFFLET 1655   J. J. Chifflet, *Anastasis Childerici I, Francorum regis; sive Thesaurus sepulchralis Tornaci Nerviorum effossus, et commentario illustratus*, Antwerp, 1655

CHRISTLEIN 1966   R. Christlein, *Das alamannische Reihengräberfeld von Marktoberdorf im Allgäu*, Materialien zur bayerische Vorgeschichte, 21, Kallmünz, 1966

CHRISTLEIN 1971   R. Christlein, *Das alamannische Gräberfeld von Dirlewang bei Mindelheim*, Materialhefte zur bayerischen Vorgeschichte, 25, Kallmünz, 1971

CICHORIUS 1896   C. Cichorius, *Die Reliefs der Traianssäule*, vol. 1, Berlin, 1896

COHEN 1966   S. L. Cohen, The Sutton Hoo whetstone, *Speculum*, 41 (Cambridge Mass., 1966), 466–70

COLES 1962   J. M. Coles, European Bronze Age shields, *Proceedings of the Prehistoric Society*, 28 (Cambridge, 1962), 156–90

COLGRAVE AND MYNORS 1969   B. Colgrave and R. A. B. Mynors, eds., *Bede's Ecclesiastical History of the English People*, Oxford, 1969

CORDER 1938   P. Corder, A Romano-British interment, with bucket and sceptres, from Brough, East Yorkshire, *The Antiquaries Journal*, 18 (London, 1938), 68–74

COUTIL 1895   L. Coutil, *Département de l'Eure. Archéologie gauloise, gallo-romaine et franque*, vol. 1, Paris, 1895

CRAMP 1968   R. Cramp, Glass finds from the Anglo-Saxon monastery of Monkwearmouth and Jarrow, *Studies in Glass History and Design* (International Conference of Glass, Committee B Publications), 1968, 16–19

CRAMP 1969   R. Cramp, Excavations at the Saxon monastic sites of Wearmouth and Jarrow, co. Durham: an interim report, *Medieval Archaeology*, 13 for 1969 (London, 1970), 21–66

CRAMP 1973   R. Cramp, The Anglo-Saxons and Rome, *Transactions of the Architectural and Archaeological Society of Durham and Northumberland*, new series, 3 (Durham, 1973), 27–37

CROWFOOT AND HAWKES 1967   E. Crowfoot and S. C. Hawkes, Early Anglo-Saxon gold braids, *Medieval Archaeology*, 11 for 1967 (London, 1968), 42–86

CUNLIFFE 1968   B. W. Cunliffe, ed., *Fifth Report on the Excavations of the Roman Fort at Richborough, Kent*, Reports of the Research Committee of the Society of Antiquaries of London, 23, Oxford, 1968

CURLE 1915   A. O. Curle, Account of excavations on Traprain Law in the parish of Prestonkirk, County of Haddington, in 1914, *Proceedings of the Society of Antiquaries of Scotland*, 49 (Edinburgh, 1915), 139–202

DANNHEIMER 1966   H. Dannheimer, Ein spätmerowingischer Eulogienbehälter aus Walda, *Germania*, 44 (Berlin, 1966), 338–54

DAREMBERG AND SAGLIO   C. Daremberg and E. Saglio, *Dictionnaire des Antiquités Grecques et Romains*, vol. IV, Paris

DÉCHELETTE 1913   J. Déchelette, *Manuel d'Archéologie préhistorique, celtique et gallo-romaine, II, Archéologie celtique ou protohistorique*, 2nd part, Paris, 1913

DEANESLY 1943   M. Deanesly, Roman traditionalist influence among the Anglo-Saxons, *English Historical Review*, 58 (London, 1943), 129–46

DELBRUECK 1929   R. Delbrueck, *Die Consulardiptychen und verwandte Denkmäler*, Studien zur spätantiken Kunstgeschichte, II, 2 vols., Berlin and Leipzig, 1929

DELBRUECK 1933   R. Delbrueck, *Spätantike Kaiserporträts von Constantinus Magnus bis zum ende des Westreichs*, Studien zur spätantiken Kunstgeschichte, VIII, Berlin and Leipzig, 1933

DEONNA 1957   W. Deonna, Cervidés et chevaux, *Ogam. Tradition Celtique*, 9 (Rennes, 1957), 5–10

DICKINSON 1974   T. M. Dickinson, *Cuddesdon and Dorchester-on-Thames*, British Archaeological Reports, I, Oxford, 1974

DOMASZEWSKY 1885   A. von Domaszewsky, *Die Fahnen im römischen Heere*, Abhandlungen des archäologisch-epigraphischen Seminares der Universität Wien, V, Vienna, 1885

DOPPELFELD 1959   O. Doppelfeld, Das fränkische Frauengrab unter dem Chor des Kölner Domes, *Kölner Domblatt*, 16/17 (Cologne, 1959), 41 ff.

DOPPELFELD 1960a   O. Doppelfeld, Das fränkische Frauengrab unter dem Chor des Kölner Domes, *Germania*, 38 (Berlin, 1960), 89–113

DOPPELFELD 1960b   O. Doppelfeld, Die Domgrabung XII. Totenbett und Stuhl des Knabengrabes, *Kölner Domblatt*, 18/19 (Cologne, 1960), 85–106

DOPPELFELD 1961/62   O. Doppelfeld, Die Domgrabung XIII. Der Helm aus dem fränkischen Knabengrab, *Kölner Domblatt*, 20 for 1961/62 (Cologne, 1962), 103–26

DOPPELFELD 1963   O. Doppelfeld, Die Domgrabung XIV. Das Inventar des fränkischen Knabengrabes, *Kölner Domblatt*, 21/22 (Cologne, 1963), 49–68

DOPPELFELD 1964   O. Doppelfeld, Das fränkische Knabengrab unter dem Chor des Kölner Domes, *Germania*, 42 (Berlin, 1964), 156–88

DOPPELFELD AND PIRLING 1966   O. Doppelfeld and R. Pirling, *Fränkische Fürsten im Rheinland*, Schriften des Rheinischen Landesmuseums Bonn, 2, Bonn, 1966

DUCANGE 1883–1887   C. Dufresne, Seigneur Du Cange, *Glossarium ad Scriptores mediae et infimae Latinitatis*, etc., ed. L. Favre, 10 vols., Niort, 1883–87

DUIGNAN 1947   M. Duignan, *The Moylough belt-shrine*, University of Galway Papers in History and Archaeology, no. 11, Galway, 1947

DUIGNAN 1951   M. Duignan, The Moylough (Co. Sligo) and other Irish belt-reliquaries, *Journal of the Galway Archaeological and Historical Society*, 24 (Galway, 1951), 83–94

DUMAS   F. Dumas, *Le Tombeau de Childeric* (guide, undated)

EBERT 1924–32   M. Ebert, *Reallexikon der Vorgeschichte*, 15 vols., Berlin, 1924–32

EKHOLM 1917   G. Ekholm, *Hjälmgraven vid Ulltuna*, Upplands fornminnesförenings tidskrift, 32, 1917

ELLIS 1969   S. E. Ellis, The petrography and provenance of Anglo-Saxon and Medieval English honestones, with notes on some other hones, *Bulletin of the British Museum (Natural History) Mineralogy*, 2, no. 3 (London, 1969), 135–87

ELLIS DAVIDSON 1958   H. R. Ellis Davidson, The ring on the sword, *The Journal of the Arms and Armour Society*, 2 (London, 1958), 211–26

ELLIS DAVIDSON 1962   H. R. Ellis Davidson, *The Sword in Anglo-Saxon England: its archaeology and literature*, Oxford, 1962

ELLIS DAVIDSON AND WEBSTER 1967   H. R. Ellis Davidson and L. Webster, The Anglo-Saxon burial at Coombe (Woodnesborough), Kent, *Medieval Archaeology*, 11 for 1967 (London, 1968), 1–41

ENGELHARDT 1863   H. C. C. Engelhardt, *Thorsbjerg Mosefund*, Copenhagen, 1863

ERÄ-ESKO 1953   A. Erä-Esko, Sutton Hoo and Finland, *Speculum*, 28 (Cambridge, Mass., 1953), 514–15

ERÄ-ESKO 1973   A. Erä-Esko, Köyliön Kjuloholmin haudan A 5 miekka, *Suomen Muinaismuistoyhdistyksen Aikakauskirja*, 74 (Helsinki, 1973), 5–24

EVISON 1951   V. I. Evison, The white material in Kentish disc brooches, *The Antiquaries Journal*, 31 (London, 1951), 197–200

EVISON 1963   V. I. Evison, Sugar-loaf shield-bosses, *The Antiquaries Journal*, 43 (London, 1963), 38–96

EVISON 1965 *a*   V. I. Evison, The Dover, Breach Downs and Birka men, *Antiquity*, 39 (Cambridge, 1965), 214–17

EVISON 1965 *b*   V. I. Evison, *The Fifth-Century Invasions South of the Thames*, London, 1965

EVISON 1967   V. I. Evison, The Dover ring-sword and other sword-rings and beads, *Archaeologia*, 101 (London, 1967), 63–118

EVISON 1968   V. I. Evison, Quoit brooch style buckles, *The Antiquaries Journal*, 48 (London, 1968), 231–46

EVISON 1975   V. I. Evison, Pagan Saxon whetstones, *The Antiquaries Journal*, 55 (London, 1975), 70–85

EVISON 1976   V. I. Evison, Sword rings and beads, *Archaeologia*, 105 (London, 1976). 303–15

FALK 1914   H. Falk, *Altnordische Waffenkunde*, Videnskapssellskapets skrifter II, Hist.-Filos. Klasse. 1914, 6, Kristiania, 1914

FETTICH 1932   N. Fettich, Der zweite Schatz von Szilágysomlyó, *Archaeologica Hungarica*, 8 (Budapest, 1932), 9–73

FORBES 1971   J. S. Forbes, Hallmarking gold and silver, *Chemistry in Britain*, 7 (London, 1971), 98–102

FOUET 1969   G. Fouet, La villa gallo-romaine de Montmaurin, xxe supplément à *Gallia*, Paris, 1969

FOX 1958   C. F. Fox, *Pattern and Purpose, a survey of early Celtic art in Britain*, Cardiff, 1958

FRANCE-LANORD 1949   A. France-Lanord, La fabrication des épées damassées aux époques mérovingienne et carolingienne, *Pays gaumais*, 10 (Virton, 1949), 1–27

FRANCE-LANORD 1952   A. France-Lanord, Les techniques métallurgiques appliquées à l'archéologie, *Revue de Metallurgie*, 49 (Paris, 1952), 411–22

FRANCE-LANORD 1961   A. France-Lanord, Die Gürtelgarnitur von Saint-Quentin, *Germania*, 39 (Berlin, 1961), 412–20

FRANCE-LANORD AND FLEURY 1962   A. France-Lanord and M. Fleury, Das Grab der Arnegundis in Saint-Denis, *Germania*, 40 (Berlin, 1962), 341–59

FREMERSDORF 1955   F. Fremersdorf, *Das fränkische Reihengräberfeld Köln-Mungersdorf*, Germanische Denkmäler der Völkerwandrungszeit, 6, 2 vols., Berlin, 1955

FUCHS 1940   S. Fuchs, Figürliche Bronzebeschläge der Langobardenzeit aus Italien, *Mitteilungen des deutschen archäologischen Instituts, roemische Abteilung*, 55 (Munich, 1940), 100–13

FUCHS AND WERNER 1950   S. Fuchs and J. Werner, *Die längobardischen Fibeln aus Italien*, Berlin, 1950

GAGE 1836   J. Gage, Recent discovery of Roman sepulchral relics in one of the greater barrows at Bartlow, in Ashdon, Essex, *Archaeologia*, 26 (London, 1836), 300–17

GAMBER 1966   O. Gamber, The Sutton Hoo military equipment—an attempted reconstruction, *Journal of the Arms and Armour Society*, 5 (London, 1966), 265–87

GAMBER 1968   O. Gamber, Kataphrakten, Clibanarier, Normannenreiter, *Jahrbuch der Kunsthistorischen Sammlung in Wien*, 64 (Vienna, 1968), 7–44

GAUERT 1954   A. Gauert, Das "Szepter" von Sutton Hoo, in P. E. Schramm and others, *Herrschaftszeichen und Staatssymbolik*, Schriften der Monumenta Germaniae Historica, 13/1, Stuttgart, 1954, 260–80

GAUERT 1972   A. Gauert, Der Ring der Königin Arnegundis aus Saint-Denis, *Festschrift für Hermann Heimpel*, vol. III, Göttingen, 1972, 328–47

GAUSTAD 1966   F. Gaustad, Til bevæpningens historie i nordisk folkevandringstid og merovingertid, *Viking*, 30 (Oslo, 1966), 97–131

GJESSING 1934   G. Gjessing, *Studier i Norsk Merovingertid*, Skrifter utgitt av Det Norske Videnskaps-Akademi i Oslo II. Hist.-Filos. Klasse 1934, 2, Oslo, 1934

GLOB 1965   P. V. Glob, *Mosefolket: Jernalderens Mennesker bevaret i 2000 År* (English edition, *The Bog People*, London, 1969), Denmark, 1965

GOODCHILD 1938   R. G. Goodchild, A priest's sceptre from the Romano-Celtic temple at Farley Heath, Surrey, *The Antiquaries Journal*, 18 (London, 1938), 391–6

GOODCHILD 1947   R. G. Goodchild, The Farley Heath sceptre, *The Antiquaries Journal*, 27 (London, 1947), 83–5

GORDON-WILLIAMS 1926   J. P. Gordon-Williams, Note on a bronze stag from Gateholm and various stray finds from Pembrokeshire, *Archaeologia Cambrensis*, 81 (Cardiff, 1926), 191–2

GÖTZE 1912   A. Götze, *Die altthuringischen Funde von Weimar*, Germanische Funde aus der Völkerwanderungszeit, Berlin, 1912

GRANSCAY 1949   S. V. Granscay, A barbarian chieftain's helmet, *Metropolitan Museum of Art Bulletin*, June 1949 (New York, 1949), 272–81

GRANT 1907   A. J. Grant, *Early Lives of Charlemagne by Eginhard and the Monk of Saint Gall*, London, 1907

GRIEG 1922–23   S. J. Grieg, Norske hjelmer fra folkevandringstiden, *Bergens Museums Aarbok 1922–23*, Historisk-antikvarisk raekke no. 3, Bergen, 1923

GRIEG 1947   S. J. Grieg, *Gjermundbufunnet en høvdingegrav fra 900-årene fra Ringerike*, Norske oldfunn VIII, Oslo, 1947

GRIERSON 1970   P. Grierson, The purpose of the Sutton Hoo coins, *Antiquity*, 44 (Cambridge, 1970), 14–18

GRIMES 1940   W. F. Grimes, The salvaging of the finds, *Antiquity*, 14 (Gloucester, 1940), 69–75

GRINSELL 1961   L. V. Grinsell, The breaking of objects as a funerary rite, *Folklore*, 72 (London, 1961), 475–91

GRÖBBELS 1905   I. W. Gröbbels, *Der Reihengräberfund von Gammertingen*, Munich, 1905

GUYAN 1958   W. U. Guyan, *Das alamannische Gräberfeld von Beggingen-Löbern*, Schriften des Instituts für Ur- und Frühgeschichte der Schweiz, 12, Basel, 1958

HABEREY 1961   W. Haberey, Ein Mädchengrab römischer Zeit aus der Josefstrasse in Bonn, *Bonner Jahrbücher*, 161 (Kevelaer, 1961), 319–32

HACKMAN 1938   A. L. F. Hackman, *Das Brandgräberfeld Pukkila*, Suomen Muinaismuistoyhdistyksen Aikakauskirja, 41, Helsinki, 1938

HAGBERG 1972–73   U. E. Hagberg, Köping på Öland, *Tor*, 1972–1973 (Uppsala, 1973), 209–56

HAGBERG 1976   U. E. Hagberg, Fundort und Fundgebiet der Modeln aus Torslunda, *Frühmittelalterliche Studien*, 10 (Münster, 1977), 323–49

HASELOFF 1951   G. Haseloff, *Der Tassilokelch*, Münchner Beiträge zur Vor- und Frühgeschichte, 1, Munich, 1951

HASELOFF 1952   G. Haseloff, Zu den Darstellungen auf der Börse von Sutton Hoo, *Nordelbingen*, 20 (Heide, 1952), 9–20

HAUCK 1954a   K. Hauck, Halsring und Ahnenstab als herrscherliche Wurdezeichen, in P. E. Schramm and others, *Herschaftszeichen und Staatssymbolik*, Schriften der Monumenta Germaniae Historica, 13/1, Stuttgart, 1954, 145–212

HAUCK 1954b K. Hauck, Herrschaftszeichen eines Wodanistischen Königtums, *Jahrbuch für fränkische Landesforschung*, 14 (Kallmünz-Opf., 1954), 9–66

HAUCK 1957a K. Hauck, Alemannische Denkmäler der vorchristlichen Adelskultur, *Zeitschrift für Württembergische Landesgeschichte*, 16 (Stuttgart, 1957), 1–39

HAUCK 1957b K. Hauck, Germanische Bilddenkmäler des frühen Mittelalters, *Deutsche Vierteljahrsschrift für Literaturwissenschaft und Geistesgeschichte*, 31 (Stuttgart, 1957), 349–79

HAWKES 1951 C. F. C. Hawkes, Bronze-workers, cauldrons, and bucket-animals in Iron Age and Roman Britain, in W. F. Grimes, ed., *Aspects of Archaeology in Britain and beyond*, London, 1951, 172–99

HAWKES, ELLIS DAVIDSON AND HAWKES 1965 S. C. Hawkes, H. R. Ellis Davidson and C. Hawkes, The Finglesham Man, *Antiquity*, 39 (Cambridge, 1965), 17–32

HAWKES AND DUNNING 1961 S. C. Hawkes and G. C. Dunning, Soldiers and settlers in Britain, fourth to fifth century, *Medieval Archaeology*, 5 for 1961 (London, 1962), 1–70

HAWKES AND DUNNING 1962–63 S. C. Hawkes and G. C. Dunning, Krieger und Siedler in Britannien während des 4. und 5. Jahrhunderts, *43.–44. Bericht der Römisch-Germanischen Kommission 1962–1963* (Berlin, 1964), 155–231

HAWKES AND GROVE 1964 S. C. Hawkes and L. R. A. Grove, Finds from a seventh century Anglo-Saxon cemetery at Milton Regis, *Archaeologia Cantiana*, 78 (London, 1963), 22–38

HAWKES AND HULL 1947 C. F. C. Hawkes and M. R. Hull, *Camulodunum, First Report on the Excavations at Colchester 1930–1939*, Reports of the Research Committee of the Society of Antiquaries of London, 14, Oxford, 1947

HAWKES, MERRICK AND METCALF 1966 S. C. Hawkes, J. M. Merrick and D. M. Metcalf, X-ray fluorescent analysis of some dark age coins and jewellery, *Archaeometry*, 9 (Oxford, 1966), 98–138

HENIG 1974 M. Henig, *A Corpus of Roman Engraved Gemstones from British Sites*, 2 parts, British Archaeological Reports 8 (i), (ii), Oxford, 1974

HENRY 1933 F. Henry, Emailleurs d'Occident, *Préhistoire*, 2, no. 1 (Paris, 1933), 65–143

HENRY 1936 F. Henry, Hanging bowls, *Proceedings of the Royal Irish Academy*, 36 (Dublin, 1936), 209–46

HENRY 1956 F. Henry, Irish enamels of the dark ages and their relation to the cloisonné techniques, in D. B. Harden, ed., *Dark Age Britain*, London, 1956, 71–88

HENRY 1965 F. Henry, *Irish Art in the Early Christian Period to 800 A.D.*, rev. ed., London, 1965

HEYNE 1903 M. Heyne, *Fünf Bücher deutscher Hausaltertümer von den ältesten geschichtlichen Zeiten bis zum 16. Jahrhundert*, 3, Körperpflege und Kleidung, Leipzig, 1903

HILDEBRAND AND HILDEBRAND 1873 B. E. Hildebrand and H. O. Hildebrand, *Teckningar ur Svenska Statens Historiska Museum*, vol. 1, Stockholm, 1873

HINZ 1971 H. Hinz, Frühgeschichtliche Untersuchungen in Rheinhausen, Kreis Moers, *Rheinische Ausgrabungen*, 9 (Düsseldorf, 1971), 134–73

HODGKIN 1952 R. H. Hodgkin, *A History of the Anglo-Saxons*, 3rd ed., 2 vols., London, 1952

HOLMES AND SITWELL 1972 M. J. R. Holmes and H. D. W. Sitwell, *The English Regalia: their history, custody and display*, London, 1972

HOLMQVIST 1939 W. E. Holmqvist, *Kunstprobleme der Merowingerzeit*, Kungl. Vitterhets Historie och Antikvitets Akademiens Handlingar, 47, Stockholm, 1939

HOLMQVIST 1951 W. Holmqvist, *Tauschierte Metallarbeiten des Nordens*, Stockholm, 1951

HOLMQVIST 1960 W. Holmqvist, The dancing gods, *Acta Archaeologica*, 31 for 1960 (Copenhagen, 1961), 101-27

HOLMQVIST AND ARRHENIUS 1961 W. Holmqvist and B. Arrhenius, *Excavations at Helgö I*, Uppsala, 1961

HOLMQVIST AND ARRHENIUS 1964 W. Holmqvist and B. Arrhenius, *Excavations at Helgö II*, Uppsala, 1964

HOOPS 1915–16 J. Hoops, *Reallexikon der Germanischen Altertumskunde*, III, Strasburg, 1915–16

HOOPS 1971 J. Hoops, *Reallexikon der Germanischen Altertumskunde*, 2nd ed., Band 1, Lieferung 3, Berlin, 1971

HOREDT AND PROTASE 1970 K. Horedt and D. Protase, Ein völkerwanderungszeitlicher Schatzfund aus Cluj-Someşeni (Siebenbürgen), *Germania*, 48 (Berlin, 1970), 85–98

HUGHES AND ODDY 1970   M. J. Hughes and W. A. Oddy, A re-appraisal of the specific gravity method for the analysis of gold alloys, *Archaeometry*, 12 (Oxford, 1970), 1–11

HUNTER 1974   M. J. Hunter, Germanic and Roman antiquity and the sense of the past in Anglo-Saxon England, *Anglo-Saxon England*, 3 (Cambridge, 1974), 29–50

HUNTER BLAIR 1947   P. Hunter Blair, The origins of Northumbria, *Archaeologia Aeliana*, 25 (Newcastle upon Tyne, 1947), 1–51

IZIKOWITZ 1931   K. G. Izikowitz, Vendelsköldarna, *Fornvännen*, 26 (Stockholm, 1931), 181–98

JACOBSTHAL 1944   P. Jacobsthal, *Early Celtic Art*, 2 vols., Oxford, 1944

JARVIS 1850   E. Jarvis, Account of the discovery of ornaments and remains, supposed to be of Danish origin, in the parish of Caenby, Lincolnshire, *Archaeological Journal*, 7 (London, 1850), 36–44

JESSUP 1950   R. Jessup, *Anglo-Saxon Jewellery*, London, 1950

KENDRICK 1933   T. D. Kendrick, Polychrome jewellery in Kent, *Antiquity*, 7 (Gloucester, 1933), 429–52

KENDRICK 1938   T. D. Kendrick, *Anglo-Saxon Art to A.D. 900*, London, 1938

KENDRICK 1939   T. D. Kendrick, The Sutton Hoo finds, *British Museum Quarterly*, 13 (London, 1939), 111–36

KENDRICK 1941   T. D. Kendrick, Portion of a basalt hone from North Wales, *The Antiquaries Journal*, 21 (London, 1941), 73

KENDRICK AND HAWKES 1937   T. D. Kendrick and C. F. C. Hawkes, Jutish jewellery from Preshaw, Hants., *The Antiquaries Journal*, 17 (London, 1937), 322–4

KESSLER 1940   P. T. Kessler, Merowingisches Fürstengrab von Planig in Rheinhessen, *Mainzer Zeitschrift*, 35 (Mainz, 1940), 1–12

KHOINOVSKI 1896   J. A. Khoinovski, Grabfunde aus Taganča, *Kratkija archaeologičeskija svedenjija o predkach Slavjan i Rusi*, 1 (1896), 118 ff

KIVIKOSKI 1947   E. Kivikoski, *Die Eisenzeit Finlands*, 1, Helsinki, 1947

KLAEBER 1941   F. Klaeber, ed., *Beowulf and the Fight at Finnsburg*, 3rd ed., New York, 1941

KLUMBACH 1973   H. Klumbach, ed., *Spätrömische Gardehelme*, Münchner Beiträge zur Vor- und Frühgeschichte, vol. 15, Munich, 1973

KÜHN 1938   H. Kühn, Die Reiterscheiben der Völkerwanderungszeit, *Jahrbuch für prähistorische und ethnographische Kunst*, 12 (Berlin, 1938), 95–115

KÜHN 1941/42   H. Kühn, Die Danielschnallen der Völkerwanderungszeit, *Jahrbuch für prähistorische und ethnographische Kunst*, 15, 16 (Berlin, 1941/42), 141–69

KUTSCH 1921   F. Kutsch, Frühfränkisches Grab aus Biebrich, *Germania*, 5 (Berlin, 1921), 27–35

LAFAURIE, JANSEN AND ZADOKS-JOSEPHUS JITTA 1961   J. Lafaurie, B. Jansen and A. N. Zadoks-Josephus Jitta, Le trésor de Wieuwerd, *Oudheidkundige Mededeelingen uit het Rijksmuseum van Oudheiden te Leiden*, 42 (Leiden, 1961), 78–107

LAING 1975   L. Laing, *Late Celtic Britain and Ireland c. 400–1200 A.D.*, London, 1975

LANTIER 1939   R. Lantier, Chevaux-enseignes celtiques, *Revue Archéologique*, 13 (Paris, 1939), 237–47

LÁSZLÓ 1938   G. László, Adatok a koronázási jogar megvilágításához (Angaben zur Klärung des Krönungsszepters), *Szent István Emlékkönyv* (St-Stephans-Gedenkbuch), 3 (Budapest, 1938), 518–58

LÁSZLO 1970   G. László, *Steppenvölker und Germanen. Kunst der Völkerwanderungszeit*, Vienna and Munich, 1970

LAUR-BELART 1938   R. Laur-Belart, Eine alamannische Goldgriffspatha aus Klein-Hünigen bei Basel, *Jahrbuch für prähistorische und ethnographische Kunst*, 12 (Berlin, 1938), 126–38

LEEDS 1924   E. T. Leeds, An Anglo-Saxon cremation burial of the seventh century in Asthall Barrow, Oxfordshire, *The Antiquaries Journal*, 4 (London, 1924), 113–25

LEEDS 1936   E. T. Leeds, *Early Anglo-Saxon Art and Archaeology*, Oxford, 1936

LEEDS AND SHORTT 1953   E. T. Leeds and H. de S. Shortt, *An Anglo-Saxon Cemetery at Petersfinger, near Salisbury, Wilts.*, Salisbury, 1953

LEROQUAIS 1940–41   V. Leroquais, *Les Psautiers manuscrits latins des bibliothèques publiques de France*, 3 vols., Macon, 1940–41

LETHBRIDGE 1951 a   T. C. Lethbridge, Bronze bowl of the Dark Ages from Hildersham, Cambs., *Proceedings of the Cambridge Antiquarian Society*, 45 for 1951 (Cambridge, 1952), 44–7

LETHBRIDGE 1951 b   T. C. Lethbridge, *A Cemetery at Lackford, Suffolk*, Cambridge, 1951

LINDQVIST 1925 a   S. Lindqvist, Vendelhjälmarnas ursprung, *Fornvännen*, 20 (Stockholm, 1925), 181–207

LINDQVIST 1925 b   S. Lindqvist, De koniska hjälmarna hos de utomnordiska germanfolken under folkvandringstiden, *Fornvännen*, 20 (Stockholm, 1925), 227–40

LINDQVIST 1932   S. Lindqvist, Vendel-time finds from Valsgärde, *Acta Archaeologica*, 3 (Copenhagen, 1932), 21–46

LINDQVIST 1936 a   S. Lindqvist, L'epoca romana dell'eta di ferro in svezia, *Istituto di Studi Romani*, 14 (Rome, 1936)

LINDQVIST 1936 b   S. Lindqvist, *Uppsala Högar och Ottarshögen*, Kungl. Vitterhets Historie och Antikvitets Akademien, 23, Stockholm, 1936

LINDQVIST 1950 a   S. Lindqvist, Vendelhjälmarna i ny rekonstruktion, *Fornvännen*, 45 (Stockholm, 1950), 1–24

LINDQVIST 1950 b   S. Lindqvist, Sköld och svärd ur Vendel I, *Fornvännen*, 45 (Stockholm, 1950), 265–80

LINS AND ODDY 1975   P. A. Lins and W. A. Oddy, The origins of mercury gilding, *Journal of Archaeological Science*, 2, no. 4 (London, 1975), 365–73

LIVERSIDGE AND BYWATERS 1955–56   J. Liversidge and F. J. Bywaters, A hoard of Romano-British ironwork from Worlington, *Proceedings of the Cambridge Antiquarian Society*, 49 (Cambridge, 1956), 89–90

LÖFGREN 1973   J. Löfgren, Die mineralogische Untersuchung der Granaten von Pariken auf Gotland, *Antikvariskt Arkiv* 53, *Early Medieval Studies*, 6 (Stockholm, 1973), 78–96

LUNDBERG 1938   O. Lundberg, ed., *Vendel i Fynd och Forskning*, *Upplands Fornminnesförenings Tidskrift*, 46, Supplement 1, Uppsala, 1938

LUNDSTRÖM 1973   P. Lundström, Almandingranaten von Pariken auf Gotland, *Antikvariskt Arkiv* 53, *Early Medieval Studies*, 6 (Stockholm, 1973), 67–77

LUNDSTRÖM 1976   A. Lundström, Bead making in Scandinavia in the Early Middle Ages, *Antikvariskt Arkiv* 61, *Early Medieval Studies*, 9 (Stockholm, 1976), 3–19

MACKEPRANG 1935   M. B. Mackeprang, Menschendarstellungen aus der Eisenzeit Dänemarks, *Acta Archaeologica*, 6 (Copenhagen, 1935), 228–49

MACKEPRANG 1952   M. B. Mackeprang, *De Nordiske Guldbrakteater*, Jysk Arkæologisk Selskabs Skrifter, 2, Aarhus, 1952

MAGOUN 1954   F. P. Magoun Jr., Review of *A History of the Anglo-Saxons* (3rd edition) by R. H. Hodgkin, *Speculum*, 29 (Cambridge, Mass., 1954), 125–6

MANN 1957   J. Mann, Arms and armour, in F. M. Stenton and others, *The Bayeux Tapestry*, London, 1957, 56–69

MANOJLOVIĆ-MARIJANSKI 1964   M. Manojlović-Marijanski, *Kasnorimski šlemovi iz Berkasova—Les casques romains tardifs de Berkasovo*, Musée de Voïvodina Monographie III, Novi Sad, 1964

MANOJLOVIĆ-MARIJANSKI 1973   M. Manojlović-Marijanski, Der Fund von Berkasovo, Jugoslavien, in H. Klumbach, ed., *Spätrömische Gardehelme*, Munich, 1973, 15–38

MARTIN 1971   M. Martin, Bemerkungen zu den frühmittelalterlichen Gürtelbeschlägen der Westschweiz, *Zeitschrift für Schweizerische Archäologie und Kunstgeschichte*, 28 (Zürich, 1971), 29–57

MARTIN-CLARKE 1950   D. E. Martin-Clarke, Significant objects at Sutton Hoo, in C. F. Fox and B. Dickens, eds., *The Early Cultures of North West Europe*, Cambridge, 1950, 109–19

MARTIN CONWAY 1915   W. Martin Conway, The Abbey of Saint-Denis and its ancient treasures, *Archaeologia*, 66 (London, 1915), 103–58

MARYON 1946   H. Maryon, The Sutton Hoo shield, *Antiquity*, 20 (Gloucester, 1946), 21–30

MARYON 1947   H. Maryon, The Sutton Hoo helmet, *Antiquity*, 21 (Gloucester, 1947), 137–44

MARYON 1948   H. Maryon, A sword of the Nydam type from Ely Fields Farm, near Ely, *Journal of the Cambridgeshire Antiquarian Society*, 41 (Cambridge, 1948), 73–6

MARYON 1960   H. Maryon, Pattern-welding and damascening of sword-blades, Parts 1 and 2, *Studies in Conservation*, 5 (Aberdeen, 1960), 25–35, 52–60

Meaney 1964   A. L. S. Meaney, *A Gazeteer of Early Anglo-Saxon Burial Sites*, London, 1964

Menghin 1973*a*   W. Menghin, Aufhängevorrichtung und Trageweise zweischneidiger Langschwerter aus germanischen Gräbern des 5. bis 7. Jahrhunderts, *Anzeiger des Germanischen Nationalmuseums 1973* (Munich, 1973), 7–56

Menghin 1973*b*   W. Menghin, Zur Trageweise frühmittelalterlicher Langschwerter, *Archäologisches Korrespondenzblatt 1973* (Mainz, 1973), 243–9

Minns 1942   E. H. Minns, The art of the northern nomads, *Proceedings of the British Academy*, 28 (London, 1942), 47–100

Moberg 1952   C.-A. Moberg, Between La Tène II and III. Studies on the fundamental relative chronology, *Acta Archaeologica*, 23 (Copenhagen, 1952), 1–29

Moosbrugger-Leu 1967   R. Moosbrugger-Leu, *Die Frühmittelalterlichen Gürtelbeschläge der Schweiz*, Monographien zur Ur- und Frühgeschichte der Schweiz, no. 14, Basle, 1967

Moosbrugger-Leu 1971   R. Moosbrugger-Leu, *Die Schweiz zur Merowingerzeit*, Band A, Bern, 1971

Mortimer 1905   J. R. Mortimer, *Forty Years' Researches in British and Saxon Burial Mounds of East Yorkshire*, London, 1905

Moss 1953*a*   A. A. Moss, Niello, *The Antiquaries Journal*, 33 (London, 1953), 75–7

Moss 1953*b*   A. A. Moss, Niello, *Studies in Conservation*, 1 (London, 1953), 42–62

Müller 1972*a*   H. H. Müller, *Die Faunenreste vom Burgberg Zehren*, Berlin, 1972

Müller 1972*b*   H. H. Müller, *Die Tierreste aus der Wiprechtsburg bei Groitzsch, kr. Borna*, Berlin, 1972

Müller-Wille 1970–71   M. Müller-Wille, Pferdegrab und Pferdeopfer im frühen Mittelalter, *Berichten van de Rijksdienst voor het Oudheidkundig Bodemonderzoek*, 20–1 (Amersfoort, 1971), 119–248

Myres and Green 1973   J. N. L. Myres and B. Green, *The Anglo-Saxon Cemeteries of Caistor-by-Norwich and Markshall, Norfolk*, Reports of the Research Committee of the Society of Antiquaries of London, no. 30, London, 1973

Nerman 1935   B. Nerman, *Die Völkerwanderungszeit Gotlands*, Kungl. Vitterhets Historie och Antikqvitets Akademien, Archäologische Monographiserien no. 21, Stockholm, 1935

Nerman 1948   B. Nerman, Sutton Hoo—en svensk kunga- eller hövdinggrav?, *Fornvännen*, 43 (Stockholm, 1948), 65–93

Nerman 1969   B. Nerman, *Die Vendelzeit Gotlands*, ii, Tafeln & provisorisiches Verzeichnis der Tafelfiguren, Stockholm, 1969

Nerman 1970   B. Nerman, Note on the 'standard' of Sutton Hoo—a torch holder?, *The Antiquaries Journal*, 50 (London, 1970), 340–1

Notker   Notker, *De Carolo Magno* in P. Jaffé, ed., *Bibliotheca Rerum Germanicarum*, iv, *Monumenta Carolina*, Berlin, 1867 (reprinted, 1961)

Obrador 1963   B. Font Obrador, Los ciervos de bronce de Lloseta (Mallorca), *Archivo Español de Arqueologia*, 36 (Madrid, 1963), 211–14

Oddy 1972   W. A. Oddy, The analysis of gold coins—a comparison of results obtained by non-destructive methods, *Archaeometry*, 14 (Oxford, 1972), 109–17

Oddy and Blackshaw 1974   W. A. Oddy and S. M. Blackshaw, The accuracy of the specific gravity method for the analysis of gold alloys, *Archaeometry*, 16 (Oxford, 1974), 81–90

Oddy and Hughes 1972   W. A. Oddy and M. J. Hughes, The specific gravity method for the analysis of gold coins, in E. T. Hall and D. M. Metcalf, eds., *Methods of Chemical and Metallurgical Investigation of Ancient Coinage*, Royal Numismatic Society Special Publication no. 8, London, 1972, 75–87

Oddy and Hughes 1975   W. A. Oddy and M. J. Hughes, The analysis of the Sutton Hood gold coins by the method of specific gravity determination, in R. L. S. Bruce-Mitford, *The Sutton Hoo Ship-Burial*, Vol. I, London, 1975, 648–53

Oddy, Schweizer and others 1972   W. A. Oddy, F. Schweizer and others, A comparative analysis of some gold coins, in E. T. Hall and D. M. Metcalf, eds., *Methods of Chemical and Metallurgical Investigation of Ancient Coinage*, Royal Numismatic Society Special Publication no. 8, London, 1972, 171–82

Odobescu 1889–1900   A. I. Odobescu, *Le Trésor de Pétrossa*, 3 vols., Paris, 1889–1900

O'KELLY 1965   M. J. O'Kelly, The belt-shrine from Moylough, Sligo, *Journal of the Royal Society of Antiquaries of Ireland*, 95 (Dublin, 1965), 149–88

O'LOUGHLIN 1964   J. N. L. O'Loughlin, Sutton Hoo—the evidence of the documents, *Medieval Archaeology*, 8 for 1964 (London, 1965), 1–19

OLSÉN 1945   P. Olsén, *Die Saxe von Valsgärde*, vol. I, Uppsala, 1945

ØRSNES-CHRISTENSEN 1966   M. Ørsnes-Christensen, *Form og still i Sydskandinaviens yngre germanske jernalder*, Nationalmuseets skrifter, Arkaeologisk-historisk raekke, vol. XI, Copenhagen, 1966

OZANNE 1962–3   A. Ozanne, The Peak dwellers, *Medieval Archaeology*, 6–7 for 1962–3 (London, 1964), 15–52

PASQUI 1918   A. Pasqui, Necropoli barbarica di Nocera Umbra, *Monumenti Antichi*, 25 (Milan, 1918), 137–351

PAULSEN 1967   P. Paulsen, *Alamannische Adelsgräber von Niederstotzingen (Kreis Heidenheim)*, Veröffentlichungen des staatlichen Amtes für Denkmalpflege, Stuttgart, Reihe A, Vor- und Frühgeschichte Heft 12/1 and 2, Stuttgart, 1967

PETCH 1957   D. F. Petch, Archaeological notes for 1956, (25) Hough-on-the-Hill, *The Architectural and Archaeological Society of the County of Lincoln Reports and Papers*, 7 (Lincoln, 1957), 17–18

PETERSSON 1958   K. G. Petersson, Ett gravfynd från Klinta, Köpings sn, Öland, *Tor*, 4 (Uppsala, 1958), 134–50

PHILLIPS 1940a   C. W. Phillips, The excavation of the Sutton Hoo ship-burial, *Antiquaries Journal*, 20 (London, 1940), 149–202

PHILLIPS 1940b   C. W. Phillips, The excavation of the Sutton Hoo ship-burial, *Antiquity*, 14 (Gloucester, 1940), 6–27

PIGGOTT 1970   S. Piggott, *Early Celtic Art*, Exhibition Catalogue, Edinburgh, 1970

PIRLING 1964   R. Pirling, Ein fränkisches Fürstengrab aus Krefeld-Gellep, *Germania*, 42 (Berlin, 1964), 188–216

PIRLING 1966   R. Pirling, *Das römisch-fränkische Gräberfeld von Krefeld-Gellep*, Germanische Denkmäler der Völkerwanderungszeit, series B, vol. II, 2 parts, Berlin, 1966

PIRLING 1973   R. Pirling, Der Fund einer Ledertasche aus Grab 2268 des fränkischen Friedhofes von Krefeld-Gellep, *Archäologisches Korrespondenzblatt 1973* (Mainz, 1973), 81–7

PIRLING 1974   R. Pirling, *Das römisch-fränkische Gräberfeld von Krefeld-Gellep 1960–1963*, Germanische Denkmäler der Völkerwanderungszeit, series B, vol. VIII, 2 parts, Berlin, 1974

POST 1944   P. Post, Ein neuer Rekonstruktionsvorschlag zum Panzerfund von Valsgärde, *Zeitschrift für historische Waffen- und Kostümkunde*, n.F.8 (Berlin, 1944), 98–123

POULÍK 1949   J. Poulík, Záhadná mohyla Žuráň (Tumulus énigmatique de Žuráň), *Arkhaeologické Rozhledy* (Prague, 1949), 10–15

DE RICCI 1910   S. de Ricci, *Catalogue of a Collection of Merovingian Antiquities belonging to J. Pierpont Morgan*, Paris, 1910

RICHARD 1971a   L. Richard, Statuettes en bronze Gallo-Romaines, *Société d'Emulation des Côtes-du-Nord*, 99 (Saint-Brieuc, 1970), 13–31

RICHARD 1971b   L. Richard, Deux massacres de cerf, *Annales de Bretagne*, 78 (Rennes, 1971), 257–66

RICHTER 1971   G. M. A. Richter, *The Engraved Gems of the Greeks and Romans, Part II, Engraved Gems of the Romans*, London, 1971

RINGQVIST 1969   P.-O. Ringqvist, Två vikingatida uppländska människofigurer i brons, *Fornvännen*, 64 (Stockholm, 1969), 287–96

ROBINS 1939   F. W. Robins, *The Story of the Lamp (and the Candle)*, Oxford, 1939

ROBINS 1953   F. W. Robins, *The Smith. The tradition and lore of an ancient craft*, London, 1953

ROBINSON 1975   H. R. Robinson, *The Armour of Imperial Rome*, London, 1975

ROMANIA 1971   *Treasures from Romania*, Catalogue of the exhibition held at the British Museum January–March 1971, London, 1971

RÖMISCH-GERMANISCHES ZENTRALMUSEUM MAINZ 1972   Römisch-Germanisches Zentralmuseum Mainz, *Führungsblatt 2: Römische Kaiserzeit*, Mainz, 1972

ROOSENS 1969   H. Roosens, Merovingische gouden sierschijf van Rosmeer. Archeologisch onderzoek, with technical appendix by D. Thomas-Goorzeckx, *Bulletin de l'Institut Royal du Patrimoine Artistique*, 11 (Brussels, 1969), 66–81

ROSENBERG 1937   G. A. T. Rosenberg with K. Jensen and F. Johannessen, *Hjortspringfundet*, Nordiske Fortidsminder, 3, no. 1, Copenhagen, 1937

ROSENQVIST 1967–68   A. M. Rosenqvist, Sverd med klinger ornert med figurer i kopperlegeringer fra eldre jernalder i Universitetets Oldsaksamling, *Universitetets Oldsaksamling Årbok 1967–1968* (Oslo, 1970), 143–200

ROSTOVTSEFF 1923   M. Rostovtseff, Commodus-Hercules in Britain, *Journal of Roman Studies*, 13 (London, 1923), 91–109

RUDENKO 1970   I. Rudenko, *Frozen Tombs of Siberia: the Pazyryk burials of Iron Age Horsemen*, trans. M. W. Thompson, London, 1970

RUPP 1937   H. Rupp, *Die Herkunft der Zelleinlage und die Almandinscheibenfibeln im Rheinland*, Rhein. Forsch. z. Vorgeschichte, II, Bonn, 1937

RYNNE 1967   R. Rynne, The Tau-Cross at Killinaboy: pagan or christian? *North Munster Studies*, ed. E. Rynne, Limerick, 1967, 146–65

SALIN 1935   B. Salin, *Die altgermanische Tierornamentik*, 2nd ed., Stockholm, 1935

SALIN 1950–59   E. Salin, *La civilisation mérovingienne*, Paris, 4 vols., 1950–59

SALIN 1960   E. Salin, Les tombes gallo-romaines et mérovingiennes de la basilique de Saint-Denis, *Mémoires de l'Institut National de France*, 44 (Paris, 1960), 169–255

SALIN AND FRANCE-LANORD 1943   E. Salin and A. France-Lanord, *Le fer à l'époque mérovingienne*, Paris, 1943

SALMO 1938   H. Salmo, *Die Waffen der Merowingerzeit in Finland*, Suomen Muinaismuistoyhdistyksen Aikakauskirja, XLII: 1, Helsinki, 1938

SALMONY 1954   A. Salmony, Antler and tongue. An essay on ancient Chinese symbolism and its implications, *Artibus Asiae*, suppl. 13, Ascona, 1954

SCHRAMM 1954, 1955   P. E. Schramm and others, *Herrschaftszeichen und Staatssymbolik*, Schriften der Monumenta Germaniae Historica, 13/1 and 2, Stuttgart, 1954, 1955

SCHRAMM 1962   P. E. Schramm, *Denkmale der deutschen Könige und Kaiser*, Veröffentlichungen des Zentralinstituts für Kunstgeschichte in München, II, Munich, 1962

SCHWEIZER 1973   F. Schweizer, Reconciliation of the specific gravity method for the analysis of gold alloys, *Archaeometry*, 15 (Oxford, 1973), 188–92

SHETELIG AND JOHANNESSEN 1930   H. Shetelig and F. Johannessen, Das Nydamschiff, *Acta Archaeologica*, 1 (Copenhagen, 1930), 1–30

SHETELIG, FALK AND GORDON 1937   H. Shetelig, H. Falk and E. V. Gordon, *Scandinavian Archaeology*, Oxford, 1937

SIEBS 1951   B. E. Siebs, Die Bildsaule von Themeln, *Jahrbuch der Männer vom Morgenstem*, 32 (1951), 1–4

SISAM 1953   K. Sisam, Anglo-Saxon royal genealogies, *Proceedings of the British Academy*, 39 (London, 1953), 287–348

SMEDLEY AND OWLES 1963   N. Smedley and E. J. Owles, Some Suffolk kilns: IV Saxon kilns in Cox Lane, Ipswich 1961, *Proceedings of the Suffolk Institute of Archaeology*, 29 for 1963 (Ipswich, 1964), 304–35

SMEDLEY AND OWLES 1967   N. Smedley and E. J. Owles, A sherd of Ipswich ware with face-mask decoration, *Proceedings of the Suffolk Institute of Archaeology*, 31 for 1967 (Ipswich, 1968), 84–7

SMITH 1923   R. A. Smith, *British Museum. A Guide to the Anglo-Saxon and Foreign Teutonic Antiquities*, London, 1923

SMITH 1947   E. A. Smith, *The Sampling and Assay of the Precious Metals*, 2nd ed., London, 1947

SMITH AND BLIN-STOYLE 1959   M. A. Smith and A. E. Blin-Stoyle, A sample analysis of British Middle and Later Bronze Age materials using optical spectrometry, *Proceedings of the Prehistoric Society*, 25 (Cambridge, 1959), 188–208

SPEAKE 1970   G. Speake, A seventh-century coin-pendant from Bacton, Norfolk and its ornament, *Medieval Archaeology*, 14 for 1970 (London, 1971), 1–16

SPEAKE 1975 G. Speake, The beginnings and development of Salin's Style II in England, University of Oxford doctoral thesis, 1975

STEINER 1906 P. Steiner, Die Dona militaria, *Bonner Jahrbücher*, 114/15 (Bonn, 1906), 1–98

STEINER 1939 P. Steiner, Römisches Brettspiel und Spielgerät aus Trier, *Saalburg Jahrbuch*, 9 (Frankfurt am Main, 1939), 34–45

STENTON 1957 F. M. Stenton and others, *The Bayeux Tapestry*, London, 1957

STENTON 1971 F. M. Stenton, *Anglo-Saxon England*, 3rd ed., Oxford, 1971

STATENS HISTORISKA MUSEUM STOCKHOLM 1968 *Sveagold und Wikingerschmuck*, Römisch-Germanisches Zentralmuseum Mainz, Ausstellungskataloge Bd III, Mainz, 1968

STOLLENMAYER 1959 P. Stollenmayer, Tassilo-Leuchter, Tassilo-Zepter, *Jahresbericht des Öffentl. Gymnasiums der Benediktiner zu Kremsmünster*, 102 (Wels, 1959), 7–72

STOLPE AND ARNE 1927 K. H. Stolpe and T. J. Arne, *La Nécropole de Vendel*, Kungl. Vitterhets Historie och Antikvitets Akademien, Archäologische Monografiserien no. 17, Stockholm 1927

SWANTON 1973 M. J. Swanton, *The Spearheads of the Anglo-Saxon Settlements*, London, 1973

SWANTON 1974a M. J. Swanton, *A Corpus of Pagan Anglo-Saxon Spear Types*, British Archaeological Reports 7, Oxford, 1974

SWANTON 1974b M. J. Swanton, Finglesham Man: a documentary postscript, *Antiquity*, 48 (Cambridge, 1974), 313–15

THOMAS 1963 C. A. Thomas, The animal art of the Scottish Iron Age and its origins, *Archaeological Journal*, 118 for 1961 (London, 1963), 14–64

THOMAS AND SZENTLÉLEKY 1959 E. Thomas and T. Szentléleky, *Führer durch die archäologischen Sammlungen des Bakonyer Museums in Veszprém. Urzeit-Römerzeit*, Budapest, 1959

THOMAS-GOORIECKX 1961 D. Thomas-Goorieckx, Examen métallographique d'une coupe transversale d'épée damassée mérovingienne, *Bulletin de l'Institut Royal du Patrimoine Artistique*, 4 (Brussels, 1961), 155–60

THORDEMAN 1939, 1940 B. Thordeman, *Armour from the Battle of Wisby 1361*, 2 vols., Uppsala, 1939, 1940

THORDEMAN 1941 B. Thordeman, Stridsdräkter under forntid och medeltid, *Nordisk Kultur*, 15 (Stockholm, 1941), 89–123

TOMTLUND 1970 J. E. Tomtlund, Hänglåsen på Helgö, *Fornvännen*, 65 (Stockholm, 1970), 238–46

TSCHUMI 1945 O. Tschumi, *Burgunder, Alamannen und Langobarden in der Schweiz*, Bern, 1945

TWINING 1960 E. F. Twining, *A History of the Crown Jewels of Europe*, London, 1960

VEECK 1931 W. Veeck, *Die Alamannen in Württemberg*, 2 vols., Germanische Denkmäler der Völkerwanderungszeit, 1, Berlin and Leipzig, 1931

VEECK 1934 W. Veeck, Neue Grabungen im Alamannenfriedhof von Oberflacht, O. A. Tuttlingen, *Hans-Seger-Festschrift*, Alt-scheslien 5, 1934, 302–8

VINSKI 1954 Z. Vinski, Ein Spangenhelmfund aus dem östlichen Syrmien, *Germania*, 32 (Berlin, 1954), 176–82

VOSS 1951 O. Voss, Der Hasselagerfund, *Acta Archaeologica*, 22 (Copenhagen, 1951), 152–65

WADDY 1934 C. Waddy (translator), A Scandinavian cremation-ceremony, by Ahmed bin Fadhlan, *Antiquity*, 8 (Gloucester, 1934), 58–62

WALLACE-HADRILL 1962 J. M. Wallace-Hadrill, *The Long-haired Kings and other Studies in Frankish History*, London, 1962

WALLACE-HADRILL 1975 J. M. Wallace-Hadrill, *Early Medieval History*, Oxford, 1975

WEBSTER 1969 G. Webster, *The Roman Imperial Army*, London, 1969

WERNER 1949/50 J. Werner, Zur Herkunft der frühmittelalterliche Spangenhelme, *Praehistorische Zeitschrift*, 34/35 (Berlin, 1950), 178–93

WERNER 1950a J. Werner, *Das alamannische Fürstengrab von Wittislingen*, Münchner Beiträge zur Vor- und Frühgeschichte, II, Berlin, 1950

WERNER 1950b J. Werner, Die Schwerter von Imola, Herbrechtingen und Endrebacke, *Acta Archaeologica*, 21 (Copenhagen, 1950), 45–81

638

WERNER 1951/52   J. Werner, Ein langobardischer Schild von Ischl an der Als, *Bayerische Vorgeschichtsblätter*, 18/19 (Munich, 1952), 45–58

WERNER 1952   J. Werner, Langobardische Grabfunde aus Reggio Emilia, *Germania*, 30 (Berlin, 1952), 190–4

WERNER 1953   J. Werner, *Das Alamannische Gräberfeld von Bülach*, Monographien zur Ur- und Frühgeschichte der Schweiz, IX, Basel, 1953

WERNER 1956   J. Werner, *Beiträge zur Archäologie des Attila-Reiches*, Abhandlungen der Bayerischen Akademie der Wissenschaften, Philosophisch- Historische Klasse, N.f.38A,B, Munich, 1956

WERNER 1958   J. Werner, Eine ostgotische Prunkschnalle von Köln-Sverinstor. Studien zur Sammlung Diergardt II, *Kölner Jahrbuch für Vor- und Frühgeschichte*, 3 (Berlin, 1958), 55–61

WERNER 1964   J. Werner, Frankish royal tombs in the cathedrals of Cologne and Saint-Denis, *Antiquity*, 38 (Cambridge, 1964), 201–16

WERNER 1970   J. Werner, Zur Verbreitung frühgeschichtlicher Metallarbeiten, *Antikvariskt Arkiv* 38, *Early Medieval Studies*, 1 (Stockholm, 1970), 65–81

WERNER 1971   J. Werner, Neue Analyse des Childerichgrabes von Tournai, *Rheinische Vierteljahrsblätter*, 35 (Kevelaer, 1971), 43–6

WEST AND OWLES 1973   S. E. West and E. Owles, Anglo-Saxon cremation burials from Snape, *Proceedings of the Suffolk Institute of Archaeology*, 33 for 1973 (Ipswich, 1974), 47–57

WHEELER AND WHEELER 1932   R. E. M. Wheeler and T. V. Wheeler, *Report on the Excavation of the Prehistoric, Roman, and Post Roman Site in Lydney Park, Gloucestershire*, Reports of the Research Committee of the Society of Antiquaries of London, 9, Oxford, 1932

WHEELER AND WHEELER 1936   R. E. M. Wheeler and T. V. Wheeler, *Verulamium. A Belgic and two Roman Cities*, Reports of the Research Committee of the Society of Antiquaries of London, 11, Oxford, 1936

WILSON 1964   D. M. Wilson, *Anglo-Saxon Ornamental Metalwork 700–1100 in the British Museum*, Catalogue of Antiquities of the Later Saxon Period, vol. 1, London, 1964

WILSON 1969   D. R. Wilson, Roman Britain in 1968: sites explored. Norfolk (2), *Journal of Roman Studies*, 59 (London, 1969), 223

WINKELMANN 1962   W. Winkelmann, Das Fürstengrab von Beckum, eine sächsische Grabstätte des 7. Jahrhunderts in Westfalen, *Die Glocke, Heimatkalender für der Kreis Beckum für 1963*, Oelde/Westfalen, 1962

WINKELMANN   W. Winkelmann, Das sächsische Fürstengrab. Eine Grabstätte des 7. Jahrhunderts in Beckum, in *Stadt Beckum*, undated

ZADOKS-JOSEPHUS JITTA, PETERS AND VAN ES 1969   A. N. Zadoks-Josephus Jitta, W. J. T. Peters and W. A. van Es, *Roman Bronze Statuettes from the Netherlands II, Statuettes found South of the Limes*, Scripta archaeologica groningana 2, Groningen, 1969

ZIMMERMANN 1916   E. H. Zimmermann, *Vorkarolingische Miniaturen*, 5 vols., Berlin, 1916

INDEX

Note: heavy type indicates figure numbers.

Abingdon (Berkshire), angon, 265
Aethelberht I, king of Kent, 351, 375, 376
Aethelfrith, Northumbrian king, 376, 597
Åker (Norway) burial, belt buckle, 79
Akerman, J. Y., Coombe sword drawing, 136
Alabanda (Asia Minor), garnet trade, 601
Alcuin, 371, 372
alderwood, on shield, 16, 22, 42, 45, 55, 67, 123, 127–8, 135, **13, 14, 15, 31, 47, 99**
Alföldi, A., sceptres, eastern, 365 & n
Alfred the Great, king, candles, 424
Altenerding (Germany), cemetery, sword belt (grave 674), 572, **419**a
Ament, H., sword belt reconstruction, 568 n, 570–2, 575–7
analyses, see gold analysis, see also individual object entries
Anastasius 1, Byzantine Emperor, 351
Anastasius dish (Inv. 76), 232, 422
angons, see spears and angons
animal art, 378–82
animal interlace
    great gold buckle, 549–54, **405–407**
    helmet, 200–2
    shield, 82–91
        bird, 85–7, **49**
        boss, 49–55, 88–9, 90–1, **33, 37, 39, 40, 41**
        dragon, 64, **51**b, c
        handgrip extensions, 77, 90, **61, 62**
        hemispherical bosses with gold foil collars, 87, **52**
        rim, rectangular panels, 82–5, **64**b, **66**
        strips, 87–8, **53**a
    shoulder-clasps, 528–9, **391**
    Vendel type, 91–2, 378, 553–4
Apahida (Romania), prince's grave
    eagle, 509–11
    purse, 517, **381**
Arlon (Belgium), sword blade, 307 n
Arnegunde, Queen, disc brooches, 477–8, **345**b, d
Arrhenius, Birgit
    classification of cloisonné backing materials, 61, 100, 105, 114–15, 123–6, 599
    Hög Edsten capsule, 560
    Preshaw necklace, 602
Arwidsson, Greta, 17, 214, 237

ash-wood, spear shafts, 241–2, 268, 272
Ashbee, Paul, excavation of site, 454
Asser, 424
Asthall (Berkshire), cremation barrow, foil fragments, 207, **154**
Augsburg (Germany), reliquary buckle, 559
Augsburg-Pfersee (Germany), helmet, 210, 223, **167**b
Augst (Switzerland), helmet, 220, **168**c
Augustus, Emperor, Prima Porta statue, 534, **394**

Barham (Kent), spear, 259
Barlaston (Staffordshire), hanging bowl, analysis, Tbl. 30
Barletta (Italy), bronze statue, 534 & n, 557 n
Barton (Cambridgeshire), hanging-bowl, 379
Barton Seagrave (Northamptonshire), disc, 92, **69**b
Barton-on-Humber (Lincolnshire), bronze die, analysis, Tbl. 30
Basel-Aeschenvorstadt (Switzerland), cemetery, buckle, 558
Bata (Hungary), bronze boar, 380 n
Batten, H. V., 114 n
Bayeux Tapestry
    mail, 234
    sceptres, 357, **262**
bears, see Vendel, grave 12 spear-head and man-between-beasts scene
Beckum (Germany), Fürstengrab
    horse-burial, 520, 522, **384**a, b
    purse, 497, 502, 520, 565, pl. 22 d
    sword, 273 n
Bede, Historia Ecclesiastica
    standards, 350, 428–30
    use of sceptrum, 350
    Wuffa, 354
beeswax
    Augsburg reliquary buckle, 559
    candles, 424
    iron lamp, 125 n, 423–4
    shield-boss, 53, 114, 125 n
Beggingen (Switzerland), cemetery, sword fittings (grave 78), **421**d
belts, late Roman, 566
Benty Grange (Derbyshire)
    boar helmet, 205–7, 220, 379–80, 382, pl. 23 a
    escutcheon, 379
    mail, 237 n

Beowulf, 150, 158, 165 *n*, 205, 224, 239
Berges, W., comments on sceptre, 371–3
Berkasovo (Yugoslavia)
    helmet 1, 220, **166** *a*
    helmet 2, 223, **166** *b*
Bernerring (Switzerland), cemetery, stag burial, 382
Bidford-on-Avon (Gloucestershire), boss, 92, **69** *a*
Biebrich (Germany)
    iron shaft, 428
    iron tripod, 426
Bifrons (Kent), cemetery, ring-swords (graves 39 and 62), 135 *n*
Bimson, Mavis, scientific reports, 100–22, 226–31, 410, 595
Biek, L., 307 *n*
bird brooches, *see* brooches, bird
bird crests, 150, 200, **164** *e*
bird heads, Style II
    great gold buckle, 552–3, 563–4
    helmet
        die 1, 189
        flying bird imagery, 169–70, 205, **125**, **126**
    shield
        bird plaque, 55–63
        grip-extension, 76
Birka (Sweden)
    iron shafts, 428
    mailcoat, 237
    whetstones, 361–2, **264**
blue glass inlays, 594, 603, *Tbl. 34*, pl. 23 *d*
    purse, 488
    pyramids, 300
    shoulder-clasps, 528, 531
boar ornament
    Bata (Hungary), 380 *n*
    Benty Grange helmet, 206–7, 379–80
    Beowulf, 150
    helmet, eyebrows, 150, 164, 169, **127–8**
    helmets, 150, 208, 220, **156** *b*, **157**, **164** *f*
    shoulder-clasps, 526–7, 529–31, **390**
body space, evidence for, 243, 439
Böhner, K., sword-rings, 134
Brampton (Norfolk), bronze stag's head, 381, **272** *c*
brass, shield, 146, 165, 227
Breach Down (Kent), bronze buckle, analysis, *Tbl. 30*
Bregnebjerg (Denmark), bronze figure, 360
bretwalda, 347, 350, 375–7, 428–9, 431 *n*, 534, 597
Brighthampton (Oxfordshire), sword type, 196 *n*
Broch of Main (Shetland), whetstone, 369, **269** *f*
brooches
    animal, 379–80
    bird, 59, 509–11, **48** *b–g*
    disc, 125–6
    penannular, 583
    quoit, 378
Brooke (Norfolk)
    bridle-ring, analysis, *Tbl. 30*
    bronze buckle, analysis, *Tbl. 30*
Broomfield (Essex)
    shield, 92
    spear, 259
bucket, iron-bound wooden no. 3 (Inv. 119), 9, 39 *n*, 335, 420
Buckland, Dover (Kent), cemetery, ferrule (grave C), 271
buckle, great gold, Sutton Hoo, *see* jewellery, gold, individual
        items

buckles
    Burgundian, 558–62
    Frisian, 553
    gold and garnet cloisonné, Sutton Hoo, *see* jewellery,
        gold, individual items
Budapest (Hungary), helmet, 220
Bulbury (Dorset), bronze ox, 380 & *n*
Bullinger, H., 566
burial chamber, 4 *n*, 7, 232, 264, 420, 439, 446
burial deposit plan, **1**
Bury St Edmunds (Suffolk), die, 81, **66** *a*

Caenby (Lincolnshire), tumulus
    foil fragments, 189, 207, 218, **153**
    mounts, 92 *n*
chainmail, *see* mail and mailcoat
Carvoran (Northumberland), angon, 265
cauldron, bronze (Inv. 113), chain, 530
Çesena (Italy) treasure, 603 *n*
Chaney, W. A., 371
Chaouilly (France), ring-sword, 133 & *n*, 134, **96** *d*
Charlemagne, Emperor, sceptre, 355
Charles the Bald, Emperor, sceptre, 356, **259**
Childeric I, Merovingian king, jewellery, 350–1, 597
chip-carving technique
    great gold buckle, 556
    shield, 77, 79, 90, 91
Christian elements in burial, 273, 304, 377, 558–60
Christlein, R., 572, 575
Church Island, Lough Currane, Ireland, whetstone, 369, **269** *g*, *h*
Cimbri, Germanic tribe, human sacrifice, 324
cleats (Inv. 219), 254
cloisonné decoration, *see* garnet, cloisonné work
Clovis, Frankish king, insignia, 351
coats, *see* helmet, dies 1 and 2
coins
    gold (Inv. 34–75), 432, 437, 440, 488
        analysis, 607–8, **439**
    Roman, **313**
Coleraine (Ireland), rath, whetstones, 369, **266**
Colgrave, B., 350, 431 *n*
Cologne Cathedral (Germany), prince's grave
    helmet, 206
    sceptre, 352–4, 402, **258**
Conçesti (Romania), helmet, 223, **167** *a*
consular diptychs, 351–2
Coombe (Kent), ring-sword, 136–7, 285 *n*, **96** *a*
copper rivets, mailcoat, 237, 240, **181**
Coptic bowl (Inv. 109), 23 *n*, 241, 243, 254, 264, 423
Cowell, M. R., jewellery gold analysis report, 618–25
Crawford, O. G. S., shield photograph, 1, 45
    sword photograph, 298 *n*
cross, Christian
    Benty Grange helmet, 206
    reliquary buckles, 559
    Spangenhelme, 206 *n*
    sword, scabbard bosses, 273, 304
Crotet (France), bronze stag, 379
Crowfoot, Elisabeth, 179, 284 *n*
Crumlin-Pedersen, Ole, comment on ship, 525
Crundale Down (Kent)
    buckle, 554, 560–2, **412–4**, **438** *d*, **441** *c*, **443**
    sword pommel and mount, 554, 560, **408** *d*, *e*, **441** *i*, **443**

Cunedda, Celtic ruler (Gwledig), 350
Cutler, D. F.
    identification of wood from shield, 21, 127–8
    report on wood from spear, angon and Inv. 211, 272

dancing warriors scene
    helmet, die 1, 173, 186–9, 208, **136, 140**
    Caenby fragment, 207, 218, **153**
    Gamla Uppsala fragment, 208, 214, 215, 218, **155**
    Valsgärde 7 version, 218, **164** c
Dannheimer, H., 560
Davis, A., 140
De Peel, see Deurne, helmet
Deanesly, Margaret, 350
Deurne (Holland), helmet, 159, 210, 223, **166** c, d, **168** d
dies, see helmet
Dirlewang (Germany), cemetery, sword-belt (grave 27), 572, **421** f
Donzdorf (Germany), cemetery
    curved scabbard mount, **420**
    sword fittings, **421** g–i
Doppelfeld, O., Cologne sceptre, 353
Dorchester (Oxfordshire)
    belt buckle, 566
    padlock with human face, 369 & n, **270**
Dover (Kent), cemetery
    composite brooch, 124, 126, **438** c, **442** c, **443**
    garnet ring, 602
    ring-sword, 135 n, **100** d
    spear, 259
dragon-heads, see helmet
drinking-horns (Inv. 120–1), 81, 580
Droxford (Hampshire), spear, 259
Dufty, A. R., 140
Durrow, see manuscripts

East, Katherine, shield, backing materials, 123–6
Echternach, see manuscripts
Edward the Confessor, king, 356, **262** a
Edwin, Northumbrian king, 350, 376, 428–30, 597
Einville-au-Jard (France), reliquary buckle, 559 n
Ekhammer (Norway), pin, 189
Ellis Davidson, H., 134
Ellis, S. E., petrography of the stone bar, 315, 360–1, 383–4
Ely Fields Farm (Cambridgeshire), cemetery, sword, 307
enamel work, 583, 595
Epsom (Surrey), necklace pendant, 602
Erquy (France), bronze stag, 379
Eurasiatic animal art, 380–2
Evans, Angela Care,
    identification of spear 6, 257
    pattern welding of sword-blade, 307
Evison, V. I., sword-rings, 134–7
excavation of Sutton Hoo site, 1968, 156, 171, 269, 454

face, human
    helmet
        face-mask, 164, **103**
        die 1, 189, **140**
        die 2, 193, **143**
    padlock, Anglo-Saxon, 369, **270**
    Scandinavian examples, 79, 126, 358, 360, **263**
    sceptre, 315–24, 357–60, 368–9, **234, 238–9**

shield
    boss, lower edge of dome, 51, **89**
    hip joint of animal on bird's wing, 87, 358, **44, 49, 63,**
        pl. 2
    lappet on bird's head, 61, pl. 2
    panel on bird's leg, 59, 358, 369, **44, 46, 63**
    whetstones, 364–9, **267–9**
fallen warrior scene, see rider and fallen warrior scene
Farley Heath (Surrey), temple, sceptre, 352 n
Farthing Down (Kent), cup, 553, **408** a
Faversham (Kent), cemetery
    bird buckle, Tbl. 36, **438** b, **441** j
    coin pendants, Tbl. 36, **441** b
    disc brooch, 296, **468** n
    rectangular ornament, 602
    ring-swords, 135 n, **100** b, c
Fenwick, Valerie H.,
    Caenby mounts, 92 n
    shield, checklist of fragments, 7 n, 127
    stag and standard, 339, 403 n
ferrules (Inv. 106–8, 211, 271), 242, 265–272, **201–206**
filigree and beaded wire, 603–9, **432–438**
    curved mount, 479
    purse frame, 494
    rod, gold strip, 398
    shield, bird's eye, 61, **76**
        ring, 132
    shoulder-clasps, 525, 527, 529–30, 532
    sword clips, 277, 299
        guards, 277, 291, 293
        pommel, 291
    triangular zoomorphic mount, 485
Finglesham (Kent)
    buckle, 189
    sword, scabbard lining, 285 n
fire-dogs, Swedish, 426, **309**
Fleury, M., 563 and n
foil
    bronze, see helmet and shield
    gold, see gold foil
Fonaby (Lincolnshire), whetstone, 383
France-Lanord, A., 563 and n
Franks Casket
    mail depicted, 237, **183**
    snake ornament, 81, **66** b
Freisen (Germany), bronze horse, 380 n
Fullerö (Sweden), mail, 237

Gallehus (Denmark), horns, 380
Gamber, O., 442 n, 564, 567, 572, 575–6
gaming pieces, ivory (Inv. 172), 422
Gamla Uppsala (Sweden), royal mounds, 208
    East mound, helmet fragment, 208, 214, 215, 218, **155**
    West mound, pyramid, 598 & n
    whetstones, 361
Gammertingen (Germany), mailcoat, 237
garnets
    backing technique, 123–6, 600–3; see also, gold foil
    cabochon, engraved, 511, 602–3
    cloisonné work
        Scandinavian, 79
        shield, 78–9, **63**
            bird, 59, 61, pl. 2

garnets (*cont.*)

    dragon, 65, **50**, pl. 3
    boss, 52, **41**, pl. 5
   sword, **229**
    pommel, 291, 303–4
    pyramids, 300, 305–6
    scabbard-bosses, 295–7, 304
   see also jewellery, under individual items
   helmet
    dragon-heads, 160, 205, pl. 9
    eyebrows, 169, 205, 228–30, **176**
   polychromy, 603
    purse, hexagonal plaques, 508
    rectangular mounts (Inv. 8, 9), 603
    scabbard-bosses, 304–5
    shoulder-clasps, 527, 530
   relief cutting, 297, 306, 601–2
   rod, filigree strip, 395, 397–8, 442
    loose cabochon setting, 442
   shield
    bird, 101
    dragon, 65, 106
    grip-extensions, 109
    rim animals, 67
   shoulder-clasps, 530
   sword, scabbard-bosses, 297
   trade, 601
   Valsgärde 7, helmet, 218
Garton (Yorkshire), warrior's grave, spear-heads, 258
Gateholm Island (Pembrokeshire), bronze stag, 379–80, **271**
Gauert, M. comments on sceptre, 371–3
gauntlet, 194 n
Gilton (Kent), ring-sword, 135 n, **100** a
Gjermundbu (Norway), helmet, 210
Glastonbury (Somerset), lake village, tin 'sceptre', 352 n
Gokstad (Norway), ship, 431 n
gold
   analysis, 306, 611–14, 618–25, *Tbls. 16, 21, 31, 35, 36*
    sampling points, **440**
    techniques, 618–9
   foil, 448, 453, 487, 595, **319**
    buckles, mounts and strap-ends, 449, 456, 459, 460, 469,
     473, 481, **344**
    purse, 487, 503, 505, 508, 511, 512, 515, 600, **373**, pl. 23 d
    pyramids, 306
    scabbard-bosses, 304
    shield, 15, 21, 22, 29–36, 125, **81**
    shoulder-clasps, 481, 523, 528, 584, **387**
    sword-pommel, 303
   jewellery, *see* jewellery, gold
Gränby (Sweden), mailcoat, 237
Greenwell, Canon W., Uncleby whetstone, 364
Gregory of Tours, *Historia Franconum*, 352
Gresin (France), pottery plaque, 567 & n, 571 n
grids, iron, 426–8
Grimes, W. F., 4, 11, 273, 307
Grumpan (Sweden), clasps, 534–5, **394**
Guido, M., 298 n
Gundestrup (Denmark), cauldron, 372 & n, 373, 379
Gutenstein (Austria), sword, 196 n

Hablainville (France), sword-blade, 307 n
Hällan (Sweden), relief brooch, 126

hanging-bowl (Inv. 110), 269, 406, 423, 563–4, 583, 594–5,
   fish, 330, 335, 354 n, 375, 376, 379, 382
   silver patch, 563, 595 n, **415**
hanging-bowls, Celtic, 378–9, 583
Hardown Hill (Wiltshire), barrow, spears, 258
harness, royal, *see* jewellery
Harold, English king, 357, **262** b
Harquency-Mulheim (France), purse-mounts, 521, **382** c
Harrold (Bedfordshire), whetstone, 383
Hauck, K., 354, 358 n, 359, 371–3
Hawnby (Yorkshire), iron fitting, 402, **237**
Haynes, Denys, comment on stag, 334
Heidenheim (Germany), disc brooch, 478 n
Helgö (Sweden), padlocks, 369 n
helmet (Inv. 93), 138–231, pls. 8, 9, 23 b
   analyses, 158, 226–31, **170–175**
   animal interlace, 200–2, *see* dies 4 and 5
   bronze foil, 146, 218, 226, *see also* dies
   cap, 149–52, 159, 220, **111**
   cheek-pieces, 149–50, 167, 171–3, 179–80, **129**
   crest, 150, 152–63, 214–5, 220, 227–8, **112–119, 174**
   dies, 146–50, 214, 224, **108–110**
    1 (dancing warriors), 173, 186–90, 195, 208, 218, **140–142**
    2 (rider and fallen warrior), 151, 193–7, 218, 237–8, **143–145**
    3 (third figural scene), 146 n, 151, 190, 197–9, **148–149**
    4 (large interlace), 150, 171–2, 200–1, **150**
    5 (small interlace), 150, 164, 172, 174–6, 201–2, **151**
   dimensions, 152, 185
   dragon heads, 140, 150, 151–2, 155–6, 159–63, 169, 171, 185,
    189, 223, 224, 228, **103, 115, 117–119, 174**
   excavation in 1939, 138
   excavation finds, 1968–9, 156, 171
   face-mask, 150, 163–71, 223–4, 228–30, **120–128**
   general description, 138
   gilding, 150, 159, 167, 169, 227, 228, 229–31, **119, 172**
   hinges, 171–2, 176–9, 185–6, 203, **133, 137–139**
   late Roman character, 210, 220–4, 330, 534
   lining, 146, 179, 203 & n , 231
   neck guard, 149, 173–9, 181, 209, 210, 214, 220, **130–133,
    135, 139**
   nostrils, 167, **122**
   replica, Tower of London, 140, 150, 152 & n, **136–138,**
    pl. 8
    compared to modern restoration, 152 n, 176 n, 181–5
    lining material, 179, 204 n
   restoration, 1947, 140, 151, 164 n, 167, 199
   restoration, 1971, 140 ff., 181, **102–107**, pls. 9, 23 b
   silver inlays, 150, 154–6, 158, 167–8, 214, 227–8, **113–115,
    121–122, 125**
   silvering, *see* tinning
   summary of features, 203
   tinning, 146, 165, 185, 205, 210, 214, 220, 226
   weight, 185
helmets, comparative; *see also* individual entries
   Anglo-Saxon, 206–8
   East Scandinavian, 152, 158, 208–20, 380
   Late Roman, 146, 152, 159, 174 n, 185, 203, 220
   Norwegian, 159 n, 206 n, 209–10
   Spangenhelme, 152, 206 n, 223, 234 n, 237
Henry, Françoise, 587, 595 n
Heorot, 382
Herpaly (Hungary), boss, 380
Hesselager (Denmark) treasure, pendant capsule, 602 n

Hicks, Carola, provenance of the stag, 333, 375, 378–82
Hildersham (Cambridgeshire), hanging-bowl, 378
Hjortspring (Denmark), boat, mailcoats, 237
Hög Edsten (Sweden)
    gold capsule, 560
    sword pommel, 303, 602 n, **230**
Högbro (Sweden), helmet eyebrows, 209
Holborough (Kent), sword, 285 n
honestones, *see* whetstones
horned head-dress, *see* helmet, die 1
horse burial, 320–22
horse harness, 193, **143**
horse ornament
    curved mount, 473–4
    helmet, 198, 199, **148** c, **149** b
    Lucca shield, 97
    purse, double plaque, 505
    shield, 49, 50, 88, 89
horse representation, *see* helmet, die 2; Pliezhausen brooch;
    Valsgärde 7 and 8 helmets
Hough-on-the-Hill (Lincolnshire), stone figure, 364, 369, 383–4,
    267
Howletts (Kent), square-headed brooches, 602
Hughes, M. J., scientific reports, 100–22, 385–93, 618–25

Ibn Fadlan, on Rus cremation, 324
Intercisa (Hungary), helmets, 220, **168**
interlace
    rectangular mounts, cloisonné, 462, **329** c, d
    shield, 64–5
    see also, animal interlace
Ipswich (Suffolk), pottery, 359 n
iron object (Inv. 210), 404, 419, 437, **304, 305**
Ischl-an-der-Als (Bavaria), shield, 27 n, 96–97
Ixworth (Suffolk), cross, 563

Jewell, Juliet, zoological study of stag, 337
jewellery, gold, pls. 13–20
    backing pastes and techniques, 599–603
    buckle and two matching strap-mounts (Inv. 12–14), 439,
        441, 445–6, 449–55, **320, 321**
        cloisonné work, 449–53, 454, 468, 567, **320**
        position on harness, 567–8, 570, 574–77, 580
    buckle, great gold (Inv. 1), 526, 536–64, **396–410, 432** i,
        pl. 20
        excavation, 435, 439, 440
        function, 556–63, 565
        gold analysis, 545, *Tbl. 31*
        interlace, 530, 548–54
        niello, 545, 549–53, 556
        position on harness, 564
        relation to purse, 488, 556, 565
        stylistic analogies, 81, 505, 553–4, 563–4
    buckle, rectangular (Inv. 11), 277, 443, 469–73, 599–600,
        318, 324 c, **336–338**, pl. 23 e
        cloisonné work, 472, **336**
        position on harness, 568, 572, 577, 579
    catalogue of items, 433
    Celtic elements, 370, 375, 497, 583–4, 595–7
    chronology, 611
    excavation, 435–47, **314–317**
    goldsmith, 563, 595–9

harness, royal, reconstruction, 257, 439, 446, 577–81,
    425–427
mount, curved (dummy buckle) (Inv. 10), 296, 437 n, 441,
    473–81, **339–342, 344, 345–348, 432** f, g, pl. 22 b
    cloisonné work, 477–78, 478–80, **340, 347**
    leather, 447 n, 481
    position on harness, 572–6, 579
mount, triangular zoomorphic (Inv. 18), 444, 445, 481–5,
    577, 607, **349–352** a, **433** a
    cloisonné work, 482–85, **349, 352**
    different style, 599
    function, 481–82, 577–79
    position on harness, 577
mounts, rectangular (mushroom cell design) (Inv. 6, 7),
    276, 303, 437, 441, 456–60, 599, **322–325, 328** a
    cloisonné work, 456–9, 322, 323
    position on harness, 568, 572
mounts, rectangular (step-pattern design) (Inv. 8, 9) 437,
    441, 460–5, 603, **326–331**
    cloisonné work, 460–3, 599, **326**
    construction, 463–5, **331**
    lidded cell technique, 463, 598–9, 600–1
    position on harness, 568–72
purse (Inv. 2, 3), 303–4, 487–522, 598, **355–380**, pls. 13,
    14, 23 d, f
    bag evidence for, 432, 441, 488, 500, 503
    bird plaques, 489, 508–12, 522, **375**
    circular studs, 489, 514–5, **364** c, **379**
    clasp and locking mechanism, 488, 516–7, **365, 380**
    cloisonné work, 491, 503, 506, 509, 514, **359, 368, 370,**
        371, 375, 376, 378
    double plaque, 49, 489, 503–5, **364** a, **369, 384** d
    excavation, 435, 439–40, 446–7, 565, **355**
    frame, 488–9, 491–500, 603, **433** e–g
    hexagonal plaques, 488–9, 505–8, **364** b–d, **372**
    lid, lining and material, 492, 494, 497–8, 501–3, 515
    man-between-beasts plaques, 489, 505, 512–4, 522, **377**;
        East Scandinavian versions, 220, 370, 522
        identification as wolves, 354
    millefiori and inlays, 488, 582–3, 590–5, 603, **429** b
    position on harness, 564–5, 577–80, **423** b
    see also coins, gold
regalia, 432, 564, 576
shoulder-clasps (Inv. 4, 5), 304, 523–35, 598, **386–393**, pls.
    15–18, 22 b, 23 c
    boars, 526–7, 529–31
    cloisonné work, 525, 601–2, **388, 389**
    differences between the two, 529–30
    excavation, 437, 439, 442
    filigree, 527, 603, 607, **432** b, c, **434–436**
    millefiori and inlays, 523, 527, 582–3, 584–90, 594, **428,**
        429 a
    pins, 525–6, 603
    zoomorphic borders, 528–9
strap-distributor, T-shaped (Inv. 17), 276, 437, 442, 455,
    465–9, **328** c, **332–335**
    cloisonné work, 466–8, 567, **332–335**
    function, 468, 491 n, 567
    position on harness, 568, 572, 574–8
strap-end, plain (Inv. 16), 300, 396 n, 444, 448, 455, 486, **354**
    position on harness, 566, 577, 580
strap-runner, plain (Inv. 15), 439, 440, 455, 485–6, **353**
    position on harness, 565–7, 577, 580

jewellery, gold (*cont.*)
    weights, *Tbl. 33*
    see also rod, wood, bone or ivory, gold fittings and sword,
        gold fittings

Kaiseraugst (Switzerland), cemetery, buckle (grave 108), 558–9,
    411 *a*
Karleby, Östergötland, ring-sword, 132
Kempston (Bedfordshire)
    fish mount, 94 *n*
    spear-head, 245, 259, 270
Kendrick, Sir T. D., 251–2, 256 *n*, 265, 373–4, 404
Kenninghall (Norfolk)
    brooch, analysis, *Tbl. 30*
    fish mount, 94 *n*, **69** *c*
Kent, J. P. C., gold fineness graph, 610, **439**
Kingston (Kent), disc brooch, 125, 296, 451, 595 *n*, 597, 614,
    Tbl. 36, **431**, **442** *a*
Kirmukarmu (Finland), sword, 359
Klinta, Öland (Denmark), boat cremation, iron shaft, 428, **310** *a*
Klumbach, H., helmets, 159, 210, 220
Köln-Müngersdorf (Germany), cemetery
    garnet backing technique, 124
    purses, 519, 565, **382** *b*
Krefeld-Gellep (Germany), cemetery
    iron spit, 426–8, **310** *b*
    purse, 502, 519–20, 565, **383**
    sword, 273 *n*
Kremsmünster (Austria), monastery, candlesticks, 355–6

lamp, iron (Inv. 66), 423
lamps, pottery, 423, **306**
lapis lazuli, 603 *n*
Laszlo, Gy., Hungarian sceptres, 356
Leeds, E. T., 207, 553
Lauterhofen (Germany), cemetery, sword-belt (grave 29), 572,
    574, **419** *d*
leather
    curved mount, 447 *n*, 481
    helmet
        cheek-pieces, 172
        lining, 146, 179, 205, 223
        neck-guard hinges, 174, 185
        Late Roman helmets, 174 *n*, 220
    mailcoat, 232
    shield
        board, 22, 27, 28, 55, 127, **13, 21, 25, 46**
        carrying strap, 69, 72, **57**
        hanging-up strap, 73, 58
    sword
        scabbard, 284, 297, **224**
        pyramids, 447 *n*
Leibenau (Germany), belt-buckle, 566
Leighton Buzzard (Bedfordshire), composite brooch, 125 *n*, 392,
    Tbl. 30
lidded cell technique, 485, 584, 598
    purse, 503, 505, 508, 512, 514, **374**
    rectangular mounts, 463, **330**
    shoulder-clasps, 525
    triangular zoomorphic mount, 483, 485
Lilleberre (Norway), iron trivet, 426, **307**
lime-wood, on shield, 16, 21–22, 127–8
limonite, 167, 180, 192, 199

Lindqvist, S., 159, 210, 423, 545
Llandudno (Wales), whetstone, 369, **269** *a–d*
Lloseta, Mallorca (Spain), bronze stag's head, 381, **272** *a*
Lochar Moss (Dumfriesshire), whetstone, 369, **268**
Lokrume (Sweden), helmet eyebrows, 158 *n*, 209
Louvre (France), cameo, 567
Lucca (Italy), shield, 35, 40, 97, **28** *b*
Lullingstone (Kent), hanging-bowl, 378
Lundström, Agneta, 362, 535 *n*
lyre, maplewood (Inv. 203), 23, 264, 285, 406, 422

Magoun, F. P., comment on sceptre, 374
mail, 196 *n*, 210, 212, 215, 237–9, **182, 183**
mailcoat (Inv. 92), 138, 232–40, **177–181**
mailcoats, 193, 196 and *n*
man-between-beasts scene
    purse, 354, 512–4, **370** *a*, **376–377**, pl. 14 *c*
    Torslunda plaque, 354, **156, 385**
    Valsgärde 7 version, 218, 220, 522, **164** *d*
Mann, Sir James, comment on mailcoat, 236 *n*
manuscripts
    Dublin, *Durrow, Book of*, 81, 462, 560, **66** *c*, **329** *a*
    London, *BM Cotton Tiberius C VI*, fs. 9 *r*, 10 *v*, 71 *v*, 581 *n*,
        426 *a, b*
    Paris, *Echternach Gospels*, f. 18 *v*, 462, **329** *b*
    St Gall, *Psalterium Aureum*, illustration of vexillum, 430,
        311
Marktoberdorf (Germany), cemetery, sword fittings (graves
    196, 197), **421** *b, c*
Maryon, H., 16, 19, 26, 31–3, 45 *n*, 73, 110, 199, 226, 338
Menghin, W., sword suspension, 567, 570–2, 575
Mikulčice (Czechoslovakia), book reliquary, 560 *n*
Mildenhall (Suffolk), fish mount, 94 *n*
millefiori, 304, 370, 582–97, *Tbl. 34*, pl. 24 *a*
    purse, 487, 489, 506, 512, 515, 590–3, **373, 429** *b*, pls. 23 *f*, 24 *a*
    shoulder-clasps, 523, 527, 530, 584–90, **428, 429** *a*, pl. 23 *c*
    sword pyramids, 300, 594, **227**
Miller, M. O., spear reconstruction, 244
Milton (Berkshire), composite brooch, 468 *n*
Mindelheim (Germany), cemetery, sword fittings (graves 11
    and 34), **421** *a, e*
Monnet-la-Ville (France), reliquary buckle, 559 *n*
Montmaurin (France), bronze stag, 379
Monza, ivory dyptych, 567
Moosbrugger-Leu, 558
Morken (Germany), chamber grave
    shield, 4 *n*, 38
    sword, 273 *n*
Moss, A. A.
    jewellery analysis, 618
    mounts, gold and garnet cloisonné, *see* jewellery, gold,
        individual items
Moylough (Ireland), belt reliquary, 558
Mucking (Essex), whetstone, 383
München-Aubing (Germany), cemetery, purse-lid (grave 812),
    517, **382** *a*
mushroom cell
    buckle and strap-mounts (Inv. 12–14), 451, 454
    curved mount (Inv. 10), 478
    purse, hexagonal plaques (Inv. 2 *c, d*), 506, 508
    rectangular buckle (Inv. 11), 472
    rectangular mounts (Inv. 6, 7), 458–9
    triangular zoomorphic mount (Inv. 18), 484, 599

Nagyszentmiklòs (Hungary), 431 n
Nerman, B., stand, 428
Niederbieber (Germany), Roman fort, dragon head, 430, **312**
Niederstotzingen (Germany), cemetery, shields, 4 n, 25 n, 94, 96
niello
    great gold buckle, 549–53, 556
    shield, grip-extensions, 77, 109
Nocera Umbra (Italy), cemetery, sword clips, 299
Notker, *De Karolo Magno I*, 355
Nydam (Denmark)
    angons, 265, 269
    sword blade, 307 n

oak-wood, associated with shield, 128
Oberflacht (Germany), cemetery, shield (grave 145), 94
Oddy, W. A., scientific reports, 100–22, 226–31, 240, 308–9, 385–93
    jewellery, gold analysis, 618–25
    millefiori, examination, 595
Old Uppsala, *see* Gamla Uppsala
Olsen, P., scramasaxes, 256
Orsay (France), ring-sword, 94
Øvre Stabu (Norway), helmet fragment, 210

padlocks, 369 n, 270
pattern welding, 282, 307, **211**
Paulsen, P., Pliezhausen disc-brooch, 194
Pazyryk (Siberia), reindeer, 302
peacock, in Scandinavian sites, 431 n
Petersfinger (Kent), cemetery, ring-sword (grave 21), 135 n
Petersson, K. G., 428
Petrossa treasure, 602
Phillips, C. W., excavation diary
    ferrules, 241, 265, 267
    helmet, 138
    iron object (Inv. 210), 419, 421–2
    jewellery, 435–7
    mailcoat, 232
    rod, gold mounts, 394–5
    sceptre, 311
    shield, 1, 4, 7–9, 11, 29–30, 36
    spears, 251
    sword, 273, 298 n
phosphate readings
    iron object (Inv. 210), 422
    rod, wood, bone or ivory (Inv. 30–33), 394
    scabbard, 394–5
Pictish art, 378 n
Piggott, Stuart
    burial deposit plans, **315, 316**, pl. 24 b
    garnet, detached, 396
    iron blade (spear 6), 254, 256
    jewellery, 439
    mailcoat, 234
    shield, 1, 7, 29, 37, 44 n
    spears, 241
    stag and stand, 404
Pirling, Renate, excavation of Krefeld-Gellep, 519
Planig (Germany), helmet, 206 n
Plenderleith, H. J., shield, 16, 19, 31–3, 110, 124 n
Pliezhausen (Germany), disc-brooch, 193, 196, 197, 218, **146**
Portsoy (Banffshire), stone with face, 369, 371 n, **269** e

Preshaw (Hampshire), necklace pendant, 602
Prittlewell (Essex), spear, 259
punched decoration
    great gold buckle, 549, 554, 556, **409**
    helmet
        dragon-heads, 159–61, 223, 224, **118, 174**
        nose and mouth casting, 167, 231, **125**
    Lombardic shields, 97
    rod, gold-foil animal, 399
    shield, 117–122, *Tbls. 18, 19*, **88, 89, 90, 92**
        bird, 59–63, 101, **44**, pl. 2
        carrying fitments, 72, **56, 58** a, pl. 7 b–d
        dragon, 64–5, 105, **50**, pl. 3
        grip-extension, 77, **60**, pl. 6
        rim animal heads, 67, **90**
purse, *see* jewellery, gold, individual items
Püspök-Szent-Erzsbét (Hungary), Avar grave, sceptre, 356
Pye, Elizabeth, shield, checklist of fragments, 7 n
pyramids, *see* sword, and shield, hanging-up strap and fittings

Raedwald, East Anglian king, 225, 347, 428–9, 563
    as *bretwalda*, 347, 351, 375–7, 597
regalia, 432, 564, 576
Reinstrup (Germany), brooch, 598
Rennes (France), bronze stag's head, 381, **272** b
Rhenen (Netherlands), cemetery, belt buckles (graves 846, 829) 566
Ribchester (Lancashire), helmet, 233, **169** a
Richborough (Kent), bronze stag, 379, 381
rider and fallen warrior scene
    helmet, die 2, 190–7, 218, **136, 143, 145**
    Pliezhausen disc-brooch, 193, **146**
    Valsgärde 7 version, 195, **163, 164** a, b
ring-mail, *see* mailcoat
ring-swords
    Anglo Saxon, 135–7, **96, 100**
    French, 133, **94, 96** d
    Scandinavian, 131–33, **95, 97**
Robinson, Russell, helmet, 140, 174 n, 204 n
rod, wood, bone or ivory (Inv. 30–33), 353–4, 394–402, **286**
    decorative features, 394–97
    fittings, gold
        animal (Inv. 32), 354 n, 396, 399, 437, 444, **281–282**
        filigree strip and ring with cabochon garnet settings (Inv. 30), 276, 394, 397–8, 437, 442, **278–280, 432** a; detached cabochon garnet setting (Inv. 302), 395–6, 432 n, 437, 442, **279** c
        fluted strip with animal head (Inv. 31), 396, 400–1, 445, **284–285**
        triangular foil mount (Inv. 33), 396, 399–400, 445–6, **283**
    phosphate analysis, 394
    substance of staff, 394–5
Roermond (Netherlands), disc, 380
Rome (Italy), bird-brooch, 509
Rosmeer (Belgium), disc-brooch, 520 n
Roundway Down (Wiltshire), linked pins, bead and pendants, 596, 614, **430, 441** k, **443**
Rude Eskilstrup (Denmark), wooden figure, 360

St Cuthbert, cross, 296, **427**
St Denis (France), cemetery, buckle (grave 11), 563
St Gall, *see* manuscripts

St Maurice d'Agaune (Switzerland), monastery, ewer, origin
   as sceptre, 356, **260**
St Sulpice (France), cemetery, sword-belt (grave 168), 572, 574,
   419 *b*
San Vitale, Ravenna (Italy), chancel mosaic, 372
Sarre (Kent), cemetery
   composite brooch, 125 *n*, *Tbl. 36*, **442** *b*, **443**
   hanging-bowl, 379
   necklace, 598 *n*
   ring-sword, 136, **96** *b*
Samur (France), bronze stag, 379
sceptre, gold mounted, *see* rod, wood, bone or ivory
sceptre, stone with metal fittings (Inv. 160 and 205), 311–77,
   236–7, pls. 10, 11
   dimensions, 312
   excavation, 7, 9, 311, 423, **235**
   function, 345–7, 370–7
      Celtic elements, 357–8, 361, 369, 374–7
      Late Antique influence, 351–2, 375, 534
      phallic symbolism, 373–4
      Scandinavian aspect, 360, 369, 374–5
      Thor's thunderbolt, 374 & *n*, 375, 376
   general description, 312–16
   metal fittings, 326–50, **274**
      analyses, 342–5, 385–93, **275–277**
      pedestal, 328–30, 339–43, 388–9, **245–247, 254, 256, 274,
         276**; *see also* sceptre, metal fittings, wire ring and stag
      saucer, 314, 324–7, 340–2, 346, 349, 357–8, 373, 389–90,
         Tbl. 30, **242–243**
      top and bottom contrasted, 326–8, **242–243**
      wire ring and stag assembly, 314, 328, 347–9, 372, 387,
         245, 247, 251; *see also* sceptre, metal fittings, pedestal
   replica, 341–2, **255**
   stag, *see* separate entry
   stone bar, 312–28
      ends contrasted, 324–8, 327–8, 349, **241, 244**
      human faces, 315–24, 357–60, 234, 238–40; beards de-
         picted, 315, 323–4; comparative faces (bronze), 358–60,
         369, **263, 270**; comparative faces (stone), 364–9,
         267–269; compared to face on shield, bird's hip, 59,
         79, 358; frames, 314, 328, 358–9, 372–3, **238–239, 244**;
         mail depicted, 234, 320; men or women, 323–4, 371,
         374; reason for number, 371, 373
      petrography, 315, 360–1, 375, 383–4, **273**
      red paint, 312, 346, 357, 373, 376, pl. 11 *a*
      staining, 315, **236**
   weight, 312
sceptres
   Anglo-Saxon, 350–57, **262**
   Carolingian, 352–6, **259**
   Eastern, 356, **260–261**
   Late Roman, 350–2, 358, 376, **257**
Schapur, king, depicted on cameo, 567
scramasax, *see* spears (spear 6, Inv. 97)
scramasaxes, 256
Selsey (Sussex), gold pyramid, 554, *Tbl. 36*, **408** *c*, **441** *g*
shield (Inv. 94), pls. 1–7
   animal ornament and interlace designs, 79–91; *see also*
      decoration in individual entries
   backing materials to garnets, 123–6
   beeswax, 53, 114
   bird, 55–63, **15, 32, 43** *d*, **44, 45–49, 74**, pl. 2
      analysis, 100–3, 125, *Tbl. 3*, **75–78**

decoration, 80, 81, 85–6, **49, 66** *d*
      East Scandinavian character, 58–9, 91, 97
      head, 55, 61
      leg, 55, 59–61, **46**
      movement in ground, 43, **32**
      position on shield, 30–1, 42–3
      tail and wing, 55, 58, 59, 554, **45, 47, 49, 74**
      underlays, 22, 55, 58, 127, **15, 47**
   board, 20
      construction, 24, 42
      curvature, 4, 11, 17, 18, 19–21
      diameter, 16, 18
      excavation, 9, 15, 16, 30
      leather covering, 22, 27–9, 44, 55, 99, **21, 25, 46**
      thickness, 27, **20**
      wood, 16, 21–2, 94 *n*, 127–8
   boss, central iron, 48–55, **18, 19, 34, 35**, pls. 4, 5
      analysis, 114–6, 125, *Tbls. 12, 13*, **87**
      cloisonné disc, 49, 52, 80, 89, 90, 124, **41, 43**, pl. 5 *b*
      decoration
         dome, 51–2, 80, 89, **39, 40, 42**
         flange, 49, 80, 88, 505, 522, 554, **36**, pl. 5 *a*
         vertical collar, 50, 80, 92, **37, 38**
      excavation, 7, 9, 11, 38–40, 50
      flange slope, 26–7, **19**
      movement in ground, 38–40
   bronze foil, *see* decoration in individual entries
   carrying-strap and anchor fittings, 44, 69, 72, **6, 56, 57,
      83**, pl. 7 *c*
      analysis of fittings, 106–7
      position in ground, 44, 45
   cloisonné work, 78, 79, **63**, pls. 2, 3, 5 *b*
   description, 11
   distribution of features and movement in the ground, 36–45,
      30, 32
   dragon, 63–5, 76, **50, 51**, pl. 3
      analysis, 103–6, **79, 80, 81**
      decoration, interlace panels, 63–5, 80, 90–1, **51**
      East Scandinavian character, 97
      movement in ground, 40, 42–4
      position on shield, 42, 98
      underlay, 128, **13**
   East Scandinavian character, 16, 17, 35, 91–99
   excavation, 1, 4–11, **2–5, 12**, pl. 24 *b*
   fragments now ascribed to lyre, 16 *n*, 23, 127
   handgrip, 24–5, **10, 16**
      bosses, 66, 75; analysis, 107–8, *Tbl. 4*
   handgrip extensions, 10, 75–8, **10, 11, 16, 43** *a–c*, **60–62**,
      pl. 6
      analysis, 108–9, *Tbls. 4–6*
      decoration, 77, 80, 90, **61, 62**
      position in ground, 1, 38–9
   hanging-up strap and fittings, 40, 44, 45, 73–5, **6, 58, 59**,
      pl. 7 *b, d, e*
      analysis of fittings, 106, **82**
   hemispherical bosses with gold foil collars, 24–6, 41–2, 44,
      66, **14, 33, 52**
      analysis, 112–3, *Tbls. 9, 10*, **86**
      decoration of collars, 87, **52**
      position in ground, 44
      underlays, 22, 42, 127, **14, 31**
   Lombardic elements, 35, 96–7, **28**
   ornamental foil strips, 67–9, **53** *a*, **54, 55**

shield (*cont.*)

    analysis, 113, *Tbl. 11*
    decoration, 80, 87–8, **53** *a*
    movement in ground, 40–2, pl. 24 *b*
    position on shield board, 40–2
    underlay, **31** *d*, *e*
  punched decoration, 59, 61, 117, *Tbls. 18, 19*, **88, 89, 90, 92**
  reconstruction, 15–29, *Tbl. 2*, **6–8, 29**
  rim, 29–36, **9, 22–26**
    animal heads, 34, 67; analysis, 110–1, **85, 90**
    movement in ground, 4, 8, 29, 39, 43–4
    number of peripheral mounts, 34, 35, 36, **29**
    rectangular foil panels, 15, 34–6, 40, 79, 81–6, **64, 65–67**;
      analysis, 112
    shape, 16, 18
    U-channelled binding, 33, **24**; gold foil, 30, 33, **26**
    underlays, lack of, 30–33
  ring (Inv. 206), 129–37, **93, 99**, pl. 7 *a*; *see also* ring-swords
    analysis, 116, *Tbl. 14*
    position on shield, 25, 46
    reasons for ascribing to shield, 45, 133–5
    Scandinavian character, 45, 134, 137
    underlay, 45–6, 89, 135
  scientific examination, 100–22; *see also* individual items
    under analysis
  unpacking list, 1, 4, *Tbl. 1*
shields
  Anglo-Saxon, 16, 27, 92
  Byzantine, 97, 99
  Carolingian, 99
  East Scandinavian, 195; *see also* Valsgärde, Vendel
  Lombardic, 35, 97, **28**
ship, 4 *n*, 29
shoulder-clasps, *see* jewellery, gold
Sidonius Apollinaris, on Frankish swords, 571
Silchester (Hampshire), hanging-bowl, 379
silver bowl, fluted (Inv. 77), 235, 422
silver bowls, set of ten (Inv. 78–87), 269, 273
Smith, E. H., 140
snake ornament
  great gold buckle, 81, 550–1
  shield, 81–4
Snape (Suffolk), ring, *Tbl. 36*, **438** *a*, **441** *f*, **443**
Snösbäck (Sweden), ring-sword, 132, **97**
Soest (Germany), brooch, 559–60
Søholdt (Denmark), wooden staff, 359–60, **263** *a*, *b*
Spangenhelme, *see* helmets
Speake, George, on Style II, 564 *n*
spears (Inv. 97, 101–5) and angons (Inv. 98–100)
  angon 1 (Inv. 98), 241, 259–61, 272, **197**
  angon 2 (Inv. 99), 261, **198**
  angon 3 (Inv. 100), 261–4, **199**
  ash-wood shafts, 241, 264–5
  date, 259
  ferrules, 242, 265, 280–1
  position in burial chamber, 242–3, 276
  spear 1 (Inv. 101), 241, 245, 259, **187**
  spear 2 (Inv. 102), 242, 245–8, 259, **188**
  spear 3 (Inv. 103), 241, 242, 248–9, 259, 272, **189**
  spear 4 (Inv. 104), 243, 249–51, **190–191**
  spear 5 (Inv. 105), 251–4, 259, 264, **192–193**
  spear 6 (Inv. 97), 'scramasax', 241–2, 254–7, 259, 273,
    194–195

spears, Anglo-Saxon, 257–9
Spontin (Belgium), belt buckle, 566
spoons, silver (Inv. 88, 89), 256, 273
Sprendlingen (Germany), brooch, 126
Stabio, Canton Tessin (Switzerland), shield, 35, 97, **28** a
stag, bronze (Inv. 205), 314, 333–9, 378–82, **248–253**, pl. 11 *c*
  analysis, 339, 342, 345, 382, 385–93
  antlers, 335–9, 380, **251** *c*, **252**
  carination, 333–4, 342, 378
  Celtic nature, 375, 378–82, 597
  damage during burial, 335
  excavation, 9, 311, 335, 340, **235**
  naturalism, 354 *n*, 378
  removal from stand to sceptre, 339–43, 346, 371, 385, 404, 406
  significance, 346–7, 376, 382
stags, 379–80, 382
stand, iron (Inv. 161), 403–31, **277, 288–303**, pl. 12
  analysis, 292–3
  associated iron object (Inv. 210), 404, 419–22, 437 & *n*, **304,
    305**
    phosphate analysis, 422
  excavation, 9, 39, 403–4
  function, 422–31
  general description, 406–11
  horned heads, 339, 409, 424
  movement in burial chamber, 405–6
  radiography and construction
    foot, 411, **294**
    grid, 417, **293, 299, 300**
    horned heads, 418, **301, 302**
    lower plate and cage, 413–7, **295–298**
    shaft, 411
    upper plate, 418, **303**
  replica, 406, **291** *b*, **296**
  stag, removal of, 339–40, 392–3
  weight, 424
standards
  Anglo-Saxon, 428–9
  Roman, 429–30, **313**
step-pattern
  buckle and matching strap-mounts (Inv. 12–14), 451–3
  curved mount (Inv. 10), 479–80
  purse
    bird plaques, 509
    hexagonal plaques, 508
  rectangular mounts (Inv. 6–9), 458–9, 461–2
  shoulder-clasps, 525, 527
  triangular zoomorphic mount, 484
Stilicho, ivory diptych, 567, **416** *a*
Stollenmayer, P., Tassilo candlesticks, 355
strap-distributor, gold and garnet cloisonné *see* jewellery, gold,
  individual items
Style II, see bird-heads; *see also* animal interlace
Swanton, Michael, spear clasification, 244 ff.
sword (Inv. 95), 273–88, **207–215**, 308
  analysis, 206, 308–9, 608–14
  blade, 282, **211, 212**
    pattern welding, 307
  East Scandinavian character, 299
  excavation, 273, 276, 435, 437, 442–3
  gold fittings, pls. 21, 22 *a*, *e*
    filigree clips (Inv. 24, 25), 276, 298–9, 603, 607, **221** *e*,
      f, **225, 226** *b*, **432**

sword (*cont.*)

    guard-plates (Inv. 20–3), 277, 288–94, **217–219, 226***a*, **423***b, c.*, pl. 21*e*

    pommel (Inv. 19), 277, 289–92, 303–4, 308–9, 448, 599, 603, **218–220, 319***i*, **432***h*, **433***d*, pls. 21*a*, 22*a*

    pyramids (Inv. 28, 29), 276, 300–6, 435, 439, 447*n*, 486, 572, 575–6, 581, 582, 594, 598, 602, **227–228, 233, 316, 423***c*, pls. 21*b*, 22*e*

        function, 581

    scabbard bosses (Inv. 26, 27), 273, 285, 287–8, 294–7, 304–5, 308, 395, 479, 570, 572, 580, **208, 222–224, 231, 232, 352***b*, pl. 21*c*

        Christian elements, 273, 304

    grip, 277, 292–3, **221**

    phosphate analysis, 394–5

    ring, *see* shield-ring

    scabbard, 284–8, 570

        fur lining, 282, 285, 307, 309, **212, 214**

    sword-belt, 564, 567–81

    textiles, associated, 273, 276–7, 282

    wooden feature on scabbard, 288, **215**

sword-rings, *see* ring-swords

sword suspension, 567, **416**

Sykes, R. L., identification of shield leather, 28*n*, 29*n*

Taganča (Kiev), tumulus, sceptre, 356, **261**

Taplow (Buckinghamshire), barrow burial

    buckle, 607, **437, 441***a*, **443**

    clasps, 534, **343, 441***a*, **443**, pl. 22*b*

    shield, 92

Tassilo III, duke of Bavaria, 355

Taunus mountains (Germany), bronze deer, 380*n*

textiles (Inv. 176–201)

    mailcoat, 232 & *n*

    SH 2, 7, 8

        on helmet, 180

        on spear, 6, 256

    SH 10, 13, 23, 24, on helmet, 180, **135**

    SH 16

        on helmet, 180

        associated with sword, 276, 284 & *n*, **213**

Theodosius, Missorium of, 372

Thetford (Norfolk), pottery lamp, 423, **306**

Thor, whetstone as emblem, 375

Thordeman, Bengt, 195*n*, 210, 234*n*

Thorsbjerg (Denmark)

    ferrule, 269

    helmet, 210

thunderbolts, whetstones as symbol of, 374–5

thuuf, *see* tufa

Tite, M. S., examination of sword, 308–9

Tongres (Belgium), mount, 598 & *n*

torcs, 372

Torslunda (Sweden), helmet dies, 208–9, **156, 157, 385, 416***b*

    analysis, 345, 393, *Tbl. 30*

    boar helmet, 176, 209–10, 215, 379

    borders, 196

    clothing represented, 196*n*, 237–8

    horned head-dress, 189

    man and bears scene, 218, 220*n*, 223, 354, 522

    spear depicted, 189, 195

    sword harness depicted, 567, 570*n*

Torslunda (Sweden), site, 208–9

Traprain Law (Scotland), antler, 381

Tressan (France), buckle, 602

tufa, 429–31

Tuna (Sweden), disc-on-bow brooch, 126

Ulltuna (Sweden)

    helmet, 208–10, 212, 220

    shield, 92

Uncleby (Yorkshire), whetstones, 362–4, **265**

Uppsala, Old, *see* Gamla Uppsala

Vaison-la-Romaine (France), statue, 534

Valerian, Emperor, depicted on cameo, 567

Vallstenarum (Sweden), burial

    shield, 27

    stand, 428, **310***c*

    sword pommel with ring, 132, **95**

    hilt clips, 299, 570, **95**

Valsgärde (Sweden), boat graves

    helmets, 208–20, 234, 237

    shields, 20, 24, 34–5, 40, 73, 92, 94, 99

        dimensions, 15, 17, 18*n*, 95

    grave 5

        fire-dog, 426, **309***b*

        helmet, 155*n*, 208, 212

        sword, 133*n*

    grave 6

        fire-dog, 426, **309***a*

        helmet, 138*n*, 155*n*, 158, 180*n*, 208, 210, 212, 220, **182***b*

        shield 1, 18*n*, 27, 34*n*, 92, 94, 96, *Tbl. 2*, **68**

        shield 3, 22*n*, 94*n*

    grave 7

        drinking horn with gilt-bronze ring, 46, 133, 134, **98, 101**

        helmet, 72, 138*n*, 208, 214–20, **159–161, 164–169**; crest, 155*n*, 158*n*; dies, 186–99, 522

        shield 1, 27, 50, 58–9, 92, 98, *Tbl. 2*, **72***b*

        shield 2, 34*n*, *Tbl. 2*

        shield 3, 24*n*, 94, *Tbl. 2*

        sword and baldric, 567–71, 575, 577, **216, 417, 426***c*

    grave 8

        helmet, 138*n*, 186, 208, 212, 223, **18***b*; crest, 155*n*, 156*n*, 158*n*, 215; die, 31, 72, 197, 199; garnet inlays, 218, **162**

        shield 1, 21*n*, 22*n*, 24, 25, 34*n*, 69*n*, 73*n*, 92, 94, 98*n*, 358, *Tbl. 2*

        shield 2, 21*n*, 22*n*, 34, 94, 98*n*, *Tbl. 2*, **27**

        shield, 3, 22*n*

        sword, 133*n*

Vegetius, 431*n*

Vendel (Sweden), boat graves

    helmets, 138*n*, 152, 158–9, 203, 208–20, 234, 237, 358

    shields, 17, 19, 40, 96, 99

    whetstones, 361

    grave 1

        bronze mount, 553, **408***b*

        helmet, 72, 155*n*, 180*n*, 199, 208, 212*n*, **17, 116***b*

        shield, 22*n*, 58, 92, 97–9, *Tbl. 2*, **72***a*

        sword, 570

        whetstone, 361

    grave 4, whetstone, 361

    grave 10, helmet, 212

    grave 11

        helmet, 208, 212, **165***b*

        shield, 24

Vendel (Sweden) (*cont.*)
  grave 12
    bridle-mount, 79, 358
    helmet, 180 *n*, 208, 212, 238, **182** *a*
    shield 1, 22 *n*, 24, 27, 69, 78, 88, 91, 92, 96, 358, **53,
      70, 71**
    shield 2, 88
    spear-head, 189, 223, 554, **152**
  grave 14
    helmet, 189, 208, 210, 212, 214–5, 220, 225, 532 *n*, **17** *a*,
      147, 158, 416 *b*; dies, 31, 72, 73, 176, 192, 195, 196 *n*,
      239, 567, 570–1
    shield, 22 *n*, 24
Veszprem (Hungary), iron grid, 426, **308**
vexillum, 429–30, **311, 312**
Vézeronce (France), helmets, 206 *n*
Vienna (Austria), rectangular mount, 451
Vimose (Denmark)
  bronze mount, 359–60, **263** *c*
  mailcoat, 237

Wahlern-Elisried (Switzerland), gravefield, belt-buckle (grave
      33), 558, **411** *b*
wala, 158, 203
Walda (Swabia), bronze strap-end, 560
Wallace-Hadrill, J. M., 350, 352 *n*, 374 *n*
Webster, Leslie, Caenby fragment, 207
Weimar (Germany), cemetery
  iron shaft, 428
  iron tripod, 426
Weinheim (Germany), belt-buckle, 566
Welbeck Hill (Lincolnshire), spear, 259
Werner, A. E. A., scientific reports, 100–22, 226–31, 240, 385–95,
      618–26

Werner, J., 210, 353, 558 *n*
whetstone (Sutton Hoo, mound 1), *see* sceptre
whetstones
    Anglo-Saxon, 362, 364 *n*, 383–4, **265**
    Celtic, 361, 369, **266, 269**
    Scandinavian, 361–2, **264**
Wiesbaden (Germany), shield, 73
Williams, Nigel, helmet reconstruction, 140
Willimer, inscription on buckle, 558
Wilton (Wiltshire), cross, 563 *n*
Wingham (Kent), pendant, *Tbl. 36*, **441** *h*
Winkelman, W., 522 *n*
Witcham Gravel, Ely (Cambridgeshire), helmet, 179, **134**
Witham (Essex), hanging-bowl, 379
Wittislingen (Germany), brooch, 559
wood and iron object (Inv. 211), *see* ferrules
wooden box, 282, 444
Worms (Germany)
    helmet, 220
    iron shaft, 428
wrist-clasps, 532
Wrotham (Kent), pendant, *Tbl. 36*, **441** *e*
Wuffingas, 354 *n*, 371–2
Wye Down (Kent), pendants, *Tbl. 36*, **441** *d*
Wynaldum (Belgium), brooch, 598

Yeavering (Northumbria), possible stand, 431 *n*
Youngs, Susan M., 193, 214 *n*, 626
Yverdon (Switzerland), buckle, 558, 559 *n*, **411** *c*

Zeus, whetstones as thunderbolt symbol, 374